CENSUS OF INDIA 1891

Census of India 1871-1951, 9 Sets In 384 Bindings (9788121258876) Rs. 700000

Census of India 1891, 28 Vols. In 49 Bindings (978-81-212-7129-5) Rs. 125000

1. General Report (9788121269834) Rs. 1450
2. General Tables For British Provinces And Feudatory States (9788121269810) Rs. 2710 (Vol. I)
3. General Tables For British Provinces And Feudatory States (9788121269797) Rs. 950 (Vol. II)
4. Assam - Report (9788121269773) Rs. 2390 (Vol. I, V.1)
5. Assam - Tables (9788121269759) Rs. 2210 (Vol. II, V.2)
6. Assam - Provincial Tables (9788121269735) Rs. 1310 (Vol. II, V.3)
7. The Lower Provinces of Bengal and their Feudatories - The Report (9788121269711) Rs. 1660 (Vol. III)
8. The Lower Provinces of Bengal and their feudatories - The Administrative Tables (9788121269698) Rs. 4200 (Vol. IV)
9. The Lower Provinces of Bengal and their feudatories - The Caste Tables (9788121269674) Rs. 2600 (Vol. V, Pt. 1)
10. Lower Provinces of Bengal - The Provincial Tables (9788121269650) Rs. 1980 (Vol. V, Pt. 2)
11. Berar or the Hyderabad Assigned Districts (9788121269636) Rs. 3360 (Vol. VI)
12. Bombay and Its Feudatories - Report (9788121269612) Rs. 4010 (Vol. VII, Pt. 1)
13. Bombay And Its Feudatories - Imperial Tables (9788121269599) Rs. 790 (Vol. VIII, Pt. 2)
14. Imperial Series - Burma Report (9788121269575) Rs. 2320 (Vol. IX-V.1)
15. Imperial Tables - Burma Report (9788121269551) Rs. 3360 (Vol. X-V.2)
16. Provincial Tables Burma Report (9788121269537) Rs. 3510 (Vol. X-V.3)
17. Provincial Tables Burma Report (9788121269513) Rs. 3630 (Vol. X-V.4)
18. The Central Provinces And Feudatories - The Report (9788121269490) Rs. 2290 (Vol. XI, Pt. 1)
19. The Central Provinces And Feudatories - Imperial tables and supplementary returns (9788121268936) Rs. 2010 (Vol. XII)
20. Madras The Report On The Census (9788121269476) Rs. 2870 (Vol. XIII)
21. Madras - Tables I to XVII-C, British Territory (9788121269452) Rs. 3490 (Vol. XIV)
22. Madras - Tables A TO E, British Territory. Tables for feudatory States and A Caste Index (9788121269438) Rs. 2820 (Vol. XV)
23. The North Western Provinces and Outh - Report and Provincial Tables (9788121268912) Rs. 3100 (Vol. XVI, Pt. 1)
24. The North - Western Provinces and Oudh- Imperial Tables (9788121269414) Rs. 2000 (Vol. XVII, Pt. 2)
25. The North - Western Provinces and Oudh- Imperial Caste Tables (9788121269391) Rs. 3020 (Vol. XVIII, Pt. 3)
26. Punjab and Its Feudatories - The Report on the Census (9788121269377) Rs. 2710 (Vol. XIX, Pt. 1)
27. Punjab and Its Feudatories - Imperial Tables and Supplementary Returns for the British Territory (9788121269353) Rs. 1370 (Vol. XX, Pt. 2)
28. Punjab and Its Feudatories - Imperial Tables and Supplementary Returns for the Native States, Together With A Caste Index (9788121269339) Rs. 4910 (Vol. XXI, Pt. 3)
29. Report on The Census of The Districts of Ajmere-Merwara (9788121269056) Rs. 720 (Vol. XXII)
30. His Highness The Nizam's Dominions - Report (9788121269315) Rs. 2240 (Vol. XXIII, Pt. 1)
31. His Highness The Nizam's Dominions - Report (9788121269292) Rs. 2410 (Vol. XXIII, Pt. 2)
32. His Highness The Nizam's Dominions - Imperial And Supplementry Tables and Caste Index (9788121269278) Rs. 3390 (Vol. XXIII, Pt. 3)
33. Baroda - Report (9788121269254) Rs. 3810 (Vol. XXIV, Pt. 1)
34. Baroda - Tables (9788121269230) Rs. 2620 (Vol. XXIV, Pt. 2)
35. Mysore - Report (9788121269216) Rs. 2590 (Vol. XXV, Pt. 1)
36. Mysore - Imperial Tables (9788121269193) Rs. 1600 (Vol. XXV, Pt. 2)
37. Mysore - Tables (9788121269179) Rs. 5320 (Vol. XXV, Pt. 3)
38. Mysore - Supplementary Tables (9788121269155) Rs. 3590 (Vol. XXV, Pt. 4)
39. Mysore- Supplement to the Mysore census report of 1891 being a list of villages in the Mysore province and : comparing the population as per Censuses of 1891, 1881 & 1871 (9788121279024) Rs. 5350 (Vol. XXV, Pt. 5)
40. Rajputana - The Report, Imperial Tables And Supplementary Returns (9788121269131) Rs. 2330 (Vol. XXVI, Pt. 1)
41. Rajputna - The Provincial Tables and Remarks (9788121269117) Rs. 550 (Vol. XXVI, Pt. 2)
42. Central India (9788121269094) Rs. 2000 (Vol. XXVII)
43. Kashmir State - The Report on the census and Imperial and supplementary Tables (9788121269070) Rs. 2290 (Vol. XXVIII)
44. The Census of Calcutta (9788121269032) Rs. 890
45. Report on the census of Cochin (9788121269018) Rs. 790 (Pt. 1)
46. Report on the census of Cochin - The Final Census Tables with Appendices (9788121268998) Rs. 910 (Pt. 2)
47. Report on the Census of Coorg (9788121268974) Rs. 730
48. Report on the census of Travancore -Report (9788121274029) Rs. 4220 (Vol. I)
49. Report on the census of Travancore -Appendix (9788121268950) Rs. 5300 (Vol. II)

Owing to the antiquity and rarity of this book, certain pages are regrettably absent, and readability is compromised due to the blurring of the original text. If you possess any insights regarding the availability of these missing sections, kindly inform us. Your assistance is crucial in ensuring the completion of this significant work for the benefit of future generations.

CENSUS OF INDIA, 1891

BOOK-10: VOL. V

CENSUS OF THE LOWER PROVINCES OF BENGAL, 1891

THE PROVINCIAL TABLES

C. J. O'DONNELL

GYAN

Published by

Gyan Publishing House
5, Ansari Road
Daryaganj, New Delhi-110002
Phone: 011-47034999, 9811692060
E-mail: books@gyanbooks.com

Distribution Network
gyanbooks.com
India, USA, Canada, UK, Australia

ISBN: 978-81-212-7129-5 (Set) 28 Vols. In 49 Bindings
978-81-212-6965-0 (PB) Book-10, Vol. V, Pt. II

First Published, 1893

2nd Impression 2024

Printed at: Gyan Press, Delhi.

CENSUS OF INDIA 1891

CENSUS

OF THE

LOWER PROVINCES OF BENGAL, 1891.

BY

C. J. O'DONNELL, M.A.,

OF THE INDIAN CIVIL SERVICE,

SUPERINTENDENT OF CENSUS OPERATIONS IN BENGAL.

The Provincial Tables.

Calcutta:

PRINTED AT THE BENGAL SECRETARIAT PRESS.

1893.

CONTENTS.

PROVINCIAL TABLE I.—SHOWING FOR EACH DISTRICT, SUBDIVISION AND THANA THE AREA, THE NUMBER OF TOWNS AND VILLAGES, OCCUPIED HOUSES IN 1891 AND 1881, THE POPULATION OF BOTH SEXES IN 1891 AND 1881, THE NUMBER OF PERSONS PER SQUARE MILE IN 1891 AND 1881, THE VARIATION OF DENSITY OF POPULATION AND ITS PERCENTAGE IN THE DECADE, THE NUMBER OF HOUSES PER SQUARE MILE AND THE NUMBER OF PERSONS PER OCCUPIED HOUSE.

Districts, of which the external boundaries have been altered since the census of 1881.

1. Bardwan.
2. Birbhum.
3. Midnapur.
4. Hugli.
5. Nadia.
6. Rajshahi.
7. Bogra.
8. Pabna.
9. Darjeeling.
10. Jalpaiguri.
11. Dacca.
12. Faridpur.
13. Maimansingh.
14. Tippera.
15. Patna.
16. Shahabad.
17. Darbhanga.
18. Saran.
19. Monghyr.
20. Bhagalpur.
21. Purnea.
22. Malda.
23. Santal Parganas.
24. Cuttack.
25. Puri.

Districts, of which the internal boundaries have been altered since the census of 1881.

1. Bardwan.
2. Birbhum.
3. Midnapur.
4. Hugli.
5. 24-Parganas.
6. Nadia.
7. Khulna.
8. Murshidabad.
9. Dinajpur.
10. Rajshahi.
11. Rangpur.
12. Bogra.
13. Pabna.
14. Darjeeling.
15. Jalpaiguri.
16. Dacca.
17. Faridpur.
18. Maimansingh.
19. Tippera.
20. Gaya.
21. Muzaffarpur.
22. Darbhanga.
23. Saran.
24. Champaran.
25. Monghyr.
26. Bhagalpur.
27. Purnea.
28. Santal Parganas.
29. Cuttack.
30. Puri.
31. Lohardaga.
32. Singhbhum.
33. Manbhum.

BARDWAN DIVISION.

BARDWAN DISTRICT.

Subdivisions and Thánas.	Area in square miles.	Number of towns and villages.	Occupied houses.		Population in 1891.			Both sexes, 1881.	Number of persons per square mile.				Number in 1891.	
			1891.	1881.	Both sexes.	Males.	Females.		1891.	1881.	Variation.	Percentage of variation.	Houses per square mile.	Persons per occupied house.
SADAR SUBDIVISION.														
Bardwan	185	102	*15,564*	14,215	*70,906*	36,408	34,498	61,904	383	335	+48	+14·3	84	4·6
Sahibganj	124	161	*18,171*	16,678	*74,279*	35,920	38,359	75,270	599	607	−8	−1·3	147	4·0
Khandaghosh	115	140	*13,794*	9,770	*55,939*	27,034	28,905	55,228	486	480	+6	+1·2	120	4·0
Baina	194	251	*22,751*	14,557	*95,339*	46,280	49,052	96,943	491	500	−9	−1·8	117	4·1
Satgachhia	181	371	*29,028*	24,459	*98,954*	48,094	50,860	102,254	547	565	−18	−3·1	160	3·4
Jamalpur	113	235	*20,369*	16,507	*71,771*	34,539	37,232	71,709	635	634	+1	+0·1	180	3·5
Bud-Bud	161	187	*20,777*	15,634	*74,749*	36,935	37,814	88,123	464	547	−83	−15·2	129	3·6
Ausgram	169	228	*21,237*	19,608	*77,938*	37,838	40,100	88,261	461	522	−61	−11·6	126	3·6
Total ...	1,242	1,675	*161,691*	130,828	*619,868*	303,048	316,820	639,692	499	515	−16	−3·1	130	3·8
RANIGANJ SUBDIVISION.														
Raniganj	218	290	*29,563*	29,827	*147,964*	73,370	74,594	146,785	679	673	+6	+8·9	136	5·0
Asansol	272	289	*23,469*	15,499	*127,341*	65,549	61,792	98,842	468	363	+105	+28·9	86	5·4
Kaksa	181	96	*7,385*	7,307	*34,968*	17,445	17,523	38,787	193	214	−21	−9·8	41	4·7
Total ...	671	675	*60,417*	52,633	*310,273*	156,364	153,909	284,414	462	424	+38	+8·9	90	5·1
KATWA SUBDIVISION.														
Katwa	142	147	*16,113*	18,449	*81,690*	39,210	42,480	82,943	575	584	−9	−1·5	113	5·0
Ketugram	136	175	*13,245*	16,662	*76,937*	37,084	39,853	76,120	566	560	+6	+1·0	97	5·8
Mungalkot	74	177	*13,527*	16,485	*71,600*	34,653	36,947	73,444	968	992	−24	−2·4	183	5·2
Total ...	352	499	*42,885*	51,596	*230,227*	110,947	119,280	232,507	654	661	−7	−1·0	122	5·3
KALNA SUBDIVISION.														
Kalna	144	286	*29,800*	23,549	*90,091*	43,544	46,547	92,484	626	642	−16	−2·4	207	3·0
Purbasthali	116	244	*18,750*	19,025	*77,098*	37,881	39,217	82,070	665	708	−43	−6·0	162	4·1
Manteswar	172	181	*13,676*	12,027	*64,323*	31,088	33,235	63,053	374	367	+7	+1·9	80	4·7
Total ...	432	711	*62,226*	54,601	*231,512*	112,513	118,999	237,607	536	550	−14	−2·5	144	3·7
DISTRICT TOTAL ...	2,697	3,560	327,219	289,658	1,391,880	682,872	709,008	1,394,220	516	517	−1	−0·1	121	4·2

DISTRICT BANKURA.

Subdivisions and Thánas.	Area in square miles.	Number of towns and villages.	Occupied houses.		Population in 1891.			Both sexes, 1881.	Number of persons per square mile.				Number in 1891.	
			1891.	1881.	Both sexes.	Males.	Females.		1891.	1881.	Variation.	Percentage of variation.	Houses per square mile.	Persons per occupied house.
SADAR SUBDIVISION.														
Bankura	332	762	*25,127*	22,468	*140,601*	69,676	70,925	127,551	423	384	+39	+10·1	76	5·6
Onda	329	756	*23,997*	10,670	*122,273*	60,669	61,604	119,321	372	363	+9	+2·4	73	5·1
Gangajalghati	} 465 {	455	*21,014*	} 30,704 {	*117,821*	58,405	59,416	} 172,607	383	371	+12	+3·2	73	5·2
*Barjora**		297	*13,005*		*60,361*	29,365	30,996							
Khatra	343	759	*19,449*	16,714	*111,948*	55,470	56,478	99,122	326	289	+37	+12·8	57	5·7
Raipura	333	662	*18,683*	6,679	*102,342*	50,173	52,169	95,802	307	288	+19	+6·5	56	5·5
Simlapal	119	296	*6,117*	5,507	*37,011*	18,470	18,541	32,683	311	275	+36	+13·0	51	6·0
Total ...	1,921	3,987	*127,385*	92,742	*699,357*	342,228	350,129	647,085	360	337	+23	+6·8	66	5·4
BISHNUPUR SUBDIVISION.														
Bishnupur	302	532	*31,027*	25,956	*135,974*	65,942	70,032	140,878	450	466	−16	−3·4	103	4·3
Sonamukhi	141	285	*16,878*	13,275	*75,489*	36,747	38,742	80,016	535	568	−33	−5·8	120	4·4
Kotalpur	133	455	*21,921*	20,674	*91,252*	44,450	46,802	94,964	686	714	−28	−3·9	165	4·1
Indas	124	238	*17,796*	15,674	*74,596*	36,574	38,022	78,809	602	636	−34	−5·3	144	4·2
Total ...	700	1,510	*87,622*	75,579	*377,311*	183,713	193,598	394,667	539	564	−25	−4·4	125	4·3
DISTRICT TOTAL ...	2,621	5,497	215,007	168,321	1,069,668	525,941	543,727	1,041,752	408	397	+11	+2·7	82	4·9

* Independent outpost.

DISTRICT BIRBHUM.

Subdivisions and Thánas.	Area in square miles.	Number of towns and villages.	Occupied houses, 1891.	Occupied houses, 1881.	Population in 1891, Both sexes.	Males.	Females.	Both sexes, 1881.	Persons per sq. mile, 1891.	1881.	Variation.	Percentage of variation.	Houses per square mile.	Persons per occupied house.
SADAR SUBDIVISION.														
Suri	311	585	*29,045*	29,701	*126,208*	62,160	64,048	126,739	406	408	−2	−0·4	93	4·3
Dubrajpur	275	430	*28,387*	27,483	*119,472*	58,207	61,265	126,566	434	460	−26	−5·8	103	4·2
Bolpur	257	415	*28,369*	27,000	*98,781*	48,631	50,150	107,893	384	420	−36	−8·5	110	3·4
Sakulipur	148	235	*16,778*	19,029	*68,145*	32,958	35,187	74,683	460	505	−45	−8·9	113	4·0
Labhpur...	117	233	*13,909*	13,406	*57,623*	28,021	29,602	52,951	493	453	+40	+8·8	119	4·1
Total ...	1,108	1,898	*116,488*	116,568	*470,229*	229,977	240,252	488,832	424	441	−17	−3·8	105	4·0

RAMPUR-HAT SUB-DIVISION.														
Rampur Ha	187	346	*20,944*	18,763	*93,434*	45,679	47,755	87,774	500	469	+31	+6·6	108	4·6
Maureswar	182	432	*19,889*	16,291	*86,428*	42,241	44,187	81,528	475	448	+27	+6·0	109	4·3
Nalhati	276	517	*31,342*	28,835	*147,742*	71,742	76,000	133,897	535	485	+50	+10·3	114	4·7
Total ...	645	1,295	*71,468*	63,889	*327,604*	159,662	167,942	303,199	508	470	+38	+8·0	111	4·5
DISTRICT TOTAL ...	1,753	3,193	187,956	180,457	797,833	389,639	408,194	792,031	455	452	+3	+0·6	107	4·2

DISTRICT MIDNAPUR.

SADAR SUBDIVISION.														
Midnapur	394	1,418	*39,007*	34,629	*179,966*	86,748	85,518	171,881	437	436	+1	+0·2	99	4·4
Jhargaon	294	638	*13,405*	11,404	*71,022*	35,381	35,641	60,605	242	206	+36	+17·4	45	5·2
Binpur	379	844	*19,578*	17,048	*102,515*	50,527	51,988	89,881	270	237	+33	+13·9	52	5·2
Salbani	215	496	*10,253*	9,361	*55,468*	27,739	27,729	54,187	258	252	+6	+2·3	48	5·4
Debra	132	708	*18,142*	15,868	*68,747*	33,847	34,900	71,646	521	543	−22	−4·0	137	3·7
Garbeta	409	879	*24,090*	20,600	*126,434*	63,404	63,030	119,668	309	293	+16	+5·4	59	5·2
Kespur	187	868	*18,177*	14,888	*83,787*	41,894	41,893	84,864	448	454	−6	−1·3	97	4·6
Sabang	262	762	*41,797*	33,736	*195,341*	97,054	98,287	198,713	746	758	−12	−1·5	159	4·6
Naraingarh	286	1,023	*26,750*	23,275	*117,441*	59,281	58,160	128,583	410	451	−41	−9·0	94	4·3
Dantun	226	681	*25,182*	21,552	*120,786*	61,218	59,568	128,046	534	567	−33	−5·8	111	4·8
Gopiballabhpur	530	1,220	*29,335*	26,431	*151,971*	75,312	76,659	139,408	287	263	+24	+9·1	55	5·1
Total ...	3,314	9,537	*265,716*	228,786	*1,265,778*	632,405	633,373	1,247,722	382	377	+5	+1·3	80	4·7
GHATAL SUBDIVISION.														
Ghatal	91	260	*15,380*	18,068	*92,521*	45,958	46,563	84,093	1,017	924	+93	+10·1	169	6·0
Chandrak	151	411	*24,999*	16,435	*101,551*	50,456	51,095	104,089	673	689	−16	−2·3	166	4·0
Daspur	130	437	*29,083*	19,937	*133,830*	64,151	69,679	124,878	1,029	961	+68	+7·0	224	4·6
Total ...	372	1,108	*69,462*	54,440	*327,909*	160,565	167,337	313,060	881	842	+39	+4·6	187	4·7
TAMLUK SUBDIVISION.														
Tamluk	85	283	*18,400*	15,621	*91,357*	44,658	46,699	84,097	1,075	989	+86	+8·6	216	4·9
Maslandpur	120	256	*17,753*	13,550	*89,561*	44,698	44,863	81,229	746	677	+69	+10·1	148	5·0
Sutahata	98	223	*11,298*	9,229	*63,299*	32,264	31,035	53,827	625	549	+76	+13·8	115	5·6
Panchkura	152	603	*30,440*	20,611	*137,752*	64,765	72,987	135,302	906	890	+16	+1·7	200	4·5
Nandigram	155	255	*20,640*	13,870	*110,459*	55,137	55,322	86,720	713	559	+154	+27·5	133	5·3
Total ...	610	1,620	*98,531*	72,881	*492,428*	241,522	250,906	441,175	807	723	+84	+11·6	162	4·9

DISTRICT MIDNAPUR—*concluded.*

Subdivisions and Thánas.	Area in square miles.	Number of towns and villages.	Occupied houses.		Population in 1891.			Both sexes, 1881.	Number of persons per square mile.				Number in 1891.	
			1891.	1881.	Both sexes.	Males.	Females.		1891.	1881.	Variation.	Percentage of variation.	Houses per square mile.	Persons per occupied house.
CONTAI SUBDIVISION.														
Contai	224	913	*27,271*	10,440	*147,370*	73,493	73,877	130,554	658	583	+75	+12·8	122	5·4
Egra	128	375	*14,304*	11,868	*73,829*	37,604	36,225	65,395	577	511	+66	+13·1	112	5·1
Pataspur	138	444	*18,404*	2,094	*93,534*	47,312	46,222	92,631	678	671	+7	+1·0	133	5·0
Ramnagar	120	391	*12,809*	11,003	*69,327*	34,194	35,133	62,124	578	518	+60	+11·5	107	5·4
Bhagabanpur	164	408	*20,730*	17,928	*111,175*	55,434	55,741	117,430	678	716	−38	−5·3	126	5·3
Khajri	75	138	*8,269*	7,212	*50,173*	25,571	24,602	45,574	669	608	+61	+10·0	110	6·0
Total ...	849	2,669	*101,773*	60,535	*545,408*	273,608	271,800	513,608	642	605	+37	+6·1	120	5·4
DISTRICT TOTAL ...	5,145*	14,934	535,482	416,642	2,631,516	1,308,100	1,323,416	2,515,665	511	489	+22	+4·4	104	4·9

*The area obtained in reference to the Bengal Office is 5,186 square miles, the difference, 41 square miles, being returned as uninhabited river-beds.

DISTRICT HUGLI.

Subdivisions and Thánas.	Area in square miles.	Number of towns and villages.	Occupied houses 1891.	Occupied houses 1881.	Population 1891 Both sexes.	Males.	Females.	Both sexes, 1881.	Persons per sq. mile 1891.	1881.	Variation.	Percentage of variation.	Houses per square mile.	Persons per occupied house.
SADAR SUBDIVISION.														
Hugli	30	68	*15,528*	17,105	*56,458*	28,616	27,842	56,425	1,882	1,881	+1	+0·05	518	3·6
Balagarh	86	170	*12,108*	12,414	*46,729*	22,658	24,071	48,218	543	561	−18	−3·2	141	3·8
Pandua	111	172	*29,017*	18,069	*65,924*	31,810	34,114	66,113	594	596	−2	−0·3	261	2·2
Dhaniakhali	135	366	*42,813*	26,631	*95,694*	46,340	49,354	93,537	709	693	+16	+2·3	317	2·2
Polba	80	202	*12,095*	12,461	*44,811*	22,256	22,555	43,924	560	549	+11	+2·0	151	3·7
Total ...	442	976	*111,561*	86,680	*309,616*	151,680	157,936	308,217	700	697	+3	+0·4	252	2·7
SERAMPUR SUBDIVISION.														
Serampur	22	11	*18,939*	17,335	*79,816*	44,054	35,762	68,344	3,628	3,107	+521	+16·7	861	4·2
Haripal	116	319	*22,176*	21,568	*95,080*	47,133	47,947	84,933	827	739	+88	+11·9	193	4·2
Krishnanagar	63	157	*14,218*	11,563	*59,938*	28,465	31,473	55,107	951	875	+76	+8·6	226	4·2
Singur	71	171	*14,940*	13,478	*67,584*	34,123	33,461	59,184	952	834	+118	+14·1	210	4·5
Chanditala	72	148	*20,373*	16,913	*97,569*	48,922	48,647	84,387	1,355	1,172	+183	+15·6	283	4·8
Total ...	343	806	*90,639*	80,837	*399,987*	202,697	197,290	351,955	1,166	1,026	+140	+13·6	264	4·4

JAHANABAD SUB-DIVISION.															
Jahanabad	147	311	*24,548*	23,517	*117,904*	56,042	61,862	110,412	802	751	+51	+6·7	167	4·8
Goghat	146	233	*27,836*	25,979	*109,416*	52,665	56,751	111,121	749	761	−12	−1·5	191	3·9
Khanakul	145	256	*30,006*	23,086	*139,787*	66,055	73,732	133,300	964	919	+45	+4·8	207	4·6
Total ...	438	800	*82,390*	71,583	*367,107*	174,762	192,345	354,833	838	810	+28	+3·4	188	4·4
DISTRICT TOTAL ...	1,223	2,582	284,590	239,039	1,076,710	529,139	547,571	1,015,006	880	830	+50	+6·0	233	3·7

DISTRICT HOWRAH.

SADAR SUBDIVISION.														
Howrah	9	1	*25,452*	24,980	*116,606*	70,477	46,129	90,813	12,956	10,090	+2,866	+28·4	2,828	4·5
Bally	2	1	*4,018*	3,360	*16,700*	9,515	7,185	14,815	8,350	7,408	+942	+12·7	2,009	4·1
Domjur	89	202	*28,078*	21,375	*147,749*	75,870	71,879	128,477	1,660	1,444	+216	+14·9	315	5·2
Jagatballabhpur	73	180	*18,016*	13,544	*85,241*	40,197	45,044	77,539	1,168	1,062	+106	+9·9	247	4·7
Total ...	173	384	*75,564*	63,259	*366,296*	196,059	170,237	311,644	2,117	1,801	+316	+17·5	437	4·8
ULUBARIA SUBDIVISION.														
Ulubaria	77	223	*17,767*	13,293	*87,696*	43,313	44,383	81,345	1,139	1,056	+83	+7·8	231	4·9
Amta	103	219	*25,390*	17,076	*120,632*	55,149	65,483	109,968	1,171	1,068	+103	+9·6	247	4·7
Bagnan	56	190	*13,484*	9,272	*68,832*	32,754	36,078	63,563	1,229	1,135	+94	+8·2	241	5·1
Shampur	67	319	*13,930*	10,144	*77,755*	37,615	40,140	68,861	1,162	1,028	+134	+13·0	208	5·5
Total ...	303	951	*70,571*	50,385	*354,915*	168,831	186,084	323,737	1,171	1,068	+103	+9·6	233	5·0
STRICT TOTAL ...	476	1,335	146,135	113,644	721,211	364,890	356,321	635,381	1,515	1,335	+180	+13·4	307	4·9
BARDWAN DIVISION TOTAL	13,915	31,101	1,696,389	1,407,761	7,688,818	3,800,581	3,888,237	7,393,954	552	531	+21	+3·9	121	4·5

PRESIDENCY DIVISION.

DISTRICT 24-PARGANAS.

Subdivisions and Thánas.	Area in square miles.	Number of towns and villages.	Occupied houses.		Population in 1891.			Both sexes, 1881.	Number of persons per square mile.				Number in 1891.	
			1891.	1881.	Both sexes.	Males.	Females.		1891.	1881.	Variation.	Percentage of variation.	Houses per square mile.	Persons per occupied house.
SADAR SUBDIVISION.														
Tollyganj	71	186	*23,495*	29,521	*128,368*	69,299	59,069	99,451	1,808	1,400	+408	+29·1	331	5·4
Baruipur	108	322	*15,893*	10,593	*86,768*	44,415	42,353	75,830	803	702	+101	+14·3	147	5·5
Sonarpur	53	142	*8,387*	6,699	*42,244*	21,005	21,239	42,434	797	801	−4	−0·4	158	5·0
Bishnupur	81	251	*13,628*	11,266	*79,080*	39,152	39,928	71,717	976	885	+91	+10·2	168	5·8
Bhangor	127	298	*14,934*	9,618	*67,937*	34,943	32,994	65,057	535	512	+23	+4·4	118	4·5
Budge-Budge	53	192	*11,880*	9,518	*72,283*	37,384	34,899	63,536	1,364	1,180	+184	+15·5	224	6·0
Canning Town	261	230	*9,683*	6,914	*56,539*	31,362	25,177	47,518	217	182	+35	+18·9	37	5·8
Jainagar	73	240	*15,244*	9,995	*91,020*	46,843	44,177	76,140	1,247	1,043	+204	+19·5	209	5·9
Baranagar	7	12	*7,380*	7,246	*34,278*	18,797	15,481	29,988	4,897	4,283	+614	+14·3	1,054	4·6
Total ...	834	1,882	*120,524*	101,372	*658,517*	343,200	315,317	570,665	790	684	+106	+15·4	145	5·4
BARASAT SUBDIVISION.														
Barasat	104	291	*15,085*	13,014	*75,576*	38,623	36,953	73,131	727	703	+24	+3·4	145	5·0
Deganga	79	143	*10,630*	8,898	*55,776*	28,359	27,417	53,516	706	677	+29	+4·2	135	5·2
Habra	108	233	*11,681*	13,158	*71,283*	36,701	34,582	75,429	660	698	−38	−5·4	108	6·1
Naihati	101	204	*18,459*	14,016	*86,076*	45,408	40,668	76,963	852	762	+90	+11·8	183	4·6
Total ...	392	871	*55,855*	49,084	*288,711*	149,091	139,620	279,038	736	712	+24	+3·3	142	5·1
DUM-DUM SUBDIVISION.														
Dum-Dum	56	181	*8,159*	8,469	*53,905*	29,008	24,897	45,378	963	810	+153	+18·8	145	6·6
Total ...	56	181	*8,159*	8,469	*53,905*	29,008	24,897	45,373	963	810	+153	+18·8	145	6·6
BARRACKPUR SUB-DIVISION.														
Barrackpur	14	56	*4,798*	7,221	*27,809*	16,371	11,438	30,629	1,986	2,188	−202	−9·2	343	5·7
Nawabganj	8	8	*3,332*	2,169	*18,437*	10,600	7,837	10,902	2,305	1,362	+943	+69·2	416	5·5
Khardaha	20	21	*4,157*	6,023	*24,211*	12,505	11,706	20,886	1,211	1,044	+167	+15·9	208	5·8
Total ...	42	85	*12,287*	15,413	*70,457*	39,476	30,981	62,417	1,678	1,486	+192	+12·9	292	5·7

BASIRHAT SUBDIVISION.														
Basirhat	99	293	*15,784*	11,387	*78,549*	38,867	39,682	76,337	793	771	+22	+2·8	159	4·9
Baduria	166	299	*24,544*	19,517	*126,466*	63,190	63,276	123,741	762	746	+16	+2·1	147	5·1
Haroa	55	218	*9,791*	7,984	*69,785*	36,001	26,784	49,393	1,142	896	+246	+27·4	177	6·4
Husainabad	40	300	*12,570*	10,096	*79,338*	42,796	36,542	67,227	1,983	1,681	+302	+18·0	317	6·2
Total ...	360	1,110	*62,519*	48,964	*347,138*	180,854	166,284	316,697	964	879	+85	+9·6	174	5·5
DIAMOND HARBOUR SUBDIVISION.														
Diamond Harbour	68	249	*13,865*	6,703	*63,430*	31,637	31,793	53,828	933	777	+156	+20·0	204	4·5
Kulpi	110	482	*20,894*	11,541	*106,544*	54,958	51,586	90,319	969	821	+148	+18·0	189	5·1
Bankipur	118	373	*5,708*	15,148	*124,453*	61,229	63,224	107,275	1,055	909	+146	+16·0	48	21·8
Debipur	50	251	*8,916*	5,893	*49,815*	24,282	25,533	43,455	996	869	+127	+14·6	178	5·5
Mathurapur	71	203	*12,135*	7,134	*58,638*	29,864	28,774	50,453	826	711	+115	+16·1	171	4·8
Total ...	417	1,558	*61,448*	46,402	*402,880*	201,970	200,910	344,330	966	825	+141	+17·0	147	6·5
DISTRICT TOTAL ...	2,101	5,687	320,785	269,694	1,821,608	943,599	878,009	1,618,420	867	770	+97	+12·5	152	5·6
SUBURBS OF CALCUTTA.														
Cossipur-Chitpur M.C.		6	*5,187*	......	*31,493*	19,424	11,999	......	......	......	......			6·0
Manicktala M.C.	7	6	*4,766*	......	*28,161*	16,418	11,743	......	......	......	......	......	......	5·9
Entally		2	*196*	......	*745*	416	329	......	......	......	......			3·8
Calcutta Canals	......	......	......	......	*3,959*	3,877	82	......	......	......	......	......	......	......
Total ...	7	14	*10,149*	......	*64,288*	40,135	24,153	......	9,184	......	......	......	1,449	6·3
Sundarbans	......	64	......	......	*6,137*	5,544	593	......	......	......	......	......	......	......
CALCUTTA ...	20	1	67,528	......	*681,560*	446,746	234,814	......	34,078	......	......	......	3,576	10·0

DISTRICT NADIA.

SADAR SUBDIVISION.														
Krishnanagar	166	174	*24,006*	23,248	*112,274*	54,897	57,377	119,469	676	720	−44	−6·1	145	4·6
Kaliganj	109	103	*10,089*	10,408	*46,845*	22,790	24,055	54,192	430	497	−67	−13·4	93	4·6
Nakasipara	135	127	*12,149*	12,281	*56,385*	27,214	29,171	59,769	418	443	−25	−5·6	90	4·6
Chapra	130	111	*11,805*	9,570	*63,481*	31,365	32,116	63,509	488	488	......	......	91	5·3
Krishnaganj	57	50	*6,890*	6,216	*32,658*	15,866	16,792	33,701	573	574	−1	−0·1	121	4·7
Hanskhali	104	89	*8,120*	8,852	*37,364*	18,599	18,765	45,340	359	436	−77	−17·6	78	4·6
Jibannagar	77	75	*7,084*	6,529	*36,146*	17,875	18,271	40,120	469	521	−52	−9·9	92	5·1
Total ...	778	729	*80,143*	77,098	*385,153*	188,606	196,547	415,093	495	534	−39	−7·2	103	4·8

DISTRICT NADIA—*concluded.*

Subdivisions and Thanas.	Area in square miles.	Number of towns and villages.	Occupied houses.		Population in 1891.			Both sexes, 1881.	Number of persons per square mile.				Number in 1891.	
			1891.	1881.	Both sexes.	Males.	Females.		1891.	1881.	Variation.	Percentage of variation.	Houses per square mile.	Persons per occupied house.
RANAGHAT SUB-DIVISION.														
Ranaghat	161	199	*17,784*	17,798	*77,307*	37,941	39,366	84,415	480	524	−44	−8·4	110	4·3
Santipur	74	63	*12,963*	12,176	*53,964*	25,700	28,264	53,864	729	728	+1	+0·1	166	4·4
Chakdaha	120	194	*14,091*	14,544	*63,923*	33,394	30,529	64,620	533	539	−6	−1·1	117	4·5
Haringhata	72	108	*8,655*	7,769	*34,842*	17,737	17,105	38,306	484	532	−48	−9·0	120	4·0
Total ...	427	564	*52,793*	52,287	*230,036*	114,772	115,264	241,205	539	565	−26	−4·6	123	4·3
KUSHTIA SUBDIVISION.														
Kushtia	30	45	*6,116*	4,216	*33,505*	16,752	16,753	27,443	1,117	915	+202	+22·0	204	5·4
Naupara	177	62	*27,746*	22,555	*140,883*	67,096	73,787	137,394	796	776	+ 20	+2·5	157	5·0
Daulatpur	144	129	*16,619*	13,419	*84,155*	40,459	43,696	80,571	584	560	+ 24	+4·2	115	5·0
Bhadalia	93	135	*13,329*	10,240	*72,377*	35,196	37,181	68,184	778	733	+ 45	+6·1	143	5·4
Kumarkhali	102	234	*20,039*	15,895	*103,124*	50,022	53,102	98,247	1,011	963	+ 48	+4·9	196	5·1
Bhaluka	51	114	*8,708*	6,505	*48,883*	23,499	25,384	41,929	958	822	+136	+16·5	171	5·6
Total ...	597	719	*92,557*	72,830	*482,927*	233,024	249,903	453,768	809	760	+ 49	+6·4	155	5·2
MIHRPUR SUBDIVISION.														
Mihrpur	133	108	*14,039*	13,930	*69,516*	33,860	35,656	71,685	523	539	− 16	−3·0	105	4·9
Karimpur	193	177	*21,323*	18,358	*106,852*	51,057	55,795	102,754	553	532	+ 21	+3·9	110	5·0
Gangni	126	147	*13,888*	12,271	*73,227*	35,533	37,694	74,955	581	595	− 14	−2·3	110	5·2
Tehata	180	136	*17,105*	14,991	*87,121*	42,314	44,807	89,169	484	495	− 11	−2·2	95	5·0
Chuadanga	33	40	*4,041*	3,230	*19,760*	9,813	9,947	21,818	599	661	− 62	−9·3	122	4·8
Damurhuda	116	112	*12,433*	9,530	*63,386*	31,058	32,328	63,014	546	543	+ 3	+0·5	107	5·0
Alamdanga	132	165	*16,335*	13,275	*89,663*	44,045	45,618	89,947	679	681	− 2	−0·2	124	5·4
Kalupol	79	85	*7,527*	5,752	*36,467*	18,065	18,402	39,396	462	499	− 37	−7·4	95	4·8
Total ...	992	970	*106,684*	91,348	*545,992*	265,745	280,247	552,739	552	558	− 6	−1·2	108	5·1
DISTRICT TOTAL ...	2,794	2,982	332,107	293,561	1,644,108	802,147	841,961	1,662,795	588	595	− 7	−1·1	119	4·9

DISTRICT JESSOR.

SADAR SUBDIVISION.														
Jessor	231	422	*39,406*	28,191	*157,939*	81,920	76,002	167,354	683	724	−41	−5·6	140	4·8
Kaliganj	141	239	*16,751*	13,423	*83,068*	42,009	41,059	89,202	589	633	−44	−6·9	119	4·9
Bagherpara	105	184	*9,495*	9,964	*57,684*	28,851	28,833	63,903	549	609	−60	−9·8	90	6·0
Gadkhali	93	137	*10,934*	11,013	*63,710*	32,240	31,470	67,420	685	725	−40	−5·5	118	5·8
Manirampur	219	330	*31,114*	24,229	*149,611*	75,959	73,652	155,611	683	710	−27	−3·8	142	4·8
Keshubpur	100	190	*16,079*	15,319	*82,840*	41,763	41,077	85,450	828	854	−26	−3·0	160	5·1
Total ...	889	1,502	*116,779*	102,138	*594,835*	302,742	292,093	628,939	669	707	−38	−5·3	131	5·0
JHENIDAHA SUB-DIVISION.														
Jhenidaha	165	256	*17,930*	14,871	*89,915*	44,462	45,453	102,627	545	622	−77	−12·3	109	5·0
Salkopa	248	475	*29,445*	23,762	*180,737*	87,229	93,508	180,170	735	732	+3	+0·4	120	6·1
Kotchandpur	64	101	*7,959*	6,035	*41,321*	21,072	20,249	44,038	646	688	−42	−6·1	124	5·1
Total ...	475	832	*55,334*	44,668	*311,973*	152,763	159,210	326,835	657	688	−31	−4·5	116	5·6
MAGURA SUBDIVISION.														
Magura	222	555	*29,360*	23,344	*166,071*	81,042	85,029	159,162	748	717	+31	+4·3	132	5·6
Muhamadpur	113	279	*14,861*	12,528	*90,767*	44,597	46,170	83,677	803	741	+62	+8·3	132	6·1
Salikha	90	134	*6,768*	7,473	*46,443*	22,312	24,131	50,464	516	561	−45	−8·0	75	6·8
Total ...	425	968	*50,989*	43,339	*303,281*	147,951	155,330	293,303	714	680	+24	+3·4	120	5·9
NARAIL SUBDIVISION.														
Narail	232	296	*29,436*	13,785	*151,514*	75,560	75,954	151,362	653	652	+ 1	+0·1	127	5·1
Lohagara	154	271	*19,273*	13,464	*115,486*	56,749	58,737	103,863	750	674	+ 76	+11·2	125	5·9
Kalia	101	155	*12,110*	10,191	*81,537*	40,662	40,875	73,947	807	722	+ 85	+11·7	120	6·7
Total ...	487	722	*60,819*	36,440	*348,537*	172,971	175,566	328,172	716	674	+ 42	+6·2	125	5·7
BANGAON SUB-DIVISION.														
Bangaon	113	154	*12,715*	12,708	*55,541*	27,907	27,634	59,668	491	528	− 37	−7·0	113	4·3
Mahespur	201	214	*20,761*	20,795	*102,980*	51,082	51,898	112,137	512	558	− 46	−8·2	103	4·9
Garapota	111	173	*11,297*	10,759	*56,187*	27,527	28,660	61,052	506	550	− 44	−8·0	102	4·9
Sarsa	130	159	*13,485*	13,465	*70,926*	35,519	34,707	79,046	540	608	− 68	−11·1	104	5·2
Gaighata	94	127	*9,779*	10,417	*45,267*	22,872	22,395	50,223	482	534	− 52	−9·7	104	4·6
Total ...	649	827	*68,030*	68,144	*330,901*	164,907	165,294	362,126	509	558	− 49	−8·7	105	4·8
DISTRICT TOTAL ...	2,925	4,851	351,944	294,729	1,888,827	941,334	947,493	1,939,375	646	663	− 17	−2·5	120	5·3

DISTRICT MURSHIDABAD.

Subdivisions and Thánás.	Area in square miles.	Number of towns an village	Occupied houses.		Population in 1891.			Both sexes, 1881.	Number of persons per square mile.				Number in 1891.	
			1891.	1881.	Both sexes.	Males.	Females.		1891.	1881.	Variation.	Percentage of variation.	Houses per square mile.	Persons per occupied house.
SADAR SUBDIVISION.														
Sujaganj	18	45	*2,073*	1,975	*9,463*	4,496	4,607	8,345	522	463	+59	+12·7	115	4·5
Gora Bazar	19	68	*3,071*	2,937	*12,018*	5,874	6,144	12,633	632	664	-32	-4·8	161	3·9
Barhampur Municipality ...	9	1	*6,384*	6,496	*23,515*	12,260	11,255	23,605	2,612	2,622	-10	-0·3	709	3·6
Burwan	108	144	*14,726*	13,127	*68,695*	33,875	34,820	67,912	636	629	+7	+1·1	136	4·8
Daulatabazar	63	117	*10,296*	8,412	*38,998*	19,108	19,890	39,568	619	628	-9	-1·4	163	3·7
Hariharpara	98	137	*12,645*	12,174	*55,058*	26,667	28,391	57,135	562	583	-21	-3·6	129	4·3
Nowada	88	81	*10,816*	7,949	*48,778*	23,707	25,071	47,559	554	540	+14	+2·5	123	4·5
Goas	157	290	*16,519*	15,670	*85,623*	41,262	44,361	78,423	545	500	+45	+9·0	105	5·1
Jalinghi	192	231	*23,894*	20,466	*112,831*	53,578	59,253	108,508	588	565	+23	+4·0	124	4·7
Total ...	752	1,114	*100,347*	89,036	*454,919*	220,827	234,092	443,688	605	590	+15	+2·6	133	4·5
LALBAGH SUB-DIVISION.														
Shahnagar	16	63	*5,187*	2,198	*11,194*	5,393	5,801	9,523	699	595	+104	+17·4	324	2·1
Manulabazar	9	4	*1,149*	407	*4,163*	2,037	2,126	1,979	463	220	+243	+110·4	127	3·6
Asanpur	12	88	*2,530*	2,842	*10,127*	5,003	5,124	11,177	844	931	-87	-9·3	210	4·0
Lalbagh Municipality	16	1	*7,263*	10,207	*35,576*	18,046	17,530	39,231	2,223	2,452	-229	-9·3	454	4·8
Bhagabangola	111	247	*12,081*	11,836	*53,590*	25,498	28,092	57,338	483	516	-33	-6·3	109	4·4
Sagardighi	86	170	*6,806*	6,069	*29,424*	14,434	14,990	27,869	342	324	+18	+5·5	79	4·3
Kaliaganj	122	172	*9,618*	8,624	*37,659*	18,398	19,254	37,206	309	305	+4	+1·3	79	3·9
Total ...	372	745	*44,627*	42,183	*181,726*	88,809	92,917	184,313	489	495	-6	-1·2	120	4·0
JANGIPUR SUB-DIVISION.														
Raghunathganj	71	161	*12,571*	11,399	*60,808*	28,874	31,934	67,456	856	950	-94	-9·8	177	4·8
Shamsherganj	104	203	*15,305*	12,588	*79,378*	37,471	41,907	69,536	763	669	+94	+14·0	147	5·1
Suti	137	228	*12,957*	10,903	*69,532*	32,917	36,615	66,556	508	486	+22	+4·5	95	5·3
Dewan Sarai	95	246	*11,572*	10,043	*60,714*	29,226	31,488	55,036	639	579	+60	+10·3	122	5·2
Mirzapur	101	166	*10,082*	9,515	*46,747*	22,424	24,323	45,496	463	450	+13	+2·8	100	4·6
Total ...	508	994	*62,487*	54,448	*317,179*	150,912	166,267	304,080	624	599	+25	+4·1	123	5·0

KANDI SUBDIVISION.														
Kandi	32	78	*7,263*	6,593	*28,375*	14,056	14,319	28,903	887	903	−16	−1·7	227	3·9
Barwa	105	231	*16,311*	22,203	*63,590*	31,198	32,392	61,417	806	585	+21	+3·5	155	3·8
Khargaon	122	157	*22,043*	11,961	*55,981*	27,226	28,755	54,018	459	443	+16	+3·6	181	2·5
Bharatpur	164	236	*19,937*	22,341	*109,240*	52,879	56,361	108,025	666	659	+7	+1·0	117	5·6
Gokarna	89	73	*9,808*	9,212	*39,936*	19,758	20,178	43,446	449	477	−28	−5·8	110	4·0
Total ...	512	774	*74,661*	72,300	*297,122*	145,117	152,005	294,809	580	576	+4	+0·6	146	3·9
DISTRICT TOTAL ...	2,144	3,627	282,122	257,967	1,250,946	605,665	645,281	1,228,790	583	572	+11	+1·9	132	4·4

DISTRICT KHULNA.

SADAR SUBDIVISION.														
Khulna	181	227	*25,084*	18,043	*142,015*	75,156	66,859	127,390	785	704	+81	+11·5	139	5·6
Dumuria	182	184	*14,744*	10,273	*79,003*	40,461	38,542	74,991	434	412	+22	+5·3	81	5·3
Baitaghata	97	146	*6,084*	4,540	*37,038*	19,870	17,168	37,501	382	387	−5	−1·2	63	6·0
Paikgachha	189	335	*13,153*	9,963	*83,437*	45,384	38,053	70,478	441	373	+68	+18·2	70	6·3
Total ...	649	892	*59,065*	42,818	*341,493*	180,871	160,622	310,360	526	478	+48	+10·0	91	5·7
BAGHERHAT SUB-DIVISION.														
Bagherhat	229	390	*28,852*	25,200	*151,778*	79,825	71,953	137,818	663	602	+61	+10·1	126	5·2
Mullahat	111	115	*9,648*	6,606	*59,124*	29,850	29,274	50,478	533	455	+78	+17·1	87	6·1
Rampal	159	210	*9,587*	7,492	*55,676*	31,054	24,622	49,827	350	313	+37	+11·8	60	5·8
Morellganj	180	234	*15,087*	9,881	*73,981*	40,795	33,186	62,670	411	348	+63	+18·1	84	4·9
Total ...	679	949	*63,174*	49,179	*340,559*	181,524	159,035	300,793	502	443	+59	+13·3	93	5·3
SATKHIRA SUB-DIVISION.														
Satkhira	138	217	*19,527*	14,676	*103,634*	52,699	50,935	96,614	751	700	+51	+7·2	142	5·3
Kalaroa	89	159	*15,633*	15,064	*79,775*	39,514	40,261	81,398	896	915	−19	−2·0	176	5·1
Magura	126	227	*16,699*	11,575	*91,044*	46,009	45,035	82,341	723	653	+70	+10·7	133	5·4
Asasuni	137	254	*10,550*	6,010	*71,694*	39,075	32,619	62,412	523	456	+67	+14·6	77	6·7
Kaliganj	259	511	*22,090*	16,901	*149,453*	78,289	71,164	146,130	577	564	+13	+2·3	85	6·7
Total ...	749	1,368	*84,499*	64,226	*495,600*	255,586	240,014	468,795	682	628	+59	+5·7	113	5·8
DISTRICT TOTAL ...	2,077	3,209	206,738	156,223	1,177,652	617,981	559,671	1,079,948	567	520	+47	+9·0	100	5·6
PRESIDENCY DIVISION TOTAL (excluding Calcutta and Suburbs)...	12,041	20,356	1,493,696	1,272,174	7,783,141	3,910,726	3,872,415	7,527,328	646	625	+21	+3·3	124	5·2

RAJSHAHI DIVISION.

DISTRICT DINAJPUR.

Subdivisions and Thánas.	Area in square miles.	Number of towns and villages.	Occupied houses.		Population in 1891.			Both sexes, 1881.	Number of persons per square mile.				Number in 1891.	
			1891.	1881.	Both sexes.	Males.	Females.		1891.	1881.	Variation.	Percentage of variation.	Houses per square mile.	Persons per occupied house.
SADAR SUBDIVISION.														
Dinajpur	394	718	*33,374*	38,830	*208,598*	108,765	99,833	212,386	529	539	−10	−1·8	85	6·2
Hemtabad	243	469	*15,900*	13,601	*84,551*	44,141	40,410	85,287	348	351	−3	−0·8	65	5·3
Kaliganj	300	546	*17,335*	17,750	*100,646*	51,689	48,957	94,883	335	316	+19	+6·0	57	5·8
Bansihari	257	631	*15,299*	14,735	*83,288*	42,891	40,397	81,965	324	319	+5	+1·6	59	5·4
Birganj	304	444	*24,536*	24,296	*138,009*	72,455	65,547	139,891	454	460	−6	−1·3	80	5·6
Patnitolla	262	634	*13,349*	12,015	*78,927*	41,319	37,608	69,238	301	264	+37	+14·0	50	5·9
Mahadevpur	171	444	*11,166*	11,534	*73,265*	37,667	35,598	67,265	428	393	+35	+8·9	65	6·5
Porsha	202	306	*8,949*	7,574	*50,634*	27,222	23,412	48,586	251	241	+10	+4·1	44	5·6
Patiram	291	686	*12,070*	12,657	*75,226*	39,621	35,605	70,661	259	243	+16	+6·6	41	6·2
Gangarampur	263	447	*14,092*	12,359	*79,594*	41,684	37,910	74,383	303	283	+20	+7·0	54	5·6
Chintaman	160	380	*9,320*	9,451	*54,164*	29,005	25,159	52,058	339	325	+14	+4·3	58	5·8
Parbatipur	166	226	*11,346*	11,196	*69,159*	36,303	32,856	66,708	417	402	+15	+3·7	68	6·0
Nawabganj	238	484	*12,234*	10,178	*66,375*	35,001	31,374	61,637	279	259	+20	+7·7	51	5·4
Total ...	3,251	6,393	*198,863*	196,175	*1,162,429*	607,763	554,666	1,124,967	358	346	+12	+3·4	61	5·8
THAKURGAON SUB-DIVISION.														
Thakurgaon	441	439	*39,696*	38,558	*224,620*	115,754	108,866	220,397	509	500	+9	+1·8	90	5·6
Ranisankail	189	397	*19,080*	16,565	*74,042*	38,192	35,850	75,102	392	397	−5	−1·2	101	3·8
Pirganj	237	447	*17,976*	17,349	*94,744*	50,338	44,406	93,880	400	396	+4	+1·0	76	5·2
Total ...	867	1,283	*76,752*	72,471	*393,406*	204,284	189,122	389,379	454	449	+5	+1·1	89	5·1
DISTRICT TOTAL ...	4,118	7,676	275,615	268,647	1,555,835	812,047	743,788	1,514,346	378	368	+10	+2·7	67	5·6

DISTRICT OF RAJSHAHI.

Subdivisions and Thánas.	Area in square miles.	Number of towns and villages.	Occupied houses, 1891.	Occupied houses, 1881.	Population 1891, Both sexes.	Males.	Females.	Both sexes, 1881.	Persons per sq. mile, 1891.	1881.	Variation.	Percentage of variation.	Houses per square mile.	Persons per occupied house.
SADAR SUBDIVISION.														
Boalia	122	422	*21,456*	17,979	*98,874*	50,629	48,245	100,887	810	827	−17	−2·0	176	4·6
Tanor	178	385	*16,282*	14,141	*86,952*	43,292	43,660	85,009	489	481	+8	+1·6	91	5·3

Godagari	173	357	*8,707*	7,282	*46,780*	24,126	22,654	43,799	270	253	+17	+6·7	60	5·3
Putia	140	309	*18,713*	16,721	*95,748*	48,514	47,234	121,238	684	866	−182	−21·0	134	5·1
Charghat	154	369	*25,028*	21,226	*124,224*	60,651	63,573	117,086	807	760	+47	+6·1	163	4·9
Baghmara	142	439	*20,137*	18,879	*119,000*	59,270	59,730	121,581	838	856	−18	−2·1	142	5·9
Total ...	909	2,281	*110,323*	96,228	*571,578*	286,482	285,096	590,200	629	649	−20	−3·1	121	5·1
NAUGAON SUB-DIVISION.														
Naugaon	139	304	*15,957*	13,454	*96,262*	48,643	47,619	85,840	693	618	+75	+12·1	115	6·0
Manda	299	569	*20,910*	17,080	*113,848*	57,230	56,618	103,308	381	346	+35	+10·1	70	5·4
Panchupur	166	356	*15,131*	12,413	*88,137*	44,209	43,928	78,902	534	478	+56	+11·7	92	5·8
Total ...	603	1,219	*51,998*	42,947	*298,247*	150,082	148,165	263,050	495	445	+50	+11·2	88	5·7
NATOR SUBDIVISION.														
Nator	199	456	*27,479*	26,713	*142,039*	68,921	73,118	153,662	714	772	−58	−7·5	138	5·1
Singra	310	649	*21,669*	20,414	*117,494*	58,844	58,650	112,743	379	364	+15	+4·1	70	5·4
Burigram	194	341	*23,477*	22,648	*116,580*	56,897	59,683	121,654	601	627	−26	−4·1	121	4·9
Lalpur	116	273	*13,446*	14,580	*67,398*	33,112	34,286	84,062	586	739	−153	−20·7	117	5·0
Total ...	818	1,719	*86,071*	84,355	*443,511*	217,774	225,737	472,921	542	578	−36	−6·2	105	5·1
DISTRICT TOTAL ...	2,330	5,219	248,392	223,530	1,313,336	654,338	658,998	1,331,171	564	571	−7	−1·2	107	5·2

DISTRICT RANGPUR.

SADAR SUBDIVISION.														
Rangpur	183	230	*28,473*	24,137	*132,081*	68,724	63,357	124,607	722	680	+42	+6·1	156	4·6
Kaliganj	264	161	*29,813*	28,848	*149,096*	77,071	72,025	155,097	565	589	−24	−4·1	113	5·0
Mahiganj	170	205	*23,202*	27,017	*110,134*	57,331	52,803	129,538	648	762	−114	−14·9	136	4·6
Badarganj	167	108	*11,866*	16,325	*87,720*	44,489	43,231	88,619	526	531	−6	−1·1	71	7·3
Mithapukhur	199	324	*19,085*	19,698	*99,341*	50,482	48,859	99,053	499	498	+1	+0·2	96	5·2
Pirganj	168	407	*13,089*	13,559	*6,8016*	35,601	32,415	69,008	430	437	−7	−1·6	83	5·1
Total ...	1,141	1,436	*125,528*	129,584	*646,388*	333,698	312,690	666,326	567	584	−17	−2·9	110	5·1
NILPHAMARI SUB-DIVISION.														
Dimla	192	239	*19,707*	17,086	*136,697*	70,383	66,314	138,760	712	723	−11	−1·5	103	6·9
Jaldhaka	242	148	*29,819*	21,480	*164,530*	84,053	80,477	163,672	680	676	+4	+0·6	123	5·5
Nilphamari	214	167	*24,932*	18,984	*146,537*	78,619	67,918	143,390	685	670	+15	+2·2	117	5·8
Total ...	648	554	*74,451*	57,550	*447,764*	233,055	214,709	445,822	691	688	+3	+0·4	116	6·0

DISTRICT RANGPUR—*concluded.*

Subdivisions and Thanas.	Area in square miles.	Number of towns and villages.	Occupied houses.		Population in 1891.			Both sexes, 1881.	Number of persons per square mile.				Number in 1891.	
			1891.	1881.	Both sexes.	Males.	Females.		1891.	1881.	Variation.	Percentage of variation.	Houses per square mile.	Persons per occupied house.
KURIGRAM SUB-DIVISION.														
Barabari	183	239	*24,975*	17,836	*120,521*	60,705	59,816	128,617	659	703	−44	−6·2	133	4·9
Kurigram	84	157	*9,361*	7,311	*58,911*	30,273	28,638	58,907	701	701	......	......	110	6·3
Nageswari	279	195	*25,455*	21,740	*141,094*	72,061	69,043	153,635	506	551	−45	−8·1	91	5·5
Ulipur	391	178	*31,641*	24,041	*187,185*	93,584	93,601	193,796	479	496	−17	−3·4	81	5·9
Total ...	937	769	*90,632*	70,828	*507,711*	256,613	251,098	534,964	542	571	−29	−5·0	97	5·6
GAIBANDA SUB-DIVISION.														
Gobindganj	351	655	*31,759*	33,514	*201,915*	104,247	97,668	189,027	575	539	+36	+6·6	90	6·3
Sadullapur	281	76	*31,037*	29,986	*175,079*	90,292	84,787	170,366	623	606	−17	−2·8	110	5·6
Sundarganj	128	48	*11,678*	15,634	*86,607*	43,907	42,700	91,469	677	715	−38	−5·3	91	7·4
Total ...	760	779	*74,467*	79,134	*463,601*	238,446	225,155	450,862	610	593	+17	+2·8	98	6·2
DISTRICT TOTAL ...	3,486	3,537	365,078	337,096	2,065,464	1,061,812	1,003,652	2,097,964	592	602	−10	−1·6	105	5·6

DISTRICT BOGRA.

Subdivisions and Thanas.	Area in square miles.	Number of towns and villages.	Occupied houses, 1891.	Occupied houses, 1881.	Population in 1891, Both sexes.	Males.	Females.	Both sexes, 1881.	Persons per sq. mile, 1891.	1881.	Variation.	Percentage of variation.	Houses per square mile.	Persons per occupied house.
Bogra	381	930	*42,107*	25,349	*254,654*	128,613	126,041	232,872	705	645	+60	+9·3	117	6·0
Shariakandi	205	455	*20,959*	12,989	*137,135*	70,409	66,726	123,825	669	599	+70	+11·6	102	6·5
Sibganj	123	462	*11,825*	9,199	*67,449*	34,712	32,737	59,170	548	481	+67	+13·9	96	5·7
Panchbibi	203	536	*13,057*	11,153	*72,936*	39,197	33,739	66,821	359	329	+30	+9·1	64	5·5
Khetlal	119	306	*7,930*	6,556	*46,274*	23,330	22,944	39,887	389	335	+54	+16·1	67	5·8
Nawabganj	85	341	*10,074*	6,511	*44,685*	23,354	21,331	39,374	526	463	+63	+13·6	119	4·4
Adamdighi	191	660	*19,349*	15,964	*109,687*	54,813	54,874	95,063	574	498	+76	+15·2	101	5·6
Sherpur	165	533	*17,946*	11,846	*84,674*	44,488	40,186	78,739	513	477	+36	+7·5	109	4·7
DISTRICT TOTAL ...	1,452	4,223	143,233	99,569	817,494	418,916	398,578	734,751	563	506	+57	+11·2	99	5·7

DISTRICT PABNA.

SADAR SUBDIVISION.														
Pabna	297	582	*36,226*	34,881	*186,927*	91,688	94,539	189,648	627	639	−12	−1·8	122	5·1
Chatmohar	211	494	*30,462*	23,390	*134,414*	66,258	68,156	133,467	637	633	+4	+0·6	144	4·4
Dulai	259	470	*35,246*	28,284	*184,145*	90,852	93,293	182,446	711	704	+7	+0·9	136	5·2
Mathura	115	260	*18,178*	15,946	*95,709*	47,300	48,402	102,486	832	891	−59	−6·6	158	5·2
Total ...	882	1,806	*120,112*	102,501	*600,488*	296,098	304,390	608,047	681	689	−8	−1·1	136	4·9
SIRAJGANJ SUB-DIVISION.														
Sirajganj	306	562	*40,129*	26,875	*238,153*	122,361	115,792	219,185	778	716	+62	+8·6	131	5·9
Shahzadpur	212	516	*40,013*	30,553	*240,756*	116,853	123,903	220,411	1,136	1,040	+98	+9·2	189	6·0
Raiganj	221	544	*17,945*	13,666	*98,910*	51,826	47,084	92,374	448	418	+30	+7·1	81	5·5
Ulapara	218	464	*27,527*	26,852	*184,085*	90,773	93,312	171,711	844	788	+56	+7·1	128	6·6
Total ...	957	2,086	*125,614*	97,946	*761,904*	381,813	380,091	703,681	796	735	+61	+8·3	131	6·0
DISTRICT TOTAL ...	1,839	3,892	245,726	200,447	1,362,392	677,911	684,481	1,311,728	741	713	+28	+3·9	134	5·5

DISTRICT DARJEELING.

Darjeeling		286	*12,735*		*60,963*	32,827	28,136							4·7
Kalimpong	726	176	*4,994*	11,801	*26,631*	14,015	12,616	65,001	145	90	+55	+61·1	30	5·3
Jor Bangala		126	*3,770*		*18,078*	9,480	8,598							4·7
Kurseong	185	331	*8,659*	5,253	*44,645*	24,856	19,789	28,179	241	152	+89	+58·5	47	5·1
Siliguri	253	400	*14,975*	11,975	*72,997*	41,868	31,129	61,465	289	247	+42	+17·0	59	4·8
DISTRICT TOTAL ...	1,164	1,319	45,126	29,028	223,314	123,046	100,268	155,645	192	134	+58	+43·2	+39	4·9

DISTRICT JALPAIGURI.

SUBDIVISIONS AND THÁNAS.	Area in square miles.	Number of towns and villages.	OCCUPIED HOUSES.		POPULATION IN 1891.			Both sexes, 1881.	NUMBER OF PERSONS PER SQUARE MILE.				NUMBER IN 1891.	
			1891.	1881.	Both sexes.	Males.	Females.		1891.	1881.	Variation.	Percentage of variation.	Houses per square mile.	Persons per occupied house.
SADAR SUBDIVISION.														
Jalpaiguri	184	365	*13,635*	12,744	*82,908*	44,130	38,778	75,418	451	410	+41	+10·0	74	6·0
Rajganj	} 324 {	229	*8,988*	} 11,598 {	*54,078*	28,131	25,947	} 79,718						
*Titalya**		92	*3,320*		*20,923*	10,677	10,246		231	246	−15	−6·0	38	6·0
Boda	381	744	*29,535*	33,187	*166,378*	86,626	79,752	178,643	437	469	−32	−6·8	78	5·6
Patgram	104	271	*12,668*	11,415	*60,101*	30,983	29,118	64,636	578	622	−44	−7·1	122	4·7
Mainaguri	360	477	*18,385*	12,368	*99,129*	53,452	45,670	77,329	275	215	+60	+27·9	51	5·3
Dam-Dim	322	539	*18,560*	5,404	*83,865*	47,727	36,138	32,453	260	101	+159	+157·4	58	4·5
Total ...	1,675	2,717	*105,091*	86,716	*567,375*	301,726	265,649	508,191	339	303	+36	+11·8	63	5·3
ALIPORE SUBDIVISION.														
Alipore	786	210	*7,408*	4,295	*41,640*	22,852	18,788	38,066	53	41	+12	+29·2	9	5·6
Salbari	501	404	*13,074*	3,784	*72,337*	40,081	32,256	40,819	144	81	+63	+77·7	26	5·5
Total ...	1,287	614	*20,482*	8,079	*113,977*	62,933	51,044	72,905	89	57	+32	+56·1	16	5·5
DISTRICT TOTAL ...	2,962	3,331	125,573	94,795	681,352	364,659	316,693	581,096	230	196	+34	+17·3	42	5·4
RAJSHAHI DIVISION TOTAL	17,551	29,197	1,448,743	1,253,112	8,019,187	4,112,729	3,906,458	7,726,701	462	445	+17	+3·8	83	5·5

* Independent outpost.

DACCA DIVISION.

DISTRICT DACCA.

Subdivisions and Thánas.	Area in square miles.	Number of towns and villages.	Occupied houses.		Population in 1891.			Both sexes, 1881.	Number of persons per square mile.				Number in 1891.	
			1891.	1881.	Both sexes.	Males.	Females.		1891.	1881.	Variation.	Percentage of variation.	Houses per square mile.	Persons per occupied house.
SADAR SUBDIVISION.														
Lalbagh	6	1	16,191	12,149	83,633	46,498	37,135	80,358	13,939	13,293	+646	+4·8	2,699	5·1
Kapasia	420	521	24,214	17,468	142,598	74,381	68,217	119,730	339	285	+54	+18·9	58	5·8
Sabhar	370	833	37,272	30,734	207,474	100,096	107,378	175,420	561	474	+87	+18·3	101	5·5
Nawabganj	160	344	33,734	22,029	170,697	81,350	89,347	155,583	1,067	972	+95	+9·7	211	5·0
Keraniganj	310	809	33,179	25,036	186,534	91,472	95,062	164,090	602	529	+73	+13·7	107	5·6
Total ...	1,266	2,508	144,590	108,016	790,936	393,797	397,139	695,181	625	549	+76	+13·8	114	5·4
NARAINGANJ SUB-DIVISION.														
Narainganj	116	715	22,143	13,742	138,205	75,950	62,255	103,760	1,191	894	+297	+33·2	191	6·2
Rupganj	227	824	33,209	13,480	197,052	100,172	96,880	163,944	868	722	+146	+20·2	146	5·9
Raipura	298	633	42,937	26,858	239,259	123,343	115,916	202,738	803	680	+123	+18·0	144	5·5
Total ...	641	2,172	98,289	54,080	574,516	299,465	275,051	470,442	896	734	+162	+22·0	153	5·8
MANIKGANJ SUB-DIVISION.														
Manikganj	208	528	37,012	35,546	200,038	98,094	101,944	184,518	962	887	+75	+8·4	178	5·4
Jafarganj	172	534	29,009	29,323	148,753	73,207	75,546	143,807	865	836	+29	+3·4	169	5·1
Harirampur	109	319	20,997	22,545	100,308	49,390	50,918	100,332	920	920	...	...	193	4·7
Total ...	489	1,381	87,011	87,414	449,099	220,691	228,408	428,657	918	877	+41	+4·6	178	5·1
MUNSHIGANJ SUB-DIVISION.														
Munshiganj	198	456	51,825	26,143	292,847	142,556	150,291	243,463	1,479	1,230	+249	+20·2	262	5·6
Srinagar	203	296	58,028	32,403	313,258	144,074	169,184	275,262	1,543	1,356	+187	+13·7	286	5·3
Total ...	401	752	109,853	58,546	606,105	286,630	319,475	518,725	1,511	1,294	+217	+16·7	274	5·5
DISTRICT TOTAL ...	2,797	6,813	439,736	308,056	2,420,656	1,200,583	1,220,073	2,113,005	865	755	+110	+14·5	157	5·5

DISTRICT FARIDPUR.

Subdivisions and Thánas.	Area in square miles.	Number of towns and villages.	Occupied houses.		Population in 1891.			Both sexes, 1881.	Number of persons per square mile.				Number in 1891.	
			1891.	1881.	Both sexes.	Males.	Females.		1891.	1881.	Variation.	Percentage of variation.	Houses per square mile.	Persons per occupied house.
SADAR SUBDIVISION.														
Faridpur	174	197	*19,288*	14,018	*96,985*	50,243	46,742	91,551	557	526	+31	+5·8	111	5·0
Bhusna	136	316	*21,494*	16,915	*102,182*	50,377	51,805	107,415	757	796	−39	−4·8	159	4·7
Awanpur	156	348	*21,646*	15,231	*102,948*	49,924	53,024	100,267	660	643	+17	+2·6	139	4·7
Bhanga	175	511	*37,058*	23,559	*187,889*	93,099	94,790	168,718	1,074	964	+110	+11·4	212	5·0
Mahsudpur	220	427	*30,529*	19,245	*176,418*	86,058	90,360	156,933	802	713	+89	+12·4	139	5·7
Total ...	860	1,798	*130,015*	88,968	*666,422*	329,701	336,721	624,874	775	727	+48	+6·6	151	5·1
MADARIPUR SUB-DIVISION.														
Madaripur	240	454	*34,109*	23,448	*193,548*	95,855	97,693	165,917	806	691	+115	+16·6	142	5·6
Gopalganj	171	179	*15,765*	11,554	*96,834*	48,573	48,261	85,341	566	499	+67	+13·4	92	6·1
Kotalipara	139	246	*15,080*	7,857	*79,129*	39,235	39,894	66,153	569	476	+93	+19·5	108	5·2
Palang	308	485	*55,968*	31,843	*279,084*	134,563	144,521	256,250	906	832	+74	+8·8	182	4·9
Sibchar	121	183	*22,241*	13,816	*131,852*	66,802	65,050	116,765	1,090	965	+125	+12·9	184	5·9
Total ...	979	1,547	*143,156*	88,518	*780,447*	385,028	395,419	690,426	797	705	+92	+13·0	146	5·4
GOALANDA SUB-DIVISION.														
Goalanda	140	323	*23,581*	15,458	*126,038*	67,055	58,983	106,050	900	757	+143	+18·8	168	5·3
Baliakandi	123	264	*19,047*	9,823	*97,798*	48,460	49,338	65,069	795	529	+266	+50·2	155	5·1
Pangsa	165	471	*23,618*	22,006	*126,615*	62,847	63,768	150,366	767	911	−144	−15·8	143	5·3
Total ...	428	1,058	*66,246*	47,287	*350,451*	178,362	172,089	321,485	819	751	+68	+9·0	155	5·2
DISTRICT TOTAL ...	2,267	4,403	339,417	224,773	1,797,320	893,091	904,229	1,636,785	793	722	+71	+9·8	150	5·3

DISTRICT BAKHARGANJ.

Subdivisions and Thánas.	Area in square miles.	Number of towns and villages.	Occupied houses, 1891.	Occupied houses, 1881.	Population in 1891, Both sexes.	Males.	Females.	Both sexes, 1881.	Persons per sq. mile, 1891.	1881.	Variation.	Percentage of variation.	Houses per square mile.	Persons per occupied house.
SADAR SUBDIVISION.														
Katwali (Barisal)	171	293	*29,775*	17,518	*133,356*	69,901	63,455	126,919	780	742	+38	+5·1	174	4·4
Bakharganj	153	253	*29,264*	15,638	*139,661*	71,408	68,253	135,396	913	885	+28	+3·1	191	4·7
Mehndiganj	292	391	*33,371*	19,490	*156,021*	81,015	75,006	145,711	534	499	+35	+7·0	114	4·6

Gaurnadi	262	508	41,384	20,974	208,148	102,483	105,665	184,192	794	705	+91	+12·9	158	5·0
Jhalakati	146	853	54,799	16,461	163,585	81,702	81,883	143,416	1,120	982	+138	+14·0	238	4·7
Nalchiti	87	245	17,675	9,753	78,406	39,510	38,896	78,961	901	908	−7	−0·7	203	4·4
Total ...	1,111	2,043	186,261	100,034	879,177	446,019	433,158	814,595	791	733	+58	+7·9	168	4·7
PATUAKHALI SUB-DIVISION.														
Patuakhali	266	278	37,373	18,634	194,465	99,861	94,604	173,801	731	653	+78	+11·9	140	5·2
Bauphal	160	224	20,935	11,050	111,034	57,432	53,602	95,188	694	595	+99	+16·6	131	5·3
Gulsakhali	511	344	20,551	12,597	112,054	58,898	53,156	98,732	219	193	+26	+13·4	40	5·4
Golachipa	294	316	15,572	7,339	79,182	42,678	36,504	59,037	269	201	+68	+33·8	53	5·1
Total ...	1,231	1,162	94,431	49,620	496,735	258,869	237,866	426,758	404	347	+57	+16·4	77	5·2
PIROJPUR SUB-DIVISION.														
Pirojpur	116	256	28,246	15,357	124,217	62,881	61,336	117,638	1,071	1,014	+57	+5·6	244	4·4
Bhandaria	114	104	20,473	8,286	94,774	47,570	47,204	73,352	831	643	+188	+29·2	180	4·6
Sarupkati	224	490	36,660	16,956	181,259	87,921	93,338	160,284	809	716	+93	+12·9	163	4·9
Matbaria	238	214	23,668	11,550	119,353	62,662	56,691	96,032	501	403	+98	+24·3	99	5·0
Total ...	692	1,064	109,047	52,049	519,603	261,034	258,569	447,306	751	646	+105	+16·2	158	4·7
DAKHIN SHAHBÁZPUR SUBDIVISION.														
Bhola	262	216	24,588	11,497	144,359	76,191	68,168	123,169	551	470	+81	+17·2	94	5·8
Barhanuddin	353	223	22,116	9,712	114,091	62,330	51,761	89,061	323	252	+71	+28·1	63	5·1
Total ...	615	439	46,704	21,209	258,450	138,521	119,929	212,230	420	345	+75	+21·7	76	5·5
DISTRICT TOTAL ...	3,649	4,708	436,443	222,912	2,153,965	1,104,443	1,049,522	1,900,889	590	521	+69	+13·2	120	4·9

DISTRICT MYMENSINGH.

Subdivisions and Thánas.	Area in square miles.	Number of towns and villages.	Occupied houses.		Population in 1891.			Both sexes, 1881.	Number of persons per square mile.				Number in 1891.	
			1891.	1881.	Both sexes.	Males.	Females.		1891.	1881.	Variation.	Percentage of variation.	Houses per square mile.	Persons per occupied house.
SADAR SUBDIVISION.														
Nasirabad	476	500	*43,180*	28,654	*231,425*	124,080	107,345	209,248	486	440	+46	+10·4	91	5·3
Phulpur	399	548	*29,430*	6,528	*139,029*	73,913	65,116	113,780	348	285	+63	+22·1	74	4·7
Gafargaon	443	356	*23,875*	14,916	*140,605*	73,024	67,581	117,759	317	266	+51	+19·1	54	5·9
Iswarganj	331	697	*47,394*	29,959	*249,232*	128,762	120,470	220,452	753	693	+60	+8·6	143	5·2
Phulbaria	200	156	*15,710*	10,079	*92,729*	48,168	44,561	73,598	464	368	+96	+26·0	79	5·9
Total ...	1,849	2,256	*159,589*	90,136	*853,020*	447,947	405,073	743,837	461	402	+59	+14·6	86	5·3
NETROKONA SUB-DIVISION.														
Netrokona	438	900	*40,806*	8,918	*249,550*	131,974	117,576	207,403	570	474	+96	+20·2	93	6·1
Durgapur	382	441	*23,748*	14,396	*115,727*	61,745	53,982	116,457	303	305	−2	−0·6	62	4·8
Kendua	569	516	*43,675*	37,366	*289,070*	149,425	139,645	264,255	508	465	+43	+9·2	77	6·6
Total ...	1,389	1,857	*108,229*	60,680	*654,347*	343,144	311,203	588,115	471	423	+48	+11·3	77	6·0
JAMALPUR SUB-DIVISION.														
Jamalpur	419	568	*44,963*	25,584	*243,631*	126,870	116,761	209,329	581	500	+81	+16·2	107	5·4
Diwanganj	342	123	*21,495*	10,429	*129,589*	67,051	62,538	101,372	379	296	+83	+28·0	63	6·0
Sherpur	242	294	*21,390*	18,642	*120,883*	62,926	57,957	119,092	500	492	+8	+1·6	88	5·6
Nalitabari	286	287	*16,227*	10,747	*85,639*	44,863	40,776	68,660	299	240	+59	+24·5	56	5·2
Total ...	1,289	1,272	*104,075*	65,402	*579,742*	301,710	278,032	498,453	450	387	+63	+16·2	81	5·5
TANGAIL SUBDIVISION.														
Tangail	446	878	*78,331*	52,385	*422,950*	209,586	213,364	367,484	948	802	+146	+18·2	176	5·4
Gopalpur	485	214	*58,750*	35,940	*306,886*	157,007	149,879	293,998	633	606	+27	+4·4	121	5·2
Kalihati	130	275	*17,692*	14,807	*129,639*	63,518	66,121	101,053	997	777	+220	+28·3	136	7·3
Total ...	1,061	1,367	*154,773*	103,132	*859,475*	430,111	429,364	762,535	810	709	+101	+14·2	146	5·5

KISORGANJ SUB-DIVISION.														
Kisorganj	151	390	25,197	24,269	159,311	76,915	75,396	185,003	1,009	898	+111	+12·3	166	6·0
Nikli	173	301	27,274	23,862	139,049	69,689	69,353	122,459	804	708	+96	+13·5	158	5·1
Bajitpur	420	516	39,728	36,308	934,249	119,100	116,149	214,235	558	510	+48	+9·4	95	5·8
Total ...	744	1,207	92,129	84,439	525,609	265,704	259,898	472,297	706	635	+71	+11·1	124	5·7
DISTRICT TOTAL ...	6,332	7,959	618,795	403,789	3,472,186	1,788,616	1,683,570	3,056,237	548	483	+65	+13·4	98	5·6
DACCA DIVISION TOTAL	15,046	23,883	1,834,391	1,159,530	9,844,127	4,986,733	4,857,394	8,705,916	654	578	+76	+13·2	121	5·3

CHITTAGONG DIVISION.

DISTRICT CHITTAGONG.

Subdivisions and Thánas.	Area in square miles.	Number of towns and villages.	Occupied houses.		Population in 1891.			Both sexes, 1881.	Number of persons per quare mile.				Number in 1891.	
			1891.	1881.	Both sexes.	Males.	Females.		1891.	1881.	Variation.	Percentage of variation.	Houses per square mile.	Persons per occupied house.
ADAR SUBDIVISION.														
Chittagong	53	64	18,429	13,961	89,666	45,353	44,313	75,152	1,692	1,418	+274	+19·3	348	4·8
Mirsorai	125	110	18,001	15,145	93,559	45,331	48,221	76,799	748	614	+134	+21·8	144	5·1
Kumira	106	93	15,847	13,056	67,394	32,596	34,798	58,611	636	553	+83	+15·0	150	4·2
Phatikchari	312	94	22,688	15,623	109,639	52,502	57,130	104,500	351	335	+16	+4·7	724	4·8
Hathasari	97	56	18,707	16,207	89,372	42,810	46,562	81,830	921	844	+77	+9·1	193	4·7
Raujan	240	121	32,773	29,553	159,843	75,762	84,081	144,380	666	602	+64	+10·6	137	4·8
Patia	252	208	41,751	34,430	206,564	96,078	110,486	180,448	820	716	+104	+14·5	166	4·9
Banskhali	196	126	26,640	22,169	127,799	59,392	68,400	101,758	655	522	+133	+25·4	137	4·8
Satkania	246	109	29,259	21,271	158,346	74,524	83,822	147,515	644	600	+44	+7·3	119	5·4
Total ...	1,626	981	224,095	181,415	1,102,161	524,348	577,813	970,993	678	597	+81	+13·5	138	4·9
COX'S BAZAR SUB-DIVISION.														
Cox's Bazar	267	78	13,897	11,726	69,105	33,597	35,508	62,817	259	235	+24	+10·2	52	5·0
Chakaria	232	55	8,777	7,524	46,584	22,480	24,104	38,825	201	167	+34	+20·3	38	5·3
Maiskal	183	49	7,177	5,563	37,691	17,960	19,731	29,158	206	159	+47	+29·5	39	5·2
Teknaf	255	71	6,014	5,159	34,626	17,483	17,143	30,548	136	120	+16	+13·3	24	5·7
Total ...	937	253	35,865	29,972	188,006	91,520	96,486	161,348	201	172	+29	+16·8	38	5·2
DISTRICT TOTAL ...	2,563	1,234	259,960	211,387	1,290,167	615,868	674,299	1,132,341	503	442	+61	+13·8	101	4·9

DISTRICT NOAKHALI.

Subdivisions and Thánas.	Area in square miles.	Number of towns and villages.	Occupied houses, 1891.	Occupied houses, 1881.	Population in 1891, Both sexes.	Males.	Females.	Both sexes, 1881.	Persons per square mile, 1891.	1881.	Variation.	Percentage of variation.	Houses per square mile.	Persons per occupied house.
SADAR SUBDIVISION.														
Sudharam	232	459	24,045	11,383	120,339	60,383	59,949	101,308	519	437	+82	+18·7	104	5·0
Hatia	185	39	9,916	4,176	49,346	26,571	22,775	40,295	267	218	+49	+22·4	54	4·9
Bamni	74	44	9,383	5,046	49,179	23,872	25,300	41,731	664	564	+100	+17·7	127	5·2
Ramganj	117	422	16,494	7,391	99,360	51,037	48,323	80,748	849	690	+159	+23·0	141	6·0
Lakshmipur	212	426	26,479	11,390	139,996	72,159	67,837	113,381	660	535	+125	+23·3	126	5·2

Begamganj	220	500	97,346	16,869	159,946	81,735	78,211	128,933	727	586	+141	+24·0	124	5·8
Sundwip	258	80	20,094	7,531	101,011	50,652	50,359	73,467	392	281	+111	+39·5	78	5·0
Total ...	1,298	1,970	133,667	63,685	719,163	366,409	352,754	578,797	554	446	+108	+24·2	103	5·4
FENNY SUBDIVISION.														
Fenny	216	422	30,575	12,542	166,242	81,945	84,297	132,697	770	614	+156	+25·4	142	5·4
Chhagalnaia	131	233	23,813	10,731	124,288	60,373	63,915	109,278	949	834	+115	+13·7	182	5·2
Total ...	347	655	54,388	23,273	290,530	142,318	148,212	241,975	837	697	+140	+20·0	157	5·3
DISTRICT TOTAL ...	1,645	2,625	188,055	86,958	1,009,693	508,727	500,966	820,772	614	499	+115	+23·0	114	5·3

DISTRICT TIPPERA.

SADAR SUBDIVISION.														
Comilla	180	713	97,179	15,414	157,905	81,893	76,012	139,385	877	774	+103	+13·3	151	5·8
Muradnagar	225	548	31,044	19,246	176,911	89,409	87,502	152,323	786	677	+109	+16·1	138	5·7
Daudkandi	205	646	28,393	16,791	173,068	87,045	86,023	143,222	844	699	+145	+20·7	139	6·1
Chandina	172	524	17,688	10,868	93,319	47,773	45,539	78,521	543	457	+86	+18·8	103	5·3
Chaudagram	163	578	22,795	11,206	116,688	59,838	56,850	103,218	716	633	+83	+13·1	140	5·1
Laksham	197	673	18,969	10,191	103,401	53,610	49,791	86,672	525	441	+84	+19·0	96	5·4
Subdivisional Total ...	1,142	3,682	146,068	83,716	821,285	419,568	401,717	703,540	719	616	+103	+16·7	128	5·6
BRAHMANBÁRIA SUB-DIVISION.														
Brahmanbaria	379	580	46,344	29,046	262,933	132,686	130,247	236,317	694	624	+70	+11·2	122	5·6
Kasba	157	420	26,918	14,137	127,318	64,187	63,131	114,153	811	727	+84	+11·5	171	4·7
Nabinagar	233	336	33,448	20,576	199,846	101,025	98,821	175,971	858	755	+103	+13·6	144	5·9
Subdivisional Total ...	769	1,336	106,710	63,759	590,097	297,898	292,199	526,440	767	685	+82	+11·9	139	5·5
CHANDPUR SUB-DIVISION.														
Chandpur	356	746	40,579	21,258	260,688	136,449	124,239	193,938	732	545	+187	+34·3	114	6·4
Hajiganj	224	554	19,125	10,014	110,865	57,884	52,981	90,393	495	404	+91	+22·5	85	5·8
Subdivisional Total ...	580	1,300	59,704	31,272	371,553	194,333	177,220	284,331	641	490	+151	+30·8	103	6·2
DISTRICT TOTAL ...	2,491	6,318	312,482	178,747	1,782,935	911,799	871,136	1,514,361	716	607	+109	+17·9	125	5·7

DISTRICT CHITTAGONG HILL TRACTS.

Subdivisions and Thánas.	Area in square miles.	Number of towns and villages.	Occupied houses.		Population in 1891.			Both sexes, 1881.	Number of persons per square mile.				Number in 1891.	
			1891.	1881.	Both sexes.	Males.	Females.		1891.	1881.	Variation.	Percentage of variation.	Houses per square mile.	Persons per occupied house.
Chakma Circle	......	419	*7,518*	4,819	*41,633*	23,753	17,880	28,843	......	......	......	+55·0	......	5·5
Mong Raja's Circle	......	178	*4,259*	6,788	*22,510*	12,096	10,414	37,989	......	......	......	−40·7	......	5·2
Bhomong's Circle	......	398 (Bhomong's Circle and Sangu Khasmahal)	*7,210*	2,980	*37,724*	20,209	17,515	19,511	......	......	......	+93·3	......	5·2
Sangu Khasmahal	......		*215*	264	*1,096*	583	513	1,374	......	......	......	−20·2	......	5·0
Head-Quarters Khasmahal ...	......	24	*1,423*	152	*3,727*	2,366	1,361	15,880 (Head-Quarters Khasmahal and Forest Reserves)	......	......	......	−72·7 (Head-Quarters Khasmahal and Forest Reserves)	......	2·6
Forest Reserves	......	10	*89*	......	*596*	559	37		......	......	......		......	6·7
DISTRICT TOTAL ...	5,419	1,029	20,714	16,003	107,286	59,566	47,720	101,597	20	19	+1	+5·2	4	5·1
CHITTAGONG DIVISION TOTAL	12,118	11,208	781,211	492,095	4,190,081	2,095,960	2,094,121	3,569,071	345	294	+51	+17·3	64	5·3
BENGAL PROPER TOTAL (excluding Calcutta and Suburbs)	70,470	115,938	7,254,430	5,584,672	37,525,354	18,906,729	18,618,625	34,922,970	532	495	+37	+7·4	102	5·1

PATNA DIVISION.

DISTRICT OF PATNA.

Subdivisions and Thánas.	Area in square miles.	Number of towns and villages.	Occupied houses.		Population in 1891.			Both sexes, 1881.	Number of persons per square mile.				Number in 1891.	
			1891.	1881.	Both sexes.	Males.	Females.		1891.	1881.	Variation.	Percentage of variation.	Houses per square mile.	Persons per occupied house.
SADAR SUBDIVISION.														
Pirbahor		4	*4,630*	3,878	*25,734*	13,604	12,130	24,744	......	......	......	+4·0	......	5·5
Sultanganj		20	*3,742*	2,726	*17,989*	8,823	9,166	16,186	......	......	......	+11·1	......	4·8
Alamganj		186	*6,767*	5,119	*29,501*	14,291	15,210	30,963	......	......	......	−4·7	......	4·3
Khwaja Kalan	46	3	*9,931*	13,307	*43,797*	21,077	22,720	42,652	......	......	......	+2·7	......	4·7
Chauk Kalan		4	*6,639*	5,248	*28,348*	13,835	14,513	32,233	......	......	......	−12·0	......	4·2
Malsalami		53	*7,345*	6,335	*34,830*	16,936	17,894	36,134	......	......	......	−3·6	......	4·7
Bankipur	94	262	*16,745*	14,163	*100,866*	49,223	51,643	97,008	1,073	1,032	+41	+3·9	178	6·0
Bikram	281	557	*27,314*	25,909	*180,519*	89,287	91,225	180,362	642	642	......	......	97	6·6
Masaudhi Basurg	193	483	*19,076*	18,397	*123,239*	60,422	62,817	120,613	639	625	+14	+2·2	99	6·4
Total ...	614	1,572	*101,489*	96,083	*584,816*	287,498	297,318	580,865	952	946	+6	+0·6	166	5·7
DINAPUR SUBDIVISION.														
Dinapur	25	109	*13,379*	12,513	*72,111*	34,963	37,148	67,612	2,884	2,704	+180	+6·6	535	5·4
Maner	118	193	*15,739*	14,528	*95,149*	44,403	50,746	98,516	806	835	−29	−3·4	133	6·0
Total ...	143	302	*29,118*	27,041	*167,260*	79,366	87,894	166,128	1,169	1,162	+7	+0·6	204	5·7
BARH SUBDIVISION.														
Barh	267	643	*30,344*	28,784	*204,871*	100,153	104,718	194,199	767	727	+40	+5·5	114	6·7
Fatuha	98	271	*14,390*	14,575	*89,266*	43,394	45,872	88,061	911	898	+13	+1·4	147	6·2
Mukameh	161	175	*13,573*	11,100	*114,119*	55,942	58,177	93,894	709	583	+126	+21·6	84	8·4
Total ...	526	1,089	*58,307*	54,459	*408,256*	199,489	208,767	376,074	776	715	+61	+8·5	111	7·0
BIHAR SUBDIVISION.														
Bihar	297	607	*43,315*	44,764	*263,066*	128,193	134,873	282,283	886	950	−64	−6·7	146	6·0
Hilsa	146	364	*16,736*	28,776	*96,915*	48,312	48,603	176,075	736	743	−7	−0·9	116	5·8
Chandi	91	219	*12,794*		*77,558*	38,455	39,103						140	6·1
Islampur or Athasarai ...	117	230	*13,920*	13,263	*81,401*	40,406	40,995	78,932	696	675	+21	+3·1	119	5·8
Sila	142	290	*14,637*	15,124	*89,732*	44,013	45,719	91,477	632	644	−12	−1·8	103	6·1
Total ...	793	1,700	*101,332*	101,927	*608,672*	299,379	309,293	628,767	768	793	−25	−3·1	128	6·0
DISTRICT TOTAL ...	2,076	4,663	290,246	278,509	1,769,004	865,732	903,272	1,751,834	852	844	+8	+0·9	140	6·1

DISTRICT OF GAYA.

Subdivisions and Thánas.	Area in square miles.	Number of towns and villages.	Occupied houses.		Population in 1891.			Both sexes, 1881.	Number of persons per square mile.				Number in 1891.	
			1891.	1881.	Both sexes.	Males.	Females.		1891.	1881.	Variation.	Percentage of variation.	Houses per square mile.	Persons per occupied house.
SADAR SUBDIVISION.														
Gaya Town	7	1	*14,580*	15,010	*80,383*	40,893	39,490	76,415	11,483	10,916	+567	+5·1	2,083	5·5
Mufassal Gaya	402	737	*35,885*	34,840	*180,017*	87,929	92,088	202,248	448	503	−55	−10·9	89	5·0
Atri	250	532	*21,358*	15,649	*123,671*	61,031	62,640	96,839	495	387	+108	+27·9	85	5·8
Tikari	283	709	*33,235*	27,534	*184,654*	90,752	93,902	176,805	652	625	+27	+4·3	117	5·5
Sherghati	547	671	*27,186*	27,499	*154,229*	73,297	80,932	156,646	282	286	−4	−1·3	50	5·6
Barachati	416	570	*21,046*	19,075	*109,488*	53,666	55,822	109,878	263	264	−1	−0·3	51	5·2
Total ...	1,905	3,220	*153,290*	139,607	*832,442*	407,568	424,874	818,831	437	430	−7	−1·6	80	5·4
NAWADA SUBDIVISION.														
Nawada	462	1,187	*51,681*	47,015	*282,923*	138,266	144,657	302,892	612	656	−44	−6·7	112	5·4
Pakribarawan	213	280	*15,303*	14,693	*81,783*	40,826	40,957	88,821	384	417	−33	−7·9	72	5·3
Rajauli	280	434	*14,867*	13,841	*74,859*	36,228	38,631	83,308	267	298	−31	−10·4	53	5·0
Total ...	955	1,901	*81,851*	75,549	*439,565*	215,320	224,245	475,021	460	497	−37	−7·4	86	5·3
JAHANABAD SUB-DIVISION.														
Jahanabad	402	1,084	*48,659*	46,300	*278,895*	139,118	139,777	283,857	694	706	−12	−1·6	121	5·7
Arwal	204	302	*18,760*	14,867	*114,922*	56,768	58,154	101,838	563	497	+66	+13·2	92	6·1
Total ...	606	1,386	*67,419*	61,167	*393,817*	195,886	197,931	385,189	650	636	+14	+2·2	111	5·8
AURANGABAD SUB-DIVISION.														
Aurangabad	667	1,263	*47,939*	39,550	*258,373*	121,221	137,152	245,429	387	368	+19	+5·1	71	5·4
Daudnagar	241	1,412	*15,373*	15,203	*106,101*	52,881	53,220	102,166	440	424	+16	+3·7	63	6·9
Nabinagar	338	913	*17,583*	15,728	*108,033*	52,135	55,898	98,046	320	290	+30	+10·3	52	6·1
Total ...	1,246	3,588	*80,095*	70,481	*472,507*	226,237	246,270	445,641	379	358	+21	+5·8	64	5·9
DISTRICT TOTAL ...	4,712	10,095	382,655	346,794	2,138,331	1,045,011	1,093,320	2,124,682	454	451	+3	+0·6	81	5·5

DISTRICT SHAHABAD.

SADAR SUBDIVISION.														
Arrah	354	472	49,607	39,774	350,119	162,932	187,180	312,640	989	883	+106	+12·0	140	7·0
Belaur	252	257	31,944	24,610	198,855	94,598	104,257	195,879	789	777	+12	+1·5	124	6·3
Piru	309	391	29,643	22,623	197,963	95,980	101,983	179,498	641	581	+60	+10·3	96	6·6
Total ...	915	1,120	110,494	87,007	746,930	363,510	393,420	688,011	816	752	+64	+8·5	121	6·7
BAXAR SUBDIVISION.														
Baxar	309	363	32,622	22,168	166,438	80,736	85,702	163,255	539	528	+11	+2·0	105	5·1
Dumraon	347	346	47,966	37,265	271,711	128,106	143,605	259,938	783	749	+34	+4·5	138	5·6
Total ...	656	709	80,588	59,433	438,149	208,842	229,307	423,193	668	645	+23	+3·5	123	5·4
SASARAM SUBDIVISION.														
Sasaram	691	552	32,920	25,018	164,074	78,351	85,723	155,760	237	225	+12	+5·3	47	5·0
Kharghar	266	413	19,796	16,494	103,555	50,671	52,884	104,647	389	393	−4	−1·0	74	5·2
Dhangain	367	543	33,371	22,692	182,346	88,672	93,674	179,916	497	490	+7	+1·4	91	5·4
Dehri	169	204	21,794	13,414	83,381	41,084	42,297	78,884	493	466	+27	+5·7	129	3·8
Total ...	1,493	1,712	107,111	77,618	533,356	258,778	274,578	519,207	357	348	+9	+2·5	72	4·9
BHABHUA SUBDIVISION.														
Bhabhua	914	785	35,547	27,212	181,965	89,658	92,307	171,883	199	188	+11	+5·8	39	5·1
Mohania	387	557	26,438	22,104	162,937	80,011	82,926	150,413	421	389	+32	+8·2	68	6·1
Total ...	1,301	1,342	61,985	49,316	344,902	169,669	175,233	322,236	265	248	+17	+6·8	48	5·5
DISTRICT TOTAL ...	4,365	4,883	360,178	273,374	2,063,337	990,799	1,072,538	1,952,647	473	447	+26	+5·8	85	5·7

DISTRICT DARBHANGA.

SADAR SUBDIVISION.														
Darbhanga	428	692	79,761	50,726	441,452	218 129	223,323	403,519	1,031	943	+88	+9·3	170	6·0
Bahera	447	476	55,984	38,331	345,559	170,033	175,526	309,875	773	693	+80	+11·5	125	6·1
Roshra	347	453	36,864	47,118	261,795	130,731	131,064	256,605	754	739	+15	+2·0	106	7·1
Total ...	1,222	1,621	165,609	136,170	1,048,806	518,893	529,913	969,999	858	794	+64	+8·0	135	6·3

DISTRICT DARBHANGA—*concluded.*

Subdivisions and Thanas.	Area in square miles.	Number of towns and villages.	Occupied houses. 1891.	Occupied houses. 1881.	Population in 1891. Both sexes.	Population in 1891. Males.	Population in 1891. Females.	Both sexes, 1881.	Number of persons per square mile. 1891.	Number of persons per square mile. 1881.	Number of persons per square mile. Variation.	Number of persons per square mile. Percentage of variation.	Number in 1891. Houses per square mile.	Number in 1891. Persons per occupied house.
MADHUBANI SUB-DIVISION.														
Madhubani	276	355	*52,218*	31,438	*244,229*	120,036	124,193	211,772	885	767	+118	+15·3	189	4·6
Benipati	292	330	*41,344*	34,507	*244,815*	119,721	125,094	247,288	838	847	−9	−1·0	141	5·9
Khajauli	323	316	*36,360*	26,301	*228,990*	113,418	115,572	177,994	709	551	+158	+28·6	112	6·2
Phulparas	458	444	*62,780*	39,669	*296,666*	146,240	150,426	267,500	648	584	+64	+10·9	137	4·7
Total ...	1,349	1,444	*192,709*	131,915	*1,014,700*	499,415	515,285	904,554	752	671	+81	+12·0	143	5·2
SAMASTIPUR SUB-DIVISION.														
Samastipur	296	374	*42,084*	37,044	*305,181*	145,336	159,845	306,493	1,031	1,035	−4	−0·3	142	7·2
Maniarpur	195	219	*23,740*	23,230	*170,992*	82,728	88,264	169,946	877	871	+6	+0·6	122	7·2
Dalsingsarai	273	232	*34,077*	33,845	*262,276*	124,613	137,663	279,504	961	1,024	−63	−6·1	125	7·6
Total ...	764	825	*99,901*	94,119	*738,449*	352,677	385,772	755,943	966	989	−23	−2·3	131	7·3
DISTRICT TOTAL ...	3,335	3,890	458,212	362,204	2,801,955	1,370,985	1,430,970	2,630,496	840	789	+51	+6·4	137	6·1

DISTRICT MUZAFFARPUR.

Subdivisions and Thanas.	Area in square miles.	Number of towns and villages.	Occupied houses. 1891.	Occupied houses. 1881.	Population in 1891. Both sexes.	Population in 1891. Males.	Population in 1891. Females.	Both sexes, 1881.	Number of persons per square mile. 1891.	Number of persons per square mile. 1881.	Number of persons per square mile. Variation.	Number of persons per square mile. Percentage of variation.	Number in 1891. Houses per square mile.	Number in 1891. Persons per occupied house.
SADAR SUBDIVISION.														
Muzaffarpur	572	939	*91,197*	80,752	*572,749*	277,442	295,307	543,347	1,001	950	+51	+5·3	159	6·2
Paru	418	556	*54,081*	41,643	*309,143*	144,095	165,048	292,456	740	700	+40	+5·7	129	5·7
Katra	228	271	*26,084*	23,286	*191,078*	93,932	97,146	186,966	838	820	+18	+2·1	114	7·3
Total ...	1,218	1,766	*171,362*	145,681	*1,072,970*	515,469	557,501	1,022,769	881	840	+41	+4·6	141	6·2
SITAMARHI SUBDIVISION.														
Sitamarhi	357	341	*53,745*	44,414	*318,084*	158,465	159,619	294,262	891	824	+67	+8·1	151	5·9
Sheohar	203	200	*29,459*	25,054	*182,757*	91,435	91,322	172,655	900	851	+49	+5·7	145	6·2
Pupri	249	210	*37,502*	28,276	*232,114*	114,502	117,612	206,429	932	829	+103	+12·4	151	6·1
Belsand	205	225	*32,853*	23,606	*191,441*	94,799	96,642	164,548	934	803	+131	+16·3	160	5·8
Total ...	1,014	976	*153,559*	121,350	*924,396*	459,201	465,195	837,894	912	826	+86	+10·4	151	6·0

HAJIPUR SUBDIVISION.														
Hajipur	286	488	*49,180*	36,125	*264,092*	122,296	141,796	270,291	923	845	−22	−2·3	172	5·3
Lalganj	171	307	*29,903*	23,418	*154,781*	70,023	84,758	157,800	905	923	−18	−1·9	175	5·1
Mahua	314	587	*56,697*	41,680	*295,206*	138,385	156,821	293,306	940	934	+6	+0·6	181	5·2
Total ...	771	1,382	*135,780*	101,223	*714,079*	330,704	383,375	721,397	926	936	−10	−1·0	176	5·2
DISTRICT TOTAL ...	3,003	4,104	460,701	368,254	2,711,445	1,305,374	1,406,071	2,582,060	903	860	+43	+5·0	153	5·8

DISTRICT SARAN.

SADAR SUBDIVISION.														
Chapra	333	488	*69,275*	52,177	*380,881*	172,606	208,275	350,790	1,144	1,053	+91	+8·6	208	5·5
Manjhi	142	216	*28,322*	19,869	*156,235*	68,665	87,570	149,671	1,100	1,054	+46	+4·3	199	5·5
Parsa	269	476	*45,308*	32,170	*236,159*	104,335	131,824	231,435	878	860	+18	+2·0	168	5·2
Mashrak	178	241	*26,579*	20,348	*145,789*	64,933	80,849	151,494	819	851	−32	−3·7	149	5·4
Sonpur	109	153	*21,281*	18,072	*113,052*	48,490	64,562	120,394	1,037	1,105	−68	−6·1	195	5·3
Total ...	1,031	1,552	*190,765*	142,636	*1,032,109*	459,029	573,080	1,003,784	1,001	974	+27	+2·7	185	5·4
GOPALGANJ SUB-DIVISION.														
Gopalganj	358	411	*48,837*	36,783	*275,023*	129,162	145,861	260,385	768	727	+41	+5·6	136	5·6
Mirganj	435	923	*63,600*	48,385	*359,607*	174,412	186,195	307,403	827	707	+120	+16·9	148	5·6
Total ..	793	1,334	*112,437*	85,168	*634,630*	303,574	331,056	567,788	800	716	+84	+11·7	142	5·6
SEWAN SUBDIVISION.														
Sewan	330	564	*59,231*	43,269	*334,366*	156,044	178,322	301,713	1,013	911	+102	+11·1	179	5·6
Darauli	253	445	*41,466*	30,859	*226,040*	107,030	119,010	213,671	893	844	+49	+5·8	164	5·4
Basantpur	246	401	*42,369*	27,273	*240,332*	108,249	132,083	210,810	977	857	+120	+14·0	172	5·6
Total ...	829	1,410	*143,066*	101,401	*800,738*	371,323	429,415	726,094	968	876	+90	+10·2	173	5·5
DISTRICT TOTAL ...	2,653	4,296	446,268	329,205	2,467,477	1,133,926	1,333,551	2,297,866	930	866	+64	+7·3	168	5·5

DISTRICT CHAMPARAN.

SUBDIVISIONS AND THÁNAS.	Area in square miles.	Number of towns and villages.	OCCUPIED HOUSES.		POPULATION IN 1891.			Both sexes, 1881.	NUMBER OF PERSONS PER SQUARE MILE.				NUMBER IN 1891.	
			1891.	1881.	Both sexes.	Males.	Females.		1891.	1881.	Variation.	Percentage of variation.	Houses per square mile.	Persons per occupied house.
SADAR SUBDIVISION.														
Motihari	288	728	*29,409*	27,342	*190,907*	97,294	92,913	178,431	660	620	+40	+6·4	102	6·4
Govindganj	272	866	*26,795*	24,398	*179,040*	88,964	90,076	164,983	658	607	+51	+8·4	99	6·7
Kesaria	269	236	*29,857*	25,924	*183,673*	88,818	94,855	177,682	683	661	+22	+3·3	111	6·1
*Madhuban**	129	342	*16,829*	16,630	*109,542*	53,427	56,115	105,066	849	815	+34	+4·1	130	6·5
Dhaka	336	420	*36,784*	35,188	*269,719*	134,364	135,355	253,998	803	756	+47	+6·2	109	7·3
Adapur	224	233	*26,069*	24,511	*167,419*	84,559	82,860	138,490	747	618	+129	+20·8	116	6·4
Total ...	1,518	2,826	*165,736*	154,067	*1,099,600*	547,426	552,174	1,018,673	724	671	+53	+7·8	109	6·6
BETTIAH SUBDIVISION.														
Bettiah	537	989	*56,306*	57,186	*334,087*	169,167	164,920	323,471	622	602	+20	+3·3	105	5·9
Hardi	766	657	*37,429*	33,106	*209,724*	108,445	101,279	182,044	274	238	+36	+15·1	49	5·6
Bagaha	710	646	*38,088*	38,440	*216,054*	111,097	104,957	197,420	304	278	+26	+9·3	54	5·6
Total ...	2,013	2,292	*131,823*	128,754	*759,865*	388,709	371,156	702,935	377	349	+28	+8·0	65	5·7
DISTRICT TOTAL ...	3,531	5,117	297,559	282,821	1,859,465	936,135	923,330	1,721,608	527	488	+39	+7·9	84	6·2
PATNA DIVISION TOTAL ...	23,675	37,048	2,695,819	2,241,161	15,811,014	7,647,962	8,163,052	15,060,993	667	636	+31	+4·8	113	5·8

* Now an independent outpost under thána Kesaria, *vide* notification, dated 26th November 1889.

BHÁGALPUR DIVISION.

DISTRICT BHÁGALPUR.

Subdivisions and Thánas.	Area in square miles.	Number of towns and villages.	Occupied houses.		Population in 1891.			Both sexes, 1881.	Number of persons per square mile.				Number in 1891.	
			1891.	1881.	Both sexes.	Males.	Females.		1891.	1881.	Variation.	Percentage of variation.	Houses per square mile.	Persons per occupied house.
SADAR SUBDIVISION.														
Bhagalpur	181	371	32,393	29,236	175,040	85,615	89,425	160,261	967	885	+ 82	+9·3	179	5·4
Sultanganj	165	218	17,510	16,591	92,278	44,749	47,529	98,427	559	597	− 38	−6·3	106	5·2
Kolgong	413	566	34,025	32,916	191,459	93,024	98,435	190,503	464	461	+ 3	+0·6	82	5·6
Bihipur	175	171	17,029	14,085	93,509	44,395	49,107	96,440	534	551	− 17	−3·0	97	5·5
Total ...	934	1,326	100,957	92,828	552,279	267,783	284,496	545,631	591	584	+ 7	+1·1	108	5·5
SUPUL SUBDIVISION.														
Supul	593	372	50,397	45,706	346,860	173,369	173,491	308,551	585	520	+ 65	+12·5	85	6·8
Pratabganj	341	224	24,195	21,715	134,702	68,401	66,301	129,468	395	380	+ 15	+3·9	71	5·6
Bangaon	263	160	28,430	20,572	163,008	80,843	82,165	148,560	620	565	+ 55	+9·7	108	5·7
Total ...	1,197	756	103,022	87,993	644,570	322,613	321,957	586,579	538	490	+ 48	+9·7	86	6·2
MADEHPURA SUB-DIVISION.														
Madehpura	547	246	47,844	48,014	287,322	143,159	144,163	279,669	525	511	+ 14	+2·7	87	6·0
Kishanganj	366	167	20,796	22,295	125,175	64,485	60,690	135,563	342	370	− 28	−7·5	57	6·0
Total ...	913	413	68,640	70,309	412,497	207,644	204,853	415,223	452	455	− 3	−0·6	75	6·0
BANKA SUBDIVISION.														
Banka	354	1,003	30,340	22,803	163,459	79,323	84,136	134,227	462	379	+ 83	+21·8	86	5·3
Amarpur	294	477	27,258	34,884	145,032	70,537	74,495	208,332	493	709	−216	−30·4	93	5·3
Katuria	534	1,092	20,490	12,497	114,859	56,965	57,894	77,644	215	145	+ 70	+48·2	38	5·6
Total ...	1,182	2,572	78,088	70,184	423,350	206,825	216,525	420,303	358	356	+ 2	+0·5	66	5·4
DISTRICT TOTAL ...	4,226	5,067	350,707	321,314	2,032,696	1,004,865	1,027,831	1,967,635	481	466	+ 15	+3·2	83	5·8

DISTRICT MONGHYR.

Subdivisions and Thánas.	Area in square miles.	Number of towns and villages.	Occupied houses.		Population in 1891.			Both sexes, 1881.	Number of persons per square mile.				Number in 1891.	
			1891.	1881.	Both sexes.	Males.	Females.		1891.	1881.	Variation.	Percentage of variation.	Houses per square mile.	Persons per occupied house.
SADAR SUBDIVISION.														
Monghyr	166	134	*26,770*	21,299	*142,637*	68,313	74,324	139,861	859	843	+16	+1·8	158	5·4
Gogri	719	579	*59,835*	47,789	*382,127*	188,151	193,976	365,954	531	509	+22	+4·3	83	6·3
Jamalpur	4	23	*4,339*	3,658	*21,698*	11,336	10,362	19,824	5,425	4,956	+469	+9·4	1,735	3·1
Surajgarha	310	257	*28,641*	21,407	*168,474*	80,402	88,072	166,263	543	536	+7	+1·3	92	5·8
Kharakpur	360	268	*25,977*	24,194	*148,971*	72,407	76,564	142,650	414	398	+18	+4·5	72	5·7
Total ...	1,559	1,261	*145,555*	118,347	*863,907*	420,609	443,298	834,552	554	535	+19	+3·5	95	5·8
BEGUSARAI SUB-DIVISION.														
Begusarai	476	619	*70,677*	47,178	*400,257*	190,963	209,294	379,794	841	798	+43	+5·3	148	5·6
Tegra	293	633	*40,905*	27,883	*217,940*	100,765	117,175	203,632	744	695	+49	+7·0	140	5·3
Total ...	769	1,252	*111,589*	75,061	*618,197*	291,728	326,469	583,426	804	759	+45	+5·9	145	5·5
JAMUI SUBDIVISION.														
Jamui	533	289	*23,547*	20,787	*125,661*	62,690	62,971	120,563	236	226	+10	+4·4	44	5·3
Shaikhpura	344	401	*34,777*	29,899	*196,656*	96,637	100,019	199,480	572	580	−8	−1·3	101	5·6
Sikandra	233	234	*20,936*	18,574	*114,459*	56,565	57,887	122,389	491	525	−34	−6·4	90	5·4
Chakai	483	430	*20,698*	17,599	*117,148*	58,843	58,305	109,540	243	227	+16	+7·0	43	5·6
Total ...	1,593	1,354	*99,958*	86,859	*553,917*	274,735	279,182	551,972	348	346	+2	+0·5	63	5·5
DISTRICT TOTAL ...	3,921	3,867	357,095	280,267	2,036,021	987,072	1,048,949	1,969,950	519	502	+17	+3·3	92	5·6

DISTRICT PURNEA.

Subdivisions and Thánas.	Area in square miles.	Number of towns and villages.	Occupied houses, 1891.	Occupied houses, 1881.	Population in 1891, Both sexes.	Males.	Females.	Both sexes, 1881.	Persons per square mile, 1891.	1881.	Variation.	Percentage of variation.	Houses per square mile.	Persons per occupied house.
SADAR SUBDIVISION.														
Purnea	424	372	*29,026*	24,969	*156,849*	79,769	77,080	153,720	370	363	+ 7	+1·9	68	5·4
Amur Kasba	279	582	*22,739*	18,363	*122,481*	61,334	61,147	121,696	439	436	+ 3	+0·6	81	5·3
Dhamdaha	519	316	*25,391*	19,763	*144,769*	76,791	67,978	110,728	279	213	+ 66	+30·9	49	5·7
...dwara	421	224	*18,605*	23,010	*115,749*	59,591	56,161	123,046	275	294	− 19	−6·4	44	6·2

Kadwa	365	707	*27,793*	24,074	*139,287*	69,262	70,025	134,275	382	368	+ 14	+3·8	76	5·0
Balarampur	323	603	*22,601*	22,419	*123,190*	62,830	60,360	115,051	381	356	+ 25	+7·0	70	5·4
Manihari	240	176	*10,203*	10,084	*58,876*	29,231	29,645	54,456	245	227	+ 18	+7·9	43	5·7
Total ...	2,571	2,980	*156,351*	142,632	*861,194*	438,808	422,386	813,746	335	316	+ 19	+6·0	61	5·5
ARARIA SUBDIVISION.														
Araria	431	576	*48,704*	30,066	*210,729*	106,195	104,534	200,012	489	464	+ 25	+5·3	113	4·3
Matiari	375	357	*24,304*	20,602	*132,024*	67,802	64,222	115,348	352	308	+ 44	+14·2	65	5·4
Raniganj	270	214	*15,900*	14,165	*89,672*	45,892	43,780	85,373	332	316	+ 16	+5·0	59	5·6
Total ...	1,076	1,147	*88,908*	65,023	*432,425*	219,889	212,536	400,733	402	372	+ 30	+8·0	83	4·8
KISHENGANJ SUB-DIVISION.														
Kishenganj	327	427	*27,297*	25,888	*157,894*	80,888	77,006	161,393	483	494	− 11	−2·2	83	5·8
Bahadurganj	393	520	*40,694*	28,720	*214,990*	109,479	105,511	196,142	547	499	+ 48	+9·6	104	5·2
Kaliaganj	626	920	*47,781*	42,800	*278,155*	144,432	133,723	277,059	444	443	+ 1	+0·2	76	5·8
Total ...	1,346	1,867	*115,772*	97,408	*651,039*	334,799	316,240	634,594	484	471	+ 13	+2·7	86	5·6
DISTRICT TOTAL ...	4,993	5,994	361,031	305,063	1,944,658	993,496	951,162	1,849,073	389	370	+ 19	+5·1	72	5·3

DISTRICT MALDA.

Malda	236	415	*11,296*	9,446	*58,866*	30,192	28,674	50,894	249	216	+33	+15·2	48	5·2
Kharba	294	583	*19,964*	18,189	*112,095*	55,346	56,749	103,051	381	351	+30	+8·5	66	5·6
Ratua	270	243	*18,560*	14,641	*107,849*	51,779	56,070	81,063	399	300	+99	+33·0	69	5·8
Gajo	272	613	*12,594*	9,496	*63,798*	33,820	29,978	54,317	235	200	+35	+17·5	46	5·0
English Bazar	128	269	*18,634*	16,571	*96,463*	47,449	49,014	85,045	754	664	+90	+13·5	146	5·1
Kaliachak	197	292	*21,319*	19,257	*129,655*	62,433	67,222	115,693	658	587	+71	+12·0	108	6·0
Sibganj	186	333	*19,999*	18,364	*114,998*	54,413	60,585	102,162	618	549	+69	+12·5	107	5·7
Gumashtapur	170	231	*13,949*	8,806	*56,575*	28,531	28,044	52,810	333	311	+22	+7·0	82	4·0
Nawabganj	149	269	*12,989*	11,632	*74,620*	35,954	38,666	66,453	501	446	+55	+12·3	87	5·7
DISTRICT TOTAL ...	1,902	3,248	149,297	126,401	814,919	399,917	415,002	711,487	428	374	+54	+14·4	78	5·4

DISTRICT SANTAL PARGANAS.

Subdivisions and Thánas.	Area in square miles.	Number of towns and villages.	Occupied houses.		Population in 1891.			Both sexes, 1881.	Number of persons per square mile.				Number in 1891.	
			1891.	1881.	Both sexes.	Males.	Females.		1891.	1881.	Variation.	Percentage of variation.	Houses per square mile.	Persons per occupied house.
DEOGHAR SUBDIVISION.														
Deoghar	422	1,142	*24,156*	20,777	*140,784*	71,058	69,726	127,846	334	303	+ 31	+10·2	57	5·8
Madhupur	300	615	*12,580*	10,189	*73,516*	36,722	36,794	61,631	245	205	+ 40	+19·5	42	5·8
Sarath	232	585	*11,859*	10,650	*69,815*	34,968	34,847	61,930	301	267	+ 34	+12·7	51	5·9
Total ...	954	2,342	*48,595*	41,616	*284,115*	142,748	141,367	251,407	298	264	+ 34	+12·8	51	5·8
GODDA SUBDIVISION.														
Godda	234	403	*20,067*	18,013	*122,781*	60,165	62,616	109,358	525	467	+ 58	+12·4	86	6·1
Mahagama	144	463	*15,055*	13,252	*88,343*	43,322	45,021	77,974	613	541	+ 72	+13·3	105	5·8
Poreya	198	200	*9,367*	9,250	*60,734*	29,467	31,267	54,570	307	276	+ 31	+11·2	47	6·4
Portion of Daminikoh	391	722	*18,478*	17,856	*113,113*	56,327	56,786	107,505	289	275	+ 14	+5·0	47	6·1
Total ...	967	1,788	*62,967*	58,371	*384,971*	189,281	195,690	349,405	398	361	+ 37	+10·2	65	6·1
PAKAUR SUBDIVISION.														
Pakaur	111	332	*11,242*	10,696	*68,249*	33,648	34,601	61,686	615	556	+ 59	+10·6	101	6·0
Mahespur	287	514	*15,857*	4,356	*97,603*	48,108	49,495	83,214	340	290	+ 50	+17·2	55	6·1
Portion of Daminikoh	285	466	*11,088*	10,841	*64,825*	32,432	32,393	60,570	227	213	+ 14	+6·5	39	5·8
Total ...	683	1,312	*38,227*	25,893	*230,677*	114,188	116,489	205,470	338	301	+ 37	+12·2	56	6·0
RAJMAHAL SUBDIVISION.														
Rajmahal	207	340	*16,931*	20,132	*100,654*	48,733	51,921	93,492	485	451	+34	+7·5	82	5·9
Sahibganj	15	12	*3,718*	2,214	*20,184*	10,677	9,507	13,686	1,346	912	+434	+47·5	248	5·4
Portion of Daminikoh	518	911	*22,365*	24,597	*155,557*	77,614	77,943	145,058	300	280	+20	+7·1	49	6·9
Total ...	740	1,263	*43,014*	46,943	*276,395*	137,024	139,371	252,236	374	341	+33	+9·6	58	6·4

DUMKA SUBDIVISION.														
Dumka	1,202	2,476	*59,209*	44,787	*362,706*	180,001	182,705	322,906	302	269	+ 33	+12·2	49	6·1
Portion of Daminikoh	227	326	*6,300*	6,758	*41,606*	20,545	21,061	40,280	183	177	+ 6	+3·3	29	6·6
Total ...	1,429	2,802	*65,509*	51,545	*404,312*	200,546	203,766	363,186	282	254	+ 28	+11·0	46	6·1
JAMTARA SUBDIVISION.														
Jamtara	696	1,759	*27,997*	22,355	*173,726*	86,780	86,946	146,263	250	210	+ 40	+19·0	40	6·2
Total ...	696	1,759	*27,997*	22,355	*173,726*	86,780	86,946	146,263	250	210	+ 40	+19·0	40	6·2
DISTRICT TOTAL ...	5,469	11,266	286,302	246,723	1,754,196	870,567	883,629	1,567,966	321	287	+ 34	+11·8	52	6·1
BHÁGALPUR DIVISION TOTAL	20,511	29,442	1,504,432	1,279,768	8,582,490	4,255,917	4,326,573	8,066,111	418	393	+ 25	+6·4	73	5·7
BIHAR TOTAL ...	44,186	66,490	4,200,251	3,520,929	24,393,504	11,903,879	12,489,625	23,127,104	552	523	+ 29	+5·5	95	5·8

ORISSA DIVISION.

DISTRICT CUTTACK.

Subdivisions and Thánas.	Area in square miles.	Number of towns and villages.	Occupied houses. 1891.	Occupied houses. 1881.	Population in 1891. Both sexes.	Population in 1891. Males.	Population in 1891. Females.	Both sexes, 1881.	Number of persons per square mile. 1891.	Number of persons per square mile. 1881.	Number of persons per square mile. Variation.	Number of persons per square mile. Percentage of variation.	Number in 1891. Houses per square mile.	Number in 1891. Persons per occupied house.
SADAR SUBDIVISION.														
Cuttack	389	593	*45,783*	40,538	*215,326*	107,887	107,439	198,574	554	510	+44	+8·6	118	4·7
Banki	116	128	*11,840*	9,181	*57,368*	28,628	28,740	56,900	495	491	+4	+0·8	102	4·8
Salepur	286	686	*54,420*	47,400	*270,568*	128,326	142,242	249,979	946	874	+72	+8·2	190	4·9
Tirtol	419	787	*33,075*	33,935	*201,309*	97,572	103,737	183,677	480	438	+42	+9·5	79	6·0
Jagatsinghpur	314	795	*49,060*	38,190	*237,420*	118,423	118,997	215,002	756	685	+71	+10·3	156	4·8
Total ...	1,524	2,989	*194,178*	169,244	*981,991*	480,836	501,155	904,132	644	593	+51	+8·5	127	5·8
KENDRAPARA SUB-DIVISION.														
Kendrapara	294	688	*39,375*	32,164	*214,954*	104,751	110,203	191,019	731	650	+81	+12·4	134	5·4
Patamundi	323	382	*20,588*	18,264	*113,446*	54,475	58,971	109,401	351	339	+12	+1·4	64	5·5
Aul or Rajabari	388	344	*18,970*	14,764	*101,370*	49,737	51,633	91,015	261	234	+27	+11·1	49	5·3
Total ...	1,005	1,414	*78,933*	65,192	*429,770*	208,963	220,807	391,435	428	389	+39	+10·0	78	5·4
JAJPUR SUBDIVISION.														
Jajpur	321	623	*49,065*	46,209	*258,400*	121,237	137,163	250,736	805	781	+24	+3·0	153	5·2
Dharmsala	783	403	*55,813*	44,972	*267,510*	129,521	137,989	248,762	342	318	+24	+7·5	71	4·7
Total ...	1,104	1,026	*104,878*	91,181	*525,910*	250,758	275,152	499,498	476	452	+24	+5·3	95	5·0
DISTRICT TOTAL ...	3,633	5,429	377,989	325,617	1,937,671	940,557	997,114	1,795,065	533	494	+39	+7·8	104	5·1

DISTRICT PURI.

Subdivisions and Thánas.	Area in square miles.	Number of towns and villages.	Occupied houses. 1891.	Occupied houses. 1881.	Population in 1891. Both sexes.	Population in 1891. Males.	Population in 1891. Females.	Both sexes, 1881.	Number of persons per square mile. 1891.	Number of persons per square mile. 1881.	Number of persons per square mile. Variation.	Number of persons per square mile. Percentage of variation.	Number in 1891. Houses per square mile.	Number in 1891. Persons per occupied house.
SADAR SUBDIVISION.														
Thána Puri	865	1,320	*37,230*	35,150	*209,273*	105,222	104,051	196,146	242	227	+ 15	+ 6·6	43	5·6
Town Puri	3	1	*6,526*	4,591	*28,794*	15,930	12,864	25,664	9,598	8,555	+1,043	+12·1	2,175	4·4

Gop	337	948	*22,389*	18,844	*134,038*	67,716	66,322	116,167	398	345	+53	+15·3	66	6·0
Pipli	325	1,336	*44,929*	33,547	*241,470*	120,607	120,863	226,783	743	698	+45	+6·4	138	5·3
Total ...	1,530	3,605	*111,060*	97,132	*613,575*	309,475	304,100	564,759	401	369	+32	+8·6	73	5·5
KHURDA SUBDIVISION.														
Khurda	583	836	*48,084*	18,580	*234,730*	116,569	118,161	233,680	403	401	+2	+0·4	82	4·8
Banpur	360	559	*18,559*	11,657	*96,693*	48,486	48,207	90,147	269	250	+19	+7·6	52	5·2
Total ...	943	1,395	*66,643*	30,237	*331,423*	165,055	166,368	323,833	351	343	+8	+2·3	71	4·9
DISTRICT TOTAL ...	2,473	5,000	177,703	127,369	944,998	474,530	470,468	888,592	382	359	+23	+6·4	72	5·3

DISTRICT BALASOR.

SADAR SUBDIVISION.														
Balasor	228	668	*25,138*	20,280	*112,570*	56,008	56,562	107,685	494	472	+22	+4·6	110	4·4
Soro	397	1,383	*35,876*	31,498	*212,002*	102,766	109,236	197,508	534	498	+36	+7·2	90	5·9
Jaleswar	139	444	*11,912*	9,146	*55,344*	27,566	27,778	55,102	398	396	+2	+0·5	81	4·9
Baliapal	204	557	*15,949*	14,684	*92,741*	46,933	45,808	88,226	455	432	+23	+5·3	78	5·8
Basta	190	477	*13,413*	12,961	*74,186*	37,308	36,878	71,186	390	375	+15	+4·0	71	5·5
Total ...	1,158	3,529	*101,588*	88,569	*546,843*	270,581	276,262	519,707	472	449	+23	+5·1	88	5·4
BHADRAK SUB-DIVISION.														
Bhadrak	287	1,107	*33,210*	30,342	*177,496*	81,598	95,898	169,972	618	592	+26	+4·3	116	5·3
Basudebpur	194	472	*12,207*	10,977	*74,229*	35,152	39,070	71,354	383	368	+15	+4·0	63	6·0
Dhamnagar	233	862	*28,088*	23,536	*138,301*	64,464	73,837	132,381	594	568	+26	+4·5	121	4·9
Chandbali	194	341	*8,643*	7,375	*57,763*	29,843	27,920	51,926	298	268	+30	+11·1	45	6·6
Total ...	908	2,782	*82,148*	72,230	*447,789*	211,057	236,725	425,573	493	469	+24	+5·1	90	5·4
DISTRICT TOTAL	2,066	6,311	183,736	160,799	994,625	481,638	512,987	945,280	481	458	+23	+5·0	89	5·4

DISTRICT ANGUL.

Angul with the Kandh Mahals	1,681	1,443	*18,840*	19,886	*170,058*	85,768	84,290	160,863	101	96	+5	+5·2	11	9·0
Total ...	1,681	1,443	*18,840*	19,886	*170,058*	85,768	84,290	160,863	101	96	+5	+5·2	11	9·0
ORISSA TOTAL ...	9,853	18,183	758,288	633,671	4,047,352	1,982,493	2,064,859	3,789,799	410	384	+26	+6·7	76	5·3

CHUTIA NAGPUR DIVISION.

DISTRICT HAZARIBAGH.

Subdivisions and Thanas.	Area in square miles.	Number of towns and villages.	Occupied houses.		Population in 1891.			Both sexes, 1881.	Number of persons per square mile.				Number in 1891.	
			1891.	1881.	Both sexes.	Males.	Females.		1891.	1881.	Variation.	Percentage of variation.	Houses per square mile.	Persons per occupied house.
SADAR SUBDIVISION.														
Hazaribagh	457	344	*15,318*	16,648	*101,342*	47,294	54,048	103,021	222	225	− 3	−1·3	33	6·6
Barhi	353	274	*9,370*	8,597	*51,593*	24,847	26,746	52,064	146	147	− 1	−0·6	27	5·5
Bagodhar	442	396	*10,234*	10,081	*64,722*	31,062	33,660	59,302	146	134	+ 12	+8·9	23	6·3
Tandwa	489	368	*10,019*	9,614	*57,311*	27,301	30,010	55,780	117	114	+ 3	+2·6	20	5·7
Ramghar	364	350	*11,720*	11,925	*79,659*	39,050	40,609	72,953	219	200	+ 19	+9·5	32	6·8
Jageswar	599	444	*10,048*	9,025	*59,962*	29,313	30,649	53,593	100	89	+ 11	+12·3	17	5·9
Kasmar	321	238	*8,427*	7,556	*50,851*	25,355	25,496	47,094	158	147	+ 11	+7·4	26	6·0
Chauparan	356	496	*12,324*	11,906	*62,912*	30,352	32,560	70,437	177	198	−21	−10·6	35	5·1
Hunterganj	480	522	*10,890*	10,792	*58,496*	28,406	30,090	56,954	122	119	+ 3	+2·5	23	5·4
Chatra	337	436	*11,653*	11,601	*61,389*	29,524	31,866	64,018	182	190	− 8	−4·2	35	5·2
Simaria	377	295	*6,901*	6,905	*36,587*	17,842	18,745	37,029	97	98	− 1	−1·0	18	5·3
Total ...	4,575	4,163	*116,904*	114,649	*684,824*	330,346	354,478	673,238	150	147	+ 3	+2·0	26	5·8
GIRIDHI SUBDIVISION.														
Giridhi	450	884	*17,698*	13,197	*107,497*	54,209	53,288	86,097	239	191	+ 48	+25·1	39	6·1
Gawan	432	461	*9,680*	9,090	*57,289*	27,909	29,380	53,375	133	124	+ 9	+7·2	22	5·9
Kodarma	442	516	*12,870*	11,496	*77,686*	37,898	39,788	73,802	176	167	+ 9	+5·3	29	6·0
Kharakdiha	613	1,308	*24,299*	24,038	*156,748*	76,815	79,933	150,545	256	246	+ 10	+4·0	40	6·4
Dumurhi	509	755	*13,276*	12,810	*80,277*	39,787	40,490	68,685	158	135	+ 23	+17·0	26	6·0
Total ...	2,446	3,924	77,823	70,631	*479,497*	236,618	242,879	432,504	196	177	+ 19	+10·7	32	6·1
DISTRICT TOTAL ...	7,021	8,087	194,727	185,280	1,164,321	566,964	597,357	1,104,742	166	157	+ 9	+5·7	28	5·9

DISTRICT LOHARDAGA.

Subdivisions and Thanas.	Area in square miles.	Number of towns and villages.	Occupied houses, 1891.	Occupied houses, 1881.	Population 1891, Both sexes.	Males.	Females.	Both sexes, 1881.	Persons per sq. mile, 1891.	1881.	Variation.	Percentage of variation.	Houses per square mile.	Persons per occupied house.
SADAR SUBDIVISION.														
Ranchi	672	463	*32,627*	27,176	*177,604*	87,945	89,659	144,723	264	215	+ 49	+22·7	49	5·4
Silli	323	199	*13,789*	11,845	*76,201*	37,788	38,413	68,835	236	212	+ 24	+11·3	43	5·5
Tamar	616	299	*21,552*	17,012	*109,222*	60,980	51,242	96,454	166	152	+ 14	+9·2	35	4·7

Karra	481	368	*17,539*	10,789	*96,671*	45,688	50,983	108,474	201	226	−25	−11·0	36	5·5
Mandar	372	241	*14,100*	12,193	*73,759*	34,068	39,691	66,666	198	179	+19	+10·6	+30	5·2
Khunti	559	401	*19,069*	17,646	*96,508*	47,925	48,583	96,593	173	173	......	......	34	5·0
Lohardaga	596	342	*28,892*	19,006	*110,574*	51,788	58,786	109,530	188	184	+2	+1·0	48	3·8
Total ...	3,619	2,303	*147,547*	124,667	*733,539*	356,182	377,357	687,764	203	190	+13	+6·8	41	4·9
PALKOT SUBDIVISION.														
Chainpur	635	255	*10,653*	11,341	*54,723*	27,526	27,197	53,791	86	85	+1	+1·1	17	5·1
Toto	573	318	*18,958*	18,385	*104,848*	50,865	53,983	98,488	183	172	+11	+6·3	33	5·6
Palkot	574	196	*12,805*	18,872	*67,177*	33,115	34,062	64,347	117	112	+5	+4·4	22	5·2
Kochdaga	877	202	*15,465*	11,593	*73,761*	37,281	36,480	63,368	84	72	+12	+16·6	18	4·7
Basia	862	304	*20,077*	16,389	*94,837*	46,904	47,933	90,411	110	105	+5	+4·7	23	4·7
Total ...	3,521	1,275	*77,958*	70,582	*395,346*	195,691	199,655	370,405	112	105	+7	+6·6	22	5·0
DISTRICT TOTAL ...	7,140	3,578	225,505	195,249	1,128,885	551,873	577,012	1,058,169	158	148	+10	+6·7	32	5·0

DISTRICT MANBHUM.

SADAR SUBDIVISION.													
Purulia	711	1,118	*39,081*	31,928	*210,079*	104,439	105,640	186,791	295	263	+32	+12·1	55	5·3
Jhalda	398	602	*18,898*	16,104	*102,320*	51,318	51,002	91,391	258	231	+27	+11·6	48	5·4
Baghmundi	178	251	*7,063*	5,762	*38,502*	19,403	19,099	33,384	219	190	+29	+15·2	40	5·4
Chandil	395	640	*18,379*	14,137	*92,673*	45,853	46,820	81,251	235	206	+29	+14·0	47	5·0
Barabhum	579	1,062	*24,997*	21,176	*136,923*	68,155	68,768	121,192	236	209	+27	+12·9	43	5·4
Manbazar	258	690	*13,667*	10,477	*77,960*	38,505	39,455	64,261	302	249	+53	+21·2	53	5·7
Raghunathpur	300	569	*21,533*	16,311	*116,832*	57,638	59,194	103,668	389	362	+27	+7·4	72	5·4
Gaurandi	173	312	*8,936*	6,840	*52,640*	26,459	26,181	45,793	304	265	+39	+14·7	52	5·8
Para	119	191	*8,831*	6,842	*43,478*	21,265	22,213	39,740	365	334	+31	+9·2	74	4·9
Chas	237	632	*17,488*	14,719	*100,487*	49,842	50,645	89,173	424	376	+48	+12·7	74	5·7
Total ...	3,344	6,067	*178,866*	147,306	*971,894*	482,877	489,017	861,644	291	258	+33	+12·7	53	5·4
GOBINDPUR SUB-DIVISION.														
Gobindpur	478	1,313	*19,521*	16,463	*109,530*	54,489	55,041	103,457	229	216	+13	+6·0	41	5·6
Nirsa	170	442	*11,240*	7,916	*58,675*	29,508	29,167	50,961	345	300	+45	+15·0	66	5·2
Topchanchi	155	495	*9,285*	6,810	*53,229*	26,325	26,904	48,166	343	272	+71	+26·1	60	5·7
Total ...	803	2,250	*40,046*	31,189	*221,434*	110,322	111,112	196,584	276	245	+31	+12·6	50	5·5
DISTRICT TOTAL ...	4,147	8,317	218,912	178,494	1,193,328	593,199	600,129	1,058,228	288	255	+33	+12·9	53	5·4

DISTRICT SINGHBHUM.

Subdivisions and Thánas.	Area in square miles.	Number of towns and villages.	Occupied houses.		Population in 1891.			Both sexes, 1881.	Number of persons per square mile.				Number in 1891.	
			1891.	1881.	Both sexes.	Males.	Females.		1891.	1881.	Variation.	Percentage of variation.	Houses per square mile.	Persons per occupied house.
Chaibasa	1,258	760	*42,145*	35,907	*229,188*	112,601	116,587	194,121	182	154	+28	+18·1	34	5·4
Chakradharpur	616	498	*16,703*	14,606	*86,954*	43,739	43,215	76,445	141	124	+17	+13·7	27	5·2
Manoharpur	732	259	*6,573*	3,389	*34,877*	19,110	15,767	17,500	48	24	+24	+100·0	9	5·3
Ghatsila or Dhalbhum	1,147	1,360	*36,718*	31,941	*194,469*	95,967	98,502	165,709	169	144	+25	+17·3	32	5·2
DISTRICT TOTAL ...	3,753	2,877	102,139	85,843	545,488	271,417	274,071	453,775	145	121	+24	+19·8	27	5·3

DISTRICT PALÁMAU.

Subdivisions and Thánas.	Area in square miles.	Number of towns and villages.	Occupied houses, 1891.	Occupied houses, 1881.	Population 1891, Both sexes.	Males.	Females.	Both sexes, 1881.	Persons per sq. mile, 1891.	1881.	Variation.	Percentage of variation.	Houses per square mile.	Persons per occupied house.
Daltonganj	590	573	*10,106*	12,918	*103,464*	50,826	52,638	77,299	175	131	+44	+33·5	17	10·2
Garhwa	588	434	*15,988*	13,246	*87,027*	42,451	44,576	79,117	148	135	+13	+9·8	27	5·4
Banka	640	251	*7,570*	8,106	*34,168*	17,106	17,062	46,546	53	73	−20	−27·3	12	4·5
Chhatrapur	350	401	*8,143*	6,355	*41,066*	20,471	20,595	36,838	117	105	+12	+11·4	23	5·0
Patan	530	871	*14,104*	12,702	*82,835*	40,937	41,898	79,408	156	150	+6	+4·0	27	5·8
Husainabad	650	509	*19,767*	16,730	*111,943*	54,744	57,199	102,515	172	58	+14	+8·8	30	5·6
Latihar	391	357	*7,853*	7,981	*42,766*	21,253	21,513	44,067	109	113	−4	−3·5	20	5·4
Mahuadanr	502	206	*5,194*	4,234	*26,153*	13,086	13,067	19,048	52	38	+14	+36·8	10	5·0
*Balumat**	664	299	*12,662*	12,383	*67,348*	33,446	33,902	66,253	101	99	+2	+2·0	19	5·3
DISTRICT TOTAL ...	4,905	3,901	101,387	94,637	596,770	294,320	302,450	551,075	122	112	+10	+8·9	21	5·9
CHUTIA NAGPUR TOTAL	26,966	26,760	842,670	739,503	4,628,792	2,277,773	2,351,019	4,225,989	171	156	+15	+9·6	31	5·4
GRAND TOTAL of all Districts (excluding Calcutta and Suburbs) ...	151,475	227,371	13,057,693	10,478,775	70,595,002	35,070,874	35,524,128	66,065,862	466	436	+30	+6·8	86	5·4

* Includes also the figures of area, &c. of portions of thánas Lohardaga and Mandar transferred to Palámau district under Government notification, dated 30th October 1891.

FEUDATORY STATES.

KUCH BIHAR.

Subdivisions and Thánas.	Area in square miles.	Number of towns and villages.	Occupied houses.		Population in 1891.			Both sexes, 1881.	Number of persons per square mile.				Number in 1891.	
			1891.	1881.	Both sexes.	Males.	Females.		1891.	1881.	Variation.	Percentage of variation.	Houses per square mile.	Persons per occupied house.
Phulbari	189	90	*12,687*	12,560	*73,106*	38,543	34,563	70,498	387	373	+14	+3·7	67	5·8
Kuch Bihar	309	261	*2,311*	27,618	*11,491*	7,417	4,074	134,673	418	435	−17	−3·9	83	5·0
Kotwali			*23,363*		*117,752*	61,413	56,339							
Matabhanga	346	264	*27,047*	30,228	*143,934*	74,512	69,422	154,292	417	447	−30	−6·7	78	5·3
Haldibari	89	66	*5,720*	6,022	*34,757*	18,272	16,485	35,411	391	398	−7	−1·7	64	6·0
Mekliganj	105	169	*8,828*	9,007	*51,004*	26,759	24,245	52,166	486	497	−11	−2·2	84	5·7
Dinhata	270	304	*27,859*	30,285	*146,824*	75,541	71,283	155,584	544	576	−32	−5·5	103	5·2
DISTRICT TOTAL ...	1,307	1,164	117,815	115,720	578,868	302,457	276,411	602,624	443	461	−18	−3·9	90	4·9

ORISSA TRIBUTARY STATES.

Subdivisions and Thánas.	Area in square miles.	Number of towns and villages.	Occupied houses, 1891.	Occupied houses, 1881.	Population in 1891, Both sexes.	Males.	Females.	Both sexes, 1881.	Persons per sq. mile, 1891.	1881.	Variation.	Percentage of variation.	Houses per square mile.	Persons per occupied house.
Athgarh	168	238	*7,117*	5,546	*36,603*	18,488	18,115	31,070	218	185	+33	+17·8	42	5·1
Talcher	399	283	*9,190*	7,693	*52,674*	26,332	26,342	35,590	132	89	+43	+48·3	23	5·7
Moharbhanj	4,243	3,493	*97,964*	71,228	*532,238*	265,880	266,358	385,737	125	91	+34	+37·3	23	5·4
Nilgiri	278	270	*10,444*	8,155	*56,198*	27,943	28,255	50,972	202	183	+19	+10·3	38	5·3
Keonjhar	3,096	1,896	*47,580*	38,213	*248,101*	125,002	123,099	215,612	80	70	+10	+14·2	15	5·2
Pal Lahara	452	202	*3,830*	2,718	*19,700*	10,012	9,688	14,887	44	33	+11	+33·3	8	5·1
Dhenkanal	1,463	1,128	*49,314*	33,726	*238,285*	118,725	119,560	208,316	163	142	+21	+14·7	34	4·8
Athmalik	730	404	*6,180*	4,024	*31,605*	16,402	15,203	21,774	43	30	+13	+43·3	8	5·1
Hindol	312	198	*7,234*	5,261	*37,973*	18,659	19,314	33,802	122	108	+14	+12·9	23	5·2
Narsinghpur	199	193	*8,129*	6,619	*33,849*	16,748	17,101	32,583	170	164	+6	+3·6	41	4·1
Baramba	134	172	*6,711*	5,663	*32,526*	16,108	16,418	29,772	243	222	+21	+9·4	50	4·8
Tigaria	46	90	*4,224*	3,059	*20,546*	10,019	10,527	19,850	447	432	+15	+3·4	92	4·8
Kandhpara	244	321	*14,737*	12,946	*63,287*	31,696	31,591	66,296	259	272	−12	−4·4	60	4·2
Nayagarh	588	718	*23,077*	22,761	*117,862*	58,629	59,233	114,622	200	195	+5	+2·5	39	5·1
Ranpur	203	316	*9,225*	6,672	*40,115*	20,139	19,976	36,539	198	180	+18	+10·0	45	4·3
Daspalla	568	508	*9,784*	8,472	*45,597*	22,804	22,793	41,608	80	73	+7	+9·5	17	4·6
Boad	1,264	955	*23,970*	14,242	*89,551*	45,864	43,687	71,144	71	56	+15	+26·7	19	3·7
Total ...	14,387	11,385	*338,710*	257,486	*1,696,710*	849,450	847,260	1,410,183	118	98	+20	+20·4	24	5·0

CHUTIA NAGPUR TRIBUTARY STATES.

Subdivisions and Thánas.	Area in square miles.	Number of towns and villages.	Occupied houses.		Population in 1891.			Both sexes, 1881.	Number of persons per square mile.				Number in 1891.	
			1891.	1881.	Both sexes.	Males.	Females.		1891.	1881.	Variation.	Percentage of variation.	Houses per square mile.	Persons per occupied house.
Chang Bhukar	906	123	*3,414*	2,733	*18,526*	9,708	8,818	13,466	20	15	+ 5	+33·3	4	5·4
Korea	1,625	257	*7,000*	5,798	*36,240*	18,586	17,654	29,846	22	18	+ 4	+22·2	4	5·1
Sirguja	6,055	1,324	*61,068*	51,132	*324,552*	165,294	159,258	270,311	54	45	+ 9	+20·0	10	5·3
Udaipur	1,055	167	*6,876*	6,135	*37,536*	19,121	18,415	33,955	36	32	+ 4	+12·5	7	5·4
Jashpur	1,963	516	*21,388*	14,780	*113,636*	57,279	56,357	90,340	58	46	+12	+26·0	11	5·3
Gangpur	2,518	832	*33,851*	6,844	*191,440*	98,480	92,960	107,965	76	43	+33	+76·7	13	5·6
Bonai	1,349	358	*6,511*	4,372	*32,120*	16,791	15,329	24,030	24	18	+ 6	+33·3	5	4·9
Kharsawan	145	402	*6,331*	5,622	*35,470*	17,707	17,763	31,187	245	215	+30	+13·9	44	5·6
Seraikela	438	699	*18,264*	15,046	*93,839*	46,717	47,122	77,062	214	176	+38	+21·5	42	5·1
Total ...	16,054	4,678	*164,703*	112,454	*883,359*	449,683	433,676	678,002	55	42	+13	+30·9	10	5·3
HILL TIPPERA ...	4,086		Not available.		137,442	71,596	65,846	95,637	33	23	+10	+43·4	......	......
FEUDATORY STATES TOTAL	25,834	17,217	621,228	485,660	3,296,379	1,673,186	1,623,193	2,786,446	91	77	+14	+18·1	17	5·3

PROVINCIAL TABLE II.—Showing the Thana Variation of population for religions with 1,000 or more adherents in each District, with percentage of variation for the principal religions.

BARDWAN

DISTRICT

Religions.	District Total.		Bardwan.		Sahibganj.		Khandaghosh.	
	Male.	Female.	Male.	Female.	Male.	Female.	Male.	Female.
HINDUS.								
1891	546,739	*571,004*	22,220	*19,709*	28,669	*30,875*	19,189	*20,686*
1881	537,124	*585,150*	23,720	*22,788*	28,552	*32,322*	18,513	*20,864*
Variation	+ 9,615	*— 14,146*	— 1,500	*— 3,086*	+ 117	*— 1,447*	+ 676	*— 178*
Percentage	+ 1·7	*— 2·4*	— 6·3	*— 13·5*	+ ·4	*— 4·4*	+ 3·6	*— ·8*
MUSALMANS.								
1891	132,622	*134,602*	7,858	*7,962*	7,251	*7,484*	7,845	*8,219*
1881	128,692	*135,923*	7,701	*7,561*	7,035	*7,361*	7,643	*8,208*
Variation	+ 3,930	*— 1,321*	+ 157	*+40 1*	+ 216	*+ 123*	+ 202	*+ 11*
Percentage	+ 3·0	*— ·9*	+ 2·0	*+ 5·3*	+ 3·0	*+ 1·6*	+ 2·6	*+ ·1*
CHRISTIANS.								
1891	739	*669*	117	*90*	...	...	...	...
1881	474	*436*	66	*68*	...	...	...	...
THE ANIMISTIC.								
1891	2,741	*2,718*	...	...	...	...	...	...
1881	3,163	*3,255*	...	...	...	...	...	...

Religions.	Raniganj.		Asansol.		Kaksa.		Katwa.	
	Male.	Female.	Male.	Female.	Male.	Female.	Male.	Female.
HINDUS.								
1891	66,160	*67,712*	60,767	*58,104*	16,064	*16,366*	31,553	*34,601*
1881	65,772	*69,367*	44,658	*45,474*	17,562	*18,945*	31,700	*35,958*
Variation	+ 388	*— 1,655*	+ 16,109	*+ 12,630*	— 1,498	*— 2,579*	— 147	*— 1,357*
Percentage	+ ·5	*— 2·3*	+ 36·0	*+ 27·7*	— 8·5	*— 13·6*	— ·4	*— 3·7*
MUSALMANS.								
1891	4,612	*4,244*	4,331	*3,261*	1,125	*944*	7,656	*7,878*
1881	4,320	*4,070*	2,692	*2,111*	1,196	*1,084*	7,346	*7,927*
Variation	+ 292	*+ 174*	+ 1,639	*+ 1,150*	— 71	*— 140*	+ 310	*— 49*
Percentage	+ 6·7	*+ 4·2*	+ 60·8	*+ 54·4*	— 5·9	*— 12·9*	+ 4·2	*— ·6*
CHRISTIANS.								
1891	133	*123*	440	*427*	23	*18*	1	*1*
1881	67	*92*	301	*262*	...	...	3	*9*
THE ANIMISTIC.								
1891	2,455	*2,509*	1	...	233	*195*	...	...
1881	1,493	*1,581*	1,670	*1,674*	...	...	...	...

DISTRICT

Religions.	District total.		Bankura.		On
	Male.	Female.	Male.	Female.	Male.
HINDUS.					
1891	452,150	*468,223*	60,555	*61,713*	53,397
1881	443,116	*467,729*	55,500	*56,544*	52,678
Variation	+ 9,034	*+ 494*	+ 5,055	*+ 5,169*	+ 719
Percentage	+ 2·0	*+ ·1*	+ 9·1	*+ 9·1*	+ 1·3

* Includes Barjora

DIVISION.

BARDWAN.

Raina.		Satgachhia.		Jamalpur.		Bud-Bud.		Ausgram.	
Male.	Female.	Male.	Female.	Male.	Female.	Male.	Female.	Male.	Female.
36,686	*39,071*	36,618	*39,184*	27,121	*28,876*	33,500	*34,899*	31,658	*33,753*
36,615	*39,772*	37,277	*41,394*	26,514	*29,038*	32,315	*35,785*	35,469	*39,168*
+ 71	− *701*	− 659	− *2,210*	+ 607	− *162*	+ 1,185	− *886*	− 3,811	− *5,415*
+ ·1	− *1·7*	− 1·7	− *5·3*	+ 2·2	− *·5*	+ 3·6	− *2·4*	− 10·7	− *13·8*
9,594	*9,981*	11,465	*11,674*	7,418	*8,356*	9,601	*9,638*	6,180	*6,347*
9,515	*11,041*	11,499	*12,079*	7,454	*8,703*	9,655	*10,368*	6,594	*7,028*
+ 79	− *1,060*	− 34	− *405*	− 36	− *347*	− 54	− *730*	− 414	− *681*
+ ·8	− *9·6*	− ·2	− *3·3*	− ·4	− *3·9*	− ·5	− *7·0*	− 6·2	− *9·6*
...	...	...	...	...	...	...	...	...	...
...	...	5	...	...	...	...	...	2	...
...	...	11	*2*	...	...	27	*12*	...	...
...	...	...	...	...	...	...	...	...	...

Ketugram.		Mungalkot.		Kalna.		Purbasthali.		Manteswar.	
Male.	Female.	Male.	Female.	Male.	Female.	Male.	Female.	Male.	Female.
28,643	*30,960*	26,394	*28,279*	32,840	*35,752*	26,704	*28,333*	21,953	*23,851*
28,331	*31,908*	26,934	*29,704*	33,319	*37,981*	28,448	*30,695*	21,425	*23,987*
+ 312	− *948*	− 540	− *1,425*	− 479	− *2,229*	− 1,744	− *2,362*	+ 528	− *136*
+ 1·1	− *2·9*	− 2·0	− *4·7*	− 1·4	− *5·8*	− 6·1	− *7·6*	+ 2·4	− *·5*
8,437	*8,889*	8,259	*8,668*	10,678	*10,789*	11,177	*10,884*	9,135	*9,384*
7,596	*8,283*	8,022	*8,784*	10,424	*10,748*	11,484	*11,442*	8,516	*9,125*
+ 841	+ *606*	+ 237	− *116*	+ 254	+ *41*	− 307	− *558*	+ 619	+ *259*
+ 11·0	+ *7·3*	+ 2·9	− *1·3*	+ 2·4	+ *·3*	− 2·6	− *4·8*	+ 7·2	+ *2·8*
4	*4*	...	...	12	*6*	...	...	...	...
1	*1*	...	...	9	*3*	...	*1*	...	...
...	...	...	...	14	...	...	...	...	...
...	...	...	...	...	...	...	...	...	...

BANKURA.

	Gangajalghati.*		Khatra.		Raipura.	
Female.	Male.	Female.	Male.	Female.	Male.	Female.
54,305	81,995	*84,783*	46,096	*46,851*	31,761	*32,751*
54,250	79,549	*83,315*	41,329	*42,269*	31,518	*32,163*
+ *55*	+ 2,446	+ *1,468*	+ 4,767	+ *4,582*	+ 243	+ *588*
+ *·1*	+ 3·0	+ *1·7*	+ 11·5	+ *10·8*	+ ·7	+ *1·8*

independent outpost.

DISTRICT

Religions.	District total.		Bankura.		On
	Male.	Female.	Male.	Female.	Male.
MUSALMANS.					
1891	22,499	*22,813*	1,809	*1,936*	945
1881	22,191	*24,083*	1,873	*1,984*	797
Variation	+ 308	— *1,970*	— 64	— *48*	+ 148
Percentage	+ 1·3	— *5·2*	— 3·4	— *2·4*	+ 18·5
THE ANIMISTIC.					
1891	51,170	*52,577*	7,267	*7,232*	6,322
1581	41,784	*42,775*	5,907	*5,703*	5,397
Variation	+ 9,386	+ *9,802*	+ 1,360	+ *1,529*	+ 925
Percentage	+ 13·3	+ *18·6*	+ 18·7	+ *21·1*	+ 14·6

Religions.	Simlapal.		Bishnupur.	
	Male.	Female.	Male.	Female.
HINDUS.				
1891	13,792	*13,955*	60,312	*64,469*
1881	12,528	*12,621*	62,549	*68,494*
Variation	+ 1,264	+ *1,334*	— 2,237	— *4,025*
Percentage	+ 10·0	+ *10·5*	— 3·5	— *5·8*
MUSALMANS.				
1891	386	*347*	3,079	*2,986*
1881	284	*263*	2,794	*3,004*
Variation	+ 102	+ *84*	+ 285	— *18*
Percentage	+ 35·9	+ *31·9*	+ 10·2	— *·5*
THE ANIMISTIC.				
1891	4,292	*4,239*	2,546	*2,570*
1881	3,448	*3,538*	1,995	*2,037*
Variation	+ 844	+ *701*	+ 551	+ *533*
Percentage	+ 19·6	+ *16·5*	+ 21·6	+ *20·7*

DISTRICT

Religions.	District total.		Suri.		Dubrajpur.		Bolpur	
	Male.	Female.	Male.	Female.	Male.	Female.	Male.	Female.
HINDUS.								
1891	289,094	*304,087*	49,198	*50,988*	46,676	*49,098*	38,766	*40,356*
1881	294,024	*317,991*	51,505	*54,232*	49,544	*53,093*	42,890	*45,966*
Variation	— 4,930	—*13,904*	— 2,307	— *3,244*	— 2,868	— *3,995*	— 4,124	— *5,610*
Percentage	— 1·6	— *4·3*	— 4·4	— *5·9*	— 5·7	— *7·5*	— 9 6	— *12·2*
MUSALMANS.								
1891	82,975	*86,777*	8,048	*8,253*	11,036	*11,697*	9,036	*9,023*
1881	79,075	*86,444*	7,766	*8,470*	11,431	*12,149*	9,276	*9,761*
Variation	+ 3,900	+ *333*	+ 282	— *217*	— 395	— *452*	— 240	— *738*
Percentage	+ 4·9	+ *·3*	+ 3·6	— *2·5*	— 3·4	— *3·7*	— 2·5	— *7·5*

* Includes Barjora

BANKURA—*concluded.*

…DA.	Gangajalghati.*		Khatra.		Raipura.	
Female.	Male.	Female.	Male.	Female.	Male.	Female.
826	1,853	*1,759*	738	*654*	306	*218*
763	1,797	*1,839*	702	*607*	763	*703*
+ *63*	+ 56	− *73*	+ 36	+ *47*	− 457	− *485*
+ *8·2*	+ 3·1	− *3·9*	+ 5·1	+ *7·7*	− 59·8	− *68·9*
6,473	3,916	*3,861*	8,611	*8,940*	18,074	*19,182*
5,435	3,052	*3,062*	7,015	*7,200*	14,907	*15,741*
+ *1,038*	+ 864	+ *799*	+ 1,596	+ *1,740*	+ 3,167	+ *3,441*
+ *16·0*	+ 22·0	+ *20·6*	+ 18·5	+ *19·4*	+ 17·5	+ *17·9*

Sonamukhi.		Kotalpur.		Indas.	
Male.	Female.	Male.	Female.	Male.	Female.
33,414	*35,390*	40,124	*41,925*	30,704	*32,081*
34,915	*37,731*	41,033	*45,207*	31,517	*35,135*
− 1,501	− *2,341*	− 909	− *3,282*	− 813	− *3,054*
− 4·2	− *6·1*	− 2·2	− *7·2*	− 2·5	− *8·6*
3,255	*3,293*	4,265	*4,854*	5,863	*5,940*
3,441	*3,809*	3,956	*4,745*	5,784	*6,373*
− 186	− *516*	+ 309	+ *109*	+ 79	− *433*
− 5·7	− *13·5*	+ 7·8	+ *2·2*	+ 1·3	− *6·7*
75	*57*	61	*23*	6	......
57	*59*	6	......	......	......
+ 18	− *2*	+ 55	+ *23*	+ 6	......
+ 24	− *3·5*	+ 90·1	+ *100*	+ 100	......

BIRBHUM.

Sakulipur.		Labhpur.		Rampur Hat.		Maureswar.		Nalhati.	
Male.	Female.	Male.	Female.	Male.	Female.	Male.	Female.	Male.	Female.
25,737	*27,584*	23,518	*24,940*	31,779	*33,631*	32,352	*34,031*	41,068	*43,459*
26,340	*29,505*	21,771	*23,859*	31,325	*34,698*	30,932	*33,695*	39,717	*42,943*
− 603	− *1,921*	+ 1,747	+ *1,081*	+ 454	− *1,067*	+ 1,420	+ *336*	+ 1,351	+ *516*
− 2·2	− *6·5*	+ 8·0	+ *4·5*	+ 1·4	− *3·0*	+ 4·5	+ *·9*	+ 3·4	+ *1·2*
7,218	*7,599*	4,435	*4,597*	9,596	*9,887*	6,786	*7,100*	26,820	*28,621*
8,959	*9,879*	3,496	*3,825*	8,135	*8,880*	6,187	*6,857*	23,825	*26,623*
− 1,741	− *2,280*	+ 939	+ *772*	+ 1,461	+ *1,007*	+ 599	+ *243*	+ 2,995	+ *1,998*
− 19·4	− *23·0*	+ 26·8	+ *20·1*	+ 17·9	+ *11·3*	+ 9·6	+ *3·5*	+ 12·5	+ *7·5*

…independent outpost.

DISTRICT

Religions.	District total.		Suri.		Dubrajpur.		Bolpur.	
	Male.	Female.	Male.	Female.	Male.	Female.	Male.	Female.
THE ANIMISTIC.								
1891	17,230	*17,059*	4,819	*4,747*	491	*467*	827	*770*
1881	7,281	*7,168*	2,421	*2,306*	180	*169*	...	...

DISTRICT

Religions.	District total.		Midnapur.		Jhargaon.	
	Male.	Female.	Male.	Female.	Male.	Female.
HINDUS.						
1891	1,155,769	*1,165,655*	71,234	*70,359*	24,716	*25,111*
1881	1,105,060	*1,128,240*	71,462	*72,547*	21,111	*21,453*
Variation	+ 50,709	+ *37,415*	— 228	— *2,188*	+ 3,605	+ *3,658*
Percentage	+ 4·5	+ *3·3*	— ·3	— *3·01*	+ 17·0	+ *17·0*
MUSALMANS.						
1891	83,980	*87,432*	10,716	*10,270*	804	*694*
1881	79,793	*84,208*	10,714	*10,697*	1,565	*1,582*
Variation	+ 4,187	+ *3,224*	+ 2	— *427*	— 761	— *888*
Percentage	+ 5·2	+ *3·8*	+ ·01	— *3·9*	— 48·6	— *56·1*
THE ANIMISTIC.						
1891	67,458	*69,471*	4,469	*4,577*	9,699	*9,669*
1881	56,233	*57,636*	3,035	*3,133*	7,290	*7,489*
Variation	+ 11,225	+ *11,835*	+ 1,434	+ *1,444*	+ 2,409	+ *2,180*
Percentage	+ 19·9	+ *20·5*	+ 47·2	+ *46·0*	+ 33·0	+ *29·1*
CHRISTIANS.						
1891	786	*759*	296	*300*	160	*166*
1881	368	*372*	109	*124*	53	*69*

Religions.	Sabang.		Naraingarh.		Dantun.		Gopiballabhpur.	
	Male.	Female.	Male.	Female.	Male.	Female.	Male.	Female.
HINDUS.								
1891	92,762	*93,596*	55,764	*54,677*	57,599	*55,887*	60,409	*61,298*
1881	93,969	*96,429*	61,483	*61,430*	61,099	*60,161*	53,870	*54,322*
Variation	— 1,207	— *2,833*	— 5,719	— *6,753*	— 3,500	— *4,274*	+ 6,539	+ *6,976*
Percentage	— 1·2	— *2·9*	— 9·3	— *10·9*	— 5·7	— *7·1*	+ 12·1	+ *12·8*
MUSALMANS.								
1891	4,280	*4,683*	1,955	*1,844*	3,054	*3,090*	496	*359*
1881	3,893	*4,422*	2,230	*2,208*	2,997	*3,104*	686	*583*
Variation	+ 387	+ *261*	— 275	— *364*	+ 57	— *14*	— 190	— *224*
Percentage	+ 9·9	+ *5·9*	— 12·3	— *16·4*	+ 1·9	— *·4*	— 27·6	— *38·4*

BIRBHUM—*concluded.*

Sakulipur.		Labhpur.		Rampur Hat.		Maureswar.		Nalhati.	
Male.	Female.	Male.	Female.	Male.	Female.	Male.	Female.	Male.	Female.
3	*4*	65	*65*	4,107	*4,064*	3,088	*3,048*	3,830	*3,894*
...	...	...	...	2,366	*2,370*	1,918	*1,930*	396	*393*

MIDNAPUR.

Binpur.		Salbani.		Debra.		Garbeta.		Kespur.	
Male.	Female.	Male.	Female.	Male.	Female.	Male.	Female.	Male.	Female.
32,689	*33,313*	21,839	*21,817*	30,481	*31,369*	46,175	*45,328*	34,251	*34,108*
28,542	*29,584*	21,153	*21,006*	31,574	*33,347*	44,266	*44,420*	34,840	*35,687*
+ 4,147	+ *3,729*	+ 686	+ *811*	— 1,093	— *1,978*	+ 1,909	+ *908*	— 589	— *1,579*
+ 14·5	+ *12·6*	+ 3·2	+ *3·8*	— 3·4	— *5·9*	+ 4·3	+ *2·4*	— 1·6	— *4·4*
488	*372*	527	*495*	3,191	*3,458*	4,509	*4,402*	6,930	*7,098*
641	*611*	551	*535*	3,143	*3,573*	4,324	*4,314*	6,654	*7,257*
— 153	— *239*	— 24	— *40*	+ 48	— *115*	+ 185	+ *88*	+ 276	— *159*
— 23·8	— *39·1*	— 4·3	— *7·4*	+ 1·5	— *3·2*	+ 3·4	+ *2·0*	+ 4·1	— *2·1*
17,309	*18,259*	5,263	*5,300*	167	*73*	12,717	*13,297*	713	*687*
14,859	*15,574*	5,421	*5,437*	8	...	11,231	*11,101*	106	*103*
+ 2,450	+ *2,685*	— 158	— *137*	+ 159	+ *73*	+ 1,486	+ *2,196*	+ 607	+ *584*
+ 15·8	+ *17·2*	— 2·9	— *2·5*	+ 1,987·5	...	+ 13·2	+ *19·7*	+ 572·6	+ *566·9*
37	*40*	103	*100*	2	...	3	*3*	...	...
24	*22*	44	*40*	...	...	1	...	1	...

Ghatal.		Chandrakona.		Daspur.		Tamluk.		Maslandpur.	
Male.	Female.	Male.	Female.	Male.	Female.	Male.	Female.	Male.	Female.
43,598	*43,089*	46,941	*47,520*	61,846	*66,921*	40,427	*41,782*	40,673	*40,796*
39,258	*40,612*	48,270	*49,843*	56,929	*63,433*	36,862	*39,113*	36,658	*37,339*
+ 4,340	+ *3,377*	— 1,329	— *2,323*	+ 4,917	+ *3,488*	+ 3,565	+ *2,669*	+ 4,015	+ *3,457*
+ 11·0	+ *8·3*	— 2·7	— *4·6*	+ 81·6	+ *5·4*	+ 9·6	+ *6·8*	+ 10·9	+ *9·2*
2,038	*2,366*	3,875	*3,530*	2,299	*2,758*	4,183	*4,864*	3,875	*3,917*
1,895	*2,321*	2,754	*2,987*	2,039	*2,474*	3,830	*4,280*	3,592	*3,443*
+ 143	+ *45*	+ 621	+ *543*	+ 260	+ *284*	+ 353	+ *584*	+ 283	+ *474*
+ 7·5	+ *1·9*	+ 22·5	+ *18·1*	+ 12·7	+ *11·4*	+ 9·2	+ *13·6*	+ 7·8	+ *13·7*

DISTRICT

Religions.	Sabang.		Naraingarh.		Dantun.		Gopiballabhpur.	
	Male.	Female.	Male.	Female.	Male.	Female.	Male.	Female.
THE ANIMISTIC.								
1891	5	*3*	1,554	*1,634*	564	*591*	14,383	*14,985*
1881	...	...	757	*775*	342	*336*	13,020	*13,549*
Variation	+ 5	+ *3*	+ 797	+ *859*	+ 222	+ *255*	+ 1,363	+ *1,436*
Percentage	...	...	+ 105·2	+ *110·8*	+ 64·9	+ *75·8*	+ 10·4	+ *10·5*
CHRISTIANS.								
1891	7	*5*	8	*5*	1	...	24	*17*
1881	...	...	...	...	3	*4*	15	*12*

Religions.	Sutahata.		Panchkura.		Nandigram.		Contai.	
	Male.	Female.	Male.	Female.	Male.	Female.	Male.	Female.
HINDUS.								
1891	28,102	*27,190*	56,354	*62,158*	49,632	*49,720*	68,963	*69,688*
1881	23,912	*23,525*	55,195	*61,659*	39,398	*39,169*	62,131	*61,385*
Variation	+ 4,250	+ *3,665*	+ 1,159	+ *499*	+ 10,234	+ *10,551*	+ 6,852	+ *8,303*
Percentage	+ 17·7	+ *15·5*	+ 2·09	+ *·8*	+ 26·1	+ *26·9*	+ 11·02	+ *13·5*
MUSALMANS.								
1891	4,102	*3,845*	8,357	*10,785*	5,426	*5,574*	4,466	*4,149*
1881	3,297	*3,093*	8,197	*10,224*	4,107	*4,044*	3,586	*3,379*
Variation	+ 805	+ *752*	+ 160	+ *561*	+ 1,319	+ *1,530*	+ 880	+ *770*
Percentage	+ 24·4	+ *24·3*	+ 1·9	+ *5·4*	+ 32·1	+ *37·8*	+ 24·5	+ *22·7*
THE ANIMISTIC.								
1891	...	...	38	*21*	15	*7*	23	*18*
1881	...	...	12	...	...	...	15	*19*
Variation	...	...	+ 26	+ *21*	+ 15	+ *7*	+ 8	− *1*
Percentage	...	...	+ 216·6	...	...	...	+ 53·3	+ *5·2*
CHRISTIANS.								
1891	...	...	6	*4*	...	...	5	...
1881	...	...	7	*8*	...	...	1	...

DISTRICT

Religions.	District Total.		Hugli.		Balagarh.	
	Male.	Female.	Male.	Female.	Male.	Female.
HINDUS.						
1891	436,307	*444,928*	23,858	*23,242*	18,570	*19,873*
1881	402,065	*423,142*	22,835	*23,511*	18,726	*20,707*
Variation	+ 34,242	+ *21,826*	+ 1,023	− *269*	− 156	− *834*
Percentage	+ 8·5	+ *5·1*	+ 4·5	− *1·1*	− ·8	− *4·2*
MUSALMANS.						
1891	91,030	*101,655*	5,124	*4,486*	4,083	*4,197*
1881	87,462	*101,338*	5,439	*4,893*	4,271	*4,514*
Variation	+ 3,568	+ *317*	− 315	− *407*	− 188	− *317*
Percentage	+ 4·0	+ *·3*	− 5·7	− *8·3*	− 4·4	− *7·0*
THE ANIMISTIC.						
1891	1,388	*665*	30	*2*	...	...
1881	24	*13*	1	...	...	...

MIDNAPUR—*concluded.*

Ghatal.		Chandrakona.		Daspur.		Tamluk.		Maslandpur.	
Male.	Female.	Male.	Female.	Male.	Female.	Male.	Female.	Male.	Female.
321	207	139	45	6	...	47	52	23	43
4	...	117	118	...	...	5	2	11	...
+ 317	+ 207	+ 22	− 73	+ 6	...	+ 42	+ 50	+ 12	...
+ 7,925	...	+ 18·8	− 61·8	...	...	+ 840	+ 2,500	+ 109·0	...
1	1	1	...	...	...	1	7	125	107
2	1	...	...	2	1	...	...	95	90

Egra.		Pataspur.		Ramnagar.		Bhagabanpur.		Khajri.	
Male.	Female.	Male.	Female.	Male.	Female.	Male.	Female.	Male.	Female.
45,237	34,673	35,979	44,049	32,282	33,273	53,303	53,531	24,382	23,509
32,067	30,695	44,104	43,792	29,436	29,578	55,389	56,277	22,082	21,434
+ 13,170	+ 3,978	− 8,125	+ 250	+ 2,846	+ 3,695	− 2,086	− 2,746	+ 2,300	+ 2,075
+ 41·07	+ 12·9	− 18·4	+ ·5	+ 9·6	+ 12·4	− 3·7	− 4·8	+ 10·4	+ 9·6
2,075	1,559	1,624	2,180	1,901	1,849	2,131	2,210	1,178	1,088
1,345	1,288	2,244	2,389	1,582	1,522	2,874	2,890	1,053	995
+ 730	+ 264	− 620	− 209	+ 319	+ 327	− 743	− 680	+ 125	+ 93
+ 54·2	+ 20·4	− 27·6	− 8·4	+ 20·1	− 21·4	− 25·8	− 23·5	+ 11·8	+ 9·3
...	...	...	...	...	...	...	...	3	3
...	...	...	...	...	...	...	...	...	...
...	...	...	...	...	...	...	...	+ 3	+ 3
...	...	...	...	...	...	...	...	...	...
...	...	1	...	...	...	...	...	5	3
...	...	5	4	...	...	...	...	6	4

HUGLI.

Pandua.		Dhaniakhali.		Polba.		Serampur.	
Male.	Female.	Male.	Female.	Male.	Female.	Male.	Female.
21,222	22,531	33,657	35,168	16,790	16,860	37,688	32,450
20,315	22,722	31,377	34,530	15,548	16,321	31,819	29,640
+ 907	− 191	+ 2,280	+ 638	+ 1,242	+ 539	+ 5,869	+ 2,810
+ 4·4	− ·8	+ 7·2	+ 1·8	+ 7·9	+ 3·3	+ 18·4	+ 9·4
10,504	11,546	12,255	13,961	5,399	5,668	6,097	3,167
10,848	12,169	12,785	14,845	5,764	6,282	3,979	2,511
− 344	− 623	− 530	− 884	− 365	− 614	+ 2,118	+ 656
− 3·1	− 5·1	− 4·1	− 5·9	− 6·3	− 9·7	+ 53·2	+ 26·1
43	17	426	224	61	24	28	11
...	...	...	...	5	4	15	9

DISTRICT

Religions.	Haripal.		Krishnanagar.		Singur.	
	Male.	Female.	Male.	Female.	Male.	Female.
HINDUS.						
1891	33,701	*38,685*	22,968	*24,629*	31,149	*30,474*
1881	33,610	*34,737*	20,621	*22,848*	26,745	*26,831*
Variation	+ 5,091	+ *3,948*	+ 2,347	+ *1,781*	+ 4,404	+ *3,643*
Percentage	+ 15·1	+ *11·3*	+ 11·3	+ *7·7*	+ 16·4	+ *13·5*
MUSALMANS.						
1891	8,025	*9,027*	5,463	*6,815*	2,919	*2,968*
1881	7,640	*8,946*	5,111	*6,527*	2,644	*2,676*
Variation	+ 385	+ *81*	+ 352	+ *288*	+ 275	+ *292*
Percentage	+ 5·0	+ *·9*	+ 6·8	+ *4·4*	+ 10·4	+ *10·9*
THE ANIMISTIC.						
1891	405	*235*	82	*29*	52	*16*
1881	...	...	...	...	...	...

DISTRICT

Religions.	District Total.		Howrah.		Bali.		Domjur.	
	Male.	Female.	Male.	Female.	Male.	Female.	Male.	Female.
HINDUS.								
1891	287,363	*278,610*	51,422	*34,797*	8,368	*6,577*	60,977	*57,319*
1881	249,689	*251,181*	38,974	*29,164*	7,011	*6,398*	52,882	*50,573*
Variation	+ 37,674	+ *27,429*	+ 12,448	+ *5,633*	+ 1,357	+ *179*	+ 8,095	+ *6,746*
Percentage	+ 15·0	+ *10·9*	+ 31·9	+ *19·3*	+ 19·3	+ *2·7*	+ 15·3	+ *13·3*
MUSALMANS.								
1891	76,154	*76,659*	17,969	*10,397*	1,086	*577*	14,723	*14,497*
1881	65,356	*66,769*	12,893	*7,621*	763	*548*	12,660	*12,264*
Variation	+ 10,798	+ *9,890*	+ 5,076	+ *2,776*	+ 323	+ *29*	+ 2,063	+ *2,233*
Percentage	+ 16·5	+ *14·8*	+ 39·3	+ *36·4*	+ 42·3	+ *5·2*	+ 16·2	+ 15·2
CHRISTIANS.								
1891	1,109	*963*	974	*893*	27	*19*	84	*49*
1881	1,184	*867*	1,088	*806*	22	*19*	50	*46*

PRESIDENCY

DISTRICT

Religions.	District Total.		Tollyganj.		Baruipur.		Sonarpur.	
	Male.	Female.	Male.	Female.	Male.	Female.	Male.	Female.
HINDUS.								
1891	619,954*	*567,850**	42,388	*34,149*	30,050	*29,052*	16,407	*16,860*
1881	511,326	*491,784*	32,410	*28,889*	26,216	*25,261*	16,734	*15,799*
Variation	+ 108,628	+ *76,066*	+ 9,978	+ *5,260*	+ 3,834	+ *3,791*	− 327	+ *1,061*
Percentage	+ 21·2	+ *15·4*	+ 30·7	+ *18·2*	+ 14·6	+ *15·0*	− 1·9	+ *6·7*
MUSALMANS.								
1891	361,528	*329,287*	26,271	*24,404*	14,274	*13,184*	4,430	*4,204*
1881	311,088	*293,635*	18,710	*18,491*	12,623	*11,419*	5,5[illegible]	*4,088*
Variation	+ 50,440	+ *35,652*	+ 7,561	+ *5,913*	+ 1,651	+ *1,765*	− 1,111	+ *116*
Percentage	+ 16·2	+ *12·1*	+ 40·4	+ *31·9*	+ 13·0	+ *15·4*	− 20·0	+ *2·8*
CHRISTIANS.								
1891	7,517	*5,465*	566	*503*	91	*117*	166	*175*
1881	5,388	*4,540*	404	*415*	126	*125*	132	*140*

* Includes Brahmos.

HUGLI—*concluded.*

Chanditala.		Jahanabad.		Goghat.		Khanakul.	
Male.	Female.	Male.	Female.	Male.	Female.	Male.	Female.
38,038	36,947	47,767	50,432	47,950	50,984	58,449	62,693
32,750	32,573	44,388	46,827	48,679	52,104	55,152	59,791
+ 5,288	+ 4,374	+ 3,379	+ 3,605	− 729	− 1,120	+ 3,297	+ 2,902
+ 16·1	+ 13·4	+ 7·6	+ 7·6	− 1·4	− 2·1	+ 5·9	+ 4·8
10,763	11,690	8,229	11,383	4,594	5,735	7,575	11,012
9,090	9,974	7,953	11,244	4,540	5,798	7,398	10,959
+ 1,673	+ 1,716	+ 276	+ 139	+ 54	− 63	+ 177	+ 53
+ 18·4	+ 17·2	+ 3·4	+ 1·2	+ 1·1	− 1·0	+ 2·3	+ ·4
113	1	46	47	121	32	31	27
...	...	...	...	...	...	...	...

HOWRAH.

Jagatballabhpur.		Ulubaria.		Amta.		Bagnan.		Shampur.	
Male.	Female.	Male.	Female.	Male.	Female.	Male.	Female.	Male.	Female.
31,046	33,260	30,029	29,691	47,037	54,008	26,322	28,685	32,162	34,273
27,766	30,985	28,311	28,124	42,138	49,757	23,967	25,909	28,640	30,271
+ 3,280	+ 2,275	+ 1,718	+ 1,567	+ 4,899	+ 4,251	+ 2,355	+ 2,776	+ 3,522	+ 4,002
+ 11·8	+ 7·3	+ 6·0	+ 5·5	+ 11·6	+ 8·5	+ 9·8	+ 10·7	+ 12·2	+ 13·2
9,149	11,784	13,253	14,683	8,094	11,460	6,428	7,387	5,452	5,867
8,254	10,534	12,038	12,838	7,603	10,470	6,335	7,347	4,810	5,140
+ 895	+ 1,250	+ 1,215	+ 1,845	+ 491	+ 990	+ 93	+ 40	+ 642	+ 727
+ 10·8	+ 11·8	+ 10·0	+ 14·3	+ 6·4	+ 9·4	+ 1·4	+ ·5	+ 13·3	+ 14·1
...	...	22	8	...	...	2	1	...	...
...	...	23	2	...	...	1	1	...	...

DIVISION.

24-PARGANAS.

Bishnupur.		Bhangor.		Budge-Budge.		Canning Town.		Jainagar.	
Male.	Female.	Male.	Female.	Male.	Female.	Male.	Female.	Male.	Female.
28,492	28,597	17,566	16,452	27,545	25,346	20,454	15,517	33,031	31,361
25,375	26,474	17,923	16,806	23,040	22,816	17,514	12,680	27,506	26,920
+ 3,117	+ 2,123	− 357	− 354	+ 4,505	+ 2,530	+ 2,940	+ 2,837	+ 5,525	+ 4,441
+ 12·3	+ 8·0	− 1·9	− 2·1	+ 19·5	+ 11·0	+ 16·7	+ 22·3	+ 20·0	+ 16·4
9,012	9,698	17,374	16,538	9,823	9,550	10,528	9,271	13,792	12,797
8,203	8,789	16,117	13,921	8,139	8,510	9,056	7,510	11,318	10,384
+ 809	+ 909	+ 1,257	+ 2,617	+ 1,684	+ 1,040	+ 1,472	+ 1,761	+ 2,474	+ 2,413
+ 9·8	+ 10·3	+ 7·7	+ 18·7	+ 20·6	+ 12·2	+ 16·2	+ 23·4	+ 21·8	+ 23·2
1,646	1,633	3	4	16	3	380	389	6	4
1,430	1,446	65	61	12		362	317	7	5

DISTRICT

Religions.	Baranagar.		Barasat.		Deganga.		Habra.	
	Male.	Female.	Male.	Female.	Male.	Female.	Male.	Female.
HINDUS.								
1891	15,169	*13,332*	16,384	*16,050*	9,312	*9,108*	15,586	*15,157*
1881	13,307	*12,446*	15,977	*16,168*	8,979	*8,796*	15,935	*15,953*
Variation	+ 1,862	+ *886*	+ 407	− *118*	+ 333	+ *312*	− 349	− *796*
Percentage	+ 13·9	+ *7·1*	+ 2·5	− *0·7*	+ 3·7	+ *3·5*	− 2·1	− 4·9
MUSALMANS.								
1891	3,572	*2,114*	22,219	*20,887*	19,047	*18,309*	21,112	*19,417*
1881	2,559	*1,585*	21,116	*19,846*	17,902	*17,839*	22,474	*21,067*
Variation	+ 1,013	+ *529*	+ 1,103	+ *1,041*	+ 1,145	+ *470*	+ 1,362	− *1,650*
Percentage	+ 39·5	+ *33·3*	+ 5·2	+ *5·2*	+ 6·3	+ *2·6*	− 6·0	− *7·8*
CHRISTIANS.								
1891	56	*35*	20	*16*	...	...	3	*8*
1881	53	*31*	7	*17*	...	...	...	...

Religions.	Basirhat.		Baduria.		Haroa.		Husainabad.	
	Male.	Female.	Male.	Female.	Male.	Female.	Male.	Female.
HINDUS.								
1891	16,581	*17,047*	25,704	*26,119*	19,808	*15,687*	31,955	*27,520*
1881	16,148	*15,861*	25,078	*25,479*	15,690	*14,248*	26,319	*22,758*
Variation	+ 433	+ *1,186*	+ 626	+ *640*	+ 4,118	+ *1,439*	+ 5,636	+ *4,769*
Percentage	+ 2·6	+ *7·4*	+ 2·4	+ *2·5*	+ 26·2	+ *10·0*	+ 21·4	+ *20·9*
MUSALMANS.								
1891	22,284	*22,635*	37,400	*37,089*	16,138	*11,049*	10,798	*8,994*
1881	22,847	*21,481*	37,013	*36,171*	10,099	*9,128*	9,955	*8,135*
Variation	− 563	+ *1,154*	+ 387	+ *918*	+ 6,039	+ *1,921*	+ 843	+ *859*
Percentage	− 2·4	+ *5·3*	+ 1·0	+ *2·5*	+ 59·7	+ *21·0*	+ 8·4	+ *10·5*
CHRISTIANS.								
1891	2	...	8	*7*	55	*48*	43	*28*
1881	...	...	4	*3*	70	*57*	34	*26*

DISTRICT

Religions.	District Total.		Krishnanagar.		Kaliganj.		Nakasipara.	
	Male.	Female.	Male.	Female.	Male.	Female.	Male.	Female.
HINDUS.								
1891	334,149	*355,075*	33,599	*35,728*	14,578	*15,734*	14,973	*16,713*
1881	351,399	*378,265*	35,864	*39,255*	16,484	*17,983*	16,326	*18,700*
Variation	− 17,250	−*23,190*	− 2,265	− *3,527*	− 1,906	− *2,249*	− 1,353	− *1,987*
Percentage	− 4·9	− *6·1*	− 6·3	− *8·9*	− 11·5	− *12·5*	− 8·3	− *10·6*
MUSALMANS.								
1891	464,081	*483,309*	20,964	*21,295*	8,206	*8,321*	12,227	*12,455*
1881	454,756	*471,939*	21,842	*21,917*	9,716	*10,000*	12,158	*12,573*
Variation	+ 9,325	+*11,370*	− 878	− *622*	− 1,510	− *1,679*	+ 69	− *118*
Percentage	+ 2·0	+ *2·4*	− 4·0	− *2·8*	− 15·5	− *16·8*	+ ·5	− *·9*

24-PARGANAS—*concluded.*

Naihati.		Dum-Dum.		Barrackpur.		Nawabganj.		Khardaha.	
Male.	Female.	Male.	Female.	Male.	Female.	Male.	Female.	Male.	Female.
29,866	*27,510*	17,127	*15,040*	10,746	*7,181*	7,620	*5,815*	9,106	*8,592*
25,132	*25,706*	12,934	*11,924*	9,348	*7,880*	4,753	*3,748*	8,387	*8,750*
+ 4,734	+ *1,804*	+ 4,193	+ *3,116*	+ 1,398	— *699*	+ 2,867	+ *2,067*	+ 719	— *228*
+ 18·8	+ *7·0*	+ 32·4	+ *26·1*	+ 14·9	— *8·8*	+ 60·3	+ *55·1*	+ 8·5	— *2·5*
15,433	*13,098*	10,626	*9,530*	5,010	*3,959*	2,908	*1,984*	3,334	*3,089*
13,646	*12,457*	10,147	*9,298*	6,636	*5,924*	1,376	*963*	1,900	*1,804*
+ 1,787	+ *641*	+ 479	+ *232*	— 1,626	— *1,965*	+ 1,532	+ *1,021*	+ 1,434	+ *1,285*
+ 13·0	+ *5·1*	+ 4·7	+ *2·4*	— 24·4	— *33·1*	+ 111·3	+ *106·0*	+ 75·4	+ *71·2*
92	*60*	1,255	*327*	586	*295*	69	*36*	60	*95*
9	*12*	826	*219*	505	*305*	12	*40*	18	*27*

Diamond Harbour.		Kulpi.		Bankipur.		Dedipur.		Mathurapur.	
Male.	Female.	Male.	Female.	Male.	Female.	Male.	Female.	Male.	Female.
23,277	*23,258*	44,216	*41,112*	39,420	*40,750*	18,250	*19,170*	23,949	*23,179*
18,997	*19,764*	37,456	*34,268*	33,539	*35,478*	15,689	*16,949*	20,931	*19,977*
+ 4,280	+ *3,494*	+ 6,760	+ *6,844*	+ 5,881	+ *5,272*	+ 2,561	+ *2,228*	+ 3,018	+ *3,202*
+ 22·5	+ *17·6*	+ 18·0	+ *19·9*	+ 17·5	+ *14·8*	+ 16·3	+ *13·1*	+ 14·4	+ *16·0*
8,333	*8,513*	10,540	*10,325*	20,839	*21,569*	6,016	*6,344*	5,442	*5,139*
6,831	*7,184*	9,236	*8,949*	17,848	*18,895*	5,222	*5,562*	4,574	*4,235*
+ 1,502	+ *1,329*	+ 1,304	+ *1,376*	+ 2,991	+ *2,674*	+ 794	+ *782*	+ 868	+ *904*
+ 21·9	+ *18·4*	+ 14·1	+ *15·3*	+ 16·7	+ *14·1*	+ 15·2	+ *14·0*	+ 18·9	+ *21·3*
27	*22*	202	*149*	970	*905*	16	*19*	423	*407*
30	*22*	158	*130*	748	*767*	23	*18*	354	*353*

NADIA.

Chapra.		Krishnaganj.		Hanskhali.		Jibannagar.		Ranaghat.	
Male.	Female.	Male.	Female.	Male.	Female.	Male.	Female.	Male.	Female.
11,230	*11,532*	8,842	*9,878*	6,721	*6,877*	8,082	*8,656*	20,429	*22,320*
11,608	*12,234*	9,552	*10,459*	8,210	*8,623*	9,344	*10,085*	22,352	*24,885*
— 378	— *702*	— 710	— *581*	— 1,489	— *1,746*	— 1,262	— *1,429*	— 1,923	— *2,565*
— 3·2	— *5·7*	— 7·4	— *5·5*	— 18·1	— *20·2*	— 13·5	— *14·1*	— 8·6	— *10·3*
19,113	*19,699*	7,016	*6,909*	11,852	*11,873*	9,792	*9,613*	17,504	*17,042*
18,583	*19,485*	6,419	*6,247*	14,004	*14,434*	10,454	*10,231*	18,770	*18,408*
+ 530	+ *214*	+ 597	+ *662*	— 2,152	— *2 561*	— 662	— *618*	— 1,266	— *1,366*
+ 2·8	+ *1·0*	+ 9·3	+ *10·5*	— 15·3	— *17·7*	— 6·3	— *6·0*	— 6·7	— *7·4*

DISTRICT

Religions.	Santipur.		Chakdaha.		Haringhata.		Kushtia.	
	Male.	Female.	Male.	Female.	Male.	Female.	Male.	Female.
HINDUS.								
1891	17,988	*19,841*	19,707	*18,606*	8,246	*8,249*	4,533	*4,168*
1881	17,750	*20,187*	19,172	*19,927*	8,849	*9,010*	3,848	*3,945*
Variation	+ 238	— *346*	+ 535	— *1,321*	— 603	— *761*	+ 685	+ *223*
Percentage	+ 1·3	— *1·7*	+ 2·7	— *6·6*	— 6·8	— *8·4*	+ 17·8	+ *5·6*
MUSALMANS.								
1891	7,706	*8,415*	13,650	*11,904*	9,491	*8,856*	12,210	*12,576*
1881	7,590	*8,296*	13,355	*12,166*	10,570	*9,877*	9,627	*9,997*
Variation	+ 116	+ *119*	+ 295	— *262*	— 1,079	— *1,021*	+ 2,583	+ *2,579*
Percentage	+ 1·5	+ *1·4*	+ 2·2	— *2·1*	— 10·2	— *10·3*	+ 26·8	+ *25·1*

Religions.	Mihrpur.		Karimpur.		Gangni.		Tehata.	
	Male.	Female.	Male.	Female.	Male.	Female.	Male.	Female.
HINDUS.								
1891	13,720	*14,989*	15,869	*17,142*	8,557	*8,870*	20,449	*21,312*
1881	14,998	*16,074*	16,673	*18,044*	9,506	*9,626*	20,782	*22,207*
Variation	— 1,278	— *1,085*	— 804	— *902*	— 949	— *756*	— 333	— *895*
Percentage	— 8·5	— *6·7*	— 4·8	— *4·9*	— 9·9	— *7·8*	— 1·6	— *4·0*
MUSALMANS.								
1891	18,997	*19,578*	35,170	*38,637*	26,707	*28,569*	21,450	*23,106*
1881	18,467	*20,026*	32,520	*35,509*	26,874	*28,483*	21,778	*23,588*
Variation	+ 530	— *448*	+ 2,650	+ *3,128*	— 167	+ *86*	— 328	— *482*
Percentage	+ 2·8	— *2·2*	+ 8·1	+ *8·8*	— ·6	+ *·3*	— 1·5	— *2·0*

DISTRICT

Religions.	District Total.		Jessor.		Kaliganj.	
	Male.	Female.	Male.	Female.	Male.	Female.
HINDUS.						
1891	362,492	*375,109*	22,989	*21,194*	15,292	*15,103*
1881	374,819	*393,503*	24,512	*23,484*	16,586	*16,588*
Variation	— 12,327	— *18,394*	— 1,523	— *2,290*	— 1,294	— *1,485*
Percentage	— 3·2	— *4·6*	— 6·2	— *9·7*	— 7·8	— *8·9*
MUSALMANS.						
1891	578,275	*571,860*	58,783	*54,697*	26,710	*25,952*
1881	584,196	*586,309*	60,891	*58,305*	28,756	*27,269*
Variation	— 5,921	— *14,449*	— 2,108	— *3,608*	— 2,046	— *1,317*
Percentage	— 1·0	— *2·4*	— 3·4	— *6·1*	— 7·1	— *4·8*

NADIA—*concluded.*

Naupara.		Daulatpur.		Bhadalia.		Kumarkhali.		Bhaluka.	
Male.	Female.	Male.	Female.	Male.	Female.	Male.	Female.	Male.	Female.
19,249	19,986	14,119	15,135	9,020	10,106	18,924	20,599	6,302	7,184
20,578	20,703	14,814	15,439	8,965	10,164	18,616	20,068	5,676	6,760
— 1,329	— 717	— 695	— 304	+ 55	— 58	+ 308	+ 531	+ 626	+ 424
— 6·0	— 2·4	— 4·6	— 1·9	+ 4·8	+ ·5	+ 1·6	+ 2·6	+ 11·0	+ 6·9
47,747	53,722	26,326	28,553	26,176	27,075	31,096	32,502	17,197	18,200
45,523	50,564	24,212	26,106	24,482	24,573	29,471	30,072	14,377	15,113
+ 2,224	+ 3,158	+ 2,114	+ 2,447	+ 1,694	+ 2,502	+ 1,625	+ 2,430	+ 2,820	+ 3,087
+ 4·8	+ 6·2	+ 8·7	+ 9·3	+ 6·9	+ 10·1	+ 5·5	+ 8·0	+ 19·6	+ 20·4

Chuadanga.		Damurhuda.		Alamdanga.		Kalupol.	
Male.	Female.	Male.	Female.	Male.	Female.	Male.	Female.
2,643	2,880	15,681	16,863	13,921	14,515	6,767	7,197
3,099	3,537	15,938	17,135	14,831	15,333	7,564	7,882
— 456	— 657	— 257	— 272	— 910	— 818	— 797	— 690
— 14·7	— 18·5	— 1·6	— 1·5	— 6·1	— 5·3	— 10·5	— 8·7
7,168	7,065	14,900	15,036	30,118	31,098	11,298	12,210
7,620	7,562	14,542	14,796	29,696	30,084	12,106	11,832
— 452	— 497	+ 358	+ 240	+ 422	+ 1,014	— 808	— 622
— 5·9	— 6·5	+ 2·4	+ 1·6	+ 1·4	+ 3·3	— 6·6	— 5·6

JESSOR.

Bagherpara.		Gadkhali.		Manirampur.		Keshudpur.	
Male.	Female.	Male.	Female	Male.	Female.	Male.	Female.
11,527	11,859	10,306	10,657	24,962	25,056	12,924	13,297
13,086	13,446	11.550	11,885	25,721	26,380	13,625	14,143
— 1,559	— 1,587	— 1,244	— 1,228	— 759	— 1,324	— 701	— 846
— 11·8	— 11·8	— 10·7	— 10·3	— 2·9	— 5·0	— 5·1	— 5·9
17,324	16,974	21,707	20,548	50,993	48,592	28,825	27,766
18,725	18,645	22,221	21,560	52,650	50,858	29,029	28,618
— 1,401	— 1,671	— 514	— 1,012	— 1,657	— 2,266	— 204	— 852
— 7·4	— 8·9	— 2·3	— 4·6	— 3·1	— 4·6	—	— 2·9

DISTRICT—

Religions.	Jhenidaha.		Salkopa.		Kotchandpur.	
	Male.	Female.	Male.	Female.	Male.	Female.
HINDUS.						
1891	16,025	*16,100*	28,755	*31,678*	8,416	*7,966*
1881	18,413	*19,213*	29,047	*32,232*	8,834	*8,158*
Variation	− 2,388	− *3,113*	− 292	− *554*	− 418	− *192*
Percentage	− 12·9	− *16·2*	− 1·0	− *1·7*	− 4·7	− *2·3*
MUSALMANS.						
1891	28,424	*29,338*	58,461	*61,822*	12,651	*12,283*
1881	32,287	*32,683*	58,284	*60,603*	13,862	*13,176*
Variation	− 863	− *3,345*	+ 177	+ *1,219*	− 1,211	− *893*
Percentage	− 11·9	− *10·2*	+ ·3	+ *2·0*	− 8·7	− *6·7*

Religions.	Lohagara.		Kalia.		Bangaon.	
	Male.	Female.	Male.	Female.	Male.	Female.
HINDUS.						
1891	25,078	*27,227*	23,994	*25,018*	11,516	*11,504*
1881	23,248	*26,905*	22,045	*22,778*	12,128	*12,582*
Variation	+ 1,830	+ *322*	+ 1,949	+ *2,240*	− 612	− *1,078*
Percentage	+ 7·8	+ *1·1*	+ 8·8	+ *9·8*	− 5·0	− *8·5*
MUSALMANS.						
1891	31,664	*31,505*	16,668	*15,857*	16,379	*16,126*
1881	25,873	*27,836*	14,231	*13,893*	17,587	*17,369*
Variation	+ 5,791	+ *3,669*	+ 2,437	+ *1,964*	− 1,208	− *1,243*
Percentage	+ 22·3	+ *13·1*	+ 17·1	+ *14·1*	− 6·8	− *7·1*

DISTRICT

Religions.	District Total.		Sujaganj, Gora Bazar, and Barhampur Municipality.		Burwan.	
	Male.	Female.	Male.	Female.	Male.	Female.
HINDUS.						
1891	303,440	*316,723*	15,410	*15,036*	18,153	*18,949*
1881	305,553	*329,243*	14,692	*15,168*	18,496	*19,580*
Variation	− 2,113	− *12,520*	+ 718	− *132*	− 343	− *631*
Percentage	− ·6	− *3·8*	+ 4·8	− *·8*	− 1·8	− *3·2*
MUSALMANS.						
1891	296,119	*322,534*	6,747	*6,803*	15,715	*15,860*
1881	279,892	*310,065*	6,963	*7,465*	14,733	*15,096*
Variation	+ 16,227	+ *12,469*	− 216	− *662*	+ 982	+ *764*
Percentage	+ 5·7	+ *4·0*	− 3·1	− *8·8*	+ 6·6	+ *5·0*
THE ANIMISTIC.						
1891	4,668	*4,636*	342	*331*	...	...
1881	431	*415*	...	...	...	...
JAINS.						
1891	1,147	*1,110*	8	*5*	...	...
1881	362	*313*	...	...	...	...

JESSOR—*concluded.*

MAGURA.		MUHAMADPUR.		SALIKHA.		NARAIL.	
Male.	Female.	Male.	Female.	Male.	Female.	Male.	Female.
36,085	*38,685*	15,549	*17,088*	11,251	*12,163*	38,348	*39,431*
34,733	*38,405*	15,332	*16,895*	12,188	*13,178*	38,808	*40,022*
+ 1,353	+ *280*	+ 217	+ *193*	— 937	— *1,015*	— 460	— *591*
+ 3·8	+ *·7*	+ 1·6	+ *1·1*	— 7·6	— *7·7*	— 1·1	— *1·4*
44,940	*46,337*	29,040	*29,080*	11,060	*11,968*	37,204	*36,518*
41,795	*44,199*	25,019	*26,423*	12,379	*12,719*	35,836	*36,672*
+ 3,145	+ *2,138*	+ 4,021	+ *2,657*	— 1,319	— *751*	+ 1,368	— *154*
+ 7·5	+ *4·8*	+ 16·5	+ *10·0*	— 10·6	— *5·9*	+ 3·8	— *·4*

MAHESPUR.		GARAPOTA.		SARSA.		GAIGHATA.	
Male.	Female.	Male.	Female.	Male.	Female.	Male.	Female.
18,964	*20,085*	10,622	*11,123*	11,610	*11,372*	8,279	*8,503*
21,086	*22,469*	11,534	*12,146*	13,014	*12,980*	9,330	*9,614*
— 2,122	— *2,384*	— 912	— *1,023*	— 1,404	— *1,608*	— 1,051	— *1,111*
— 10·0	— *10·6*	— 7·9	— *8·3*	— 10·7	— *12·3*	— 11·2	— *11·5*
32,110	*31,809*	16,853	*17,484*	23,886	*23,312*	14,593	*13,892*
34,852	*34,215*	18,088	*19,284*	26,633	*26,401*	15,698	*15,581*
— 2,242	— *2,406*	— 1,235	— *1,800*	— 2,747	— *3,089*	— 1,105	— *1,689*
— 6·2	— *7·0*	— 6·8	— *9·3*	— 10·3	— *11·7*	— 7·0	— *10·8*

MURSHIDABAD.

DAULATABAZAR.		HARIHARPARA.		NOWADA.		GOAS.	
Male.	Female.	Male.	Female.	Male.	Female.	Male.	Female.
7,323	*7,343*	10,837	*11,588*	11,468	*11,966*	12,917	*12,907*
7,387	*8,060*	11,946	*13,058*	11,343	*12,094*	12,502	*12,840*
— 64	— *717*	— 1,109	— *1,470*	+ 125	— *128*	+ 415	+ *67*
— ·8	— *8·8*	— 9·2	— *11·2*	+ 1·1	— *1·0*	+ 3·3	+ *·5*
11,785	*12,547*	15,828	*16,803*	12,235	*13,105*	28,342	*31,453*
11,500	*12,621*	15,658	*16,469*	11,846	*12,270*	25,153	*27,895*
+ 285	— *74*	+ 170	+ *334*	+ 389	+ *835*	+ 3,189	+ *3,558*
+ 2·4	— *·5*	+ 1·0	+ *2·0*	+ 3·2	+ *6·8*	+ 12·1	+ *12·7*
...	...	...	...	...	...	...	...
...	...	...	...	...	...	...	...
...	...	1	...	...	...	...	...
...	...	2	...	...	...	...	...

DISTRICT

Religions.	Jalinghi.		Shahnagar, Manulabazar, Asanpur, and Lalbagh Municipality.		Bhagabangola.	
	Male.	Female.	Male.	Female.	Male.	Female.
HINDUS.						
1891	14,847	*15,856*	17,780	*17,019*	9,528	*9,553*
1881	14,974	*16,907*	18,116	*17,985*	10,098	*10,854*
Variation	— 127	— *1,051*	— 386	— *973*	— 570	— *1,301*
Percentage	— ·8	— *6·2*	— 2·1	— *5·4*	— 5·6	— *11·9*
MUSALMANS.						
1891	38,725	*43,393*	11,079	*11,839*	15,951	*18,523*
1881	35,434	*41,191*	11,788	*13,086*	16,499	*19,781*
Variation	+ 3,291	+ *2,202*	— 709	— *1,247*	— 548	— *1,258*
Percentage	+ 9·2	+ *5·3*	— 6·0	— *9·5*	— 3·3	— *6·3*
THE ANIMISTIC.						
1891	...	1	...	...	8	*9*
1881	...	...	123	121	...	...
JAINS.						
1891	·1	...	1,052	*1,080*	4	*3*
1881	...	...	337	*307*	...	...

Religions.	Suti.		Dewansarai.		Mirzapur.	
	Male.	Female.	Male.	Female.	Male.	Female.
HINDUS.						
1891	17,201	*18,825*	8,930	*8,957*	14,293	*15,440*
1881	16,349	*17,980*	8,334	*9,383*	14,081	*15,864*
Variation	+ 852	+ *845*	+ 596	— *426*	+ 212	— *424*
Percentage	+ 5·2	+ *4·1*	+ 7·1	— *4·5*	+ 1·5	— *2·6*
MUSALMANS.						
1891	15,691	*17,787*	20,291	*22,531*	7,961	*8,728*
1881	15,352	*16,863*	17,314	*20,005*	7,441	*8,079*
Variation	+ 339	+ *924*	+ 2,977	+ *2,526*	+ 520	+ *649*
Percentage	+ 2·2	+ *5·4*	+ 17·1	+ *12·1*	+ 6·9	+ *8·0*
THE ANIMISTIC.						
1891	...	...	...	...	75	*67*
1881	...	...	...	...	17	*13*
JAINS.						
1891	23	*2*	4	...	1	...
1881	1	*3*	...	...	...	...

DISTRICT

Religions.	District Total.		Khulna.		Dumuria.	
	Male.	Female.	Male.	Female.	Male.	Female.
HINDUS.						
1891	300,045	*272,620*	36,964	*33,722*	19,618	*18,654*
1881	275,116	*248,541*	32,294	*32,218*	16,873	*15,980*
Variation	+ 24,929	+ *24,079*	+ 4,670	+ *1,504*	+ 2,745	+ *2,724*
Percentage	+ 9·3	+ *9·6*	+ 14·0	+ *4·6*	+ 16·2	+ *17·0*

MURSHIDABAD—*concluded.*

Sagardighi.		Kaliaganj.		Raghunathganj.		Shamsherganj.	
Male.	Female.	Male.	Female.	Male.	Female.	Male.	Female.
7,690	7,981	11,151	11,817	10,784	11,141	17,878	19,793
8,403	8,926	11,700	12,737	12,934	12,210	17,468	18,390
− 713	− 945	− 549	− 920	− 2,150	− 1,069	+ 410	+ 1,403
− 8·4	− 10·5	− 4·7	− 7·2	− 16·6	− 8·7	+ 2·3	+ 7·6
5,309	5,607	6,504	6,717	18,046	20,780	18,884	21,444
4,917	5,435	6,060	6,585	20,064	22,227	15,538	17,961
+ 392	+ 172	+ 444	+ 132	− 2,018	− 1,447	+ 3,346	+ 3,483
+ 7·0	+ 3·1	+ 7·3	+ 2·0	− 10·0	− 6·5	+ 21·5	+ 19·3
1,423	1,395	735	714	17	7	685	658
97	80	...	...	...	...	83	87
10	5	1	...	25	6	17	9
...	...	...	...	14	2	8	1

Kandi.		Barwa.		Khargaon.		Bharatpur.		Gokarna.	
Male.	Female.	Male.	Female.	Male.	Female.	Male.	Female.	Male.	Female.
10,379	10,086	23,329	24,361	18,700	19,910	33,462	35,739	11,430	11,863
10,446	11,367	22,592	24,571	18,176	20,456	32,755	37,129	12,761	13,684
− 67	− 681	+ 737	− 210	+ 524	− 546	+ 707	− 1,390	− 1,331	− 1,821
− ·6	− 5·9	+ 3·2	− ·8	+ 2·8	− 2·6	+ 2·1	− 3·7	− 10·4	− 13·3
3,618	3,545	7,716	7,878	8,130	8,408	19,395	20,602	8,167	8,181
3,554	3,536	6,954	7,300	7,284	7,887	17,926	20,205	7,884	8,108
+ 64	+ 9	+ 762	+ 578	+ 846	+ 521	+ 1,469	+ 397	+ 283	+ 73
+ 1·8	+ ·2	+ 10·9	+ 7·9	+ 11·6	+ 6·6	+ 8·1	+ 1·9	+ 3·5	+ ·9
59	88	153	153	396	437	18	14	159	134
...	...	...	...	101	114	...	...	...	...
...	...	...	...	...	...	...	...	...	...
...	...	...	...	...	...	...	...	...	...

KHULNA.

Baitaghata.		Paikgachha.		Bagherhat.		Mullahat.	
Male.	Female.	Male.	Female.	Male.	Female.	Male.	Female.
11,965	10,435	26,404	22,199	44,284	40,682	15,187	14,817
11,352	9,451	21,016	16,817	39,971	38,484	13,525	13,512
+ 613	+ 984	+ 5,388	+ 5,382	+ 4,313	+ 2,198	+ 1,662	+ 1,305
+ 5·3	+ 10·4	+ 25·6	+ 32·0	+ 10·7	+ 5·7	+ 12·3	+ 9·6

DISTRICT

Religions.	District Total.		Khulna.		Dumuria.	
	Male.	Female.	Male.	Female.	Male.	Female.
MUSALMANS.						
1891	317,378	*286,617*	38,084	*33,055*	20,843	*19,888*
1881	292,883	*262,661*	31,914	*30,836*	21,251	*20,936*
Variation	+ 24,495	+ *23,956*	+ 6,170	+ *2,219*	— 408	— *1,048*
Percentage	+ 8·3	+ *9·1*	+ 19·3	+ *7·1*	— 1·9	— *5·0*

Religions.	Rampal.		Morrellganj.		Satkhira.	
	Male.	Female.	Male.	Female.	Male.	Female.
HINDUS.						
1891	15,544	*11,990*	14,740	*11,509*	20,763	*19,743*
1881	13,810	*10,675*	13,882	*10,917*	19,406	*18,397*
Variation	+ 1,734	+ *1,315*	+ 858	+ *1,255*	+ 1,357	+ *1,346*
Percentage	+ 12·5	+ *12·3*	+ 6·1	+ *12·2*	+ 6·9	+ *7·3*
MUSALMANS.						
1891	15,123	*12,393*	26,054	*21,681*	31,933	*31,199*
1881	13,549	*11,915*	21,352	*17,189*	29,276	*29,530*
Variation	+ 1,574	+ *1,108*	+ 4,703	+ *4,492*	+ 2,657	+ *1,669*
Percentage	+ 11·6	+ *9·8*	+ 22·0	+ *26·1*	+ 9·0	+ *5·6*

RAJSHAHI

DISTRICT

Religions.	District Total.		Dinajpur.		Hemtabad.	
	Male.	Female.	Male.	Female.	Male.	Female.
HINDUS.						
1891	388,623	*351,819*	50,265	*44,190*	26,219	*24,451*
1881	371,422	*345,208*	50,001	*45,661*	25,586	*23,804*
Variation	+ 17,201	+ *6,611*	+ 264	— *1,471*	+ 633	+ *647*
Percentage	+ 4·6	+ *1·9*	+ ·5	— *3·2*	+ 2·4	+ *2·7*
MUSALMANS.						
1891	416,670	*385,927*	58,375	*55,569*	17,902	*15,946*
1881	409,749	*386,075*	59,388	*57,239*	18,852	*17,045*
Variation	+ 6,921	— *148*	— 1,013	— *1,670*	— 950	— *1,099*
Percentage	+ 1·6	— *0·3*	— 1·7	— *2·9*	— 5·0	— *6·4*
THE ANIMISTIC.						
1891	5,597	*5,097*	...	...	...	...
1881	859	*576*	...	...	...	...

KHULNA—*concluded.*

Baitaghata.		Paikgachha.		Bagherhat.		Mullahat.	
Male.	Female.	Male.	Female.	Male.	Female.	Male.	Female.
7,903	*6,732*	18,939	*15,822*	35,528	*31,267*	14,663	*14,457*
10,236	*6,429*	18,973	*13,672*	30,356	*29,007*	11,705	*11,736*
— 2,333	+ *303*	— 34	+ *2,150*	+ 5,172	+ *2,260*	+ 2,958	+ *2,721*
— 22·7	+ *4·7*	— ·1	+ *15·7*	+ 17·0	+ *7·7*	+ 25·2	+ *23·0*

Kalaroa.		Magura.		Asasuni.		Kaliganj.	
Male.	Female.	Male.	Female.	Male.	Female.	Male.	Female.
10,249	*11,308*	19,946	*20,289*	20,443	*17,215*	43,938	*40,064*
11,218	*11,736*	19,678	*19,160*	18,110	*15,023*	43,981	*36,891*
— 969	— *428*	+ 268	+ *1,129*	+ 2,333	+ *2,192*	— 43	+ *3,173*
— 8·6	— *3·6*	+ 1·3	+ *5·8*	+ 12·8	+ *14·5*	— ·0	+ *8·6*
29,265	*28,953*	26,063	*24,746*	18,632	*15,404*	34,348	*31,097*
29,080	*29,364*	21,989	*21,414*	15,894	*13,383*	37,308	*27,950*
+ 185	— *411*	+ 4,074	+ *3,332*	+ 2,738	+ *2,021*	— 2,960	+ *3,147*
+ ·6	— *1·4*	+ 18·5	+ *15·5*	+ 17·2	+ *15·1*	— 7·9	+ *11·2*

DIVISION.

DINAJPUR.

Kaliganj.		Bansihari.		Birganj.		Patnitolla.		Mahadebpur.	
Male.	Female.	Male.	Female.	Male.	Female.	Male.	Female.	Male.	Female.
35,562	*33,592*	22,890	*21,265*	40,029	*37,018*	18,621	*16,647*	13,931	*12,848*
33,831	*32,193*	22,483	*21,165*	38,842	*36,961*	14,953	*13,698*	13,513	*12,749*
+ 1,731	+ *1,399*	+ 407	+ *100*	+ 1,187	+ *57*	+ 3,668	+ *2,949*	+ 418	+ *99*
+ 5·1	+ *4·3*	+ 1·8	+ *·4*	+ 3·0	+ *·1*	+ 24·5	+ *21·5*	+ 3·0	+ *·7*
15,634	*14,916*	19,855	*18,995*	32,426	*28,529*	22,480	*20,777*	23,699	*22,710*
14,709	*14,148*	19,569	*18,731*	33,884	*30,204*	20,565	*20,003*	20,632	*20,344*
+ 925	+ *768*	+ 286	+ *264*	— 1,458	— *1,675*	+ 1,915	+ *774*	+ 3,067	+ *2,366*
+ 6·2	+ *5·4*	+ 1·4	+ *1·4*	— 4·3	— *5·5*	+ 9·3	+ *3·8*	+ 4·8	+ *11·6*
478	*445*	100	*87*	...	*184*	218	...	35	*40*
...	...	13	*9*	...	...	4	*6*	...	...

DISTRICT

Religions.	Porsha.		Patiram.		Gangarampur.		Chintaman.	
	Male.	Female.	Male.	Female.	Male.	Female.	Male.	Female.
HINDUS.								
1891	9,748	*7,018*	18,257	*16,128*	23,003	*20,767*	11,895	*9,611*
1881	8,473	*6,646*	19,278	*17,330*	21,633	*19,641*	9,370	*8,271*
Variation	+ 1,275	+ *379*	− 1,021	− *1,909*	+ 1,370	+ *1,126*	+ 2,525	+ *1,340*
Percentage	+ 15·0	+ *5·5*	− 5·2	− *6·9*	+ 6·3	+ *5·7*	+ 26·9	+ *16·2*
MUSALMANS.								
1891	17,292	*16,255*	17,262	*15,735*	18,143	*16,639*	17,077	*15,534*
1881	16,894	*16,414*	17,409	*16,404*	17,134	*15,965*	17,184	*16,265*
Variation	+ 398	− *159*	− 147	− *669*	+ 1,009	+ *674*	− 107	− *731*
Percentage	+ 2·3	− *·9*	− ·8	− *4·0*	+ 5·8	+ *4·2*	− 6·2	− *4·4*
THE ANIMISTIC.								
1891	159	*128*	3,479	*3,195*	531	*496*	19	*9*
1881	86	*73*	...	...	...	...	601	*367*

DISTRICT

Religions.	District Total.		Boalia.		Tanor.	
	Male.	Female.	Male.	Female.	Male.	Female.
HINDUS.						
1891	143,367	*135,571*	12,724	*10,539*	5,923	*5,485*
1881	144,415	*142,760*	12,483	*11,057*	5,695	*5,663*
Variation	− 1,048	− *7,189*	+ 241	− *518*	+ 228	− *178*
Percentage	− ·7	− *5·0*	+ 1·9	− *4·6*	+ 4·0	− *3·1*
MUSALMANS.						
1891	510,688	*523,239*	37,835	*37,656*	37,334	*38,149*
1881	511,904	*531,903*	38,169	*39,069*	36,167	*38,084*
Variation	− 1,216	− *8,664*	− 334	− *1,413*	+ 1,167	+ *65*
Percentage	− ·2	− *1·6*	− ·8	− *3·6*	+ 3·2	+ *·1*

Religions.	Naugaon.		Manda.		Panchupur.	
	Male.	Female.	Male.	Female.	Male.	Female.
HINDUS.						
1891	10,716	*9,418*	15,819	*14,824*	9,804	*9,107*
1881	9,607	*9,102*	14,114	*13,551*	8,695	*8,335*
Variation	+ 1,109	+ *316*	+ 1,705	+ *1,273*	+ 1,109	+ *772*
Percentage	+ 11·5	+ *3·4*	+ 12·0	+ *9·3*	+ 12·7	+ *9·2*
MUSALMANS.						
1891	37,923	*38,199*	41,276	*41,697*	34,405	*34,821*
1881	33,747	*33,383*	37,127	*38,511*	30,887	*30,977*
Variation	+ 4,176	+ *4,816*	+ 4,149	+ *3,186*	+ 3,518	+ *3,844*
Percentage	+ 12·3	+ *14·4*	+ 11·1	+ *8·2*	+ 11·3	+ *12·4*

DINAJPUR—*concluded.*

Parbatipur.		Nawabganj.		Thakurgaon.		Ranisankail.		Pirganj.	
Male.	Female.	Male.	Female.	Male.	Female.	Male.	Female.	Male.	Female.
11,398	*9,368*	8,996	*7,363*	51,723	*48,866*	17,667	*16,894*	28,419	*25,793*
10,547	*9,154*	7,114	*6,043*	50,659	*48,889*	17,522	*16,984*	27,617	*26,019*
+ 851	+ *214*	+ 1,882	+ *1,320*	+ 1,064	— *23*	+ 145	— *90*	+ 802	— *226*
+ 8·0	+ *2·3*	+ 26·4	+ *21·8*	+ 2·1	— *0·4*	+ ·8	— *·5*	+ 2·9	— *·8*
24,892	*23,481*	25,250	*23,369*	64,031	*60,000*	20,524	*18,956*	21,822	*18,516*
24,004	*22,913*	24,643	*23,639*	62,658	*58,190*	20,768	*19,828*	21,456	*18,743*
+ 888	+ *568*	+ 607	— *270*	+ 1,373	+ *1,810*	— 244	— *872*	+ 366	— *227*
+ 3·6	+ *2·4*	+ 2·4	— *1·1*	+ 2·1	+ *3·1*	— 1·1	— *4·3*	+ 1·7	— *1·2*
...	...	511	*459*	...	...	...	...	67	*61*
46	*39*	109	*89*	...	...	...	...	...	...

RAJSHAHI.

Godagari.		Putia.		Charghat.		Baghmara.	
Male.	Female.	Male.	Female.	Male.	Female.	Male.	Female.
10,836	*9,411*	6,593	*6,437*	14,754	*14,766*	5,377	*5,062*
11,059	*9,245*	8,704	*8,728*	14,166	*14,144*	5,668	*5,598*
— 223	+ *166*	— 2,111	— *2,291*	+ 588	+ *622*	— 291	— *536*
— 2·0	+ *1·7*	— 24·2	— *26·2*	+ 4·1	+ *4·3*	— 5·1	— *9·6*
13,286	*13,243*	41,914	*40,792*	45,890	*48,802*	53,885	*54,668*
11,592	*11,903*	51,144	*52,661*	42,838	*45,879*	54,693	*55,622*
+ 1,694	+ *1,340*	— 9,230	— *11,869*	+ 3,052	+ *2,923*	— 808	— *954*
+ 14·6	+ *11·2*	— 18·0	— *22·5*	+ 7·1	+ *6·3*	— 1·4	— *1·7*

Nator.		Singra.		Burigram.		Lalpur.	
Male.	Female.	Male.	Female.	Male.	Female.	Male.	Female.
16,454	*16,656*	14,650	*14,265*	9,362	*9,920*	10,355	*9,681*
17,525	*18,722*	13,905	*14,452*	10,638	*11,562*	12,156	*12,601*
— 1,071	— *2,066*	+ 745	— *187*	— 1,276	— *1,642*	— 1,801	— *2,920*
— 6·1	— *11·0*	+ 5·3	— *1·2*	— 11·9	— *14·2*	— 14·8	— *23·1*
52,457	*56,459*	44,194	*44,385*	47,535	*49,763*	22,754	*24,605*
55,991	*61,418*	42,040	*42,346*	48,602	*50,752*	28,907	*31,298*
— 3,534	— *4,959*	+ 2,154	+ *2,039*	— 1,067	— *989*	— 6,153	— *6,693*
— 6·3	— *8·0*	+ 5·1	+ *4·8*	— 2·1	— *1·9*	— 21·2	— *21·3*

DISTRICT

Religions.	District Total.		Rangpur.		Kaliganj.	
	Male.	Female.	Male.	Female.	Male.	Female.
HINDUS.						
1891	396,671	*371,569*	24,546	*21,761*	45,573	*43,592*
1881	414,244	*402,288*	22,448	*22,616*	48,809	*47,403*
Variation	— 17,573	— *30,726*	+ 2,098	— *855*	— 3,236	— *3,811*
Percentage	— 4·2	— *7·4*	+ 9·3	— *3·7*	— 6·6	— *8·7*
MUSALMANS.						
1891	663,897	*631,514*	44,002	*41,548*	31,498	*28,433*
1881	652,383	*627,222*	40,553	*38,868*	30,957	*28,437*
Variation	+ 11,514	+ *4,292*	+ 3,449	+ *2,680*	+ 541	— *4*
Percentage	+ 1·7	+ *·6*	+ 8·5	+ *6·8*	+ 1·7	— *·0*

Religions.	Jaldhaka.		Nilphamari.		Barabari.		Kurigram.	
	Male.	Female.	Male.	Female.	Male.	Female.	Male.	Female.
HINDUS.								
1891	40,933	*40,231*	31,132	*26,210*	25,767	*27,157*	9,717	*8,536*
1881	41,980	*40,809*	30,036	*27,843*	29,111	*29,745*	10,362	*10,784*
Variation	— 1,047	— *578*	+ 1,096	— *1,633*	— 3,344	— *2,588*	— 645	— *2,248*
Percentage	— 2·4	— *1·4*	+ 3·6	— *5·8*	— 11·4	— *8·7*	— 6·2	— *20·8*
MUSALMANS.								
1891	43,089	*40,246*	47,290	*41,573*	34,844	*32,635*	20,529	*20,089*
1881	41,649	*39,123*	44,473	*40,976*	35,811	*33,941*	19,007	*18,742*
Variation	+ 1,440	+ *1,123*	+ 2,817	+ *597*	— 967	— *1,306*	+ 1,522	+ *1,347*
Percentage	+ 3·4	+ *2·8*	+ 6·3	+ *1·4*	— 2·7	— *3·8*	+ 8·0	+ *6·7*

DISTRICT

Religions.	District Total.		Bogra.		Shariakandi.		Sirganj.	
	Male.	Female.	Male.	Female.	Male.	Female.	Male.	Female.
HINDUS.								
1891	83,822	*70,474*	19,003	*15,569*	11,627	*9,387*	5,438	*4,371*
1881	74,066	*66,594*	16,213	*14,659*	10,609	*9,022*	4,792	*4,161*
Variation	+ 9,756	+ *3,880*	+ 2,790	+ *910*	+ 1,018	+ *365*	+ 646	+ *210*
Percentage	+ 13·1	+ *5·8*	+ 17·2	+ *6·2*	+ 9.5	+ *4·0*	+ 13·4	+ *5·0*
MUSALMANS.								
1891	334,004	*327,096*	109,565	*110,457*	58,763	*57,339*	29,272	*28,366*
1881	298,733	*295,271*	100,116	*101,823*	52,401	*50,781*	25,382	*24,835*
Variation	+ 35,271	+ *31,825*	+ 9,449	+ *8,634*	+ 6,362	+ *6,558*	+ 3,890	+ *3,531*
Percentage	+ 11·8	+ *10·7*	+ 9·4	+ *8·4*	+ 12·1	+ *12·9*	+ 15·3	+ *14·2*
THE ANIMISTIC.								
1891	1,008	*992*	...	...	...	...	...	...
1881	...	...	...	...	...	...	...	...

RANGPUR.

Mahiganj.		Badarganj.		Milapukhur.		Pirganj.		Dimla.	
Male.	Female.	Male.	Female.	Male.	Female.	Male.	Female.	Male.	Female.
18,942	*16,675*	12,802	*11,289*	9,926	*8,661*	6,814	*5,169*	39,925	*37,864*
23,433	*21,023*	12,385	*11,826*	10,500	*9,661*	6,433	*5,602*	41,496	*39,264*
− 4,491	− *4,348*	+ 417	− *537*	− 574	− *1,000*	+ 381	− *433*	− 1,571	− *1,400*
− 19·1	− *20·6*	+ 3·3	− *4·5*	− 5·4	− *10·3*	+ 5·9	− *7·7*	− 3·7	− *3·5*
38,310	*36,112*	31,687	*31,942*	40,556	*40,198*	28,778	*27,238*	30,410	*28,432*
43,123	*41,619*	33,032	*1,376*	39,719	*38,468*	28,832	*27,750*	30,106	*27,842*
− 4,813	− *5,507*	− 1,345	+ *566*	+ 837	+ *1,730*	− 54	− *512*	+ 304	+ *590*
− 11·1	− *13·2*	− 4·0	+ *1·8*	+ 2·1	+ *4·4*	− ·1	− *1·8*	+ 1·0	+ *2·1*

Nageswari.		Ulipur.		Gobindganj.		Sadullapur.		Sundarganj.	
Male.	Female.	Male.	Female.	Male.	Female.	Male.	Female.	Male.	Female.
34,018	*34,681*	26,798	*26,165*	25,519	*22,175*	29,221	*26,888*	15,038	*14,508*
38,361	*38,101*	29,562	*30,570*	24,164	*22,525*	29,426	*28,423*	15,738	*16,093*
− 4,343	− *3,420*	− 2,764	− *4,405*	+ 1,355	− *350*	− 205	− *1,535*	− 700	− *1,585*
− 11·3	− *8·9*	− 9·3	− *14·4*	+ 5·6	− *1·5*	− ·6	− *5·3*	− 4·4	− *9·8*
37,928	*34,352*	66,691	*67,408*	78,456	*75,258*	61,000	*57,858*	28,829	*28,185*
39,500	*37,656*	66,293	*67,353*	72,434	*69,901*	56,922	*55,549*	29,972	*29,614*
− 1,572	− *3,304*	+ 398	+ *55*	+ 6,022	+ *5,357*	+ 4,078	+ *2,309*	− 1,143	− *1,429*
− 3·9	− *8·7*	+ ·6	...	+ 8·3	+ *7·6*	+ 7·1	+ *4·1*	− 3·8	− *4·8*

BOGRA.

Panchbibi.		Khetlal.		Nawabganj.		Adamdighi.		Sherpur.	
Male.	Female.	Male.	Female.	Male.	Female.	Male.	Female.	Male.	Female.
14,476	*11,956*	3,533	*3,171*	7,560	*6,525*	11,057	*10,176*	11,128	*9,319*
12,571	*11,027*	3,043	*2,237*	6,073	*5,648*	10,102	*9,353*	10,663	*9,787*
+ 1,905	+ *929*	+ 490	+ *934*	+ 1,487	+ *877*	+ 955	+ *823*	+ 465	− *468*
+ 15·1	+ *8·4*	+ 16·1	+ *7·9*	+ 24·4	+ *15·5*	+ 9·4	+ *8·7*	+ 4·3	− *4·7*
23,783	*20,871*	19,747	*19,722*	15,792	*14,805*	43,730	*44,669*	33,352	*30,867*
22,452	*20,762*	16,792	*17,111*	14,328	*13,324*	37,444	*38,164*	29,818	*28,471*
+ 1,331	+ *109*	+ 2,955	+ *2,611*	+ 1,464	+ *1,481*	+ 6,286	+ *6,505*	+ 3,534	+ *2,396*
+ 5·9	+ *·5*	+ 17·6	+ *15·2*	+ 10·2	+ *11·1*	+ 16·7	+ *17·0*	+ 11·8	+ *8·4*
934	*912*	50	*51*	...	...	24	*22*	...	...
...	...	...	..	...	...	...	...	...	...

DISTRICT

Religions.	District Total.		Pabna.		Chatmohar.		Dulai.	
	Male.	Female.	Male.	Female.	Male.	Female.	Male.	Female.
HINDUS.								
1891	179,668	*189,495*	23,331	*23,219*	16,844	*17,804*	26,979	*28,770*
1881	175,956	*185,593*	24,061	*24,176*	17,758	*19,446*	27,166	*29,467*
Variation	+ 3,712	— *3,098*	— 730	— *957*	— 914	— *1,642*	— 187	— *697*
Percentage	+ 2·1	+ *1·6*	— 3·03	— *3·9*	— 5·1	— *8·4*	— 6·8	— *2·3*
MUSALMANS.								
1891	497,856	*501,953*	68,272	*71,241*	49,414	*50,352*	63,867	*64,518*
1881	472,089	*477,819*	69,170	*72,170*	47,346	*48,915*	62,886	*62,927*
Variation	+ 25,767	+ *24,134*	— 898	— *929*	+ 2,068	+ *1,437*	+ 981	+ *1,591*
Percentage	+ 5·4	+ *5·0*	— 1·2	— *1·2*	+ 4·3	+ *2·9*	+ 1·5	+ *2·5*

DISTRICT

Religions.	District Total.		Darjeeling.*	
	Male.	Female.	Male.	Female.
HINDUS.				
1891	94,876	*76,295*	39,934	*34,412*
1881	73,233	*53,948*	27,401	*20,771*
Variation	+ 21,643	+ *22,347*	+ 12,533	+ *13,641*
Percentage	+ 29·5	+ *41·4*	+ 45·7	+ *65·6*
MUSALMANS.				
1891	6,582	*3,429*	1,292	*339*
1881	5,109	*3,097*	798	*163*
Variation	+ 1,473	+ *332*	+ 494	+ *176*
Percentage	+ 28·8	+ *10·7*	+ 61·9	+ *107·9*
BUDDHISTS.				
1891	20,610	*19,910*	14,310	*14,120*
1881	10,095	*8,680*	8,065	*7,160*
Variation	+ 10,515	+ *11,230*	+ 6,245	+ *6,960*
Percentage	+ 104·1	+ *129·2*	+ 77·4	+ *97·2*
CHRISTIANS.				
1891	874	*628*	693	*473*
1881	539	*303*	410	*212*

* Includes Kalimpong

DISTRICT

Religions.	District Total.		Jalpaiguri.		Rajganj, including Titalya.		Boda.	
	Male.	Female.	Male.	Female.	Male.	Female.	Male.	Female.
HINDUS.								
1891	241,957	*207,581*	26,379	*22,521*	20,136	*18,637*	47,740	*44,322*
1881	193,971	*173,456*	23,788	*21,350*	20,765	*19,729*	51,069	*48,998*
Variation	+ 47,986	+ *34,125*	+ 2,591	+ *1,171*	— 629	— *1,092*	— 3,329	— *4,676*
Percentage	+ 24·7	+ *19·6*	+ 10·8	+ *5·4*	— 3·0	— *5·5*	— 6·5	— *9·5*
MUSALMANS.								
1891	117,595	*104,880*	17,571	*16,138*	18,663	*17,550*	38,874	*35,430*
1881	108,485	*100,026*	15,492	*14,739*	20,055	*19,136*	40,907	*37,667*
Variation	+ 9,110	+ *4,854*	+ 2,079	+ *1,406*	— 1,392	— *1,586*	— 2,033	— *2,237*
Percentage	+ 8·3	+ *4·8*	+ 13·4	+ *9·5*	— 6·9	— *8·2*	— 4·9	— *5·9*
THE BUDDHISTS.								
1891	1,384	*1,125*	17	...	...	...	...	...
1881	276	*210*	...	...	...	...	...	...
THE ANIMISTIC.								
1891	3,301	*2,994*	83	*85*	3	*2*	...	...
1881	1,608	*1,604*	...	...	...	...	...	...

PABNA.

Mathura.		Sirajganj.		Shahzadpur.		Raiganj.		Ulapara.	
Male.	Female.	Male.	Female.	Male.	Female.	Male.	Female.	Male.	Female.
17,573	*18,583*	31,236	*27,535*	27,092	*30,327*	15,239	*13,375*	21,374	*22,812*
19,465	*19,899*	28,142	*27,700*	26,350	*30,291*	13,242	*13,181*	19,772	*21,363*
— 1,892	— *1,316*	+ 3,094	— *165*	+ 742	+ *36*	+ 1,997	+ *194*	+ 1,602	+ *1,449*
— 9·7	— *6·6*	+ 10·9	— *·5*	+ 2·8	+ *·1*	+ 15·0	+ *1·4*	+ 8·1	+ *6·7*
29,702	*29,813*	90,856	*88,244*	89,761	*93,576*	36,585	*33,709*	69,399	*70,500*
31,595	*31,521*	82,052	*81,084*	80,297	*83,418*	33,874	*32,077*	64,869	*65,707*
— 1,893	— *1,708*	+ 8,804	+ *7,160*	+ 9,464	+ *10,158*	+ 2,711	+ *1,632*	+ 4,530	+ *4,793*
— 5·9	— *5·7*	+ 10·7	+ *8·8*	+ 11·7	+ *12·1*	+ ·80	+ *5·0*	+ 6·9	+ *7·5*

DARJEELING.

Kurseong.		Siliguri.	
Male.	Female.	Male.	Female.
18,642	*14,299*	36,300	*27,654*
15,469	*9,101*	30,363	*24,076*
+ 3,173	+ *5,198*	+ 5,937	+ *3,578*
+ 20·5	+ *56·3*	+ 19·5	+ *14·8*
415	*102*	4,875	*2,988*
557	*111*	3,754	*2,823*
— 142	— *9*	+ 1,121	+ *165*
— 25·4	— *8·1*	+ 29·8	+ *5·8*
5,677	*5,371*	623	*419*
1,546	*1,202*	484	*318*
+ 4,131	+ *4,169*	+ 139	+ *101*
+ 267·2	+ *346·8*	+ 28·7	+ *31·7*
115	*87*	66	*68*
113	*77*	1 6	*7*

and Jor-Bangala thánas.

JALPAIGURI.

Patgram.		Mainaguri.		Dam-Dim.		Alipore.		Salbari.	
Male.	Female.	Male.	Female.	Male.	Female.	Male.	Female.	Male.	Female.
18,580	*17,573*	42,128	*35,564*	38,289	*29,218*	18,688	*15,222*	30,017	*24,524*
20,422	*18,913*	32,381	*27,974*	14,484	*10,356*	13,713	*11,571*	17,349	*14,565*
— 1,842	— *1,340*	+ 9,747	+ *7,590*	+ 23,805	+ *18,862*	+ 4,975	+ *3,651*	+ 12,668	+ *9,959*
— 9·0	— *7·0*	+ 30·1	+ *37·1*	+ 164·3	+ *182·1*	+ 36·2	+ *31·5*	+ 73·0	+ *68·3*
12,374	*11,545*	10,728	*9,798*	7,784	*5,658*	2,647	*1,998*	8,954	*6,763*
13,006	*12,295*	8,709	*8,237*	3,875	*2,994*	1,463	*1,060*	4,978	*3,896*
— 632	— *750*	+ 2,019	+ *1,561*	+ 3,909	+ *2,664*	+ 1,184	+ *929*	+ 3,976	+ *2,867*
— 4·8	— *6·1*	+ 23·1	+ *18·9*	+ 100·8	+ *88·9*	+ 80·9	+ *86·9*	+ 79·8	+ *73·3*
...	...	259	*178*	361	*241*	701	*662*	46	*44*
...	...	5	...	249	*185*	21	*25*	1	...
...	...	253	*111*	1,163	*977*	797	*900*	1,002	*919*
...	...	...	...	130	*149*	1,459	*1,455*	19	*7*

f 3

DACCA

DISTRICT

Religions.	District Total.		Lalbagh.		Kapasia.	
	Male.	Female.	Male.	Female.	Male.	Female.
HINDUS.						
1891	460,544	*475,021*	25,068	*16,945*	24,820	*22,368*
1881	412,804	*444,020*	23,506	*16,951*	22,589	*20,478*
Variation	+ 47,740	+ *31,001*	+ 1,582	— *6*	+ 2,231	+ *1,890*
Percentage	+ 15·1	+ *6·9*	+ 6·7	...	+ 9·8	+ *8·8*
MUSALMANS.						
1891	734,663	*739,136*	20,948	*19,879*	48,924	*45,211*
1881	614,981	*632,219*	19,070	*20,298*	39,347	*36,475*
Variation	+ 119,682	+ *106,917*	+ 1,878	— *419*	+ 9,577	+ *8,736*
Percentage	+ 19·4	+ *16·9*	+ 9·8	— *2·0*	+ 24·3	+ *23·9*
CHRISTIANS.						
1891	4,900	*5,576*	248	*219*	451	*598*
1881	4,214	*4,583*	262	*213*	414	*497*
Variation	+ 686	+ *993*	— 14	+ *6*	+ 37	+ *101*
Percentage	+ 16·2	+ *21·6*	— 5·3	+ *2·8*	+ 8·9	+ *20·3*

Religions.	Rupganj.		Raipura.		Manikganj.	
	Male.	Female.	Male.	Female.	Male.	Female.
HINDUS.						
1891	27,987	*27,496*	26,517	*24,186*	34,388	*36,123*
1881	24,164	*24,866*	23,947	*22,758*	32,687	*35,759*
Variation	+ 3,823	+ *2,630*	+ 2,570	+ *1,428*	+ 1,701	+ *364*
Percentage	+ 15·8	+ *10·5*	+ 10·7	+ *6·2*	+ 5·2	+ *1·0*
MUSALMANS.						
1891	70,388	*67,580*	96,818	*91,726*	63,704	*66,521*
1881	56 792	*54,965*	79,602	*76,431*	56,778	*59,906*
Variation	+ 13,596	+ *12,615*	+ 17,216	+ *15,295*	+ 6,926	+ *6,615*
Percentage	+ 23·9	+ *22·9*	+ 21·6	+ *20·0*	+ 12·1	+ *11·1*
CHRISTIANS.						
1891	1,790	*1,800*	7	3	2	...
1881	1,582	*1,575*	...	...	...	...
Variation	+ 208	+ *225*	...	...	...	...
Percentage	+ 13·1	+ *14·3*	...	...	...	...

DISTRICT

Religions.	District Total.		Faridpur.		Bhusna.	
	Male.	Female.	Male.	Female.	Male.	Female.
HINDUS.						
1891	338,319	*359,350*	17,849	*16,667*	17,761	*19,085*
1881	314,839	*339,845*	17,996	*17,348*	18,817	*20,681*
Variation	+ 23,480	+ *19,505*	— 147	— *681*	— 1,056	— *1,596*
Percentage	+ 7·4	+ *5·7*	— 0·8	— *3·9*	— 5·6	— *7·7*

DIVISION.

DACCA.

Sabhar.		Nawabganj.		Keraniganj.		Naraingan.j.	
Male.	Female.	Male.	Female.	Male.	Female.	Male.	Female.
47,018	50,591	32,053	36,337	43,265	44,148	27,716	19,810
41,433	46,376	29,663	34,642	38,347	40,482	20,395	16,807
+ 5,585	+ 4,145	+ 2,390	+ 1,695	+ 4,918	+ 3,666	+ 7,321	+ 3,003
+ 13·4	+ 8·9	+ 8·0	+ 4·8	+ 12·8	+ 9·0	+ 35·8	+ 17·8
53,051	56,837	47,517	50,564	48,046	50,766	48,118	42,398
41,906	45,659	41,598	45,585	41,115	44,034	34,121	32,360
+ 11,145	+ 11,178	+ 5,919	+ 4,979	+ 6,931	+ 6,732	+ 13,997	+ 10,038
+ 6·5	+ 24·4	+ 14·2	+ 10·8	+ 16·8	+ 10·7	+ 41·0	+ 31·0
26	20	1,779	2,442	153	143	100	38
30	16	1,824	2,271	57	55	27	12
— 4	+ 4	— 45	+ 171	+ 96	+ 88	+ 73	+ 26
— 13·3	+ 25·0	— 2·4	+ 7·5	+ 168·4	+ 160·0	+ 270·3	+ 216·6

Jafarganj.		Harirampur.		Munshiganj.		Srinagar.	
Male.	Female.	Male.	Female.	Male.	Female.	Male.	Female.
27,004	28,880	19,059	20,291	52,078	57,580	73,551	90,406
27,798	29,600	19,219	20,697	44,330	50,955	64,726	83,649
— 794	— 720	— 160	— 406	+ 7,748	+ 6,625	+ 8,825	+ 6,757
— 2·8	— 2·4	— 0·8	— 1·9	+ 17·4	+ 13·0	+ 13·6	+ 8·0
46,176	46,634	30,319	30,626	90,440	92,685	70,214	78,409
42,985	43,422	29,622	30,794	72,847	75,302	59,198	67,688
+ 3 191	+ 3,212	+ 697	— 168	+ 17,593	+ 17,383	+ 11,016	+ 10,721
+ 7·4	+ 7·3	+ 2·3	— 0·5	+ 24·1	+ 23·0	+ 18·6	+ 15·8
2	...	12	1	21	13	309	369
1	1	...	...	16	13	1	...
+ 1	...	...	...	+ 5	...	+ 308	...
+ 100·0	...	...	...	+ 31·2	...	+ 30,800·0	...

FARIDPUR.

Awanpur.		Bhanga.		Maksudpur.		Madaripur.	
Male.	Female.	Male.	Female.	Male.	Female.	Male.	Female.
13,978	15,835	28,810	31,916	42,218	45,125	38,425	40,114
14,293	16,100	26,726	30,105	36,922	40,775	33,465	36,111
— 315	— 265	+ 2,084	+ 1,111	+ 5,296	+ 4,350	+ 4,960	+ 4,003
— 2·2	— 1·0	+ 7·7	+ 3·6	+ 14·3	+ 10·6	+ 14·8	+ 11·0

DISTRICT

Religions.	District Total.		Faridpur.		Bhusna.	
	Male.	Female.	Male.	Female.	Male.	Female.
MUSALMANS.						
1891	552,918	*543,119*	32,349	*30,039*	32,615	*32,720*
1881	492,328	*487,019*	28,915	*27,234*	33,585	*34,339*
Variation	+ 60,590	+ *56,100*	+ 3,434	+ *2,805*	— 970	— *1,619*
Percentage	+ 12·3	+ *11·5*	+ 11·8	+ *10·2*	— 2·8	— *4·6*
CHRISTIANS.						
1891	1,803	*1,736*	24	*27*	...	...
1881	1,385	*1,358*	23	*30*	...	...

Religions.	Gopalganj.		Kotalipara.		Palang.	
	Male.	Female.	Male.	Female.	Male.	Female.
HINDUS.						
1891	29,389	*29,696*	27,250	*28,300*	43,331	*52,129*
1881	26,576	*26,709*	22,784	*24,500*	41,970	*49,751*
Variation	+ 2,813	+ *2,987*	+ 4,466	+ *3,800*	+ 1,361	+ *2,378*
Percentage	+ 10·5	+ *11·1*	+ 19·6	+ *15·5*	+ 3·2	+ *4·7*
MUSALMANS.						
1891	19,126	*18,493*	10,853	*10,443*	91,228	*92,392*
1881	16,170	*15,822*	8,551	*8,504*	82,163	*82,365*
Variation	+ 2,956	+ *2,671*	+ 2,302	+ *1,939*	+ 9,065	+ *10,027*
Percentage	+ 18·2	+ *16·8*	+ 26·9	+ *22·8*	+ 11·0	+ *12·1*
CHRISTIANS.						
1891	58	*72*	1,132	*1,151*	2	...
1881	28	*36*	898	*916*	1	...

DISTRICT

Religions.	District Total.		Katwali (Barisal).		Bakarganj.		Mehndiganj.	
	Male.	Female.	Male.	Female.	Male.	Female.	Male.	Female.
HINDUS.								
1891	349,074	*331,307*	22,895	*18,893*	22,693	*21,306*	18,357	*16,325*
1881	320,220	*304,377*	20,995	*17,787*	22,587	*21,430*	17,898	*16,083*
Variation	+ 28,854	+ *26,930*	+ 1,900	+ *1,106*	+ 106	— *124*	+ 459	+ *242*
Percentage	+ 9·0	+ *8·8*	+ 9·0	+ *6·2*	+ 0·4	— *0·5*	+ 2·5	+ *1·5*
MUSALMANS.								
1891	749,690	*713,022*	46,679	*44,394*	48,333	*46,557*	62,656	*58,681*
1881	648,797	*618,897*	44,734	*43,039*	45,886	*44,765*	56,568	*55,149*
Variation	+100,893	+ *94,125*	+ 1,945	+ *1,222*	+ 2,447	+ *1,792*	+ 6,088	+ *3,532*
Percentage	+ 15·5	+ *15·2*	+ 4·3	+ *3·0*	+ 5·3	+ *4·0*	+ 10·7	+ *6·4*
CHRISTIANS.								
1891	2,396	*2,263*	248	*187*	381	*390*	2	...
1881	1,836	*1,881*	189	*109*	340	*387*	5	...
BUDDHISTS.								
1891	8,205	*2,875*	14	...	...	...	...	...
1881	2,552	*2,215*	...	...	1	...	8	...

FARIDPUR—*concluded.*

Awanpur.		Bhanga.		Muksudpur.		Madaripur.	
Male.	Female.	Male.	Female.	Male.	Female.	Male.	Female.
35,946	37,189	64,265	63,554	43,525	44,939	57,253	57,436
34,328	35,536	55,785	56,100	38,716	40,087	47,976	48,127
+ 1,618	+ 1,653	+ 8,480	+ 7,454	+ 4,809	+ 4,852	+ 9,277	+ 9,309
+ 4·7	+ 4·6	+ 15·2	+ 13·2	+ 12·4	+ 12·1	+ 19·3	+ 19·3
...	...	5	1	315	296	177	143
...	...	2	...	217	216	113	125

Sibchar.		Goalanda.		Baliakandi.		Pangsa.	
Male.	Female.	Male.	Female.	Male.	Female.	Male.	Female.
15,410	16,427	22,006	19,723	22,453	23,745	19,439	21,288
13,999	15,794	20,276	18,297	13,574	14,613	27,441	29,061
+ 1,411	+ 633	+ 1,730	+ 1,426	+ 8,879	+ 9,132	— 8,002	— 7,773
+ 10·0	+ 4·0	+ 8·5	+ 7·7	+ 65·4	+ 62·4	— 29·1	— 26·7
51,392	48,623	44,954	39,214	26,007	25,593	43,405	42,477
44,112	42,859	35,666	31,673	18,860	18,022	47,501	46,351
+ 7,280	+ 5,764	+ 9,288	+ 7,541	+ 7,147	+ 7,571	— 4,096	— 3,874
+ 16·5	+ 13·4	+ 26·0	+ 23·8	+ 37·8	+ 42·0	— 8·6	— 8·3
...	...	87	43	...	...	3	3
1	...	94	31	...	...	8	4

BAKHARGANJ.

Gaurnadi.		Jhalakati.		Nalchiti.		Patuakhali.	
Male.	Female.	Male.	Female.	Male.	Female.	Male.	Female.
52,153	56,660	38,007	39,556	12,877	13,480	20,198	17,298
45,955	51,031	33,344	35,983	15,079	13,313	19,189	16,418
+ 6,198	+ 5,629	+ 4,663	+ 3,573	— 2,202	+ 167	+ 1,009	+ 880
+ 13·4	+ 11·0	+ 13·9	+ 9·9	— 14·6	+ 1·2	+ 5·2	+ 5·3
48,766	47,485	43,677	42,314	26,587	25,394	79,567	77,222
42,682	42,161	37,306	36,750	25,632	24,822	69,452	68,576
+ 6,084	+ 5,324	+ 6,371	+ 5,564	+ 955	+ 572	+ 10,115	+ 8,646
+ 14·2	+ 12·6	+ 17·0	+ 15·1	+ 3·7	+ 2·3	+ 14·5	+ 12·6
1,563	1,520	17	13	35	22	94	84
1,116	1,247	23	10	41	24	86	80
...	...	...	...	11	...	...	...
...	...	...	...	50	...	...	...

DISTRICT

Religions.	Bauphal.		Gulsakhali.		Golachipa.		Pirojpur.	
	Male.	Female.	Male.	Female.	Male.	Female.	Male.	Female.
HINDUS.								
1891	12,202	*10,335*	8,049	*5,764*	7,256	*4,739*	27,904	*27,294*
1881	10,843	*9,561*	8,232	*5,316*	6,216	*3,974*	26,870	*25,906*
Variation	+ 1,359	+ *774*	— 183	+ *448*	+ 1,040	+ *765*	+ 1,034	+ *1,388*
Percentage	+ 12·5	+ *8·0*	— 2·2	+ *8·4*	+ 16·7	+ *19·2*	+ 3·8	+ *5·3*
MUSALMANS.								
1891	45,226	*43,267*	48,159	*44,920*	34,965	*31,369*	34,971	*34,037*
1881	38,655	*36,129*	42,264	*38,069*	26,238	*22,129*	32,875	*31,983*
Variation	+ 6,571	+ *7,138*	+ 5,895	+ *6,251*	+ 8,727	+ *9,233*	+ 2,096	+ *2,054*
Percentage	+ 16·9	+ *19·7*	+ 13·9	+ *16·1*	+ 33·2	+ *41·7*	+ 6·3	+ *6·4*
CHRISTIANS.								
1891	...	...	3	...	...	...	6	*5*
1881	...	...	5	*3*	...	...	4	...
BUDDHISTS.								
1891	4	...	2,686	*2,479*	457	*403*	...	...
1881	...	...	2,252	*1,991*	256	*224*	...	...

DISTRICT

Religions.	District Total.		Nasirabad.		Phulpur.		Gafargaon.	
	Male.	Female.	Male.	Female.	Male.	Female.	Male.	Female.
HINDUS.								
1891	548,473	*497,093*	37,511	*27,055*	24,186	*20,413*	20,320	*17,442*
1881	498,474	*477,439*	35,872	*26,902*	21,154	*19,336*	17,810	*15,841*
Variation	+ 49,999	+ *19,654*	+ 1,639	+ *153*	+ 3,032	+ *1,077*	+ 2,510	+ *1,601*
Percentage	+ 1·0	+ *4·1*	+ 4·5	+ *0·5*	+ 14·3	+ *5·5*	+ 14·9	+ *10·1*
MUSALMANS.								
1891	1,224,694	*1,171,789*	85,338	*79,223*	43,673	*38,823*	52,367	*49,805*
1881	1,004,630	*972,326*	75,211	*70,287*	34,443	*30,966*	42,917	*40,935*
Variation	+ 220,064	+ *199,456*	+ 10,127	+ *8,936*	+ 9,230	+ *7,857*	+ 9,450	+ *8,870*
Percentage	+ 21·9	+ *20·5*	+ 13·4	+ *12·7*	+ 26·7	+ *25·3*	+ 22·0	+ *21·6*
THE ANIMISTIC.								
1891	15,070	*14,539*	1,086	*998*	6,034	*5,855*	329	*332*
1881	13,348	*12,607*	461	*440*	4,087	*3,794*	118	*136*
Variation	+ 1,722	+ *1,932*	+ 625	+ *558*	+ 1,947	+ *2,061*	+ 211	+ *196*
Percentage	+ 12·9	+ *15·3*	+ 13·5	+ *126·8*	+ 47·6	+ *54·3*	+ 178·8	+ *144·1*

Religions.	Jamalpur.		Diwanganj.		Sherpur.		Nalitabari.	
	Male.	Female.	Male.	Female.	Male.	Female.	Male.	Female.
HINDUS.								
1891	23,012	*17,820*	9,281	*7,009*	13,349	*11,217*	18,548	*16,744*
1881	20,393	*18,531*	7,484	*6,581*	15,807	*13,800*	13,542	*14,785*
Variation	+ 2,619	— *711*	+ 1,797	+ *428*	— 2,458	— *2,583*	+ 5,006	+ *1,959*
Percentage	+ 12·8	— *3·8*	+ 24·0	+ *6·5*	— 15·5	— *18·7*	+ 36·9	+ *13·2*

BAKHARGANJ—*concluded.*

Bhandaria.		Surupkati.		Matbaria.		Bhola.		Barhanuddin.	
Male.	Female.	Male.	Female.	Male.	Female.	Male.	Female.	Male.	Female.
15,567	*14,598*	51,936	*55,983*	16,629	*13,402*	10,694	*7,358*	11,657	*8,316*
12,777	*12,083*	46,414	*50,551*	14,694	*11,386*	9,755	*6,835*	9,372	*6,720*
+ 2,790	+ *2,515*	+ 5,522	+ *5,432*	+ 1,935	+ *2,016*	+ 939	+ *523*	+ 2,285	+ *1,596*
+ 21·8	+ *20·8*	+ 11·8	+ *10·7*	+ 13·1	+ *17·7*	+ 9·6	+ *7·6*	+ 24·3	+ *23·7*
32,002	*32,605*	35,946	*37,319*	46,028	*43,287*	65,462	*60,810*	50,666	*43,438*
24,422	*24,070*	31,100	*32,124*	36,191	*33,744*	55,307	*51,250*	39,425	*33,544*
+ 7,580	+ *8,535*	+ 4,786	+ *5,195*	+ 9,837	+ *9,543*	+ 10,155	+ *9,560*	+ 11,241	+ *9,894*
+ 31·0	+ *35·4*	+ 15·3	+ *16·1*	+ 27·1	+ *28·3*	+ 18·3	+ *18·6*	+ 28·5	+ *29·4*
1	*1*	34	*32*	5	*2*	2	...	5	*7*
...	...	12	*12*	9	*8*	6	*1*	...	...
...	...	...	...	...	...	33	...	...	...
...	...	...	...	...	...	15	...	...	...

MAIMANSINGH.

Iswarganj.		Phulbaria.		Netrokona.		Durgapur.		Kendua.	
Male.	Female.	Male.	Female.	Male.	Female.	Male.	Female.	Male.	Female.
31,732	*27,170*	13,758	*12,057*	48,640	*42,767*	31,015	*27,748*	55,636	*51,284*
30,896	*27,449*	10,938	*11,739*	40,192	*37,362*	31,628	*28,762*	52,904	*48,851*
+ 836	— *279*	+ 2,820	+ *318*	+ 8,448	+ *5,405*	— 613	— *1,014*	+ 2,732	+ *2,433*
+ 2·7	— *1·0*	+ 25·7	+ *2·7*	+ 21·0	+ *14·4*	— 1·9	— *3·5*	+ 5·1	+ *4·9*
96,968	*93,259*	34,069	*32,155*	83,075	*74,583*	26,651	*22,325*	93,789	*88,361*
86,763	*84,061*	25,819	*24,739*	67,423	*61,951*	25,247	*21,677*	83,053	*79,373*
+ 10,205	+ *9,198*	+ 8,250	+ *7,416*	+ 15,652	+ *12,632*	+ 1,404	+ *648*	+ 10,736	+ *8,988*
+ 11·7	+ *10·9*	+ 31·9	+ *29·9*	+ 23·2	+ *20·3*	+ 5·5	+ *2·9*	+ 12·9	+ *11·3*
63	*41*	335	*349*	246	*216*	4,072	*3,895*	...	...
143	*141*	163	*200*	238	*218*	4,680	*4,459*	43	*27*
— 80	— *100*	+ 172	+ *149*	+ 8	— *2*	— 608	— *564*	— 43	— *27*
— 56·3	— *70·9*	+ 105·5	+ *74·5*	+ 3·3	— *0·9*	— 12·9	— *12·6*	— 100·0	— *100·0*

Tangail.		Gopalpur.		Kalihati.		Kisorganj.		Nikli.		Bajitpur.	
Male.	Female.	Male.	Female.	Male.	Female.	Male.	Female.	Male.	Female.	Male.	Female.
75,076	*77,516*	28,972	*32,058*	21,263	*22,936*	23,951	*22,793*	17,602	*17,529*	47,621	*45,535*
63,106	*70,667*	22,395	*29,925*	18,602	*18,892*	22,930	*22,296*	16,650	*17,356*	49,171	*48,364*
+ 11,970	+ *6,849*	+ 6,577	+ *2,133*	+ 2,661	+ *4,044*	+ 1,021	+ *497*	+ 952	+ *173*	— 1,550	— *2,829*
+ 18·9	+ *9·6*	+ 22·3	+ *7·1*	+ 14·3	+ *21·4*	+ 4·4	+ *2·2*	+ 5·7	+ *0·9*	— 3·1	— *5·8*

DISTRICT

Religions.	Jamalpur.		Diwanganj.		Sherpur.		Nalitabari.	
	Male.	Female.	Male.	Female.	Male.	Female.	Male.	Female.
MUSALMANS.								
1891	103,340	98,448	57,652	55,489	48,932	46,133	24,737	22,423
1881	86,613	83,068	43,980	43,206	45,387	42,596	19,299	17,867
Variation	+ 16,727	+ 15,380	+ 13,672	+ 12,283	+ 3,545	+ 3,537	+ 5,438	+ 4,556
Percentage	+ 19·3	+ 18·4	+ 31·0	+ 28·4	+ 7·8	+ 8·3	+ 28·1	+ 25·4
THE ANIMISTIC.								
1891	505	499	42	37	613	607	1,576	1,549
1881	384	330	62	59	792	708	1,607	1,500
Variation	+ 121	+ 169	— 20	— 22	— 179	— 101	— 31	+ 49
Percentage	+ 31·5	+ 49·0	— 32·2	— 37·2	— 22·6	— 14·2	— 1·9	+ 3·3

CHITTAGONG

DISTRICT

Religions.	District Total.		Chittagong.		Mirsarai.		Kumira.		Phattikchari.		Hathazari.	
	Male.	Female.	Male.	Female.	Male.	Female.	Male.	Female.	Male.	Female.	Male.	Female.
HINDUS.												
1891	145,673	156,660	9,980	6,333	13,725	14,549	8,121	8,112	11,731	12,949	9,048	10,093
1881	129,930	145,247	8,497	5,498	11,110	12,449	7,094	7,326	11,574	12,718	8,468	9,506
Variation	+ 15,743	+ 11,413	+ 1,483	+ 835	+ 2,615	+ 2,100	+ 1,027	+ 786	+ 157	+ 231	+ 580	+ 587
Percentage	+ 12·1	+ 7·8	+ 17·4	+ 15·1	+ 23·5	+ 16·3	+ 14·4	+ 10·7	+ 1·3	+ 1·8	+ 6·8	+ 6·1
MUSALMANS.												
1891	440,893	483,956	34,251	37,296	30,720	32,883	24,320	26,562	39,134	42,296	32,951	35,687
1881	376,770	425,216	28,468	31,332	25,521	27,033	20,856	23,036	36,530	40,621	29,710	33,342
Variation	+ 64,123	+ 58,740	+ 5,783	+ 5,964	+ 5,199	+ 5,850	+ 3,464	+ 3,526	+ 2,604	+ 1,675	+ 3,241	+ 2,345
Percentage	+ 17·0	+ 13·8	+ 20·3	+ 19·0	+ 20·3	+ 21·6	+ 16·6	+ 15·3	+ 7·1	+ 4·1	+ 10·9	+ [illegible]
BUDDHISTS.												
1891	28,535	33,080	442	228	884	789	147	124	1,636	1,875	744	727
1881	24,318	29,792	292	167	356	330	159	135	1,402	1,645	633	660
Variation	+ 4,217	+ 3,288	+ 150	+ 61	+ 528	+ 459	— 12	— 11	+ 234	+ 230	+ 111	+ 67
Percentage	+ 17·7	+ 11·0	+ 51·3	+ 36·5	+ 148·3	+ 136·0	— 7·5	— 8·1	+ 16·6	+ 13·9	+ 17·5	+ 10·1
CHRISTIANS.												
1891	661	530	553	456	...	...	8	...	6	6	7	6
1881	623	432	523	368	...	...	...	...	8	2	4	7
Variation	+ 38	+ 98	+ 30	+ 88	...	...	+ 8	...	— 2	+ 4	+ 3	— 1
Percentage	+ 6·0	+ 22·6	+ 5·7	+ 23·9	...	...	...	...	— 25	+ 200	+ 75	— 14·3

DISTRICT

Religions.	District Total.		Sudharam.		Hatia.		Bamni.	
	Male.	Female.	Male.	Female.	Male.	Female.	Male.	Female.
HINDUS.								
1891	126,105	122,018	11,586	10,534	5,571	4,634	5,060	4,911
1881	107,723	103,753	10,114	8,951	4,926	3,851	4,558	4,586
Variation	+ 18,382	+ 18,265	+ 1,472	+ 1,583	+ 645	+ 783	+ 502	+ 325
Percentage	+ 17·0	+ 17·6	+ 14·5	+ 17·6	+ 13·0	+ 20·3	+ 11·0	+ 7·0

MAIMANSING—*concluded.*

Tangail.		Gopalpur.		Kalihati.		Kisorganj.		Nikly.		Bajitpur.	
Male.	Female.	Male.	Female.	Male.	Female.	Male.	Female.	Male.	Female.	Male.	Female.
134,499	135,847	120,855	117,651	42,250	43,185	52,936	52,575	52,087	51,824	71,476	69,614
111,926	111,783	78,973	78,277	30,877	32,682	44,856	45,494	43,922	44,531	57,921	58,773
+ 22,573	+ 24,064	+ 41,882	+ 39,374	+ 11,373	+ 10,503	+ 8,080	+ 7,081	+ 8,165	+ 7,293	+ 13,555	+ 10,841
+ 20·1	+ 21·5	+ 53·0	+ 50·3	+ 36·8	+ 32·1	+ 18·0	+ 15·5	+ 18·5	+ 16·3	+ 23·4	+ 18·4
2	...	168	168	...	...	...	...	...	...	...	...
...	...	571	595	...	...	...	...	...	...	...	...
+ 2	...	− 403	− 427	...	...	...	...	...	...	...	...
...	...	− 70·5	− 71·7	...	...	...	...	...	...	...	...

DIVISION.

CHITTAGONG.

Raujan.		Patia.		Banskhali.		Satkania.		Cox's Bazar.		Chakaria.		Maiskal.		Teknaf.	
Male.	Female.	Male.	Female.	Male.	Female.	Male.	Female.	Male.	Female.	Male.	Female.	Male.	Female.	Male.	Female.
23,360	26,933	32,423	38,272	16,581	18,341	12,475	14,481	2,713	2,160	2,409	2,310	2,464	1,943	543	184
21,154	25,401	29,265	35,785	13,415	15,801	12,150	14,299	2,507	2,240	2,285	2,275	1,999	1,803	412	146
+ 2,206	+ 1,532	+ 3,158	+ 2,487	+ 3,166	+ 2,540	+ 325	+ 182	+ 206	− 80	+ 124	+ 35	+ 465	+ 140	+ 131	+ 38
+ 10·4	+ 6·0	+ 10·7	+ 6·9	+ 23·6	+ 16·0	+ 2·6	+ 1·2	+ 8·2	− 3·5	+ 5·4	+ 1·5	+ 23·2	+ 7·7	+ 31·7	+ 26·0
45,420	48,831	59,279	66,183	42,037	48,940	59,975	66,955	26,836	28,161	18,414	20,044	13,823	16,364	13,733	13,754
39,897	44,257	49,564	56,580	31,517	39,346	53,730	63,109	23,740	25,499	14,879	16,827	9,884	12,798	12,465	11,936
+ 5,523	+ 4,574	− 285	+ 9,603	+ 10,520	+ 9,594	+ 6,245	+ 3,846	+ 3,087	+ 2,662	+ 3,535	+ 3,217	+ 3,939	+ 3,566	+ 1,268	+ 1,818
+ 13·8	+ 10·3	− ·5	+ 16·9	+ 33·3	+ 24·3	+ 11·6	+ 6·0	+ 12·9	+ 10·4	+ 23·7	+ 19·1	+ 39·8	+ 27·8	+ 10·1	+ 15·2
6,952	8,296	4,346	6,013	859	1,099	2,073	2,386	4,040	5,182	1,543	1,736	1,662	1,420	3,207	3,205
6,011	7,615	3,737	5,454	701	962	1,970	2,251	3,708	5,106	1,185	1,371	1,375	1,296	2,789	2,800
+ 941	+ 681	+ 609	+ 559	+ 158	+ 137	+ 103	+ 135	+ 332	+ 76	+ 358	+ 365	+ 287	+ 124	+ 418	+ 405
+ 15·6	+ 8·9	+ 16·2	+ 10·2	+ 22·5	+ 14·2	+ 5·2	+ 5·9	+ 8·9	+ 1·4	+ 30·1	+ 26·6	+ 20·8	+ 9·5	+ 14·9	+ 14·4
30	21	30	18	12	14	1	...	8	5	1	...	5	4	...	...
24	21	37	25	13	3	3	3	5	3	3	...	3	...	...	...
+ 6	...	− 7	− 7	− 1	+ 11	− 2	+ 3	+ 3	+ 2	− 2	...	+ 2	...	...	...
+ 25	...	− 18·9	− 28	− 7·6	+ 366·6	− 66·6	...	+ 60	+ 66·6	− 66·6	...	+ 66·6	...	...	...

NOAKHALI.

Ramganj.		Lakshmipur.		Begamganj.		Sundwip.		Fenny.		Chhagalnaia.	
Male.	Female.	Male.	Female.	Male.	Female.	Male.	Female.	Male.	Female.	Male.	Female.
12,683	12,291	15,383	13,629	20,837	20,489	13,110	12,072	21,227	21,448	20,648	22,080
10,929	10,249	13,793	11,928	17,677	17,585	[illegible]	8,169	17,718	18,151	19,050	20,290
+ 1,754	+ 1,979	+ 1,590	+ 1,701	+ 3,160	+ 2,904	+ 4,152	+ 3,903	+ 3,509	+ 3,297	+ 1,598	+ 1,790
+ 16·0	+ 19·3	+ 11·5	+ 14·2	+ 17·8	+ 16·5	+ 46·3	+ 47·7	+ 19·8	+ 18·1	+ 8·3	+ 8·8

DISTRICT [NOAKHALI]

Religions.	District Total.		Sudharam.		Hatia.		Bamni.	
	Male.	Female.	Male.	Female.	Male.	Female.	Male.	Female.
MUSALMANS.								
1891	382,076	*378,521*	48,496	*49,136*	20,998	*18,141*	18,811	*20,389*
1881	307,151	*301,441*	41,476	*40,233*	17,136	*14,382*	15,800	*16,772*
Variation	+ 74,925	+ *77,080*	+ 7,020	+ *8,903*	+ 3,862	+ *3,759*	+ 3,011	+ *3,617*
Percentage	+ 24·3	+ *25·5*	+ 16·9	+ *22·1*	+ 22·5	+ *26·2*	+ 19·0	+ *21·5*

DISTRICT [TIPPERA]

Religions.	District total.		Comilla.		Muradnagar.		Daudkandi.		Chandina.	
	Male.	Female.	Male.	Female.	Male.	Female.	Male.	Female.	Male.	Female.
HINDUS.										
1891	284,058	*273,021*	22,298	*19,553*	29,798	*30,071*	19,815	*19,393*	12,658	*11,961*
1881	256,110	*252,956*	21,086	*18,334*	26,861	*28,377*	17,468	*17,484*	11,369	*11,070*
Variation	+ 27,948	+ *20,065*	+ 1,212	+ *1,219*	+ 2,937	+ *1,694*	+ 2,347	+ *1,909*	+ 1,289	+ *891*
Percentage	+ 10·9	+ *7·9*	+ 5·7	+ *6·6*	+ 10·9	+ *5·9*	+ 13·4	+ *10·9*	+ 10·4	+ *8·0*
MUSALMANS.										
1891	626,945	*597,391*	59,490	*56,379*	59,579	*57,407*	67,226	*66,630*	35,075	*33,537*
1881	512,035	*492,687*	50,678	*49,101*	49,200	*47,862*	54,267	*54,000*	28,414	*27,664*
Variation	+ 114,910	+ *104,704*	+ 8,812	+ *7,278*	+ 10,379	+ *9,545*	+ 12,959	+ *12,630*	+ 6,661	+ *5,873*
Percentage	+ 22·4	+ *21·2*	+ 17·3	+ *14·8*	+ 21·0	+ *19·9*	+ 23·8	+ *23·3*	+ 23·4	+ *21·2*
BUDDHISTS.										
1891	611	*606*	31	*26*	...	...	...	...	40	*41*
1881	202	*179*	22	*28*	...	...	...	...	2	*2*

CHITTAGONG [HILL TRACTS]

Religions.	District Total.		Chakma Circle.		Mong Raja's Circle.	
	Male.	Female.	Male.	Female.	Male.	Female.
HINDUS.						
1891	14,709	*11,093*	2,268	*788*	6,905	*5,869*
1881	11,461	*8,824*	7,432	*6,458*	1,555	*617*
Variation	+ 3,248	+ *2,269*	— 5,164	— *5,670*	+ 5,350	+ *5,252*
Percentage...	+ 28·3	+ *25·7*	— 69·4	— *87·7*	+ 344·0	+ *851·2*
MUSALMANS.						
1891	4,577	*291*	2,244	*203*	226	...
1881	6,226	*1,066*	928	*616*	2,140	*434*
Variation	— 1,649	— *775*	+ 1,316	— *413*	— 1,914	— *434*
Percentage...	— 26·4	— *72·7*	+ 141·8	— *67·0*	— 89·4	— *100*
BUDDHISTS.						
1891	38,901	*35,227*	19,119	*16,783*	4,965	*4,545*
1881	38,833	*35,137*	5,969	*5,439*	17,703	*15,502*
Variation	+ 68	+ *90*	+ 13,150	+ *11,344*	—12,738	— *10,957*
Percentage...	+ 0·1	+ *0·2*	+ 220·3	+ *208·5*	— 71·9	— *70·6*

NOAKHALI—*concluded.*

Ramganj.		Lakshmipur.		Begamganj.		Sandwip.		Feny.		Chhagalnaia.	
Male.	Female.	Male.	Female.	Male.	Female.	Male.	Female.	Male.	Female.	Male.	Female.
38,340	*36,088*	56,750	*54,196*	60,814	*57,665*	37,506	*38,287*	60,647	*62,784*	39,714	*41,835*
31,057	*28,495*	44,870	*42,698*	48,164	*45,422*	27,096	*28,240*	47,857	*48,958*	33,695	*36,241*
+ 7,283	+ *7,593*	+ 11,880	+ *11,498*	+ 12,650	+ *12,243*	+ 10,410	+ *10,047*	+ .12,790	+ *13,826*	+ 6,019	+ *5,594*
+ 23·4	+ *26·6*	+ 26·4	+ *26·9*	+ 26·3	+ *26·9*	+ 38·4	+ *35·5*	+ 26·7	+ *28·2*	+ 17·8	+ *15·4*

TIPPERA.

Chaudagram.		Laksham.		Brahmanbaria.		Kasba.		Nabinagar.		Chandpur.		Hajiganj.	
Male.	Female.	Male.	Female.	Male.	Female.	Male.	Female.	Male.	Female.	Male.	Female.	Male.	Female.
13,051	*12,517*	9,522	*8,649*	60,065	*60,429*	29,216	*30,238*	32,263	*32,198*	40,845	*35,201*	14,527	*12,818*
12,555	*11,938*	8,879	*8,109*	56,129	*58,599*	28,188	*28,864*	29,690	*30,742*	31,146	*28,423*	12,739	*11,023*
+ 496	+ *579*	+ 643	+ *540*	+ 3,936	+ *1,830*	+ 1,028	+ *1,374*	+ 2,573	+ *1,456*	+ 9,699	+ *6,778*	+ 1,788	+ *1,795*
+ 3·9	+ *4·8*	+ 7·2	+ *6·6*	+ 7·0	+ *3·1*	+ 3·6	+ *4·7*	+ 8·6	+ *4·7*	+ 31·1	+ *23·8*	+ 14·0	+ *16·3*
46,729	*44,285*	43,610	*40,648*	72,571	*69,802*	34,971	*32,893*	68,761	*66,623*	95,576	*89,024*	43,357	*40,163*
40,605	*38,114*	36,351	*33,278*	60,924	*60,613*	29,098	*28,002*	58,159	*57,380*	69,380	*65,001*	34,959	*31,672*
+ 6,124	+ *6,171*	+ 7,259	+ *7,370*	+ 11,647	+ *9,189*	+ 5,873	+ *4,891*	+ 10,602	+ *9,243*	+ 26,196	+ *24,023*	+ 8,398	+ *8,491*
+ 15·0	+ *16·1*	+ 19·9	+ *22·1*	+ 19·1	+ *15·1*	+ 20·1	+ *17·4*	+ 18·2	+ *16·1*	+ 37·7	+ *36·9*	+ 24·0	+ *26·8*
41	*38*	478	*501*	20	...	...	...	...	...	1	...	...	...
1	*5*	125	*137*	52	...	...	...	...	...	...	...	...	...

HILL TRACTS.

Bhomong's Circle.		Sangu Khasmahal.		Head-Quarters Khasmahal.		Forest Reserves.	
Male.	Female.	Male.	Female.	Male.	Female.	Male.	Female.
3,620	*3,116*	Detailed religion figures of 1891 are not separately shown, but included with Bhomong's circle.		1,916	*1,320*	Not shown in the Census Report of 1881, and figures therefore are not available. It has been added to Khasmahal in 1891.	
402	*162*			2,072	*1,587*		
+ 3,218	+ *2,954*			− 156	− *267*		
+ 800·4	+ *1,823·4*			− 7·5	− *16·8*		
1,558	*86*			549	*2*		
110	*5*			3,048	*11*		
+ 1,448	+ *81*			− 2,499	− *9*		
+ 1,316·3	+ *162·0*			− 81·9	− *81·8*		
14,629	*13,828*			188	*71*		
10,293	*9,903*			4,868	*4,293*		
+ 4,336	+ *3,925*			− 4,680	− *4,222*		
+ 42·1	+ *39·6*			− 96·1	− *98·3*		

PATNA DISTRICT

Religions.	District Total.		Pirbahor.		Sultanganj.		Alamganj.	
	Male.	Female.	Male.	Female.	Male.	Female.	Male.	Female.
HINDUS.								
1891	772,623	*792,180*	10,390	*9,146*	6,771	*6,907*	11,352	*12,074*
1881	757,718	*778,410*	9,613	*9,072*	5,849	*5,943*	11,777	*12,855*
Variation	+ 14,905	+ *13,770*	+ 777	+ *74*	+ 922	+ *964*	— 425	— *781*
Percentage	+ 1·9	+ *1·7*	+ 8·0	+ *0·8*	+ 15·7	+ *16·2*	— 3·6	— *6·0*
MUSALMANS.								
1891	91,231	*109,855*	3,198	*2,795*	2,051	*2,259*	2,911	*3,107*
1881	97,155	*115,897*	2,986	*2,802*	2,094	*2,299*	2,925	*3,330*
Variation	— 5,924	— *6,042*	+ 212	— *7*	— 43	— *40*	— 14	— *223*
Percentage	— 6·0	— *5·2*	+ 7·0	— *0·2*	— 2·0	— *1·7*	— 0·4	— *6·6*
CHRISTIANS.								
1891	1,738	*1,095*	16	*189*	1	...	28	*29*
1881	1,718	*875*	38	*910*	...	*1*	34	*41*

Religions.	Dinapur.		Maner.		Barh.		Fatuha.	
	Male.	Female.	Male.	Female.	Male.	Female.	Male.	Female.
HINDUS.								
1891	27,442	*29,465*	40,410	*44,878*	93,199	*95,988*	39,769	*41,159*
1881	25,114	*27,332*	41,321	*46,246*	87,817	*90,558*	38,827	*40,351*
Variation	+ 2,328	+ *2,133*	— 911	— *1,368*	+ 5,382	+ *5,430*	+ 942	+ *808*
Percentage	+ 9·3	+ *7·7*	— 2·2	— *2·9*	+ 6·1	+ *5·9*	+ 2·4	+ *2·0*
MUSALMANS.								
1891	6,309	*7,103*	3,991	*5,868*	6,899	*8,690*	3,621	*4,702*
1881	6,051	*7,122*	4,562	*6,387*	7,210	*8,580*	3,892	*4,981*
Variation	+ 258	— *19*	— 571	— *519*	— 311	+ *110*	— 271	— *279*
Percentage	+ 4·3	— *0·3*	— 12·5	— *8·1*	— 4·3	+ *1·3*	— 6·9	— *5·4*
CHRISTIANS.								
1891	1,205	*566*	2	...	25	*18*	2	*3*
1881	1,452	*533*	...	...	13	*8*	...	...

DISTRICT

Religions.	District Total.		Gaya Town.		Mufassal Gaya.	
	Male.	Female.	Male.	Female.	Male.	Female.
HINDUS.						
1891	944,964	*966,290*	32,467	*30,579*	80,107	*82,121*
1881	937,275	*954,209*	31,678	*30,179*	87,283	*89,615*
Variation	+ 7,689	+ *12,081*	+ 789	+ *400*	— 7,176	— *7,494*
Percentage	+ 0·8	+ *1·2*	+ 2·4	+ *1·3*	— 8·2	— *8·3*
MUSALMANS.						
1891	99,857	*126,848*	8,324	*8,823*	7,821	*9,964*
1881	106,108	*126,990*	6,810	*7,741*	12,474	*12,807*
Variation	— 6,251	— *142*	+ 1,514	+ *1,082*	— 4,653	— *2,843*
Percentage	— 5·8	— *0·1*	+ 22·2	+ *13·9*	— 37·3	— *22·1*

DIVISION.

PATNA.

Khwaja Kalan.		Chauk Kalan.		Malsalami.		Bankipur.		Bikram.		Masaudhi Bazurg.	
Male.	Female.	Male.	Female.	Male.	Female.	Male.	Female.	Male.	Female.	Male.	Female.
13,465	14,033	11,282	11,817	15,423	16,161	43,083	45,464	83,243	83,967	54,837	55,704
13,477	14,050	12,405	12,611	16,323	16,255	41,355	43,617	82,080	84,477	52,763	54,606
− 12	− 17	− 1,123	− 794	− 900	− 94	+ 2,328	+ 1,847	+ 1,163	− 510	+ 2,074	+ 1,098
...	− 0·1	− 9·0	− 6·2	− 5·5	− 0·5	+ 5·6	+ 4·2	+ 1·4	− 0·6	+ 3·9	+ 2·0
7,597	8,675	2,520	2,666	1,511	1,729	5,240	6,021	6,043	7,257	5,575	7,107
6,799	8,280	3,457	3,743	1,748	1,801	5,495	6,371	6,363	7,442	6,000	7,240
+ 798	+ 395	− 937	− 1,077	− 237	− 72	− 255	− 350	− 320	− 185	− 425	− 133
+ 11·7	+ 4·7	− 27·1	− 28·7	− 13·5	− 3·9	− 4·6	− 5·4	− 5·0	− 2·4	− 7·8	− 1·8
7	9	12	3	2	4	296	153	1	1	2	2
7	9	5	4	4	3	118	50	...	...	2	2

Mukameh.		Bihar.		Hilsa including Chandi.		Islampur or Athasarai.		Silao.	
Male.	Female.	Male.	Female.	Male.	Female.	Male.	Female.	Male.	Female.
52,851	54,692	112,579	114,610	79,858	79,429	36,332	36,074	39,737	40,612
43,987	43,980	120,472	119,714	79,798	80,394	34,784	35,367	39,956	40,982
+ 8,864	+ 10,712	− 7,893	− 5,104	+ 60	− 965	+ 1,548	+ 707	− 219	− 370
+ 20·1	+ 24·3	− 6·5	− 4·2	...	− 1·1	+ 4·4	+ 1·9	− 0·5	− 0·9
3,012	3,445	15,558	20,200	6,908	8,277	4,011	4,840	4,276	5,107
2,764	3,036	18,799	23,291	7,301	8,582	4,051	4,729	4,658	5,881
+ 248	+ 409	− 3,241	− 3,091	− 393	− 305	− 40	+ 111	− 382	− 774
+ 8·9	+ 13·4	− 17·2	− 13·2	− 5·3	− 3·5	− 0·9	+ 2·3	− 8·2	− 13·1
71	37	4	...	1	...	63	81	...	..
41	11	4	2	...	...	...	1	...	..

GAYA.

Atri.		Tikari.		Sherghati.		Barachati.		Nawada.	
Male.	Female.	Male.	Female.	Male.	Female.	Male.	Female.	Male.	Female.
55,557	55,829	81,801	82,646	64,324	68,915	40,591	50,833	126,004	128,950
43,230	43,556	77,279	78,177	65,165	69,007	49,605	50,491	135,960	136,604
+ 12,327	+ 12,273	+ 4,522	+ 4,469	− 841	− 92	− 14	+ 342	− 9,956	− 7,654
+ 28·5	+ 28·1	+ 5·8	+ 5·7	− 1·2	− 0·1	...	+ 0·6	− 7·3	− 5·6
5,471	6,811	8,950	11,253	8,969	12,002	4,072	4,984	12,201	15,655
4,609	5,444	9,623	11,726	9,981	12,493	4,636	5,146	14,038	16,290
+ 862	+ 1,367	− 673	− 473	− 1,012	− 491	− 564	− 162	− 1,837	− 635
+ 18·4	+ 25·1	− 6·9	− 4·0	− 10·1	− 3·9	− 12·1	− 3·1	− 18·0	− 3·9

DISTRICT

Religions.	Pakribarawan.		Rajauli.		Jahanabad.	
	Male.	Female.	Male.	Female.	Male.	Female.
HINDUS.						
1891	36,447	*36,016*	33,086	*34,406*	127,484	*125,104*
1881	39,750	*39,256*	37,543	*37,883*	128,681	*126,820*
Variation	− 3,303	− *3,240*	− 4,507	− *3,477*	− 1,197	− *1,716*
Percentage	− 8·3	− *8·2*	− 12·0	− *9·1*	− 0·9	− *1·3*
MUSALMANS.						
1891	4,379	*4,941*	3,190	*4,223*	11,634	*14,673*
1881	4,789	*5,026*	3,665	*4,215*	13,011	*15,343*
Variation	− 410	− *85*	− 475	+ *8*	− 1,377	− *670*
Percentage	− 8·5	− *1·6*	− 12·9	+ *0·1*	− 10·5	− *4·3*

DISTRICT

Religions.	District Total.		Arrah.		Belauti.		Piru.		Baxar.	
	Male.	Female.	Male.	Female.	Male.	Female.	Male.	Female.	Male.	Female.
HINDUS.										
1891	923,221	*990,889*	150,183	*171,085*	89,795	*98,200*	90,986	*96,175*	75,087	*79,681*
1881	877,285	*929,456*	135,135	*150,525*	89,017	*95,889*	83,088	*86,154*	73,697	*77,909*
Variation	+ 45,936	+ *61,433*	+ 15,048	+ *20,560*	+ 778	+ *2,311*	+ 7,898	+ *10,091*	+ 1,390	+ *1,772*
Percentage	+ 5·2	+ *6·6*	+ 11·1	+ *13·6*	+ 0·8	+ *2·4*	+ 9·5	+ *11·6*	+ 1·8	+ *2·2*
MUSALMANS.										
1891	67,197	*81,262*	12,503	*15,812*	4,801	*6,053*	4,991	*5,806*	5,543	*5,938*
1881	67,018	*78,592*	12,202	*14,733*	4,963	*5,995*	4,996	*5,253*	5,431	*6,048*
Variation	+ 179	+ *2,670*	+ 301	+ *1,079*	− 162	+ *58*	− 5	+ *553*	+ 112	− *110*
Percentage	+ 0·2	+ *3·3*	+ 2·4	+ *7·0*	− 3·2	+ *0·9*	− 0·1	+ *10·5*	+ 2·0	− *1·8*

DISTRICT

Religions.	District Total.		Darbhanga.		Bahera.		Roshra.		Madhubani.	
	Male.	Female.	Male.	Female.	Male.	Female.	Male.	Female.	Male.	Female.
HINDUS.										
1891	1,207,352	*1,254,956*	171,301	*179,221*	147,015	*151,594*	122,412	*122,658*	105,634	*109,532*
1881	1,144,172	*1,177,121*	155,775	*159,275*	131,881	*134,055*	120,753	*119,704*	92,031	*95,576*
Variation	+ 63,180	+ *77,835*	+ 15,526	+ *19,946*	+ 15,134	+ *16,369*	+ 1,659	+ *2,954*	+ 13,603	+ *13,956*
Percentage	+ 5·5	+ *6·6*	+ 9·9	+ *8·1*	+ 11·4	+ *12·5*	+ 1·3	+ *2·4*	+ 14·7	+ *14·5*
MUSALMANS.										
1891	163,136	*175,531*	46,633	*50,884*	23,008	*23,995*	8,299	*8,376*	14,371	*14,633*
1881	149,890	*158,830*	42,584	*45,765*	21,257	*22,074*	7,900	*8,237*	12,001	*12,164*
Variation	+ 13,246	+ *16,701*	+ 4,049	+ *5,119*	+ 1,751	+ *1,921*	+ 399	+ *139*	+ 2,370	+ *2,469*
Percentage	+ 8·8	+ *10·5*	+ 9·5	+ *11·1*	+ 8·2	+ *8·7*	+ 5·0	+ *1·6*	+ 19·7	+ *20·2*

GAYA—*concluded.*

Arwal.		Aurangabad.		Daudnagar.		Nabinagar.	
Male.	Female.	Male.	Female.	Male.	Female.	Male.	Female.
52,434	53,003	108,427	118,165	48,681	48,083	48,604	51,640
46,154	46,515	102,968	111,609	46,034	46,626	43,891	46,949
+ 6,280	+ 6,488	+ 5,459	+ 6,556	+ 2,647	+ 1,457	+ 4,713	+ 4,698
+ 13·6	+ 13·9	+ 5·3	+ 5·8	+ 5·7	+ 3·1	+ 10·7	+ 10·0
4,322	5,138	12,793	18,987	4,200	5,136	3,531	4,258
4,003	4,647	12,947	17,909	4,329	5,173	3,247	3,966
+ 319	+ 491	— 154	+ 1,085	— 129	— 37	+ 284	+ 292
+ 7·9	+ 10·5	— 1·1	+ 6·0	— 2·9	— 0·7	+ 8·7	+ 7·3

SHAHABAD.

Dumraon.		Sasaram.		Kharghar.		Dhangain.		Dehri.		Bhabhua.		Mohania.	
Male.	Female.	Male.	Female.	Male.	Female.	Male.	Female.	Male.	Female.	Male.	Female.	Male.	Female.
120,656	134,419	69,928	74,244	48,417	50,489	83,383	87,448	37,524	38,154	82,495	84,252	74,767	76,749
116,466	127,081	66,725	69,447	49,378	50,537	82,346	86,014	35,456	35,492	77,110	80,099	68,867	70,309
+ 4,190	+ 7,331	+ 3,203	+ 4,797	— 961	— 48	+1,037	+1,434	+ 2,068	+2,662	+ 5,385	+4,153	+ 5,900	+6,440
+ 3·5	+ 5·7	+ 4·8	+ 6·9	— 1·9	...	+ 2·2	+ 1·6	+ 5·8	+ 7·5	+ 6·9	+ 5·1	+ 8·5	+ 9·1
7,447	9,193	8,416	11,474	2,254	2,395	5,289	6,926	3,549	4,134	7,161	8,054	5,243	6,177
7,548	8,842	8,303	11,282	2,339	2,393	5,348	6,170	3,820	4,093	6,737	7,877	5,331	5,906
— 101	+ 351	+ 113	+ 192	— 85	+ 2	— 59	+ 56	— 271	+ 41	+ 424	+ 177	— 88	+ 271
— 1·3	+ 3·9	+ 1·3	+ 1·7	— 3·6	...	— 1·1	+ 0·9	— 7·0	+ 1·0	+ 6·2	+ 2·2	— 1·6	+ 4·5

DARBHANGA.

Benipati.		Khajauli.		Phulparas.		Samastipur.		Maniarpur.		Dalsingsarai.	
Male.	Female.	Male.	Female.	Male.	Female.	Male.	Female.	Male.	Female.	Male.	Female.
100,029	104,043	104,181	106,252	131,565	135,559	132,077	144,034	75,486	80,216	117,652	128,917
103,219	105,796	81,964	83,147	119,452	122,537	134,914	142,455	75,997	78,601	128,186	135,375
— 3,190	— 1,753	+ 22,217	+ 23,105	+ 12,113	+ 13,022	— 2,837	+ 1,579	— 511	+ 1,615	— 10,534	— 6,458
— 3·0	— 1·6	+ 27·1	+ 27·7	+ 10·1	+ 10·6	— 2·1	+ 1·1	— 0·6	+ 2·0	— 8·2	— 4·8
19,681	21,032	9,225	9,309	14,670	14,862	13,103	15,682	7,219	8,029	6,927	8,729
18,915	19,339	6,437	6,434	12,742	12,766	13,409	15,620	7,414	7,923	7,231	8,508
+ 766	+ 1,693	+ 2,788	+ 2,875	+ 1,928	+ 2,096	— 306	+ 62	— 195	+ 106	— 304	+ 221
+ 4·0	+ 8·7	+ 43·3	+ 44·6	+ 15·1	+ 16·4	— 2·2	+ 0·3	— 2·6	+ 1·3	— 4·2	+ 2·5

DISTRICT

Religions.	District Total.		Muzaffarpur.		Paru.		Katra.		Sitamarhi.	
	Male.	Female.	Male.	Female.	Male.	Female.	Male.	Female.	Male.	Female.
HINDUS.										
1891	1,148,733	*1,229,168*	240,626	*253,545*	130,710	*149,028*	80,599	*83,071*	138,767	*139,960*
1881	1,114,219	*1,151,161*	232,351	*236,339*	128,610	*135,646*	80,432	*81,677*	130,376	*127,500*
Variation	+ 34,514	+ *78,007*	+ 8,275	+*17,906*	+ 2,100	+*13,382*	+ 167	+ *1,394*	+ 8,391	+*12,460*
Percentage	+ 3·0	+ *6·7*	+ 3·5	+ *7·2*	+ 1·6	+ *9·8*	+ 0·2	+ *1·7*	+ 6·4	+ *9·7*
MUSALMANS.										
1891	156,284	*176,589*	36,624	*41,581*	13,365	*16,012*	13,317	*14,056*	19,683	*19,651*
1881	151,300	*165,008*	35,427	*48,982*	13,385	*14,763*	11,995	*12,853*	18,286	*18,096*
Variation	+ 4,984	+*11,581*	+ 1,197	+ *2,599*	— 20	+ *1,249*	+ 1,322	+ *1,203*	+ 1,396	+ *1,555*
Percentage	+ 3·2	+ *7·0*	+ 3·3	+ *6·6*	— 0·1	+ *8·4*	+ 11·0	+ *9·3*	+ 7·6	+ *8·5*

DISTRICT

Religions.	District Total.		Chapra.		Manjhi.		Parsa.		Mashrak.	
	Male.	Female.	Male.	Female.	Male.	Female.	Male.	Female.	Male.	Female.
HINDUS.										
1891	1,003,144	*1,172,069*	154,894	*184,873*	63,278	*80,057*	96,078	*120,037*	59,351	*73,253*
1881	965,443	*1,061,073*	145,310	*166,078*	63,203	*73,856*	97,903	*113,016*	64,925	*72,270*
Variation	+ 37,701	+ *110,996*	+ 9,584	+ *18,795*	+ 75	+ *6,201*	— 1,825	+ *7,021*	— 5,574	+ *983*
Percentage	+ 3·9	+ *10·4*	+ 6·5	+ *11·3*	+ 0·1	+ *8·3*	— 1·8	+ *6·2*	— 8·5	+ *1·3*
MUSALMANS.										
1891	130,573	*160,440*	17,614	*23,316*	5,384	*7,510*	8,249	*11,779*	5,575	*7,586*
1881	125,929	*144,039*	17,627	*21,667*	5,703	*6,902*	9,084	*11,420*	6,431	*7,847*
Variation	+ 4,644	+ *16,401*	— 13	+ *1,649*	— 319	+ *608*	— 835	+ *359*	— 856	— *261*
Percentage	+ 3·6	+ *11·3*	...	+ *7·6*	— 5·5	+ *8·8*	— 9·1	+ *3·1*	— 13·3	— *3·3*

DISTRICT

Religions.	District Total.		Motihari.		Govindganj.		Kesaria.	
	Male.	Female.	Male.	Female.	Male.	Female.	Male.	Female.
HINDUS.								
1891	802,375	*787,669*	82,068	*77,670*	79,872	*80,914*	80,584	*85,478*
1881	748,216	*728,769*	77,224	*73,025*	73,947	*73,913*	79,795	*80,844*
Variation	+ 54,159	+ *58,900*	+ 4,844	+ *4,645*	+ 5,925	+ *7,001*	+ 789	+ *4,634*
Percentage	+ 7·2	+ *8·0*	+ 6·2	+ *6·3*	+ 8·0	+ *9·4*	+ 0·9	+ *5·7*
MUSALMANS.								
1891	132,790	*134,529*	15,186	*15,221*	9,088	*9,161*	8,229	*9,373*
1881	121,558	*121,129*	14,148	*13,974*	8,681	*8,442*	8,351	*8,675*
Variation	+ 11,232	+ *13,400*	+ 1,038	+ *1,247*	+ 407	+ *719*	— 122	+ *698*
Percentage	+ 9·2	+ *11·0*	+ 7·3	+ *8·9*	+ 4·6	+ *8·5*	— 1·4	+ *8·0*
CHRISTIANS.								
1891	968	*1,132*	38	*22*	4	*1*	5	*4*
1881	853	*1,083*	29	*31*	...	...	10	*7*
Variation	+ 115	+ *49*	+ 9	— *9*	+ 4	+ *1*	— 5	— *3*
Percentage	+ 13·4	+ *4·5*	+ 31·0	— *29·0*	...	...	— 50·0	— *42·8*

MUZAFFARPUR.

Sitamarhi.		Pupri.		Belsand.		Hajipur.		Lalganj.		Mahua.	
Male.	Female.	Male.	Female.	Male.	Female.	Male.	Female.	Male.	Female.	Male.	Female.
79,397	78,976	92,248	93,476	83,736	85,480	115,499	132,708	64,418	76,887	122,733	136,037
75,299	73,799	81,559	82,062	72,774	72,341	120,957	133,036	68,082	75,737	123,779	133,024
+ 4,098	+ 5,177	+ 10,689	+ 11,414	+ 10,962	+13,139	— 5,458	— 328	— 3,664	+ 1,150	— 1,046	+ 3,013
+ 5·4	+ 7·0	+ 13·0	+ 13·9	+ 15·0	+ 18·1	— 4·5	— 0·2	— 5·3	+ 1·5	— 0·8	+ 2·2
12,031	12,337	22,208	24,086	11,054	11,154	6,781	9,080	5,600	7,868	15,622	20,764
11,734	11,810	20,771	22,029	9,725	9,704	7,221	9,063	6,259	7,705	16,497	20,003
+ 297	+ 527	+ 1,437	+ 2,057	+ 1,329	+ 1,450	— 440	+ 17	— 659	+ 163	— 875	+ 761
+ 2·5	+ 4·4	+ 6·9	+ 9·3	+ 13·6	+ 14·9	— 6·0	+ 0·1	— 10·5	+ 2·1	— 5·3	+ 3·8

SARAN.

Sonpur.		Gopalganj.		Mirganj.		Sewan.		Darauli.		Basantpur.	
Male.	Female.	Male.	Female.	Male.	Female.	Male.	Female.	Male.	Female.	Male.	Female.
45,616	60,569	111,435	125,331	151,943	161,174	126,591	142,927	98,037	108,540	95,921	116,215
50,804	63,069	111,092	113,914	131,695	136,530	117,138	125,740	94,494	100,156	88,879	97,351
— 5,188	— 2,500	+ 343	+ 11,417	+ 20,248	+ 24,644	+ 9,453	+ 17,187	+ 3,543	+ 8,384	+ 7,042	+ 18,864
— 10·2	— 3·9	+ 0·3	+ 10·0	+ 15·3	+ 18·0	+ 8·0	+ 13·6	+ 3·7	+ 8·3	+ 7·9	+ 19·3
2,840	3,989	17,710	20,525	22,463	24,017	29,437	35,391	8,987	10,467	12,314	15,860
2,732	3,796	17,206	18,162	19,206	19,966	27,577	31,204	8,897	10,008	11,466	13,067
+ 108	+ 193	+ 504	+ 2,363	+ 3,257	+ 4,051	+ 1,860	+ 4,187	+ 90	+ 459	+ 848	+ 2,793
+ 3·9	+ 5·0	+ 2·9	+ 13·0	+ 16·9	+ 20·2	+ 6·7	+ 13·4	+ 1·0	+ 4·5	+ 7·3	+ 21·3

CHAMPARAN.

Madhuban.		Dhaka.		Adapur.		Bettiah.		Hardi.		Bagaha.	
Male.	Female.	Male.	Female.	Male.	Female.	Male.	Female.	Male.	Female.	Male.	Female.
46,666	50,826	113,793	113,252	68,403	67,158	140,388	135,718	88,846	82,372	99,755	94,281
47,971	46,580	108,346	106,013	57,606	55,499	134,985	132,822	76,533	73,205	91,809	86,868
+ 695	+ 4,246	+ 5,447	+ 7,239	+ 10,797	+ 11,659	+ 5,403	+ 2,896	+ 12,313	+ 9,167	+ 7,946	+ 7,413
+ 1·4	+ 9·1	+ 5·0	+ 6·8	+ 18·7	+ 21·0	+ 4·0	+ 2·2	+ 16·0	+ 12·5	+ 8·6	+ 8·5
4,759	5,288	20,556	22,092	16,156	15,702	28,058	28,177	19,578	18,902	11,180	10,613
5,255	5,273	19,514	20,102	11,784	12,600	26,802	27,239	16,234	15,986	9,789	8,838
— 496	+ 15	+ 1,042	+ 1,990	+ 3,372	+ 3,102	+ 1,256	+ 938	+ 3,344	+ 2,916	+ 1,391	+ 1,775
— 9·4	+ 0·2	+ 5·3	+ 9·8	+ 26·3	+ 24·6	+ 4·6	+ 3·4	+ 20·5	+ 18·2	+ 14·2	+ 20·0
2	1	15	11	...	...	721	1,025	21	5	162	68
4	3	13	4	9	1	625	998	76	10	87	29
— 2	— 2	+ 2	+ 7	— 9	— 1	+ 96	+ 27	— 55	— 5	+ 75	+ 39
— 50·0	— 66·6	+ 15·3	+ 175·0	...	...	+ 15·3	+ 2·7	— 72·3	— 50·0	+ 86·2	+ 135·4

BHAGALPUR

DISTRICT

Religions.	District Total.		Bhagalpur.		Sultanganj.		Kolgong.		Bihipur.		Supul.	
	Male.	Female.	Male.	Female.	Male.	Female.	Male.	Female.	Male.	Female.	Male.	Female.
HINDUS.												
1891	895,891	*915,528*	68,857	*70,580*	39,810	*41,885*	80,553	*85,753*	39,965	*43,837*	155,904	*156,319*
1881	879,810	*887,004*	64,225	*63,598*	42,400	*43,728*	84,129	*85,193*	42,415	*43,536*	139,508	*139,963*
Variation	+ 16,012	*+ 28,524*	+ 4,632	*+ 6,982*	— 2,680	*— 1,843*	— 3,576	*+ 560*	— 2,450	*+ 301*	+ 1,664	*+ 2,008*
Percentage	+ 1·8	*+ 3·2*	+ 7·2	*+ 10·9*	— 6·3	*— 4·2*	— 4·2	*+ 0·6*	— 5·7	*+ 0·6*	+ 1·0	*+ 1·3*
MUSALMANS.												
1891	96,152	*99,439*	16,414	*18,008*	4,935	*5,642*	8,555	*8,742*	4,427	*5,269*	17,379	*17,115*
1881	92,291	*93,800*	15,349	*16,042*	5,938	*6,262*	8,363	*8,487*	5,049	*5,434*	14,714	*14,339*
Variation	+ 3,861	*+ 5,639*	+ 1,065	*+ 1,966*	— 1,003	*— 620*	+ 192	*+ 255*	— 1,622	*— 165*	— 122,129	*— 122,848*
Percentage	+ 4·1	*+ 6·0*	+ 6·9	*+ 11·8*	— 16·8	*— 9·9*	+ 2·2	*+ 3·0*	— 12·3	*— 3·0*	— 87·5	*— 87·7*
THE ANIMISTIC.												
1891	12,271	*12,469*	41	*4*	3	*1*	3,902	*3,921*	...	...	3	*5*
1881	7,982	*7,750*	50	...	...	...	2,947	*2,902*	...	...	...	...
Variation	+ 4,289	*+ 4,719*	— 9	*+ 4*	+ 3	*+ 1*	+ 955	*+ 1,019*	...	...	...	...
Percentage	+ 53·7	*+ 60·8*	— 18·0	...	...	...	+ 32·4	*+ 3·5*	...	...	...	...

DISTRICT

Religions.	District Total.		Monghyr.		Gogri.		Jamalpur.		Surajgarha.	
	Male.	Female.	Male.	Female.	Male.	Female.	Male.	Female.	Male.	Female.
HINDUS.										
1891	896,067	*943,092*	59,518	*64,190*	171,112	*175,531*	9,179	*8,424*	75,164	*81,347*
1881	876,819	*897,363*	59,294	*62,270*	166,198	*165,386*	8,349	*7,500*	75,580	*78,126*
Variation	+ 19,248	*+ 45,729*	+ 224	*+ 1,920*	+ 4,914	*+ 10,145*	+ 830	*+ 924*	— 416	*+ 3,221*
Percentage	+ 2·1	*+ 5·0*	+ 0·3	*+ 3·0*	+ 2·9	*+ 6·1*	+ 9·9	*+ 12·3*	— 0·5	*+ 4·1*
MUSALMANS.										
1891	88,411	*103,359*	8,608	*9,902*	17,028	*18,439*	1,740	*1,638*	5,238	*6,724*
1881	88,266	*99,258*	8,497	*9,553*	16,721	*17,646*	1,738	*1,567*	5,834	*6,713*
Variation	+ 145	*— 4,101*	+ 111	*+ 349*	+ 307	*+ 793*	+ 2	*+ 71*	— 596	*+ 11*
Percentage	+ 0·1	*— 4·1*	+ 1·3	*+ 3·6*	+ 1·8	*+ 4·4*	+ 0·1	*+ 4·5*	— 10·2	*+ 10·1*
CHRISTIANS.										
1891	723	*601*	145	*182*	11	*6*	417	*300*	...	*1*
1881	589	*502*	105	*133*	2	*1*	371	*299*	7	*3*
Variation	+ 134	*+ 99*	+ 40	*+ 49*	+ 9	*+ 5*	+ 46	*+ 1*	— 7	*— 2*
Percentage	+ 22·7	*+ 19·7*	+ 38·0	*+ 36·8*	+ 475·0	*+ 500·0*	+ 12·3	*+ 0·3*	— 100·0	*— 66·6*
THE ANIMISTIC.										
1891	1,840	*1,866*	11	*10*	...	...	...	...	...	...
1881	3,564	*3,589*	...	...	...	...	...	...	...	...
Variation	— 1,724	*— 1,723*	+ 11	*+ 10*	...	...	...	...	...	...
Percentage	— 48·3	*— 48·0*	...	...	...	...	...	...	...	...

DIVISION.

BHAGALPUR.

Pratabganj.		Bangaon.		Madhipura.		Kishanganj.		Banka.		Amarpur.		Katuria.	
Male.	Female.	Male.	Female.	Male.	Female.	Male.	Female.	Male.	Female.	Male.	Female.	Male.	Female.
60,726	59,179	71,748	72,818	133,421	135,014	60,123	56,671	69,128	73,452	65,020	69,177	49,976	50,843
58,325	56,484	66,098	66,238	180,327	132,474	62,966	62,428	60,837	62,652	94,043	97,623	33,856	33,087
+ 2,401	+ 2,695	+ 5,650	+6,580	— 5,497	— 5,727	— 2,843	— 5,757	+ 8,291	+10,800	— 29,023	—28,446	+ 16,120	+ 17,756
+ 4·1	+ 4·7	+ 8·5	+ 9·9	— 3·9	— 4·0	— 4·5	— 9·2	+ 13·6	+ 17·2	— 30·6	— 29·1	+ 47·6	+ 53·6
7,482	6,975	9,069	9,328	9,604	9,144	4,357	4,019	7,281	7,095	4,621	5,036	1,938	1,866
7,353	7,274	8,023	8,194	8,585	8,258	5,100	5,060	4,416	4,244	7,888	8,134	1,513	1,479
+ 129	— 299	+ 1,046	+1,134	—120,633	—123,330	— 743	— 1,041	+ 2,865	+ 3,451	— 3,267	— 3,008	+ 425	+ 394
+ 1·7	— 4·1	+ 13·0	+ 13·8	— 92·5	— 93·0	— 14·5	— 20·5	+ 64·8	+ 81·3	— 41·3	— 38·0	+ 28·0	+ 26·7
63	82	...	...	...	...	...	...	2,914	2,989	296	282	5,049	5,185
...	...	...	...	...	...	...	...	1,022	1,052	23	20	3,940	3,776
+ 63	+ 82	...	...	...	...	...	...	+ 1,892	+ 1,937	+ 273	+ 262	+ 1,109	+ 1,409
...	...	...	...	...	...	...	...	+ 185·1	+ 184·1	+ 118·6	+ 131·0	+ 28·1	+ 3·73

MONGHYR.

Kharakpur.		Begusarai.		Teghra.		Jamui.		Shaikhpura.		Sikandra.		Chakai.	
Male.	Female.	Male.	Female.	Male.	Female.	Male.	Female.	Male.	Female.	Male.	Female.	Male.	Female.
66,394	69,571	174,277	189,717	91,467	104,871	58,590	58,911	84,550	84,628	51,384	52,049	54,432	53,844
64,631	65,860	168,228	177,600	87,504	95,808	55,566	54,909	86,017	85,446	55,448	55,245	50,004	49,204
+ 1,763	+ 3,711	+ 6,049	+ 12,117	+ 3,963	+ 9,063	+ 3,024	+ 4,002	— 1,467	— 818	— 4,064	— 3,196	+ 4,428	+ 4,640
+ 2·7	+ 5·6	+ 3·5	+ 6·8	+ 4·5	+ 9·4	+ 5·4	+ 7·2	— 1·7	— 0·9	— 7·3	— 5·7	+ 8·8	+ 9·4
4,828	5,806	16,658	19,555	9,275	12,296	4,098	4,058	12,086	15,390	5,175	5,832	3,677	3,719
4,866	5,630	15,894	18,055	8,836	11,475	3,812	3,717	12,843	15,174	5,584	6,112	3,641	3,616
— 38	+ 176	+ 764	+ 1,500	+ 439	+ 821	+ 286	+ 341	— 757	+ 216	— 409	— 280	+ 36	+ 103
— 0·7	+ 3·1	+ 4·8	+ 8·3	+ 4·9	+ 7·1	+ 7·5	+ 9·1	— 5·8	+ 1·4	— 7·3	— 4·5	+ 0·9	+ 2·8
4	...	28	22	23	8	2	2	1	1	6	6	86	73
5	...	11	6	6	3	38	31	...	...	...	...	44	26
— 1	...	+ 17	+ 16	+ 17	+ 5	— 36	— 29	+ 1	+ 1	+ 6	+ 6	+ 42	+ 47
— 20·0	...	+ 154·5	+ 266·6	+ 283·3	+ 166·6	— 94·7	— 93·5	...	...	...	...	+ 95·4	+ 180·7
1,181	1,187	...	...	...	...	...	...	...	...	...	...	648	669
828	830	...	...	...	...	1,248	1,242	...	...	...	...	1,488	1,517
+ 353	+ 357	...	...	...	...	— 1,248	— 1,242	...	...	...	...	— 840	— 848
+ 42·6	+ 43·0	...	...	...	...	— 100·0	— 100·0	...	...	...	...	— 56·4	— 55·8

DISTRICT

RELIGIONS.	District Total.		Purnea.		Amur-kasba.	
	Male.	Female.	Male.	Female.	Male.	Female.
HINDUS.						
1891	583,845	*554,893*	53,725	*51,619*	23,877	*23,742*
1881	545,170	*531,755*	51,918	*50,900*	23,819	*24,361*
Variation	+ 38,675	+ *23,138*	+ 1,807	+ *719*	+ 58	— *619*
Percentage	+ 7·0	+ *4·3*	+ 3·4	+ *1·4*	+ 0·2	— *2·5*
MUSALMANS.						
1891	409,212	*396,055*	25,886	*25,361*	37,457	*37,405*
1881	391,729	*379,401*	25,605	*25,088*	36,852	*36,530*
Variation	+ 17,483	+ *16,654*	+ 281	+ *273*	+ 575	+ *875*
Percentage	+ 4·4	+ *4·3*	+ 1·0	+ *1·0*	+ 1·5	+ *2·4*

RELIGIONS.	Manihari.		Araria.		Matiari.	
	Male.	Female.	Male.	Female.	Male.	Female.
HINDUS.						
1891	23,695	*23,617*	60,148	*58,662*	55,664	*52,723*
1881	21,115	*22,183*	57,017	*57,288*	46,764	*46,203*
Variation	+ 2,580	+ *1,434*	+ 3,131	+ *1,374*	+ 8,900	+ *6,520*
Percentage	+ 12·2	+ *6·4*	+ 5·4	+ *2·3*	+ 19·0	+ *14·1*
MUSALMANS.						
1891	5,507	*6,002*	46,032	*45,867*	12,054	*11,465*
1881	5,376	*5,772*	42,898	*42,805*	11,277	*11,100*
Variation	+ 131	+ *230*	+ 3,134	+ *3,062*	+ 777	+ *365*
Percentage	+ 2·4	+ *3·9*	+ 7·3	+ *7·1*	+ 6·8	+ *3·2*

DISTRICT

RELIGIONS.	District Total.		Malda.		Kharba.		Ratua.	
	Male.	Female.	Male.	Female.	Male.	Female.	Male.	Female.
HINDUS.								
1891	204,300	*204,836*	16,726	*15,173*	32,345	*32,259*	38,099	*41,968*
1881	189,359	*190,811*	17,975	*16,714*	30,535	*30,786*	29,144	*32,180*
Variation	+ 14,941	+ *14,025*	— 1,249	— *1,541*	+ 1,810	+ *1,473*	+ 9,555	+ *9,788*
Percentage	+ 7·8	+ *7·3*	— 6·9	— *9·2*	+ 5·9	+ *4·7*	+ 32·7	+ *30·4*
MUSALMANS.								
1891	184,718	*199,933*	8,144	*8,612*	22,878	*24,369*	13,069	*14,017*
1881	157,228	*172,319*	7,201	*7,781*	19,732	*21,998*	9,229	*10,501*
Variation	+ 27,490	+ *27,614*	+ 943	+ *831*	+ 3,146	+ *2,371*	+ 3,840	+ *3,516*
Percentage	+ 17·4	+ *16·0*	+ 13·0	+ *10·6*	+ 15·9	+ *10·7*	+ 41·6	+ *33·4*
THE ANIMISTIC.								
1891	10,842	*10,192*	5,305	*4,877*	121	*116*	7	*83*
1881	902	*832*	638	*585*	...	...	...	...

PURNEA.

Dhamdaha.		Gondwara.		Kadwa.		Balarampur.	
Male.	Female.	Male.	Female.	Male.	Female.	Male.	Female.
70,624	62,643	52,190	49,438	47,376	47,822	36,157	34,644
53,195	48,847	55,577	52,431	44,197	45,787	33,555	33,332
+ 17,429	+ 13,796	— 3,387	— 2,993	+ 3,179	+ 2,035	+ 2,602	+ 1,312
+ 32.7	+ 28.2	— 6.0	— 5.7	+ 7.1	+ 4.4	+ 7.7	+ 3.9
6,118	5,325	7,379	6,698	21,860	22,190	26,670	25,712
4,416	4,250	8,507	7,382	21,504	22,115	24,159	23,955
+ 1,702	+ 1,075	— 1,128	— 684	+ 356	+ 75	+ 2,481	+ 1,757
+ 38.5	+ 25.2	— 13.2	— 9.2	+ 1.6	+ 0.3	+ 10.2	+ 7.3

Raniganj.		Kishenganj.		Bahadurganj.		Kaliaganj.	
Male.	Female.	Male.	Female.	Male.	Female.	Male.	Female.
37,472	35,474	24,212	22,770	44,996	42,417	53,709	49,322
36,052	35,043	25,312	24,517	41,886	39,756	54,763	51,107
+ 1,420	+ 431	— 1,100	— 1,747	+ 3,110	+ 2,661	— 1,054	— 1,785
+ 3.9	+ 1.2	— 4.3	— 7.1	+ 7.4	+ 6.6	— 1.9	— 3.4
8,409	8,305	56,642	54,233	64,478	63,092	90,720	84,400
7,091	7,174	57,025	54,529	57,809	56,662	89,150	82,039
+ 1,318	+ 1,131	— 383	— 296	+ 6,669	+ 6,430	+ 1,570	+ 2,361
+ 18.5	+ 15.7	— 0.6	— 0.5	+ 11.5	+ 11.3	+ 1.7	+ 2.8

MALDA.

Gajol.		English Bazar.		Kaliachak.		Sibaganj.		Gumashtapur.		Nawabganj.	
Male.	Female.	Male.	Female.	Male.	Female.	Male.	Female.	Male.	Female.	Male.	Female.
20,740	18,320	28,280	28,513	29,992	32,313	12,808	13,663	11,427	9,807	13,283	12,820
20,980	19,209	25,791	27,112	27,723	30,257	13,011	12,927	11,372	9,634	12,828	11,922
— 240	— 889	+ 2,489	+ 1,401	+ 2,269	+ 2,056	— 203	+ 736	+ 55	+ 173	+ 455	+ 898
— 1.1	— 4.6	+ 9.6	+ 5.1	+ 8.1	+ 6.7	— 1.5	+ 5.6	+ 0.4	+ 1.7	+ 3.5	+ 6.9
7,715	6,588	19,158	20,496	32,429	34,896	41,600	46,919	17,054	18,190	22,671	25,846
7,055	6,562	15,528	16,593	27,657	30,055	36,070	40,148	15,428	16,376	19,328	22,305
+ 660	+ 26	+ 3,630	+ 3,903	+ 4,772	+ 4,841	+ 5,530	+ 6,771	+ 1,626	+ 1,814	+ 3,343	+ 3,541
+ 9.3	+ 0.3	+ 23.3	+ 23.5	+ 17.2	+ 16.1	+ 15.3	+ 16.8	+ 10.5	+ 11.0	+ 17.2	+ 15.8
5,353	5,060	2	9	10	7	2	3	42	44	...	...
264	247	...	...	...	...	...	...	...	...	...	...

Religions.	District Total.		Deoghar.		Madhupur.		Sarath.	
	Male.	Female.	Male.	Female.	Male.	Female.	Male.	Female.
HINDUS.								
1891	445,089	*455,731*	63,485	*62,151*	27,458	*27,533*	23,780	*23,792*
1881	423,421	*423,702*	58,714	*56,297*	25,993	*24,703*	23,276	*22,287*
Variation	+ 21,668	+ *32,029*	+ 4,771	+ *5,854*	+ 1,465	+ *2,830*	+ 504	+ *1,505*
Percentage	+ 5·1	+ *7·5*	+ 8·1	+ *10·3*	+ 5·6	+ *11·0*	+ 2·1	+ *6·7*
MUSALMANS.								
1891	60,372	*60,714*	4,031	*3,751*	4,537	*4,568*	2,765	*2,723*
1881	54,124	*55,116*	3,404	*3,216*	3,859	*3,389*	2,254	*2,193*
Variation	+ 6,248	+ *5,598*	+ 627	+ *535*	+ 678	+ *1,179*	+ 511	+ *530*
Percentage	+ 11·5	+ *10·1*	+ 18·4	+ *16·6*	+ 17·5	+ *34·7*	+ 22·6	+ *24·1*
THE ANIMISTIC.								
1891	362,089	*364,195*	3,539	*3,808*	4,710	*4,671*	8,416	*8,329*
1881	304,633	*300,884*	3,116	*3,094*	1,813	*1,753*	6,019	*5,811*
Variation	+ 57,456	+ *63,311*	+ 423	+ *714*	+ 2,897	+ *2,918*	+ 2,397	+ *2,518*
Percentage	+ 18·8	+ *21·0*	+ 13·5	+ *23·0*	+ 159·7	+ *166·4*	+ 39·8	+ *43·3*
CHRISTIANS.								
1891	2,979	*2,964*	3	*6*	17	*22*	5	*2*
1881	1,543	*1,513*	3	*2*	86	*35*	9	*9*

Religions.	Maheshpur.		Portion of Damin-i-koh (Pakaur Sub-Division).		Rajmahal.		Sahibganj.	
	Male.	Female.	Male.	Female.	Male.	Female.	Male.	Female.
HINDUS.								
1891	13,596	*14,245*	3,531	*3,631*	31,639	*33,523*	8,726	*7,775*
1881	12,220	*12,823*	5,568	*5,345*	34,185	*36,034*	5,509	*5,362*
Variation	+ 1,376	+ *1,422*	— 2,037	— *1,714*	— 2,546	— *2,511*	+ 3,217	+ *2,413*
Percentage	+ 11·3	+ *11·0*	— 3·6	— *32·0*	— 7·4	— *6·9*	+ 58·3	+ *45·0*
MUSALMANS.								
1891	4,249	*4,563*	853	*848*	5,756	*6,195*	1,861	*1,667*
1881	4,028	*4,401*	992	*902*	6,417	*7,512*	1,282	*1,220*
Variation	+ 221	+ *162*	— 139	— *54*	— 661	— *1,317*	+ 579	+ *447*
Percentage	+ 5·4	+ *3·6*	— 14·0	— *5·9*	— 10·3	— *17·5*	+ 45·1	+ *36·6*
THE ANIMISTIC.								
1891	29,965	*30,422*	27,941	*27,833*	11,207	*12,051*	1	...
1881	24,855	*24,614*	23,908	*23,788*	4,604	*4,720*	133	*20*
Variation	+ 5,110	+ *5,808*	+ 4,033	+ *4,045*	+ 6,603	+ *7,331*	— 132	— *20*
Percentage	+ 20·5	+ *23·5*	+ 16·8	+ *17·0*	+ 143·4	+ *155·3*	— 99·2	— *100·0*
CHRISTIANS.								
1891	308	*265*	107	*81*	151	*151*	71	*61*
1881	150	*193*	40	*27*	6	*2*	45	*48*

SANTAL PARGANAS.

Godda.		Mahagama.		Poreya.		Portion of Damini-koh (Godda Sub-Division).		Pakaur.	
Male.	Female.	Male.	Female.	Male.	Female.	Male.	Female.	Male.	Female.
42,600	45,110	30,026	31,815	17,359	18,934	10,162	10,458	12,271	12,455
39,795	40,480	26,824	28,105	16,958	17,978	10,597	10,713	10,949	11,638
+ 2,805	+ 4,630	+ 3,202	+ 3,710	+ 401	+ 956	— 435	— 255	+ 1,322	+ 817
+ 7·0	+ 11·4	+ 11·9	+ 13·2	+ 2·3	+ 5·3	— 4·1	— 2·3	+ 12·0	+ 7·0
5,672	5,669	7,449	7,433	905	916	1,651	1,518	8,445	8,965
4,458	4,449	5,745	6,078	920	896	1,581	1,508	7,379	8,110
+ 1,214	+ 1,220	+ 1,704	+ 1,355	— 15	+ 20	+ 70	+ 10	+ 1,066	+ 855
+ 27·2	+ 27·4	+ 29·6	+ 22·2	— 1·6	+ 2·2	+ 4·4	+ 0·6	+ 14·4	+ 10·5
11,853	11,804	5,844	5,770	11,192	11,405	44,262	44,586	12,861	13,130
10,180	9,932	5,661	5,561	8,999	8,819	40,421	40,166	11,652	11,919
+ 1,672	+ 1,872	+ 183	+ 209	+ 2,193	+ 2,586	+ 3,841	+ 4,420	+ 1,209	+ 1,211
+ 16·4	+ 18·8	+ 3·2	+ 3·7	+ 24·4	+ 29·3	+ 9·5	+ 11·0	+ 10·3	+ 10·1
41	33	8	3	11	12	252	294	71	51
10	7	...	...	...	...	84	33	20	19

Portion of Damini-koh (Rajmahal Sub-Division).		Dumka.		Portion of Damini-koh (Dumka Sub-Division).		Jamtara.	
Male.	Female.	Male.	Female.	Male.	Female.	Male.	Female.
16,745	17,644	90,316	92,257	5,470	5,747	47,945	48,661
16,968	15,326	86,442	87,146	6,865	6,745	42,558	42,720
— 223	+ 2,318	+ 3,874	+ 5,111	— 1,395	— 998	+ 5,387	+ 5,941
— 1·3	+ 15·1	+ 4·4	+ 5·8	— 20·3	— 14·9	+ 12·6	+ 13·9
1,801	1,746	4,548	4,347	276	286	5,573	5,500
2,592	2,420	4,139	3,806	358	300	4,716	4,716
— 791	— 674	+ 409	+ 541	— 82	— 14	+ 857	+ 793
— 30·5	— 27·8	+ 9·8	+ 14·2	— 22·9	— 4·6	+ 18·1	+ 16·8
58,434	57,913	84,048	84,914	14,635	14,861	33,192	32,698
53,378	53,294	70,873	69,226	13,018	12,854	25,931	25,253
+ 5,056	+ 4,619	+ 13,175	+ 15,688	+ 1,617	+ 2,007	+ 7,261	+ 7,445
+ 9·4	+ 8·6	+ 18·5	+ 22·6	+ 12·4	+ 15·6	+ 28·0	+ 29·4
634	640	1,073	1,168	164	167	68	78
525	555	583	617	7	1	25	35

ORISSA

DISTRICT

Religions.	District Total.		Cuttack.		Banki.		Salepur.		Tirtol.	
	Male.	Female.	Male.	Female.	Male.	Female.	Male.	Female.	Male.	Female.
HINDUS.										
1891	914,498	*967,415*	101,177	*100,310*	28,443	*28,604*	123,125	*135,415*	81,830	*83,663*
1881	853,729	*890,498*	92,894	*93,227*	28,296	*28,323*	115,550	*123,488*	89,343	*90,983*
Variation	+ 60,769	+ *76,917*	+ 8,283	+ *7,083*	+ 147	+ *281*	+ 7 575	+ *11,927*	— 7,513	— *7,320*
Percentage	+ 7·1	+ *8·6*	+ 8·9	+ *7·5*	+ 0·5	+ *0·9*	+ 6·5	+ *9·6*	— 8·5	— *8·0*
MUSALMANS.										
1891	24,649	*28,246*	5,504	*5,814*	181	*133*	5,179	*6,814*	1,506	*1,846*
1881	22,425	*25,104*	4,871	*5,512*	145	*125*	4,804	*6,081*	1,576	*1,769*
Variation	+ 2,224	+ *3,142*	+ 633	+ *302*	+ 36	+ *8*	+ 375	+ *733*	— 70	+ *77*
Percentage	+ 9·9	+ *12·5*	+ 12·9	+ *5·4*	+ 24·8	+ *6·4*	+ 7·8	+ *12·0*	— 4·4	+ *4·3*
CHRISTIANS.										
1891	1,339	*1,384*	1,163	*1,269*	4	*3*	22	*13*	11	*5*
1881	1,071	*1,271*	878	*1,145*	7	*4*	1	...	4	*2*
Variation	+ 268	+ *113*	+ 285	+ *124*	— 3	— *1*	+ 21	+ *13*	+ 7	+ *3*
Percentage	+ 25·0	+ *8·8*	+ 32·4	+ *10·8*	— 42·8	— *25·0*	+ 2,100	+ *1,300*	+ 175	+ *150*

DISTRICT

Religions.	District Total.		Thana Puri.		Town Puri.	
	Male.	Female.	Male.	Female.	Male.	Female.
HINDUS.						
1891	465,799	*461,715*	104,610	*103,548*	15,684	12,792
1881	439,264	*434,505*	98,368	*96,940*	13,524	11,882
Variation	+ 26,535	+ *27,210*	+ 6,242	+ *6,608*	+ 2,160	+ 910
Percentage	+ 6·0	+ *6·2*	+ 6·3	+ *6·7*	+ 15·9	+ 7·6
MUSALMANS.						
1891	7,822	*7,775*	570	*459*	220	49
1881	7,017	*6,986*	490	*297*	153	97
Variation	+ 805	+ *789*	+ 80	+ *162*	+ 67	— 48
Percentage	+ 11·4	+ *11·2*	+ 16·3	+ *54·5*	+ 43·7	— 49·4

DISTRICT

Religions.	District Total.		Balasor.		Soro.		Jaleswar.	
	Male.	Female.	Male.	Female.	Male.	Female.	Male.	Female.
HINDUS.								
1891	468,798	*500,413*	53,045	*53,485*	101,398	*107,999*	27,042	*27,288*
1881	446,830	*468,962*	50,778	*51,401*	95,125	*100,043*	24,728	*24,727*
Variation	+ 21,968	+ *31,451*	+ 2,267	+ *2,084*	+ 6,273	+ *7,956*	+ 2,314	+ *2,561*
Percentage	+ 4·9	+ *6·7*	+ 4·4	+ *4·0*	+ 6·5	+ *7·9*	+ 9·3	+ *10·3*

DIVISION.

CUTTACK.

Jagatsinghpur.		Kendrapara.		Patamundi.		Aul or Rajabari.		Jajpur.		Dharmsala.	
Male.	Female.	Male.	Female.	Male.	Female.	Male.	Female.	Male.	Female.	Male.	Female.
129,922	133,920	102,419	107,743	53,893	58,373	48,999	50,822	118,293	133,995	126,397	134,510
104,109	105,973	91,374	95,693	53,236	54,758	44,366	44,806	116,545	128,691	118,016	124,496
+ 25,813	+ 27,947	+ 11,045	+ 12,050	+ 657	+ 3,615	+ 4,633	+ 6,016	+ 1,748	+ 5,304	+ 8,381	+ 10,014
+ 24·7	+ 26·3	+ 12·0	+ 12·5	+ 1·2	+ 6·6	+ 10·4	+ 13·4	+ 1·5	+ 4·1	+ 7·1	+ 8·0
2,707	3,298	2,269	2,426	555	567	732	746	2,930	3,160	3,086	3,442
2,170	2,721	1,860	2,063	787	481	680	636	2,657	2,807	2,875	2,909
+ 537	+ 577	+ 409	+ 363	− 232	+ 86	+ 52	+ 110	+ 273	+ 353	+ 211	+ 533
+ 24·7	+ 21·2	+ 21·9	+ 17·5	− 29·4	+ 17·8	+ 7·6	+ 17·2	+ 10·2	+ 12·5	+ 7·3	+ 18·3
19	2	50	21	27	31	...	1	5	2	38	37
14	14	20	9	104	35	...	...	5	1	38	61
+ 5	− 12	+ 30	+ 12	− 77	− 4	...	+ 1	...	+ 1	...	− 24
+ 35·7	− 85·7	+ 150	+ 133·3	− 74·0	− 11·4	...	+ 100	...	+ 100	...	− 39·3

PURI.

Gop.		Pipli.		Khurda.		Arnpur.	
Male.	Female.	Male.	Female.	Male.	Female.	Male.	Female.
66,026	64,556	118,308	118,640	113,556	114,845	47,615	47,334
57,445	55,941	111,411	111,565	113,871	114,028	44,645	44,149
+ 8,581	+ 8,615	+ 6,897	+ 7,075	− 315	+ 817	+ 2,970	+ 3,185
+ 14·9	+ 15·3	+ 6·1	+ 6·3	− ·2	+ ·7	+ 6·6	+ 7·2
1,659	1,740	1,974	1,880	2,722	2,976	677	671
1,347	1,434	1,585	1,691	2,752	2,812	690	655
+ 312	+ 306	+ 389	+ 189	− 30	+ 164	− 13	+ 16
+ 23·1	+ 21·3	+ 24·5	+ 11·1	− 1·0	+ 5·8	− 1·8	+ 2·4

BALASOR.

Baliapal.		Basta.		Bhadrak.		Basudebpur.		Dhamnagar.		Chandbali.	
Male.	Female.	Male.	Female.	Male.	Female.	Male.	Female.	Male.	Female.	Male.	Female.
45,856	44,829	36,542	36,187	77,814	91,481	34,703	38,696	63,336	72,763	29,062	27,685
43,532	42,515	34,792	33,674	76,161	86,450	33,873	36,465	61,844	68,524	25,997	25,163
+ 2,324	+ 2,314	+ 1,750	+ 2,513	+ 1,653	+ 5,031	+ 830	+ 2,231	+ 1,492	+ 4,239	+ 3,065	+ 2,522
+ 5·3	+ 5·4	+ 5·0	+ 7·4	+ 2·1	+ 5·8	+ 2·4	+ 6·1	+ 2·4	+ 6·1	+ 11·7	+ 10·0

DISTRICT

Religions.	District Total.		Balasor.		Soro.		Jaleswar.	
	Male.	Female.	Male.	Female.	Male.	Female.	Male.	Female.
MUSALMANS.								
1891	12,232	*12,018*	2,602	*2,742*	1,359	*1,232*	384	*341*
1881	11,798	*12,006*	2,390	*2,644*	1,141	*1,199*	461	*435*
Variation	+ 434	+ *12*	+ 212	+ *98*	+ 218	+ *33*	— 77	— *94*
Percentage	+ 3·6	+ *·0*	+ 8·8	+ *3·7*	+ 19·1	+ *2·7*	— 16·7	— *21·6*
CHRISTIANS.								
1891	549	*526*	306	*305*	8	*5*	140	*149*
1881	470	*345*	281	*188*	...	...	142	*136*

DISTRICT

Religion.
HINDUS.
1891 ... ...
1881 ... ...
Variation ... ...
Percentage ... ...

CHUTIA NAG

DISTRICT

Religions.	District Total.		Hazaribagh.		Barhi.		Bagodhar.	
	Male.	Female.	Male.	Female.	Male.	Female.	Male.	Female.
HINDUS.								
1891	466,411	*493,776*	40,662	*46,466*	21,484	*23,330*	26,536	*29,002*
1881	455,405	*469,406*	42,644	*45,847*	22,184	*23,277*	24,594	*26,439*
Variation	+ 11,006	+*24,370*	— 1,982	+ *619*	— 700	+ *53*	+ 1,942	+ *2,563*
Percentage	+ 2·4	+ *5·1*	— 4·6	+ *1·3*	— 3·1	+ *·2*	+ 7·8	+ *9·6*
MUSALMANS.								
1891	56,168	*58,605*	6,018	*7,005*	2,656	*2,719*	3,282	*3,427*
1881	52,857	*53,240*	6,432	*6,870*	2,757	*2,798*	2,887	*3,025*
Variation	+ 3,311	+ *5,365*	— 414	+ *135*	— 101	— *79*	+ 395	+ *402*
Percentage	+ 6·2	+ *10·0*	— 6·4	+ *1·9*	— 3·6	— *2·8*	+ 13·6	+ *13·2*
THE ANIMISTIC.								
1891	43,593	*44,273*	398	*340*	694	*686*	1,237	*1,229*
1881	36,352	*36,929*	455	*460*	518	*516*	1,148	*1,209*
Variation	+ 7,241	+ *7,344*	— 57	— *120*	+ 176	+ *170*	+ 89	+ *20*
Percentage	+ 19·9	+ *19·8*	— 12·5	— *26·0*	+ 33·9	+ *32·9*	+ 7·7	+ *1·6*

BALASOR—*concluded.*

Baliapal.		Basta.		Bhadrak.		Basudebpur.		Dhamnagar.		Chandbali.	
Male.	Female.	Male.	Female.	Male.	Female.	Male.	Female.	Male.	Female.	Male.	Female.
1,073	*976*	762	*690*	3,766	*4,386*	444	*371*	1,117	*1,058*	725	*222*
1,117	*1,036*	1,227	*1,176*	3,461	*3,872*	541	*474*	946	*967*	514	*203*
− 44	− *60*	− 465	− *486*	+ 305	+ *514*	− 97	− *103*	+ 171	+ *91*	+ 211	+ *19*
− 3·9	− *5·7*	− 37·9	− *41·3*	+ 8·8	+ *13·2*	− 17·9	− *21·7*	+ 18·0	+ *9·4*	+ 41·0	+ *9·3*
4	*3*	4	*1*	18	*31*	5	*3*	11	*16*	53	*13*
1	...	1	...	9	*19*	1	...	4	...	31	*2*

ANGUL.

Angul.	
Male.	Female.
85,445	*84,056*
62,076	*60,226*
+ 23,369	+ *23,830*
+ 37·6	+ *39·5*

PUR DIVISION.

HAZARIBAGH.

Tandwa.		Ramghar.		Jageswar.		Kasmar.	
Male.	Female.	Male.	Female.	Male.	Female.	Male.	Female.
23,476	*25,880*	29,328	*30,607*	21,698	*22,994*	16,601	*16,843*
23,867	*25,275*	27,306	*28,287*	18,528	*20,053*	15,698	*16,375*
− 391	+ *605*	+ 2,022	+ *2,320*	+ 3,170	+ *2,941*	+ 903	+ *468*
− 1·6	+ *2·3*	+ 7·4	+ *8·2*	+ 17·1	+ *14·6*	+ 5·7	+ *2·8*
2,300	*2,411*	3,141	*3,055*	1,972	*1,925*	1,468	*1,376*
2,223	*2,287*	3,062	*2,905*	1,574	*1,576*	1,255	*1,201*
+ 77	+ *124*	+ 79	+ *150*	+ 398	+ *349*	+ 213	+ *175*
+ 3·4	+ *5·4*	+ 2·5	+ *5·1*	+ 2·5	+ *22·1*	+ 16·4	+ *14·5*
1,525	*1,719*	6,580	*6,944*	5,597	*5,699*	7,286	*7,277*
1,039	*1,089*	5,515	*5,878*	5,872	*5,931*	6,196	*6,369*
+ 486	+ *630*	+ 1,065	+ *1,066*	− 275	− *232*	+ 1,090	+ *908*
+ 46·7	+ *57·8*	+ 19·3	+ *18·1*	− 4·6	− *3·9*	+ 17·5	+ *14·2*

DISTRICT

Religions.	Chauparan.		Hunterganj.		Chatra.		Simaria.	
	Male.	Female.	Male.	Female.	Male.	Female.	Male.	Female.
HINDUS.								
1891	27,910	*29,959*	26,266	*27,492*	26,881	*28,703*	16,091	*16,990*
1881	31,955	*32,689*	26,060	*26,221*	28,329	*29,096*	16,716	*17,148*
Variation	— 4,045	— *2,730*	+ 206	+ *1,271*	— 1,448	— *393*	— 625	— *158*
Percentage	— 12·6	— *8·3*	+ ·7	+ *4·8*	— 5·1	— *1·3*	— 3·7	— *·9*
MUSALMANS.								
1891	2,410	*2,545*	2,140	*2,597*	2,627	*3,150*	1,426	*1,448*
1881	2,938	*2,860*	2,256	*2,416*	3,105	*3,473*	1,432	*1,444*
Variation	— 528	— *315*	— 116	+ *181*	— 478	— *323*	— 6	+ *4*
Percentage	— 18·0	— *11·0*	— 5·1	+ *7·4*	— 15·3	— *9·3*	— ·4	+ *·3*
THE ANIMISTIC.								
1891	25	*60*	...	...	7	...	325	*307*
1881	...	...	1	1	10	*5*	137	*152*
Variation	+ 25	+ *60*	— 1	— 1	— 3	— *5*	+ 188	+ *155*
Percentage	...	...	— 100	— 100	— 30·0	— *100*	+ 137·2	+ *101·9*

DISTRICT

Religions.	District Total.		Ranchi.		Sili.		Tamar.		Karra.		Mandar.	
	Male.	Female.	Male.	Female.	Male.	Female.	Male.	Female.	Male.	Female.	Male.	Female.
HINDUS.												
1891	222,215	*222,751*	37,686	*36,996*	28,458	*28,748*	22,571	*22,663*	12,658	*12,989*	13,258	*13,842*
1881	206,868	*204,615*	31,184	*30,166*	25,332	*25,168*	20,770	*21,336*	14,536	*14,261*	11,881	*12,001*
Variation	+ 15,347	+ *18,136*	+ 6,502	+ *6,830*	+ 3,126	+ *3,580*	+ 1,801	+ *1,327*	— 1,878	— *1,272*	+ 1,377	+ *1,841*
Percentage	+ 7·4	+ *8·8*	+ 20·8	+ *22·6*	+ 12·3	+ *14·2*	+ 8·6	+ *6·2*	— 12·9	— *8·9*	+ 11·5	+ *15·3*
MUSALMANS.												
1891	18,513	*17,608*	7,794	*7,792*	426	*273*	329	*251*	1,178	*1,192*	2,400	*2,315*
1881	15,796	*15,662*	6,355	*6,460*	356	*265*	206	*192*	1,203	*1,191*	1,958	*1,935*
Variation	+ 2,717	+ *1,946*	+ 1,439	+ *1,332*	+ 70	+ *8*	+ 123	+ *59*	— 25	+ *1*	+ 442	+ *380*
Percentage	+ 17·2	+ *12·4*	+ 22·6	+ *20·6*	+ 19·6	+ *3·0*	+ 59·7	+ *30·7*	— 2·0	+ *·0*	+ 22·5	+ *19·6*
CHRISTIANS.												
1891	37,682	*38,011*	2,814	*2,455*	45	*57*	1,155	*1,148*	4,198	*4,227*	969	*1,069*
1881	18,192	*18,071*	1,277	*1,090*	28	*25*	1,012	*890*	2,349	*2,335*	630	*649*
THE ANIMISTIC.												
1891	273,463	*298,649*	39,651	*42,416*	8,859	*9,335*	26,925	*27,180*	27,654	*32,575*	17,441	*22,465*
1881	282,466	*296,449*	33,723	*34,537*	8,515	*8,646*	24,481	*24,567*	34,963	*37,636*	17,886	*19,715*
Variation	— 9,003	+ *2,200*	+ 5,928	+ *7,879*	+ 344	+ *689*	+ 2,444	+ *2,613*	— 7,309	— *5,061*	— 445	+ *2,750*
Percentage	— 3·1	+ *7·1*	+ 14·6	+ *22·8*	+ 4·0	+ *8·1*	+ 9·9	+ *10·6*	+ 20·9	— *13·4*	— 2·4	+ *13·9*

HAZARIBAGH—*concluded.*

Giridhi.		Gawan.		Kodarma.		Kharakdiha.		Dunurhi.	
Male.	Female.	Male.	Female.	Male.	Female.	Male.	Female.	Male.	Female.
38,538	37,863	23,555	24,764	33,561	35,308	65,126	68,081	28,698	29,501
32,895	31,999	23,012	22,409	32,330	33,312	64,206	64,359	25,081	26,627
+ 5,643	+ 5,864	+ 543	+ 2,355	+ 1,231	+ 1,996	+ 920	+ 3,722	+ 3,617	+ 2,874
+ 17·1	+ 18·3	+ 2·3	+ 10·5	+ 3·8	+ 5·9	+ 1·4	+ 5·7	+ 14·4	+ 10·7
5	6,868	2,369	2,553	4,191	4,347	9,394	9,603	3,709	3,576
4,673	4,272	2,275	2,315	3,869	4,018	8,862	8,762	3,057	3,018
+ 2,192	+ 2,596	+ 94	+ 238	+ 322	+ 329	+ 532	+ 841	+ 652	+ 558
+ 44·9	+ 60·7	+ 4·1	+ 10·2	+ 8·3	+ 8·1	+ 6·0	+ 9·5	+ 21·3	+ 18·4
8,336	8,320	1,985	2,063	142	133	2,290	2,249	7,166	7,247
6,035	5,853	1,717	1,647	145	128	2,202	2,154	5,362	5,538
+ 2,301	+ 2,467	+ 268	+ 416	— 3	+ 5	+ 88	+ 95	+ 1,804	+ 1,709
+ 38·1	+ 42·1	+ 15·6	+ 25·2	— 2·0	+ 3·9	+ 3·9	+ 4·4	+ 33·6	+ 30·8

LOHARDAGA.

Khunti.		Lohardaga.		Chainpur.		Toto.		Palkot.		Kochdaga.		Basia.	
Male.	Female.	Male.	Female.	Male.	Female.	Male.	Female.	Male.	Female.	Male.	Female.	Male.	Female.
13,429	13,589	17,129	17,858	9,280	9,071	15,350	15,036	15,262	15,256	17,455	16,755	19,679	19,948
12,788	12,834	16,025	16,670	8,810	8,601	13,968	13,740	15,430	14,946	13,926	13,409	22,218	21,483
+ 641	+ 755	+ 1,104	+ 1,188	+ 470	+ 470	+ 1,382	+ 1,296	— 168	+ 310	+ 3,529	+ 3,346	— 2,539	— 1,535
+ 5·0	+ 5·8	+ 6·8	+ 7·1	+ 5·3	+ 5·4	+ 9·8	+ 9·4	— 1·0	+ 2·0	+ 25·3	+ 24·9	— 11·4	— 7·1
326	175	3,445	3,527	367	301	1,315	1,006	363	277	263	191	307	308
186	182	3,285	3,426	297	254	1,049	1,022	370	307	227	158	304	270
+ 140	— 7	+ 160	+ 101	+ 70	+ 47	+ 266	— 16	— 7	— 30	+ 36	+ 33	+ 3	+ 38
+ 75·3	— 3·8	+ 4·8	+ 2·9	+ 23·5	+ 18·5	+ 25·3	— 1·5	— 1·8	— 9·7	+ 15·8	+ 20·8	+ ·9	+ 14·0
8,829	8,924	833	894	6,864	7,124	1,336	1,459	2,994	2,955	1,451	1,447	6,194	6,252
9,505	9,649	365	433	3	...	45	58	201	212	...	...	2,777	2,807
25,341	25,895	30,381	36,507	11,015	10,701	32,864	36,482	14,406	15,574	18,112	18,087	20,724	21,425
25,274	26,182	31,951	37,319	18,100	17,726	33,329	35,277	16,356	16,525	17,911	17,737	19,977	20,575
+ 67	— 287	— 1,570	— 812	— 7,085	— 7,025	— 465	+ 1,205	— 1,860	— 951	+ 201	+ 350	+ 747	+ 850
+ ·3	— 1·0	— 4·9	— 2·1	— 39·1	— 39·6	— 1·3	+ 3·4	— 11·3	— 5·7	+ 1·1	+ 1·9	+ 3·7	+ 4·0

DISTRICT

Religions.	District Total.		Purulia.		Jhalda.		Baghmundi.		Chandil.		Barabhum.	
	Male.	Female.	Male.	Female.	Male.	Female.	Male.	Female.	Male.	Female.	Male.	Female.
HINDUS.												
1891	482,238	*490,271*	89,885	*91,442*	45,627	*45,470*	16,803	*16,851*	38,770	*39,570*	53,949	*54,484*
1881	468,689	*477,558*	87,708	*90,307*	43,266	*43,409*	16,026	*16,327*	38,378	*39,268*	58,863	*59,557*
Variation	+ 13,549	+ *12,713*	+ 2,177	+ *1,135*	+ 2,361	+ *2,061*	+ 777	+ *524*	+ 392	+ *302*	— 4,914	— *5,073*
Percentage	+ 2·8	+ *2·6*	+ 2·4	+ *10·2*	+ 5·4	+ *4·7*	+ 4·8	+ *3·2*	+ 1·0	+ *·7*	— 8·3	— *8·5*
MUSALMANS.												
1891	27,658	*25,597*	5,279	*4,774*	2,536	*2,301*	538	*434*	797	*564*	1,544	*1,346*
1881	23,277	*22,176*	4,231	*4,003*	2,097	*1,937*	442	*414*	534	*443*	1,204	*1,115*
Variation	+ 4,381	+ *3,421*	+ 1,048	+ *771*	+ 439	+ *364*	+ 96	+ *20*	+ 263	+ *121*	+ 340	+ *231*
Percentage ...	+ 18·8	+ *15·4*	+ 24·7	+ *19·2*	+ 20·9	+ *18·7*	+ 21·7	+ *4·8*	+ 49·2	+ *27·3*	+ 28·2	+ *20·7*
CHRISTIANS.												
1891	783	*749*	316	*301*	86	*101*	60	*73*	51	*23*	13	*3*
1881	283	*269*	148	*166*	4	...	48	*42*	31	*28*	2	...
THE ANIMISTIC.												
1891	82,517	*83,512*	8,959	*9,123*	3,067	*3,130*	2,002	*1,741*	6,235	*6,663*	12,648	*12,935*
1881	21,669	*21,520*	103	*97*	346	*339*	40	*45*	1,291	*1,278*	2	*69*

DISTRICT

Religions.	District Total.		Chaibasa.	
	Male.	Female.	Male.	Female.
HINDUS.				
1891	115,958	*115,041*	31,700	*31,335*
1881	223,614	*224,196*	96,957	*96,952*
Variation	— 107,656	— *109,155*	— 64,257	— *65,617*
Percentage	— 48·1	— *48·6*	— 66·9	— *67·6*
MUSALMANS.				
1891	1,853	*1,369*	602	*516*
1881	1,239	*1,090*	527	*436*
Variation	+ 614	+ *279*	+ 75	+ *80*
Percentage	+ 49·5	+ *24·9*	+ 14·2	+ *18·3*
CHRISTIANS.				
1891	2,491	*2,373*	524	*543*
1881	1,505	*1,483*	120	*129*
THE ANIMISTIC.				
1891	151,115	*155,295*	79,778	*84,193*
1881	323	*328*	...	...

MANBHUM.

Manbazar.		Raghunathpur.		Gaurandi.		Para.		Chas.		Gobindpur.		Nirsa.		Topchanchi.	
Male.	Female.	Male.	Female.	Male.	Female.	Male.	Female.	Male.	Female.	Male.	Female.	Male.	Female.	Male.	Female.
30,088	30,826	45,157	46,838	18,567	18,400	18,734	19,601	44,100	44,847	37,112	37,997	21,564	21,544	21,882	22,401
28,312	29,137	46,564	47,896	17,139	17,130	17,472	17,833	39,599	40,168	38,541	39,199	19,615	19,607	17,206	17,720
+ 1,776	+ 1,689	− 1,407	− 1,058	+ 1,428	+ 1,270	+ 1,262	+ 1,768	+ 4,501	+ 4,679	− 1,429	− 1,202	+ 1,949	+ 1,937	+ 4,676	+ 4,681
+ 6·2	+ 5·7	− 3·0	− 2·2	+ 8·3	+ 7·4	+ 7·2	+ 9·9	+ 11·3	+ 11·6	− 3·7	− 3·0	+ 9·9	+ 9·8	+ 27·1	+ 26·4
829	748	1,994	1,910	622	503	1,739	1,787	3,027	3,027	4,425	4,312	2,100	1,766	2,228	2,125
633	585	1,712	1,741	750	681	1,579	1,640	2,506	2,522	3,944	3,839	1,770	1,559	1,875	1,697
+ 196	+ 163	+ 282	+ 169	− 128	− 178	+ 160	+ 147	+ 521	+ 505	+ 481	+ 473	+ 330	+ 207	+ 353	+ 428
+ 30·9	+ 27·8	+ 16·4	+ 9·7	− 17·0	− 26·1	+ 10·1	+ 8·9	+ 20·7	+ 20·0	+ 12·1	+ 12·3	+ 18·6	+ 13·2	+ 18·8	+ 25·2
3	2	13	5	1	...	1	...	2	2	229	230	6	3	...	...
...	...	7	...	...	...	...	...	3	3	32	24	8	0	...	...
7,585	7,873	10,472	10,441	7,269	7,278	791	825	2,718	2,760	12,723	12,502	5,838	5,854	9,215	2,378
...	...	5,425	5,323	5,077	5,016	599	617	2,160	2,212	4,571	4,534	183	190	1,792	1,807

SINGHBHUM.

Chakradharpur.		Manoharpur.		Ghatsila or Dhalbhum.	
Male.	Female.	Male.	Female.	Male.	Female.
13,377	12,885	8,256	6,383	62,625	64,438
36,868	36,514	8,857	8,600	81,932	82,130
− 23,491	− 23,629	− 601	− 2,217	− 19,307	− 17,692
− 63·7	− 64·7	− 6·7	− 25·7	− 23·5	− 21·5
374	224	334	103	543	519
191	184	14	21	507	449
+ 183	+ 40	+ 320	+ 82	+ 36	+ 70
+ 95·8	+ 21·7	+ 2,285·7	+ 39·4	+ 7·1	+ 15·5
1,713	1,644	201	135	53	51
1,357	1,331	5	3	23	20
28,275	28,402	10,319	9,146	32,746	33,494
...	...	...	...	323	325

DISTRICT

Religions.	District Total.		Daltonganj.		Garhwa.		Ranka.	
	Male.	Female.	Male.	Female.	Male.	Female.	Male.	Female.
HINDUS.								
1891	244,482	*251,936*	43,767	*45,309*	34,999	*36,859*	13,248	*13,975*
1881	226,737	*230,622*	32,739	*33,475*	32,202	*33,430*	18,735	*18,438*
Variation	+ 17,745	+ *21,314*	+ 11,028	+ *11,834*	+ 2,797	+ *3,429*	— 5,487	— *5,163*
Percentage	+ 7·8	+ *9·2*	+ 33·6	+ *35·3*	+ 8·6	+ *10·2*	— 29·2	— *28·0*
MUSALMANS.								
1891	25,337	*25,108*	4,423	*4,675*	5,071	*5,372*	876	*809*
1881	22,841	*23,104*	3,880	*3,905*	4,678	*4,883*	1,212	*1,051*
Variation	+ 2,496	+ *2,004*	+ 543	+ *770*	+ 393	+ *489*	— 336	— *242*
Percentage	+ 10·9	+ *8·6*	+ 13·9	+ *19·7*	+ 8·4	+ *10·0*	— 27·7	— *23·0*
CHRISTIANS.								
1891	3,337	*3,339*	8	*6*	1	...	7	*3*
1881	13	*5*	10	*3*	1	*2*	...	...
THE ANIMISTIC.								
1891	21,159	*22,064*	2,628	*2,648*	2,375	*2,349*	2,975	*2,975*
1881	23,558	*23,850*	1,682	*1,605*	1,798	*1,779*	3,566	*3,544*
Variation	— 2,399	— *1,786*	+ 946	+ *1,043*	+ 577	+ *570*	— 591	— *569*
Percentage	— 10·1	— *7·4*	+ 56·2	+ *64·9*	+ 32·0	+ *32·0*	— 16·5	— *16·0*

FEUDATORY

KUCH

Religions.	Total.		Phulbari.		Kuch Bihar and Kotwali.	
	Male.	Female.	Male.	Female.	Male.	Female.
HINDUS.						
1891	212,035	*94,493*	27,859	*25,016*	51,709	*45,325*
1881	220,672	*206,806*	27,711	*25,782*	53,508	*47,963*
Variation	— 8,637	— *12,313*	+ 148	— *706*	— 1,799	— *2,633*
Percentage	— 3·9	— *5·9*	+ 0·5	— *2·9*	— 3·3	— *5·5*
MUSALMANS.						
1891	89,471	*81,275*	10,237	*9,127*	16,769	*14,885*
1881	90,609	*83,930*	8,633	*8,091*	17,058	*15,902*
Variation	— 1,138	— *2,655*	+ 1,604	+ *1,036*	— 289	— *1,017*
Percentage	— 1·2	— *3·1*	+ 18·5	+ *12·8*	— 1·1	— *6·3*
THE ANIMISTIC.						
1891	530	*481*	388	*420*	57	*61*
1881	219	*196*	134	*134*	64	*60*

ORISSA TRIBU

Religions.	Total.		Athgarh.		Talcher.		Moharbhanj.	
	Male.	Female.	Male.	Female.	Male.	Female.	Male.	Female.
HINDUS.								
1891	766,992	*764,817*	18,166	*17,823*	26,230	*26,226*	205,954	*208,444*
1881	544,575	*532,706*	15,489	*15,054*	18,757	*16,709*	95,877	*93,417*
Variation	+ 222,417	+ *232,111*	+ 2,677	+ *2,769*	+ 7,473	+ *9,517*	+ 110,077	+ *115,027*
Percentage	+ 40·8	+ *43·5*	+ 17·2	+ *18·3*	+ 39·8	+ *56·9*	+ 114·8	+ *123·1*

PALAMAU.

Chhatrapur.		Patan.		Husainabad.		Latehar.		Mahuadanr.		Balumat.	
Male.	Female.	Male.	Female.	Male.	Female.	Male.	Female.	Male.	Female.	Male.	Female.
19,192	*19,312*	36,679	*37,614*	47,967	*50,740*	16,701	*16,790*	7,984	*7,891*	23,511	*23,699*
17,252	*16,978*	35,080	*35,993*	44,327	*46,429*	17,328	*17,005*	5,191	*4,956*	23,883	*23,918*
+ 1,940	+ *2,334*	+ 1,609	+ *1,621*	+ 3,640	+ *4,311*	— 627	— *215*	+ 2,793	+ *2,935*	— 372	— *219*
+ 11·2	+ *13·7*	+ 4·5	+ *4·5*	+ 8·2	+ *9·2*	— 3·6	— *1·2*	+ 53·8	+ *59·2*	— 1·5	— *·9*
1,065	*1,079*	3,596	*3,586*	6,457	*6,167*	1,585	*1,535*	448	*467*	1,759	*1,357*
1,091	*1,090*	3,319	*3,327*	5,377	*5,717*	1,449	*1,471*	311	*335*	1,524	*1,325*
— 26	— *11*	+ 277	+ *259*	+ 1,080	+ *450*	+ 136	+ *64*	+ 137	+ *132*	+ 235	+ *32*
— 2·3	— *1·0*	+ 8·3	+ *7·7*	+ 20·0	+ *7·8*	+ 9·3	+ *4·3*	+ 44·0	+ *39·4*	+ 15·4	+ *2·4*
1	*1*	4	*2*	4	*3*	2	*3*	3,276	*3,302*	22	*2*
...	...	...	...	...	...	2	...	...	...	...	...
213	*203*	658	*696*	316	*289*	2,965	*3,185*	1,378	*1,407*	7,057	*7,655*
235	*192*	810	*879*	354	*310*	3,216	*3,586*	4,278	*3,971*	7,619	*7,984*
— 22	+ *11*	— 152	— *183*	— 83	— *21*	— 251	— *401*	— 2,900	— *2,564*	— 562	— *329*
— 9·3	+ *5·7*	— 18·7	— *20·8*	— 10·7	— *6·7*	— 7·8	— *11·1*	— 67·7	— *64·5*	— 7·3	— *4·1*

STATES.

BIHAR.

Mathabhanga.		Haldibari.		Mekliganj.		Dinhata.	
Male.	Female.	Male.	Female.	Male.	Female.	Male.	Female.
56,625	*53,128*	8,873	*7,973*	17,425	*15,591*	49,544	*47,460*
60,284	*56,816*	8,932	*8,281*	18,312	*16,587*	51,925	*51,377*
— 3,659	— *3,688*	— 59	— *308*	— 887	— *996*	— 2,381	— *3,917*
— 6·0	— *6·4*	— 0·6	— *3·7*	— 4·8	— *6·0*	— 4·5	— *7·6*
17,850	*16,288*	9,390	*8,506*	9,318	*8,649*	25,907	*23,820*
19,481	*17,694*	9,455	*8,742*	9,014	*8,242*	26,968	*25,259*
— 1,631	— *1,406*	— 65	— *236*	+ 304	+ *407*	— 1,061	— *1,439*
— 8·3	— *7·9*	— 0·6	— *2·6*	+ 3·3	+ *4·9*	— 3·9	— *5·6*
...	...	...	...	...	...	85	...
3	*1*	...	...	...	...	18	*1*

TARY STATES.

Nilgiri.		Keonjhar.		Pal Lahara.		Dhenkanal.		Athmalik.	
Male.	Female.	Male.	Female.	Male.	Female.	Male.	Female.	Male.	Female.
26,518	*26,874*	114,209	*113,138*	8,394	*7,082*	114,089	*114,319*	14,018	*11,348*
21,977	*21,928*	98,635	*97,060*	7,203	*6,799*	63,596	*64,762*	8,542	*7,843*
+ 4,541	+ *4,946*	+ 15,574	+ *16,078*	+ 1,191	+ *283*	+ 50,493	+ *49,557*	+ 5,476	+ *3,505*
+ 20·6	+ *22·5*	+ 15·7	+ *16·5*	+ 16·5	+ *4·1*	+ 79·3	+ *76·5*	+ 64·1	+ *44·6*

ORISSA TRIBUTARY

Religions.	Total.		Athgarh.		Talcher.		Mohabbhanj.	
	Male.	Female.	Male.	Female.	Male.	Female.	Male.	Female.
MUSALMANS.								
1891	3,367	2,824	103	83	61	80	1,570	1,412
1881	3,053	2,679	110	88	70	51	1,192	1,058
Variation	+ 314	+ 152	— 7	— 5	— 9	+ 29	+ 378	+ 354
Percentage	+ 10·2	+ 5·6	— 6·3	— 5·6	— 12·8	+ 56·8	+ 31·7	+ 33·4
THE ANIMISTIC.								
1891	77,376	77,918	44	42	40	34	57,334	55,464
1881	104,341	161,751	...	...	...	...	97,717	96,402
Variation	— 86,965	— 83,833	+ 44	+ 42	+ 40	+ 34	— 40,383	— 40,938
Percentage	— 52·9	— 51·8	...	...	...	...	— 41·3	— 24·4

Religions.	Hindol.		Narsinghpur.		Baramba.		Tigaria.	
	Male.	Female.	Male.	Female.	Male.	Female.	Male.	Female.
HINDUS.								
1891	18,567	19,222	16,700	17,057	15,716	16,041	9,854	10,349
1881	15,872	15,765	16,326	16,147	13,102	12,967	9,711	9,864
Variation	+ 2,695	+ 3,457	+ 374	+ 910	+ 2,614	+ 3,074	+ 143	+ 485
Percentage	+ 17·0	+ 21·9	+ 2·2	+ 5·6	+ 19·9	+ 23·7	+ 1·4	+ 4·9
MUSALMANS.								
1891	89	88	48	44	53	46	165	178
1881	441	412	52	58	66	52	137	138
Variation	— 352	— 324	— 4	— 14	— 13	— 6	+ 28	+ 40
Percentage	— 79·8	— 78·6	— 7·6	— 24·1	— 19·6	— 11·5	+ 20·4	+ 28·9
THE ANIMISTIC.								
1891	...	...	...	...	6	5	...	...
1881	671	637	...	...	1,573	1,520	...	...
Variation	— 671	— 637	...	...	— 1,567	— 1,515	...	...
Percentage	— 100·0	— 100·0	...	...	— 99·6	— 93·0	...	...

CHUTIA NAGPUR

Religions.	Total.		Chang Bhukar.		Korba.		Sirguja.		Udaipur.	
	Male.	Female.	Male.	Female.	Male.	Female.	Male.	Female.	Male.	Female.
HINDUS.										
1891	293,240	280,608	9,697	8,810	18,401	17,527	98,415	94,117	15,379	14,801
1881	341,673	329,453	6,803	6,618	15,039	14,599	136,215	131,812	17,030	16,753
Variation	— 48,433	— 48,845	+ 2,894	+ 2,192	+ 3,362	+ 2,928	— 37,800	— 37,695	— 1,651	— 1,952
Percentage ...	— 14·1	— 14·8	+ 42·5	+ 33·1	+ 22·3	+ 20·2	— 27·7	— 28·5	— 9·6	— 11·6
MUSALMANS.										
1891	3,505	3,228	11	8	137	95	1,796	1,581	43	57
1881	2,327	2,177	23	22	123	85	1,174	1,110	81	91
Variation	+ 1,178	+ 1,051	— 12	— 14	+ 14	+ 10	+ 622	+ 471	— 38	— 34
Percentage ...	+ 50·6	+ 48·2	— 52·1	— 63·6	+ 11·3	+ 11·7	+ 52·9	+ 42·4	— 46·9	— 37·3
THE ANIMISTIC.										
1891	152,678	149,579	...	...	48	32	65,083	63,560	3,699	3,557
1881	1,177	1,078	...	...	...	...	...	...	...	...

STATES—*concluded.*

Nilgiri.		Keonjhar.		Pal Lahara.		Dhenkanal.		Athmalik.	
Male.	Female.	Male.	Female.	Male.	Female.	Male.	Female.	Male.	Female.
50	10	252	229	25	18	371	238	61	46
25	7	228	219	4	4	276	259	38	40
+ 25	+ 3	+ 24	+ 10	+ 21	+ 14	+ 95	− 21	+ 23	+ 6
+ 100·0	+ 42·8	+ 10·5	+ 4·5	+ 525·0	+ 350·0	+ 34·4	− 8·1	+ 60·5	+ 15·0
1,326	1,317	10,538	9,732	1,593	2,588	4,148	4,894	2,323	3,809
3,446	3,553	10,152	9,256	458	419	39,616	39,731	2,776	2,535
− 2,120	− 2,236	+ 386	+ 476	+ 1,135	+ 2,169	− 35,468	− 34,837	− 453	+ 1,274
− 61·5	− 62·9	+ 3·8	+ 5·1	+ 247·8	+ 517·6	− 89·5	− 87·6	− 16·3	+ 50·2

Kandhpara.		Nayagarh.		Ranpur.		Daspalla.		Boad.	
Male.	Female.	Male.	Female.	Male.	Female.	Male.	Female.	Male.	Female.
31,670	31,561	58,356	59,073	19,995	19,857	22,775	22,758	45,781	43,645
33,834	32,362	57,135	56,177	17,212	17,048	14,622	14,414	36,685	34,390
− 2,164	− 801	+ 1,221	+ 2,896	+ 2,783	+ 2,809	+ 8,153	+ 8,344	+ 9,096	+ 9,255
− 6·3	− 2·4	+ 2·1	+ 5·1	+ 16·1	+ 16·4	+ 55·7	+ 57·8	+ 24·7	+ 26·9
26	30	251	160	142	119	22	4	78	39
39	21	221	140	94	92	22	2	38	31
− 13	+ 9	+ 30	+ 20	+ 48	+ 27	...	+ 2	+ 40	+ 8
− 33·3	+ 42·8	+ 13·5	+ 14·2	+ 51·0	+ 29·3	...	+ 100·0	+ 105·2	+ 25·8
...	...	22	...	...	...	...	30	2	3
18	22	505	444	1,076	1,017	6,333	6,215	...	...
− 18	− 22	− 483	− 444	− 1,076	− 1,017	− 6,333	− 6,185	+ 2	+ 3
− 100·0	− 100·0	− 95·6	− 100·0	− 100·0	− 100·0	− 100·0	− 99·5	...	...

TRIBUTARY STATES.

Jashpur.		Gangpur.		Bonai.		Kharsawan.		Seraikela.	
Male.	Female.	Male.	Female.	Male.	Female.	Male.	Female.	Male.	Female.
30,452	29,931	76,671	71,472	13,516	12,328	7,457	7,476	23,253	23,146
45,717	43,979	54,908	50,972	12,146	11,299	15,356	15,478	38,459	37,943
− 15,265	− 14,048	+ 21,763	+ 20,500	+ 1,370	+ 1,029	− 7,899	− 8,002	− 15,206	− 14,797
− 33·3	− 31·9	+ 39·6	+ 42·1	+ 11·2	+ 9·9	− 51·4	− 51·6	− 39·5	− 38·9
457	477	404	396	23	24	172	165	462	425
282	262	143	124	19	12	140	153	342	318
+ 175	+ 215	+ 261	+ 272	+ 4	+ 12	+ 32	+ 12	+ 120	+ 107
+ 62·0	+ 82·0	+ 182·5	+ 219·3	+ 21·0	+ 100·0	+ 22·8	+ 7·8	+ 35·0	+ 33·6
26,370	25,049	21,201	19,882	3,196	2,919	10,078	10,122	23,003	23,551
...	...	897	804	280	274	...	...	...	...

PROVINCIAL TABLE III—Showing for every thana in each district the number of Immigrants, distinguishing between those from contiguous districts and from other districts and provinces, when their total number exceeds 1,000 persons.

The statistics of emigration by *thánás* was not recorded in the Census schedules, but its more important District totals are presented in the marginal tables in the District Analyses in Chapter VII of the Report.

BARDWAN

DISTRICT

	Total for the District.		Bardwan.		Sahibganj.		Khandaghosh.		Raina.		Satgachhia.		Jamalpur.		Bud-Bud.	
	Male.	Female.	Male.	Female.	Male.	Female.	Male.	Female.	Male.	Female.	Male.	Female.	Male.	Female.	Male.	Female.
IMMIGRANTS.																
(a) From contiguous districts—																
Santal Parganas	2,878	3,368	28	139	24	11	...	...	1	...	30	14	57	10	...	94
Nadia	4,590	5,639	154	95	102	3	5	...	10	4	168	101	7	14	237	1
Hugli	2,577	4,956	441	247	27	6	82	215	236	1,868	155	163	19	211	137	124
Bankura	9,724	11,904	1,026	751	24	39	731	2,233	351	795	223	792	392	181	787	1,378
Birbhum	4,135	6,707	286	288	37	79	...	19	15	18	114	56	69	69	104	70
Murshidabad	1,654	2,594	58	58	13	26	...	...	10	33	42	28	17	17	15	8
Manbhum	8,200	7,632	712	105	...	15	16	10	...	...	16	10	4	4	8	13
Total ...	33,813	42,830	2,705	1,685	227	179	834	2,477	623	2,718	748	1,164	565	506	1,278	1,787
(b) From other districts in Bengal Proper	2,315	2,227	406	266	36	30	37	57	66	103	100	53	95	220	134	189
(c) From Bihar	8,513	3,633	1,947	488	94	10	44	...	50	7	103	21	138	20	187	40
Patna	721	482	131	50	12	...	2	...	5	2	16	1	2	1	...	6
Gaya	2,456	1,642	259	183	26	10	6	...	2	2	22	...	16	5	106	3
Shahabad	1,462	517	84	31	13	...	1	...	5	3	12	8	16	1	...	9
Saran	1,234	96	969	22	1	...	11	...	...	...	13	...	...	2	...	1
Monghyr	1,212	663	228	49	1	...	...	...	...	...	10	10	6	9	37	21
(d) From Orissa	459	77	245	9	...	...	7	...	6	1	5	30	1	2	2	2
(e) From Chutia Nagpur ...	1,928	1,172	216	57	...	1	8	7	4	4	11	...	17	1	69	2
Hazaribagh	1,628	1,092	170	39	...	1	8	1	2	2	3	...	4	1	22	1
(f) From other Provinces and countries	4,022	2,403	820	358	58	10	26	1	40	20	147	87	88	36	101	67
North-Western Provinces	2,383	1,625	484	208	34	10	11	1	9	13	130	76	52	25	73	62
TOTAL IMMIGRANTS ...	51,050	52,342	6,339	2,863	415	230	956	2,522	789	2,853	1,114	1,355	904	785	1,771	2,087

DISTRICT

	Total for the District.		Bankura.		Onda.		Gangajalghati.		Barjora.	
	Male.	Female.	Male.	Female.	Male.	Female.	Male.	Female.	Male.	Female.
IMMIGRANTS.										
(a) From contiguous districts—										
Midnapur	4,490	7,390	185	80	298	558	25	16	4	15
Manbhum	6,526	8,819	702	1,452	106	41	687	1,364	21	56
Hugli	1,027	2,483	50	62	28	15	9	8	8	7
Bardwan	2,569	5,433	157	102	44	16	605	1,512	271	776
Total ...	14,612	24,118	1,094	1,696	476	630	1,326	2,900	304	858

DIVISION.

BARDWAN.

Ausgram.		Raniganj.		Asansol.		Kaksa.		Katwa.		Ketugram.		Mungalkot.		Kalna.		Purbasthali.		Manteswar.	
Male.	Female.	Male.	Female.	Male.	Female.	Male.	Female.	Male.	Female.	Male.	Female.	Male.	Female.	Male.	Female.	Male.	Female.	Male.	Female.
7	...	358	408	2,129	2,542	162	130	2	2	6	...	...	...	68	15	1	3	...	...
121	171	32	14	63	30	11	6	359	558	230	512	36	38	737	805	2,205	3,164	123	122
8	2	61	17	248	124	57	16	33	12	194	181	39	17	805	1,567	4	59	31	25
226	294	3,415	2,518	1,548	1,672	338	781	22	108	14	19	30	49	472	226	43	34	82	36
428	919	1,176	1,630	473	498	254	682	28	173	582	899	333	1,090	190	159	20	23	26	39
23	40	4	1	18	8	6	1	85	168	1,050	1,884	42	80	124	65	125	135	22	42
10	72	617	826	6,657	6,376	48	47	48	48	6	6	3	4	41	15	74	91	...	20
823	1,494	5,663	5,414	1,136	11,250	876	1,663	577	1,069	2,082	3,501	483	1,278	2,437	2,852	2,472	3,509	284	284
84	48	427	394	378	379	3	25	59	105	24	13	25	39	221	161	99	144	71	21
190	7	710	108	4,299	2,653	351	61	28	86	11	7	76	8	194	72	71	41	20	4
...	...	28	7	469	401	23	7	...	...	...	...	2	3	27	...	4	4	...	...
...	...	174	84	1,733	1,287	70	26	18	3	...	...	...	...	2	18	22	21	...	...
14	...	47	17	1,083	395	82	10	5	1	4	1	...	...	81	45	5	1	...	...
...	...	33	...	91	64	87	5	1	1	1	...	...	...	27	1	...	...	...	...
5	7	46	...	677	559	74	10	...	77	6	...	74	5	25	...	23	2	...	4
29	19	6	...	57	4	9	...	43	1	12	2	8	...	22	...	5	...	2	7
5	...	172	100	1,362	965	23	1	...	1	...	...	...	...	14	1	27	32	...	...
5	...	164	88	1,193	929	20	1	...	1	...	...	...	...	10	1	27	26	...	...
12	6	240	112	1,805	1,428	256	42	72	22	25	8	59	9	202	167	45	24	1	6
10	3	154	38	1,112	1,006	140	23	38	16	19	8	36	3	41	136	24	1	7	6
1,143	1,574	7,227	6,128	19,037	16,679	1,568	1,792	779	1,284	2,154	3,531	651	1,334	3,090	3,253	2,719	3,750	394	322

BANKURA.

Khatra.		Raipura.		Simlapal.		Bishnupur.		Sonamukhi.		Katalpur.		Indas.	
Male.	Female.	Male.	Female.	Male.	Female.	Male.	Female.	Male.	Female.	Male.	Female.	Male.	Female.
120	99	2,527	3,595	476	835	469	1,012	22	25	329	1,102	35	56
834	1,568	3,801	4,016	175	127	77	67	40	32	51	41	32	63
86	27	111	63	11	7	100	131	42	218	518	1,694	114	351
35	16	35	41	2	2	145	134	463	838	137	357	675	1,6[illegible]9
1,025	1,700	6,474	7,715	664	971	791	1,344	587	1,113	1,035	3,194	856	1,999

DISTRICT

	Total for the District.		Bankura.		Onda.		Gangajalghati.		Barjora.	
	Male.	Female.	Male.	Female.	Male.	Female.	Male.	Female.	Male.	Female.
(b) From other districts in Bengal Proper	545	500	137	125	62	12	65	142	29	43
(c) From Bihar	788	194	266	120	61	8	80	26	22	1
(d) From Orissa	175	25	15	7	14	...	28	1	3	...
(e) From Chutia Nagpur	360	357	27	25	25	14	33	57	4	4
(f) From other Provinces and countries ...	714	265	201	89	54	10	96	35	45	...
TOTAL IMMIGRANTS ...	17,194	25,459	1,740	2,062	702	674	1,628	3,161	407	904

DISTRICT

	Total for the District.		Suri.		Dubrajpur.		Bolpur.	
	Male.	Female.	Male.	Female.	Male.	Female.	Male.	Female.
IMMIGRANTS.								
(a) From contiguous districts—								
Santal Parganas ...	6,623	7,653	2,042	2,251	558	1,087	613	479
Bardwan	3,813	7,985	361	2,111	778	2,096	1,058	2,405
Murshidabad	4,669	7,725	126	71	15	21	59	54
Total ...	15,105	23,363	2,529	2,533	1,345	3,204	1,730	2,938
(b) From other districts in Bengal Proper	1,245	1,122	396	259	51	202	142	129
(c) From Bihar	2,368	834	423	212	116	17	113	6
Shahabad	966	338	142	28	31	2	50	1
(d) From Orissa	128	12	16	3	6	6	15	...
(e) From Chutia Nagpur ...	253	271	67	69	64	127	19	30
(f) From other Provinces and countries	1,645	292	111	31	128	7	109	32
North-Western Provinces	1,334	205	47	18	110	1	50	1
TOTAL IMMIGRANTS	20,744	25,894	3,542	3,107	1,710	3,563	2,128	3,135

BANKURA—*concluded.*

Khatra.		Raipura.		Simlapul.		Bishnupur.		Sonamukhi.		Katalpur.		Indas.	
Male.	Female.	Male.	Female.	Male.	Female.	Male.	Female.	Male.	Female.	Male.	Female.	Male.	Female.
19	4	13	14	1	...	70	57	37	51	50	34	62	18
16	5	65	11	13	2	140	5	67	13	14	...	44	3
6	...	20	10	6	...	30	1	4	...	32	1	17	5
16	26	157	164	1	3	27	16	12	17	38	30	10	1
46	13	46	23	24	11	114	55	34	17	22	...	32	12
1,128	1,748	6,775	7,937	709	987	1,172	1,478	721	1,211	1,190	3,259	1,021	2,038

BIRBHUM.

Sakulipur.		Labhpur.		Rampur Hat.		Maureswar.		Nalhati.	
Male.	Female.	Male.	Female.	Male.	Female.	Male.	Female.	Male.	Female.
28 1,055 315	21 2,848 835	31 137 210	22 197 688	967 179 825	923 109 1,402	464 116 617	431 57 984	1,926 129 2,502	2,439 62 3,670
1,398	3,704	378	907	1,971	2,434	1,197	1,472	4,557	6,171
91	86	89	36	211	186	100	30	165	194
41 21	15 5	44 6	2 ...	684 245	234 124	216 98	29 18	[illegible] 873	319 164
14	...	33	...	28	3	5	...	11	...
8	13	...	...	23	5	42	4	30	23
16 10	... ...	458 410	2 2	353 302	100 83	123 99	22 16	347 306	98 83
1,568	3,818	1,002	947	3,270	2,962	1,683	1,557	5,841	6,805

	Total for the District.		Midnapur.		Jhargaon.		Binpur.		Sabani.	
	Male.	Female.	Male.	Female.	Male.	Female.	Male.	Female.	Male.	Female.
IMMIGRANTS.										
(a) From contiguous districts—										
Balasor	2,932	4,488	193	48	33	26	16	...	10	9
24-Parganas	789	347	60	49	1	...	102	3	...	...
Bankura	3,064	5,326	226	87	117	137	1,851	2,712	143	159
Howrah	348	298	31	15	...	...	3	...	...	...
Singhbhum	1,720	2,377	105	10	432	553	471	649	...	2
Hugli	3,259	5,644	353	160	13	4	93	62	19	17
Bardwan	466	319	146	82	6	2	47	18	3	4
Total ...	12,528	18,799	1,114	451	602	722	2,583	3,444	175	191
(b) From other districts in Bengal Proper	889	435	242	82	6	...	20	...	13	11
(c) From Bihar	1,909	615	483	182	148	67	87	37	110	16
Shahabad	997	241	298	89	135	63	46	19	55	5
(d) From Orissa	2,482	791	276	93	28	12	23	35	21	7
Cuttack	2,116	570	240	35	26	7	21	8	11	3
(e) From Chutia Nagpur ...	944	839	116	31	183	144	389	484	97	91
Manbhum	824	340	78	23	178	139	382	15	82	76
(f) From other Provinces and countries	1,653	471	393	49	50	10	86	23	38	47
North-Western Provinces	933	210	163	14	23	4	53	8	27	2
TOTAL IMMIGRANTS	20,405	21,950	2,624	888	1,017	955	3,188	4,023	454	363

	Chandrakona.		Daspur.		Tamluk.		Maslandpur.		Sutahata.	
	Male.	Female.	Male.	Female.	Male.	Female.	Male.	Female.	Male.	Female.
IMMIGRANTS.										
(a) From contiguous districts—										
Balasor	25	1	20	1	7	...	196	4	121	31
24-Parganas	6	9	35	28	57	10	90	52	152	113
Bankura	209	491	22	8	12	10	5	2	2	...
Howrah	13	8	39	82	91	23	40	45	19	37
Singhbhum	...	2	3	...	...	...	...	...	...	...
Hugli	642	1,651	338	1,017	225	152	157	114	87	64
Bardwan	19	70	7	9	25	13	14	6	10	...
Total ...	914	2,232	454	1,095	417	217	502	223	391	245
(b) From other districts in Bengal Proper	20	25	34	23	62	38	37	18	28	4
(c) From Bihar	71	22	65	1	58	• 5	94	...	27	2
Shahabad	41	17	23	...	37	1	19	...	15	...
(d) From Orissa	39	8	20	6	15	6	60	7	239	12
Cuttack	35	5	20	1	12	...	45	4	229	12
(e) From Chutia Nagpur ...	2	14	2	1	11	...	5	...	2	...
Manbhum	...	14	1	1	8	...	...	...	...	...
(f) From other Provinces and countries	103	16	75	36	52	6	170	35	89	39
North-Western Provinces	52	10	55	9	28	1	131	13	83	35
TOTAL IMMIGRANTS	1,149	2,317	650	1,162	615	272	868	283	976	302

MIDNAPUR.

Debra.		Garbeta.		Kespur.		Sabang.		Narain-garh.		Dantun.		Gopiballabh-pur.		Ghatal.	
Male.	Female.	Male.	Female.	Male.	Female.	Male.	Female.	Male.	Female.	Male.	Female.	Male.	Female.	Male.	Female.
10	5	6	8	58	...	15	...	96	26	291	1,201	830	1,147	13	8
7	1	18	14	2	1	42	...	9	...	1	...	...	...	19	28
2	...	261	1,605	44	18	6	...	1	...	9	4	...	21	104	70
1	...	...	...	...	...	1	...	2	...	1	...	...	...	25	27
4	...	4	39	...	...	...	...	15	7	12	2	661	1,113	12	...
37	6	43	98	56	67	43	6	19	3	13	13	...	...	727	1,900
15	3	28	45	15	10	1	1	5	6	4	2	1	2	41	23
76	15	360	1,809	175	96	108	7	147	42	331	1,222	1,492	2,283	941	2,046
12	2	42	69	1	2	50	...	1	8	29	27	4	60	43	15
13	...	29	58	38	3	56	11	98	16	50	15	137	119	70	2
6	...	9	13	29	...	45	...	25	3	26	1	28	16	31	1
43	8	4	19	8	4	36	17	59	4	146	20	344	361	25	18
31	3	4	14	7	...	31	6	39	3	128	10	329	347	18	2
1	1	18	63	...	2	2	...	4	1	20	...	16	6	14	1
...	...	17	63	...	...	...	...	2	1	10	...	15	6	7	1
11	2	36	106	38	6	22	7	61	28	59	12	56	13	42	1
5	1	22	81	20	1	13	7	39	6	27	9	45	2	22	...
156	28	489	2,124	260	113	274	42	370	99	635	1,296	2,049	2,842	1,135	2,083

Panchkura.		Nandigram.		Contai.		Egra.		Pataspur.		Ramnagar.		Bagabanpur.		Khajri.	
Male.	Female.	Male.	Female.	Male.	Female.	Male.	Female.	Male.	Female.	Male.	Female.	Male.	Female.	Male.	Female.
41	4	61	10	240	30	86	302	42	19	360	1,545	7	1	140	67
21	19	33	3	40	9	15	2	...	...	20	2	3	...	16	...
35	2	1	...	8	...	3	...	1	...	...	...	2	...	...	...
41	106	32	5	...	...	1	...	...	...	...	...	3	...	5	...
...	...	...	...	...	...	1	...	...	...	...	...	...	...	...	...
184	245	45	9	93	37	13	5	23	1	6	5	14	7	16	1
16	8	31	4	14	7	6	...	1	...	...	...	6	...	5	4
338	384	203	31	404	83	122	309	67	20	395	1,552	35	8	182	72
34	5	38	...	87	40	6	...	5	4	11	...	36	2	28	...
95	9	45	23	44	9	12	2	2	...	17	...	38	18	22	...
40	5	20	2	34	6	2	...	1	...	6	...	15	...	11	...
33	8	221	47	324	39	210	10	60	4	28	12	93	7	127	27
25	7	212	45	256	32	99	6	55	3	27	7	90	1	126	9
23	...	3	...	8	...	...	...	...	...	2	...	8	...	18	...
19	...	...	...	1	...	...	...	...	...	...	...	...	...	15	...
40	12	64	4	75	4	7	4	19	...	12	...	35	10	20	1
34	1	43	3	46	1	4	...	14	...	9	...	20	2	10	...
563	418	574	105	942	175	357	325	153	28	465	1,564	245	43	397	100

DISTRICT

	Total for the District.		Hugli.		Balagarh.		Pandua.		Dhaniakhali.		Polba.	
	Male.	Female.	Male.	Female.	Male.	Female.	Male.	Female.	Male.	Female.	Male.	Female.
IMMIGRANTS.												
(a) From contiguous districts —												
Bardwan	8,577	13,209	1,634	1,933	538	1,260	1,498	3,081	1,402	2,840	230	187
Bankura	14,324	11,597	1,036	772	388	880	1,736	1,148	1,979	1,196	1,287	775
Nadia	2,891	3,165	806	633	1,252	1,981	262	323	44	36	146	33
Calcutta	450	845	180	391	11	16	21	41	16	38	3	7
24-Parganas	1,742	2,169	607	1,093	86	168	101	125	58	68	48	99
Midnapur	5,675	9,370	215	193	121	127	144	96	1,046	696	390	336
Howrah	1,462	3,661	68	36	5	4	10	13	8	12	8	4
Total ...	35,121	44,016	4,546	5,051	2,401	3,936	3,772	4,827	4,553	4,886	2,062	1,481
(b) From other districts in Bengal Proper	2,704	2,061	670	401	217	240	433	251	243	229	139	37
Birbhum	754	638	45	71	11	90	319	186	160	129	38	18
(c) From Bihar	4,463	1,677	1,861	536	234	87	352	122	103	52	110	15
Patna	972	536	378	156	8	4	47	13	21	7	11	3
Gaya	955	195	380	119	61	...	116	9	31	5	68	8
Saran	837	204	225	64	10	10	44	15	6	35	16	...
(d) From Orissa	1,828	822	535	338	51	8	94	15	54	89	74	...
Cuttack	1,331	136	482	37	48	8	93	15	44	7	70	...
Balasor	592	686	53	299	3	...	1	...	10	82	4	...
(e) From Chutia Nagpur	3,094	596	544	105	285	140	206	54	323	9	142	18
Chutia Nagpur Tributary States ...	2,483	252	500	54	170	20	115	23	301	...	126	...
(f) From Other Provinces and countries	2,352	1,160	871	637	90	5	122	10	45	12	21	2
North-Western Province	1,689	755	645	354	46	3	95	1	13	...	8	...
TOTAL IMMIGRANTS ...	49,662	50,332	9,027	7,066	3,278	4,416	4,979	5,279	5,321	5,277	2,548	1,553

DISTRICT

	Total for the District.		Howrah.		Bally.	
	Male.	Female.	Male.	Female.	Male.	Female.
IMMIGRANTS.						
(a) From contiguous districts—						
Hugli	16,314	18,145	11,603	10,931	1,043	1,157
24-Parganas	2,097	4,400	1,560	1,743	247	503
Calcutta	632	850	524	735	39	49
Midnapur	6,718	5,254	2,912	2,543	235	146
Total ...	26,661	28,649	16,599	15,952	1,564	1,855
(b) From other districts in Bengal Proper	5,600	3,008	3,675	2,118	585	338
Bardwan	1,458	1,086	1,134	855	167	143
Bankura	1,436	636	553	343	125	56
Nadia	893	519	687	417	98	62
(c) From Bihar	13,942	4,049	11,629	3,652	953	182
Patna	2,537	865	2,037	736	236	43
Gya	1,546	446	1,276	404	142	41
Shahabad	3,031	1,171	2,767	1,139	110	23
Muzaffarpur	1,506	296	986	239	166	30
Saran	3,316	844	2,859	792	78	3
Monghyr	1,386	327	1,212	312	117	10
(d) From Orissa	3,899	284	2,240	189	165	8
Cuttack	2,991	254	1,835	165	153	6
(e) From Chutia Nagpur ...	1,793	382	323	103	317	88
Lohardaga ...	1,050	195	15	21	266	79
(f) From other Provinces and countries	16,176	5,759	13,838	5,106	1,057	288
North-Western Provinces	13,611	4,765	12,428	4,292	748	216
Oudh	1,068	222	805	171	137	36
TOTAL IMMIGRANTS	68,071	42,131	48,304	27,136	4,641	2,767

HUGLI.

Serampur.		Haripal.		Krishnanagar.		Singur.		Chanditala.		Jahanabad.		Goghat.		Khanakul.	
Male.	Female.	Male.	Female.	Male.	Female.	Male.	Female.	Male.	Female.	Male.	Female.	Male.	Female.	Male.	Female.
1,917	1,289	314	800	48	48	171	56	42	33	523	1,512	246	647	14	23
456	199	2,303	1,340	611	368	918	415	1,516	476	1,110	1,087	982	3,402	52	39
244	32	39	13	5	7	44	9	15	7	21	26	6	3	7	3
192	289	9	24	2	5	1	1	7	13	8	16	...	4	...	...
517	99	67	63	32	23	41	107	115	209	31	32	17	30	22	62
118	148	887	517	175	144	381	230	179	59	366	592	1,075	4,017	578	2,295
425	257	60	82	128	202	13	20	263	1,214	13	20	6	21	455	1,767
3,869	2,313	3,679	2,339	1,001	797	1,569	847	2,137	2,011	2,072	3,215	2,332	8,124	1,128	4,189
667	785	100	23	41	1	67	28	70	19	29	31	18	9	10	5
139	104	28	13	5	1	2	2	2	...	7	8	6	7	2	4
840	700	233	21	58	2	104	15	433	90	75	26	43	10	17	1
355	298	42	6	3	...	22	6	62	16	20	20	3	6	...	1
122	8	66	9	13	...	...	...	59	30	20	4	15	3	10	...
233	80	31	...	23	...	43	...	190	...	3	...	9	...	4	...
237	308	292	1	38	...	96	3	236	3	120	54	55	4	46	1
112	59	84	1	33	...	86	3	212	3	20	2	9	...	38	1
125	249	208	...	2	...	10	...	24	...	100	52	46	4	6	...
272	113	283	86	225	1	326	5	253	8	131	39	96	17	8	1
230	53	226	40	205	...	316	5	28	2	122	38	82	7	8	...
558	373	135	1	116	1	88	4	149	93	94	17	20	5	45	...
362	292	121	1	94	...	63	1	141	92	59	6	12	5	24	...
8,441	4,592	4,722	2,471	1,479	801	2,250	904	3,278	2,224	2,521	3,382	2,584	8,189	1,254	4,198

HOWRAH.

Domjár.		Jagatballabhpur.		Ulubaria.		Amta.		Bagnan.		Shampur.	
Male.	Female.	Male.	Female.	Male.	Female.	Male.	Female.	Male.	Female.	Male.	Female.
2,008	2,463	254	494	431	229	790	2,514	128	203	57	64
349	750	32	77	435	588	40	68	42	94	292	577
43	54	7	6	14	...	5	2	...	3	...	1
1,341	202	66	37	537	226	303	780	584	780	740	540
3,741	3,469	359	614	1,417	1,043	1,138	3,364	754	1,170	1,088	1,182
923	242	102	137	211	123	39	35	45	12	20	3
91	33	14	7	31	28	10	10	9	8	2	2
675	161	38	40	26	19	9	16	1	1	11	...
76	26	4	1	15	9	6	2	4	1	3	1
810	63	62	4	348	118	60	20	43	1	37	1
163	...	...	...	91	85	5	1	4	...	1	...
85	...	12	...	2	...	8	...	10	1	11	...
111	8	15	1	4	...	5	...	16	...	3	...
159	11	7	...	161	...	23	16	1	...	3	...
267	27	17	3	67	14	10	...	8	...	10	1
36	2	3	...	...	...	8	3	3	...	7	...
785	14	115	...	459	13	67	49	42	11	26	...
605	14	64	...	232	11	60	49	19	7	23	...
1,115	152	31	40	2	...	4	...	1	1	...	...
737	58	30	40	2	...	...	...	...	...	...	...
571	249	109	18	236	4	53	26	139	32	173	36
304	174	44	13	232	3	32	8	84	27	139	32
42	12	8	4	6	...	14	...	43	...	13	...
7,945	4,189	778	813	2,673	1,299	1,361	3,478	1,024	1,227	1,345	1,222

PRESIDENCY

DISTRICT

	Total for the District.		Tollyganj.		Baruipur.		Sonarpur.		Bishnupur.		Bhangar.		Budge-Budge.	
	Male.	Female.	Male.	Female.	Male.	Female.	Male.	Female.	Male.	Female.	Male.	Female.	Male.	Female.
IMMIGRANTS.														
(a) From contiguous districts—														
Khulna	5,542	4,600	235	...	35	7	1	...	...	...	35	47	88	3
Nadia	5,492	4,421	323	323	42	5	12	7	14	2	182	38	98	10
Hugli	9,157	7,586	961	512	44	14	17	52	59	32	265	14	849	1,082
Howrah	5,838	420	527	29	1	45	28	16	...	...	7	19	148	18
Total ...	26,029	17,027	2,046	864	122	71	58	75	73	34	489	118	1,183	1,113
(b) From other districts in Bengal Proper ...	22,127	10,966	1,513	895	578	286	207	251	146	215	461	260	273	781
Bardwan	3,533	3,300	290	54	3	1	15	40	29	1	45	...	45	29
Bankura	2,277	1,571	346	176	12	2	22	5	...	...	10	13	6	498
Jessor	9,405	3,120	317	298	466	276	116	198	100	204	172	257	130	58
Murshidabad ...	923	655	127	115	...	...	...	...	...	...	1	...	3	...
Dacca	1,464	397	23	100	7	...	16	2	...	...	12	...	38	3
Faridpur	2,554	847	89	44	62	...	7	...	14	...	215	...	58	283
(c) From Bihar	19,271	9,870	2,765	1,853	240	508	130	169	60	227	115	105	408	534
Patna	5,492	3,074	1,740	450	53	313	22	118	30	205	35	56	66	129
Gaya	2,940	1,355	360	442	86	3	19	9	...	...	36	...	30	...
Shahabad	651	2,145	...	446	...	3	...	...	...	...	...	4	...	...
Muzaffarpur ...	2,500	383	280	98	20	56	37	16	...	9	3	15	57	...
Darbhanga	1,029	510	...	119	10	112	15	9	...	13	...	5	...	...
Saran	4,639	1,274	16	19	36	21	22	17	20	...	33	6	227	323
Monghyr	1,468	735	366	377	32	...	15	...	10	...	8	...	12	5
(d) From Orissa	11,771	3,790	880	323	405	67	194	86	186	24	147	138	412	14
Cuttack	7,182	2,965	328	153	317	38	134	16	179	1	114	88	200	14
Balasor	4,431	629	552	85	88	29	58	59	...	14	33	50	201	...
(e) From Chutia Nagpur ...	6,604	4,268	4	150	20	219	244	275	145	298	270	405	453	356
Hazaribagh	2,148	1,090	2	128	17	14	...	5	...	6	56	...	210	30
Lohardaga	2,477	1,720	...	...	...	...	220	156	145	99	198	290	243	194
Manbhum	1,562	1,106	...	...	...	198	...	102	...	185	...	95	...	120
(f) From other Provinces and countries	20,579	9,369	4,015	2,300	301	250	232	252	278	360	180	282	1,106	378
North-Western Provinces	13,205	5,978	3,032	1,906	132	115	84	125	90	199	40	126	668	150
Oudh	2,388	2,226	832	218	12	90	13	88	20	125	6	116	218	159
Central Provinces	1,337	637	32	20	38	22	29	20	42	28	30	27	28	99
Assam	2,028	136	98	49	101	16	91	3	112	2	89	...	78	...
England	1,336	119	...	...	...	...	...	...	1	...	...	...	...	...
TOTAL IMMIGRANTS	106,381	55,290	11,223	6,485	1,666	1,401	1,065	1,108	895	1,158	1,662	1,308	3,835	3,115

DIVISION.

24-PARGANAS.

Canning Town.		Jainagar.		Baranagar.		Barasat.		Deganga.		Habra.		Naihati.		Dum-Dum.		Barrackpur.	
Male.	Female.	Male.	Female.	Male.	Female.	Male.	Female.	Male.	Female.	Male.	Female.	Male.	Female.	Male.	Female.	Male.	Female.
97	10	33	...	168	7	35	8	25	18	47	5	298	625	68	...	1	...
151	11	2	...	258	219	108	76	4	2	293	592	1,029	1,223	68	279	159	151
136	...	126	10	1,297	1,622	110	83	5	2	53	45	1,785	1,792	78	47	449	339
8	25	2	36	32	12	3	10	...	18	...	20	3	28	37	22	...	25
392	46	162	46	1,755	1,860	256	177	34	40	393	662	3,115	3,668	246	348	609	515
1,822	282	305	322	1,302	614	1,014	480	302	118	257	60	2,501	2,465	359	347	925	586
15	22	5	4	403	466	33	35	29	7	8	13	1,275	1,803	21	49	147	49
546	...	...	2	171	37	11	...	8	...	1	1	465	369	...	36	68	15
224	125	226	99	429	106	726	145	247	98	242	16	614	120	246	209	614	229
...	49	4	159	146	...	123	125	...	9	...	...	...	...	84	19	...	98
8	...	10	...	42	...	5	1	...	1	...	...	117	140	55	7	37	17
739	...	57	17	53	...	88	77	6	...	2	...	9	1	...	...	85	3
1,017	590	65	109	2,337	1,312	334	92	25	29	50	444	3,621	721	507	272	1,504	763
108	208	8	98	576	159	18	50	...	...	8	426	1,030	...	51	40	151	229
18	10	36	...	518	225	44	5	...	8	2	...	294	231	181	9	180	5
...	6	...	2	...	414	150	8	...	...	...	...	180	341	...	161	100	378
98	18	9	3	156	59	52	9	12	5	18	...	599	14	55	15	104	19
101	10	9	...	...	8	8	10	6	13	...	10	605	15	51	26	62	28
568	303	...	...	1,050	425	23	2	5	3	19	5	586	35	115	20	845	45
7	3	3	6	53	22	23	2	1	...	3	3	318	83	15	1	49	45
2,352	1,262	633	39	449	136	142	27	30	33	36	10	387	31	239	126	53	13
703	1,178	410	36	442	48	121	2	30	6	29	...	381	31	239	17	53	13
1,636	79	199	...	5	85	21	19	...	18	7	...	4	...	...	109	...	...
94	204	70	177	1	13	172	138	225	107	299	194	95	220	70	58	289	264
73	16	49	1	...	...	39	20	...	1	1	8	27	31	...	48	88	113
4	56	4	60	...	...	129	90	225	87	298	104	68	95	70	...	200	125
...	100	...	110	...	...	...	...	...	...	...	68	...	80	...	...	...	26
2,176	527	139	437	977	454	198	320	181	176	179	166	2,424	720	1,504	412	2,153	405
1,040	270	32	298	650	259	60	198	45	60	54	72	2,018	559	476	298	1,546	214
283	220	6	99	210	129	10	78	15	89	12	67	222	129	101	88	40	25
40	26	25	22	46	47	38	29	42	15	39	20	71	26	25	23	29	32
125	9	70	...	61	19	88	12	78	9	69	7	99	4	78	3	81	2
...	...	...	...	...	...	...	...	...	...	...	...	...	...	814	...	429	108
7,853	2,911	1,374	1,130	6,871	4,391	2,116	1,234	797	503	1,214	1,536	12,069	7,825	2,925	1,563	5,533	2,546

	Nawabganj.		Khardaha.		Basirhat.		Baduria.		Haroa.		Husainabad.		Diamond Harbour.	
	Male.	Female.	Male.	Female.	Male.	Female.	Male.	Female.	Male.	Female.	Male.	Female.	Male.	Female.
IMMIGRANTS.														
(a) From Contiguous districts—														
Khulna	8	...	18	2	329	687	791	1,932	583	30	1,488	961	...	5
Nadia	175	118	14	1	20	27	113	114	298	80	34	11	56	19
Hugli	465	849	21	70	5	31	25	27	101	23	25	18	208	14
Howrah	40	19	3	6	...	9	...	8	144	12	...	7	468	2
Total ...	683	986	56	79	354	754	929	2,081	1,126	145	1,547	997	732	40
(b) From other districts in Bengal Proper	945	687	236	186	673	323	840	250	1,011	253	965	269	180	...
Bardwan	139	130	1	6	182	125	211	88	165	69	99	16	13	...
Bankura	185	178	...	...	...	29	7	29	125	40	197	52	13	...
Jessor	447	198	217	189	453	98	559	16	648	10	252	82	125	...
Murshidabad ...	153	56	10	9	...	...	1	...	18	...	123	...	...	...
Dacca	17	12	...	...	2	48	1	29	4	10	83	8	3	...
Faridpur	3	3	...	8	2	25	23	43	31	44	46	98	14	...
(c) From Bihar	1,339	448	37	121	160	348	381	114	372	116	231	80	94	20
Patna	214	198	18	99	2	24	15	26	67	38	41	14	20	5
Gaya	120	8	7	...	23	70	8	46	84	49	22	40	26	...
Shahabad	3	145	...	...	...	219	210	3	7	5	1	4	...	...
Muzaffarpur ...	81	8	3	5	122	...	125	3	140	4	135	3	41	...
Darbhanga	25	25	3	17	...	16	2	8	...	3	...	3	2	...
Saran	631	3	4	...	13	9	23	4	15	2	20	1	1	4
Monghyr	241	59	1	...	...	10	...	20	47	15	3	15	3	9
(d) From Orissa	551	52	58	16	105	100	37	141	118	290	840	120	444	118
Cuttack	390	5	57	...	105	95	37	129	82	280	361	110	244	115
Balasor	138	39	...	16	...	2	...	8	36	5	477	4	190	...
(e) From Chutia Nagpur ...	148	337	155	113	208	69	382	62	433	72	1,011	65	12	22
Hazaribagh	13	184	21	...	13	29	...	46	109	53	707	46	...	4
Lohardaga	123	128	100	95	92	20	80	14	60	19	11	18	...	7
Manbhum	...	10	...	...	102	...	300	...	200	...	226	...	...	6
(f) From other Provinces and countries	1,069	398	131	139	419	126	446	225	399	156	291	104	59	19
North-Western Provinces	904	318	7	92	322	45	368	125	298	86	186	69	25	...
Oudh	15	14	2	19	26	53	24	71	39	42	50	33	3	16
Central Provinces	25	25	19	27	12	26	10	29	11	28	12	2	2	3
Assam	79	1	99	...	50	...	39	...	45	...	84	...	10	...
England	28	11	...	...	...	...	...	...	...	...	...	...	15	...
TOTAL IMMIGRANTS	4,735	2,908	673	654	1,119	1,720	3,017	2,873	3,459	1,032	4,885	1,635	1,521	219

24-PARGANAS—*concluded.*

Kulpi.		Bankipur.		Debipur.		Mathurapur.		Cossipur-Chitpur M. C.		Maniktala M. C.		Entally.		Calcutta Canals.		Sundarbans.	
Male.	Female.	Male.	Female.	Male.	Female.	Male.	Female.	Male.	Female.	Male.	Female.	Male.	Female.	Male.	Female.	Male.	Female.
19	79	25	85	3	20	...	9	...	20	565	25	1	...	329	5	223	10
10	125	12	229	14	287	14	316	1,097	66	755	49	...	4	68	2	84	35
317	225	129	181	182	184	115	161	347	48	779	75	48	6	154	6	132	2
514	5	401	4	330	8	501	5	550	5	2,070	6	11	...	8	...	2	1
760	434	567	499	529	499	630	491	1,994	139	4,169	175	60	10	559	13	441	48
619	239	357	228	449	87	222	82	636	148	1,301	110	1	32	1,172	30	389	102
77	71	66	45	69	5	74	4	20	71	32	52	1	14	9	6	5	25
59	18	2	45	2	34	1	32	...	16	21	14	...	...	...	...	...	...
248	24	246	48	269	16	110	10	425	10	329	14	...	...	201	20	13	3
40	...	26	...	29	...	7	6	38	...	25	...	...	...	20	...	1	10
3	8	9	3	2	4	2	4	...	1	472	4	...	...	380	...	168	1
11	40	4	16	21	28	4	23	...	19	250	40	...	7	503	2	158	18
494	77	238	88	329	72	247	34	702	217	1,024	239	6	21	291	37	90	10
148	15	102	49	158	24	118	11	236	19	212	42	2	4	209	22	39	3
105	25	39	27	24	30	12	18	167	40	480	29	...	4	17	...	7	4
...	...	...	...	...	...	...	...	...	...	...	4	...	2	...	...	...	...
80	...	35	...	52	...	69	...	42	4	30	20	1	...	24	...	2	...
...	5	...	7	1	6	...	2	...	10	110	6	...	4	...	...	28	...
80	7	15	3	25	...	13	2	90	8	98	2	2	5	21	...	14	...
79	25	36	2	66	3	33	1	12	14	14	10	...	2	1	...	...	3
724	86	271	85	85	23	218	29	808	112	694	200	89	11	19	17	166	59
177	82	211	75	60	19	121	21	795	109	642	198	47	10	17	11	166	59
528	...	44	1	21	2	96	5	10	...	37	...	41	...	...	...	...	...
180	50	99	41	138	65	196	27	304	122	674	90	...	11	134	11	79	34
69	26	1	36	3	51	79	...	82	88	537	65	...	9	2	...	...	34
8	19	7	3	8	2	2	4	52	19	68	10	...	2	43	9	19	...
99	...	88	...	123	...	115	...	96	3	60	3	...	...	89	...	53	...
113	71	143	129	87	125	92	48	306	138	338	159	78	34	384	61	179	40
59	14	52	60	48	72	41	10	210	89	210	84	32	20	308	45	159	20
8	45	4	58	8	48	6	28	58	24	66	39	29	8	39	3	6	6
8	6	8	4	5	5	9	8	7	25	8	36	9	2	...	2	1	14
33	...	35	...	19	...	33	...	28	...	36	...	2	...	30	...	8	...
1	...	40	...	2	...	...	...	...	...	...	...	...	...	...	...	5	...
2,890	957	1,675	1,070	1,617	871	1,605	709	4,750	874	8,200	973	234	119	2,559	169	1,544	293

	Total for the District.		Krishnanagar.		Kaliganj.		Nakasipara.		Chapra.		Krishnaganj.	
	Male.	Female.	Male.	Female.	Male.	Female.	Male.	Female.	Male.	Female.	Male.	Female.
IMMIGRANTS.												
(a) From contiguous districts—												
Calcutta	111	259	26	164	1	1	2	5	3	2	5	8
24-Parganas ...	1,306	1,844	123	59	5	3	12	23	11	7	3	14
Jessor	7,291	9,502	297	220	11	4	7	7	9	4	85	150
Khulna	169	62	27	14	...	...	...	...	...	...	11	...
Pabna	3,035	2,962	93	185	...	5	15	1	...	...	3	5
Hugli	1,531	1,704	215	201	3	4	11	33	18	2	21	13
Bardwan	2,847	4,216	890	1,396	559	953	306	565	32	25	13	33
Rajshahi	3,057	3,321	89	50	4	3	3	2	9	...	5	...
Murshidabad ...	3,991	6,058	215	165	625	1,190	85	95	12	9	10	14
Total ...	23,388	29,928	1,925	2,454	1,208	2,163	441	731	94	49	156	232
(b) From other districts in Bengal Proper	4,144	4,992	602	817	100	149	6	45	8	77	41	24
Dacca	700	735	295	384	36	32	...	...	1	2	5	...
Faridpur	2,626	1,903	113	152	2	6	4	3	3	1	4	4
(c) From Bihar	3,839	936	940	103	120	56	92	13	351	13	56	29
(d) From Orissa	254	55	96	29	...	...	7	1	2	...	2	3
(e) From Chutia Nagpur ...	746	608	101	69	143	136	8	9	5	...	2	...
(f) From other Provinces and countries ...	3,127	928	893	289	28	8	140	17	139	38	37	9
TOTAL IMMIGRANTS	35,498	37,447	4,557	3,761	1,599	2,512	694	816	599	177	294	297

	Naupara.		Daulatpur.		Bhadalia.		Kumarkhali.		Bhaluka.		Mihrpur.	
	Male.	Female.	Male.	Female.	Male.	Female.	Male.	Female.	Male.	Female.	Male.	Female.
IMMIGRANTS.												
(a) From contiguous districts—												
Calcutta	14	6	1	...	...	...	...	2	16	10	1	1
24-Parganas ...	6	6	...	3	1	4	25	6	2	...	11	9
Jessor	99	76	7	6	664	1,127	1,053	1,334	558	928	44	46
Khulna	2	...	1	...	1	2	6	...	7	...	6	2
Pabna	173	339	111	21	72	28	724	875	158	109	...	...
Hugli	5	5	...	...	...	...	9	3	13	10	17	14
Bardwan	22	16	13	6	37	22	8	16	17	25	...	10
Rajshahi	38	91	2,669	2,788	17	10	24	31	15	28	...	1
Murshidabad ...	89	98	174	7	17	228	23	20	13	...	67	66
Total ...	446	637	2,976	2,831	809	1,421	1,872	2,287	797	1,110	146	149
(b) From other districts in Bengal Proper	109	112	61	36	83	40	1,511	2,218	247	182	18	20
Dacca	24	11	28	13	6	...	29	24	24	4	2	...
Faridpur	3	44	3	...	17	28	1,385	2,094	146	167	6	9
(c) From Bihar	64	37	18	14	265	85	39	2	59	40	279	56
(d) From Orissa	1	...	2	...	24	...	1	...	12	...	8	...
(e) From Chutia Nagpur ...	9	4	102	57	2	...	3	...	8	1	4	8
(f) From other Provinces and countries	75	34	11	6	94	17	17	14	92	9	298	85
TOTAL IMMIGRANTS	706	824	3,170	2,944	1,247	1,563	3,443	4,521	1,215	1,342	753	318

NADIA.

Hanskhali.		Jibannagar.		Ranaghat.		Santipur.		Chakdaha.		Haringhata.		Kushtia.	
Male.	Female.	Male.	Female.	Male.	Female.	Male.	Female.	Male.	Female.	Male.	Female.	Male.	Female.
9	7	1	...	11	29	3	3	3	4	...	6	10	8
15	...	8	7	96	104	103	130	382	434	461	974	12	27
148	236	736	1,227	811	921	122	86	851	608	300	708	114	75
7	1	1	...	47	24	14	6	22	6	9	3	...	1
9	9	3	...	8	7	30	39	9	1	...	...	1,641	1,318
24	6	3	7	260	376	241	343	537	523	55	122	2	7
21	22	19	21	130	146	423	649	81	73	22	34	30	18
1	...	1	1	3	3	13	13	4	1	...	...	29	29
6	1	8	2	49	46	19	7	26	13	2	2	35	7
240	282	780	1,265	1,415	1,656	971	1,276	1,915	1,663	939	1,849	1,873	1,490
56	94	40	24	132	152	254	141	169	139	62	55	279	161
13	12	...	...	14	7	25	28	41	3	...	1	17	5
6	6	2	2	11	4	31	44	10	1	1	2	76	38
127	17	21	1	121	65	222	103	257	54	120	41	149	108
2	6	1	1	21	1	36	10	6	1	3	1	16	...
93	70	7	1	54	79	75	64	8	18	25	13	2	7
99	55	13	8	203	50	147	25	29	13	294	34	145	197
617	524	862	1,300	1,946	2,003	1,705	1,619	2,384	1,888	1,443	1,993	2,464	1,963

Karimpur.		Gangni.		Tehata.		Chuadanga.		Damurhuda.		Alamdanga.		Kalupol.	
Male.	Female.	Male.	Female.	Male.	Female.	Male.	Female.	Male.	Female.	Male.	Female.	Male.	Female.
1	1	...	...	...	...	1	...	2	7	1	...	...	...
5	1	...	...	...	1	8	8	5	11	9	10	3	3
35	4	19	6	20	3	68	45	92	78	444	653	607	920
...	1	...	...	...	...	2	...	1	...	5	2	...	...
3	5	5	3	1	...	5	2	3	5	16	3	5	2
10	4	4	10	42	2	10	7	18	7	7	3	3	2
9	16	13	18	88	83	37	2	24	16	57	46	6	5
163	244	5	...	10	9	...	...	4	6	1	10	...	1
1,632	2,773	58	26	719	1,223	...	1	47	44	57	9	3	7
1,858	3,049	104	63	880	1,326	121	65	196	174	597	766	627	940
28	12	36	33	173	267	30	21	34	8	30	22	25	43
2	...	4	...	162	207	5	...	...	...	2	2	2	...
2	...	1	...	1	...	14	12	26	7	1	14	1	2
34	21	42	3	284	21	42	7	78	30	30	12	29	5
1	...	...	...	3	...	3	2	4	...	2	...	1	...
22	13	41	45	...	...	14	8	9	2	2	1	7	3
21	6	182	11	19	4	45	11	78	66	15	14	13	8
1,974	3,101	435	155	1,359	1,618	255	114	399	280	676	815	702	999

	Total for the District.		Jessor.		Kaliganj.		Bagherpara.		Gadkhali.	
	Male.	Female.	Male.	Female.	Male.	Female.	Male.	Female.	Male.	Female.
IMMIGRANTS.										
(a) From contiguous districts—										
Khulna	3,707	5,919	404	44	36	3	29	1	136	538
Faridpur	5,192	6,156	176	19	46	10	127	3	15	...
Nadia	8,720	11,123	358	239	257	279	62	5	55	71
Total ...	17,619	23,198	938	302	339	292	218	9	206	609
(b) From other districts in Bengal Proper ...	3,031	3,940	287	383	162	48	39	107	77	270
24-Parganas ...	682	1,968	54	50	31	8	8	2	32	66
(c) From Bihar	1,693	322	222	84	63	15	28	21	121	6
(d) From Orissa	300	25	92	1	2	...	...	...	21	...
(e) From Chutia Nagpur ...	179	135	6	3	8	16	...	...	...	...
(f) From other Provinces and countries	1,261	217	138	41	64	6	61	14	46	4
TOTAL IMMIGRANTS	24,083	27,837	1,623	814	638	377	346	151	471	889

	Muhamadpur.		Salikha.		Narail.		Lohagara.	
	Male.	Female.	Male.	Female.	Male.	Female.	Male.	Female.
IMMIGRANTS.								
(a) From contiguous districts—								
Khulna	56	13	4	3	195	46	421	718
Faridpur	853	1,687	21	45	175	82	988	1,474
Nadia	116	37	65	10	173	22	245	28
Total ...	1,025	1,737	90	58	543	150	1,654	2,220
(b) From other districts in Bengal Proper	89	89	39	44	167	55	97	128
24-Parganas ...	10	14	1	1	17	12	15	27
(c) From Bihar	68	23	13	7	147	7	48	...
(d) From Orissa	16	9	8	2	2	...	35	...
(e) From Chutia Nagpur ...	6	20	...	2	2	...	...	2
(f) From other Provinces and countries	45	11	23	1	37	6	34	5
TOTAL IMMIGRANTS	1,249	1,889	173	114	898	218	1,868	2,355

JESSOR.

Manirampur.		Keshubpur.		Jhenidaha.		Salkopa.		Kotchandpur.		Magura.	
Male.	Female.	Male.	Female.	Male.	Female.	Male.	Female.	Male.	Female.	Male.	Female.
399	994	983	2,404	16	3	40	4	55	2	76	20
19	3	70	9	84	38	370	294	10	1	1,428	1,491
96	37	38	22	1,768	2,826	1,440	2,115	795	699	643	243
514	1,034	1,091	2,435	1,868	2,867	1,850	2,413	860	702	2,147	1,754
22	61	213	51	181	270	256	200	106	43	286	210
7	29	28	64	22	14	5	3	15	16	9	14
38	1	24	6	91	30	29	29	127	12	126	17
16	4	46	...	8	...	5	2	1	...	7	...
...	...	1		23	28	18	12	18	...	58	33
48	20	45	4	68	16	43	2	76	2	92	2
638	1,120	1,420	2,497	2,239	3,211	2,201	2,658	1,188	759	2,716	2,016

Kalia.		Bangaon.		Mahespur.		Garapata.		Sarsa.		Gaighata.	
Male.	Female.	Male.	Female.	Male.	Female.	Male.	Female.	Male.	Female.	Male.	Female.
414	757	168	16	36	7	21	1	161	286	57	59
772	986	14	2	9	7	5	2	2	3	8	...
113	2	583	795	1,255	2,582	204	367	284	362	170	382
1,299	1,745	765	813	1,300	2,596	230	370	447	651	235	441
379	64	243	218	167	104	69	63	110	550	102	982
...	2	42	154	1	25	27	24	93	521	45	922
33	7	192	29	111	22	128	2	65	2	19	2
11	1	6	3	13	...	4	2	6	...	1	...
3	1	9	2	4	1	16	...	7	6	...	8
69	8	209	64	38	2	38	2	75	5	12	3
1,794	1,826	1,424	1,129	1,633	2,725	485	439	710	1,214	369	1,436

	Total for the District.		Sujaganj.		Gora Bazar.		Burwan.		Daulata Bazar.		Hariharpara.	
	Male.	Female.	Male.	Female.	Male.	Female.	Male.	Female.	Male.	Female.	Male.	Female.
IMMIGRANTS.												
(a) From Contiguous districts—												
Nadia	7,847	9,923	59	33	850	775	587	886	129	148	339	447
Bardwan	11,752	2,593	10	5	401	244	134	105	7	10	11	18
Birbhum	4,016	7,306	17	21	502	304	32	38	5	4	10	...
Malda	3,264	3,657	...	...	29	10	...	...	4	...	1	3
Rajshahi	504	737	2	8	170	182	4	2	...	...	4	6
Total ...	27,383	24,516	88	67	1,952	1,515	757	1,031	145	162	365	474
(b) From other districts in Bengal Proper	2,201	2,018	24	8	582	608	14	...	19	...	18	2
(c) From Bihar	6,589	4,280	30	8	1,361	670	45	16	54	1,518	38	8
Patna	1,065	603	1	...	384	188	...	...	2	3	...	3
Shahabad	859	313	...	...	158	63	18	4	3	1	2	...
Musaffarpur ...	1,001	284	4	...	222	46	7	...	13	...	12	...
Saran	890	1,670	5	2	98	36	13	...	16	1,500	...	...
Bhagalpur	755	597	5	1	95	39	...	1	12	2	1	...
Monghyr	1,005	287	7	5	162	38	7	2	4	8	4	...
(d) From Orissa	230	54	8	...	40	10	...	3	6	2	11	2
(e) From Chutia Nagpur ...	4,835	3,102	27	21	360	146	48	39	57	...	8	4
Santal Parganas	3,627	2,558	20	10	231	125	...	...	12	...	6	...
Hazaribagh ...	880	296	6	11	94	17	8	3	16	...	1	4
(f) From other Provinces and countries	3,605	1,459	135	43	368	65	21	...	73	76	7	14
North-Western Provinces	2,774	1,060	120	16	179	52	8	...	69	72	...	...
TOTAL IMMIGRANTS	44,843	35,429	312	147	4,663	2,914	885	1,088	354	1,758	447	504

	Sagardighi.		Kaliaganj.		Raghunathganj.		Shamsherganj.		Suti.		Dewan Sarai.	
	Male.	Female.	Male.	Female.	Male.	Female.	Male.	Female.	Male.	Female.	Male.	Female.
IMMIGRATNS.												
(a) From contiguous districts—												
Nadia	80	18	47	7	43	11	94	59	39	10	74	30
Bardwan	27	10	37	3	10	...	18	8	12	12	21	11
Birbhum	357	413	372	600	30	24	73	117	429	1,342	9	7
Malda	5	2	6	9	59	98	2,581	2,938	309	362	85	72
Rajshahi	7	8	2	...	11	17	14	16	5	18	30	40
Total ...	426	451	464	619	153	150	2,780	3,133	794	1,744	219	160
(b) From other districts in Bengal Proper	20	...	26	3	6	1	97	63	10	25	19	63
(c) From Bihar	144	39	98	64	164	87	843	616	262	139	474	38
Patna	18	3	3	5	37	35	115	100	48	42	6	2
Shahabad	35	7	14	1	48	22	90	24	65	17	50	23
Muzaffarpur ...	9	...	12	2	17	...	119	59	23	11	15	...
Saran	11	...	6	1	11	8	67	25	47	12	347	6
Bhagalpur	46	27	28	39	4	4	288	271	47	41	15	1
Monghyr	14	2	12	4	27	16	141	92	17	14	23	6
(d) From Orissa	4	2	...	...	3	...	5	...	...	...	4	...
(e) From Chutia Nagpur ...	1,047	828	534	471	...	21	824	100	124	320	4	88
Santal Parganas	1,032	827	533	469	...	21	803	62	77	320	4	88
Hazaribagh ...	12	1	...	...	...	...	...	...	5	...	...	...
(f) From other Provinces and countries	227	17	37	22	70	70	233	83	77	31	93	26
North-Western Provinces	186	10	34	8	6	50	192	60	58	30	67	20
TOTAL IMMIGRANTS	1,868	1,337	1,159	1,179	396	329	4,782	3,995	1,267	2,259	813	375

MURSHIDABAD.

Nawada.		Goas.		Jalinghi.		Shahnagar.		Manula Bazar.		Asanpur.		Bhagbangola.	
Male.	Female.	Male.	Female.	Male.	Female.	Male.	Female.	Male.	Female.	Male.	Female.	Male.	Female.
1,968	2,993	243	188	1,568	2,557	469	370	17	16	533	513	89	50
25	28	9,621	71	93	9	270	197	3	3	104	72	36	4
8	28	2	11	22	132	153	159	2	1	68	106	8	10
2	...	6	9	37	45	63	40	2	2	8	8	16	21
2	6	...	19	90	138	76	123	3	8	22	45	38	68
2,005	3,055	9,872	298	1,810	2,881	1,031	889	27	29	735	744	187	153
53	57	20	2	283	149	724	805	6	3	48	80	12	37
49	19	99	41	364	134	1,701	562	52	32	139	107	192	98
2	...	3	2	31	5	301	147	2	9	38	20	10	16
6	1	17	11	56	25	116	39	...	2	...	30	43	22
9	...	46	...	105	69	302	75	15	7	7	2	11	7
...	...	13	15	42	3	114	36	...	...	12	4	43	4
...	...	...	...	46	17	82	67	...	3	19	11	28	38
6	...	7	6	30	6	401	37	17	11	20	18	28	4
4	...	8	9	61	...	14	18	8	2	2	4	...	...
4	2	140	207	29	58	1,094	416	53	27	161	197	18	6
1	...	139	202	28	53	484	147	29	24	58	122	13	5
...	...	...	5	...	...	542	148	24	3	103	75	...	1
32	96	22	66	66	146	1,180	471	113	10	177	26	64	31
12	92	16	...	49	81	973	402	96	8	162	20	14	30
2,147	3,229	10,161	629	2,613	3,368	5,744	3,161	259	103	1,262	1,158	473	325

Mirzapur.		Kandi.		Barwa.		Khargaon.		Bharatpur.		Gokarna.	
Male.	Female.	Male.	Female.	Male.	Female.	Male.	Female.	Male.	Female.	Male.	Female.
28	32	47	24	20	10	18	4	378	614	178	129
23	18	123	61	95	167	31	31	568	1,752	72	54
424	1,005	116	121	468	962	626	1,445	205	338	79	118
35	29	7	6	2	...	2	2	5	6	...	...
...	7	7	10	...	...	2	...	10	9	5	7
510	1,091	299	222	585	1,139	679	1,482	1,166	2,719	334	308
46	7	77	40	25	15	14	4	27	43	31	3
122	45	111	32	33	13	47	1	75	16	92	72
30	9	7	5	7	4	2	...	10	3	8	2
29	3	41	2	12	1	24	...	18	3	20	12
19	3	13	...	2	1	5	...	3	...	11	2
20	11	14	4	...	...	3	...	16	3	1	...
6	13	12	16	3	3	1	...	13	3	4	...
6	6	12	...	4	2	1	...	14	...	41	10
2	...	14	...	10	2	12	...	12	...	2	...
129	70	53	15	2	3	27	28	26	1	66	34
104	70	12	6	2	3	27	28	4	...	8	6
...	...	9	...	...	...	...	...	2	1	58	28
68	32	188	88	72	20	152	22	99	4	31	...
57	3	176	80	60	20	140	6	76	...	24	...
877	1,245	742	397	727	1,192	931	1,537	1,405	2,783	558	417

DISTRICT

	Total for the District.		Khulna.		Dumuria.		Baitaghata.		Paikgachha.		Bagherhat.	
	Male.	Female.	Male.	Female.	Male.	Female.	Male.	Female.	Male.	Female.	Male.	Female.
IMMIGRANTS.												
(a) From Contiguous districts—												
Jessor	17,470	11,258	4,817	2,808	1,716	3,115	738	53	1,111	383	2,896	665
Faridpur	6,367	2,141	1,383	215	104	14	244	34	97	10	1,600	461
Nadia	1,791	380	459	98	37	27	31	...	67	3	350	46
24-Parganas ...	4,087	5,079	91	59	110	102	11	7	1,021	659	82	48
Bakharganj ...	16,483	8,039	311	125	111	24	47	7	67	41	2,975	1,546
Total ...	44,398	26,897	7,091	3,305	2,078	3,282	1,071	101	2,363	1,096	7,903	2,763
(b) From other districts in Bengal Proper	3,872	630	964	122	34	6	199	45	175	34	834	90
Dacca	1,373	102	278	28	1	3	125	11	51	3	279	35
Pabna	1,099	5	279	...	8	1	34	...	18	...	216	1
(c) From Bihar	1,790	158	544	63	96	4	55	6	133	2	234	12
(d) From Orissa	359	31	70	4	33	...	...	2	26	...	31	2
(e) From Chutia Nagpur ...	461	173	45	19	...	...	...	...	139	97	...	...
(f) From other Provinces and countries ...	992	118	272	64	18	1	26	2	58	...	175	9
TOTAL IMMIGRANTS	51,872	28,007	8,986	3,577	2,259	3,293	1,351	157	2,894	1,229	9,177	2,876

RAJSHAHI

DISTRICT

	Total for the District.		Dinajpur.		Hemtabad.		Kaliganj.		Bansihari.		Birganj.		Patnitala.		Mahadebpur.	
	Male.	Female.	Male.	Female.	Male.	Female.	Male.	Female.	Male.	Female.	Male.	Female.	Male.	Female.	Male.	Female.
IMMIGRANTS.																
(a) From Contiguous districts—																
Purnea	10,529	5,185	7,213	1,128	731	770	221	279	73	40	203	47	19	17	65	—
Rangpur	3,388	4,920	347	1,241	21	18	...	...	5	2	496	961	85	7	9	33
Malda	3,080	2,166	78	147	124	11	843	1,197	292	260	76	38	119	124	120	13
Jalpaiguri	1,007	1,701	23	105	...	...	...	...	1	...	258	505	...	...	...	...
Bogra	972	841	27	11	...	...	...	...	3	4	6	6	213	...	153	318
Rajshahi	3,694	4,006	83	12	14	3	5	3	12	1	8	1	211	43	225	3,256
Total ...	22,670	18,819	7,721	2,644	890	802	1,069	1,479	386	307	1,047	1,558	647	191	571	3,620
(b) From other districts in Bengal Proper	9,308	5,894	396	322	473	400	460	440	461	260	177	147	800	234	1,234	149

KHULNA.

Mullahat.		Rampal.		Morellganj.		Satkhira.		Kalaroa.		Magura.		Asasuni.		Kaliganj.	
Male.	Female.	Male.	Female.	Male.	Female.	Male.	Female.	Male.	Female.	Male.	Female.	Male.	Female.	Male.	Female.
636	473	1,114	69	455	61	579	192	910	2,653	426	478	786	59	1,286	226
1,065	1,347	324	14	618	30	208	4	7	8	18	2	157	15	542	7
55	12	105	5	70	13	137	22	39	102	21	17	183	4	207	31
1	2	72	1	18	10	468	1,592	390	933	47	61	640	86	1,136	1,525
335	364	552	57	9,263	5,813	309	29	14	2	19	1	191	1	489	29
2,092	2,198	2,167	146	10,424	5,927	1,701	1,839	1,360	3,698	531	559	1,957	165	3,660	1,818
51	10	113	2	434	75	305	78	86	12	15	9	239	80	423	67
28	...	29	...	210	15	118	3	...	...	3	...	123	...	128	4
...	1	46	...	217	...	178	1	...	...	1	...	71	...	33	1
34	10	150	8	73	3	53	8	125	12	21	...	120	26	152	4
...	1	2	...	11	3	27	4	47	2	31	1	17	2	64	10
32	1	2	...	11	1	37	2	40	5	38	2	49	24	68	22
8	2	46	...	147	9	84	21	22	6	27	...	19	2	90	1
2,217	2,222	2,480	156	11,100	6,018	2,207	1,952	1,680	3,735	663	571	2,401	299	4,457	1,922

DIVISION.

DINAJPUR.

Parsa.		Patiram.		Gangarampur.		Chintaman.		Parbatipur.		Nawabganj.		Thakurgaon.		Ranisankail.		Pirganj.	
Male.	Female.	Male.	Female.	Male.	Female.	Male.	Female.	Male.	Female.	Male.	Female.	Male.	Female.	Male.	Female.	Male.	Female.
52	74	82	59	226	53	...	...	20	7	13	11	1,081	1,869	460	731	70	100
8	10	79	31	8	31	483	170	685	574	1,124	1,023	...	727	3	3	35	89
901	114	125	79	264	129	7	8	6	5	6	...	61	1	33	10	25	30
...	...	8	...	3	1	3	...	...	...	...	...	589	1,006	1	4	126	80
3	2	283	284	11	2	68	13	19	6	182	190	3	1	2	4	...	...
103	192	2,276	75	149	109	86	40	47	24	460	136	20	10	5	1	40	100
1,067	392	2,848	528	661	325	647	231	777	616	1,785	1,360	1,754	3,614	504	753	296	399
1,353	789	803	498	110	144	416	316	449	559	508	164	392	284	254	304	1,024	884

DISTRICT

	TOTAL FOR THE DISTRICT.		DINAJPUR.		HEMTABAD.		KALIGANJ.		BANSHIHARI.		BIRGANJ.		PANITALA.		MAHADEBPUR.	
	Male.	Female.	Male.	Female.	Male.	Female.	Male.	Female.	Male.	Female.	Male.	Female.	Male.	Female.	Male.	Female.
(c) From Bihar	13,000	5,563	3,027	1,888	619	500	659	283	348	239	658	50	346	266	319	70
Muzaffarpur ...	1,603	324	513	4	50	7	93	4	22	8	66	8	17	2	10	...
Saran	4,059	207	1,201	11	108	12	45	18	52	14	496	5	43	8	88	1
Monghyr	1,492	2,203	348	1,278	...	294	273	199	105	62	12	1	16	10	25	...
Bhagalpur	3,546	1,872	523	176	147	176	144	55	90	86	18	33	189	136	20	7
(d) From Orissa	208	152	10	...	1	...	4	...	1	...	1	20	...	...	4	...
(e) From Chutia Nagpur ...	15,295	12,410	672	444	160	69	894	958	481	384	...	...	2,307	2,030	890	779
Hazaribagh	1,012	902	13	5	40	2	...	...	...	...	...	...	123	97	530	564
Manbhum	847	419	298	108	20	...	116	194	...	...	...	...	20	4	...	...
Santal Parganas ...	11,043	10,533	345	321	100	67	778	764	160	90	...	...	2,150	1,929	80	59
(f) From other Provinces and countries ...	5,531	3,188	389	262	188	4	194	72	205	33	68	3	746	480	542	147
North-Western Provinces	3,389	1,058	249	136	151	3	184	69	126	8	15	2	230	80	410	134
Central Provinces	1,144	1,620	122	112	...	1	...	...	5	12	...	...	487	363	...	...
TOTAL IMMIGRANTS	66,012	46,024	12,215	5,560	2,231	1,775	3,280	3,232	1,882	1,203	1,951	1,778	4,846	3,201	3,560	4,765

DISTRICT

	TOTAL FOR THE DISTRICT.		BOALIA.		TANOR.		GODAGARI.		PUTIA.		CHARGHAT.	
	Male.	Female.	Male.	Female.	Male.	Female.	Male.	Female.	Male.	Female.	Male.	Female.
IMMIGRANTS.												
(a) From contiguous districts—												
Bogra	1,012	1,135	...	41	5	7	11	13	1	...	5	6
Pabna	7,865	3,588	4,044	85	16	7	26	11	29	26	54	56
Nadia	4,432	2,335	346	27	155	22	121	63	83	24	635	366
Murshidabad ...	7,071	8,280	322	3,111	464	60	4,305	4,007	41	28	415	443
Malda	4,034	2,102	870	332	210	109	945	1,035	1	...	11	17
Dinajpur	3,143	1,417	12	9	6	3	13	10	...	...	2	...
Total ...	27,557	18,917	5,594	3,656	856	208	5,421	5,139	155	78	1,122	888
(b) From other districts in Bengal Proper	2,627	2,083	665	577	70	29	136	101	68	73	72	83
(c) From Bihar	4,007	2,485	103	919	110	16	1,364	663	69	8	127	73
Purnea	1,242	1,322	...	416	1	1	742	604	...	4	13	11
(d) From Orissa	221	5	51	...	6	1	9	4	18	...	22	...
(e) From Chutia Nagpur ...	3,778	2,759	295	353	433	286	305	269	10	150	16	13
Santal Parganas ...	1,763	1,528	72	227	210	162	151	12	5	149	8	1
Lohardaga	1,427	867	72	77	158	87	...	200	...	...	...	13
(f) From other Provinces and countries ...	4,520	1,786	361	293	212	15	755	93	141	52	156	48
North-Western Provinces	3,003	1,071	270	272	83	14	650	69	129	5	103	31
Central Provinces	902	584	...	...	118	...	48	11	...	41	1	...
TOTAL IMMIGRANTS	42,710	28,034	7,069	5,797	1,687	555	7,990	6,269	481	361	1,515	1,065

DINAJPUR—*concluded.*

Parsa.		Patiram.		Gangarampur.		Chintaman.		Parbatipur.		Nawabganj.		Thakurgaon.		Ranisankail.		Pirganj.	
Male.	Female.	Male.	Female.	Male.	Female.	Male.	Female.	Male.	Female.	Male.	Female.	Male.	Female.	Male.	Female.	Male.	Female.
518	268	1,464	701	844	222	1,328	375	1,115	229	724	63	329	40	454	129	348	240
5	65	92	2	58	33	198	3	223	2	93	1	...	11	113	1	50	85
170	...	152	2	106	9	409	2	478	25	455	4	137	18	79	5	40	73
29	2	133	81	100	88	93	14	95	57	15	2	48	11	103	34	97	70
117	101	944	591	457	72	517	293	203	82	60	7	11	4	61	53	40	...
2	...	33	17	15	...	7	1	8	1	6	...	6	2	3	...	107	111
410	167	3,337	2,842	841	612	2,090	1,671	747	613	1,669	1,767	...	...	669	94	128	...
29	34	53	37	59	78	64	4	43	44	58	47	...	...	...	...	...	...
...	...	16	13	...	...	87	10	1	2	...	...	...	...	169	88	120	...
85	133	2,939	2,634	767	534	1,939	1,657	693	567	1,601	1,720	...	...	...	6	8	...
979	249	276	801	611	328	227	54	206	134	152	51	228	25	162	18	358	525
853	100	210	75	108	67	216	40	110	32	58	1	68	25	72	18	323	268
121	102	...	722	297	252	...	...	46	12	28	14	1	...	2	...	35	30
4,329	1,865	8,761	5,387	3,082	1,631	4,715	2,648	3,302	2,152	4,842	3,405	2,709	3,965	2,046	1,298	2,261	2,159

RAJSHAHI.

Baghmara.		Naugaon.		Manda.		Panchupur.		Nator.		Singra.		Burigram.		Lalpur.	
Male.	Female.	Male.	Female.	Male.	Female.	Male.	Female.	Male.	Female.	Male.	Female.	Male.	Female.	Male.	Female.
3	...	8	72	40	58	37	8	6	5	880	910	9	8	7	7
490	95	62	382	92	23	86	96	174	96	913	450	1,564	1,764	315	497
76	265	786	284	332	57	241	181	242	87	427	52	180	69	808	838
117	7	222	347	562	117	320	3	88	46	103	48	24	12	83	51
348	...	570	91	762	504	311	16	3	1	6	3	1	1	2	3
3	1	1,011	33	1,120	1,350	959	...	2	4	4	4	2	2	0	1
1,031	368	2,659	1,209	2,908	2,109	1,954	304	515	239	2,338	1,467	1,780	1,856	1,224	1,397
247	102	98	59	297	284	223	239	148	2	289	284	149	70	165	200
63	6	319	200	518	361	342	9	320	90	470	97	67	10	135	33
9	2	234	53	214	223	...	...	19	2	3	...	1	0	6	...
38	...	2	...	4	...	7	...	15	...	38	...	11	...	...	...
18	3	34	120	1,365	1,017	987	393	29	95	264	57	14	...	8	3
9	2	17	50	071	747	493	164	8	1	114	11	1	...	4	2
6	1	7	24	647	226	403	185	...	...	44	44	...	...	...	1
554	100	191	248	722	85	716	487	190	251	383	29	144	55	195	29
139	98	149	228	313	77	377	173	135	13	336	28	125	37	144	26
6	...	4	...	404	...	319	313	...	219	...	...	2	...	2	...
1,751	579	3,303	1,836	5,814	3,856	4,229	1,432	1,217	677	3,782	1,934	2,165	1,991	1,727	1,662

DISTRICT

	Total for the District.		Rangpur.		Kaliganj.		Mahiganj.		Badarganj.		Mithapukhur.		Pirganj.		Dimla.	
	Male.	Female.	Male.	Female.	Male.	Female.	Male.	Female.	Male.	Female.	Male.	Female.	Male.	Female.	Male.	Female.
IMMIGRANTS.																
(a) From contiguous Districts—																
Dinajpur	381	377	29	13	...	2	11	8	...	...	79	104	56	92	41	20
Jalpaiguri ...	398	735	41	...	...	183	3	...	...	...	...	...	...	...	273	323
Bogra	1,432	1,451	34	5	16	5	7	5	...	...	16	...	7	9	6	...
Maimansingh ...	3,859	2,312	150	35	45	6	35	11	1	...	22	6	17	4	9	3
Kuch Bihar ...	2,689	3,654	18	18	614	857	...	3	...	...	...	...	...	...	316	146
Assam	801	718	27	33	78	...	10	...	...	...	5	...	1	...	9	1
Total ...	9,560	9,247	299	104	753	1,053	66	27	1	...	122	110	81	105	654	1,394
(b) From other districts in Bengal Proper ...	7,423	2,791	1,853	769	435	116	513	124	24	2	185	31	301	48	174	43
Pabna	2,245	1,319	296	133	...	29	107	9	8	...	45	...	56	1	35	16
Dacca	1,395	391	387	168	59	...	61	17	2	...	17	...	22	4	30	1
(c) From Bihar	22,549	1,420	2,171	245	774	17	1,906	156	1,688	130	1,121	39	1,245	32	588	46
Musaffarpur ...	2,831	69	533	6	46	1	237	1	209	5	284	25	385	3	115	1
Saran	15,701	670	947	158	559	10	1,186	27	1,341	85	462	3	417	7	346	5
Champaran ...	1,507	88	85	...	5	...	202	12	32	...	340	2	360	...	9	...
(d) From Orissa	165	7	52	4	15	...	29	2	...	...	1	...	9	...	7	...
(e) From Chutia Nagpur ...	468	306	27	2	2	...	12	5	75	...	12	...	48	45	2	...
(f) From other Provinces and countries	2,905	417	437	34	144	1	156	43	90	43	157	9	108	14	182	20
TOTAL IMMIGRANTS	43,070	14,188	4,839	1,158	2,123	1,187	2,682	357	1,878	175	1,598	189	1,792	244	1,607	1,503

DISTRICT

	Total for the District.		Bogra.		Shariakandi.		Shibganj.	
	Male.	Female.	Male.	Female.	Male.	Female.	Male.	Female.
IMMIGRANTS.								
(a) From Contiguous Districts—								
Rangpur	880	1,035	73	92	297	394	193	344
Pabna	6,300	3,810	686	240	1,514	756	188	6
Dinajpur	1,036	1,127	28	26	3	1	4	11
Maimansingh ...	1,081	700	97	61	866	551	7	7
Rajshahi	3,733	4,358	264	280	27	39	39	17
Total ...	13,030	11,030	1,148	699	2,707	1,741	436	444
(b) From other districts in Bengal Proper	6,372	1,545	954	321	461	62	231	74
Nadia	2,029	541	316	61	46	16	87	14
Murshidabad ...	1,235	333	30	46	81	8	40	25

RANGPUR.

Jaldhaka.		Nilphamari.		Barabari.		Kurigram.		Nageswari.		Ulipur.		Gobindganj.		Sadullapur.		Sundraganj.	
Male.	Female.	Male.	Female.	Male.	Female.	Male.	Female.	Male.	Female.	Male.	Female.	Male.	Female.	Male.	Female.	Male.	Female.
8	8	33	...	13	1	5	...	...	9	10	3	78	110	18	7	...	...
2	13	6	1	6	3	2	...	60	...	2	7	3	1	...	5	...	...
1	...	575	467	...	1	16	...	18	...	...	...	735	958	...	...	1	1
6	2	3,313	2,142	23	6	41	16	37	...	47	...	95	80	2	1	16	...
...	...	10	10	347	412	10	5	1,337	1,492	5	6	...	...	32	3	...	...
25	...	92	26	48	8	23	7	388	619	43	21	8	...	31	3	18	...
42	23	4,029	2,646	437	431	97	28	1,835	2,120	107	37	919	1,149	83	19	35	1
107	14	1,256	786	180	33	447	165	748	65	117	11	865	523	102	44	116	17
3	...	809	654	42	...	36	9	80	8	45	1	631	449	32	5	21	5
7	2	164	82	30	7	190	81	380	19	17	...	14	1	7	9	8	...
540	13	2,026	32	1,218	67	1,077	94	908	38	1,228	21	981	173	3,839	279	1,239	38
205	...	105	2	57	1	63	3	164	10	23	2	213	5	17	2	172	...
163	...	1,806	18	954	22	600	29	621	18	1,150	4	560	3	3,589	253	1,001	23
86	...	43	12	21	18	...	...	49	...	33	12	55	...	136	24	31	8
11	...	...	...	10	...	12	1	...	...	...	...	8	...	...	...	11	...
18	8	12	...	10	...	5	88	...	...	...	...	236	158	2	...	7	...
114	...	74	13	147	20	371	127	279	16	112	2	346	35	63	1	125	39
832	58	7,397	3,477	2,002	551	2,009	503	3,770	2,239	1,564	71	3,355	2,038	4,089	343	1,533	95

BOGRA.

Panchbibi.		Khetlal.		Nawabganj.		Adamdighi.		Sherpur.	
Male.	Female.	Male.	Female.	Male.	Female.	Male.	Female.	Male.	Female.
135	111	53	48	47	2	29	14	48	30
262	58	14	3	90	21	180	63	3,366	2,604
619	541	7	6	329	487	39	50	7	5
14	4	1	...	11	3	14	11	71	63
710	270	46	13	783	913	1,316	2,550	548	276
1,740	984	121	70	1,260	1,426	1,578	2,688	4,040	2,978
1,962	462	282	17	1,118	228	688	209	676	172
1,111	229	147	7	463	56	372	87	387	71
443	101	67	1	400	57	117	60	57	39

DISTRICT

	Total for the District.		Bogra.		Shariakandi.		Shirganj.	
	Male.	Female.	Male.	Female.	Male.	Female.	Male.	Female.
(c) From Bihar	6,737	880	1,853	236	1,131	86	784	52
Saran	3,526	100	1,207	43	590	10	575	2
(d) From Orissa	80	1	24	...	6	...	12	...
(e) From Chutia Nagpur ...	4,874	3,739	58	22	8	...	54	14
Santal Parganas ...	1,888	1,296	14	7	...	...	2	...
Hazaribagh	1,096	445	16	1	8	...	9	5
Lohardaga	1,963	1,634	28	14	...	...	36	2
(f) From Other Provinces and countries	5,560	726	1,822	258	1,216	84	299	27
North-Western Provinces	4,609	596	1,475	206	1,151	70	264	26
TOTAL IMMIGRANTS	36,653	17,921	5,859	1,536	5,529	1,973	1,816	611

DISTRICT

	Total for the District.		Pabna.		Chatmohar.		Dulai.	
	Male.	Female.	Male.	Female.	Male.	Female.	Male.	Female.
IMMIGRANTS.								
(a) From contiguous Districts—								
Faridpur	2,823	1,385	245	149	104	28	844	779
Dacca	2,272	763	217	73	140	18	245	85
Maimansingh ...	2,503	1,570	86	40	69	25	54	50
Nadia	6,780	3,693	3,326	3,017	482	87	734	311
Rajshahi	3,924	3,478	1,015	1,781	1,099	1,092	206	15
Bogra	712	921	17	14	9	18	4	9
Total ...	19,013	11,805	4,906	5,074	1,903	1,268	2,087	1,249
(b) From other districts in Bengal Proper ...	3,253	951	899	427	133	41	618	131
Jessor	1,308	240	196	64	44	13	479	88
(c) From Bihar	5,316	758	1,080	309	179	12	253	20
Muzaffarpur ...	1,515	160	119	20	52	...	40	1
Saran	1,666	135	141	42	23	2	58	...
(d) From Orissa	340	5	123	2	51	...	10	...
(e) From Chutia Nagpur ...	2,182	775	104	91	77	25	...	...
Hazaribagh	1,553	488	5	7	50	4	...	...
(f) From other Provinces and countries	7,606	1,496	756	230	162	33	251	38
North-Western Provinces	6,733	1,358	616	168	107	29	181	15
TOTAL IMMIGRANTS	37,710	15,790	7,868	6,133	2,505	1,379	3,219	1,438

BOGRA—*concluded.*

Fanchbibi.		Khetlal.		Nawabganj.		Adamdighi.		Sherpur.	
Male.	Female.	Male.	Female.	Male.	Female.	Male.	Female.	Male.	Female.
948	208	284	80	555	88	638	84	544	46
301	28	135	5	173	2	290	8	255	2
3	...	1	...	14	...	14	1	6	...
2,631	2,382	179	93	852	775	896	313	696	140
1,172	1,132	42	47	150	106	6	4	2	...
358	279	...	...	11	24	7	5	686	131
909	817	113	26	574	526	302	249	1	...
473	85	127	38	308	52	596	117	719	65
390	62	121	35	274	46	489	92	645	60
7,757	4,121	994	298	4,107	2,569	3,910	3,412	6,881	3,401

PABNA.

Mathura.		Sirajganj.		Shahzadpur.		Raiganj.		Ulapaar.	
Male.	Female.	Male.	Female.	Male.	Female.	Male.	Female.	Male.	Female.
787	323	453	45	121	27	95	19	173	15
497	317	790	88	199	126	86	25	98	31
261	81	1,492	724	360	529	87	21	94	100
258	27	1,047	150	310	33	344	29	279	39
220	7	51	28	79	30	1,193	494	61	26
14	5	369	594	30	26	232	237	37	18
2,037	760	4,202	1,029	1,099	771	2,037	825	742	229
358	48	724	190	249	53	179	28	93	33
210	8	223	25	82	10	40	10	85	22
248	4	1,864	325	618	27	507	52	467	9
47	1	835	123	214	10	103	3	105	2
101	...	607	77	213	3	272	8	252	3
8	...	59	3	38	...	29	...	22	...
4	...	350	58	28	...	1,425	585	194	16
...	...	233	43	2	...	1,080	418	183	16
289	9	3,964	1,026	423	33	597	80	1,164	47
229	...	3,519	1,005	391	24	568	71	1,127	46
2,944	821	11,263	3,231	2,455	884	4,774	1,570	2,382	334

DISTRICT

	Total for the District.		Darjeeling.	
	Male.	Female.	Male.	Female.
IMMIGRANTS.				
(a) From contiguous Districts—				
Jalpaiguri	2,097	1,808	5	3
Purnea	6,271	4,832	55	11
Total ...	8,368	6,640	60	14
(b) From other districts in Bengal Proper	1,688	691	333	123
(c) From Bihar	8,060	1,324	2,139	255
Darbhanga	845	193	108	9
Muzaffarpur	2,045	314	530	23
Saran	3,191	272	1,013	77
Purnea	6,271	4,832	55	11
(d) From Orissa	65	4	14	3
(e) From Chutia Nagpur	2,818	2,192	9	2
Lohardaga	1,871	1,726	5	2
Chutia Nagpur Tributary States	732	309	1	...
(f) From other Provinces and countries	57,979	47,228	19,634	17,063
Central Provinces ...	2,604	2,469	15	5
North-Western Provinces	1,565	414	589	106
Nipal	47,799	40,228	15,595	14,333
Sikkim	3,110	2,946	1,878	1,923
Bhutan	540	571	333	350
TOTAL IMMIGRANTS ...	78,978	58,079	22,189	17,480

DISTRICT

	Total for the District.		Jalpaiguri.		Rajganj.		Titalya.	
	Male.	Female.	Male.	Female.	Male.	Female.	Male.	Female.
IMMIGRANTS.								
(a) From Contiguous Districts—								
Darjeeling	1,347	894	14	17	281	265	37	42
Dinajpur	2,127	2,629	66	41	139	89	125	112
Rangpur	7,361	8,109	710	516	77	25	2	...
Kuch Bihar	20,085	16,203	562	555	6	8	...	...
Total ...	30,920	27,835	1,352	1,129	503	377	164	154
(b) From Other districts in Bengal Proper ...	12,431	7,641	4,765	1,393	682	46	1,188	5
(c) From Bihar	12,529	4,216	2,257	307	1,198	604	979	1,203
Saran	3,430	158	807	15	212	8	49	...
Darbhanga	920	181	193	7	33	...	10	22
Muzaffarpur ...	2,505	209	731	62	196	2	29	...
Bhagalpur	1,145	547	77	28	43	20	13	6
Purnea	2,537	2,273	102	16	612	505	756	1,083

DARJEELING.

Kalimpong.		Kurseong.		Siliguri.		Jorbangala.	
Male.	Female.	Male.	Female.	Male.	Female.	Male.	Female.
8	...	33	15	2,051	1,787	...	3
4	...	145	16	6,066	4,414	1	391
12	...	178	31	8,117	6,201	1	394
32	74	194	83	892	350	237	61
160	38	1,137	202	4,495	777	129	52
23	...	67	4	647	180	...	...
36	1	325	110	1,154	180	...	...
81	35	528	43	1,569	...	...	...
4	...	145	16	6,066	4,414	1	391
4	...	7	...	2	1	38	...
99	83	433	383	2,232	1,722	45	2
...	...	394	348	1,472	1,376	...	...
98	83	20	19	578	205	55	2
7,207	6,129	15,736	12,424	8,915	6,125	6,488	5,487
1	...	448	300	2,140	2,164	...	...
27	3	198	33	741	236	10	36
5,778	4,986	14,766	11,920	5,552	3,585	6,108	5,398
1,087	429	111	86	19	...	15	8
173	153	29	21	5	2	...	45
7,514	6,324	17,684	13,123	24,653	15,176	6,938	5,996

JALPAIGURI.

Boda.		Patgram.		Mainaguri.		Dam-Dim.		Alipur.		Salbari.	
Male.	Female.	Male.	Female.	Male.	Female.	Male.	Female.	Male.	Female.	Male.	Female.
...	7	...	...	122	...	851	573	...	...	42	...
1,341	2,308	19	11	85	30	176	38	171	...	5	...
653	1,159	974	1,253	610	351	502	1,159	3,700	3,572	133	74
...	...	1,269	1,664	1,214	928	1,232	966	10,954	8,104	4,818	3,978
1,994	3,474	2,262	2,928	2,031	1,309	2,761	2,736	14,855	11,676	4,998	4,052
258	55	258	58	2,040	2,601	1,875	1,807	383	963	982	713
802	504	330	70	1,762	245	2,638	493	1,843	736	720	54
240	2	177	59	727	18	509	...	264	56	445	...
82	5	19	...	163	62	284	28	130	57	7	...
196	...	31	7	372	11	597	32	194	89	160	6
...	...	9	...	35	...	217	95	739	356	12	12
200	480	2	4	81	24	576	166	192	45	16	...

DISTRICT

	Total for the District.		Jalpaiguri.		Rajganj.		Titalya.	
	Male.	Female.	Male.	Female.	Male.	Female.	Male.	Female.
(d) From Orissa	171	154	28	5	...	...	...	...
(e) From Chutia Nagpur ...	11,500	10,954	776	750	72	129	196	...
Santal Parganas ...	2,832	239	685	14	9	13	2	...
Lohardaga	8,093	10,715	387	736	63	116	194	...
(f) From other Provinces and Countries	20,363	9,813	1,149	264	723	327	60	32
Nipal	13,449	7,056	106	35	237	158	16	1
Bhutan	911	856	5	1	...	...	...	...
North-Western Provinces ...	2,363	606	562	23	242	37	...	8
Punjab	1,205	135	45	35	...	7	...	2
TOTAL IMMIGRANTS	87,914	60,613	10,327	3,848	3,178	1,483	2,607	1,394

DACCA

DISTRICT

	Total for the District.		Lalbagh.		Kapasia.		Sabhar.		Nawabganj.		Keraniganj.	
	Male.	Female.	Male.	Female.	Male.	Female.	Male.	Female.	Male.	Female.	Male.	Female.
IMMIGRANTS.												
(a) From contiguous Districts—												
Faridpur	7,268	4,731	2,238	306	70	13	75	831	452	371	121	63
Maimansingh ...	16,790	15,990	3,259	703	2,851	2,696	3,141	3,147	12	10	1,204	723
Pabna	3,945	2,206	1,108	31	41	11	32	17	220	3	74	63
Tippera	6,459	4,188	2,723	80	112	103	...	37	2	4	220	347
Total ...	34,462	27,110	9,328	1,120	3,074	2,823	3,248	4,032	686	388	1,619	1,155
(b) From other districts in Bengal Proper	6,324	2,447	1,125	565	815	148	485	165	433	124	230	126
Bakharganj ...	1,043	351	549	100	7	3	20	5	85	36	28	19
Nadia	1,757	251	417	73	39	9	32	6	175	6	12	6
(c) From Bihar	15,484	1,579	6,055	955	565	71	506	17	396	5	922	168
Patna	1,287	317	687	215	9	10	18	2	55	2	95	30
Musaffarpur	2,106	148	820	75	161	33	178	2	6	...	7	4
Saran	3,315	103	585	84	159	19	154	4	121	...	341	91
Shahabad	885	387	712	282	43	4	4	...	15	...	29	7
Monghyr	6,317	378	2,474	261	197	...	144	7	168	1	369	15
(d) From Orissa	339	82	82	25	24	3	...	...	7	1	22	2
(e) From Chutia Nagpur ...	55	38	23	2	2	...	1	...	...	...	14	6
(f) From other Provinces and countries ...	12,239	1,682	5,744	615	1,167	131	320	45	73	58	471	161
North-Western Provinces	6,681	1,056	2,602	494	379	111	216	22	22	10	287	79
Assam	4,030	416	2,227	82	777	2	90	19	34	33	113	34
TOTAL IMMIGRANTS	68,903	32,938	22,357	3,282	5,647	3,176	4,560	4,259	1,595	576	3,278	1,618

JALPAIGURI—*concluded.*

Boda.		Patgram.		Mainaguri.		Dam-Dim.		Alipore.		Salbari.	
Male.	Female.	Male.	Female.	Male.	Female.	Male.	Female.	Male.	Female.	Male.	Female.
...	...	...	...	18	3	104	146	18	...	3	...
78	62	50	...	3,068	2,568	5,653	5,740	1,402	757	205	948
...	62	...	...	903	72	894	28	505	30	134	20
78	...	50	...	2,165	2,496	4,088	5,712	877	727	71	928
829	152	141	128	3,860	2,182	10,805	5,214	1,018	430	1,758	1,088
2	...	...	...	2,921	1,517	8,808	4,715	846	387	513	240
...	...	...	...	224	181	190	164	...	...	492	510
580	132	...	94	400	168	171	39	...	43	808	62
...	...	...	...	100	32	1,060	26	...	...	...	34
3,961	4,247	3,041	3,182	12,779	8,908	23,836	16,138	19,519	14,582	8,666	6,853

DIVISION.

DACCA.

Narainganj.		Rupganj.		Raipura.		Manikganj.		Jafarganj.		Harirampur.		Munshiganj.		Srinagar.	
Male.	Female.	Male.	Female.	Male.	Female.	Male.	Female.	Male.	Female.	Male.	Female.	Male.	Female.	Male.	Female.
515	55	46	...	67	15	110	34	264	302	324	341	2,569	2,103	417	297
189	96	4,674	6,127	119	86	384	996	690	1,194	17	36	130	52	20	65
212	33	89	2	158	1	212	34	110	1,936	181	53	1,256	12	302	10
1,441	604	754	1,104	352	747	18	9	...	...	4	...	749	1,107	84	141
2,357	788	5,513	7,233	696	849	724	1,073	1,064	3,432	526	430	4,704	3,274	923	513
230	120	431	92	366	197	323	201	169	152	343	184	798	210	577	183
60	5	8	...	10	8	16	5	10	...	16	8	130	105	66	84
189	41	39	4	85	...	95	20	12	54	119	12	289	9	211	11
1,917	152	983	44	647	3	471	16	497	75	485	3	716	49	1,324	21
148	24	23	17	100	...	25	3	9	...	14	2	84	11	70	11
452	4	222	6	22	...	8	1	48	...	7	...	101	18	79	...
221	16	291	13	219	1	230	2	245	11	416	...	150	9	183	...
29	74	7	8	...	...	17	6	2	...	2	...	24	6	1	...
776	20	399	...	276	1	167	2	179	60	34	...	306	4	898	7
32	...	4	...	15	4	12	2	84	28	6	1	40	8	11	8
6	7	...	2	...	1	4	6	...	5	1	3	4	2	...	4
1,860	255	479	60	221	24	457	56	469	121	255	44	469	54	254	58
1,463	170	290	50	96	7	390	24	409	63	120	11	299	11	102	4
174	57	178	8	107	9	28	23	89	40	5	31	127	34	136	51
6,402	1,322	7,410	7,431	1,944	1,078	1,991	1,354	2,283	3,813	1,616	665	6,731	3,597	3,089	767

DISTRICT

	TOTAL FOR THE DISTRICT.		FARIDPUR.		BHUSNA.		AWANPUR.		BHANGA.		MAKSUDPUR.	
	Male.	Female.	Male.	Female.	Male.	Female.	Male.	Female.	Male.	Female.	Male.	Female.
IMMIGRANTS.												
(a) From contiguous districts—												
Dacca	8,782	5,751	964	411	104	68	133	50	717	576	222	185
Pabna	6,987	6,394	262	106	68	76	19	10	75	16	43	30
Jessor	6,258	7,876	273	129	1,450	2,643	130	100	148	81	1,058	1,788
Khulna	758	578	27	8	30	9	12	5	14	1	134	58
Tippera	450	904	26	...	1	...	9	1	12	...	3	3
Bakharganj	3,563	4,152	104	24	17	15	14	26	160	55	76	103
Total ...	26,798	25,655	1,656	678	1,670	2,811	317	192	1,126	679	1,536	2,088
(b) From other districts in Bengal Proper	8,079	4,616	721	248	327	114	139	48	389	69	348	62
Nadia	5,271	3,039	363	115	296	70	111	1	146	3	296	11
(c) From Bihar	4,282	440	657	74	78	13	96	4	407	4	132	3
Saran	1,398	71	172	16	7	...	37	...	280	...	78	...
Monghyr	1,279	35	234	12	27	...	21	...	85	1	22	...
(d) From Orissa	191	17	12	...	17	2	24	4	6	...	6	3
(e) From Chutia Nagpur ...	144	115	11	4	31	24	1	2	1	2	9	5
(f) From other Provinces and countries	2,143	852	120	43	39	13	25	5	49	2	24	5
North-Western Provinces	1,271	439	80	16	19	8	9	1	21	...	15	3
TOTAL IMMIGRANTS	41,637	31,695	3,177	1,047	2,162	2,977	602	255	1,978	758	2,055	2,166

DISTRICT

	TOTAL FOR THE DISTRICT.		BARISAL.		BAKHARGANJ.		MEHNAGANJ.		GAURNADI.		JHALAKATI.		NALCHITI.		PATUAKHALI.	
	Male.	Female.	Male.	Female.	Male.	Female.	Male.	Female.	Male.	Female.	Male.	Female.	Male.	Female.	Male.	Female.
IMMIGRANTS.																
(a) From contiguous districts—																
Faridpur	21,566	6,020	1,774	280	2,101	26	2,356	699	2,517	3,144	1,462	159	785	103	1,449	71
Khulna	1,545	1,597	94	39	20	...	5	1	38	16	82	33	22	13	20	...
Noakhali	5,633	978	145	27	69	...	1,238	431	83	2	90	44	42	...	73	...
Tippera	809	233	59	18	15	...	152	85	31	15	109	50	294	35	16	1
Total ...	29,553	8,828	2,072	364	2,205	26	3,751	1,216	2,669	3,177	1,743	291	1,143	151	1,551	74
(b) From other districts in Bengal Proper ...	17,895	3,148	2,612	792	1,314	61	1,422	110	652	250	1,987	199	808	145	1,112	135
Jessor	3,055	780	162	32	317	3	77	6	117	54	547	55	67	10	187	19
Dacca	12,236	1,814	1,908	508	721	21	1,249	76	898	102	1,034	58	...	39	829	59

FARIDPUR.

Madaripur.		Gopalganj.		Kotalipara.		Palang.		Sibchar.		Goalanda.		Baliakandi.		Pangsa.	
Male.	Female.	Male.	Female.	Male.	Female.	Male.	Female.	Male.	Female.	Male.	Female.	Male.	Female.	Male.	Female.
514	245	47	18	69	28	3,563	3,199	660	237	1,594	559	54	69	141	125
61	11	1	...	6	...	5	2	23	...	4,821	4,118	234	312	1,369	1,723
103	63	843	729	105	90	8	12	51	1	725	188	588	1,035	776	1,117
18	7	291	350	160	124	29	2	1	...	26	13	2	1	14	...
13	3	2	1	...	...	287	182	8	645	74	69	...	...	15	...
1,297	1,625	237	270	590	1,293	688	725	327	12	32	4	1	...	20	...
2,006	1,954	1,421	1,368	930	1,535	4,580	4,122	1,070	895	7,272	4,951	879	1,417	2,335	2,965
357	88	340	85	24	102	25	95	720	115	2,295	821	640	294	1,754	2,465
131	19	210	31	14	3	10	6	3	...	1,618	379	384	168	1,689	2,232
408	19	96	7	33	...	397	35	721	11	1,071	246	56	6	129	18
248	1	2	...	29	...	193	9	62	4	311	37	5	2	24	2
65	3	3	...	1	...	118	2	391	...	276	17	14	...	22	...
1	2	5	...	...	...	12	...	...	...	77	2	9	1	22	3
...	...	3	5	2	1	1	...	...	...	75	57	5	7	5	8
60	8	9	2	8	3	276	119	48	14	1,330	598	58	5	97	35
29	4	5	...	6	2	115	25	23	11	841	333	24	4	84	32
2,833	2,071	1,874	1,477	997	1,641	5,291	4,371	2,559	1,035	12,120	6,675	1,647	1,730	4,342	5,494

BAKHARGANJ.

Bauphal.		Gulsakhali.		Golachipa.		Pirojpur.		Bhandaria.		Sahupkati.		Matbaria.		Bhola.		Barhanuddin.	
Male.	Female.	Male.	Female.	Male.	Female.	Male.	Female.	Male.	Female.	Male.	Female.	Male.	Female.	Male.	Female.	Male.	Female.
967	44	683	13	1,112	61	810	98	340	31	1,131	1,044	631	48	2,004	158	1,435	40
6	...	...	...	1	...	635	789	35	5	507	631	62	6	15	8	3	1
239	...	46	...	325	2	32	...	1	...	7	1	37	3	719	89	2,488	379
2	...	7	...	5	...	23	14	...	...	2	3	1	...	44	2	55	9
1,214	44	736	13	1,443	63	1,500	901	385	36	1,647	1,729	731	57	2,782	257	3,981	429
636	47	469	29	506	33	1,267	350	465	28	549	490	518	60	1,749	217	1,809	202
42	5	69	...	67	...	571	186	264	13	388	367	118	26	13	3	40	1
546	39	349	5	420	18	598	94	131	12	135	56	335	18	1,481	152	1,544	36

DISTRICT

	Total for the District.		Barisal.		Bakharganj.		Mehndiganj.		Gaurnadi.		Jhalakati.		Nalchiti.		Patuakhali.	
	Male.	Female.	Male.	Female.	Male.	Female.	Male.	Female.	Male.	Female.	Male.	Female.	Male.	Female.	Male.	Female.
(c) From Bihar	2,161	293	267	78	198	43	73	23	51	4	336	16	8	8	176	28
(d) From Orissa	484	20	113	5	41	...	2	2	28	1	75	5	28	...	12	1
(e) From Chutia Nagpur ...	17	4	5	4	1	...	3	...	1	...	...	...	4	...	...	...
(f) From other Provinces and countries	1,615	295	425	85	31	3	117	4	56	70	275	13	125	6	71	13
TOTAL IMMIGRANTS	51,725	12,586	5,494	1,328	3,790	133	5,368	1,855	3,457	5,502	4,414	524	2,190	310	2,922	249

DISTRICT

	Total for the District.		Nasirabad.		Phulpur.		Gafargaon.	
	Male.	Female.	Male.	Female.	Male.	Female.	Male.	Female.
IMMIGRANTS.								
(a) From contiguous districts—								
Dacca	14,822	6,285	2,562	585	893	5	1,011	363
Pabna	7,502	4,705	471	51	171	3	38	5
Bogra	1,339	1,027	7	12	...	...	...	...
Rangpur...	840	326	...	16	...	1	...	...
Tippera	3,939	61	...	17	2,685	...	115	...
Assam	5,734	5,893	65	2	...	16	3,704	1
Total ...	34,176	18,297	3,105	613	3,249	25	4,868	269
(b) From other districts in Bengal Proper	5,105	1,062	942	188	371	39	405	17
Faridpur	2,029	319	414	46	105	11	109	4
(c) From Bihar	15,626	977	692	259	116	48	481	5
Saran	13,118	500	...	145	...	25	...	1
Muzaffarpur	1,350	29	439	29	96	...	462	...
(d) From Orissa	183	22	33	13	...	2	...	...
(e) From Chutia Nagpur ...	231	25	41	9	9	1	3	...
(f) From other Provinces and countries	23,462	2,824	3,307	67	120	8	8,435	2
North-Western Provinces	18,151	2,081	...	...	...	...	8,396	...
TOTAL IMMIGRANTS	78,783	23,207	8,120	1,129	3,885	123	18,182	393

BAKHARGANJ—*concluded.*

BAUPHAL.		GULSAKHALI.		GOLACHIPA.		PIROJPUR.		BHANDARIA.		SARUPKATI.		MATBARIA.		BHOLA.		BARHANUDDIN.	
Male.	Female.	Male.	Female.	Male.	Female.	Male.	Female.	Male.	Female.	Male.	Female.	Male.	Female.	Male.	Female.	Male.	Female.
67	1	84	3	54	7	122	2	108	4	10	5	334	7	113	23	86	43
50	...	18	...	36	...	15	...	15	...	28	4	5	...	19	2	21	...
...	...	...	...	...	...	1	...	...	...	...	...	2	...	...	...	...	...
39	2	46	15	71	8	3	26	25	4	171	...	47	7	81	21	32	18
1,996	94	1,353	60	2,110	111	2,908	1,279	1,018	72	2,405	2,228	1,637	131	4,744	520	5,929	692

MAIMANSINGH.

ISWARGANJ.		PHULBARIA.		NETROKONA.		DURGAPUR.		KENDUA.	
Male.	Female.	Male.	Female.	Male.	Female.	Male.	Female.	Male.	Female.
456	60	...	5	1,338	128	478	36	319	34
27	13	...	...	...	...	54	...	55	10
1	...	...	...	1	...	1	1	1	...
...	3	...	...	15	...	...	...	...	...
...	...	...	...	...	28	...	...	139	16
36	...	...	...	30	...	128	1,305	463	2,336
520	76	...	5	1,384	156	658	1,342	977	2,396
363	74	131	26	91	126	230	10	246	97
110	15	...	4	257	23	52	1	69	...
11	71	146	2	261	18	7,183	35	76	38
...	61	...	...	45	...	7,118	23	...	34
...	...	137	...	182	...	16	...	...	...
...	...	6	...	6	2	2	...	...	...
14	9	...	...	...	...	...	1	...	...
6,628	10	4	81	2,136	518	796	13	652	2
6,615	...	...	...	1,573	...	532	...	137	...
7,536	240	287	114	3,878	820	8,867	1,401	1,851	2,533

DISTRICT

	Jamalpur.		Diwnganj.		Sherpur.		Nalitabari.	
	Male.	Female.	Male.	Female.	Male.	Female.	Male.	Female.
IMMIGRANTS.								
(a) From contiguous districts—								
Dacca	615	72	146	1,256	297	33	73	3
Pabna	1,023	540	...	344	137	31	82	8
Bogra	366	601	12	288	752	...	21	...
Rangpur	766	16	3	255	53	...	...	8
Tippera	107	...	43	...	310	...	67	...
Assam	348	9	41	...	302	284	92	4
Total ...	3,225	1,238	245	2,143	1,851	348	340	23
(b) From other districts in Bengal Proper	317	34	68	31	267	15	99	4
Faridpur	193	8	42	9	118	6	37	4
(c) From Bihar	96	87	1,469	122	58	77	1,206	35
Saran	...	20	1,392	12	8	33	1,185	17
Muzaffarpur	13	...	15	...	...	...	...	...
(d) From Orissa	5	...	2	...	20	2	3	...
(e) From Chutia Nagpur ...	56	2	12	2	58	...	...	...
(f) From other provinces and countries	581	1	179	86	68	40	42	5
North-Western Provinces	563	...	174	68	15	32	27	...
TOTAL IMMIGRANTS	4,280	1,362	1,975	2,384	2,322	482	1,690	67

CHITTAGONG

DISTRICT

	Total for the District.		Chittagong.		Mirserai.		Kumira.		Phatikchari.		Hathazari.	
	Male.	Female.	Male.	Female.	Male.	Female.	Male.	Female.	Male.	Female.	Male.	Female.
IMMIGRANTS.												
(a) From contiguous districts—												
Aracan	356	261	27	5	...	...	2	...	4	1	1	1
Chittagong Hill Tracts	287	282	...	...	...	...	...	...	...	...	...	...
Noakhali	1,495	669	433	71	714	543	120	27	6	13	19	3
Tippera	733	226	358	27	251	163	15	8	25	8	6	6
Total ...	2,871	1,438	818	103	965	706	137	35	35	22	26	10
(b) From other districts in Bengal Proper	2,042	1,047	779	243	82	11	78	35	240	225	100	101
(c) From Bihar	754	169	235	57	2	2	31	14	92	30	28	16
(d) From Orissa	109	36	32	14	...	...	18	12	6	2	10	...
(e) From Chutia Nagpur ...	620	476	18	1	9	...	20	70	235	140	139	119
(f) From other Provinces and countries	1,428	706	395	162	24	87	128	60	275	211	209	83
TOTAL IMMIGRANTS	7,824	3,872	2,277	580	1,082	806	412	226	883	630	512	329

MAIMANSINGH—*concluded.*

Tangail.		Gopalpur.		Kalihati.		Kisorganj.		Nikli.		Bajitpur.	
Male.	Female.	Male.	Female.	Male.	Female.	Male.	Female.	Male.	Female.	Male.	Female.
3,516	1,748	388	60	98	89	287	21	310	247	2,535	1,590
2,665	1,980	2,593	1,612	168	128	3	...	5	...	10	...
1	23	173	97	3	4	...	...	...	1	...	...
...	25	...	2	3	...	...	...	...	...	...	...
140	...	125	...	35	...	125	...	25	...	13	...
30	82	280	94	155	...	25	...	19	24	16	1,736
6,352	3,858	3,559	1,865	462	221	440	21	369	272	2,574	3,326
318	292	314	82	209	27	395	7	246	1	93	12
74	67	113	8	15	8	49	4	32	1	210	...
405	60	358	38	12	58	...	8	38	17	3,018	1
375	37	20	19	5	7	...	8	...	13	3,015	...
...	...	...	...	...	...	...	...	...	...	...	...
...	...	17	...	...	3	...	...	...	...	89	...
5	...	21	...	5	...	...	1	5	...	2	...
17	499	49	60	18	327	105	182	391	511	34	412
13	495	17	59	14	327	17	182	45	509	8	409
7,097	4,709	4,318	2,043	706	636	840	219	1,049	801	5,810	3,751

DIVISION.

CHITTAGONG.

Raujan.		Patia.		Banskhali.		Satkania.		Cox's Bazar.		Chakaria.		Maiskal.		Teknaf.	
Male.	Female.	Male.	Female.	Male.	Female.	Male.	Female.	Male.	Female.	Male.	Female.	Male.	Female.	Male.	Female.
...	...	...	...	...	...	...	...	23	7	7	2	...	1	293	244
85	...	13	48	...	...	...	...	170	...	19	212	...	22	...	...
75	...	12	...	23	...	2	...	54	12	12	...	2	...	23	...
6	2	11	2	...	4	5	...	16	6	38	...	2	...	...	...
166	2	36	50	23	4	7	...	263	25	76	214	4	23	315	244
120	88	170	67	313	257	87	5	45	8	7	6	14	...	7	1
114	8	206	18	13	3	2	2	11	...	1	19	19	...	...	...
28	5	6	...	9	3	...	...	...	...	...	...	...	...	...	...
88	42	31	41	80	63	...	...	...	...	...	...	...	...	...	...
210	12	56	7	64	67	22	5	2	...	1	2	35	6	7	4
726	157	505	183	502	397	118	12	321	33	85	241	72	29	329	249

DISTRICT

	Total for the District.		Sudharam.		Hatia.		Bamni.	
	Male.	Female.	Male.	Female.	Male.	Female.	Male.	Female.
IMMIGRANTS.								
(a) From contiguous districts—								
Tippera	2,901	4,061	286	111	38	83	33	9
Chittagong	2,275	1,966	266	73	240	581	81	56
Bakharganj	1,263	482	71	29	368	150	33	...
Total ...	6,439	6,509	623	213	646	814	147	65
(b) From other districts in Bengal Proper	3,959	1,119	976	422	518	64	81	29
Dacca	2,153	607	620	267	320	12	31	3
Faridpur	1,516	308	280	101	186	32	41	...
(c) From Bihar	149	20	57	1	15	8	...	2
(d) From Orissa	50	4	3	...	2	...	...	...
(e) From Chutia Nagpur ...	3	...	1	...	...	...	...	...
(f) From other Provinces and countries	376	91	102	16	12	4	7	12
TOTAL IMMIGRANTS	10,976	7,743	1,762	652	1,193	890	236	108

DISTRICT

	Total for the District.		Comilla.		Muradnagar.		Daudkandi.		Chandina.	
	Male.	Female.	Male.	Female.	Male.	Female.	Male.	Female.	Male.	Female.
IMMIGRANTS.										
(a) From contiguous districts—										
Noakhali	8,140	4,431	769	57	610	...	90	6	355	21
Hill Tippera	75	46	27	24	...	...	...	...	...	...
Dacca	12,053	4,795	858	268	599	155	1,377	421	198	22
Faridpur	3,451	890	157	31	40	9	75	17	27	6
Bakharganj	574	278	32	7	5	...	17	5	7	3
Maimansingh	1,484	1,813	50	16	37	7	67	15	2	2
Assam	4,394	5,422	208	15	349	4	168	3	71	6
Total ...	30,180	17,675	2,101	418	1,640	175	1,784	467	660	60
(b) From other districts in Bengal Proper	1,814	353	535	129	182	5	51	17	45	8
Chittagong	1,132	81	377	36	151	...	27	3	22	1
(c) From Bihar	3,974	185	229	68	952	8	500	2	59	...
Saran	1,939	29	91	25	384	2	315	...	31	...
(d) From Orissa	176	2	28	2	20	...	14	...	5	...
(e) From Chutia Nagpur ...	68	2	33	2	5	...	1	...	...	...
(f) From other Provinces and countries	1,754	480	301	141	316	107	58	14	46	3
North-Western Provinces	1,589	427	227	119	316	107	54	14	46	3
TOTAL IMMIGRANTS	37,965	18,697	3,227	760	3,115	295	2,408	500	815	71

NOAKHALI.

Ramganj.		Lakshmipur.		Begamganj.		Sundwip.		Fenny.		Chhagalnaia.	
Male.	Female.	Male.	Female.	Male.	Female.	Male.	Female.	Male.	Female.	Male.	Female.
619	1,758	707	686	373	406	48	8	435	527	362	473
16	10	116	18	30	16	290	292	530	399	706	521
33	11	601	267	33	8	85	12	26	5	13	...
668	1,779	1,424	971	436	430	423	312	991	931	1,081	994
221	57	1,391	327	211	37	284	62	215	107	62	14
94	23	635	197	112	13	168	23	151	62	22	7
106	21	680	108	65	16	88	19	49	11	21	...
2	...	27	...	8	...	16	5	15	4	9	...
13	...	12	1	9	...	...	...	4	1	7	2
...	...	...	...	...	...	...	...	2	...	...	...
47	2	32	15	45	5	32	15	46	10	53	12
951	1,838	2,886	1,314	709	472	755	394	1,273	1,053	1,212	1,022

TIPPERA.

Chaudagram.		Laksham.		Brahmanbaria.		Kasba.		Nabinagar.		Chandpur.		Hajiganj.	
Male.	Female.	Male.	Female.	Male.	Female.	Male.	Female.	Male.	Female.	Male.	Female.	Male.	Female.
629	1,102	692	758	272	3	820	...	31	1	2,943	1,661	938	823
2	...	...	...	3	5	29	13	...	...	14	4	...	...
57	13	268	63	1,064	194	192	44	900	341	5,920	3,223	620	51
18	3	76	3	104	10	36	...	77	6	2,495	790	346	15
4	...	11	...	4	4	3	...	30	...	427	244	34	15
7	2	11	4	1,075	1,592	27	31	67	118	101	25	50	1
14	1	14	2	2,432	5,057	337	112	567	142	170	52	64	28
731	1,121	1,072	830	4,954	6,865	1,444	200	1,672	608	12,070	5,999	2,052	932
175	30	78	5	272	66	42	7	114	5	247	60	73	21
160	20	67	4	121	7	32	1	81	...	67	6	27	3
13	2	12	3	476	29	136	9	668	37	782	9	145	18
1	...	2	...	225	1	96	...	270	...	476	1	48	...
2	...	...	...	29	...	33	...	1	...	8	...	25	...
3	...	...	...	21	...	...	...	1	...	4	...	...	...
13	15	20	7	331	87	72	27	212	51	227	19	158	9
13	15	16	7	253	64	72	25	211	50	224	14	157	9
937	1,168	1,182	845	6,085	7,047	1,727	243	2,688	701	13,338	6,087	2,463	980

DISTRICT CHITTA

	Total for the District.		Chakma circle.		Mong Raja's circle.	
	Male.	Female.	Male.	Female.	Male.	Female.
IMMIGRANTS.						
(a) From contiguous districts—						
Chittagong	5,661	377	3,615	139	250	...
Hill Tippera	325	249	27	21	284	225
Arakan	78	69	...	...	...	...
Total ...	6,064	695	3,642	160	534	225
(b) From other districts in Bengal Proper	591	37	77	15	457	...
(c) From Bihar	78	7	54	7	4	...
(d) From Orissa	5	...	4	...	...	...
(e) From Chutia Nagpur ...	324	55	51	55	...	...
(f) From other provinces and countries	534	191	184	94	27	2
TOTAL IMMIGRANTS ...	7,594	985	4,012	331	1,022	227

PATNA

DISTRICT

	Total for the District.		Pirbahor.		Sultanganj.		Alamganj.	
	Male.	Female.	Male.	Female.	Male.	Female.	Male.	Female.
IMMIGRANTS.								
(a) From contiguous districts—								
Gaya	11,836	33,694	498	214	85	49	178	69
Musaffarpur ...	10,929	5,869	225	107	228	101	635	287
Saran	7,684	16,894	340	146	164	150	392	184
Shahabad	3,759	6,781	240	101	45	25	121	76
Monghyr	10,600	9,380	148	54	48	28	40	69
Darbhanga	3,106	589	31	33	21	23	45	24
From other provinces and countries—								
Balia	295	...	16	...	10	...	...	...
Total ...	48,209	73,207	1,498	655	601	376	1,408	709
(b) From other districts in Bihar	338	362	45	9	7	5	24	...
(c) From Bengal Proper ...	1,508	1,382	421	258	33	205	30	51
Calcutta	417	609	48	60	17	176	1	...
(d) From Orissa	...	68	...	...	...	...	...	26
(e) From Chutia Nagpur ...	173	177	37	...	...	8	3	...
(f) From other provinces and countries ...	7,240	2,830	894	861	36	517	591	176
North-Western Provinces	3,360	1,492	880	850	20	205	35	15
Oudh	868	416	...	...	...	...	508	103
Panjab...	1,141	469	...	...	...	301	...	33
TOTAL IMMIGRANTS	57,468	78,024	2,895	1,783	677	1,111	2,056	982

GONG HILL TRACTS.

Bhomong's circle.		Sangu Khas Mahal.		Head-quarters Khas Mahal and Forest Reserves.	
Male.	Female.	Male.	Female.	Male.	Female.
1,637	231	159	7	...	...
...	...	14	3	...	...
78	69	...	...	...	...
1,715	300	173	10	...	...
...	...	47	22	10	...
4	...	14	...	...	...
...	...	1	...	...	...
...	...	14	...	259	...
...	...	313	95	10	...
1,719	300	582	127	279	...

DIVISION.

PATNA.

Khwaja Kalan.		Chauk Kalan.		Malsalami.		Bankipur.		Bikram.		Masaudhi Bazurg.	
Male.	Female.	Male.	Female.	Male.	Female.	Male.	Female.	Male.	Female.	Male.	Female.
420	323	243	84	141	31	265	206	1,457	4,407	1,074	1,879
1,067	561	260	704	39	301	151	84	89	62	129	138
245	206	2,275	113	199	80	388	198	140	270	151	78
140	65	106	43	143	37	377	128	702	2,558	184	147
119	128	86	32	28	15	35	12	18	17	27	10
132	88	16	11	99	26	35	19	...	...	7	4
4	...	9	...	15	...	19	...	18	...	15	...
2,127	1,371	2,995	987	664	490	1,270	647	2,473	7,314	1,587	2,256
37	16	38	4	17	35	30	7	3	6	4	130
24	115	23	58	104	36	80	71	4	10	15	16
22	71	2	1	1	...	30	22	...	10	6	8
...	28	...	3	...	3	...	...	...	...	...	...
19	...	...	...	...	21	...	21	...	...	...	12
344	52	836	234	266	123	226	18	84	3	...	22
105	7	730	12	164	1	...	...	84	...	...	...
89	13	11	195	10	5	...	...	...	...	...	...
...	8	...	10	...	117	...	...	...	...	...	...
2,551	1,582	3,892	1,286	1,051	708	1,606	764	2,564	7,333	1,606	2,436

DISTRICT

	Dinapur.		Maner.		Barh.		Fatuha.	
	Male.	Female.	Male.	Female.	Male.	Female.	Male.	Female.
IMMIGRANTS.								
(a) From contiguous districts—								
Gaya	406	787	106	330	584	1,713	217	30
Musaffarpar ..	208	246	30	120	4,932	1,036	1,440	27
Saran	1,161	7,459	1,176	2,958	251	...	130	4
Shahabad	592	1,061	458	2,301	85	32	15	34
Monghyr	62	67	9	8	2,528	2,522	67	1,869
Darbhanga	42	8	4	7	1,065	88	208	44
From other Provinces and countries—								
Balia	98	...	36	...	11	...	4	...
Total ...	2,569✓	9,628	1,849	5,724	9,456	5,391	2,081	1,999
(b) From other districts in Bihar	9	26	2	...	9	6	1	40
(c) From Bengal Proper ...	237	292	93	39	159	77	40	9
Calcutta	149	162	4	19	11	12	5	4
(d) From Orissa	...	...	...	...	...	...	...	...
(e) From Chutia Nagpur ...	4	38	3	5	24	3	2>	1
(f) From other Provinces and countries ...	1,119	84	395	131	138	35	439	134
North-Western Provinces	83	2	300	80	80	22	430	46
Oudh	105	52	95	46	7	...	8	...
Panjab	...	...	...	...	46	...	...	...
TOTAL IMMIGRANTS	3,938	10,068	2,342	5,899	9,786	5,512	2,583	2,183

DISTRICT

	Total for the District.		Town Gaya.		Mufassal Gaya.		Atri.		Tikari.		Sherghati.		Barachati.	
	Male.	Female.	Male.	Female.	Male.	Female.	Male.	Female.	Male.	Female.	Male.	Female.	Male.	Female.
IMMIGRANTS.														
(a) From contiguous districts—														
Lohardaga	656	1,433	33	12	32	11	4	...	...	...	...	119	...	8
Hasaribagh	1,434	2,273	119	72	75	19	5	5	5	49	278	556	204	399
Monghyr	2,027	4,481	141	55	30	6	36	71	12	1	4	3	19	3
Patna	7,956	15,474	1,154	592	212	90	1,047	1,485	164	90	75	17	70	31
Shahabad	2,427	4,106	373	275	62	7	31	18	38	9	54	28	41	17
Total ...	14,500	27,767	1,820	1,006	411	133	1,123	1,579	219	149	411	723	334	440
(b) From other districts in Bihar	1,752	708	716	204	136	21	70	50	71	21	98	51	56	38
(c) From Bengal Proper ...	939	403	571	215	37	16	14	4	11	39	11	67	6	27
(d) From Orissa	51	20	17	16	1	...	...	...	...	...	...	...	...	...
(e) From Chutia Nagpur ...	209	529	17	2	30	...	20	...	20	...	50	55	40	...
(f) From other Provinces and countries	4,263	2,923	550	363	384	141	204	160	132	114	13,	197	76	47
TOTAL IMMIGRANTS	21,714	32,350	3,691	1,806	999	311	1,431	1,793	453	323	701	1,093	512	552

PATNA—*concluded.*

Mukameh.		Bihar.		Hilsa.		Chandi.		Islampur or Athasarai.		Silao.	
Male.	Female.	Male.	Female.	Male.	Female.	Male.	Female.	Male.	Female.	Male.	Female.
726	11,745	1,537	3,424	416	693	159	301	2,667	5,852	657	1,557
1,079	1,512	91	56	96	49	74	78	200	94	16	6
279	...	155	4,926	108	99	22	5	90	12	9	2
129	93	93	38	20	14	19	3	94	29	69	4
6,414	860	708	3,101	31	149	60	209	74	52	89	185
1,238	93	48	66	15	4	26	25	68	20	6	4
14	...	...	...	16	...	2	...	8	...	...	...
9,879	14,603	2,632	11,611	702	1,008	371	621	3,201	6,059	846	1,758
40	...	44	27	2	5	26	6	...	18	...	22
130	67	60	52	2	13	1	...	16	5	38	8
62	19	35	34	2	...	1	...	14	2	7	6
...	...	...	3	...	2	...	1	...	...	...	...
9	2	41	36	...	1	7	...	20	16	4	13
315	32	229	218	923	33	215	6	160	77	30	74
287	8	113	210	24	18	3	...	66	12	7	39
5	...	35	...	7	...	7	...	28	...	3	...
...	...	...	...	841	...	205	...	29	...	20	...
10,373	14,704	3,006	11,947	1,629	1,062	620	634	3,397	6,175	916	1,875

GAYA.

Nawada.		Pakribarawan.		Rajauli.		Jahanabad.		Arwal.		Aurangabad.		Daudnagar.		Nabinagar.	
Male.	Female.	Male.	Female.	Male.	Female.	Male.	Female.	Male.	Female.	Male.	Female.	Male.	Female.	Male.	Female.
12	21	...	13	...	...	...	...	1	20	105	113	...	17	460	1,099
66	206	190	311	422	534	9	2	5	97	43	15	6	15	7	...
590	1,821	1,131	2,455	24	14	34	31	...	...	6	9	...	...	...	13
1,384	2,236	311	549	92	31	2,408	9,230	711	1,002	187	26	111	90	30	15
22	22	...	4	12	4	177	243	634	1,658	561	680	231	426	191	715
2,074	4,306	1,632	3,332	550	583	2,628	9,506	1,351	2,777	902	843	348	548	697	1,842
86	77	71	18	23	9	134	116	135	73	58	9	42	14	56	7
97	8	66	9	6	1	7	5	15	...	46	...	16	8	38	4
1	...	...	...	...	...	...	...	...	...	...	4	2	...	30	...
6	1	...	...	...	...	...	...	...	...	1	22	18	5	7	444
208	125	160	14	205	20	594	79	242	123	493	300	477	194	407	1,046
2,472	4,517	1,929	3,373	784	613	3,363	9,706	1,743	2,973	1,500	1,178	903	769	1,233	3,343

DISTRICT

	Total for the District.		Arrah.		Belauti.		Piru.		Buxar.	
	Male.	Female.	Male.	Female.	Male.	Female.	Male.	Female.	Male.	Female.
IMMIGRANTS.										
(a) From contiguous districts—										
Saran	13,326	20,356	695	438	108	2,290	563	661	1,030	2,455
Gaya	6,677	5,861	2,512	475	8	265	407	1,088	476	851
Patna	2,589	3,807	847	328	149	341	184	135	710	737
Other Provinces—										
Balia	11,784	7,746	2,577	750	12	2,692	104	108	3,034	747
Ghasipur	3,702	1,413	129	225	41	252	86	149	1,508	342
Total ...	38,078	39,183	6,760	2,216	318	5,840	1,344	2,141	6,758	5,122
(b) From other districts in Bihar	17,016	3,002	3,402	438	54	135	57	90	1,756	529
Champaran	7,048	582	619	9	2	54	8	26	45	18
Musaffarpur ...	2,652	1,127	1,242	212	8	29	15	20	321	92
Bhagalpur	715	688	440	216	20	7	11	5	173	319
Purnea	793	188	220	...	8	10	4	15	347	16
Darbhanga	3,036	44	445	...	6	...	16	...	162	1
Monghyr	2,772	373	436	1	10	35	3	24	708	83
(c) From Bengal Proper ...	3,389	1,813	1,012	767	39	72	42	63	357	119
Calcutta	883	240	440	7	14	21	3	4	256	23
(d) From Orissa	139	2	1	...	2	...	...	...	...	...
(e) From Chutia Nagpur ...	5,218	1,574	1,845	219	20	1	17	4	519	612
Chutia Nagpur Tributary States ...	2,005	83	83	...	7	1	5	4	99	...
Lohardaga	2,367	1,075	1,727	219	1	...	2	...	370	612
(f) From other Provinces and countries	9,344	5,674	2,252	270	736	279	45	123	686	255
North-Western Provinces	5,108	4,663	1,577	134	612	71	19	100	532	118
Punjab	942	208	353	1	43	27	1	75	28	21
Rajputana States ...	1,223	37	4	15	2	1	2	...	...	...
TOTAL IMMIGRANTS	73,184	51,048	15,272	3,910	1,169	6,327	1,505	2,421	10,076	6,637

DISTRICT

	Total for the District.		Darbhanga.		Bahera.		Roshra.		Madhubani.	
	Male.	Female.	Male.	Female.	Male.	Female.	Male.	Female.	Male.	Female.
IMMIGRANTS.										
(a) From contiguous districts—										
Musaffarpur	15,948	23,160	5,029	5,666	534	117	835	624	702	207
Patna	1,631	2,727	569	369	...	43	45	92	108	34
Monghyr	4,743	10,800	198	106	200	198	2,519	5,219	228	45
Bhagalpur	2,335	3,437	108	66	205	257	284	269	65	46
Total ...	24,657	40,133	5,924	6,207	939	615	3,683	6,204	1,103	332

SHAHABAD.

Dumraon.		Sassaram.		Kharghar.		Dhangain.		Dehri.		Bhabhua.		Mohania.	
Male.	Female.	Male.	Female.	Male.	Female.	Male.	Female.	Male.	Female.	Male.	Female.	Male.	Female.
6,351	10,277	1,186	1,662	787	193	588	508	714	977	502	655	802	240
408	1,620	304	234	1,004	144	404	385	92	177	270	422	792	200
89	1,460	71	196	426	99	15	265	38	69	3	59	57	118
3,343	2,352	568	231	1,154	120	284	260	324	132	123	182	261	172
980	455	160	...	302	...	3	...	115	...	26	...	352	...
11,171	16,164	2,289	2,323	3,673	556	1,294	1,418	1,283	1,355	924	1,318	2,264	730
2,003	178	186	450	199	419	2,317	270	498	178	2,588	208	3,956	109
119	10	51	114	20	300	18	9	14	10	2,432	17	3,720	15
274	1	53	262	9	19	504	115	97	150	49	173	81	54
71	141	...	...	...	...	...	...	...	...	...	...	...	...
109	10	7	37	10	76	3	4	76	1	9	6	...	13
57	...	4	12	8	...	1,785	7	311	3	90	8	152	13
1,373	16	72	25	152	24	7	135	...	14	8	2	3	14
137	88	233	99	17	152	250	42	954	123	252	40	96	48
76	13	43	9	6	126	9	3	7	...	12	...	17	23
9	2	86	...	5	...	7	...	13	...	8	...	8	...
344	62	699	143	22	9	561	158	294	185	582	30	315	151
80	...	565	23	16	...	412	...	139	...	445	5	154	1
231	62	30	32	...	...	5	12	...	54	...	7	1	77
413	195	1,745	1,940	212	804	1,609	364	348	205	961	760	337	479
257	59	1,032	1,836	25	707	400	301	115	165	412	715	127	427
26	6	178	31	16	...	16	19	2	13	182	5	97	10
6	21	220	...	10	...	781	...	108	...	79	...	13	...
14,077	16,689	5,238	4,955	4,128	1,940	6,038	2,252	3,390	2,046	5,315	2,354	6,976	1,517

DARBHANGA.

Benipati.		Khajauli.		Phulparas.		Samastipur.		Maniarpur.		Dalsingh Sarai.	
Male.	Female.	Male.	Female.	Male.	Female.	Male.	Female.	Male.	Female.	Male.	Female.
1,054	1,822	760	410	1,596	730	2,947	6,631	1,112	1,688	1,379	5,274
...	...	21	12	87	73	359	550	40	28	382	1,526
34	13	10	1	76	...	385	1,519	90	107	1,003	3,592
6	9	19	15	1,537	2,646	64	51	18	14	29	64
1,094	1,844	810	438	3,296	3,449	3,755	8,751	1,260	1,837	2,793	10,458

DISTRICT

	Total for the District.		Darbhanga.		Bahera.		Roshra.		Madhubani.	
	Male.	Female.	Male.	Female.	Male.	Female.	Male.	Female.	Male.	Female.
(b) From other districts in Bihar	4,880	1,242	1,497	359	229	23	216	29	674	112
Saran	3,777	793	1,109	287	190	...	173	20	509	46
(c) From Bengal Proper ...	741	420	234	180	24	4	217	43	21	17
(d) From Orissa	8	4	8	...	...	...	...	...	...	...
(e) From Chutia Nagpur ...	6	2	4	2	...	...	...	...	...	...
(f) From other Provinces and countries	6,089	5,998	1,441	739	202	26	72	66	581	258
North-Western Provinces	1,650	556	672	216	65	9	27	5	360	189
Nipal	2,996	4,938	148	147	10	6	...	...	130	74
TOTAL IMMIGRANTS ...	36,381	47,799	8,106	7,487	1,394	668	4,188	6,342	2,379	719

DISTRICT

	Total for the District.		Muzaffarpur.		Paru.		Katra.		Sitamarhi.	
	Male.	Female.	Male.	Female.	Male.	Female.	Male.	Female.	Male.	Female.
IMMIGRANTS.										
(a) From contiguous districts—										
Saran	7,969	6,009	1,288	702	1,824	1,780	218	62	1,248	443
Champaran	4,533	13,462	421	486	1,604	6,309	26	32	304	690
Patna	2,160	4,292	1,144	891	66	74	20	16	72	33
Darbhanga	5,962	19,709	1,315	1,047	58	83	935	4,767	569	498
Other Provinces—										
Nipal	2,508	7,835	67	137	41	38	24	75	1,230	3,407
Total ...	23,132	51,307	4,235	3,263	3,593	8,344	1,223	4,952	3,417	5,071
(b) From other districts in Bihar	1,294	1,567	567	393	74	90	31	40	91	106
Monghyr	338	766	165	91	10	25	8	23	13	35
(c) From Bengal Proper... ...	781	546	467	268	48	129	4	...	80	70
(d) From Orissa	21	9	12	5	2	...	...	...	...	1
(e) From Chutia Nagpur ...	56	53	24	9	1	28	...	...	12	3
(f) From other Provinces and countries	2,517	1,703	1,201	646	182	514	59	16	299	18
North-Western Provinces	1,633	966	563	281	130	322	48	16	249	8
TOTAL IMMIGRANTS ...	27,803	55,185	6,506	4,584	3,880	9,106	1,317	5,008	3,899	5,267

DARBHANGA—*concluded.*

Benipati.		Khajauli.		Phulparas.		Samastipur.		Maniarpur.		Dalsingh Sarai.	
Male.	Female.	Male.	Female.	Male.	Female.	Male.	Female.	Male.	Female.	Male.	Female.
164	68	528	186	717	150	568	214	132	23	155	78
131	50	501	180	618	118	328	93	106	4	112	45
20	5	1	5	19	12	169	129	9	7	27	18
...	...	...	...	...	...	...	...	1	...	1	4
...	...	...	...	2	...	...	...	...	...	...	...
470	956	1,191	1,851	1,451	1,948	502	111	86	3	93	40
14	6	77	10	79	18	280	96	18	2	49	25
389	950	1,071	1,841	1,220	1,909	24	3	1	3	3	5
1,748	2,873	2,530	2,480	5,485	5,559	4,994	9,205	1,488	1,870	3,069	10,596

MUZAFFARPUR.

Sitamarhi.		Pupri.		Belsand.		Hajipur.		Lalganj.		Mahua.	
Male.	Female.	Male.	Female.	Male.	Female.	Male.	Female.	Male.	Female.	Male.	Female.
1,380	652	360	83	175	45	573	885	385	794	524	563
1,877	5,410	57	70	139	336	30	27	53	34	17	8
34	21	27	10	22	5	649	2,709	83	272	43	261
123	245	1,197	3,896	173	308	748	4,492	48	133	796	4,240
632	2,290	443	1,817	53	60	2	3	7	2	9	6
4,046	8,618	2,084	5,876	562	754	2,002	8,116	581	1,235	1,389	5,078
79	47	61	25	23	12	235	531	41	87	92	236
7	...	13	8	6	2	65	318	12	50	33	214
4	16	14	8	11	10	29	23	20	15	104	7
...	...	1	...	1	...	4	3	...	...	1	...
...	3	9	...	...	...	11	9	...	...	1	1
159	258	109	28	132	96	239	57	59	23	98	49
122	193	92	17	120	38	195	45	44	12	70	34
4,288	8,942	2,278	5,937	729	872	2,520	8,739	701	1,360	1,685	3,571

DISTRICT

	Total for the District.		Chapra.		Manjhi.		Parsa.		Mashrak.	
	Male.	Female.	Male.	Female.	Male.	Female.	Male.	Female.	Male.	Female.
IMMIGRANTS.										
(a) From contiguous districts—										
Shahabad	515	7,105	12	20	106	242	49	81	50	...
Musaffarpur	1,185	8,613	...	2	16	145	449	3,022	2	10
Patna	629	3,378	10	35	41	89	81	328	6	10
Champaran	353	1,178	40	50	14	30	149	76	10	130
Other Provinces—										
Gorakhpur (North-Western Provinces)	1,603	6,319	2	2	194	62	5	6	...	10
Azimgarh (ditto) ...	173	163	...	1	22	11	4	2	10	...
Balia (ditto) ...	1,669	2,862	9	10	276	422	25	12	102	10
Total ...	6,124	29,628	73	120	669	1,001	762	3,527	180	170
(b) From other districts in Bihar	211	910	4	39	11	61	51	68	7	25
(c) From Bengal Proper... ...	47	51	...	...	1	2	1	13	...	9
(d) From Orissa	2	...	...	...	...	...	...	...	...	...
(e) From Chutia Nagpur ...	9	5	...	...	...	...	...	...	...	...
(f) From other Provinces and countries	1,210	1,429	24	43	199	158	49	72	14	36
TOTAL IMMIGRANTS ...	7,603	32,023	101	202	880	1,222	863	3,680	201	240

DISTRICT

	Total for the District.		Matihari.		Govindganj.		Kesaria.		Madhuban.	
	Male.	Female.	Male.	Female.	Male.	Female.	Male.	Female.	Male.	Female.
IMMIGRANTS.										
(a) From contiguous districts—										
Saran	49,278	83,963	3,295	1,056	3,099	3,152	805	2,553	2,060	2,855
Musaffarpur	27,232	28,844	1,319	573	496	363	5,749	4,403	8,299	9,465
Other Provinces—										
Gorakhpur (N.-W. P.)	26,298	14,364	108	44	108	53	10	93	12	10
Total ...	102,808	77,171	4,722	1,673	3,703	3,568	6,564	7,049	10,371	12,330
(b) From other districts in Bihar	8,941	3,350	562	212	157	101	43	91	1,275	2,105
Shahabad	875	426	171	44	91	56	32	6	10	1
Gaya	4,184	324	58	42	42	30	...	...	8	1
Darbhanga	3,051	2,328	88	20	6	5	...	76	1,233	2,089
(c) From Bengal Proper ...	2,305	581	140	70	8	10	...	...	10	...
(d) From Orissa	127	3	6	1	...	...	...	...	...	...
(e) From Chutia Nagpur ...	398	2	7	2	...	...	...	...	2	...
(f) From other Provinces and countries	26,413	26,612	876	363	325	93	300	179	2,091	2,749
North-Western Provinces	8,002	3,522	225	86	103	61	5	...	30	5
Oudh	1,561	1,201	92	35	11	6	...	...	19	...
Nipal	18,561	21,075	396	174	164	20	292	77	1,971	2,572
TOTAL IMMIGRANTS ...	140,992	107,519	6,313	2,321	4,193	3,772	6,907	7,319	13,749	17,184

SARAN.

Sonpur.		Gopalganj.		Mirganj.		Sewan.		Darauli.		Basantpur.	
Male.	Female.	Male.	Female.	Male.	Female.	Male.	Female.	Male.	Female.	Male.	Female.
108	356	50	20	70	12	10	6,200	23	117	37	57
550	5,096	5	2	9	3	...	5	26	52	128	276
414	2,237	10	6	...	28	...	612	44	16	23	17
17	14	20	15	...	6	...	598	34	32	69	227
74	2	...	3	...	...	...	1,505	1,273	4,675	55	64
9	...	1	...	3	3	...	...	104	143	17	3
56	14	20	10	36	60	30	50	1,013	2,188	102	86
1,228	7,719	106	56	118	112	40	8,970	2,517	7,223	431	730
72	90	18	40	1	21	...	534	16	19	31	13
15	7	3	...	6	...	...	...	18	15	3	5
1	...	...	...	...	...	1	...	...	...	...	...
7	1	...	...	...	...	2	...	...	4	...	...
306	117	25	...	86	61	...	378	438	503	69	61
1,629	7,934	152	96	211	194	43	9,882	2,989	7,764	534	809

CHAMPARAN.

Dhaka.		Adapur.		Bettia.		Hardi.		Bagaha.	
Male.	Female.	Male.	Female.	Male.	Female.	Male.	Female.	Male.	Female.
1,304	3,632	7,392	5,405	5,282	4,372	16,685	5,435	9,356	5,503
5,177	7,903	5,045	5,444	385	292	499	312	263	89
21	5	52	12	7,293	299	5,443	1,182	13,251	12,666
6,502	11,540	12,489	10,861	12,960	4,963	22,627	6,929	27,870	18,258
3,697	197	1,847	132	848	338	225	5	287	169
45	21	36	49	251	110	7	...	232	139
3,587	66	267	41	132	119	12	5	28	20
29	95	1,536	29	85	14	74	...	...	...
43	62	21	...	1,967	23	75	...	41	216
1	2	...	...	120	...	...	...	...	...
...	...	...	...	389	...	...	...	...	...
991	2,956	8,317	11,337	4,932	4,100	4,832	4,381	3,749	454
40	9	1,855	304	2,242	1,013	746	503	2,756	641
22	7	67	29	1,039	921	235	32	184	171
903	2,899	4,895	10,678	700	896	3,728	3,713	512	46
11,234	14,757	22,674	22,330	21,216	9,424	27,759	11,315	26,847	19,097

BHAGALPUR

DISTRICT

	Total for the District.		Bhagalpur.		Sultanganj.		Kolgong.		Bihipur.	
	Male.	Female.	Male.	Female.	Male.	Female.	Male.	Female.	Male.	Female.
IMMIGRANTS.										
(a) From contiguous districts—										
Monghyr	25,196	29,124	2,119	1,932	2,501	4,668	3,022	2,843	2,208	3,603
Santal Parganas ...	4,181	6,023	183	128	51	34	1,928	2,740	11	19
Darbhanga	13,061	15,988	371	120	142	74	196	44	209	75
Purnea	8,945	2,120	305	164	18	50	612	885	177	385
Total ...	51,383	60,255	2,978	2,344	2,712	4,826	5,758	6,512	2,600	4,082
(b) From other districts in Bihar	16,124	9,447	2,960	1,502	487	320	2,948	1,374	403	113
Shahabad	3,818	2,331	627	390	180	111	1,262	701	56	39
Patna	2,079	1,300	911	578	42	116	419	307	62	20
Gaya	1,064	2,767	356	205	102	67	156	118	11	22
Muzaffarpur	6,344	2,357	695	254	87	17	651	141	195	25
Saran	2,819	667	371	70	76	9	460	107	79	7
(c) From Bengal Proper	4,721	1,309	754	452	63	40	135	119	37	2
Bardwan	3,119	87	89	26	3	8	10	2	4	2
(d) From Orissa	60	14	41	13	2	...	2	1	1	...
(e) From Chutia Nagpur	536	569	23	30	1	1	186	180	...	1
(f) From other Provinces and countries	8,640	4,406	2,150	1,058	358	105	1,400	818	251	294
North-Western Provinces	4,172	1,774	1,133	428	304	58	1,255	596	189	251
Rajputana	1,053	856	491	510	26	19	18	137	57	22
Nipal	2,113	1,377	1	...	1	...	...	...	...	...
TOTAL IMMIGRANTS ...	81,464	76,000	8,906	5,399	3,623	5,292	10,425	9,004	3,292	4,492

DISTRICT

	Total for the District.		Monghyr.		Gogri.		Jamalpur.		Surajgarha.	
	Male.	Female.	Male.	Female.	Male.	Female.	Male.	Female.	Male.	Female.
IMMIGRANTS.										
(a) From contiguous districts—										
Patna	6,961	12,000	895	165	393	174	...	...	2,601	2,892
Gaya	3,972	6,397	162	156	46	41	...	15	114	163
Santal Parganas ...	325	551	17	53	9	3	...	...	2	...
Darbhanga	8,171	11,111	55	242	5,711	6,917	...	10	65	63
Bhagalpur	8,167	17,251	295	2,904	3,179	9,573	45	...	75	170
Hazaribagh	941	2,530	2	...	1	...	...	...	1	3
Total ...	28,537	49,860	1,426	3,520	9,339	16,708	45	25	2,858	3,291
(b) From other districts in Bihar	7,113	4,840	920	529	3,197	895	70	122	274	177
Shahabad	1,613	838	465	419	428	209	15	...	39	12
Saran	1,426	399	355	1	484	96	5	25	96	64
Muzaffarpur	3,884	3,424	91	31	2,207	560	50	97	137	99

DIVISION.

BHAGALPUR.

Supul.		Pratabganj.		Bangaon.		Madhepura.		Kishanganj.		Banka.		Amarpur.		Katuria.	
Male.	Female.	Male.	Female.	Male.	Female.	Male.	Female.	Male.	Female.	Male.	Female.	Male.	Female.	Male.	Female.
595	350	408	276	1,282	2,269	1,828	1,384	5,783	4,581	819	689	1,772	3,213	2,864	3,316
7	4	4	2	4	2	...	...	12	2	1,079	3,004	85	85	817	3
5,972	7,445	1,144	626	3,366	6,105	997	937	437	515	66	18	10	16	151	13
281	280	630	629	44	85	6,454	6,118	359	471	25	36	14	...	26	17
6,855	8,079	2,186	1,533	4,696	8,461	9,279	8,439	6,591	5,569	1,989	3,747	1,881	3,314	3,858	3,349
3,624	1,461	1,765	529	592	517	1,406	521	452	206	717	399	356	202	414	2,303
157	53	122	58	196	188	242	144	127	75	446	284	180	109	223	179
170	67	92	23	30	25	126	22	33	27	103	41	52	53	39	21
71	55	52	53	8	7	57	18	57	30	81	65	40	29	73	2,098
2,371	1,077	1,032	268	293	267	680	251	158	43	61	8	61	6	60	...
855	199	467	117	65	30	301	86	77	31	26	1	23	5	19	5
173	71	142	34	8	4	66	29	63	...	182	187	2,935	37	183	334
31	15	30	6	...	...	16	9	9	...	9	13	2,905	6	13	...
3	...	...	...	...	...	...	...	...	...	5	...	6	...	...	...
1	...	...	1	...	...	2	1	1	...	144	108	15	15	163	232
1,582	1,278	1,457	367	205	48	487	111	206	115	190	102	225	68	129	42
423	129	133	30	183	29	226	72	106	82	55	46	106	36	59	17
132	41	129	37	4	4	78	7	58	29	49	23	...	23	11	4
571	1,056	1,160	291	11	13	31	16	27	...	2	1	9	...	...	...
12,238	10,889	5,550	2,464	5,501	9,030	11,240	9,101	7,313	5,890	3,227	4,543	5,418	3,836	4,727	6,260

MONGHYR.

Kharakpur.		Begusarai.		Teghra.		Jamui.		Shaikhpura.		Sikandra.		Chakai.	
Male.	Female.	Male.	Female.	Male.	Female.	Male.	Female.	Male.	Female.	Male.	Female.	Male.	Female.
191	74	...	...	342	1,755	64	...	2,082	6,662	255	266	138	102
119	92	...	...	13	21	277	...	2,679	4,847	394	956	168	36
17	21	70	...	3	1	90	...	...	1	7	16	110	456
137	72	...	...	1,958	3,775	93	17	42	13	54	2	56	...
22	3,330	...	55	13	50	280	25	3,911	25	90	233	257	886
20	7	...	...	...	...	...	...	5	27	3	20	909	2,473
506	3,596	70	55	2,329	5,602	804	42	8,719	11,575	803	1,493	1,638	3,953
916	237	92	45	911	2,495	298	12	100	130	69	55	266	143
146	78	17	...	7	6	260	...	22	11	14	3	200	100
278	102	40	25	76	63	21	2	31	3	15	18	25	...
463	47	35	20	794	2,422	17	10	47	101	34	32	9	5

DISTRICT

	Total for the District.		Monghyr.		Gogri.		Jamalpur.		Surajgarha.	
	Male.	Female.	Male.	Female.	Male.	Female.	Male.	Female.	Male.	Female.
(c) From Bengal Proper	1,999	2,039	477	636	169	78	180	33	48	28
Birbhum	281	922	40	179	13	16	20	20	9	6
(d) From Orissa	29	5	...	5	...	...	...	...	4	...
(e) From Chutia Nagpur ...	130	102	80	76	4	2	...	...	...	...
(f) From other Provinces and countries	4,709	1,911	802	879	874	274	88	130	552	174
North-Western Provinces	2,871	1,057	539	433	518	130	73	120	310	55
Rajputana States ...	936	487	45	140	256	130	...	...	203	95
TOTAL IMMIGRANTS ...	42,517	58,757	3,705	5,645	13,583	17,957	383	310	3,736	3,670

DISTRICT

	Total for the District.		Purnea.		Amurkasba.		Dhamdaha.		Gondwara.		Kadwa.	
	Male.	Female.	Male.	Female.	Male.	Female.	Male.	Female.	Male.	Female.	Male.	Female.
IMMIGRANTS.												
(a) From contiguous districts—												
Bhagalpur	32,439	25,332	968	540	72	24	18,136	14,391	4,238	3,266	611	256
Dinajpur	1,670	2,299	4	...	7	4	...	...	44	45	11	23
Malda	1,542	1,833	65	24	4	3	13	6	290	28	15	123
Jalpaiguri	528	700	...	...	2	2	...	...	23	...	18	35
Darjeeling	327	230	...	...	4	4	...	...	15	9	23	79
Santal Parganas ...	367	454	40	52	...	...	104	105	45	54	4	14
Total ...	36,873	30,848	1,077	616	89	37	18,253	14,502	4,655	3,402	682	530
(b) From other districts in Bihar	35,299	14,591	5,629	2,644	1,122	323	6,346	3,746	4,429	1,741	1,906	1,252
Saran	4,259	905	574	196	125	17	195	16	446	82	228	138
Musaffarpur	7,506	1,837	1,386	359	456	89	447	96	753	227	625	257
Gaya	2,621	2,066	609	595	28	12	277	319	366	266	325	128
Patna	1,319	630	237	146	37	6	88	18	47	80	126	40
Darbhanga	6,164	1,555	837	234	139	17	528	92	377	55	246	244
Shahabad	2,202	839	297	75	50	41	260	74	241	71	132	118
Monghyr	11,098	6,686	1,662	1,039	257	141	4,495	3,131	2,171	950	223	312
(c) From Bengal Proper	1,992	1,244	224	299	122	21	94	126	290	181	150	82
(d) From Orissa	3	6	...	...	2	...	...	...	1	...	...	...
(e) From Chutia Nagpur	194	230	4	6	17	...	134	144	8	8	3	18
(f) From other Provinces and countries	8,952	5,016	969	472	194	25	537	354	979	302	911	257
North-Western Provinces	3,987	1,635	751	273	167	15	274	220	716	140	331	104
Nipal	3,296	2,716	79	100	8	5	28	25	11	85	395	126
TOTAL IMMIGRANTS ...	83,313	51,935	7,903	4,037	1,546	406	25,364	18,871	10,362	5,634	3,652	2,139

MONGHYR—*concluded.*

Kharakpur.		Begusarai.		Tegra.		Jamui.		Shaikhpura.		Sikandra.		Chakai.	
Male.	Female.	Male.	Female.	Male.	Female.	Male.	Female.	Male.	Female.	Male.	Female.	Male.	Female.
40	32	269	180	69	47	284	102	71	18	114	94	278	791
10	10	80	45	14	19	10	3	11	5	25	18	49	601
7	...	...	...	5	...	6	...	...	...	...	...	7	...
10	4	10	...	1	...	17	...	12	10	4	...	2	10
467	99	591	141	96	27	629	35	219	41	110	29	281	82
406	38	251	120	41	11	261	35	180	17	82	22	210	77
20	45	62	25	51	10	230	...	29	24	20	7	20	5
1,946	3,968	1,032	421	3,411	8,171	2,038	191	8,111	11,774	1,100	1,671	2,472	4,979

PURNEA.

Balarampur.		Manihari.		Araria.		Matiari.		Raniganj.		Kishenganj.		Bahadurganj.		Kaliaganj.	
Male.	Female.	Male.	Female.	Male.	Female.	Male.	Female.	Male.	Female.	Male.	Female.	Male.	Female.	Male.	Female.
308	177	1,091	1,192	421	213	3,555	3,107	2,410	2,030	142	72	291	35	196	29
670	809	123	4	...	...	25	54	...	...	139	220	9	9	638	1,131
313	510	781	1,078	16	1	25	25	2	4	...	29	13	...	5	2
3	...	18	...	...	...	...	35	...	...	23	3	...	...	441	625
...	...	145	...	...	...	...	15	...	...	8	2	...	2	132	119
9	15	113	170	14	3	9	19	3	3	21	10	...	2	5	7
1,303	1,511	2,271	2,444	451	217	3,614	3,256	2,415	2,037	333	336	313	48	1,417	1,913
1,363	681	2,216	854	2,948	891	3,209	1,263	1,030	304	1,398	359	2,029	402	1,675	131
183	19	418	148	532	98	636	99	143	34	207	36	244	22	328	...
222	28	269	67	598	114	867	350	287	101	368	28	641	95	587	26
67	73	148	69	341	276	169	184	44	34	...	25	97	77	30	8
83	67	192	4	188	86	134	54	32	12	...	64	81	41	74	12
88	36	185	155	868	182	907	310	249	40	400	40	823	135	457	15
117	34	165	105	228	68	340	112	173	48	75	54	59	21	65	18
578	424	815	235	188	52	140	140	83	35	284	97	69	9	133	52
198	100	153	137	104	58	242	79	38	1	137	65	98	45	144	51
...	...	...	2	...	...	...	4	...	...	...	...	...	...	...	...
8	...	8	10	6	14	...	15	...	...	5	3	...	...	1	12
428	131	652	306	390	224	1,323	1,202	66	17	528	202	1,498	1,271	477	253
399	93	496	218	196	136	220	220	29	6	209	118	122	54	157	38
60	15	3	48	98	82	1,000	838	15	4	227	54	1,285	1,194	157	12
3,300	2,423	5,299	3,753	3,899	1,404	8,388	5,818	3,547	2,359	2,401	965	3,938	1,766	3,714	2,360

DISTRICT

	Total for the District.		Malda.		Kharba.		Batua.	
	Male.	Female.	Male.	Female.	Male.	Female.	Male.	Female.
IMMIGRANTS.								
(a) From contiguous districts—								
Santal Parganas	12,088	7,369	4,704	592	...	216	1,211	1,077
Murshidabad	8,681	7,558	755	527	144	130	589	547
Rajshahi	1,907	1,975	24	...	...	14	...	...
Purnea	3,876	4,180	108	115	1,904	2,277	878	975
Dinajpur	1,695	2,082	95	56	364	576	60	42
Total ...	28,247	23,164	5,686	1,290	2,412	3,213	2,738	2,641
(b) From other districts in Bengal	3,616	3,204	872	2,161	221	30	137	168
Bardwan	345	760	108	630	45	...	...	...
Pabna	423	587	203	535	...	1	33	...
(c) From Bihar	10,417	5,254	868	623	1,708	1,101	2,182	1,435
Shahabad	1,009	706	43	56	36	15	192	196
Muzaffarpur	1,389	375	227	30	237	124	202	81
Saran	1,083	108	66	1	156	...	170	...
Bhagalpur	3,896	2,714	236	230	579	502	1,107	987
Monghyr	1,760	1,041	227	181	519	422	296	171
(d) From Orissa	130	8	...	...	47	...	...	...
(e) From Chutia Nagpur	1,569	2,113	...	1,262	120	193	39	10
Lohardaga	830	1,587	...	1,200	...	...	39	...
(f) From other Provinces and countries	5,814	2,588	888	553	613	221	474	504
North-Western Provinces	4,768	284	530	293	529	161	436	504
TOTAL IMMIGRANTS ...	49,793	38,331	8,314	5,889	5,121	4,758	5,570	4,758

DISTRICT SANTAL

	Total for the District.		Deoghar.		Madhupur.		Sarath.		Godda.		Mahagama.		Poreya.		Portion of Daminikoh (Godda Sub-division).	
	Male.	Female.	Male.	Female.	Male.	Female.	Male.	Female.	Male.	Female.	Male.	Female.	Male.	Female.	Male.	Female.
IMMIGRANTS.																
(a) From contiguous districts—																
Manbhum	806	729	34	36	21	12	23	27	30	20	12	6	6	11	38	17
Birbhum	1,472	1,656	61	74	40	27	38	32	159	41	30	17	19	12	148	34
Bhagalpur	3,341	3,212	103	148	52	55	80	61	109	79	51	35	23	10	97	72
Monghyr	6,311	3,311	200	157	103	62	159	70	231	101	98	72	51	17	170	181
Malda	3,140	5,273	111	98	47	59	71	76	89	131	62	53	50	19	37	102
Bardwan	750	904	32	142	20	58	11	17	29	101	62	8	1	2	52	12
Purnea	890	1,004	72	152	31	68	13	22	32	106	106	8	19	7	112	12
Hazaribagh ...	1,008	1,303	77	187	33	74	17	98	40	118	19	88	20	11	191	23
Total ...	17,718	17,392	690	989	347	415	412	403	719	697	440	282	189	89	829	453

MALDA.

Gajol.		English Bazar.		Kaliachak.		Sibganj.		Gumashtapur.		Nawabganj.	
Male.	Female.	Male.	Female.	Male.	Female.	Male.	Female.	Male.	Female.	Male.	Female.
3,880	3,498	384	164	146	154	727	440	585	842	501	386
234	96	1,070	889	398	298	2,576	364	806	2,873	2,109	1,834
...	...	25	...	20	18	489	434	315	381	1,084	1,133
134	24	42	82	...	...	161	66	46	31	608	610
963	1,209	...	...	18	2	139	161	14	19	22	17
5,231	4,827	1,521	1,135	582	467	4,042	1,465	1,716	4,146	4,319	3,980
278	98	925	373	200	65	240	73	427	121	316	115
46	43	18	45	17	...	9	5	14	8	88	29
...	80	102	...	29	...	33	16	15	4	9	1
965	582	2,229	635	705	258	551	261	575	74	634	285
81	8	218	321	90	43	254	46	53	5	42	21
94	...	224	33	225	56	73	19	53	23	55	9
12	39	262	1	61	18	89	22	157	9	110	18
541	376	633	120	212	116	56	154	270	18	262	211
170	141	342	68	78	23	29	2	23	13	76	20
...	...	81	...	...	...	...	7	...	...	2	1
493	33	42	175	223	2	95	60	323	182	234	196
307	33	19	175	223	...	...	...	211	152	31	27
414	200	1,090	618	125	22	311	190	1,204	114	694	166
413	196	803	618	124	22	222	188	1,129	47	583	155
7,381	5,740	5,888	2,936	1,836	814	5,239	2,056	4,245	4,837	6,199	4,743

PARGANAS.

Pakaur.		Mahespur.		Portion of Daminikoh (Pakaur Sub-division).		Rajmahal.		Sahibganj.		Portion of Daminikoh (Rajmahal Sub-division).		Dumka.		Portion of Daminikoh (Dumka Sub-division).		Jamtara.	
Male.	Female.	Male.	Female.	Male.	Female.	Male.	Female.	Male.	Female.	Male.	Female.	Male.	Female.	Male.	Female.	Male.	Female.
103	102	94	72	48	58	52	60	10	12	74	65	44	20	10	4	217	207
51	191	187	104	39	21	106	131	19	11	161	189	21	156	10	99	390	517
412	351	319	200	94	139	213	305	37	95	290	373	599	377	151	11	711	901
942	331	594	191	139	175	440	198	100	12	529	388	853	247	202	197	1,510	912
399	211	322	193	92	172	210	479	35	72	290	617	597	1,632	120	308	608	1,196
141	61	96	18	32	11	98	71	7	4	51	213	19	74	8	11	91	106
35	82	51	15	27	23	157	16	11	9	97	225	65	75	35	91	27	90
51	61	19	85	80	16	187	29	6	13	83	247	72	185	43	15	120	53
2,134	1,390	1,682	808	491	615	1,462	1,289	225	228	1,575	2,320	2,270	2,766	579	736	3,874	3,912

DISTRICT SANTAL

	TOTAL FOR THE DISTRICT.		DEOGHAR.		MADHUPUR.		SARATH.		GODDA.		MAHAGAMA.		POREYA.		PORTION OF DAMINIKOH (GODDA SUB-DIVISION).	
	Male.	Female.	Male.	Female.	Male.	Female.	Male.	Female.	Male.	Female.	Male.	Female.	Male.	Female.	Male.	Female.
(b) From Bengal Proper ...	29,615	29,779	2,311	2,244	1,445	1,074	1,897	2,257	1,560	1,327	581	909	311	1,491	1,494	1,377
Murshidabad ...	2,880	3,050	247	228	79	154	45	327	181	254	37	29	11	120	299	16
Dinajpur	5,374	5,525	136	311	52	285	80	493	111	68	61	29	23	127	95	175
Hugli	6,750	8,136	517	272	211	25	306	339	206	120	79	493	111	541	191	781
Bankura	5,385	8,362	247	119	71	272	241	587	298	411	72	285	17	493	173	311
24-Parganas ..	1,916	1,879	305	212	217	72	733	91	10	82	16	17	6	19	24	6
Nadia	3,465	3,423	253	412	498	94	175	212	335	144	127	44	52	100	421	12
Midnapur	3,895	4,404	606	690	317	172	512	208	410	248	189	12	91	91	291	78
(c) From Bihar	24,772	25,034	1,354	1,297	451	807	1,207	891	712	696	553	655	303	931	763	1,116
Patna	5,338	5,268	287	391	72	643	240	285	199	257	57	48	68	122	172	198
Saran	7,006	8,139	517	273	247	25	611	339	340	121	160	493	89	541	252	781
Shahabad	1,316	1,725	21	206	40	47	41	106	12	72	17	22	3	50	8	6
Gaya	9,565	8,673	288	304	54	72	28	10	101	167	99	74	100	200	188	100
Muzaffarpur ...	1,218	937	182	106	18	12	225	91	30	72	205	4	43	7	122	6
(d) From other Provinces and countries... ...	5,291	3,486	1,458	337	227	53	257	122	232	190	91	201	207	59	279	110
North-Western Provinces	1,793	950	312	104	72	18	49	32	105	12	15	17	105	6	10	8
Oudh	2,023	1,932	990	206	100	11	122	48	7	111	2	106	19	40	9	92
Central Provinces...	957	416	28	11	22	8	45	32	105	60	48	72	65	9	237	4
TOTAL IMMIGRANTS	77,396	75,691	5,813	4,867	2,470	2,349	3,773	3,673	3,223	2,910	1,665	2,047	1,010	2,570	3,365	3,056

ORISSA

DISTRICT

	TOTAL FOR THE DISTRICT.		CUTTACK.		BANKI.		SALEPUR.		TIRTOL.	
	Male.	Female.	Male.	Female.	Male.	Female.	Male.	Female.	Male.	Female.
IMMIGRANTS.										
(a) From Contiguous districts—										
Puri	2,926	9,006	1,157	3,035	506	2,506	79	57	94	110
Balasor	1,111	4,390	202	109	1	2	20	15	4	19
Orissa Tributary States	1,158	5,607	220	578	568	4,115	35	3	1	2
Total ...	5,195	19,003	1,579	3,722	1,075	6,623	134	75	99	131
(b) From Bengal Proper ...	671	656	397	481	1	...	9	26	21	13
(c) From Bihar	248	59	176	5	4	...	5	...	2	...
(d) From Chutia Nagpur ...	47	2	8	2	13	...	...	...	4	...
(e) From other Provinces and countries	2,656	1,397	1,727	779	116	[illegible]	60	22	80	37
Madras	1,116	638	779	498	85	26	33	14	34	13
TOTAL IMMIGRANTS	8,817	21,117	3,887	5,036	1,209	6,709	208	123	216	181

PARGANAS—*concluded.*

Pakaur.		Maheshpur.		Portion of Daminikoh (Pakaur Sub-division).		Rajmahal.		Sahibganj.		Portion of Daminikoh (Rajmahal Sub-division).		Dumka.		Portion of Daminikoh (Dumka Sub-division).		Jamtara.	
Male.	Female.	Male.	Female.	Male.	Female.	Male.	Female.	Male.	Female.	Male.	Female.	Male.	Female.	Male.	Female.	Male.	Female.
2,133	2,192	1,483	1,385	778	1,333	1,176	1,573	640	550	2,112	4,433	7,142	4,769	1,873	1,057	2,879	1,808
95	81	61	184	11	81	208	85	10	45	197	801	747	695	221	205	381	245
321	931	324	254	180	730	201	387	38	59	292	1,095	2,452	187	398	113	610	283
873	923	510	872	200	364	191	493	130	132	383	1,489	1,551	735	402	265	890	292
632	41	280	17	286	12	197	85	301	67	325	391	1,250	163	306	37	600	71
63	35	15	12	35	15	35	80	10	41	85	738	112	306	145	38	100	106
141	95	93	34	59	27	212	422	83	200	609	116	289	693	11	198	107	620
9	86	200	12	8	104	132	12	68	6	221	303	741	1,990	100	201	191	191
1,872	1,543	1,119	1,185	1,103	648	959	1,186	1,142	361	1,807	3,616	5,560	6,328	3,236	1,962	2,631	1,812
639	182	437	153	178	34	203	117	211	88	383	699	1,281	903	199	853	717	295
952	827	512	872	697	461	308	493	405	132	820	1,489	196	735	10	265	890	292
41	52	8	17	21	9	115	211	196	100	140	58	253	360	199	99	201	310
201	411	187	111	199	95	308	317	328	12	364	1,168	3,562	4,091	2,798	702	812	809
38	36	20	29	12	44	22	4	2	9	91	186	190	204	10	38	10	89
129	263	300	124	31	51	277	50	136	124	1,037	575	232	492	82	64	336	681
41	36	225	12	14	34	121	20	18	10	439	189	98	242	2	40	167	170
14	200	20	92	13	12	47	8	81	103	295	273	106	209	51	19	147	402
36	7	35	10	4	5	60	...	35	1	212	81	15	24	5	2	5	90
6,288	5,378	4,584	3,502	2,403	2,647	3,874	4,098	2,143	1,283	6,531	10,944	15,204	14,355	5,550	3,819	9,520	8,213

DIVISION.

CUTTACK.

Jagatsinghpur.		Kendrapara.		Patamundi.		Aul or Rajbari.		Jajpur.		Dharmsala.	
Male.	Female.	Male.	Female.	Male.	Female.	Male.	Female.	Male.	Female.	Male.	Female.
934	3,244	36	14	7	...	19	3	44	27	50	10
...	5	189	35	10	2	100	317	421	3,319	164	567
11	6	24	17	2	...	...	...	45	45	252	841
945	3,255	249	66	19	2	119	320	510	3,391	466	1,418
25	41	75	6	5	...	18	8	83	38	37	43
4	...	13	...	2	...	...	2	15	3	27	3
17	...	...	...	...	...	...	...	...	...	5	...
75	47	266	250	29	21	32	18	83	72	178	85
32	10	49	18	19	11	13	13	11	4	61	31
1,066	3,343	603	322	55	23	169	348	691	3,504	713	1,529

DISTRICT

	Total for the district.		Puri.		Puri Town.	
	Male.	Female.	Male.	Female.	Male.	Female.
IMMIGRANTS.						
(a) From contiguous districts—						
Cuttack	7,128	12,272	458	136	1,876	730
Orissa Tributary States	2,195	6,994	221	161	209	220
Total ...	9,323	19,266	679	297	2,085	950
(b) From other districts in Orissa	209	132	5	2	75	78
(c) From Bengal Proper ...	381	276	37	36	129	175
(d) From Bihar...	273	75	51	6	130	40
(e) From Chutia Nagpur ...	155	3	12	...	40	3
(f) From other Provinces and countries	5,456	4,380	1,287	978	1,049	944
Madras	3,854	3,765	898	877	713	695
TOTAL IMMIGRANTS	15,797	24,132	2,071	1,319	3,508	2,190

DISTRICT

	Total for the District.		Balasor.		Soro.		Jaleswar.		Baliapal.	
	Male.	Female.	Male.	Female.	Male.	Female.	Male.	Female.	Male.	Female.
IMMIGRANTS.										
(a) From contiguous districts—										
Cuttack	5,167	7,130	1,552	309	327	91	127	9	78	26
Midnapur	2,940	4,398	197	157	647	2	986	1,767	788	2,313
Orissa Tributary States	2,203	2,881	1,701	2,803	209	...	148	...	19	...
Total ...	10,310	14,409	3,450	3,269	1,183	93	1,261	1,776	885	2 339
(b) From other districts in Orissa	351	455	22	11	49	24	...	...	3	...
(c) From Bengal Proper ...	796	623	216	334	51	64	25	42	46	2
(d) From Bihar	318	184	198	135	17	...	10	10	1	2
(e) From Chutia Nagpur ...	309	138	281	106	...	...	1	29	...	...
(f) From other Provinces and countries	2,922	4,108	1,558	1,480	160	525	78	104	170	214
North-Western Provinces and Oudh	865	1,308	405	118	67	9	26	5	5	...
TOTAL IMMIGRANTS	15,006	19,917	5,725	5,335	1,460	706	1,375	1,961	2,105	2,557

PURI.

Gop.		Pipli.		Khurda.		Banpur.	
Male.	Female.	Male.	Female.	Male.	Female.	Male.	Female.
1,400	2,953	1,595	4,089	1,563	4,146	236	218
20	6	96	37	1,233	5,627	416	943
1,420	2,959	1,691	4,126	2,796	9,773	652	1,161
6	2	64	33	52	15	7	2
19	...	104	48	77	9	15	8
1	2	70	19	20	8	1	...
7	...	96	...	...	...	...	...
308	37	367	165	689	272	1,756	1,984
79	4	147	74	504	168	1,513	1,947
1,761	3,000	2,392	4,391	3,834	10,077	2,431	3,155

BALASOR.

Basta.		Bhadrak.		Basudebpur.		Dhamnagar.		Chandbali.	
Male.	Female.	Male.	Female.	Male.	Female.	Male.	Female.	Male.	Female.
192	31	930	915	135	11	1,108	5,139	718	599
277	120	8	28	6	...	23	9	8	
101	...	23	56	...	...	1	21	1	1
570	151	961	999	141	11	1,132	5,169	727	602
97	335	50	65	9	...	12	4	109	16
59	10	29	13	3	1	30	21	337	136
31	5	17	13	...	...	16	5	28	14
12	...	9	...	...	...	...	2	6	1
104	154	385	1,381	13	10	105	118	349	122
67	117	134	1,050	7	...	58	7	101	2
873	655	1,451	2,471	168	22	1,295	5,319	1,556	891

ANGUL WITH THE

IMMIGRANTS.
(a) From contiguous districts—
Cuttack ... ...
Sambalpur (Central Provinces)
Madras ... ...
Total ...
(b) From other districts in Bengal Proper
(c) From Bihar ... ...
(d) From Chutia Nagpur ... ...
(e) From other Provinces and countries ...
TOTAL IMMIGRANTS ...

CHUTIA

DISTRICT

	Total for the District.		Hazaribagh.		Barhi.	
	Male.	Female.	Male.	Female.	Male.	Female.
IMMIGRANTS.						
(a) From contiguous districts—						
Gaya	11,454	11,173	929	630	353	161
Lohardaga	2,987	18,291	224	168	20	13
Monghyr	2,516	3,521	32	12	14	5
Manbhum	2,482	4,697	31	17	9	...
Santal Parganas	948	1,804	9	...	2	...
Total ...	20,387	39,486	1,225	827	398	179
(b) From other districts in Chutia Nagpur	...	2	...	...	...	2
(c) From Bengal Proper	1,324	1,008	185	86	37	74
(d) From Bihar	2,424	5,377	391	307	97	49
Shahabad	814	4,182	179	138	65	18
Patna	895	685	122	88	20	14
(e) From Orissa	45	1	30	...	3	...
(f) From other Provinces and countries	2,132	758	372	153	132	39
North-Western Provinces	1,235	329	271	81	101	21
TOTAL IMMIGRANTS ...	26,312	46,632	2,203	1,373	667	343

KANDH MAHALS.

Total for the District.	
Male.	Female.
2,507	1,055
1,089	972
1,139	2,466
4,735	4,493
76	7
3	18
41	6
84	45
4,939	4,569

NAGPUR DIVISION.

HAZARIBAGH.

Bagodhar.		Tandwa.		Ramghar.		Jageswar.		Kasmar.	
Male.	Female.	Male.	Female.	Male.	Female.	Male.	Female.	Male.	Female.
168	53	161	103	185	70	171	57	88	10
28	9	745	984	493	910	104	91	69	103
6	5	2	2	...	1	17	9	8	8
...	6	2	...	145	4	41	393	868	125
3	4	...	...	1	1	22	7	12	4
205	77	900	1,089	824	992	355	557	1,045	250
...	...	...	...	...	...	...	...	...	...
6	4	9	1	13	8	52	26	35	7
106	61	46	9	55	19	58	39	30	10
41	40	9	9	24	17	26	14	13	7
88	14	3	...	13	1	14	4	1	2
3	...	...	...	...	...	1	...	...	...
90	42	30	14	92	12	41	17	79	14
87	25	26	2	23	8	25	5	21	1
410	184	985	1,113	984	1,031	507	639	1,189	281

DISTRICT

	Chauparan.		Huntarganj.		Chatra.		Simaria.	
	Male.	Female.	Male.	Female.	Male.	Female.	Male.	Female.
IMMIGRANTS.								
(a) From contiguous districts ...								
Gaya	678	406	3,481	4,889	905	876	388	170
Lohardaga	7	15	344	344	212	14,954	631	594
Monghyr	3	2	1	...	6	5	...	...
Manbhum	...	1,935	...	3	2	...	...	2
Santal Parganas	...	...	...	...	...	...	2	...
Total ...	688	2,358	3,826	5,236	1,125	15,835	1,021	766
(b) From other districts in Chutia Nagpur	...	...	...	...	...	...	...	...
(c) From Bengal Proper	17	10	2	1	25	6	5	1
(d) From Bihar	94	34	68	66	127	3,764	14	5
Shahabad	30	18	21	36	40	3,718	4	...
Patna	33	3	28	13	56	28	2	5
(e) From Orissa	1	...	...	...	...	1	...	...
(f) From other Provinces and countries	73	44	74	16	116	153	59	23
North-Western Provinces	48	6	23	14	62	19	23	4
TOTAL IMMIGRANTS ...	873	2,446	3,970	5,319	1,393	19,759	1,099	795

DISTRICT

	Total for the District.		Ranchi.		Sili.		Tamar.		Karra.		Mandar.	
	Male.	Female.	Male.	Female.	Male.	Female.	Male.	Female.	Male.	Female.	Male.	Female.
IMMIGRANTS.												
(a) From contiguous districts—												
Hazaribagh	3,060	4,498	757	1,754	406	644	981	891	103	86	434	539
Shahabad	1,120	883	99	189	28	37	151	141	35	4	67	42
Singhbhum	134	129	78	43	37	45	...	21	...	...	...	1
Gaya	2,589	1,839	484	536	203	76	45	24	74	30	58	36
Manbhum	1,292	2,901	120	114	1,105	2,542	21	191	15	3	10	14
Chutia Nagpur Tributary States ...	1,373	1,443	24	15	8	...	13	86	18	14	...	1
Total ...	10,168	11,693	1,562	2,671	1,877	3,344	1,211	1,354	245	137	569	633
(b) From other districts in Chutia Nagpur	57	14	48	1	1	...	...	...	...	2	...	...
(c) From Bengal Proper ...	364	119	167	99	48	...	33	...	19	1	35	...
(d) From Bihar	640	236	211	125	12	3	3	13	27	6	35	...
(e) From Orissa	17	9	17	1	...	...	...	...	...	...	...	...
(f) From other Provinces and countries	1,280	908	702	471	13	...	158	305	...	7	28	12
TOTAL IMMIGRANTS	12,528	12,979	2,707	3,368	1,940	3,347	1,405	1,672	291	153	667	645

HAZARIBAGH—*concluded.*

GIRIDHI.		GAWAN.		KODARMA.		KHARAKDIHA.		DUMURHI.	
Male.	Female.	Male.	Female.	Male.	Female.	Male.	Female.	Male.	Female.
55	878	1,094	2,163	405	314	358	299	2,045	99
6	13	7	3	1	...	...	2	96	82
1,763	1,701	187	269	43	34	359	1,435	76	33
471	866	...	6	5	18	37	...	871	1,322
766	1,544	14	11	5	9	65	172	47	62
3,060	4,997	1,302	2,452	459	375	819	1,908	3,135	1,588
...	...	...	...	...	...	...	...	...	...
809	708	54	3	9	8	30	50	36	15
786	515	105	144	66	22	308	311	73	22
239	110	10	5	26	9	59	42	30	6
286	227	80	132	24	6	149	144	26	4
4	...	2	...	...	...	1	...	...	...
277	76	352	57	68	25	104	27	173	48
161	58	237	47	14	...	54	18	60	21
4,936	6,296	1,815	2,656	602	430	1,262	2,298	3,417	1,671

LOHARDAGA.

KHUNTI.		LOHARDAGA.		CHAINPUR.		TOTO.		PALKOT.		KOCHDAGA.		BASIA.	
Male.	Female.	Male.	Female.	Male.	Female.	Male.	Female.	Male.	Female.	Male.	Female.	Male.	Female.
121	185	285	170	15	...	97	74	116	10	150	74	102	62
207	188	131	62	69	19	121	73	53	11	150	89	9	28
...	1	3	5	1	...	...	1	1	...	1	...	13	12
752	661	304	160	97	40	166	110	120	44	170	17	116	85
1	1	18	23	...	3	...	...	2	6	...	1	...	3
3	4	16	8	84	52	...	2	18	2	...	1,132	1,189	127
1,084	1,040	757	428	266	114	384	260	310	82	474	1,313	1,429	317
...	1	8	...	...	...	...	8	...	2	...	...	...	...
6	2	38	4	3	...	...	...	4	3	1	8	12	2
32	...	94	13	1	1	156	...	5	1	64	60	...	14
...	...	...	...	...	...	...	...	...	...	...	...	...	8
198	34	34	13	1	...	18	4	30	11	19	37	79	14
1,320	1,077	931	458	271	115	558	272	349	99	558	1,418	1,520	355

DISTRICT

	TOTAL FOR THE DISTRICT.		PURULIA.		JHALDA.		BAGHMANDI.		CHANDIL.		BARABHUM.	
	Male.	Female.	Male.	Female.	Male.	Female.	Male.	Female.	Male.	Female.	Male.	Female.
IMMIGRANTS.												
(a) From contiguous districts—												
Singhbhum	846	936	40	56	22	35	...	13	386	475	289	282
Bankura	5,828	6,308	1,103	1,528	474	210	371	42	248	99	752	416
Bardwan	2,068	1,552	736	124	136	36	3	10	32	8	57	13
Lohardaga	2,155	3,225	339	868	51	604	292	21	865	1,555	267	26
Hazaribagh	4,799	6,153	352	124	859	987	77	722	213	158	27	7
Total ...	15,696	18,174	543	2,700	1,542	1,872	743	808	1,744	2,295	1,386	744
(b) From other districts in Chutia Nagpur	1,062	1,621	65	169	...	8	...	11	1	4	4	4
Santal Parganas	1,029	1,588	65	165	...	2	...	...	1	1	1	1
(c) From Bengal Proper ...	1,346	1,161	274	186	57	61	33	11	77	58	221	142
(d) From Bihar	3,923	1,782	602	172	248	126	120	28	378	87	192	40
Gaya	2,654	1,322	435	124	175	26	90	17	277	53	97	25
(e) From Orissa	103	74	56	15	5	2	2	2	23	9	5	41
(f) From other Provinces and countries	1,599	540	357	...	430	270	12	2	134	25	203	45
North-Western Provinces	777	246	310	...	200	200	...	...	100	...	100	...
TOTAL IMMIGRANTS ...	23,729	23,352	3,897	3,242	2,282	2,339	910	882	2,357	2,478	2,010	1,016

DISTRICT

	TOTAL FOR THE DISTRICT.		CHAIBASA.	
	Male.	Female.	Male.	Female.
IMMIGRANTS.				
(a) From continguous districts—				
Manbhum	8,158	3,199	317	611
Lohardaga	6,293	6,110	...	996
Midnapur	3,768	6,096	114	31
Total ...	13,219	15,405	431	1,638
(b) From other districts in Chutia Nagpur	764	511	167	270
Hazaribagh	757	479	164	240
(c) From Bengal Proper ...	1,250	777	439	108
Bankura	619	539	283	70
(d) From Bihar	1,155	434	338	118
(e) From Orissa	2,068	2,445	853	1,323
Cuttack	1,967	2,323	851	1,201
(f) From other Provinces and countries	1,079	202	492	34
TOTAL IMMIGRANTS	18,535	18,774	2,720	3,491

MANBHUM.

Manbazar.		Raghunathpur.		Gaurandi.		Para.		Chas.		Gobindpur.		Nirsa.		Topchanchi.	
Male.	Female.	Male.	Female.	Male.	Female.	Male.	Female.	Male.	Female.	Male.	Female.	Male.	Female.	Male.	Female.
33	39	53	...	30	10	...	6	...	11	...	7	...	...	...	2
1,445	2,112	734	1,030	479	725	38	11	42	38	83	22	91	60	18	15
13	21	434	758	48	50	38	27	37	13	70	36	423	434	41	22
16	17	185	26	2	13	121	60	11	21	...	14	9	...	4	...
24	7	147	237	24	13	24	17	519	964	902	1,017	316	206	1,245	1,694
1,531	2,196	1,553	2,051	583	811	221	121	609	1,047	1,095	1,096	839	700	1,308	1,733
2	2	...	92	...	...	...	6	52	36	548	557	361	683	29	49
1	1	...	92	...	...	...	2	35	35	536	557	361	683	29	49
120	76	137	52	42	115	23	7	20	11	180	221	128	181	34	40
47	24	197	132	210	206	65	19	117	57	491	191	940	588	316	112
40	22	151	84	47	196	49	18	90	29	159	78	807	545	237	105
2	1	4	...	1	...	...	1	1	...	1	3	3	...	...	...
66	43	59	28	2	3	6	4	100	27	3	3	227	90	...	...
2	...	...	2	2	3	6	4	54	...	3	3	...	34	...	...
1,766	2,342	1,950	2,366	838	1,135	315	158	899	1,178	2,318	2,071	2,498	2,242	1,687	1,934

SINGHBHUM.

Chakradharpur.		Manoharpur.		Ghatsila or Dhalbhum.	
Male.	Female.	Male.	Female.	Male.	Female.
249	248	677	422	1,915	1,918
2,884	3,119	3,315	1,860	94	135
3	...	8	2	3,643	6,063
3,136	3,367	4,000	2,284	5,652	8,116
167	59	352	113	78	69
164	59	351	111	78	69
497	24	124	30	190	615
323	4	13	1	...	464
349	203	265	75	213	38
147	22	261	109	807	991
51	22	261	109	804	991
302	77	89	51	196	40
4,598	3,752	5,081	2,662	7,136	9,869

DISTRICT

	Total for the District.		Daltonganj.		Garhwa.		Ranka.		Chhatrapur.	
	Male.	Female.	Male.	Female.	Male.	Female.	Male.	Female.	Male.	Female.
IMMIGRANTS.										
(a) From contiguous districts—										
Hazaribagh ...	3,811	3,579	530	1,245	42	31	25	37	45	25
Shahabad	3,119	2,540	691	27	878	611	100	46	101	142
Singhbhum	4	6	...	1	...	2	...	...	...	...
Gaya	6,755	8,198	451	309	48	386	77	40	2,795	3,510
Manbhum	40	55	35	41	...	...	2	...	...	1
Chutia Nagpur Tributary States ...	8	17	...	4	...	2	...	...	1	1
Total ...	13,737	14,390	1,707	1,627	968	1,032	204	123	2,942	3,680
(b) From Bengal Proper ...	1,266	161	896	34	...	43	8	3	2	2
(c) From Bihar	2,128	52	1,935	2	32	19	...	4	52	3
Muzaffarpur ...	1,007	6	1,001	1	1	...	...	...	3	1
(d) From other Provinces and countries	2,220	1,544	1,337	171	110	718	50	4	25	4
North-Western Provinces	1,569	1,363	910	14	81	712	26	...	14	3
TOTAL IMMIGRANTS	19,351	16,147	5,875	1,834	1,110	1,812	262	134	3,021	3,689

FEUDATORY

KUCH

	Total.		Phulbari.		Kuch Bihar.	
	Male.	Female.	Male.	Female.	Male.	Female.
IMMIGRANTS.						
(a) From contiguous districts—						
Rangpur	8,156	9,360	677	580	122	61
Jalpaiguri	4,841	5,832	322	304	...	9
Total ...	12,997	15,192	999	884	122	70
(b) From other districts in Bengal Proper	3,282	1,201	840	230	797	534
(c) From Bihar	6,494	529	541	50	1,774	157
Muzaffarpur	1,140	95	147	5	436	48
(d) From Orissa	68	2	2	...	45	2
(e) From Chutia Nagpur	54	106	4	...	16	4
(f) From other provinces and countries	5,115	2,189	2,054	1,521	999	208
TOTAL IMMIGRANTS ..	27,990	19,219	4,440	2,685	3,753	975

PALAMAU.

Patan.		Husainabad.		Latihar.		Mahuadanr.		Balumat.	
Male.	Female.	Male.	Female.	Male.	Female.	Male.	Female.	Male.	Female.
348	405	21	...	292	55	56	24	2,452	1,756
233	207	913	1,406	64	36	20	22	119	43
...	1	1	1	1	...	2	...	...	1
1,332	1,116	1,421	2,325	328	186	206	93	97	228
...	1	3	1	...	1	...	...	...	10
4	3	2	2	1	1	...	...	...	4
1,917	1,733	2,361	3,735	686	279	284	139	2,668	2,042
7	2	18	13	11	...	...	...	324	64
40	2	...	20	3	2	...	...	66	...
...	1	...	1	2	2	...	...	...	...
5	106	573	501	50	19	4	3	66	18
1	103	443	500	38	14	2	1	49	16
1,969	1,843	2,952	4,269	750	300	288	142	3,124	2,124

STATES.

BIHAR.

Kotwali.		Matabhanga.		Haldibari.		Mekliganj.		Dinhata.	
Male.	Female.	Male.	Female.	Male.	Female.	Male.	Female.	Male.	Female.
394	259	1,592	1,389	1,902	2,324	843	1,207	2,626	3,540
50	28	46	1,110	1,144	1,961	1,384	2,410	1,895	10
444	287	1,638	2,499	3,046	4,285	2,227	3,617	4,521	3,550
178	61	463	125	167	61	425	78	402	112
1,093	148	1,094	56	435	35	439	39	1,118	44
145	11	142	13	66	8	65	2	130	8
2	...	6	...	...	...	11	...	2	...
25	100	1	...	...	...	2	...	6	2
732	253	488	59	164	26	184	72	494	50
2,474	849	3,680	2,739	3,812	4,407	3,283	3,806	6,543	3,758

	TOTAL.		ATHGARH.		TALCHER.		MOHARBHANJ.	
	Male.	Female.	Male.	Female.	Male.	Female.	Male.	Female.
IMMIGRANTS.								
(a) From contiguous districts—								
Cuttack	16,928	17,077	1,742	2,490	278	55	7,199	6,533
Puri	3,947	7,179	159	201	36	13	56	9
Balasor	9,064	13,884	8	...	1	...	5,368	5,370
Singhbhum	7,999	8,483	...	...	...	...	4,338	4,721
Midnapur	7,876	7,487	...	...	...	...	7,840	7,480
From other Provinces—								
Sambalpur (Central Provinces)	19,279	18,325	96	...	314	496	7,626	6,910
Madras	3,381	2,404	26	19	20	4	62	49
Total ...	68,474	74,929	2,026	2,710	649	568	32,489	31,072
(b) From Bengal Proper ...	3,978	3,756	...	...	14	...	3,629	3,567
(c) From Bihar	328	183	...	...	...	...	164	18
(d) From Chutia Nagpur ...	4,955	4,061	4	...	71	...	3,400	2,848
Lohardaga	2,461	2,367	...	...	...	...	2,421	2,345
Chutia Nagpur Tributary States	1,634	1,467	4	...	7	...	169	264
(e) From other Provinces and countries	825	286	3	...	121	56	180	36
TOTAL IMMIGRANTS	78,560	83,215	2,033	2,710	791	624	39,862	37,539

	HINDOL.		NARSINGHPUR.		BARAMBA.		TIGARIA.	
	Male.	Female.	Male.	Female.	Male.	Female.	Male.	Female.
IMMIGRANTS.								
(a) From contiguous districts—								
Cuttack	445	327	109	121	545	1,294	288	1,105
Puri	38	21	83	87	168	329	117	237
Balasor	5	2	1	1	6	3	...	...
From other Provinces—								
Sambalpur (Central Provinces)	31	43	141	9	64	...	2	...
Madras	37	16	55	15	31	28	2	11
Total ...	556	409	389	233	814	1,654	409	1,353
(b) From Bengal Proper ...	10	4	88	...	...	...	1	...
(c) From Bihar	...	...	...	...	...	...	...	...
(d) From Chutia Nagpur ...	...	1	1	...	3	...	...	...
Lohardaga	...	...	...	...	3	...	...	...
Chutia Nagpur Tributary States	...	1	1	...	...	...	...	...
(e) From other Provinces and countries	4	...	4	2	4	...	82	39
TOTAL IMMIGRANTS	570	414	482	235	821	1,654	492	1,392

TARY STATES.

Nilgiri.		Keonjhar.		Pal Lahera.		Dhenkanal.		Athmalik.	
Male.	Female.	Male.	Female.	Male.	Female.	Male.	Female.	Male.	Female.
289	104	991	1,864	118	7	3,383	2,295	424	27
6	6	16	1	1	...	308	140	44	8
2,888	6,697	747	1,797	...	...	36	12	4	1
...	3,762	3,661	...	...	...	...	...	...	...
...	...	34	5	...	...	2	...	...	...
39	45	95	111	515	482	197	165	2,880	2,652
4	2	25	19	...	...	153	40	84	58
3,226	10,616	5,569	3,797	634	489	4,079	2,652	3,436	2,746
85	87	5	...	...	...	19	13	1	2
...	...	22	13	...	...	1	1	...	...
1,446	...	...	1,160	2	...	39	24	...	4
...	...	...	...	...	...	35	22	...	...
1,446	...	...	1,160	2	...	4	2	...	4
38	9	81	61	15	...	20	12	3	...
4,795	10,712	5,677	5,031	651	489	4,158	2,702	3,440	2,752

Kandhpara.		Nayagarh.		Rampur.		Daspalla.		Boad.	
Male.	Female.	Male.	Female.	Male.	Female.	Male.	Female.	Male.	Female.
175	602	307	121	110	107	156	7	369	18
139	927	991	1,852	1,567	3,305	69	20	149	23
...	...	3	1	1	...	1	...	...	...
136	25	249	312	30	43	60	8	6,795	7,024
135	25	1,388	1,474	110	77	285	150	955	507
585	1,579	2,938	3,760	1,836	3,532	571	185	8,268	7,572
3	2	7	3	46	46	48	20	22	12
...	...	...	...	...	...	33	151	108	...
1	...	4	1	...	...	35	20	13	5
...	...	2	...	...	...	...	...	...	...
1	...	2	1	...	...	35	20	13	5
23	2	3	...	12	5	70	15	162	51
612	1,583	2,952	3,764	1,894	3,583	757	391	8,573	7,640

	TOTAL.		CHANG BHUKAR.		KOREA.		SIRGUJA.	
	Male.	Female.	Male.	Female.	Male.	Female.	Male.	Female.
IMMIGRANTS.								
(a) From contiguous districts—								
Manbhum	1,750	2,408	...	...	...	...	...	...
Singhbhum	4,581	4,958	...	450	...	...	...	...
Lohardaga	49,899	47,341	18	1	2,009	1,885	25,478	24,592
Orissa Tributary States	3	9	...	...	...	...	...	...
From other Provinces—								
Sambalpur (Central Provinces)	6,555	6,244	...	...	51	1	25	14
Total ...	62,788	60,955	13	451	2,060	1,886	25,503	24,606
(b) From other districts in Chutia Nagpur	464	519	...	...	...	...	4	2
(c) From Bengal Proper ...	308	335	...	...	...	...	2	2
(d) From Bihar	1,835	1,153	2	...	61	4	933	643
Shahabad	711	621	2	...	45	4	558	517
Gaya	1,049	500	...	...	16	...	368	126
(e) From Orissa	1,390	1,542	...	...	...	...	48	32
Cuttack	1,365	1,494	...	...	...	...	48	32
(f) From other Provinces and countries	11,904	9,877	2,775	2,471	2,684	2,123	4,401	3,657
North-Western Provinces	5,019	4,083	227	145	1,040	699	3,635	3,111
Central Provinces ...	6,419	5,457	2,547	2,316	1,612	1,420	698	582
TOTAL IMMIGRANTS ...	78,689	74,381	2,790	2,922	4,805	4,013	30,891	28,942

HILL

IMMIGRANTS.
(a) From contiguous districts—
Chittagong ... ...
Noakhali ... ...
Tippera ... ...
Other Provinces—
Sylhet ... ...
Cachar ... ...
Total ...
(b) From other districts in Bengal Proper ...
(c) From Bihar ... ...
(d) From Orissa ... ...
(e) From Chutia Nagpur ... ...
(f) From other Provinces and countries ...
TOTAL IMMIGRANTS ...

TRIBUTARY STATES.

Udaipur.		Jashpur.		Gangpur.		Bonai.		Kharsawan.		Seraikela.	
Male.	Female.	Male.	Female.	Male.	Female.	Male.	Female.	Male.	Female.	Male.	Female.
...	1	...	...	349	926	23	12	...	150	1,378	1,319
...	...	...	...	492	450	574	492	20	...	3,495	3,561
315	198	5,838	5,857	13,464	11,861	388	419	2,015	2,173	329	355
...	...	...	4	3	5	...	...	...	...	...	...
16	30	80	98	6,339	5,995	42	55	...	50	2	1
331	229	5,968	5,959	20,647	19,237	1,027	978	2,035	2,373	5,204	5,236
2	7	260	254	154	87	1	...	...	150	43	19
...	2	18	4	9	29	30	8	9	41	240	249
25	8	363	283	216	158	9	2	10	1	216	54
2	...	53	49	42	45	3	1	...	...	6	5
15	1	310	234	128	92	6	1	10	...	196	46
1	...	...	...	289	401	73	56	5	...	974	1,053
1	...	...	...	288	401	73	55	5	...	950	1,006
107	83	116	32	1,058	871	144	474	597	140	23	26
16	2	27	19	33	7	...	27	22	50	19	23
90	54	85	6	728	627	109	422	550	80	...	...
466	329	6,724	6,532	22,373	27,083	1,284	1,518	2,656	2,705	6,700	6,637

TIPPERA.

Total.	
Male.	Female.
5,064	4,209
2,279	1,252
4,320	2,525
6,024	5,267
43	45
17,730	13,298
685	271
80	43
11	......
12	11
744	443
19,262	14,066

PROVINCIAL TABLE IV—Showing the Statistics of Education by Thanas for Religions with 1,000 or more Adherents in each District and 100 or more Literates, including Pupils.

BARDWAN DIVISION.

DISTRICT BARDWAN.

Thanas.	Hindus.				Musalmans.			
	Pupils.		Literate.		Pupils.		Literate.	
	Male.	Female.	Male.	Female.	Male.	Female.	Male.	Female.
SADAR SUBDIVISION.								
Bardwan	2,291	*57*	6,270	*348*	438	*38*	5,029	*56*
Sahibganj	1,897	*95*	4,130	*197*	287	*30*	515	*59*
Khandaghosh	1,538	*15*	2,931	*40*	451	*3*	661	*11*
Raina	3,359	*38*	5,767	*159*	721	*7*	989	*9*
Satgachhia	2,209	*19*	4,057	*137*	293	*9*	523	*6*
Jamalpur	1,895	*68*	3,918	*208*	458	*22*	632	*7*
Bud-Bud	1,269	*31*	3,784	*71*	658	*18*	739	*9*
Ausgram	1,664	*23*	4,198	*65*	277	*24*	541	*5*
Total ...	16,122	*340*	35,064	*1,155*	3,583	*144*	5,629	*155*
RANIGANJ SUBDIVISION.								
Raniganj	3,248	*83*	7,647	*113*	202	*8*	506	*14*
Asansol	1,695	*13*	5,281	*62*	90	*4*	615	*6*
Kaksa	748	*4*	1,857	*22*	31	...	113	*1*
Total ...	5,691	*100*	14,785	*197*	323	*12*	1,234	*21*
KATWA SUBDIVISION.								
Katwa	1,724	*9*	2,878	*117*	663	*5*	410	*18*
Ketugram	1,712	*23*	2,854	*89*	288	*1*	495	*7*
Mungalkot	1,800	*15*	3,242	*41*	770	*7*	563	*5*
Total ...	5,236	*47*	8,974	*247*	1,721	*13*	1,468	*30*
KALNA SUBDIVISION.								
Kalna	1,883	*43*	4,490	*248*	246	*1*	527	*8*
Purbasthali	1,129	*23*	2,747	*161*	171	*1*	453	*3*
Manteswar	1,727	*13*	3,349	*102*	222	*2*	501	*15*
Total ...	4,739	*79*	10,586	*511*	639	*4*	1,481	*26*
DISTRICT TOTAL ...	31,788	572	69,409	2,110	6,266	173	9,812	232

Thanas.	Christians.			
	Pupils.		Literate.	
	Male.	Female.	Male.	Female.
SADAR SUBDIVISION.				
Bardwan	11	*18*	83	*51*
RANIGANJ SUBDIVISION.				
Raniganj	11	*14*	85	*78*
Asansol	72	*97*	322	*232*
Kaksa	...	*1*	17	*12*
DISTRICT TOTAL ...	94	130	507	373

DISTRICT BANKURA.

Thanas.	Hindus.				Musalmans.			
	Pupils.		Literate.		Pupils.		Literate.	
	Male.	Female.	Male.	Female.	Male.	Female.	Male.	Female.
SADAR SUBDIVISION.								
Bankura	3,637	*51*	9,004	*127*	80	*8*	225	*9*
Onda	2,987	*59*	7,766	*99*	41	...	92	...
Gangajalghati	2,231	*27*	5,648	*25*	11	*9*	56	*3*
Barjora	1,507	*24*	3,530	*81*	38	...	111	*1*
Khatra	3,258	*45*	5,372	*52*	18	*1*	65	*1*
Raipura	1,646	*20*	3,696	*47*	10	...	69	...
Simlapal	792	*72*	2,001	*30*	18	...	52	*3*
Total ...	16,058	*298*	37,017	*461*	216	*11*	670	*17*
BISHNUPUR SUB-DIVISION.								
Bishnupur	4,338	*203*	10,823	*208*	147	*2*	344	*3*
Sonamukhi	2,290	*41*	4,753	*85*	119	*3*	276	*1*
Kotalpur	3,200	*111*	7,797	*133*	196	*4*	440	*4*
Indas	2,326	*104*	4,759	*142*	375	*10*	613	*23*
Total ...	12,204	*459*	28,132	*568*	837	*19*	1,673	*31*
DISTRICT TOTAL ...	28,262	757	65,149	1,029	1,053	30	2,343	48

Thanas.	Christians.				The Animistic.			
	Pupils.		Literate.		Pupils.		Literate.	
	Male.	Female.	Male.	Female.	Male.	Female.	Male.	Female.
SADAR SUBDIVISION.								
Bankura	14	*22*	16	*17*	81	...	48	...
Onda	...	...	1	...	11	...	47	...
Gangajalghatti	...	...	1	...	13	...	6	*1*
Barjora	...	...	...	...	...	...	...	...
Khatra	...	...	...	...	61	*2*	60	...
Raipura	8	*2*	8	...	79	*1*	172	*1*
Simlapal	...	...	...	...	14	...	33	*1*
Total ...	22	*24*	26	*17*	259	*3*	366	*3*
BISHNUPUR SUB-DIVISION.								
Bishnupur	...	*1*	5	*2*	4	...	12	...
Sonamukhi	...	...	2	*1*	...	*1*	...	...
Kotalpur	...	...	...	...	...	...	...	...
Indas	...	...	1	...	...	...	...	...
Total ...	...	*1*	8	*3*	4	*1*	12	...
DISTRICT TOTAL ...	22	25	34	20	263	4	378	3

DISTRICT BIRBHUM.

THANAS.	HINDUS.				MUSALMANS.			
	PUPILS.		LITERATE.		PUPILS.		LITERATE.	
	Male.	Female.	Male.	Female.	Male.	Female.	Male.	Female.
SADAR SUBDIVISION.								
Suri	2,846	*58*	6,789	*189*	407	*22*	818	*27*
Dubrajpur	2,268	*42*	5,718	*119*	450	*11*	1,002	*22*
Bolpur	1,628	*16*	5,540	*78*	239	*7*	821	*6*
Sakulipur	1,406	*19*	2,957	*34*	209	*3*	528	*6*
Labhpur	1,061	*8*	2,731	*29*	137	*4*	287	*4*
Total ...	8,709	*143*	23,735	*449*	1,492	*47*	3,451	*65*
RAMPURHAT SUB-DIVISION.								
Rampur Hat	3,061	*53*	8,191	*126*	1,553	*11*	2,998	*25*
Maureswar	1,605	*20*	3,847	*48*	236	*9*	445	*27*
Nalhati	1,489	*21*	4,378	*63*	1,873	*13*	2,043	*22*
Total ...	6,155	*94*	16,416	*237*	3,662	*33*	5,486	*74*
DISTRICT TOTAL ...	14,864	237	40,161	679	5,154	80	8,937	139

THANAS.	CHRISTIANS.				THE ANIMISTIC.			
	PUPILS.		LITERATE.		PUPILS.		LITERATE.	
	Male.	Female.	Male.	Female.	Male.	Female.	Male.	Female.
SADAR SUBDIVISION.								
Suri	3	*1*	19	*7*	26	...	18	...
Dubrajpur	...	...	...	...	...	...	...	...
Bolpur	...	...	...	...	...	...	...	...
Sakulipur	...	...	...	...	...	...	...	...
Labhpur	...	...	...	...	...	...	...	...
Total ...	8	*1*	19	*7*	26	...	18	...
RAMPUR HAT SUB-DIVISION.								
Rampur Hat	13	*11*	57	*40*	21	...	18	...
Maureswar	...	...	2	...	7	...	6	...
Nalhati	...	...	8	*9*	7	...	30	...
Total ...	18	*11*	67	*49*	35	...	54	...
DISTRICT TOTAL ...	16	12	86	49	61	...	72	...

DISTRICT MIDNAPUR.

Thanas.	Hindus.				Musalmans.			
	Pupils.		Literate.		Pupils.		Literate.	
	Male.	Female.	Male.	Female.	Male.	Female.	Male.	Female.
SADAR SUBDIVISION.								
Midnapur	2,928	*148*	11,440	*671*	327	*28*	1,218	*76*
Jhargon	632	*16*	1,714	*33*	24	...	115	...
Binpur	1,132	*8*	2,666	*23*	18	...	67	*1*
Salbani	712	*4*	1,789	*7*	19	...	66	*3*
Debra	1,786	*13*	5,902	*72*	99	*3*	251	*4*
Garbeta	2,285	*113*	6,194	*297*	97	*4*	252	*8*
Kespur	1,629	*17*	4,733	*50*	267	*3*	656	*9*
Sabang	5,271	*66*	15,612	*234*	146	*2*	371	*6*
Naraingarh	1,892	*22*	6,924	*137*	32	*3*	172	*4*
Dantun	1,398	*18*	5,521	*133*	38	*1*	131	...
Gopibullabpur	775	*12*	4,746	*41*	2	...	49	...
Total ...	20,440	*437*	67,241	*1,688*	1,069	*44*	3,348	*104*
GHATAL SUBDIVISION.								
Ghatal	3,191	*63*	7,590	*118*	92	*1*	298	*4*
Chandrakona	3,598	*103*	7,690	*130*	183	*10*	342	*10*
Daspur	5,136	*67*	10,469	*128*	91	...	186	*7*
Total ...	11,925	*233*	25,749	*376*	366	*11*	826	*21*
TAMLUK SUBDIVISION.								
Tamluk	3,577	*99*	9,158	*255*	248	*14*	512	*15*
Maslandpur	3,814	*81*	9,789	*205*	135	*3*	387	*6*
Sutahata	3,134	*64*	7,647	*159*	230	*5*	649	*11*
Panchkura	4,852	*49*	11,225	*169*	489	*2*	862	*19*
Nandigram	4,517	*67*	8,253	*115*	221	*4*	539	*4*
Total ...	19,894	*360*	46,072	*903*	1,323	*28*	2,949	*55*
CONTAI SUBDIVISION.								
Contai	5,398	*169*	11,932	*376*	185	*5*	397	*11*
Egra	1,536	*29*	4,700	*131*	36	...	78	*2*
Pataspur	2,079	*32*	5,236	*152*	63	*1*	145	*2*
Ramnagar	1,591	*46*	2,190	*51*	44	*3*	63	...
Bhagabanpur	3,380	*44*	6,776	*134*	28	..	80	...
Khajri	1,648	*23*	4,070	*68*	5	*5*	10	*10*
Total ...	15,632	*343*	34,904	*912*	361	*14*	773	*25*
DISTRICT TOTAL ...	67,891	1,373	173,906	3,879	3,119	97	7,896	205

DISTRICT MIDNAPUR—*concluded.*

THANAS.	CHRISTIANS.				THE ANIMISTIC.			
	PUPILS.		LITERATE.		PUPILS.		LITERATE.	
	Male	Female.	Male.	Female.	Male.	Female.	Male.	Female.
SADAR SUBDIVISION.								
Midnapur	42	*23*	93	*66*	15	*2*	33	...
Jhargon	19	*12*	10	*6*	34	*2*	46	...
Binpur	4	*2*	18	*10*	78	*9*	132	*2*
Salbani	35	*31*	22	*15*	42	*7*	40	...
Debra	...	...	2	...	...	...	...	...
Garbeta	...	...	2	*3*	17	*1*	82	...
Keshpur	...	...	...	...	...	...	...	...
Sabang	...	...	...	...	...	...	...	...
Naraingurh	1	*1*	2	*1*	...	...	1	...
Dantun	...	...	1	...	...	...	...	...
Gopiballabpur	4	...	2	...	...	...	...	...
Total ...	105	*69*	152	*101*	186	*21*	334	*2*
GHATAL SUBDIVISION.								
Ghatal	...	...	1	*1*	...	...	...	...
Chandrakona	...	...	...	...	...	...	...	...
Daspur	...	...	...	...	...	...	...	...
Total ...	...	...	1	*1*	...	...	...	...
TAMLUK SUBDIVISION.								
Tamluk	...	...	1	...	...	...	...	...
Maslandpur	...	*16*	33	*21*	...	...	...	...
Sutahata	...	...	...	...	...	...	...	...
Panchkura	...	...	1	*1*	...	...	...	...
Nandigram	...	...	...	...	...	...	...	...
Total ...	...	*16*	35	*22*	...	...	...	...
CONTAI SUBDIVISION.								
Contai	...	...	5	...	...	...	...	...
Egra	...	...	1	...	...	...	...	...
Pataspur	...	...	...	...	...	...	...	...
Ramnagar	...	...	...	...	...	...	...	...
Bhagabanpur	...	...	...	...	...	...	...	...
Khajri	...	...	1	...	...	...	...	...
Total ...	...	...	7	...	...	...	...	...
DISTRICT TOTAL ...	105	85	195	124	186	21	334	2

DISTRICT HUGLI.

Thanas.	Hindus.				Musalmans.				Christians.			
	Pupils.		Literate.		Pupils.		Literate.		Pupils.		Literate.	
	Male.	Female.	Male.	Female.	Male.	Female.	Male.	Female.	Male.	Female.	Male.	Female.
SADAR SUBDIVISION.												
Hugli	2,689	*166*	5,721	*812*	220	*8*	738	*6*	20	*13*	58	*63*
Balagarh	747	*10*	2,447	*238*	53	*7*	267	*7*	...	...	2	*1*
Pandua	1,341	*48*	3,419	*199*	455	*8*	1,240	*9*	6	*4*	29	*10*
Dhantakhali	4,121	*75*	5,214	*287*	842	*3*	113	*2*	...	...	...	
Polba	1,169	*45*	2,790	*95*	600	*4*	729	*13*	...	...	1	...
Total ...	10,067	*344*	19,591	*1,694*	2,170	*30*	3,087	*37*	26	*17*	90	*74*
SERAMPUR SUB-DIVISION.												
Serampur	3,351	*254*	9,286	*1,150*	103	*2*	808	*7*	83	*9*	98	*76*
Haripal	2,645	*34*	6,079	*114*	525	*3*	971	*10*	...	...	...	...
Krishnanagar	1,785	*26*	4,330	*99*	455	*2*	820	*4*	...	...	...	...
Singur	1,821	*19*	4,298	*141*	141	*4*	256	*1*	...	...	1	...
Chanditala	3,072	*54*	8,557	*181*	556	*1*	805	*22*	...	...	...	*3*
Total ...	12,674	*387*	32,559	*1,678*	1,780	*19*	3,660	*53*	83	*9*	99	*79*
JAHANABAD SUB-DIVISION.												
Jahanabad	4,177	*85*	8,021	*142*	860	*2*	889	*21*	...	...	...	...
Goghat	3,604	*63*	8,473	*135*	300	*2*	619	*10*	...	...	...	...
Khanakul	4,713	*47*	9,723	*120*	723	*6*	750	*4*	...	...	...	...
Total ...	12,494	*195*	26,217	*397*	1,883	*10*	2,258	*44*	...	...	...	...
DISTRICT TOTAL ...	35,235	926	78,367	3,699	5,833	52	9,005	134	109	26	189	153

DISTRICT HOWRAH.

Thanas.	Hindus.				Musalmans.				Christians.			
	Pupils.		Literate.		Pupils.		Literate.		Pupils.		Literate.	
	Male.	Female.	Male.	Female.	Male.	Female.	Male.	Female.	Male.	Female.	Male.	Female.
SADAR SUBDIVISION.												
Howrah	3,301	*157*	14,367	*851*	336	*19*	2,495	*65*	121	*92*	708	*585*
Bally	839	*37*	2,281	*203*	21	*2*	138	*3*	1	...	19	*4*
Domjur	3,935	*36*	10,287	*104*	416	*6*	1,443	*6*	7	*5*	22	*10*
Jagatballabhpur	2,287	*4*	5,308	*52*	455	...	1,154	*20*	...	...	...	...
Total ...	10,362	*264*	32,243	*1,210*	1,227	*27*	5,230	*94*	120	*97*	749	*599*
ULUBARIA SUB-DIVISION.												
Ulubaria	1,546	*8*	4,933	*46*	471	*12*	1,302	*16*	...	...	16	*2*
Amta	4,785	*126*	7,675	*156*	653	*3*	1,204	*11*	...	...	...	...
Bagnan	2,434	*32*	4,466	*72*	327	*8*	591	*8*	...	...	1	*1*
Shampur	3,330	*59*	6,259	*101*	315	*2*	678	*5*	...	...	...	...
Total ...	12,104	*225*	23,333	*375*	1,766	*25*	3,775	*40*	...	...	17	*3*
DISTRICT TOTAL ...	22,466	489	55,576	1,585	2,993	52	9,005	134	129	97	766	602

PRESIDENCY DIVISION.

DISTRICT 24-PARGANAS.

THANAS.	HINDUS.				MUSALMANS.				CHRISTIANS.			
	PUPILS.		LITERATE.		PUPILS.		LITERATE.		PUPILS.		LITERATE.	
	Male.	Female.	Male.	Female.	Male.	Female.	Male.	Female.	Male.	Female.	Male.	Female.
SADAR SUBDIVISION.												
Tollyganj	1,854	*211*	8,253	*735*	801	*38*	3,421	*195*	53	*45*	136	*75*
Baruipur	1,575	*189*	4,494	*725*	610	*9*	1,712	*75*	11	*9*	20	*13*
Sonarpur	1,368	*293*	3,079	*492*	114	...	352	*5*	22	*11*	22	*9*
Bishnupur	1,704	*163*	4,655	*359*	310	*6*	912	*11*	133	*63*	242	*81*
Bhangor	627	*4*	2,084	*37*	508	*4*	1,392	*7*	...	...	...	...
Budge-Budge	1,822	*179*	5,088	*381*	259	*3*	720	*9*	2	...	3	*1*
Canning Town	509	*11*	2,334	*78*	224	*3*	972	*7*	11	*9*	60	*18*
Jainagar	2,897	*415*	8,781	*1,483*	779	*3*	2,355	*138*	...	...	1	...
Baranagar	1,311	*207*	2,958	*103*	332	*5*	1,320	*17*	3	*6*	8	*8*
Total ...	13,667	*1,595*	41,726	*4,393*	3,937	*64*	13,186	*387*	235	*136*	492	*205*
BARASAT SUBDIVISION.												
Barasat	1,184	*205*	2,726	*561*	665	*9*	2,359	*27*	3	*7*	9	*7*
Deganga	497	*11*	1,333	*93*	515	*3*	1,801	*23*	...	...	...	...
Habra	908	*54*	2,635	*240*	547	*2*	2,124	*4*	...	*1*	2	*3*
Naihati	1,528	*256*	4,974	*951*	367	*2*	1,399	*9*	8	*5*	60	*41*
Total ...	4,207	*526*	11,688	*1,845*	2,094	*16*	7,683	*63*	11	*13*	71	*51*
DUM-DUM SUBDIVISION.												
Dum-Dum	985	*39*	2,835	*389*	276	*3*	1,088	*5*	30	*38*	1,026	*129*
BARACKPUR SUBDIVISION.												
Barackpur	478	*43*	2,292	*186*	95	...	728	*27*	39	*37*	487	*192*
Nawabganj	423	*29*	1,744	*84*	55	*1*	372	*8*	4	*5*	44	*26*
Khardaha	951	*229*	2,232	*326*	75	*2*	424	*4*	7	*47*	9	*24*
Total ...	1,852	*301*	6,318	*596*	225	*3*	1,524	*39*	50	*89*	540	*242*
BASIRHAT SUBDIVISION.												
Basirhat	1,324	*172*	2,565	*145*	483	*1*	1,518	*16*	...	...	...	...
Baduria	1,415	*197*	3,129	*509*	294	*22*	2,605	*55*	1	...	4	*2*
Haroa	603	*11*	2,086	*25*	363	*1*	1,696	*8*	1	...	6	*3*
Husainabad	996	*26*	2,752	*454*	182	*1*	638	*2*	...	...	6	...
Total ...	4,318	*406*	11,132	*1,126*	1,321	*25*	6,457	*81*	2	...	16	*5*
DIAMOND HARBOUR SUBDIVISION.												
Diamond Harbour	2,118	*200*	5,229	*491*	637	*4*	1,479	*8*	6	...	11	*9*
Kulpi	4,570	*184*	10,696	*431*	825	*2*	2,298	*21*	10	*6*	48	*6*
Bankipur	3,169	*171*	8,377	*432*	1,220	*25*	3,477	*18*	90	*45*	251	*77*
Debipur	1,726	*142*	3,709	*344*	280	*11*	611	*10*	...	...	3	...
Mathurapur	1,967	*176*	4,861	*378*	800	...	881	*10*	14	*3*	42	*17*
Total ...	13,550	*873*	32,862	*2,076*	3,762	*42*	8,746	*67*	120	*54*	355	*109*

DISTRICT 24-PARGANAS—*concluded.*

THANAS.	HINDUS.				MUSALMANS.				CHRISTIANS.			
	PUPILS.		LITERATE.		PUPILS.		LITERATE.		PUPILS.		LITERATE.	
	Male.	Female.	Male.	Female.	Male.	Female.	Male.	Female.	Male.	Female.	Male.	Female.
SUBURBS, CALCUTTA.												
Cossipur-Chitpur M. C. ...	718	41	3,022	449	69	1	436	5	17	4	86	64
Maniktola M. C.	1,158	13	2,900	89	105	10	564	21	30	14	25	46
Entally	8	...	81	2	1	...	2	...	...	...	...	...
Calcutta Canals	3	...	156	1	3	...	105	...	...	...	...	...
Total ...	1,887	54	6,159	541	178	11	1,107	26	47	18	111	110
Sundarbans	25	1	183	4	...	...	111	...	...	...	5	2
DISTRICT TOTAL ...	40,521	3,788	112,903	10,970	11,793	164	39,872	668	495	348	2,616	853

DISTRICT NADIA.

THANAS.	HINDUS.				MUSALMANS.				CHRISTIANS.			
	PUPILS.		LITERATE.		PUPILS.		LITERATE.		PUPILS.		LITERATE.	
	Male.	Female.	Male.	Female.	Male.	Female.	Male.	Female.	Male.	Female.	Male.	Female.
SADAR SUBDIVISION.												
Krishnanagar	2,080	241	6,328	864	324	4	952	27	72	102	70	76
Kaliganj	564	10	1,269	61	41	1	196	6	...	...	...	...
Nakasipara	702	49	1,765	172	68	11	306	2	...	...	3	...
Chapra	353	4	1,125	42	211	...	565	2	79	54	150	114
Krishnanganj	473	27	1,177	95	64	...	234	3	...	...	...	2
Hanskhali	187	2	851	24	134	...	676	3	1	1	17	3
Jibannagar	338	7	906	27	85	...	367	...	...	...	...	...
Total ...	4,696	333	13,421	1,285	927	16	3,299	43	152	157	240	195
RANAGHAT SUBDIVISION.												
Ranaghat	1,178	144	3,061	359	160	...	754	3	...	...	3	...
Santipur	1,349	79	3,353	457	193	...	563	15	...	1	1	3
Chakdaha	908	11	3,030	157	119	9	752	9	3	1	27	13
Haringhata	276	12	575	83	153	14	554	18	...	..	...	...
Total ...	3,711	246	10,019	1,056	625	23	2,623	45	3	2	31	16
KUSHTIA SUBDIVISION.												
Kushtia	351	21	901	46	109	...	337	15	2	1	2	3
Naupara	815	16	2,458	111	344	16	1,130	10	5	1	33	8
Daulatpur	400	6	1,182	32	128	...	481	1	...	...	3	...
Bhadalia	588	25	1,102	31	230	...	638	2	...	...	...	...
Kumarkhali	983	38	2,332	140	324	...	713	7	...	...	...	...
Bhaluka	309	20	805	70	104	...	489	2	...	...	...	...
Total ...	3,506	126	8,840	430	1,329	16	3,788	37	7	2	38	11

DISTRICT NADIA—*concluded.*

Thanas.	Hindus.				Musalmans.				Christians.			
	Pupils.		Literate.		Pupils.		Literate.		Pupils.		Literate.	
	Male.	Female.	Male.	Female.	Male.	Female.	Male.	Female.	Male.	Female.	Male.	Female.
MIHRPUR SUBDIVISION.												
Mihrpur	507	9	1,463	99	112	...	414	1	84	98	101	89
Karimpur	428	5	1,900	51	211	...	723	2	...	1	13	6
Gangni	289	...	822	4	156	...	531	...	10	4	31	19
Tehata	610	1	1,664	11	149	...	520	...	28	25	39	40
Chuadanga	152	11	343	23	124	...	321	2	...	...	1	...
Damurhuda	668	30	1,438	78	53	...	386	2	25	47	55	51
Alamdanga	573	1	1,756	49	290	9	943	12	...	...	1	...
Kalupol	222	1	679	14	101	...	388	...	...	...	...	...
Total ...	3,449	58	10,064	329	1,196	9	4,226	19	97	175	241	198
DISTRICT TOTAL ...	15,362	763	42,344	3,093	4,077	57	13,936	144	259	336	550	420

DISTRICT JESSOR.

Thanas.	Hindus.				Musalmans.				Christians.			
	Pupils.		Literate.		Pupils.		Literate.		Pupils.		Literate.	
	Male.	Female.	Male.	Female.	Male.	Female.	Male.	Female.	Male.	Female.	Male.	Female.
SADAR SUBDIVISION.												
Jessor	905	139	4,448	578	835	25	4,052	15	24	10	50	33
Kaliganj	511	63	2,009	222	356	...	2,199	5	...	...	4	3
Bagherpara	390	60	1,505	215	177	2	975	3	...	...	...	...
Gadkhali	509	68	1,396	208	226	1	1,040	4	39	47	8	6
Monirampur	1,065	138	3,643	260	505	16	3,032	26	...	...	1	...
Keshubpur	851	158	2,564	350	284	3	1,609	19	3	2	5	4
Total ...	4,231	626	15,625	1,833	2,383	47	12,907	72	66	59	68	46
JHENIDAHA SUBDIVISION.												
Jhenidaha	514	52	2,135	242	269	24	1,890	13	...	1	10	5
Sailkopa	1,215	240	3,776	296	683	3	2,363	14	...	...	5	4
Kotchandpur	252	4	988	177	116	22	916	2	...	...	5	...
Total ...	1,981	296	6,899	715	1,068	49	5,169	29	...	1	20	9
MAGURA SUBDIVISION.												
Magura	909	89	4,479	383	365	...	1,875	26	...	...	9	5
Muhamadpur	787	81	2,198	262	359	19	1,030	7	...	...	5	2
Salikha	127	...	1,028	186	32	15	553	7	...	...	...	...
Total ...	1,823	170	7,705	831	756	34	3,458	40	...	...	14	7

DISTRICT JESSOR—*concluded.*

THANAS.	HINDUS.				MUSALMANS.				CHRISTIANS.			
	PUPILS.		LITERATE.		PUPILS.		LITERATE.		PUPILS.		LITERATE.	
	Male.	Female.	Male.	Female.	Male.	Female.	Male.	Female.	Male.	Female.	Male.	Female.
NARAIL SUBDIVISION.												
Narail	2,061	*108*	5,042	*367*	275	*2*	1,421	*18*	...	...	3	*3*
Lohagara	1,387	*89*	3,941	*253*	321	*1*	1,248	*37*	...	...	2	...
Kalia	1,056	*77*	2,491	*323*	152	...	862	*5*	...	...	...	...
Total ...	4,504	*267*	11,474	*943*	748	*3*	3,531	*60*	...	...	5	*3*
BANGAON SUBDIVISION.												
Bangaon	406	*68*	1,615	*238*	177	*4*	865	*4*	...	...	4	*1*
Mahespur	667	*69*	2,090	*254*	355	*3*	1,821	*14*	4	...	2	*1*
Garapota	341	*59*	1,168	*181*	183	...	766	*9*	...	...	...	...
Sarsa	233	*53*	1,220	*176*	154	...	1,122	*6*	...	...	...	...
Gaighata	287	*53*	993	*46*	143	*2*	663	*4*	...	...	...	...
Total ...	1,934	*302*	7,086	*895*	1,012	*9*	5,242	*37*	4	...	6	*2*
DISTRICT TOTAL ...	14,473	1,661	48,789	5,217	5,967	142	30,307	238	70	60	113	67

DISTRICT MURSHIDABD.

THANAS.	HINDUS.				MUSALMANS.			
	PUPILS.		LITERATE.		PUPILS.		LITERATE.	
	Male.	Female.	Male.	Female.	Male.	Female.	Male.	Female.
SADAR SUBDIVISION.								
Sujaganj ... ... *Gora Bazar* ... ... *Berhampur Municipality* ...	1,166	*140*	3,242	*509*	121	*15*	448	*18*
Bardwan	565	*1*	1,586	*18*	171	*1*	583	*9*
Daulatabazar	265	*1*	869	*16*	77	...	365	*3*
Hariharpara	374	*4*	1,244	*41*	116	...	418	...
Nowada	390	*4*	1,125	*16*	91	*1*	276	...
Goas	371	*8*	1,325	*15*	273	*3*	851	*6*
Jalinghi	599	*20*	1,777	*65*	269	*2*	1,111	*6*
Total ...	3,730	*178*	11,168	*680*	1,118	*22*	4,052	*49*
LALBAGH SUBDIVISION.								
Shahnagar ... ... *Manulabazar* ... ... *Asanpur* ... ... *Lalbagh Municipality*	1,043	*97*	3,316	*289*	347	*14*	935	*44*
Bhagabangola	213	*1*	807	*9*	191	...	533	*1*
Sagardighi	181	*4*	538	*8*	134	*2*	270	*2*
Kaliaganj	319	*2*	708	*3*	131	*1*	310	*3*
Total ...	1,756	*104*	5,309	*309*	803	*17*	2,048	*50*

DISTRICT MURSHIDABAD—*continued.*

Thanas.	Hindus.				Musalmans.			
	Pupils.		Literate.		Pupils.		Literate.	
	Male.	Female.	Male.	Female.	Male.	Female.	Male.	Female.
JANGIPUR SUBDIVISION.								
Raghunathganj	803	46	1,644	92	321	4	783	7
Shamsherganj	453	6	1,544	26	306	2	954	6
Suti	567	6	1,382	18	261	...	597	4
Dewan Sarai	313	2	838	17	300	6	652	7
Mirzapur	433	3	1,254	24	114	...	363	2
Total ...	2,269	63	6,662	177	1,302	12	3,349	26
KANDI SUBDIVISION.								
Kandi	739	18	1,558	126	43	1	100	2
Barwa	1,043	29	2,306	85	266	1	501	6
Khargaon	768	6	1,562	22	268	3	429	4
Bharatpur	1,737	21	3,312	91	742	80	1,310	115
Gokarna	284	4	830	13	96	1	286	...
Total ...	4,571	78	9,568	337	1,415	86	2,626	127
DISTRICT TOTAL ...	12,326	423	32,767	1,503	4,638	137	12,075	245

Thanas.	Christians.				Jains.			
	Pupils.		Literate.		Pupils.		Literate.	
	Male.	Female.	Male.	Female.	Male.	Female.	Male.	Female.
SADAR SUBDIVISION.								
Sujaganj ... . / *Gora Bazar* ... ... / *Barhampur Municipality* ...	9	7	50	41	1	...	5	...
Burwan	...	...	7	6	...	...	...	...
Daulatabazar	...	...	...	...	...	...	...	...
Hariharpara	1	...	...	...	...	...	...	...
Nowada	...	...	4	...	...	...	...	...
Goas	...	...	3	1	...	...	...	...
Jalinghi	...	1	5	2	...	...	1	...
Total ...	10	8	69	50	1	...	6	...
LALBAGH SUBDIVISION.								
Shahnagar ... ... / *Manulabazar* ... ... / *Azanpur* ... ... / *Lalbagh Municipality* ...	2	5	10	6	83	9	663	27
Bhagabangola	1	...	5	1	...	...	4	...
Sagardighi	...	...	2	1	1	...	5	...
Kaliaganj	1	...	...	...	...	...	1	...
Total ...	4	5	17	8	84	9	673	27

DISTRICT MURSHIDABAD—*concluded.*

Thanas.	Christians.				Jains.			
	Pupils.		Literate.		Pupils.		Literate.	
	Mal	Female.	Male.	Female.	Male.	Female.	Male.	Female.
JANGIPUR SUBDIVISION.								
Raghunathganj	...	...	2	...	3	...	20	*1*
Shamsherganj	...	...	...	*1*	4	...	11	...
Suti	...	...	...	...	3	...	16	...
Dewan Sarai	...	...	1	...	...	...	...	...
Mirzapur	...	...	...	...	...	...	4	...
Total ...	...	...	3	*1*	10	...	51	*1*
KANDI SUBDIVISION.								
Kandi	...	...	...	...	...	...	...	...
Barwa	...	...	...	...	...	...	...	...
Khargaon	...	...	...	...	...	...	...	...
Bharatpur	1	*3*	...	*3*	...	...	...	...
Gokarna	...	...	...	...	...	...	...	...
Total ...	1	*3*	...	*3*	...	...	...	...
DISTRICT TOTAL ...	15	16	89	62	95	9	730	28

DISTRICT KHULNA.

Thanas.	Hindus.				Musalmans.				Christians.			
	Pupils.		Literate.		Pupils.		Literate.		Pupils.		Literate.	
	Male.	Female.	Male.	Female.	Male.	Female.	Male.	Female.	Male.	Female.	Male.	Female.
SADAR SUBDIVISION.												
Khulna	2,329	*87*	6,111	*425*	476	*3*	2,129	*26*	20	*4*	44	*26*
Dumuria	1,132	*48*	2,634	*126*	344	*9*	1,225	*7*	...	...	...	...
Baitaghata	167	*3*	801	*5*	166	*1*	308	*1*	...	...	2	*1*
Paikgacha	656	*44*	2,129	*109*	208	*1*	732	*10*	4	*2*	5	*7*
Total ...	4,284	*182*	11,675	*665*	1,194	*7*	4,454	*44*	24	*6*	51	*30*
BAGHERHAT SUBDIVISION.												
Bagherhat	3,039	*93*	8,981	*296*	724	*7*	2,392	*44*	...	...	4	...
Mullahat	191	...	1,185	*9*	116	*6*	708	*7*	...	...	...	...
Rampal	275	...	1,455	*8*	151	...	705	*2*	16	*9*		*27*
Morellganj	9	...	284	...	3	...	208	*1*	...	...	1	*3*
Total ...	3,514	*93*	11,905	*313*	994	*13*	4,013	*54*	16	*9*	91	*30*
SATKHIRA SUBDIVISION.												
Satkhira	946	*67*	2,646	*77*	654	*2*	2,288	*21*	...	...	2	...
Kalaroa	657	*5*	1,797	*51*	423	*6*	1,719	*14*	...	...	...	...
Magura	781	*70*	1,612	*156*	186	...	696	*8*	...	...	...	...
Asasuni	431	*11*	1,968	*37*	299	*4*	1,138	*2*	...	...	...	...
Kaliganj	1,975	*75*	5,451	*229*	644	*9*	2,301	*13*	...	...	3	*3*
Total ...	4,790	*228*	13,474	*543*	2,206	*21*	8,142	*58*	...	...	5	*3*
DISTRICT TOTAL ...	12,588	503	37,054	1,521	4,394	41	6,609	156	40	8	147	63

RAJSHAHI DIVISION.

DISTRICT DINAJPUR.

Thanas.	Hindus.				Musalmans.				Christians.			
	Pupils.		Literate.		Pupils.		Literate.		Pupils.		Literate.	
	Male.	Female.	Male.	Female.	Male.	Female.	Male.	Female.	Male.	Female.	Male.	Female.
SADAR SUBDIVISION.												
Dinajpur	930	*10*	4,410	*60*	1,457	*18*	6,789	*60*	6	*12*	24	*13*
Hemtabad	1,184	...	5,172	...	864	*1*	2,290	...	...	...	1	...
Kaliganj	568	*9*	1,881	*26*	397	*23*	1,111	*12*	...	...	...	...
Bansihari	211	*11*	1,176	*4*	580	*16*	2,277	*25*	...	...	1	...
Birganj	398	*5*	2,553	*21*	419	*15*	2,338	*32*	...	...	...	...
Patnitolla	161	...	937	*10*	399	*6*	1,287	*3*	...	...	...	...
Mahadevpur	318	*8*	1,386	*36*	439	*9*	1,405	*16*	...	...	...	...
Porsha	90	*3*	700	*10*	402	*10*	1,127	*9*	...	...	...	...
Patiram	407	*3*	1,957	*30*	394	*18*	1,724	*16*	1	*1*	18	*3*
Gangarampur ...	328	*9*	1,797	*15*	405	*9*	2,311	*10*	...	...	...	...
Chintaman	284	*4*	1,290	*27*	349	*9*	1,264	*9*	...	...	...	...
Parbatipur	95	*1*	1,029	*7*	417	*2*	2,560	*10*	...	...	11	*5*
Nawabganj	92	...	593	*7*	364	*4*	1,611	*3*	...	...	...	...
Total ...	5,066	*56*	24,881	*253*	6,936	*140*	28,084	*205*	7	*13*	55	*21*
THAKURGAON SUBDIVISION.												
Thakurgaon	784	*12*	2,903	*16*	1,037	*13*	4,401	*56*	...	...	...	...
Ranisankail	874	*12*	1,234	*41*	396	*8*	1,340	*15*	...	...	...	...
Pirganj	400	*11*	1,693	*21*	455	*9*	1,746	*16*	...	...	5	*2*
Total ...	1,558	*35*	5,920	*78*	1,888	*30*	7,487	*87*	...	...	5	*2*
DISTRICT TOTAL ...	6,624	91	30,801	331	8,824	170	35,571	292	7	13	60	23

DISTRICT RAJSHAI.

Thanas.	Hindus.				Musalmans.			
	Pupils.		Literate.		Pupils.		Literate.	
	Male.	Female.	Male.	Female.	Male.	Female.	Male.	Female.
SADAR SUBDIVISION.								
Boalia	1,001	*110*	2,555	*305*	584	*15*	1,983	*17*
Tanor	180	*2*	697	*14*	350	*27*	1,454	*16*
Godagari	74	...	640	*3*	198	*24*	723	*5*
Putia	495	*48*	1,423	*251*	10	...	144	...
Charghat	686	*59*	1,987	*133*	519	*2*	1,702	*12*
Baghmara	134	*2*	768	*28*	706	*6*	2,249	*18*
Total ...	2,570	*214*	8,070	*734*	2,326	*74*	8,248	*68*
NAUGAON SUBDIVISION.								
Naugaon	304	*7*	1,536	*51*	696	*3*	1,998	*13*
Manda	252	*71*	1,322	*224*	375	*24*	1,912	*18*
Panchupur	382	*12*	1,230	*44*	843	*9*	2,465	*33*
Total ...	1,928	*90*	4,088	*319*	1,913	*36*	6,375	*59*

DISTRICT RAJSHAHI—*concluded.*

Thanas.	Hindus.				Musalmans.			
	Pupils.		Literate.		Pupils.		Literate.	
	Male.	Female.	Male.	Female.	Male.	Female.	Male.	Famale.
NATOR SUBDIVISION.								
Nator	931	*38*	2,242	*179*	775	*23*	2,048	*27*
Singra	455	*6*	1,849	*79*	488	*8*	2,352	*9*
Burigram	288	*9*	1,102	*24*	270	*2*	1,405	*4*
Lalpur	317	*12*	1,105	*33*	241	*28*	682	*13*
Total ...	1,991	*65*	6,298	*315*	1,774	*61*	487	*53*
DISTRICT TOTAL ...	5,598	369	18,456	1,368	6,013	171	21,110	180

DISTRICT RANGPUR.

Thanas.	Hindus.				Musalmans.			
	Pupils.		Literate.		Pupils.		Literate.	
	Male.	Female.	Male.	Female.	Male.	Female.	Male.	Female.
SADAR SUBDIVISION.								
Rangpur	767	*37*	2,678	*130*	672	*1*	2,306	*26*
Kaliganj	808	*15*	3,057	*60*	524	*11*	1,456	*16*
Mahiganj	803	*15*	2,042	*44*	350	*4*	1,790	*7*
Badarganj	183	*3*	1,016	*11*	565	*9*	2,217	*16*
Mithapukhur	196	*4*	671	*11*	484	*7*	1,553	*20*
Pirganj	133	*1*	448	*7*	383	*3*	1,251	*11*
Total ...	2,889	*75*	9,912	*263*	2,978	*35*	10,573	*96*
NILPHAMARI SUB-DIVISION.								
Dimla	932	*12*	2,975	*24*	849	*20*	2,189	*31*
Jaldhaka	658	*4*	2,277	*22*	579	*1*	2,079	*10*
Nilphamari	404	*16*	2,735	*54*	557	*9*	3,099	*15*
Total ...	1,994	*32*	7,987	*100*	1,985	*39*	7,367	*56*
KURIGRAM SUB-DIVISION.								
Barabari	612	*3*	2,561	*19*	476	*4*	1,555	*14*
Kurigram	214	...	624	*3*	197	...	674	*7*
Nageswari	511	*3*	2,286	*23*	235	...	768	*3*
Ulipur	615	*9*	2,159	*27*	556	*4*	1,905	*9*
Total ...	1,952	*15*	7,630	*72*	1,404	*8*	4,902	*33*
GAIBANDA SUB-DIVISION.								
Gobindganj	250	*2*	976	*5*	426	*6*	1,712	*6*
Sadullapur	490	*11*	2,364	*50*	621	*1*	2,203	*15*
Sundarganj	185	...	689	...	245	...	537	*2*
Total ...	925	*13*	4,029	*55*	1,292	*7*	4,452	*23*
DISTRICT TOTAL ...	7,260	135	29,558	490	7,719	89	27,294	208

DISTRICT RANGPUR—*concluded.*

THANAS.	CHRISTIANS.				JAINS.			
	PUPILS.		LITERATE.		PUPILS.		LITERATE.	
	Male.	Female.	Male.	Female.	Male.	Female.	Male.	Female.
SADAR SUBDIVISION.								
Rangpur	7	*3*	13	*4*	5	...	70	...
Kaliganj	...	...	...	...	...	...	...	...
Mahiganj	...	...	...	...	...	...	24	...
Badarganj	...	...	...	...	...	...	...	...
Mithapukhur	...	...	...	...	...	...	...	...
Pirganj	...	...	...	...	...	...	...	*4*
Total ...	7	*3*	13	*4*	5	...	94	*4*
NILPHAMARI SUB-DIVISION.								
Dimla	...	...	...	...	3	...	38	...
Jaldhaka	...	...	...	...	3	...	20	...
Nilphamari	35	*20*	79	*79*	...	...	39	...
Total ...	85	*20*	79	*79*	6	...	97	...
KURIGRAM SUB-DIVISION.								
Barabari	...	...	...	...	1	...	8	...
Kurigram	...	...	5	...	1	*1*	8	*1*
Nageswari	...	...	...	...	...	...	105	...
Ulipur	...	...	...	...	6	...	49	...
Total ...	...	...	5	...	8	*1*	170	*1*
GAIBANDA SUB-DIVISION.								
Gobindganj	...	...	...	...	1	...	16	*2*
Sadullapur	...	...	...	...	2	...	56	*1*
Sundarganj	...	...	...	...	3	...	31	...
Total ...	...	...	...	...	6	...	103	*3*
DISTRICT TOTAL ...	42	23	97	83	25	1	464	8

DISTRICT BOGRA.

THANAS.	HINDUS.				MUSALMANS.			
	PUPILS.		LITERATE.		PUPILS.		LITERATE.	
	Male.	Female.	Male.	Female.	Male.	Female.	Male.	Female.
Bogra	903	*69*	2,751	*149*	3,040	*45*	8,165	*61*
Shariakandi	358	*4*	1,241	*16*	1,065	*17*	2,596	*6*
Sibganj	177	*3*	647	*8*	532	*1*	1,648	*9*
Panchbibi	226	*6*	1,364	*22*	326	*4*	1,282	*9*
Khetlal	94	*6*	300	*9*	719	*6*	1,806	*19*
Nawabganj	229	*5*	753	*29*	301	...	1,111	*4*
Adamdighi	480	*3*	1,760	*49*	1,319	*11*	3,337	*14*
Sherpur	434	*7*	1,403	*69*	488	*7*	1,555	*3*
DISTRICT TOTAL ...	2,901	98	10,225	330	7,790	91	21,519	118

DISTRICT PABNA.

THANAS.	HINDUS.				MUSALMANS.			
	PUPILS.		LITERATE.		PUPILS.		LITERATE.	
	Male.	Female.	Male.	Female.	Male.	Female.	Male.	Female.
SADAR SUBDIVISION.								
Pabna	1,630	*99*	4,220	*340*	862	*8*	2,441	*49*
Chatmohar	808	*10*	2,582	*126*	494	*4*	1,956	*9*
Dulai	1,702	*21*	4,088	*169*	755	*10*	2,226	*15*
Mathura	1,067	*9*	3,008	*111*	357	...	1,117	*5*
Total ...	5,207	*139*	13,898	*746*	2,468	*22*	7,740	*78*
SIRAJGANJ SUB-DIVISION.								
Sirajganj	1,626	*26*	5,429	*119*	1,506	*19*	4,614	*43*
Shahzadpur	1,939	*38*	4,396	*143*	1,180	*17*	2,956	*29*
Raiganj	574	*4*	2,028	*67*	349	...	1,393	*2*
Ulapara	533	*10*	1,148	*79*	893	*14*	2,852	*6*
Total ...	4,672	*78*	13,001	*408*	3,928	*50*	11,815	*80*
DISTRICT TOTAL ...	9,879	210	26,899	1,154	6,396	72	19,555	158

THANAS.	CHRISTIANS.				JAINS.			
	PUPILS.		LITERATE.		PUPILS.		LITERATE.	
	Male.	Female.	Male.	Female.	Male.	Female.	Male.	Female.
SADAR SUBDIVISION.								
Pabna	...	*8*	38	*24*	1	...	18	...
Chatmohar	...	...	...	...	...	...	...	...
Dulai	...	...	1	...	...	...	...	...
Mathura	...	...	3	*3*	...	...	16	...
Total ...	...	*8*	42	*27*	1	...	34	...
SIRAJGANJ SUB-DIVISION.								
Sirajganj	1	...	*44*	*8*	5	...	205	...
Shahzadpur	...	...	...	...	...	...	...	...
Raiganj	...	...	...	...	...	...	...	...
Ulapara	...	...	...	...	...	...	...	...
Total ...	1	...	*44*	*8*	5	...	205	...
DISTRICT TOTAL ...	1	8	86	35	6	...	239	...

DISTRICT DARJEELING.

Thanas.	Hindus.				Musalmans.			
	Pupils.		Literate.		Pupils.		Literate.	
	Male.	Female.	Male.	Female.	Male.	Female.	Male.	Female.
Darjeeling	670	*41*	4,584	*95*	28	*4*	414	*10*
Kalimpong	237	*19*	1,448	*93*	5	*1*	23	*3*
Jor Bangala	255	*6*	1,433	*13*	4	...	33	*1*
Kurseong	352	*24*	1,401	*43*	47	*3*	79	*8*
Siliguri	305	*10*	1,747	*49*	53	*4*	294	*4*
DISTRICT TOTAL ...	1,819	93	10,613	216	137	12	843	26

Thanas.	Christians.				Buddhists.			
	Pupils.		Literate.		Pupils.		Literate.	
	Male.	Female.	Male.	Female.	Male.	Female.	Male.	Female.
Darjeeling	23	*25*	309	*85*	137	*2*	999	*26*
Kalimpong	37	*19*	72	*91*	72	...	462	*8*
Jor Bangala	3	*2*	23	*14*	57	*9*	260	*16*
Kurseong	23	*4*	54	*38*	68	*2*	270	*23*
Siliguri	3	*10*	84	*28*	7	*4*	39	*26*
DISTRICT TOTAL ...	89	53	492	186	341	10	2,030	99

DISTRICT JALPAIGURI.

Thanas.	Hindus.				Musalmans.			
	Pupils.		Literate.		Pupils.		Literate.	
	Male.	Female.	Male.	Female.	Male.	Female.	Male.	Female.
SADAR SUBDIVISION.								
Jalpaiguri	634	*43*	2,756	*110*	470	*15*	1,651	*40*
Rajganj	159	*3*	710	*29*	349	*15*	814	*16*
Titalya	123	*6*	878	*36*	115	*13*	318	*5*
Boda	1,177	*23*	2,289	*65*	1,041	*54*	3,251	*65*
Patgram	467	*3*	1,741	*20*	217	*3*	865	*20*
Mainaguri	591	*9*	3,009	*34*	266	*1*	723	*16*
Dam-Dim	170	*9*	2,517	*44*	99	*2*	707	*7*
Total ...	3,321	*96*	13,394	*329*	2,557	*103*	8,323	*169*
ALIPORE SUBDIVISION.								
Alipore	239	...	1,150	*9*	60	...	247	*1*
Salbari	246	*3*	1,871	*19*	83	*1*	551	*8*
Total ...	485	*3*	3,021	*28*	142	*1*	798	*9*
DISTRICT TOTAL ...	3,806	99	16,415	357	2,699	104	9,121	178

DISTRICT JALPAIGURI—*concluded.*

THANAS.	CHRISTIANS.				BUDDHISTS.				JAINS.			
	PUPILS.		LITERATE.		PUPILS.		LITERATE.		PUPILS.		LITERATE.	
	Male.	Female.	Male.	Female.	Male.	Female.	Male.	Female.	Male.	Female.	Male.	Female.
SADAR SUBDIVISION.												
Jalpaiguri	1	*3*	33	*15*	...	...	3	...	5	...	16	...
Rajganj	...	...	...	...	...	...	...	...	...	...	...	...
Titalya	1	*1*	1	...	...	...	...	...	...	...	3	...
Boda	...	...	...	...	...	...	...	...	...	...	10	...
Patgram	...	...	...	...	...	...	...	...	1	...	23	...
Mainaguri	1	...	27	*5*	...	...	17	...	...	...	7	...
Dam-Dim	1	*2*	95	*16*	6	...	51	...	...	...	...	...
Total ...	4	*6*	156	*36*	6	...	71	...	6	...	59	...
ALIPORE SUBDIVISION.												
Alipore	2	*3*	9	*3*	4	...	55	*2*	1	...	3	...
Salbari	...	*1*	14	*4*	...	...	...	...	1	...	38	...
Total ...	2	*4*	23	*7*	4	...	55	*2*	2	...	41	...
DISTRICT TOTAL ...	**6**	**10**	**179**	**43**	**10**	...	**126**	**2**	**8**	...	**100**	...

DACCA DIVISION.

DISTRICT DACCA.

THANAS.	HINDUS.				MUSALMANS.				CHRISTIANS.			
	PUPILS.		LITERATE.		PUPILS.		LITERATE.		PUPILS.		LITERATE.	
	Male.	Female.	Male.	Female.	Male.	Female.	Male.	Female.	Male.	Female.	Male.	Female.
SADAR SUBDIVISION.												
Lalbagh	4,075	*221*	10,501	*840*	1,459	*170*	3,521	*277*	31	*28*	191	*123*
Kapasia	807	*44*	2,555	*98*	454	*4*	1,207	*21*	23	*25*	9	*5*
Sabhar	2,061	*42*	5,545	*191*	404	*3*	1,376	*19*	...	...	9	*4*
Nawabganj	1,829	*44*	4,978	*179*	609	*15*	1,808	*51*	51		121	*4*
Keraniganj	1,679	*64*	5,484	*375*	721	*20*	2,228	*75*	11	*9*	10	...
Total	10,511	*415*	29,063	*1,683*	3,647	*219*	10,140	*443*	116	*70*	340	*136*
NARAINGANJ SUB-DIVISION.												
Naraingan	1,516	*32*	5,532	*247*	679	*14*	1,648	*17*	3	*1*	51	*16*
Rupganj	1,716	*87*	4,505	*369*	734	*7*	2,094	*27*	89	*48*	42	*18*
Raipura	1,049	*43*	3,915	*193*	887	*6*	3,007	*32*	2	...	2	...
Total	4,281	*162*	13,952	*739*	2,300	*27*	6,749	*76*	94	*40*	95	*34*

DISTRICT DACCA—*concluded.*

THANAS.	HINDUS.				MUSALMANS.				CHRISTIANS.			
	PUPILS.		LITERATE.		PUPILS.		LITERATE.		PUPILS.		LITERATE.	
	Male.	Female.	Male.	Female.	Male.	Female.	Male.	Female.	Male.	Female.	Male.	Female.
MANIKGANJ SUB-DIVISION.												
Manikganj	1,806	*68*	5,143	*347*	429	*6*	1,251	*16*	...	...	2	...
Jaffarganj	1,378	*38*	4,209	*217*	318	*4*	899	*10*	...	...	...	*2*
Harirampar	1,012	*11*	3,192	*117*	255	*7*	708	*9*	...	...	...	...
Total	4,196	*117*	12,544	*681*	1,002	*17*	2,858	*35*	...	...	2	*2*
MUNSHIGANJ SUB-DIVISION.												
Munshiganj	5,677	*296*	10,316	*1,408*	1,508	*25*	3,689	*56*	1	...	1	...
Srinagar	6,865	*337*	12,694	*1,622*	1,071	*41*	2,783	*46*	2	...	7	...
Total	12,542	*633*	23,010	*3,030*	2,579	*66*	6,472	*102*	3	...	8	...
DISTRICT TOTAL ...	31,530	1,327	78,569	6,133	8,528	322	26,219	656	213	119	445	172

DISTRICT FARIDPUR.

THANAS.	HINDUS.				MUSALMANS.				CHRISTIANS.			
	PUPILS.		LITERATE.		PUPILS.		LITERATE.		PUPILS.		LITERATE.	
	Male.	Female.	Male.	Female.	Male.	Female.	Male.	Female.	Male.	Female.	Male.	Female.
SADAR SUBDIVISION.												
Faridpur	1,235	*57*	3,547	*291*	276	*9*	914	*18*	9	...	12	*17*
Bhusna	1,034	*26*	3,203	*88*	300	*3*	1,110	*14*	...	...	...	...
Awanpur	755	*34*	2,473	*98*	268	*3*	1,152	*13*	...	...	...	...
Bhunga	1,673	*36*	4,359	*180*	432	*29*	2,090	*35*	...	...	4	*1*
Maksudpur	1,853	*69*	4,059	*178*	620	*8*	1,688	*21*	10	*1*	8	*4*
Total	6,550	*222*	18,831	*765*	1,896	*52*	6,954	*101*	19	*1*	24	*22*
MADARIPUR SUB-DIVISION.												
Madaripur	2,287	*74*	5,885	*290*	634	*14*	2,223	*24*	9	*2*	26	*8*
Gopalganj	923	*43*	3,829	*205*	289	*11*	1,312	*46*	12	*18*	16	*15*
Kotalipara	1,049	*36*	3,603	*162*	71	...	448	*4*	38	*11*	140	*44*
Palang	3,731	*149*	9,927	*829*	796	*42*	3,214	*83*	...	...	1	...
Sibchar	857	*16*	2,567	*96*	373	*4*	1,531	*12*	...	...	...	...
Total	8,847	*318*	25,811	*1,582*	2,163	*71*	8,728	*169*	59	*31*	183	*67*

DISTRICT FARIDPUR—*concluded.*

THANAS.	HINDUS.				MUSALMANS.				CHRISTIANS.			
	PUPILS.		LITERATE.		PUPILS.		LITERATE.		PUPILS.		LITERATE.	
	Male.	Female.	Male.	Female.	Male.	Female.	Male.	Female.	Male.	Female.	Male.	Female.
GOALANDA SUB-DIVISION.												
Goalanda	1,294	*80*	4,416	*931*	387	*1*	1,489	*11*	5	*11*	74	*28*
Baliakandi	1,151	*48*	2,449	*196*	278	*2*	573	*6*	...	...	...	...
Pangsa	1,149	*37*	2,874	*112*	539	*8*	1,089	*13*	1	*1*	1	*2*
Total	3,594	*165*	9,739	*539*	1,204	*11*	3,151	*30*	6	*12*	75	*30*
DISTRICT TOTAL ...	18,991	705	53,881	2,886	5,263	134	18,833	300	84	44	282	119

DISTRICT BAKHARGANJ.

THANAS.	HINDUS.				MUSALMANS.			
	PUPILS.		LITERATE.		PUPILS.		LITERATE.	
	Male.	Female.	Male.	Female.	Male.	Female.	Male.	Female.
SADAR SUBDIVISION.								
Katwali (Barisal) ...	2,783	*185*	6,624	*533*	1,067	*19*	3,897	*66*
Bakharganj	1,366	*50*	5,142	*120*	821	*31*	3,307	*46*
Mehndiganj	1,008	*12*	3,302	*53*	1,190	*22*	2,935	*42*
Gaurnadi	4,173	*168*	9,136	*613*	851	*27*	2,856	*13*
Jhalakati	3,750	*238*	9,470	*648*	1,241	*33*	4,259	*67*
Nalchiti	1,418	*98*	3,850	*213*	443	*11*	2,032	*17*
Total ...	14,498	*751*	37,524	*2,180*	5,613	*143*	19,286	*251*
PATUAKHALI SUB-DIVISION.								
Patuakhali	477	*12*	3,871	*88*	671	*17*	4,729	*53*
Bauphal	558	*21*	2,597	*38*	1,235	*16*	3,808	*44*
Gulsakhali	99	*2*	1,646	*10*	874	*8*	2,335	*18*
Golachipa	162	*2*	1,956	*7*	531	*8*	1,850	*9*
Total ...	1,296	*37*	10,070	*143*	2,811	*49*	12,812	*124*
PIROJPUR SUBDIVISION.								
Pirojpur	1,728	*53*	7,287	*171*	1,088	*34*	4,634	*111*
Bhandaria	436	*6*	2,310	*15*	527	*3*	2,315	*37*
Saruphati	8,574	*152*	11,704	*713*	916	*28*	3,976	*56*
Matbaria	260	*3*	2,384	*10*	623	*9*	2,600	*32*
Total ...	6,007	*214*	23,775	*909*	3,153	*74*	13,525	*236*

DISTRICT BAKHARGANJ—*concluded.*

THANAS.	HINDUS.				MUSALMANS.			
	PUPILS.		LITERATE.		PUPILS.		LITERATE.	
	Male.	Female.	Male.	Female.	Male.	Female.	Male.	Female.
DAKHIN SHAHBAZPUR SUBDIVISION.								
Bhola	491	*20*	2,402	*54*	1,628	*51*	3,561	*56*
Barhanuddin	431	*4*	2,213	*6*	1,178	*31*	3,170	*25*
Total ...	922	*24*	4,615	*60*	2,806	*89*	6,751	*81*
DISTRICT TOTAL ...	22,723	1,026	75,984	3,292	14,383	348	52,374	692

THANAS.	CHRISTIANS.				BUDDHISTS.			
	PUPILS.		LITERATE.		PUPILS.		LITERATE.	
	Male.	Female.	Male.	Female.	Male.	Female.	Male.	Female.
SADAR SUBDIVISION.								
Katwali (Barisal) ...	33	*67*	80	*54*	...	...	14	...
Bakharganj	12	...	57	*5*	...	...	...	...
Mehndiganj	...	...	...	...	...	...	...	...
Gournadi	77	*9*	170	*54*	...	...	...	...
Jhalakati	5	...	8	...	...	...	...	...
Nalchiti	...	...	7	*1*	...	...	11	...
Total ...	127	*76*	322	*114*	...	...	25	...
PATUAKHALI SUBDIVISION.								
Patuakhali	...	...	6	...	...	...	...	...
Bauphal	...	...	...	...	...	...	...	...
Gulsakhali	...	...	1	...	36	*2*	968	*40*
Golachipa	...	...	...	...	18	...	65	*3*
Total ...	...	...	7	...	54	*2*	1,033	*43*
PIROJPUR SUBDIVISION.								
Pirojpur	1	...	3	*2*	...	...	...	...
Bhandaria	...	...	...	...	...	...	...	...
Sarupkati	2	...	10	*4*	...	...	...	...
Matbaria	1	...	4	...	...	...	...	...
Total ...	4	...	17	*6*	...	...	...	...
DAKHIN SHAHBAZPUR SUBDIVISION.								
Bhola	...	...	2	...	...	...	...	...
Barhanuddin	...	*3*	2	*1*	...	...	...	...
Total ...	...	*3*	4	*1*	...	...	...	...
DISTRICT TOTAL ...	131	79	350	121	54	2	1,058	43

DISTRICT MAIMANSINGH.

THANAS.	HINDUS.				MUSALMANS.			
	PUPILS.		LITERATE.		PUPILS.		LITERATE.	
	Male.	Female.	Male.	Female.	Male.	Female.	Male.	Female.
SADAR SUBDIVISION.								
Nasirabad	1,672	*93*	5,945	*347*	751	*46*	2,965	*103*
Phulpur	422	*11*	2,212	*57*	332	*6*	1,343	*18*
Gafargaon	500	*26*	1,963	*52*	665	*28*	1,719	*30*
Iswarganj	1,193	*64*	4,919	*211*	899	*13*	3,157	*50*
Phulbaria	152	*16*	839	*12*	251	*3*	1,160	*13*
Total ...	3,939	*210*	15,878	*679*	2,898	*96*	10,344	*214*
NETRAKONA SUB-DIVISION.								
Netrakona	1,819	*89*	6,043	*215*	709	*14*	2,609	*40*
Durgapur	705	*51*	3,002	*79*	178	*2*	624	*12*
Kendua	1,452	*55*	5,132	*123*	698	*30*	2,807	*107*
Total ...	3,976	*195*	14,177	*417*	1,585	*46*	6,040	*159*
JAMALPUR SUB-DIVISION.								
Jamalpur	1,034	*14*	3,638	*87*	1,263	*6*	3,412	*33*
Diwanganj	225	*1*	1,352	*24*	491	*6*	1,696	*23*
Sherpur	455	*9*	1,750	*60*	386	*3*	1,260	*9*
Nalitabari	251	*4*	1,072	*5*	214	*2*	729	*6*
Total ...	1,965	*28*	7,862	*176*	2,354	*17*	7,097	*71*
TANGAIL SUBDIVISION.								
Tangail	4,092		10,556	*137*	1,306	*15*	3,995	*80*
Gopalpur	987	*9*	4,596	*96*	867	*9*	4,289	*76*
Kalihati	1,005	*13*	3,036	*94*	354	*3*	1,162	*21*
Total ...	6,084	*213*	18,188	*327*	2,527	*27*	9,446	*183*
KISORGANJ SUB-DIVISION.								
Kisorganj	1,325	*118*	3,679	*171*	756	*71*	1,680	*42*
Nikli	1,210	*27*	3,208	*133*	619	*32*	1,439	*38*
Bajitpur	1,517	*72*	6,116	*157*	779	*18*	2,866	*95*
Total ...	4,052	*217*	13,003	*461*	2,154	*121*	5,985	*175*
DISTRICT TOTAL ...	20,016	863	69,108	2,060	11,518	307	38,912	802

DISTRICT MAIMANSINGH—*concluded.*

THANAS.	CHRISTIANS.				JAINS.			
	PUPILS.		LITERATE.		PUPILS.		LITERATE.	
	Male.	Female.	Male.	Female.	Male.	Female.	Male.	Female.
SADAR SUBDIVISION.								
Nasirabad	9	*17*	29	*18*	6	...	25	...
Phulpur	3	...	6	...	...	...	...	...
Gafargaon	...	...	4	*1*	...	...	...	...
Iswarganj	...	...	...	...	...	...	...	...
Phulbaria	...	...	...	...	...	...	3	...
Total ...	12	*17*	39	*19*	6	...	28	...
NETRAKONA SUB-DIVISION.								
Netrakona	1	...	2	...	...	...	...	...
Durgapur	...	...	4	*2*	...	...	...	...
Kendua	...	...	...	...	...	...	...	...
Total ...	1	...	6	*2*	...	...	...	...
JAMALPUR SUB-DIVISION.								
Jamalpur	...	...	2	...	1	...	10	...
Diwanganj	...	...	...	...	2	...	35	...
Sherpur	...	...	...	...	2	...	27	...
Nalitabari	...	...	1	...	...	...	...	...
Total ...	...	...	3	...	5	...	72	...
TANGAIL SUB-DIVISION.								
Tangail	...	...	...	*1*	...	...	1	...
Gopalpur	6	*1*	4	*2*	...	...	...	...
Kalihati	...	...	...	...	...	...	...	...
Total ...	6	*1*	4	*3*	...	...	1	...
KISORGANJ SUB-DIVISION.								
Kisorganj	1	*1*	4	*2*	...	...	...	...
Nikli	...	...	...	...	...	...	...	...
Bajitpur	...	...	...	...	...	...	...	...
Total ...	1	*1*	4	*2*	...	...	...	...
DISTRICT TOTAL ...	20	19	56	26	11	...	101	...

CHITTAGONG DIVISION.

DISTRICT CHITTAGONG.

Thanas.	Hindus.				Musalmans.			
	Pupils.		Literate.		Pupils.		Literate.	
	Male.	Female.	Male.	Female.	Male.	Female.	Male.	Female.
SADAR SUBDIVISION.								
Chittagong	979	20	2,943	98	2,169	88	3,617	134
Mirserai	808	93	1,620	19	1,287	59	1,812	28
Kumira	550	9	1,414	24	1,123	27	1,989	50
Phatikchari	569	20	1,861	31	1,023	26	2,680	35
Hathazari	934	10	1,920	44	1912	29	2,230	29
Baujan	1,446	49	3,938	99	1,125	39	3,648	44
Patia	3,428	87	6,495	253	2,064	57	4,433	40
Banskhali	660	13	2,708	43	884	93	2,624	45
Satkania	819	111	2,411	27	1,767	28	4,229	153
Total ...	10,193	244	25,310	624	12,354	389	27,262	558
COX'S BAZAR SUB-DIVISION.								
Cox's Bazar	93	3	659	10	232	20	661	20
Chakaria	59	2	349	1	431	45	710	21
Maiskal	45	3	377	...	102	1	379	5
Teknaf	10	...	143	...	340	13	444	8
Total ...	207	8	1,528	11	1,105	79	2,194	63
DISTRICT TOTAL ...	10,400	252	26,838	635	13,459	468	29,456	621

Thanas.	Christians.				Buddhists.			
	Pupils.		Literate.		Pupils.		Literate.	
	Male.	Female.	Male.	Female.	Male.	Female.	Male.	Female.
SADAR SUBDIVISION.								
Chittagong	70	57	148	93	25	...	129	...
Mirserai	...	...	...	...	15	...	24	...
Kumira	...	...	7	...	2	...	19	...
Phatikchari	1	...	4	4	39	1	225	2
Hathazari	1	...	4	1	44	...	104	...
Baujan	...	...	8	1	291	2	952	13
Patia	...	...	4	1	380	2	741	9
Banskhali	...	1	6	9	5	...	65	...
Satkania	...	...	1	..	62	...	226	6
Total ...	72	58	182	109	863	5	2,485	30
COX'S BAZAR SUB-DIVISION.								
Cox's Bazar	...	...	3	1	249	11	367	56
Chakaria	...	...	...	...	64	5	323	17
Maiskal	...	...	2	...	43	...	397	5
Teknaf	...	...	...	...	107	8	539	54
Total ...	...	...	5	1	463	24	1,626	139
DISTRICT TOTAL ...	72	58	187	110	1,326	29	4,111	162

DISTRICT NOAKHALI.

Thanas.	Hindus.				Musalmans.			
	Pupils.		Literate.		Pupils.		Literate.	
	Male.	Female.	Male.	Female.	Male.	Female.	Male.	Female.
SADAR SUBDIVISION.								
Sudharam	1,064	*58*	2,856	*148*	1,604	*82*	3,191	*66*
Hatia	276	*10*	973	*23*	846	*14*	1,322	*20*
Bamni	221	*3*	784	*9*	636	*7*	1,492	*19*
Ramganj	1,463	*52*	2,987	*63*	2,053	*65*	2,944	*41*
Lakshmipur	1,242	*48*	3,154	*64*	2,314	*82*	4,139	*49*
Begamganj	1,553	*26*	4,022	*53*	1,763	*72*	3,324	*25*
Sundwip	650	*3*	1,541	*20*	1,073	*22*	2,235	*29*
Total ...	6,469	*200*	16,317	*373*	10,289	*344*	18,647	*249*
FENNY SUBDIVISION.								
Fenny	1,081	*12*	3,010	*45*	2,041	*63*	4,235	*47*
Chhagalnaia	814	*12*	2,610	*19*	1,237	*25*	3,255	*34*
Total ...	1,895	*24*	5,620	*64*	3,278	*88*	7,490	*81*
DISTRICT TOTAL ...	8,364	224	21,937	437	13,567	432	26,137	323

DISTRICT TIPPERA.

Thanas.	Hindus.				Musalmans.				Christians.			
	Pupils.		Literate.		Pupils.		Literate.		Pupils.		Literate.	
	Male.	Female.	Male.	Female.	Male.	Female.	Male.	Female.	Male.	Female.	Male.	Female.
SADAR SUBDIVISION.												
Comilla	1,704	*106*	5,548	*221*	2,481	*63*	7,415	*191*	10	*7*	29	*21*
Muradnagar	2,575	*130*	6,800	*151*	2,144	*21*	4,653	*46*	1	...	2	*1*
Daudkandi	1,157	*51*	4,198	*92*	1,278	*12*	6,156	*35*	...	...	...	...
Chandina	697	*38*	2,280	*58*	516	*17*	1,470	*13*	...	...	...	...
Chaudagram	682	*13*	2,405	*45*	867	*24*	2,850	*34*	...	...	...	...
Laksham	641	*17*	2,125	*34*	879	*38*	2,433	*29*	...	...	...	...
Total ...	7,446	*355*	23,356	*601*	8,165	*175*	21,977	*278*	11	*7*	31	*22*
BRAHMANBARIA SUBDIVISION.												
Brahmanbaria	2,703	*132*	8,058	*328*	1,107	*47*	3,024	*61*	1	...	11	*4*
Kasba	14,62	*50*	4,697	*109*	810	*6*	2,445	*25*	...	...	...	...
Nabinagar	1,743	*29*	5,288	*168*	1,571	*26*	3,616	*49*	...	...	1	...
Total ...	5,908	*211*	18,043	*605*	3,488	*79*	9,085	*135*	1	...	12	*4*
CHANDPUR SUB-DIVISION.												
Chandpur	2,983	*118*	7,902	*240*	3,143	*131*	5,388	*53*	9	...	3	...
Hajiganj	825	*45*	2,938	*51*	1,117	*27*	2,593	*14*	...	...	...	...
Total ...	3,808	*163*	10,840	*300*	4,260	*158*	7,981	*67*	9	...	3	...
DISTRICT TOTAL ...	17,162	729	52,239	1,506	15,913	412	39,043	480	21	7	46	26

NOTE—Details regarding education are not available for the Chittagong Hill Tracts. (*See* note on title-page of Imperial Table VII.)

PATNA DIVISION.

DISTRICT PATNA.

THANAS.	HINDUS.				MUSALMANS.				CHRISTIANS.			
	PUPILS.		LITERATE.		PUPILS.		LITERATE.		PUPILS.		LITERATE.	
	Male.	Female.	Male.	Female.	Male.	Female.	Male.	Female.	Male.	Female.	Male.	Female.
SADAR SUBDIVISION.												
Pirbahor	938	*29*	2,253	*208*	520	*19*	795	*49*	5	*56*	10	*118*
Sultanganj	240	*3*	1,185	*78*	98	*7*	331	*24*	...	...	1	...
Alamganj	/ 286	*7*	2,275	*52*	117	*8*	495	*31*	3	*3*	20	*16*
Khwaja Kalan	419	*6*	2,338	*59*	406	*15*	1,309	*124*	...	...	2	*4*
Chauk Kalan	359	*5*	2,367	*51*	107	*6*	405	*21*	3	...	8	*3*
Malsalami	171	...	1,670	*88*	48	*3*	165	*3*	...	...	...	*9*
Bankipur	903	*10*	4,484	*198*	80	*1*	438	*10*	117	*28*	178	*107*
Bikram	671	*7*	6,817	*200*	60	*1*	392	*7*	...	...	1	...
Masaudhi Basrug	888	*38*	4,822	*130*	162	*2*	529	*3*	...	*1*	...	*2*
Total ...	4,875	*107*	28,211	*1,054*	1,598	*55*	4,859	*272*	128	*88*	220	*252*
DINAPUR SUBDIVISION.												
Dinapur	686	*14*	4,408	*139*	260	*26*	1,146	*74*	120	*37*	304	*289*
Maner	1,009	*13*	3,806	*203*	226	*4*	517	*8*	...	...	1	...
Total ...	1,695	*27*	8,214	*342*	486	*30*	1,663	*82*	120	*37*	305	*289*
BARH SUBDIVISION.												
Barh	1,858	*149*	9,444	*233*	186	*2*	618	*13*	2	...	20	*2*
Fatuha	708	*2*	4,236	*45*	118	...	397	*4*	1	...	3	*1*
Mukameh	729	*34*	4,372	*205*	46	...	307	*3*	1	*4*	61	*23*
Total ...	3,295	*185*	18,052	*483*	350	*2*	1,322	*20*	4	*4*	84	*26*
BIHAR SUBDIVISION.												
Bihar	1,264	*16*	7,010	*99*	344	*52*	863	*86*	...	...	1	...
Hilsa	668	*2*	3,903	*41*	94	*2*	330	*10*	...	...	1	...
Chandi	734	*24*	3,746	*247*	74	*1*	273	*10*	...	...	...	...
Islampur or Athasarai ...	517	*1*	3,036	*39*	60	...	343	*13*	11	*13*	44	*37*
Silao	473	*24*	3,027	*86*	89	...	360	*8*	...	...	...	...
Total ...	3,656	*67*	20,722	*512*	661	*55*	2,178	*127*	11	*13*	46	*37*
DISTRIOT TOTAL ...	13,521	386	75,199	2,391	3,095	142	10,022	501	263	142	655	604

DISTRICT GAYA.

THANAS.	HINDUS.				MUSALMANS.			
	PUPILS.		LITERATE.		PUPILS.		LITERATE.	
	Male.	Female.	Male.	Female.	Male.	Female.	Male.	Female.
SADAR SUBDIVISION.								
Gaya Town	953	*26*	6,337	*231*	273	*6*	1,267	*54*
Mufassal Gaya	546	*7*	4,897	*63*	137	*1*	543	*3*
Atri	179	...	1,795	*17*	12	...	192	...
Tikari	697	*12*	7,636	*109*	103	*2*	868	*15*
Sherghati	184	...	3,065	*29*	44	...	740	*3*
Barachati	64	...	949	*4*	20	...	154	...
Total ...	2,623	*45*	24,679	*453*	589	*9*	3,754	*75*

DISTRICT GAYA—*concluded.*

THANAS.	HINDUS.				MUSALMANS.			
	PUPILS.		LITERATE.		PUPILS.		LITERATE.	
	Male.	Female.	Male.	Female.	Male.	Female.	Male.	Female.
NAWADA SUBDIVISION.								
Nawada	734	*17*	7,486	*160*	92	*5*	446	*20*
Pakribarawan	224	*11*	1,673	*45*	34	...	224	...
Rajauli	91	*1*	1,634	*11*	13	...	128	*9*
Total ...	1,049	*29*	10,793	*216*	139	*5*	798	*29*
JAHANABAD SUBDIVISION.								
Jahanabad	1,794	*61*	9,711	*197*	288	*10*	1,018	*37*
Arwal	465	*6*	3,322	*65*	51	*3*	283	*6*
Total ...	2,259	*67*	13,033	*262*	339	*13*	1,301	*43*
AURANGABAD SUBDIVISION.								
Aurangabad	898	*4*	7,808	*114*	212	*1*	1,193	*51*
Daudnagar	320	...	3,638	*45*	71	...	492	*37*
Nabinagar	419	*8*	2,682	*61*	34	*4*	161	...
Total ...	1,637	*12*	14,128	*220*	317	*5*	1,846	*88*
DISTRICT TOTAL ...	7,568	153	62,633	1,151	1,384	32	7,699	228

DISTRICT SHAHABAD.

THANAS.	HINDUS.				MUSALMANS.			
	PUPILS.		LITERATE.		PUPILS.		LITERATE.	
	Male.	Female.	Male.	Female.	Male.	Female.	Male.	Female.
SADAR SUBDIVISION.								
Arrah	2,708	*55*	14,976	*370*	671	*18*	1,804	*85*
Belauti	595	*1*	6,275	*167*	100	...	400	*2*
Piru	459	*2*	5,312	*99*	32	...	213	*2*
Total ...	3,762	*58*	26,563	*635*	803	*18*	2,417	*89*
BUXAR SUBDIVISION.								
Buxar	615	*16*	4,834	*126*	86	*1*	499	*12*
Dumraon	1,200	*28*	8,300	*335*	107	*8*	470	*15*
Total ...	1,815	*44*	13,134	*461*	193	*9*	969	*27*
SASARAM SUBDIVISION.								
Sasaram	461	*11*	3,568	*46*	471	*17*	855	*36*
Kharghar	161	*1*	1,891	*28*	23	...	123	*1*
Dhangain	359	*2*	4,321	*71*	160	*2*	369	*5*
Dehri	336	*5*	2,184	*53*	54	...	260	*4*
Total ...	1,317	*19*	11,964	*198*	708	*19*	1,607	*48*

DISTRICT SHAHABAD—*concluded.*

Thanas.	Hindus.				Musalmans.			
	Pupils.		Literate.		Pupils.		Literate.	
	Male.	Female.	Male.	Female.	Male.	Female.	Male.	Female.
BHABHUA SUBDIVISION.								
Bhabhua	258	*11*	3,657	*107*	37	...	376	*19*
Mohania	431	*1*	2,967	*36*	24	...	169	...
Total ...	689	*12*	6,624	*143*	61	...	545	*19*
DISTRICT TOTAL ...	7,583	133	58,285	1,437	1,765	46	5,538	183

Thanas.	Christians.				Jains.			
	Pupils.		Literate.		Pupils.		Literate.	
	Male.	Female.	Male.	Female.	Male.	Female.	Male.	Female.
SADAR SUBDIVISION.								
Arrah	...	*2*	23	*19*	34	*1*	116	*9*
Belauti	...	...	5	*8*	...	...	...	...
Piru	...	...	...	*6*	...	...	...	...
Total ...	...	*2*	28	*33*	34	*1*	116	*9*
BUXAR SUBDIVISION.								
Buxar	18	*5*	65	*48*	...	...	1	...
Dumraon	...	...	3	...	...	...	...	...
Total ...	18	*5*	68	*48*	...	...	1	...
SASARAM SUBDIVISION.								
Sasaram	1	...	5	*3*	...	...	...	...
Kharghar	...	...	...	...	...	...	...	...
Dhangain	...	...	...	...	...	...	...	...
Dehri	...	...	17	*14*	...	...	...	...
Total ...	1	...	22	*17*	...	...	...	...
BHABHUA SUBDIVISION.								
Bhabhua	1	...	1	*1*	...	...	...	...
Mohania	...	...	...	...	...	...	...	...
Total ...	1	...	1	*1*	...	...	...	...
DISTRICT TOTAL ...	20	7	119	99	34	1	117	9

DISTRICT DARBHANGA.

Thanas.	Hindus.				Musalmans.				Christians.			
	Pupils.		Literate.		Pupils.		Literate.		Pupils.		Literate.	
	Male.	Female.	Male.	Female.	Male.	Female.	Male.	Female.	Male.	Female.	Male.	Female.
SADAR SUBDIVISION.												
Darbhanga	2,218	*74*	12,471	*122*	711	*12*	2,292	*35*	5	*8*	43	*38*
Bahera	796	...	8,487	*51*	82	...	595	*2*	...	...	9	*1*
Roshra	586	*3*	6,369	*94*	35	*1*	291	*10*	...	...	2	...
Total ...	3,600	*77*	27,327	*267*	828	*13*	3,178	*47*	5	*8*	54	*39*
MADHUBANI SUB-DIVISION.												
Madhubani	827	*3*	6,787	*53*	100	...	379	*5*	...	...	10	*7*
Benipati	668	*9*	5,494	*48*	132	...	447	*7*	...	...	1	...
Khajauli	356	...	4,029	*7*	41	...	219	...	...	...	4	*3*
Phulparas	364	*1*	6,675	*24*	36	*1*	306	...	...	...	1	*1*
Total ...	2,215	*13*	22,985	*132*	309	*1*	1,351	*12*	...	...	16	*11*
SAMASTIPUR SUB-DIVISION.												
Samastipur	1,251	*85*	9,848	*229*	186	*3*	794	*11*	10	*13*	81	*47*
Maniarpur	591	*6*	4,651	*61*	54	*1*	226	*11*	...	...	9	*6*
Dalsingsarai	710	*5*	7,991	*186*	84	...	338	*4*	...	...	15	*3*
Total ...	2,552	*96*	22,490	*476*	324	*4*	1,358	*26*	10	*13*	105	*56*
DISTRICT TOTAL ...	8,367	186	72,802	875	1,461	18	5,887	85	15	21	175	106

DISTRICT MUZAFFARPUR.

Thanas.	Hindus.				Musalmans.				Christians.			
	Pupils.		Literate.		Pupils.		Literate.		Pupils.		Literate.	
	Male.	Female.	Male.	Female.	Male.	Female.	Male.	Female.	Male.	Female.	Male.	Female.
SADAR SUBDIVISION.												
Muzaffarpur	9,867	*102*	32,945	*234*	479	*22*	1,683	*13*	14	*2*	89	*70*
Paru	1,163	*11*	7,538	*576*	72	*2*	336	*3*	...	...	7	*2*
Khatra	2,640	*42*	1,882	*189*	30	*1*	972	*6*	...	...	...	...
Total ...	13,670	*155*	42,365	*1,049*	581	*25*	2,991	*22*	14	*2*	96	*72*
SITAMARHI SUB-DIVISION.												
Sitamarhi	551	*35*	4,882	*109*	350	*5*	1,239	*4*	...	...	5	...
Siuhar	522	*2*	4,132	*63*	244	*4*	1,719	*18*	...	...	...	...
Pupri	624	*8*	3,012	*50*	120	*1*	948	*45*	...	...	1	...
Belsand	294	*22*	14,401	*51*	131	...	1,044	*4*	1	...	5	*3*
Total ...	1,991	*67*	26,427	*273*	845	*10*	4,950	*71*	1	...	11	*3*
HAJIPUR SUBDIVISION.												
Hajipur	1,603	*54*	6,342	*20*	301	*4*	1,250	*7*	...	...	10	*7*
Lalganj	659	*33*	5,186	*401*	51	*3*	336	*9*	...	..	4	*1*
Mahua	1,393	*53*	7,033	*72*	128	*2*	1,202	*6*	1	...	25	*9*
Total ...	3,655	*140*	18,561	*502*	480	*9*	2,788	*22*	1	...	30	*17*
DISTRICT TOTAL ...	19,316	362	87,353	1,824	1,906	44	10,729	115	16	2	146	92

DISTRICT SARAN.

Thanas.	Hindus.				Musalmans.				Christians.			
	Pupils.		Literate.		Pupils.		Literate.		Pupils.		Literate.	
	Male.	Female.	Male.	Female.	Male.	Female.	Male.	Female.	Male.	Female.	Male.	Female.
SADAR SUBDIVISION.												
Chapra	2,579	*30*	15,634	*379*	514	*21*	1,615	*81*	6	*4*	40	*28*
Manjhi	511	*2*	5,156	*213*	42	*1*	213	*9*	...	...	3	*2*
Parsa	1,211	*19*	6,145	*353*	76	...	358	*7*	2	*1*	5	*4*
Mashrak	369	*11*	2,943	*66*	22	...	216	*5*	...	...	7	*7*
Sonpur	754	*22*	4,323	*52*	32	*4*	180	*2*	4	*1*	21	*5*
Total ...	5,424	*93*	34,201	*1,063*	686	*26*	2,582	*104*	12	*6*	76	*46*
GOPALGANJ SUB-DIVISION.												
Gopalganj	1,041	*5*	4,696	*119*	50	*12*	360	*13*	...	...	12	*3*
Mirganj	849	*3*	5,614	*69*	74	*6*	423	*3*	...	...	6	*1*
Total ...	1,890	*8*	10,310	*188*	124	*18*	783	*16*	..	...	18	*4*
SEWAN SUBDIVISION.												
Sewan	965	*11*	6,320	*142*	335	*23*	1,290	*61*	2	...	12	*3*
Darauli	499	*12*	5,470	*205*	75	*5*	424	*3*	...	...	5	*3*
Basantpur	816	...	4.949	*137*	62	*6*	329	*23*	...	...	12	*6*
Total ...	2,270	*23*	16.739	*484*	472	*34*	2,043	*87*	2	...	29	*12*
DISTRICT TOTAL ...	9,584	124	61,250	1,735	1,282	78	5,408	207	14	6	123	62

DISTRICT CHAMPARAN.

Thanas.	Hindus.				Musalmans.				Christians.			
	Pupils.		Literate.		Pupils.		Literate.		Pupils.		Literate.	
	Male.	Female.	Male.	Female.	Male.	Female.	Male.	Female.	Male.	Female.	Male.	Female.
SADAR SUBDIVISION.												
Motihari	628	*8*	4,268	*95*	104	*3*	635	*17*	1	*2*	25	*12*
Govindganj	301	*4*	3,005	*25*	27	...	131	...	...	...	4	*1*
Kesaria	434	...	3,341	*42*	28	...	177	*1*	...	...	5	*4*
Madhuban	223	*7*	1,660	*22*	15	...	103	*6*	...	...	2	*1*
Dhaka	659	*6*	4,785	*49*	40	*2*	540	*15*	...	...	12	*8*
Adapur	341	*1*	2,590	*15*	75	*3*	417	*10*	...	...	...	...
Total ...	2,586	*26*	19,649	*248*	289	*8*	2,003	*49*	1	*2*	48	*26*
BETTIAH SUBDIVISION.												
Bettiah	757	*6*	5,919	*76*	169	*4*	760	*22*	65	*3*	140	*76*
Hardi	345	...	3,138	*53*	58	...	447	*1*	2	*1*	8	*4*
Bagaha	342	*3*	2.649	*40*	15	...	194	*5*	23	*1*	34	*9*
Total ...	1,444	*9*	11,706	*169*	242	*4*	1,401	*28*	90	*5*	182	*89*
DISTRICT TOTAL ...	4,030	35	31,355	417	531	12	3,404	77	91	7	230	115

BHAGALPUR DIVISION.

DISTRICT BHAGALPUR.

THANAS.	HINDUS.				MUSALMANS.			
	PUPILS.		LITERATE.		PUPILS.		LITERATE.	
	Male.	Female.	Male.	Female.	Male.	Female.	Male.	Female.
SADAR SUBDIVISION.								
Bhagalpur	1,758	*65*	6,401	*301*	620	*22*	1,800	*67*
Sultanganj	592	*2*	2,975	*20*	25	*1*	198	*1*
Colgong	601	*4*	5,259	*55*	29	*2*	333	...
Bihipur	285	*3*	2,921	*30*	23	...	116	*3*
Total ...	3,236	*74*	17,556	*406*	697	*25*	2,447	*75*
SUPUL SUBDIVISION.								
Supul	581	*10*	6,323	*60*	83	*1*	504	*2*
Pratabganj	162	*1*	2,824	*10*	22	...	221	*7*
Bangaon	382	...	3,107	*20*	31	...	291	...
Total ...	1,125	*11*	12,254	*90*	136	*1*	1,016	*9*
MADEHPURA SUBDIVISION.								
Madehpura	570	*18*	5,040	*52*	43	*2*	305	*4*
Kishangunj	324	*6*	3,040	*46*	16	...	144	*1*
Total ...	894	*24*	8,080	*98*	59	*2*	449	*5*
BANKA SUBDIVISION.								
Banka	472	*24*	3,702	*80*	60	...	350	*1*
Amarpur	758	*13*	4,473	*39*	34	...	133	...
Katuria	197	*4*	2,200	*18*	10	...	56	*1*
Total ...	1,427	*41*	10,375	*137*	104	...	539	*2*
DISTRICT TOTAL ...	6,682	150	48,265	731	996	28	4,451	91

THANAS.	CHRISTIANS.				JAINS.			
	PUPILS.		LITERATE.		PUPILS.		LITERATE.	
	Male.	Female.	Male.	Female.	Male.	Female.	Male	Female.
SADAR SUBDIVISION.								
Bhagalpur	62	*20*	72	*61*	8	...	34	...
Sultanganj	...	...	1	*1*	...	...	...	...
Colgong	2	*4*	11	*5*	...	...	1	...
Bihipur	...	...	2	...	...	...	...	...
Total ...	64	*24*	86	*67*	8	...	35	...

DISTRICT BHAGALPUR—*concluded.*

Thanas.	Christians.				Jains.			
	Pupils.		Literate.		Pupils.		Literate.	
	Male.	Female.	Male.	Female.	Male.	Female.	Male.	Female.
SUPUL SUBDIVISION.								
Supul	2	*9*	25	*11*	...	...	21	...
Pratabganj	1	...	9	*9*	...	...	57	*1*
Bangaon	...	...	5	*1*	...	...	...	...
Total ...	3	*9*	39	*21*	...	...	78	*1*
MADEHPURA SUBDIVISION.								
Madehpura	...	...	4	*3*	2	...	31	...
Kishanganj	...	...	2	...	...	...	...	...
Total ...	...	...	6	*3*	2	...	31	...
BANKA SUBDIVISION.								
Banka	...	*4*	...	*5*	...	...	...	...
Amarpur	...	...	...	...	...	...	...	...
Katuria	...	...	2	...	...	...	...	...
Total ...	...	*4*	2	*5*	...	...	...	...
DISTRICT TOTAL ...	67	30	133	96	10	...	144	1

DISTRICT MONHYR.

Thanas.	Hindus.				Musalmans.				Christians.			
	Pupils.		Literate.		Pupils.		Literate.		Pupils.		Literate.	
	Male.	Female.	Male.	Female.	Male.	Female.	Male.	Female.	Male.	Female.	Male.	Female.
SADAR SUBDIVISION.												
Monghyr	1,516	*47*	6,289	*210*	531	*8*	1,184	*53*	45	*26*	71	*120*
Gogri	629	*26*	7,026	*63*	75	...	756	*4*	...	...	7	*2*
Jamalpur	409	*32*	1,586	*139*	42	...	205	*5*	30	*47*	296	*160*
Surajgarha	943	*32*	6,347	*103*	103	*7*	349	*7*	...	...	...	...
Kharakpur	608	*24*	4,498	*71*	27	*1*	203	*2*	...	...	4	...
Total ...	4,105	*161*	25,741	*586*	778	*16*	2,697	*71*	95	*73*	378	*282*

DISTRICT MONGHYR—*concluded.*

Thanas.	Hindus.				Musalmans.				Christians.			
	Pupils.		Literate.		Pupils.		Literate.		Pupils.		Literate.	
	Male.	Female.	Male.	Female.	Male.	Female.	Male.	Female.	Male.	Female.	Male.	Female.
BEGUSARAI SUB-DIVISION.												
Begusarai	1,022	*35*	8,988	*188*	111	*4*	559	*7*	...	*2*	20	*11*
Tegra	543	*27*	5,786	*125*	124	...	414	*11*	1	...	12	*5*
Total ...	1,565	*62*	14,774	*313*	235	*4*	973	*18*	1	*2*	32	*16*
JAMUI SUBDIVISION.												
Jamui	420	*7*	3,833	*75*	19	...	197	*4*	...	...	2	*2*
Shaikhpura	1,301	*55*	7,201	*165*	328	*1*	1,208	*14*	...	...	...	...
Sikandra	449	...	3,451	*125*	48	...	260	*3*	3	*1*	2	*6*
Chakai	513	*30*	2,454	*136*	31	*1*	131	*5*	5	*6*	56	*32*
Total ...	2,683	*92*	16,939	*501*	426	*2*	1,796	*26*	8	*78*	60	*40*
DISTRICT TOTAL ...	8,353	315	57,454	1,400	1,439	22	5,466	115	104	82	470	336

DISTRICT PURNEA.

Thanas.	Hindus.				Musalmans.			
	Pupils.		Literate.		Pupils.		Literate.	
	Male.	Female.	Male.	Female.	Male.	Female.	Male.	Female.
SADAR SUBDIVISION.								
Purnea	869	*32*	4,317	*102*	419	*6*	1,789	*11*
Amur Kasba	312	*5*	1,479	*7*	505	*1*	2,372	*6*
Dhamdaha	310	*14*	2,514	*17*	36	...	201	...
Gondwara	226	*11*	2,809	*3*	46	*1*	367	...
Kadwa	208	...	2,118	*10*	181	...	1,387	*6*
Balarampur	236	...	1,569	*13*	227	*2*	1,456	*8*
Manihari	206	*9*	1,619	*20*	78	...	460	...
Total ...	2,367	*71*	16,425	*172*	1,492	*10*	8,032	*31*
ARARIA SUBDIVISION.								
Araria	648	*3*	3,973	*12*	773	*9*	2,841	*28*
Matiari	274	*1*	2,959	*2*	76	...	453	*4*
Raniganj	210	...	1,837	*3*	64	*1*	450	*1*
Total ...	1,132	*4*	8,769	*17*	913	*10*	3,744	*33*

DISTRICT PURNEA—*concluded.*

Thanas.	Hindus.				Musalmans.			
	Pupils.		Literate.		Pupils.		Literate.	
	Male.	Female.	Male.	Female.	Male.	Female.	Male.	Female.
KISHENGANJ SUB-DIVISION.								
Kishenganj	227	*3*	1,476	*8*	689	*8*	3,466	*17*
Bahadurganj	422	*1*	2,475	*11*	1,118	*4*	4,077	*8*
Kaliaganj	543	*1*	2,834	*11*	966	*6*	4,422	*16*
Total ...	1,192	*5*	6,785	*30*	2,773	*18*	11,965	*41*
DISTRICT TOTAL ...	4,691	80	31,979	219	5,178	38	23,741	105

Thanas.	Christians.				Jains.			
	Pupils.		Literate.		Pupils.		Literate.	
	Male.	Female.	Male.	Female.	Male.	Female.	Male.	Female.
SADAR SUBDIVISION.								
Purnea	9	*6*	30	*55*	...	...	62	...
Amur Kasba	...	...	...	...	...	...	...	...
Dhamdaha	...	...	4	*3*	...	...	34	...
Gondwara	5	*2*	14	*12*	...	...	1	...
Kadwa	9	...	17	*9*	...	...	1	...
Balarampur	...	...	3	*3*	...	...	...	...
Manihari	8	*2*	17	*20*	...	...	...	...
Total ...	31	*10*	85	*102*	...	...	98	...
ARARIA SUBDIVISION.								
Araria	1	...	3	*2*	1	...	3	...
Matiari	...	...	13	*5*	2	...	35	...
Raniganj	...	...	1	...	...	...	9	...
Total ...	1	...	17	*7*	3	...	47	...
KISHENGANJ SUB-DIVISION.								
Kishenganj	...	...	...	...	...	...	32	...
Bahadurganj	...	...	1	...	...	...	2	...
Kaliaganj	1	...	1	*1*	...	...	...	...
Total ...	1	...	2	*1*	...	...	34	...
DISTRICT TOTAL ...	33	10	104	110	3	...	179	...

DISTRICT MALDA.

Thanas.	Hindus.				Musalmans.			
	Pupils.		Literate.		Pupils.		Literate.	
	Male.	Female.	Male.	Female.	Male.	Female.	Male.	Female.
Malda	405	...	1,136	26	121	1	314	2
Kharba	1,031	35	2,390	29	457	8	1,043	3
Ratua	856	36	2,152	14	178	3	362	5
Gajol	174	2	933	1	205	10	685	1
English Bazar	1,315	51	3,727	105	391	7	987	14
Kallia Chak	933	19	1,953	23	487	5	1,066	5
Sibganj	401	26	1,325	41	593	9	1,459	14
Gumashtapur	231	1	888	2	138	...	551	7
Nawabganj	249	7	1,159	36	362	1	804	5
DISTRICT TOTAL ...	5,595	177	15,663	277	2,922	44	7,301	56

DISTRICT SANTAL PARGANAS.

Thanas.	Hindus.				Musalmans.			
	Pupils.		Literate.		Pupils.		Literate.	
	Male.	Female.	Male.	Female.	Male.	Female.	Male.	Female.
DEOGHAR SUBDIVISION.								
Deoghar	471	14	3,534	132	16	...	97	2
Madhupur	336	9	2,007	42	21	...	210	6
Sarath	275	4	1,284	5	6	...	52	...
Total ...	1,082	27	6,825	179	43	...	359	8
GODDA SUBDIVISION.								
Godda	721	29	2,020	38	109	4	290	3
Mahagama	486	5	1,440	11	167	1	306	...
Poreya	188	5	731	2	8	...	26	...
Portion of Daminikoh ...	110	2	326	4	...	...	...	...
Total ...	1,505	41	4,517	55	284	5	622	3
PAKAUR SUBDIVISION.								
Pakaur	381	4	1,050	33	204	...	435	1
Mahespur	200	5	614	10	100	2	167	2
Portion of Daminikoh ...	58	...	200	9	74	...	100	...
Total ...	639	9	1,864	52	378	2	702	3

DISTRICT SANTAL PARGANAS—*continued.*

THANAS.	HINDUS.				MUSALMANS.			
	PUPILS.		LITERATE.		PUPILS.		LITERATE.	
	Male.	Female.	Male.	Female.	Male.	Female.	Male.	Female.
RAJMAHAL SUB-DIVISION.								
Rajmahal	717	*14*	2,098	*30*	786	*6*	664	*5*
Sahibganj	119	*4*	1,108	*20*	25	...	466	*4*
Portion of Daminikoh ...	100	*2*	281	*2*	3	...	51	...
Total ...	936	*20*	3,487	*52*	814	*6*	1,181	*9*
DUMKA SUBDIVISION.								
Dumka	210	*1*	806	*9*	76	...	50	...
Portion of Daminikoh ...	108	...	321	*1*	20	...	59	...
Total ...	318	*1*	1,127	*10*	96	...	109	...
JAMTARA SUBDIVISION.								
Jamtara	1,588	*51*	2,311	*44*	166	*3*	891	*1*
Total ...	1,388	*51*	2,311	*44*	166	*3*	891	*1*
DISTRICT TOTAL ...	6,068	149	20,131	392	1,781	16	3,864	24

THANAS.	CHRISTIANS.				THE ANIMISTIC.			
	PUPILS.		LITERATE.		PUPILS.		LITERATE.	
	Male.	Female.	Male.	Female.	Male.	Female.	Male.	Female.
DEOGHAR SUBDIVISION.								
Deoghar	...	...	2	*3*	...	...	6	...
Madhupur	2	*1*	5	...	2	...	14	...
Sarath	...	...	...	...	...	...	12	...
Total ...	2	*1*	7	*3*	2	...	32	...

DISTRICT SANTAL PARGANAS—*concluded.*

THANAS.	CHRISTIANS.				THE ANIMISTIC.			
	PUPILS.		LITERATE.		PUPILS.		LITERATE.	
	Male.	Female.	Male.	Female.	Male.	Female.	Male.	Female.
GODDA SUBDIVISION.								
Godda	1	3	3	10	15	1	30	...
Mahagama	...	...	1	...	8	...	...	...
Poreya	2	...	5	...	6	1	63	...
Portion of Daminikoh ...	1	...	8	...	18	...	28	2
Total ...	4	3	17	10	47	2	121	2
PAKAUR SUBDIVISION.								
Pakaur	11	...	19	6	44	...	39	1
Mahespur	10	...	8	...	10	...	23	...
Portion of Daminikoh ...	3	2	8	4	35	...	...	...
Total ...	24	2	35	10	89	...	62	1
RAJMAHAL SUBDIVISION.								
Rajmahal	7	1	9	5	11	1	38	1
Shahibganj	6	...	8	...	...	...	...	...
Portion of Daminikoh ...	12	10	16	2	92	1	36	1
Total ...	25	11	33	7	103	2	74	2
DUMKA SUBDIVISION.								
Dumka	...	...	...	...	100	...	43	2
Portion of Daminikoh ...	...	2	...	2	...	...	4	...
Total ...	...	2	...	2	100	...	47	2
JAMTARA SUBDIVISION.								
Jamtara	...	...	3	...	18	8	12	3
Total ...	...	...	3	...	18	8	12	3
DISTRICT TOTAL ...	55	19	88	31	359	12	348	10

ORISSA DIVISION.

DISTRICT CUTTACK.

THANAS.	HINDUS.				MUSALMANS.				CHRISTIANS.			
	PUPILS.		LITERATE.		PUPILS.		LITERATE.		PUPILS.		LITERATE.	
	Male.	Female.	Male.	Female.	Male.	Female.	Male.	Female.	Male.	Female.	Male.	Female.
SADAR SUBDIVISION.												
Cuttack	4,178	139	13,380	471	444	39	1,285	85	268	186	450	576
Banki	437	5	1,748	32	2	...	25	...	...	1	3	...
Salepur	5,016	80	12,688	114	304	5	590	29	1	...	11	6
Tirtol	1,995	24	7,858	67	73	3	140	11	...	...	3	1
Jagatsinghpur	4,180	62	13,191	188	91	...	275	13	...	...	12	1
Total ...	15,805	310	48,855	872	914	40	2,315	138	269	187	479	584
KENDRAPARA SUB-DIVISION.												
Kendrapara	4,006	82	11,796	98	141	3	235	5	...	4	44	12
Patamundi	2,069	15	5,490	44	14	...	35	1	...	...	10	11
Aul or Rajabari	1,546	25	4,817	74	11	...	70	...	...	...	...	...
Total ...	7,681	122	22,103	216	166	3	340	6	...	4	54	23
JAJPUR SUBDIVISION.												
Jajpur	4,470	107	15,735	257	108	4	290	3	...	...	2	...
Dharmsala	3,255	48	12,367	224	59	2	259	13	...	...	23	21
Total ...	7,725	155	28,102	481	167	6	568	16	...	...	25	21
DISTRICT TOTAL ...	31,211	587	99,060	1,569	1,247	49	3,243	160	269	191	558	628

DISTRICT PURI.

THANAS.	HINDUS.				MUSALMANS.				CHRISTIANS.			
	PUPILS.		LITERATE.		PUPILS.		LITERATE.		PUPILS.		LITERATE.	
	Male.	Female.	Male.	Female.	Male.	Female.	Male.	Female.	Male.	Female.	Male.	Female.
SADAR SUBDIVISION.												
Thana Puri	2,791	53	10,327	115	5	...	66	3	...	1	5	...
Town Puri	816	122	5,326	228	1	...	86	3	1	4	12	19
Gop	1,744	24	4,043	46	50	1	108	1	...	1	2	...
Pipli	3,649	107	12,364	154	48	...	188	...	33	41	89	68
Total ...	9,000	306	32,660	543	104	1	448	7	34	47	108	80

DISTRICT PURI—*concluded.*

THANAS.	HINDUS.				MUSALMANS.				CHRISTIANS.			
	PUPILS.		LITERATE.		PUPILS.		LITERATE.		PUPILS.		LITERATE.	
	Male.	Female.	Male.	Female.	Male.	Female.	Male.	Female.	Male.	Female.	Male.	Female.
KHURDA SUBDIVISION.												
Khurda	2,176	*49*	6,745	*123*	49	...	230	*3*	29	*21*	41	*55*
Banpur	984	*30*	3,133	*44*	6	...	52	...	...	...	1	...
Total ...	3,160	*79*	9,878	*167*	55	...	282	*3*	29	*21*	42	*55*
DISTRICT TOTAL ...	12,160	385	42,538	710	159	1	730	10	63	68	160	135

DISTRICT BALASOR.

THANAS.	HINDUS.				MUSALMANS.				CHRISTIANS.			
	PUPILS.		LITERATE.		PUPILS.		LITERATE.		PUPILS.		LITERATE.	
	Male.	Female.	Male.	Female.	Male.	Female.	Male.	Female.	Male.	Female.	Male.	Female.
SADAR SUBDIVISION.												
Balasor	2,289	*164*	5,673	*42*	118	*17*	309	*26*	102	*113*	115	*92*
Saro	3,241	*68*	8,147	*127*	45	*1*	69	...	...	...	7	*5*
Jaleswar	1,059	*45*	2,208	*60*	1	*1*	129	*11*	48	*32*	23	*35*
Baliapal	1,674	*51*	3,525	*98*	7	...	59	...	...	...	3	*9*
Basta	1,028	*31*	2,259	*344*	12	*13*	44	*5*	...	...	3	...
Total ...	9,291	*359*	21,812	*671*	183	*32*	610	*49*	150	*145*	151	*134*
BHADRAK SUBDIVISION.												
Bhadrak	2,565	*54*	8,244	*173*	277	*14*	811	*15*	2	*4*	8	*10*
Basudebpur	921	*24*	3,039	*18*	9	...	35	...	...	...	4	...
Dhamnagar	1,889	*52*	7,234	*101*	16	*3*	99	*23*	3	*4*	6	*5*
Chandbali	953	*17*	3,903	*29*	10	...	204	...	3	...	39	*7*
Total ...	6,328	*147*	22,420	*21*	312	*17*	1,149	*38*	8	*8*	57	*29*
DISTRICT TOTAL ...	15,619	506	44,232	692	495	49	1,759	80	158	153	208	156

DISTRICT ANJUL.

THANAS.	HINDUS.			
	PUPILS.		LITERATE.	
	Male.	Female.	Male.	Female.
Angul and Kandh Mahals	867	*18*	2,134	*33*

CHUTIA NAGPUR DIVISION.

DISTRICT HAZARIBAGH.

THANAS.	HINDUS.				MUSALMANS.			
	PUPILS.		LITERATE.		PUPILS.		LITERATE.	
	Male.	Female.	Male.	Female.	Male.	Female.	Male.	Female.
SADAR SUBDIVISION.								
Hazaribagh	989	*42*	2,618	*159*	1,181	*23*	1,201	*75*
Barhi	171	*26*	842	*18*	17	...	78	*1*
Bagodhar	169	*25*	1,040	*15*	15	...	101	*2*
Tandwa	236	*5*	885	*5*	34	*1*	74	*2*
Ramghar	418	*52*	1,175	*25*	56	*3*	181	*1*
Jageswar	189	*22*	801	*22*	15	*3*	84	*2*
Kasmar	379	*48*	817	*22*	13	...	54	*1*
Chauparan	278	*13*	1,120	*20*	27	*5*	102	...
Hunterganj	208	*39*	800	*25*	35	*2*	133	*2*
Chatra	269	*8*	1,267	*29*	48	*9*	174	*10*
Simari	67	...	461	*5*	2	...	33	...
Total ...	3,373	*280*	11,826	*345*	1,443	*46*	2,215	*96*
GIRIDHI SUBDIVISION.								
Giridhi	760	*23*	2,550	*82*	131	*11*	293	*2*
Gawan	254	*1*	1,000	*10*	22	...	81	...
Kodarma	300	*8*	889	*6*	18	...	96	...
Kharakdiha	777	*19*	3,313	*60*	25	...	144	*5*
Dumurhi	262	*3*	1,155	*16*	16	...	91	*4*
Total ...	2,353	*54*	8,907	*174*	212	*11*	705	*11*
DISTRICT TOTAL ...	**5,726**	**334**	**20,733**	**519**	**1,655**	**57**	**2,920**	**107**

THANAS.	CHRISTIANS.				JAINS.				THE ANIMISTIC.			
	PUPILS.		LITERATE.		PUPILS.		LITERATE.		PUPILS.		LITERATE.	
	Male.	Female.	Male.	Female.	Male.	Female.	Male.	Female.	Male.	Female.	Male.	Female.
SADAR SUBDIVISION.												
Hazaribagh	33	*32*	55	*81*	9	...	13	...	...	...	1	...
Barhi	1	*2*	8	*2*	...	...	...	...	...	...	2	...
Bagodhar	...	...	1	...	...	...	...	...	...	...	2	...
Tandwa	...	...	...	...	...	...	...	...	...	...	1	...
Ramghar	...	...	1	*1*	...	...	...	...	6	*1*	10	...
Jageswar	...	...	10	*1*	...	...	...	...	8	*7*	17	...
Kasmar	...	...	...	...	...	...	...	...	63	*6*	35	...
Chauparan	...	...	...	...	...	...	5	...	...	...	...	...
Hunterganj	...	...	...	...	...	...	...	...	...	...	...	...
Chatra	...	...	...	...	2	...	3	...	...	...	...	...
Simaria	...	...	...	...	...	...	...	...	...	...	...	...
Total ...	34	*34*	75	*85*	11	...	21	...	77	*14*	68	...

DISTRICT HAZARIBAGH—*concluded.*

Thanas.	Christians.				Jains.				The Animistic.			
	Pupils.		Literate.		Pupils.		Literate.		Pupils.		Literate.	
	Male.	Female.	Male.	Female.	Male.	Female.	Male.	Female.	Male.	Female.	Male.	Female.
GIRIDHI SUBDIVISION.												
Giridhi	40	*34*	69	*53*	2	...	63	*2*	90	*40*	46	*1*
Gawan	...	...	...	...	...	...	...	...	...	...	6	...
Kodarma	...	...	4	...	...	...	...	...	...	...	...	...
Kharakdiha	...	...	4	...	...	...	...	...	32	*1*	20	...
Dumurhi	...	...	13	*4*	1	...	129	...	...	...	...	...
Total ...	40	*34*	90	*57*	3	...	192	*2*	122	*41*	72	*1*
DISTRICT TOTAL ...	74	68	165	142	14	...	213	2	199	55	140	1

DISTRICT LOHARDAGA (INCLUDING PALAMAU).

Thanas.	Hindus.				Musalmans.			
	Pupils.		Literate.		Pupils.		Literate.	
	Male.	Female.	Male.	Female.	Male.	Female.	Male.	Female.
SADAR SUBDIVISION.								
Ranchi	579	*83*	2,958	*678*	185	*17*	706	*93*
Sili	314	*4*	982	*28*	6	...	39	...
Tamar	265	*7*	982	*38*	7	...	31	*1*
Karra	40	*1*	903	*31*	8	...	80	...
Mandar	255	*9*	810	*8*	...	...	32	...
Khunti	49	...	757	*8*	7	...	46	*3*
Lohardaga	119	*9*	1,183	*145*	36	...	207	*99*
Total ...	1,621	*106*	8,555	*956*	249	*17*	1,141	[illegible]
PALKOT SUBDIVISION.								
Chainpur	2	...	392	*3*	...	...	29	...
Toto	259	*1*	1,402	*135*	21	...	84	*1*
Palkot	135	*1*	897	*35*	4	...	26	...
Koohdaga	31	...	684	*3*	...	...	11	...
Basia	64	*1*	764	*6*	...	...	16	...
Total ...	491	*3*	4,109	*189*	25	...	166	*1*

DISTRICT LOHARDAGA (INCLUDING PALAMAU)—*continued.*

THANAS.	HINDUS.				MUSALMANS.			
	PUPILS.		LITERATE.		PUPILS.		LITERATE.	
	Male.	Female.	Male.	Female.	Male.	Female.	Male.	Female.
PALAMAU.								
Daltonganj	119	*4*	305	*14*	19	...	82	*8*
Garhwa	191	*3*	1,331	*117*	21	...	107	*4*
Ranka	65	*5*	262	*17*	4	*3*	35	...
Chhatrapur	112	*9*	549	*25*	7	...	37	*1*
Patan	121	...	1,268	*19*	6	*1*	180	*4*
Husainabad	347	*9*	1,897	*133*	71	...	287	*1*
Latihar	33	...	360	*7*	9	...	68	...
Mahuadanr	7	...	164	*1*	...	...	26	...
Balumat	76	...	482	*6*	...	...	70	...
Total ...	1,071	*16*	6,618	*339*	137	*4*	892	*18*
DISTRICT TOTAL ...	3,183	125	19,282	1,457	411	21	2,199	138

THANAS.	CHRISTIANS.				THE ANIMISTIC.			
	PUPILS.		LITERATE.		PUPILS.		LITERATE.	
	Male.	Female.	Male.	Female.	Male.	Female.	Male.	Female.
SADAR SUBDIVISION.								
Ranchi	701	*244*	813	*259*	74	...	339	*25*
Silli	...	...	3	*1*	47	*10*	144	*13*
Tamar	10	...	87	*6*	230	*5*	365	*23*
Karra	...	...	42	...	6	...	74	*12*
Mandar	26	*1*	79	*6*	34	...	74	*1*
Khunti	174	*45*	625	*98*	51	...	229	*9*
Lohardaga	63	*50*	91	*38*	12	...	118	*1*
Total ...	974	*340*	1,740	*408*	454	*15*	1,339	*84*
PALKOT SUBDIVISION.								
Chainpur	...	...	2	*6*	...	...	46	...
Toto	16	*2*	59	*10*	116	...	383	*1*
Palkot	2	...	10	...	14	...	45	*1*
Kochdaga	...	...	11	...	3	...	37	...
Basia	35	*9*	237	*19*	1	...	59	*1*
Total ...	53	*11*	319	*38*	134	...	570	*3*

DISTRICT LOHARDAGA (INCLUDING PALAMAU)—*concluded.*

Thanas.	Christians.				The Animistic.			
	Pupils.		Literate.		Pupils.		Literate.	
	Male.	Female.	Male.	Female.	Male.	Female.	Male.	Female.
PALAMAU.								
Daltonganj	1	...	5	*5*	...	...	...	...
Garhwa	...	...	1	...	...	...	...	...
Ranka	...	...	...	...	...	...	5	...
Chhatrapur	...	...	1	...	...	...	5	...
Patan	...	...	4	*1*	...	...	2	...
Husainabad	...	...	...	*1*	...	...	1	...
Latihar	...	...	2	...	1	...	2	...
Mahuadanr	...	...	12	*4*	...	...	6	...
Balumat	...	...	...	...	...	...	4	...
Total ...	1	...	25	*11*	1	...	25	...
DISTRICT TOTAL ...	1,028	351	2,084	447	589	15	1,934	87

DISTRICT MANBHUM.

Thanas.	Hindus.				Musalmans.			
	Pupils.		Literate.		Pupils.		Literate.	
	Male.	Female.	Male.	Female.	Male.	Female.	Male.	Female.
SADAR SUBDIVISION.								
Purulia	2,017	*66*	5,578	*227*	78	*4*	359	*7*
Jhalda	732	*22*	2,065	*39*	18	...	111	...
Baghmundi	179	*20*	716	*23*	8	...	52	...
Chandil	433	*2*	1,313	*25*	9	...	123	...
Barabhum	773	*16*	2,170	*23*	13	...	135	...
Manbazar	924	*13*	1,758	*19*	5	...	23	...
Raghunathpur	1,837	*33*	4,063	*58*	61	*5*	164	*2*
Gaurandi	550	*6*	1,665	*21*	29	...	60	...
Para	578	*11*	1,346	*16*	47	...	102	...
Chas	860	*10*	2,582	*16*	37	...	148	...
Total ...	8,883	*199*	23,256	*467*	305	*9*	1,277	*9*
GOBINDPUR SUB-DIVISION.								
Gobindpur	730	*35*	1,830	*39*	62	...	188	*3*
Nirsa	532	*12*	1,325	*21*	35	...	117	*1*
Topchanchi	325	*1*	1,042	*12*	19	...	92	*1*
Total ...	1,587	*48*	4,197	*65*	116	...	397	*5*
DISTRICT TOTAL ...	10,470	247	27,453	532	421	9	1,674	14

DISTRICT MANBHUM—*concluded.*

Thanas.	Christians.				The Animistic.			
	Pupils.		Literate.		Pupils.		Literate.	
	Male.	Female.	Male.	Female.	Male.	Female.	Male.	Female.
SADAR SUBDIVISION.								
Purulia	35	*34*	100	*65*	9	...	27	...
Jhalda	3	...	24	*9*	9	...	19	...
Baghmundi	2	...	13	*3*	2	...	9	...
Chandil	3	...	18	*1*	10	...	26	...
Barabhum	2	...	3	*2*	50	*1*	50	...
Manbazar	...	*1*	2	*3*	121	...	30	...
Raghunathpur	2	...	5	*2*	31	...	88	...
Gaurandi	...	...	1	...	7	...	34	...
Para	...	...	1	...	3	...	2	...
Chas	1	*1*	1	...	8	*4*	11	*1*
Total ...	48	*36*	168	*85*	250	*5*	296	*1*
GOBINDPUR SUBDIVISION.								
Gobindpur	55	*42*	20	*6*	40	*3*	39	...
Nirsa	1	...	4	*3*	7	...	18	...
Topchanchi	...	...	...	*1*	2	...	13	...
Total ...	56	*42*	24	*10*	49	*3*	70	...
DISTRICT TOTAL ...	104	78	192	94	299	8	366	1

DISTRICT SINGHBHUM.

Thanas.	Hindus.				Musalmans.			
	Pupils.		Literate.		Pupils.		Literate.	
	Male.	Female.	Male.	Female.	Male.	Female.	Male.	Female.
Chaibasa	846	*108*	2,357	*106*	36	*7*	135	*6*
Chakradharpur	181	*3*	984	*27*	...	...	86	...
Manoharpur	172	...	845	*16*	1	...	60	...
Ghatsila or Dhalbhum ...	1,640	*171*	3,212	*141*	22	...	67	*1*
DISTRICT TOTAL ...	2,939	282	7,398	290	59	7	344	7

Thanas.	Christians.				The Animistic.			
	Pupils.		Literate.		Pupils.		Literate.	
	Male.	Female.	Male.	Female.	Male.	Female.	Male.	Female.
Chaibasa	115	*100*	102	*81*	1,083	*36*	987	*27*
Chakradharpur	22	*4*	162	*34*	148	*8*	155	*5*
Manoharpur	1	*2*	39	*24*	17	...	62	*1*
Ghatsila or Dhalbhum ...	...	*1*	6	*13*	132	*5*	229	*8*
DISTRICT TOTAL ...	138	107	309	152	1,380	49	1,433	41

FEUDATORY STATES.

KUCH BIHAR.

States.	Hindus.				Musalmans.				Christians.				Jains.			
	Pupils.		Literate.		Pupils.		Literate.		Pupils.		Literate.		Pupils.		Literate.	
	Male.	Female.	Male.	Female.	Male.	Female.	Male.	Female.	Male.	Female.	Male.	Female.	Male.	Female.	Male.	Female.
Phulbari ...	295	*6*	1,896	*19*	72	*1*	376	*1*	...	...	...	...	3	...	36	...
Kuch Bihar ...	626	*69*	1,514	*201*	104	*3*	324	*11*	5	*4*	34	*15*	7	...	34	2
Kotwali ...	1,127	*17*	4,508	*76*	238	...	770	*8*	4	*3*	25	*11*	1	...	5	...
Matabhanga ...	1,064	*15*	4,748	*69*	296	*19*	1,086	*13*	...	...	1	...	...	...	6	...
Haldibari ...	202	*2*	927	*6*	341	*20*	921	*33*	2	*2*	4	*3*	...	...	...	...
Mekliganj ...	479	*19*	1,702	*23*	274	*11*	632	*9*	...	...	...	...	...	...	3	...
Dinhata ...	1,223	*49*	4,126	*40*	585	*10*	1,300	*19*	...	...	...	...	9	...	7	...
TOTAL ...	5,016	163	19,421	427	1,910	64	5,409	87	11	9	64	29	20	...	81	2

ORISSA TRIBUTARY STATES.

States.	Hindus.				Musalmans.			
	Pupils.		Literate.		Pupils.		Literate.	
	Male.	Female.	Male.	Female.	Male.	Female.	Male.	Female.
Athgarh	199	*23*	1,279	*57*	...	...	5	*1*
Talcher	343	*21*	1,496	*58*	1	...	13	...
Moharbhanj	1,970	*45*	7,288	*182*	10	*1*	144	*1*
Nilgiri	595	*14*	1,724	*27*	...	...	13	...
Keonjhar	1,318	*20*	7,807	*118*	5	*1*	27	...
Pal Lahara	36	*2*	215	*8*	...	...	6	...
Dhenkanal	1,753	*57*	6,811	*220*	11	*1*	57	*1*
Athmalik	92	*1*	719	*19*	5	...	5	*3*
Hindol	248	*4*	418	*9*	6	...	11	...
Narsinghpur	191	*3*	919	*7*	...	...	8	*2*
Baramba	242	*9*	1,201	*62*	...	...	5	...
Tigaria	71	*1*	889	*17*	...	...	23	...
Kandhpara	114	*2*	2,168	*102*	...	...	...	...
Nayagarh	406	*11*	3,447	*94*	1	...	12	...
Ranpur	226	*6*	1,289	*47*	4	...	7	...
Daspalla	204	*6*	762	*19*	...	...	1	...
Boad	238	*6*	988	*30*	...	...	10	...
TOTAL ...	8,246	231	39,420	1,076	43	3	347	8

ORISSA TRIBUTARY STATES—*concluded*.

States.	Christians.				The Animistic.				Buddhists.			
	Pupils.		Literate.		Pupils.		Literate.		Pupils.		Literate.	
	Male.	Female.	Male.	Female.	Male.	Female.	Male.	Female.	Male.	Female.	Male.	Female.
Athgarh	...	...	34	*66*	...	...	...	...	...	...	...	...
Talcher	...	*1*	1	...	...	...	...	...	...	...	...	...
Moharbhanj	1	...	35	*12*	49	...	180	*1*	...	...	...	...
Nilgiri	6	*5*	11	*19*	2	...	13	...	...	...	...	...
Keonjhar	...	...	...	...	20	...	131	...	...	...	...	...
Pal Lahara	...	...	...	...	8	...	23	...	...	...	...	...
Dhenkanal	2	*1*	5	...	9	...	78	...	15	*2*	53	*2*
Athmalik	...	...	...	...	10	...	38	...	...	...	...	...
Hindol	...	...	...	...	...	...	...	...	...	...	...	...
Narsinghpur	...	...	...	...	...	...	...	...	...	...	...	...
Baramba	...	...	2	*3*	...	...	...	...	30	*5*	166	*14*
Tigaria	...	...	...	...	...	...	...	...	...	...	...	...
Kandhpara	...	...	...	...	...	...	...	...	...	...	...	...
Nayagarh	...	...	...	...	...	...	...	...	...	...	...	...
Ranpur	1	...	1	...	...	...	...	...	...	...	...	...
Daspalla	...	...	1	...	...	...	...	...	...	...	...	...
Boad	...	...	3	...	...	...	...	...	...	...	...	...
TOTAL ...	10	7	93	93	98	...	461	1	45	7	218	16

CHUTIA NAGPUR TRIBUTARY STATES.

States.	Hindus.				Musalmans.				The Animistic.			
	Pupils.		Literate.		Pupils.		Literate.		Pupils.		Literate.	
	Males.	Female.	Male.	Female.	Male.	Female.	Male.	Female.	Male.	Female.	Male.	Female.
Chang Bhukar	2	...	63	*3*	...	...	...	...	...	...	...	...
Korea	7	...	45	*6*	...	...	5	...	...	...	...	...
Sirguja	30	*1*	577	*26*	3	...	47	...	1	...	28	...
Udaipur	25	...	123	*1*	3	...	4	...	...	...	...	...
Jashpur	23	...	422	*15*	...	...	30	...	...	...	...	...
Gangpur	99	*1*	2,096	*55*	1	...	43	...	2	...	62	...
Bonai	14	*1*	517	*25*	...	...	5	...	...	...	...	...
Kharsawan	66	*1*	665	*41*	9	...	33	...	5	...	70	*1*
Seraikela	92	*14*	2,134	*104*	3	...	43	...	7	*1*	79	*4*
TOTAL ...	358	18	6,642	276	16	...	210	...	15	1	230	5

NOTE.—Figures for Hill Tippera are not available—See note on title page of Imperial Table VII.

PROVINCIAL TABLE V—Showing for each Thana the castes of Hindus, the Animistic tribes and the divisions of Musalmans which contribute 1,000 or more persons to the District Population.

BARDWAN

DISTRICT

Caste or Group.	District Total.			Bardwan.		Sahibganj.		Khandaghosh.	
	Total.	Male.	Female.	Male.	Female.	Male.	Female.	Male.	Female.
Aguri	62,249	29,808	32,441	1,965	2,060	3,214	3,684	2,217	2,377
Bagdi	149,461	73,446	76,015	3,912	4,257	5,306	5,503	5,900	5,870
Baidya	3,420	1,641	1,779	157	151	40	45	27	25
Baiti	2,091	1,012	1,079	44	35	39	49	26	28
Baniya	29,782	14,249	15,533	1,254	1,008	610	725	552	786
(i) Gandha Banik	5,408	2,363	3,045	...	...	102	111	...	...
(ii) Khatri	4,301	2,489	1,812	354	198	39	25	25	21
(iii) Subarna Banik ...	1,619	732	887	54	63	25	36	31	45
Barui	3,906	1,928	1,978	19	19	130	120	94	87
Bauri	92,322	44,951	47,371	981	1,061	458	457	700	733
Bediya	1,852	900	952	2	6	...	...	...	...
Bhuiya	4,147	2,255	1,892	...	...	11	6	3	1
Brahman	103,749	48,986	54,763	3,684	2,494	2,576	3,234	1,343	1,611
Chamar and Muchi ...	51,280	25,124	26,156	1,282	1,408	2,090	2,161	1,088	1,041
Dhopa	3,845	1,921	1,924	187	177	56	57	41	41
Dom and Kaora	39,689	19,931	19,758	982	935	1,363	1,356	774	721
Goala	62,479	32,009	30,470	992	1,043	2,786	2,743	659	744
Hari and Mihtar ...	22,976	11,635	11,341	692	739	827	902	163	172
Jugi	4,261	2,067	2,194	32	31	16	19	1	...
Kahar	1,464	858	606	...	...	2	...	1	...
Kaibartta	26,656	12,877	13,779	253	287	166	173	195	218
Kamar and Lohar ...	20,371	10,174	10,197	611	515	1,286	1,506	841	850
Kayastha	31,861	14,312	17,549	1,225	793	583	879	951	1,449
Kewat	3,315	1,654	1,661	36	38	7	18	...	...
Kora	5,336	2,660	2,676	49	51	31	42	14	12
Kumhar	11,092	5,376	5,716	333	529	221	233	220	249
Kurmi	2,012	1,176	836	160	81	5	1	14	10
Maira and Halwai ...	11,104	5,451	5,653	567	472	208	227	145	156
Mal	1,729	817	912	14	17	48	48	23	21
Malakar	2,506	1,295	1,211	149	132	49	35	24	28
Namasudra or Chandal	18,075	9,428	8,647	504	494	774	746	434	417
Napit and Hajjam ...	15,756	7,576	8,180	505	562	276	298	332	399
Rajput	4,268	2,177	2,091	282	305	11	2	6	4
Sadgop	106,674	52,234	54,440	1,687	1,846	1,266	1,358	1,542	1,744
Santal	22,256	11,508	10,748	41	36	...	...	8	4
Sonar	7,053	3,362	3,691	307	336	137	199	42	36
Sunri and Kalwar ...	20,294	9,863	10,431	412	480	275	295	142	135
Sutradhar	8,916	4,407	4,509	271	243	198	190	127	135
Tambuli	5,535	2,482	3,053	254	328	154	193	104	140
Tanti	17,524	8,535	8,989	548	627	587	665	159	152
Teli and Kalu	49,890	24,027	25,863	945	894	1,215	1,290	742	733
Religious devotees and persons returned by sect.									
Baisnab	24,033	10,975	13,058	627	931	716	860	282	384
Hindus returned by title or common sub-caste.									
Buna	2,807	1,412	1,395	56	49	220	190	45	10
Malik	2,575	1,274	1,301	1	4	...	...	...	...
Rajbansi	3,595	1,746	1,849	...	...	...	...	...	...
Hindus returned by actual occupation.									
Dulia	17,325	8,563	8,762	68	73	21	29	173	180
Jaliya	2,977	1,498	1,479	25	11	3	...	11	7
Kotal	9,684	4,854	4,830	388	390	281	308	...	...
Matiya	9,405	4,655	4,750	281	318	146	137	313	310

DIVISION.

BARDWAN.

Raina.		Satgachhia.		Jamalpur.		Bud-Bud.		Ausgram.	
Male.	Female.	Male.	Female.	Male.	Female.	Male.	Female.	Male.	Female.
4,227	4,642	3,703	4,073	217	191	3,292	3,483	456	449
9,658	9,928	5,500	5,709	6,009	6,408	5,445	5,575	3,377	3,407
49	41	111	124	24	86	15	31	112	120
23	20	118	134	79	110	34	40	22	6
834	933	702	865	860	471	550	750	404	481
...	...	194	240	...	...	215	312	70	56
16	18	95	86	114	110	50	69	7	3
21	22	71	117	14	19	57	110	74	116
23	41	86	85	194	179	270	152	137	147
68	78	...	...	408	328	707	628	1,884	1,960
...	...	3	5	...	...	16	20	3	6
...	...	...	...	...	...	...	...	1	...
2,268	2,626	3,632	4,396	1,936	2,323	2,393	2,530	2,979	3,790
1,760	1,794	1,783	1,704	1,060	1,271	1,452	1,612	1,500	1,607
124	114	112	112	120	106	53	58	72	102
934	937	564	627	562	577	1,558	1,577	2,943	2,872
1,589	1,734	2,240	2,216	1,539	1,555	2,343	1,315	1,309	1,651
494	572	1,598	1,462	689	631	398	375	382	389
86	74	213	234	285	330	33	35	55	64
...	...	...	...	38	5	8	8	110	51
107	139	629	646	2,246	2,284	277	282	139	138
673	626	677	725	336	335	643	576	1,137	1,171
1,721	2,486	659	930	1,012	1,536	428	440	639	860
...	...	...	...	...	...	34	...	55	71
66	54	174	143	157	158	310	284	69	79
187	244	374	407	297	348	155	161	262	269
2	1	51	34	19	8	84	18	23	19
163	187	281	277	226	273	213	214	321	323
30	37	34	62	...	...	193	195	46	48
57	66	93	95	17	31	33	35	28	53
1,321	1,247	932	927	1,015	894	110	106	203	158
693	728	556	582	422	588	306	364	394	408
491	499	46	21	56	41	57	69	15	14
1,288	1,339	4,391	4,674	2,400	2,641	1,927	1,987	6,236	6,309
89	78	107	19	122	106	14	3	107	124
...	...	261	294	228	253	62	65	140	203
162	187	138	112	104	112	216	222	605	650
236	282	263	348	145	140	251	377	261	230
106	144	291	469	224	331	254	282	398	359
143	140	1,153	1,171	426	359	178	170	290	364
4,564	4,718	651	811	743	840	709	703	78	99
417	433	524	582	363	391	871	820	799	863
37	31	32	22	30	35	11	5	40	31
24	24	535	538	...	...	...	...	...	...
1	1	16	...	...	...	6	...	...	...
1,611	1,557	2,037	2,201	2,572	2,530	120	69	...	...
45	44	146	157	519	462	10	3	31	28
153	173	420	426	...	...	138	145	195	230
...	...	...	...	7	2	733	748	2,761	2,901

Caste or Group.	Raniganj.		Asansol.		Kaksa.		Katwa.	
	Male.	Female.	Male.	Female.	Male.	Female.	Male.	Female.
Aguri	1,086	1,156	852	864	929	1,020	1,265	1,439
Bagdi	2,606	2,485	342	360	1,563	1,687	3,744	4,108
Baidya	95	97	232	223	56	55	272	241
Baiti	...	8	...	...	3	6	93	96
Baniya	1,765	1,783	2,319	1,551	270	296	1,252	1,663
(i) Gandha Banik	740	923	4	6	80	93	42	58
(ii) Khatri	373	250	837	408	79	58	...	...
(iii) Subarna Banik ...	227	167	...	...	59	74	14	17
Barui	158	236	109	67	191	301	131	133
Bauri	17,283	18,380	17,185	18,278	1,272	1,340	732	827
Bediya	738	780	37	37	...	...	33	33
Bhuiya	133	98	2,066	1,761	7	9	1	...
Brahman	7,607	8,535	3,764	3,253	1,464	1,674	3,208	3,927
Chamar and Muchi ...	1,658	1,740	1,353	1,315	987	938	1,437	1,487
Dhopa	241	177	246	192	34	35	134	165
Dom and Kaora	2,933	2,928	1,778	1,657	970	991	660	701
Goala	3,784	2,978	4,168	3,980	854	882	1,741	1,683
Hari and Mihtar ...	1,248	1,132	851	727	424	486	680	661
Jugi	254	254	26	22	17	17	124	131
Kahar	202	151	413	318	25	9	...	...
Kaibartta	950	892	1	1	375	347	1,073	1,260
Kamar and Lohar ...	1,169	1,155	1,059	953	577	567	237	248
Kayastha	896	679	474	262	216	295	1,340	1,537
Kewat	669	730	633	603	101	103	...	...
Kora	583	578	963	986	79	83	12	9
Kumhar	454	475	655	664	157	128	574	620
Kurmi	178	102	524	448	27	...	12	10
Maira and Halwai ...	860	900	736	633	151	177	277	346
Mal	19	13	19	5	232	259	35	39
Malakar	515	415	52	46	16	22	20	21
Namasudra or Chandal	117	107	1	...	51	56	19	20
Napit and Hajjam ...	823	881	654	587	148	150	484	576
Rajput	666	597	186	158	27	32	114	136
Sodgop	3,888	4,028	941	855	2,466	2,362	4,450	4,556
Santal	2,358	2,399	8,442	7,796	214	180	3	1
Sonar	401	415	240	290	80	95	357	340
Sunri and Kalwar ...	2,368	2,535	2,149	2,288	245	233	1,068	1,148
Sutradhar	574	541	354	282	192	159	270	291
Tambuli	193	176	81	56	217	286	2	5
Tanti	786	852	667	595	239	204	1,399	1,518
Teli and Kalu	5,202	5,609	2,399	2,498	489	512	1,075	1,195
Religious devotees and persons returned by sect.								
Baisnab	1,256	1,362	817	896	261	259	1,149	1,415
Hindus returned by title or common sub-caste.								
Buna	281	308	432	461	26	23	8	12
Malik	19	19	182	209	...	...	...	...
Rajbansi	95	106	448	452	...	...	536	542
Hindus returned by actual occupation.								
Dulia	12	9	4	...	5	5	...	...
Jaliya	188	172	28	27	1	...	...	...
Kotal	47	42	...	...	7	14	1,303	1,237
Matiya	...	...	...	...	101	108	...	...

BARDWAN—*continued.*

Ketugram.		Mungalkot.		Kalna.		Purbasthali.		Manteswar.	
Male.	Female.	Male.	Female.	Male.	Female.	Male.	Female.	Male.	Female.
16	17	2,076	2,347	501	501	224	234	3,568	4,004
4,274	4,392	4,710	4,060	4,357	4,477	3,337	3,326	3,406	3,563
122	192	34	32	127	181	108	171	60	14
115	98	20	21	158	150	186	207	52	71
795	1,035	149	199	809	869	596	866	1,028	1,303
490	730	81	112	61	73	103	143	181	188
35	36	68	87	214	204	162	221	21	18
64	78	...	...	11	9	...	...	10	14
50	56	12	7	106	132	217	217	1	...
845	853	1,121	1,167	717	736	266	273	324	263
55	53	7	...	...	...	11	13	...	...
2	...	1	...	27	12	3	5	...	...
2,415	3,349	2,042	2,451	3,698	3,584	1,864	2,504	2,113	2,482
1,846	1,868	1,884	1,982	1,196	1,262	1,309	1,468	1,450	1,558
129	142	64	75	134	171	111	131	63	69
1,138	1,056	1,313	1,318	701	760	622	612	136	133
958	970	1,262	1,308	2,215	2,163	1,561	1,497	2,009	2,008
873	894	403	401	737	674	847	353	829	771
89	70	7	9	404	434	421	464	4	6
18	12	...	...	5	...	36	52	...	...
840	859	431	447	2,457	2,730	2,630	2,987	108	89
209	177	279	258	410	423	261	252	269	300
1,403	1,711	388	540	993	1,312	1,166	1,477	218	354
14	10	81	86	24	2	...	...	...	...
84	96	...	...	51	49	18	22	...	...
397	435	334	370	361	388	263	273	112	123
38	34	2	...	36	14	48	50	3	5
159	169	291	320	415	423	323	347	115	209
...	...	...	...	...	...	74	107	48	61
39	38	58	74	67	63	116	25	26	29
540	536	511	472	1,835	1,414	923	915	138	133
455	517	368	284	579	611	273	359	308	337
24	21	9	8	187	104	...	...	...	...
5,882	6,062	3,743	3,925	3,417	3,699	5,402	5,561	1,248	1,444
...	...	...	...	...	...	2	2	1	...
218	235	194	189	297	316	257	262	141	163
1,073	1,156	403	369	164	165	105	120	235	224
424	380	211	214	244	304	230	244	136	149
10	6	41	45	88	152	9	4	46	77
758	870	277	232	216	253	417	419	292	348
711	762	1,410	1,603	1,108	1,301	735	833	1,251	1,337
806	1,181	753	1,099	664	809	351	473	229	300
5	8	5	6	99	110	54	54	31	40
...	...	...	...	371	360	142	147	...	...
135	142	33	36	61	79	398	485	17	6
6	2	10	7	1,725	1,799	103	114	106	187
104	126	1	...	342	405	1	3	43	34
314	281	356	341	44	52	211	178	997	1,013
...	...	313	226	...	...	...	...	...	...

DISTRICT

Group.	District total.			Bardwan.		Sahibganj.		Khandaghosh.	
	Total.	Male.	Female.	Male.	Female.	Male.	Female.	Male.	Female.
Musalmans returned by sect.									
Sunni	4,565	2,318	2,247	10	3	252	267	...	...
Musalmans returned by title.									
Pathan	6,190	3,428	2,762	440	242	103	73	47	56
Sayyid	5,362	2,599	2,763	240	206	50	60	132	151
Shaikh	235,931	116,352	119,579	8,195	7,191	8,530	8,823	7,593	7,965
Musalmans returned by actual occupation.									
Nikari	1,271	598	673	...	...	24	25	...	...

Group.	Raniganj.		Asansol.		Kaksa.		Katwa.	
	Male.	Female.	Male.	Female.	Male.	Female.	Male.	Female.
Musalmans returned by sect.								
Sunni	9	1	217	166	...	...	2	...
Musalmans returned by title.								
Pathan	469	368	524	277	77	68	231	239
Sayyid	241	185	308	203	73	77	169	186
Shaikh	5,224	5,111	4,963	4,362	929	773	6,767	7,500
Musalmans returned by actual occupation.								
Nikari	...	...	...	...	...	...	70	73

DISTRICT

Caste.	District Total.			Bankura.		Onda.		Gangajalghati.		Barjora.	
	Total.	Male.	Female.	Male.	Female.	Male.	Female.	Male.	Female.	Male.	Female.
Aguri	10,936	5,576	5,360	19	7	181	153	295	328	968	898
Bagdi	49,729	24,305	25,424	993	1,006	982	1,059	1,071	1,249	1,478	1,443
Baidya	3,451	1,569	1,882	214	189	131	139	461	664	117	155
Baniya	25,066	12,193	12,873	1,556	1,490	748	670	1,457	1,444	1,226	1,350
(i) Baisya	1,993	964	1,029	170	179	52	55	2	2	571	620
(ii) Ghandha Banik ...	9,232	4,502	4,730	244	252	301	270	756	712	185	216
(iii) Khatri	3,770	1,866	1,904	290	220	...	...	243	287	153	172
(iv) Subarna Banik ...	7,392	3,482	3,910	632	629	142	147	123	104	317	342
Barui	2,911	1,477	1,434	1	...	684	637	...	...	178	198

BARDWAN—*concluded.*

Raina.		Satgachhia.		Jamalpur.		Bud-Bud.		Ausgram.	
Male.	Female.	Male.	Female.	Male.	Female.	Male.	Female.	Male.	Female.
...	...	...	...	69	81	1,277	1,188	90	97
150	145	132	88	95	98	177	155	101	97
35	30	200	229	217	261	89	238	165	125
7,000	7,550	7,205	8,000	6,910	7,657	5,894	6,174	4,888	5,126
...	...	...	...	4	1	...	...	...	...

Ketugram.		Mungalkot.		Kalna.		Purbasthali.		Manteswar.	
Male.	Female.	Male.	Female.	Male.	Female.	Male.	Female.	Male.	Female.
...	...	...	...	383	436	4	3	5	5
263	242	282	303	67	60	103	85	157	166
196	234	72	105	166	156	107	142	139	175
7,435	8,503	7,432	7,870	9,405	9,571	9,783	9,166	8,199	8,217
57	69	...	...	160	178	249	279	34	43

BANKURA.

Khatra.		Raipura.		Simlapal.		Bisnupur.		Sonamukhi.		Kotalpur.		Indas.	
Male.	Female.	Male.	Female.	Male.	Female.	Male.	Female.	Male.	Female.	Male.	Female.	Male.	Female.
2	3	123	131	13	11	357	335	289	240	530	547	2,799	2,698
390	407	57	77	40	33	3,813	4,138	4,140	4,223	5,351	5,704	5,981	6,065
93	86	18	5	6	3	218	270	145	194	66	70	100	107
671	660	434	364	375	364	2,148	2,347	1,623	1,990	947	1,068	1,008	1,117
156	168	8	3	...	...	...	...	2	2	3	...	...	...
467	451	269	243	348	346	529	582	673	760	436	510	294	388
...	...	...	...	...	...	353	358	178	237	238	239	411	391
48	46	87	71	27	18	993	1,126	757	989	177	213	179	225
2	...	8	...	...	...	123	143	235	230	250	226	2	...

Caste or Group.	District Total.			Bankura.		Onda.		Gangajalghati.		Barjora.	
	Total.	Male.	Female.	Male.	Female.	Male.	Female.	Male.	Female.	Male.	Female.
Bauri	123,197	58,417	64,780	12,931	14,333	5,752	6,413	12,585	13,184	4,150	5,003
Bhuiya	3,481	1,680	1,801	132	139	...	...	6	...	...	...
Bhumij	20,798	9,942	10,856	988	1,092	90	95	6	1	9	7
Brahman	85,002	41,892	43,110	5,022	4,728	5,016	5,110	5,598	5,693	3,206	3,233
Chamar and Muchi ...	5,450	2,273	3,177	234	356	132	220	294	412	251	319
Chasa	2,437	1,235	1,202	109	108	10	6	233	232	77	83
Dhopa	4,297	2,173	2,124	376	322	131	126	142	159	140	148
Dom and Kaora	18,048	9,006	9,042	552	589	626	677	976	1,098	857	839
Goala	62,062	31,883	30,179	4,432	3,289	4,367	4,147	5,880	5,671	1,998	2,010
Hari	6,725	3,259	3,406	410	521	69	53	412	387	161	166
Kaibartta	18,434	9,339	9,095	872	773	689	630	1,905	1,976	1,791	1,691
Kamar and Lohar ...	41,149	20,159	20,990	2,200	2,277	2,898	2,980	2,078	2,156	1,441	1,550
Kayastha	18,494	8,405	10,089	683	610	1,159	1,380	332	349	433	579
Kewat	1,996	1,027	969	250	241	49	43	209	182	284	289
Khaira	28,359	13,717	14,642	2,492	2,711	4,945	5,205	1,873	1,888	1,158	1,268
Koiri	5,283	2,540	2,743	2	1	...	...	...	...	...	...
Kora	4,746	2,287	2,459	336	402	...	...	649	686	4	4
Kumhar	9,496	4,766	4,730	542	532	502	445	733	736	255	258
Kurmi	13,724	6,690	7,034	429	410	...	...	...	...	5	8
Maira	6,007	2,919	3,088	574	577	193	170	421	462	176	178
Mal	12,958	6,218	6,740	1,956	2,102	2,630	2,867	152	160	5	3
Munda	1,327	642	685	16	23	77	74	265	260	...	...
Namasudra or Chandal	1,695	802	893	...	...	...	...	10	8	22	24
Napit	11,655	5,779	5,876	930	939	908	865	746	718	288	349
Rajput	16,766	8,405	8,361	2,901	2,941	822	738	1,045	1,069	1,233	1,358
Sadgop	45,747	22,602	23,145	1,131	1,059	3,273	3,183	352	389	1,616	1,546
Santal	101,537	50,143	51,394	7,217	7,185	6,318	6,453	3,578	3,476	8,434	8,779
Sarak	1,707	879	828	140	135	95	71	55	45	50	55
Sunri and Kalwar ...	22,265	11,266	10,999	2,354	2,215	503	503	3,256	3,207	704	726
Sutradhar	6,050	2,982	3,068	316	322	279	309	389	414	246	264
Tambuli	16,707	8,246	8,461	2,761	2,876	948	930	591	549	117	147
Tanti	30,298	15,808	14,490	1,983	1,901	1,395	1,297	1,186	1,133	378	361
Teli and Kalu	92,197	46,384	45,813	4,875	4,735	6,437	6,284	5,996	5,949	2,385	2,353
Religious devotees and persons returned by sect.											
Baisnab	19,941	9,482	10,459	1,010	1,142	1,011	1,091	1,035	1,093	641	740
Hindus returned by title or common sub-caste.											
Mahat	1,179	614	565	17	...	27	10	...	...	...	...
Naik	10,524	4,933	5,591	6	3	2,043	2,283	...	...	54	60
Samanta	5,203	2,598	2,605	2,465	2,455	56	50	18	22	1	...
Hindus returned by actual occupation.											
Jaliya	2,430	1,222	1,208	94	92	225	212	276	303	...	...
Mala	3,408	1,634	1,774	498	510	267	268	328	391	1	4
Manjhi	24,557	11,837	12,720	62	70	1,746	1,730	8	6	87	96
Matiya	12,390	5,865	6,525	583	639	1,061	1,080	34	37	84	93
Poddar	1,003	476	527	27	14	123	127	105	168	...	...
Musalmans returned by title.											
Shaikh	40,423	19,976	20,447	1,444	1,589	939	821	495	417	950	778

BANKURA—*concluded.*

Khatra.		Raipura.		Simlapal.		Bisnupur.		Sonamukhi.		Kotalpur.		Indas.	
Male.	Female.	Male.	Female.	Male.	Female.	Male.	Female.	Male.	Female.	Male.	Female.	Male.	Female.
10,820	11,660	3,754	4,259	2,084	2,318	3,469	4,213	2,723	3,230	61	64	88	103
924	1,017	542	562	65	80	...	...	...	...	...	...	11	3
5,724	6,242	2,611	2,847	287	345	21	23	29	26	177	178	...	...
4,600	4,544	1,833	1,695	2,262	2,287	6,006	6,314	2,527	2,797	3,600	4,237	2,222	2,472
94	110	62	145	63	62	373	470	40	78	560	803	170	208
32	26	210	211	...	...	563	536	1	...	...	...	...	...
294	288	298	282	87	84	396	399	119	137	55	78	105	106
609	520	678	589	295	281	844	896	887	851	1,172	1,201	1,610	1,501
2,485	2,353	1,803	1,820	705	654	3,198	3,212	3,811	3,690	1,547	1,621	1,657	1,712
379	381	491	547	109	124	433	444	254	262	351	394	190	187
180	168	82	75	8	3	1,423	1,409	1,568	1,571	347	333	494	476
1,323	1,402	1,150	1,192	418	444	5,128	5,547	2,069	2,171	897	773	497	408
384	321	466	445	112	108	2,185	2,655	504	684	521	651	1,626	2,307
...	...	56	40	11	7	109	100	56	58	3	9	...	...
885	978	460	501	799	855	...	...	1,029	1,149	...	...	76	87
...	...	...	...	...	...	2,538	2,742	...	...	...	...	...	...
685	713	570	602	32	40	...	...	...	...	...	...	11	12
608	574	609	624	159	174	447	463	276	309	425	404	205	206
2,085	2,238	3,223	3,475	910	903	13	...	3	...	16	...	6	...
350	326	152	176	3	3	371	402	325	373	165	213	169	208
716	800	419	437	285	324	10	2	...	...	23	24	22	15
...	...	214	255	...	...	70	73	...	...	...	...	...	...
67	68	74	71	...	...	118	150	67	89	189	151	255	332
522	402	268	256	108	123	689	726	280	298	602	620	432	400
1,125	1,026	235	228	194	167	340	343	279	242	123	128	90	121
1,300	1,170	1,883	1,962	386	358	2,926	2,030	2,146	2,298	6,148	6,783	1,441	1,462
...	...	17,703	18,696	4,200	4,160	2,539	2,559	75	57	73	23	6	...
114	105	88	75	63	65	69	67	75	80	55	50	75	80
2,523	2,409	632	579	183	185	429	395	417	464	109	109	156	217
51	53	69	53	5	5	546	600	360	371	467	454	254	223
648	664	534	536	109	148	1,099	1,123	750	786	307	322	322	380
925	869	1,425	1,175	219	170	3,931	3,479	1,997	1,830	1,605	1,554	764	721
1,104	1,081	1,541	1,472	958	901	8,689	8,685	1,999	2,036	3,327	8,271	4,073	4,046
950	972	886	902	432	410	1,048	1,239	784	946	775	910	910	994
217	196	319	339	...	...	34	20	...	...	...	...	...	...
3	...	73	70	81	89	2,608	3,022	9	11	56	53	...	...
56	78	1	...	...	...	...	...	...	...	1	...	...	...
11	8	89	100	...	...	338	310	44	38	119	116	26	29
...	...	...	...	...	...	292	349	162	165	...	...	36	87
659	7[illegible]8	2,357	2,548	1,719	1,768	1,817	1,997	38	34	2,629	3,044	715	710
56	56	123	128	165	187	1,137	1,344	663	765	972	1,126	987	1,070
26	20	85	92	35	27	...	...	...	...	74	85	1	...
...	...	300	218	386	347	2,079	2,986	3,255	3,293	4,265	4,058	5,863	5,940

Caste or Group.	District Total.			Suri.		Dubrajpur.		Bolpur.	
	Total.	Male.	Female.	Male.	Female.	Male.	Female.	Male.	Female.
Aguri	3,059	1,482	1,577	10	4	264	285	658	710
Bagdi	76,080	36,673	39,407	4,843	5,158	5,526	5,933	3,648	3,866
Baidya	1,239	545	694	123	163	152	175	113	137
Baniya	14,294	6,854	7,440	1,374	1,531	867	1,008	772	793
(i) Gandha Banik ...	10,082	4,850	5,232	800	916	305	335	678	648
(ii) Subarna Banik ..	2,915	1,346	1,569	186	193	524	630	94	145
Barui	2,070	1,008	1,062	186	213	97	110	90	86
Bauri	30,137	15,237	14,900	3,877	3,934	6,804	6,652	1,509	1,128
Bhuiya	1,505	691	814	387	442	6	2	...	...
Brahman	37,457	18,384	19,073	2,911	2,477	3,227	3,547	2,886	3,163
Chamar and Muchi ...	37,164	18,717	18,447	2,323	2,349	1,910	1,920	3,321	3,536
Chero	2,003	1,133	870	650	596	...	...	69	35
Dhopa	3,820	1,895	1,925	1,165	1,174	205	223	140	121
Dom	36,159	17,921	18,238	4,592	4,598	3,999	3,969	3,580	3,733
Goala	11,794	5,933	5,861	1,488	1,444	1,776	1,786	729	671
Hari	28,539	13,629	14,910	3,616	3,770	1,080	1,513	2,363	2,829
Jugi	1,659	794	865	98	116	128	125	281	301
Kahar	1,248	607	641	175	183	8	...	4	7
Kaibartta	7,172	3,453	3,719	947	1,049	597	633	228	215
Kamar and Lohar ...	10,195	5,061	5,134	746	765	705	707	1,483	1,575
Kayastha	8,452	4,072	4,380	716	642	765	995	458	505
Kewat	3,736	1,827	1,909	315	359	580	609	247	267
Kora	10,267	4,857	5,410	423	457	276	299	320	340
Kumhar	7,428	3,106	4,322	413	614	466	694	291	478
Maira	9,523	4,556	4,967	1,643	1,684	919	1,002	425	493
Mal	29,525	14,549	14,976	2,334	2,477	602	657	1,003	1,118
Malo	4,465	2,106	2,359	...	...	...	...	...	...
Namasudra or Chandal	5,777	2,789	2,988	9	10	13	11	183	180
Napit	9,712	4,648	5,064	441	466	516	601	453	472
Pod	6,132	2,938	3,194	25	57	...	...	1	...
Rajput	6,606	3,330	3,276	960	864	55	65	90	53
Sadgop	80,175	39,087	41,088	6,052	6,421	6,605	6,907	6,995	6,856
Santal	21,770	11,204	10,566	2,901	2,685	...	...	726	648
Sonar	4,838	2,468	2,370	201	291	277	232	173	107
Sunri and Kalwar ...	16,600	8,219	8,381	1,853	1,906	1,406	1,517	970	985
Sutradhar	6,409	3,077	3,332	403	450	628	616	427	437
Tambuli	1,724	825	899	30	24	371	455	365	369
Tanti	15,073	7,364	7,709	1,388	1,388	1,134	1,186	962	998
Teli and Kalu	31,079	15,166	15,913	1,639	2,096	2,766	2,721	2,230	2,030
Tiyar	1,004	440	555	49	55	50	69	79	88
Religious devotees and persons returned by sect.									
Baisnab	19,629	8,809	10,820	1,710	2,276	1,064	1,281	1,150	1,344
Hindus returned by title or common sub-caste.									
Buna	6,361	3,112	3,249	1,101	1,129	396	464	199	228
Rajbansi	2,659	1,283	1,376	...	...	4	...	...	...
Hindus returned by actual occupation.									
Matiya...	1,509	754	755	...	...	98	81	606	683
Musalmans returned by title.									
Pathan	12,643	6,233	6,410	443	454	2,978	3,398	348	327
Sayyid	4,068	2,311	2,357	164	148	333	371	207	211
Shaikh	130,005	65,840	64,165	662	665	7,485	7,475	8,064	8,072
Musalmans returned by actual occupation.									
Jolaha	2,853	1,428	1,425	187	253	180	140	169	162

BIRBHUM.

Sakulipur.		Labhpur.		Rampur Hat.		Maureswar.		Nalhati.	
Male.	Female.	Male.	Female.	Male.	Female.	Male.	Female.	Male.	Female.
484	494	55	75	11	9	...	...	...	...
4,188	4,364	3,217	3,370	5,746	6,401	5,250	5,705	4,265	4,610
33	50	20	21	33	33	5	3	66	112
755	909	597	677	717	684	785	823	987	1,015
709	841	493	570	491	481	533	570	841	871
46	68	92	91	139	163	140	144	125	136
...	...	...	...	217	242	141	159	277	252
467	544	628	635	946	950	645	682	361	375
...	...	...	...	175	209	74	105	49	56
1,733	1,939	1,882	2,035	1,846	1,791	2,235	2,463	1,664	1,658
1,960	2,044	2,543	2,531	1,154	1,120	2,917	2,938	2,589	2,009
19	18	28	29	141	107	67	30	159	65
75	76	48	59	137	126	...	...	125	146
1,588	1,653	1,060	1,043	967	998	1,199	1,281	936	1,063
846	899	226	230	71	73	229	204	568	554
1,421	1,406	914	939	585	585	1,218	1,334	2,432	2,534
...	...	96	88	33	38	26	30	132	167
...	...	...	...	123	124	47	35	250	292
287	317	531	562	127	128	25	29	711	786
320	304	140	138	524	518	208	230	935	897
443	561	197	220	327	260	610	580	556	617
95	120	75	78	...	...	515	476	...	...
136	111	346	317	2,477	2,883	660	698	249	305
301	427	246	245	368	470	630	860	391	540
263	333	267	354	417	428	443	454	179	214
129	121	...	...	4,077	4,155	325	373	6,079	6,075
...	...	145	125	...	...	...	...	1,961	2,234
80	70	7	3	3	5	5	1	2,484	2,708
296	353	262	334	379	438	518	548	1,783	1,852
...	...	...	...	626	642	542	639	1,744	1,856
73	74	114	115	736	834	694	677	608	594
5,566	5,997	6,012	6,443	2,126	2,488	4,697	4,828	1,034	1,148
2	2	33	28	2,459	2,227	2,217	2,176	2,866	2,800
280	248	313	314	335	333	235	233	564	562
1,292	1,330	792	854	636	556	770	753	500	480
363	402	285	308	313	348	326	379	332	392
13	3	6	6	3	1	33	55	4	6
424	441	625	643	1,581	1,692	430	489	820	872
991	972	800	818	1,983	2,390	3,861	4,033	896	853
46	53	29	25	75	90	70	80	51	95
801	1,020	974	1,152	752	906	1,591	1,795	767	1,046
...	...	32	37	277	291	858	851	249	249
...	...	...	...	5	8	...	...	1,274	1,373
26	27	...	...	15	15	...	...	9	9
457	452	466	238	306	316	349	319	886	906
194	189	192	191	778	817	129	154	314	276
6,5[illegible]0	5,862	3,830	3,891	8,189	8,125	6,046	6,006	24,984	24,069
137	124	150	181	200	225	107	115	298	225

DISTRICT

Caste.	District Total.			Midnapur.		Jhargaon.		Binpur.		Saldani.	
	Total.	Male.	Female.	Male.	Female.	Male.	Female.	Male.	Female.	Male.	Female.
Bagdi	75,469	37,176	38,293	2,017	2,017	6	11	105	190	664	686
Baidya	1,993	1,012	981	180	150	4	...	17	6	1	...
Baniya	28,051	14,166	13,885	2,172	2,063	143	142	672	645	33	37
(i) Baisya	4,885	2,484	2,401	73	70	...	...	3	...	...	...
(ii) Gandha Banik	6,657	3,287	3,370	495	437	5	2	253	279	14	16
(iii) Khatri	3,736	1,938	1,798	479	459	...	...	...	...	...	...
(iv) Subarna Banik	8,304	4,147	4,157	898	857	10	7	157	153	10	6
Barui	7,662	3,831	3,831	230	229	294	293	1	3	...	...
Bauri	13,193	6,566	6,627	701	747	80	76	1,517	1,572	1,006	1,055
Bhat	3,031	1,458	1,573	46	51	2	2	121	112	...	...
Bhuiya	10,628	5,149	5,479	118	145	727	803	...	...	32	21
Bhumij	38,804	18,731	20,073	1,287	1,348	2,234	2,420	2,674	3,006	1,879	1,960
Brahman	121,888	61,886	60,002	4,065	3,897	440	379	753	676	318	306
Chamar and Muchi	7,379	3,893	3,481	380	405	139	122	112	118	83	89
Dhopa	39,351	19,476	19,875	1,588	1,575	391	410	414	449	286	275
Dom and Kaora	23,560	11,795	11,765	1,169	1,007	444	488	499	620	194	178
Goala	54,565	28,170	26,395	3,324	2,401	1,193	1,200	704	725	321	311
Hari and Mihtar	26,421	13,145	13,276	1,190	1,232	414	427	291	344	59	71
Jugi	4,585	2,253	2,332	11	16	11	9	51	61	9	5
Kadma	27,211	13,533	13,678	66	46	...	...	63	80	20	13
Kahar	1,529	779	750	57	49	31	15	78	70	2	3
Kaibartta	803,998	399,746	404,252	3,399	3,193	1,123	1,097	1,364	1,345	1,918	1,894
Kamar and Lohar	38,777	19,517	19,260	1,607	1,545	794	789	796	776	443	434
Kansari	1,149	580	569	...	...	...	...	...	...	...	...
Karanga	6,079	2,979	3,100	43	32	12	20	26	30	99	103
Kastha	22,889	11,416	11,473	2,867	2,821	29	25	...	...	24	13
Kayastha and Karan	82,526	40,578	41,948	3,867	3,606	1,113	1,055	1,309	1,268	1,686	1,725
Kewat	2,853	1,415	1,438	53	66	...	...	...	...	34	46
Khadal	2,562	1,304	1,258	...	...	1	...	...	...	...	...
Khaira	7,236	3,597	3,639	68	95	208	221	203	199	42	41
Khandait	1,467	727	740	13	...	88	101	...	...	...	...
Kharia	3,296	1,617	1,679	...	...	...	...	968	1,057	...	...
Kora	8,845	4,433	4,412	912	927	438	432	309	404	76	75
Kumhar	26,326	13,271	13,055	993	1,014	718	631	474	513	110	117
Kurmi	55,327	28,906	26,421	3,003	2,951	8,337	7,597	3,045	3,123	5,564	4,768
Mahili	3,112	1,543	1,569	120	150	66	69	265	240	131	134
Maira and Halwai	6,057	3,049	3,008	442	420	113	93	164	151	10	11
Mal	4,317	2,103	2,214	20	...	131	157	499	611	433	445
Malakar	8,002	4,015	3,987	427	437	3	5	11	6	38	25
Munda	2,388	1,168	1,220	252	265	156	139	262	295	...	...
Namasudra or Chandal ...	41,939	21,030	20,900	2,388	2,422	...	...	2	3	...	...
Napit	43,551	21,440	22,102	1,674	1,728	309	303	387	406	254	241
Pan	1,452	596	856	...	...	...	...	...	...	1	15
Pod	22,930	11,780	11,150	56	36	...	...	...	...	...	...
Rajput	17,692	9,068	8,624	1,366	1,258	56	68	201	215	253	233
Raju	57,749	28,809	28,940	199	78	61	44	...	...	93	82
Rajwar	2,324	1,141	1,183	156	141	446	432	64	78	33	39
Sadgop	118,923	59,600	59,323	10,622	10,545	490	417	2,219	1,064	2,561	2,566
Sankhari	1,360	708	652	...	...	...	...	...	...	..	...
Santal	119,159	56,609	62,550	3,808	3,803	8,861	8,915	11,517	15,397	5,835	5,919
Savar	2,808	1,376	1,432	82	92	51	44	76	78	...	...
Sonar	7,164	3,550	3,614	234	224	...	...	...	...	...	...
Sukli	30,325	15,225	15,100	3,222	3,159	8	6	...	...	217	187
Sunri	8,555	4,237	4,318	287	243	68	72	593	632	553	544

MIDNAPUR.

Debra.		Garhbeta.		Keshpur.		Sabang.		Narayangarh.		Dantun.		Gopiballabhpur.		Ghatal.	
Male.	Female.	Male.	Female.	Male.	Female.	Male.	Female.	Male.	Female.	Male.	Female.	Male.	Female.	Male.	Female.
963	1,009	927	958	7,137	7,219	498	558	2,522	2,458	147	143	299	296	6,916	7,005
146	149	1	...	173	177	68	76	15	17	2	...	16	11	17	19
193	235	1,559	1,461	373	331	418	437	858	875	369	362	671	651	936	959
...	...	177	130	...	...	129	159	127	130	3	5	3	6	2	...
51	65	744	726	90	70	113	130	165	152	9	8	133	136	238	223
...	...	7	10	98	91	34	20	262	283	26	21	216	202	...	...
95	125	487	453	146	137	68	60	314	310	125	129	262	270	668	697
50	60	469	481	112	77	170	155	188	166	463	468	129	138	127	157
8	...	1,502	1,515	312	262	129	138	21	19	20	24	269	284	502	502
...	1	...	...	62	99	73	95	...	...	356	345	25	66	...	...
21	26	367	355	12	9	4	...	234	247	737	780	729	816	...	...
49	...	485	500	117	177	9	1	710	707	52	72	9,095	9,788	3	...
1,430	1,424	4,128	4,286	2,351	2,393	3,855	3,995	2,743	2,639	3,345	2,989	2,123	1,957	3,855	4,062
150	136	204	158	250	138	225	221	101	108	48	47	75	58	791	581
564	565	612	602	265	285	1,866	1,866	1,305	1,324	1,075	1,161	12	14	462	460
294	308	505	508	317	318	589	663	419	384	671	677	995	993	459	445
340	233	1,879	1,826	1,489	1,459	751	724	1,154	1,163	1,486	1,447	2.783	2,795	2,389	1,511
246	260	680	692	568	584	1,199	1,163	1,016	1,002	954	934	353	414	605	611
15	7	1	...	2	...	245	234	40	51	63	64	55	52	31	30
1	2	...	...	...	...	...	...	773	785	3,114	3,080	231	251	...	...
...	...	2	...	16	6	6	7	27	51	5	2	15	12	33	29
11,794	11,909	3,699	3,367	2,688	2,575	61,093	60,677	9,584	9,167	9,937	9,845	3,842	3,737	8,264	8,712
320	370	...	...	409	388	665	726	1,101	913	804	748	2,140	2,146	1,736	1,794
...	...	...	...	...	...	...	...	117	109	82	66	4	...	19	19
66	91	145	130	123	138	376	437	321	272	200	197	34	37	...	...
1,363	1,469	53	48	156	185	1,793	1,829	3,257	3,199	515	472	...	...	115	109
2,124	2,356	1,056	1,065	584	701	3,363	3,613	1,920	1,920	893	934	1,724	1,686	3,072	3,564
1	...	...	...	234	220	...	...	184	179	219	223	...	...	289	270
...	...	...	...	...	...	31	19	214	196	148	142	12	14	...	...
1	...	1,632	1,563	...	...	1	2	123	119	...	...	...	2	...	...
5	...	...	...	...	...	...	...	...	...	49	47	534	556	...	...
...	...	...	...	...	...	...	...	...	...	178	166	43	45	...	...
3	...	...	...	...	...	821	813	...	...	...	...	121	122	...	...
205	211	775	659	268	258	1,362	1,384	693	644	572	527	501	521	371	332
13	...	1,135	986	387	420	15	11	1,081	1,086	3	13	5,906	5,069	16	...
...	...	449	439	5	5	...	...	121	127	7	7	269	285	...	...
246	242	395	396	73	74	60	52	199	174	115	115	118	108	171	152
...	...	461	508	23	7	1	...	...	...	3	3	103	91	429	392
90	86	119	100	89	36	240	258	210	180	158	173	1,178	1,227	87	100
226	258	...	...	...	...	...	...	...	...	...	...	239	248	...	...
663	706	195	196	1,640	1,565	3,434	3,454	1,649	1,610	376	369	222	123	1,551	1,351
1,016	1,034	1,184	1,199	580	556	1,289	1,465	1,023	1,003	972	904	807	826	855	877
4	15	47	65	...	...	...	...	...	...	...	...	496	630	13	43
3	1	...	...	...	...	...	...	...	...	...	...	2	3	...	...
114	109	118	117	1,189	1,077	307	288	369	407	1,247	1,123	1,292	1,178	854	856
3	1	...	...	...	...	5	3	4,052	4,021	11,964	11,613	2,253	2,250	...	...
1	...	72	73	43	54	...	...	2	...	1	...	323	366	...	...
1,100	1,080	5,254	5,300	7,244	7,486	980	1,084	1,810	1,848	1,374	1,337	4,082	3,778	4,612	4.821
...	...	...	...	...	...	29	22	...	...	...	...	18	22	...	...
190	83	...	...	12,015	12,757	614	690	20	24	626	714	12,103	13,453	170	164
...	...	...	...	...	...	42	44	44	54	62	72	401	420	...	...
324	333	256	260	42	43	366	369	28	38	...	...	...	...	2	2
1,858	1,940	...	...	328	324	624	630	1,939	1,926	2,654	2,551	91	106	361	359
70	76	900	938	...	...	12	16	293	272	70	72	25	23	228	284

DISTRICT

Caste.	Chandrakona.		Daspur.		Tamluk.		Maslandpur.		Sutahata.		Panchkura.	
	Male.	Female.	Male.	Female.	Male.	Female.	Male.	Female.	Male.	Female.	Male.	Female.
Bagdi	4,445	4,416	4,195	4,585	105	111	842	949	852	847	1,476	1,679
Baidya	151	154	28	14	7	4	8	...	5	3	30	62
Baniya	1,086	1,275	476	532	266	264	210	197	77	28	481	570
(i) Baisya	59	52	98	98	36	48	6	6	...	...	171	133
(ii) Gandha Banik...	353	455	226	261	36	33	47	30	6	1	71	81
(iii) Khatri	117	192	...	...	112	79	112	78	67	22	166	171
(iv) Subarna Banik	437	448	86	109	82	104	33	13	...	...	119	115
Barui	354	358	280	300	274	256	129	123	6	8	1	...
Bauri	236	213	...	...	...	...	188	136	7	13	...	...
Bhat	60	57	123	126	8	5	112	155	...	...	40	39
Bhuiya	9	11	331	348	427	477	23	36	551	601	...	1
Bhumij	82	90	...	...	...	...	...	...	...	...	6	4
Brahman	3,493	3,684	3,758	4,056	1,956	2,098	2,007	1,644	1,271	908	2,745	2,761
Chamar and Muchi	156	142	168	125	102	96	155	157	76	73	271	277
Dhopa	373	369	1,043	1,160	1,306	1,101	901	1,050	578	602	763	809
Dom and Kaora	918	900	1,332	1,372	452	462	208	210	172	186	767	783
Goala	1,070	1,046	1,875	1,906	477	559	1,270	1,247	246	260	1,718	1,755
Hari and Mihtar...	529	561	811	765	163	151	452	439	86	86	381	347
Jugi	23	16	6	9	56	49	216	217	163	194	62	63
Kadma	...	...	28	29	...	...	1	...	74	41	...	...
Kahar	10	...	114	148	32	25	30	5	72	63	93	93
Kaibartta	3,093	2,907	27,678	29,564	2,8325	29,471	30,788	31,107	18,425	18,159	35,814	30,778
Kamar and Lohar	720	669	2,153	2,142	452	443	353	306	201	126	472	566
Kansari	...	...	178	220	...	...	...	...	6	8	5	1
Karanga	3	5	248	231	74	88	126	106	193	219	129	133
Kastha	4	...	238	271	31	26	19	27	4	...	156	130
Kayastha and Karan	555	668	3,037	3,328	1,698	1,644	556	483	256	199	2,087	1,985
Kewat	...	...	...	...	167	206	36	31	...	...	...	...
Khadal	146	133	...	...	...	...	1	1	...	1	...	...
Khaira	5	4	238	309	...	...	947	945	1	1	...	...
Khandait	1	...	...	...	...	...	...	...	...	...	31	33
Kharia	...	...	...	...	...	...	...	...	...	...	...	...
Kora	44	264	...	...	435	413	...	...	...	...	...	...
Kumhar	617	610	899	986	422	426	209	234	183	186	799	823
Kurmi	5	...	3	1	...	...	6	...	4	1	4	...
Mahili	...	...	...	...	...	...	...	...	...	...	...	...
Maira and Halwai	203	225	129	131	147	111	1	...	2	1	33	54
Mal	...	...	...	...	...	...	...	...	...	...	...	...
Malakar	191	129	392	369	104	90	71	76	47	39	197	207
Munda	...	...	...	...	...	...	...	...	...	...	...	...
Namasudra or Chandal ...	563	579	510	544	286	305	1,662	1,743	590	572	803	844
Napit	757	706	1,334	1,452	640	636	665	673	509	539	867	1,038
Pan	...	...	...	...	...	...	...	...	...	...	...	...
Pod	...	...	...	...	...	...	...	...	...	...	...	...
Rajput	159	113	178	198	118	117	117	26	114	136	163	185
Raju	...	...	...	...	...	...	...	...	1	1	...	...
Rajwar	...	...	...	...	...	...	...	...	...	...	...	...
Sadgop	14,508	14,387	1,811	1,390	8	15	65	11	94	92	185	160
Sankhari	178	167	297	308	5	...	20	...	5	...	23	13
Santal	338	253	121	39	5	...	52	47	23	43	...	...
Savar	...	...	...	...	57	59	53	47	46	39	20	22
Sonar	165	173	943	976	248	247	356	351	124	103	336	354
Sukli	532	487	583	624	21	23	53	41	4	2	39	25
Sunri	336	363	57	67	...	...	76	80	47	37	30	28

MIDNAPUR—*continued.*

Nandigram.		Contai.		Egra.		Pataspur.		Ramnagar.		Bhagabanpur.		Khajri.	
Male.	Female.	Male.	Female.	Male.	Female.	Male.	Female.	Male.	Female.	Male.	Female.	Male.	Female.
653	622	1,018	1,208	40	31	120	125	59	60	724	737	446	443
2	...	29	39	1	...	3	3	71	90	16	8	1	...
864	877	337	310	67	77	118	118	122	105	1,060	1,003	475	416
656	699	2	1	14	14	1	...	...	...	924	850	...	...
125	125	48	56	...	...	...	...	32	29	43	53	...	...
83	53	87	96	...	...	5	...	8	...	23	5	36	16
...	...	47	28	7	7	10	12	16	20	70	95	...	...
20	20	62	60	68	62	20	6	75	66	305	341	4	4
1	...	65	67	...	...	2	4	...	...	...	...	...	...
151	169	83	45	59	70	78	69	50	56	3	...	1	...
12	17	...	...	71	57	673	634	91	95	...	...	...	...
...	...	1	...	8	...	...	...	...	...	...	...	...	...
2,795	2,657	4,229	3,597	2,348	1,949	2,349	2,183	2,497	2,625	2,232	2,328	800	569
143	172	50	64	8	2	87	76	6	4	103	109	5	3
802	830	1,451	1,555	637	603	929	927	657	660	838	835	369	338
372	267	286	212	201	214	268	280	114	97	102	119	48	54
639	797	1,141	1,161	201	193	285	261	584	682	367	361	390	372
460	423	661	670	342	359	460	449	209	232	930	942	125	118
177	177	424	431	130	152	55	57	122	148	215	226	70	66
175	255	2,372	2,528	1,635	1,654	1,351	1,285	1,645	1,706	1,310	1,314	674	610
62	95	4	...	71	68	2	...	5	3	3	...	9	7
21,167	21,271	30,835	31,528	11,719	11,016	22,722	22,129	11,048	11,001	31,374	31,075	8,053	7,848
816	781	903	921	720	718	472	475	625	584	689	733	226	228
...	...	...	...	...	...	92	65	51	58	...	...	26	23
98	102	192	188	147	160	...	...	88	92	181	225	56	43
27	25	283	321	66	63	98	101	9	12	274	257	5	11
720	871	1,702	1,780	1,086	1,081	2,803	2,800	181	209	3,114	3,120	72	50
...	...	75	58	...	...	121	135	2	5	...	...	...	...
238	258	...	...	...	...	432	433	8	5	73	56	...	...
28	39	...	...	99	99	1	...	...	...	...	...	...	...
...	...	...	...	4	1	...	2	2	...	...	...	...	...
...	...	...	...	87	95	341	316	...	...	...	...	...	...
...	...	908	899	...	...	...	...	...	...	76	63	...	...
498	500	440	487	670	646	720	660	150	131	310	252	307	284
93	108	...	2	...	...	271	271	...	...	15	17	...	...
110	113	...	...	...	...	...	...	...	...	...	...	...	...
28	34	33	24	140	189	16	8	76	90	101	110	34	43
...	...	...	...	...	...	...	...	...	...	...	...	...	...
89	152	22	12	40	28	78	73	11	5	112	101	61	65
...	...	...	...	...	...	33	15	...	...	...	...	...	...
1,191	1,217	338	360	...	...	11	4	370	318	2,448	2,493	139	125
1,141	1,100	1,246	1,377	1,162	1,109	642	650	577	636	1,038	1,070	571	574
...	...	...	...	...	...	...	...	35	88	...	..	...	...
2,840	2,686	829	829	...	...	2	5	...	...	2	...	8,046	7,590
85	59	97	85	111	110	113	113	131	145	100	106	210	202
44	...	2,098	2,288	3,638	3,687	26	30	4,289	4,819	25	14	58	44
...	...	...	...	...	...	...	...	...	...	...	...	...	...
202	187	207	212	75	73	474	488	55	42	70	95	8	4
7	...	3	1	111	102	6	11	...	1	4	...	2	...
38	25	21	4	...	...	...	...	209	202	...	...	...	...
298	308	54	50	...	...	...	...	39	30	51	67	...	...
136	136	...	...	2	4	...	...	...	...	...	...	4	1
196	216	839	340	1,192	1,148	808	803	137	189	2	2	17	14
3	2	271	293	72	53	47	45	188	161	9	13	...	...

DISTRICT

Caste or Group.	District Total.			Midnapur.		Jhargaon.		Binpur.		Salbani.	
	Total.	Male.	Female.	Male.	Female.	Male.	Female.	Male.	Female.	Male.	Female.
Sutradhar	9,825	4,809	5,016	155	199	72	89	21	14	5	5
Tambuli	11,480	5,677	5,803	894	941	9	10	229	210	389	370
Tanti and Tatwa	95,523	48,076	47,447	1,680	1,663	1,575	1,617	1,683	1,577	929	[illegible]
Teli and Kalu	70,558	35,319	35,239	1,572	1,511	256	243	1,253	1,105	469	447
Tiyar	8,093	4,192	3,901	4	...	...	...	78	73	...	...
Religious devotees and persons returned by sect.											
Baisnab	75,287	36,294	38,993	2,087	2,417	386	432	934	941	323	307
Hindus returned by title or common sub-caste.											
Mahat	3,971	1,999	1,972	89	48	254	246	1,360	1,376	...	...
Malik	5,533	2,637	2,896	325	336	75	64	175	229	275	[illegible]
Naik	7,869	3,810	4,059	314	326	1	...	...	...	534	[illegible]
Raut	1,277	609	668	3	1	...	...	...	...	...	...
Hindus returned by actual occupation.											
Dulia	8,914	4,393	4,521	130	196	...	...	...	...	...	...
Jaliya	8,345	4,190	4,155	...	...	21	22	141	108	...	...
Machhua	2,399	1,148	1,251	282	359	...	...	...	...	...	...
Manjhi	46,472	22,822	23,650	1,835	1,859	1,319	1,371	2,223	2,243	1,540	[illegible]
Matiya	1,293	660	633	132	120	...	...	75	60	...	...
Hindus returned by locality.											
Hindustanis	3,936	1,971	1,965	490	480	...	...	107	106	165	209
Uriyas	27,100	13,533	13,567	3	3	159	144	82	62	112	137
Musalmans returned by sect.											
Sunni	2,837	1,401	1,436	444	480	45	53	3	3	6	[illegible]
Musalmans returned by title.											
Moghul	3,222	1,584	1,638	62	47	19	17	24	21	2	...
Pathan	28,065	14,090	13,975	1,684	1,679	48	53	96	76	99	[illegible]
Sayyid	8,080	4,003	4,077	281	276	33	30	4	15	6	4
Shaikh	119,439	58,135	61,304	3,137	3,553	596	507	143	112	405	[illegible]
Musalmans returned by actual occupation.											
Jolaha	3,983	2,073	1,910	191	205	4	5	30	35	56	[illegible]
Soria	2,093	922	1,171	118	164	69	5	53	84	56	[illegible]

MIDNAPUR—*continued.*

Debra.		Garbeta.		Keshpur.		Sabang.		Narayangarh.		Dantun.		Gopiballabhpur.		Ghatal.	
Male.	Female.	Male.	Female.	Male.	Female.	Male.	Female.	Male.	Female.	Male.	Female.	Male.	Female.	Male.	Female.
208	211	416	407	51	54	140	138	189	179	199	194	219	209	393	418
107	107	1,422	1,437	192	201	103	81	147	131	96	87	200	185	687	729
870	868	1,066	1,126	847	853	3,050	3,097	3,356	3,277	2,960	2,851	3,202	3,198	1,306	1,363
1,095	1,055	2,385	2,183	589	503	2,613	2,706	1,407	1,378	4,357	4,294	2,500	2,486	1,322	1,379
...	...	...	...	...	...	834	780	...	...	...	...	3	2	300	304
647	725	1,568	1,588	401	436	872	995	3,586	3,581	2,166	2,790	2,827	2,775	1,174	1,263
1	...	276	291	3	1	...	...	...	1	...	...	9	8	...	...
125	140	90	95	10	5	112	115	78	66	110	119	352	384	95	96
...	...	1,706	1,893	1,157	1,241	...	...	6	5	...	...	...	...	22	3
6	7	...	...	...	...	14	11	93	67	233	305	48	44	...	...
142	159	10	11	322	347	133	132	1	2	94	110	12	15	366	368
78	93	498	472	169	157	493	471	98	91	26	23	43	39	348	381
44	50	...	...	659	685	...	...	...	...	...	...	...	...	...	...
87	67	1,858	2,032	2,401	2,530	12	16	1,655	1,704	820	869	5,975	6,292	411	362
45	48	...	...	...	...	10	15	25	28	...	...	...	...	...	...
...	...	360	307	175	179	40	60	9	15	105	108	...	...	138	136
43	56	1	3	2	...	207	271	553	533	1,234	1,229	1,396	1,332	...	...
239	249	378	379	...	...	85	86	...	...	157	141	3	1	40	39
20	10	46	32	61	67	144	141	6	...	...	...	...	...	152	154
467	520	468	461	411	400	523	554	418	380	988	923	221	117	272	298
118	136	128	152	221	231	340	362	167	152	33	28	51	41	95	90
2,261	2,405	2,802	2,639	7,594	7,736	2,625	2,854	1,178	1,525	1,620	1,661	212	127	1,328	1,594
35	39	95	76	42	51	14	13	59	48	75	62	9	4	45	51
85	45	...	...	96	86	...	...	...	...	80	95	...	...	76	92

Caste or Group.	Chandrakona.		Daspur.		Tamluk.		Maslandpur.		Sutahata.		Panchkura.	
	Male.	Female.	Male.	Female.	Male.	Female.	Male.	Female.	Male.	Female.	Male.	Female.
Sutradhar	355	352	435	452	119	144	61	*48	10	7	207	193
Tambuli	475	518	388	427	23	30	4	...	...	...	129	156
Tanti and Tatwa	1,706	1,553	1,856	1,936	693	707	552	591	725	764	1,177	1,256
Teli and Kalu	1,281	1,184	1,686	1,872	615	681	622	759	399	491	1,340	1,416
Tiyar	...	...	397	347	434	268	597	510	121	115	574	534
Religious devotees and persons returned by sect.												
Baisnab	921	1,044	1,437	1,341	515	688	369	351	394	402	1,319	1,704
Hindus returned by title or common sub-caste.												
Mahat	6	1	1	...	...	...	...	...	...	...	...	...
Malik	153	220	120	187	76	66	...	...	24	34	...	...
Naik	22	13	...	...	...	...	...	...	...	...	...	...
Raut	1	...	...	...	...	...	74	92	...	...	...	...
Hindus returned by actual occupation.												
Dulia	1,101	1,095	340	382	110	104	154	148	854	832	256	255
Jaliya	460	537	700	744	235	191	44	48	78	75	223	222
Machhua	...	...	147	135	...	...	...	...	...	...	16	22
Manjhi	2,604	2,819	78	79	2	...	...	...	...	...	...	...
Matiya	...	...	60	65	...	...	...	...	78	85	...	...
Hindus returned by locality.												
Hindustanis	...	...	...	...	211	206	...	...	...	...	56	59
Uriyas	...	1	4	...	182	210	73	83	71	56	12	12
Musalmans returned by sect.												
Sunni	...	...	...	...	...	1	...	...	3	1	...	...
Musalmans returned by title.												
Moghul	83	81	54	102	51	48	84	89	71	40	41	62
Pathan	184	187	181	201	383	340	274	266	198	154	2,161	2,589
Sayyid	165	154	107	129	207	218	197	198	169	187	433	434
Shaikh	2,430	2,572	833	913	3,796	3,886	3,656	3,833	2,640	3,019	9,249	9,983
Musalmans returned by actual occupation.												
Jolaha	20	30	48	45	10	15	258	223	230	195	425	394
Soria	...	...	25	45	...	...	115	180	...	...	...	...

MIDNAPUR—*concluded.*

Nandigram.		Contai.		Egra.		Pataspur.		Ramnagar.		Bhagabanpur.		Khajri.	
Male.	Female.	Male.	Female.	Male.	Female.	Male.	Female.	Male.	Female.	Male.	Female.	Male.	Female.
191	253	285	343	347	344	198	185	245	264	135	148	159	166
...	...	1	...	86	86	74	76	22	21	...	...	...	...
2,306	2,141	5,546	5,588	2,580	2,461	2,689	2,487	2,025	2,061	2,363	2,212	1,374	1,378
1,018	1,033	1,494	1,498	2,749	2,689	1,608	1,634	1,133	1,183	1,173	1,184	378	375
523	568	127	199	157	168	...	...	22	20	17	19	4	...
1,505	1,538	1,526	1,603	1,918	1,945	3,364	3,356	1,304	1,315	2,321	2,794	2,430	2,652
...	...	...	...	...	...	...	...	...	...	...	...	...	...
80	76	...	...	92	88	203	216	...	...	67	100	...	...
6	4	23	20	10	10	3	2	...	...	...	...	6	7
2	...	...	...	...	...	117	120	...	...	18	21	...	...
50	43	18	9	43	53	134	142	67	50	...	...	56	68
213	229	125	125	...	...	19	13	21	32	67	82	...	...
...	...	...	...	...	...	...	...	...	...	...	...	...	...
...	...	2	...	...	...	...	...	...	...	...	...	...	...
...	...	...	...	216	202	...	...	...	...	...	...	19	10
...	...	11	25	...	...	104	75	...	...	...	...	...	...
281	288	3,909	4,055	1,263	1,248	691	632	3,123	3,082	132	130	...	...
...	...	...	...	...	...	...	...	...	...	...	...	...	...
403	425	102	95	36	42	21	19	98	110	4	7	...	...
1,003	1,082	2,035	1,784	543	496	385	391	431	372	518	511	99	94
526	538	186	167	75	73	107	108	211	192	132	145	11	17
2,596	2,577	3,390	3,647	761	760	1,433	1,427	1,181	1,206	1,292	1,373	977	1,035
136	122	189	131	39	48	33	29	20	15	14	10	6	9
69	68	...	...	...	...	45	60	...	...	...	...	85	122

DISTRICT

Caste or Group.	District Total.			Hugli.		Balagarh.		Pandua.		Dhaniakhali.		Polba.	
	Total.	Male.	Female.	Male.	Female.	Male.	Female.	Male.	Female.	Male.	Female.	Male.	Female.
Aguri	6,001	2,952	3,049	196	157	26	34	111	107	494	520	227	218
Bagdi	157,304	78,849	78,455	5,068	5,575	2,447	2,402	4,338	4,352	2,012	2,176	2,855	2,930
Baidya	4,509	2,296	2,213	295	301	206	279	43	32	201	121	10	9
Baiti	5,077	2,404	2,673	73	59	29	36	98	88	1,020	1,049	93	67
Baniya	21,398	9,829	11,569	1,495	1,896	665	720	368	435	2,283	2,467	461	578
(i) Baisya	1,396	604	792	366	491	2	...	14	15	52	49	...	...
(ii) Gandha Banik	7,536	3,405	4,131	201	183	297	372	133	195	733	730	295	318
(iii) Khatri	3,433	1,647	1,786	41	40	2	1	64	52	504	610	62	150
(iv) Subarna Banik	7,837	3,517	4,320	862	1,169	179	234	76	138	732	806	104	110
Barui	2,795	1,366	1,429	415	457	57	57	...	...	238	248	44	70
Bauri	6,081	2,850	3,231	153	152	96	103	1,009	1,208	580	652	555	565
Bhuiya	1,658	854	804	37	19	...	...	...	...	319	310	86	109
Brahman	74,991	35,482	39,509	2,532	2,651	1,686	2,148	2,108	2,753	1,085	1,322	1,612	1,718
Chamar and Muchi	20,534	10,221	10,313	1,163	909	692	739	865	782	910	1,001	409	402
Dhopa	7,960	3,821	4,139	184	272	158	176	126	142	498	460	122	128
Dom and Kaora	26,419	13,248	13,171	452	516	183	180	969	924	1,415	1,435	257	285
Goala	38,602	19,472	19,130	1,206	980	1,748	1,730	1,853	1,984	991	1,076	879	986
Hari and Mihtar	12,967	6,895	6,072	487	307	312	232	873	795	600	542	427	451
Jugi	4,831	2,344	2,487	80	81	79	107	78	102	873	904	27	31
Kahar	2,843	1,596	1,247	155	27	150	100	13	...	207	209	67	64
Kaibartta	143,780	71,158	72,622	1,732	1,742	3,286	3,122	762	963	1,058	1,089	603	628
Kamar and Lohar	13,841	7,031	6,810	272	298	579	624	230	277	1,068	1,118	416	451
Kansari	2,539	1,261	1,278	328	353	11	9	65	62	469	497	252	209
Kayastha	29,177	13,360	15,817	1,332	1,413	842	902	651	920	1,068	1,333	434	522
Khaira	1,800	926	874	21	16	9	9	111	107	220	252	439	453
Kora	2,049	1,015	1,034	22	19	100	90	275	254	75	50	55	74
Kumhar	10,883	5,831	5,052	214	193	167	126	225	140	878	853	385	325
Kurmi	2,346	1,360	986	128	38	49	40	27	14	471	496	89	114
Maira aad Halwai	9,728	5,033	4,695	337	296	327	371	184	176	196	181	239	221
Mal	1,978	1,011	967	7	5	...	...	...	...	489	546	84	93
Malakar	5,474	3,008	2,466	106	54	14	19	78	76	583	571	162	137
Namasudra or Chandal ...	14,042	7,072	6,970	511	549	1,159	1,169	1,229	1,023	889	938	178	179
Napit and Hajjam	14,147	6,555	7,592	415	454	269	289	250	253	985	1,063	414	457
Oraon	1,993	1,501	492	63	4	1	...	93	...	49	...	124	121
Pod	2,685	1,400	1,285	16	10	5	8	22	11	87	64	165	147
Rajput	5,275	2,557	2,718	96	69	49	61	136	112	731	853	186	189
Sadgop	56,288	27,211	29,077	1,660	1,897	1,300	1,529	2,034	2,428	908	944	473	727
Sankhari	1,276	635	641	6	8	...	...	...	...	312	307	128	108
Santal	4,109	2,336	1,773	34	3	71	40	76	23	616	652	233	207
Sonar	8,794	4,500	4,294	150	156	96	105	186	175	925	1,018	226	261
Sukli	3,893	1,995	1,898	...	...	...	...	...	...	...	...	...	...
Sunri and Kalwar	4,966	2,254	2,712	206	214	11	22	53	79	687	698	297	252
Sutradhar	6,361	3,086	3,275	193	178	45	56	74	78	801	868	227	263
Tambuli	8,218	3,777	4,441	297	288	...	...	145	189	840	1,012	184	212
Tanti and Tatwa	24,571	12,774	11,797	614	691	373	300	189	151	932	784	283	190
Teli and Kalu	54,603	27,256	27,347	938	932	844	477	665	879	2,027	2,135	633	897
Tiyar	9,233	4,627	4,606	79	98	296	321	...	...	161	184	154	102
Religious devotees and persons returned by sect.													
Baisnab	12,803	5,939	6,864	315	399	312	372	177	218	1,209	1,224	361	325
Gosain	2,711	1,304	1,407	19	14	10	15	3	2	742	848	239	253
Hindus returned by title or common sub-caste.													
Buna	1,632	1,014	618	18	2	71	69	...	...	369	360	136	155
Naik	1,099	545	554	2	2	12	14	21	17	289	309	98	119

HUGLI.

Serampur.		Haripal.		Krishnanagar.		Singur.		Chanditala.		Jahanabad.		Goghat.		Khanakul.	
Male.	Female.	Male.	Female.	Male.	Female.	Male.	Female.	Male.	Female.	Male.	Female.	Male.	Female.	Male.	Female.
106	135	179	159	3	13	17	17	3	1	1,504	1,610	86	78	...	...
2,619	2,177	10,115	9,870	5,775	5,826	6,102	6,708	7,928	7,496	10,059	9,955	9,930	9,409	9,601	9,579
1,045	1,005	31	29	15	19	11	9	52	58	256	207	33	33	98	111
273	477	101	67	58	73	29	20	27	78	342	403	126	120	135	136
492	379	498	585	463	569	324	385	327	316	1,015	1,155	811	1,164	697	920
...	...	56	79	...	...	...	...	7	22	...	...	107	126	...	...
332	292	244	289	102	211	162	211	111	105	327	426	324	526	144	273
...	...	144	145	191	167	68	57	102	80	276	265	...	...	193	219
90	87	40	67	125	128	94	117	107	109	410	461	368	489	330	405
...	...	51	58	...	...	...	...	313	317	...	...	243	222	...	...
...	...	64	85	96	102	120	117	4	5	360	429	13	13	...	...
...	...	18	8	4	...	16	8	11	11	228	230	...	...	135	109
4,876	4,196	2,799	3,323	2,243	2,763	1,828	2,538	3,124	4,133	2,616	3,013	4,681	4,221	3,993	4,731
5	9	1,001	913	384	404	989	927	365	532	1,551	1,693	1,368	1,483	519	519
810	1,000	119	116	166	174	946	770	172	153	244	323	100	182	176	243
3,067	2,762	689	678	478	482	625	573	1,162	1,152	1,220	1,274	1,487	1,556	1,244	1,354
1,130	827	1,756	1,712	1,769	1,496	86	91	3,481	3,359	1,385	1,396	2,021	2,124	1,167	1,370
499	420	792	779	530	546	296	137	234	191	730	658	491	454	624	560
150	94	111	128	151	128	121	120	204	323	385	421	59	22	31	26
250	225	37	11	38	29	113	9	44	49	412	422	1	2	109	100
3,777	3,578	11,706	12,393	2,141	2,013	12,878	13,130	7,318	7,411	3,166	3,026	1,375	923	21,356	22,604
978	670	504	561	153	171	376	381	403	394	633	663	921	731	493	481
...	...	79	79	...	...	5	7	40	49	...	...	...	...	12	13
3,346	2,925	634	925	421	625	481	623	643	837	1,327	1,857	982	1,315	1,197	1,620
...	...	38	22	19	3	16	9	46	...	1	...	6	3	...	...
100	145	26	26	56	58	146	185	67	84	15	24	18	17	...	8
732	665	353	271	260	178	299	282	458	366	784	739	412	373	664	539
11	2	43	10	10	...	17	...	227	6	254	262	33	4	1	...
1,830	1,459	289	267	201	201	211	257	210	224	482	477	233	271	294	304
...	...	55	51	33	27	66	38	98	24	146	146	14	13	19	24
1,172	716	16	25	45	59	89	88	64	91	293	333	302	209	134	138
721	654	73	49	593	679	81	59	105	154	533	585	440	449	560	483
630	800	474	502	306	369	399	447	496	569	877	1,023	372	454	668	822
70	30	22	2	93	20	137	43	443	2	18	...	150	75	238	195
...	...	8	...	...	...	70	83	1,026	955	1	1	...	...	...	...
542	560	150	175	14	17	122	140	49	51	294	277	119	123	67	91
1,684	1,241	1,597	1,678	1,406	1,543	1,335	1,379	3,395	3,358	2,830	3,157	7,318	7,740	1,272	1,456
...	...	...	...	5	5	...	...	...	...	141	154	19	23	24	36
28	12	616	417	94	45	81	19	208	101	134	137	145	117	...	...
1,338	969	204	197	243	238	120	111	170	195	420	427	79	90	341	332
...	...	9	5	5	...	8	3	10	15	2	3	...	1	1,961	1,871
40	130	123	209	145	288	6	8	12	85	432	480	235	242	7	5
100	100	152	160	91	97	55	72	65	57	629	669	490	464	164	223
...	...	169	175	219	329	15	11	220	362	403	558	865	884	361	421
476	598	1,587	1,526	2,359	2,157	145	150	984	723	462	458	3,155	2,965	1,265	1,104
5,694	3,751	681	674	1,430	1,148	348	308	696	730	4,916	5,854	6,354	6,607	2,530	2,946
742	744	2	...	...	...	536	529	597	599	...	...	...	...	2,060	2,029
98	99	389	357	166	195	332	254	214	243	786	820	697	784	883	1,074
90	85	19	25	86	55	33	36	11	9	2	20	25	20	25	25
10	6	48	25	...	...	50	...	317	1	...	...	...	...	...	...
...	...	40	20	1	...	5	3	...	...	61	52	16	18	...	...

DISTRICT

Group.	District Total.			Hugli.		Balagarh.		Pandua.		Dhaniakhali.		Polba.	
	Total.	Male.	Female.	Male.	Female.	Male.	Female.	Male.	Female.	Male.	Female.	Male.	Female.
Hindus returned by actual occupation.													
Jaliya	13,955	6,742	7,213	224	268	444	534	372	374	695	706	359	358
Hindus returned by locality.													
Uriyas	1,018	555	463	27	7	1	...	25	...	197	201	191	218
Musalmans returned by sect.													
Sunni	2,536	1,221	1,315	16	7	33	25	677	724	166	172	91	68
Musalmans returned by title.													
Pathan	8,012	4,293	3,719	101	79	41	39	41	33	756	794	179	204
Sayyid	5,197	2,734	2,463	63	56	18	19	62	87	769	839	236	227
Shaikh	147,581	67,827	79,754	4,371	4,849	3,140	4,153	8,796	9,729	2,495	2,598	1,796	2,832
Musalmans returned by actual occupation.													
Jolaha	13,383	6,517	6,866	677	760	356	373	277	279	692	711	397	410

DISTRICT

Caste.	District Total.			Howrah.		Bally.		Domjur.	
	Total.	Male.	Female.	Male.	Female.	Male.	Female.	Male.	Female.
Bagdi	59,621	29,760	29,861	1,929	1,620	536	862	8,371	7,764
Baidya	1,005	566	439	204	104	97	98	50	32
Baiti	1,020	518	502	100	120	52	40	58	45
Baniya	7,955	3,804	4,151	1,483	1,782	149	119	630	731
(i) Gandha Banik ...	3,283	1,638	1,645	617	510	22	14	361	456
(ii) Subarna Banik	2,856	1,355	1,501	845	970	15	11	140	131
Barui	4,741	2,521	2,220	281	100	52	24	827	757
Brahman	42,733	21,216	21,517	5,207	3,815	2,541	2,848	3,854	4,236
Chamar and Muchi	3,764	2,412	1,352	743	310	250	64	269	145
Dhopa	9,277	4,431	4,846	1,105	783	383	579	534	557
Dom and Kaora ...	20,980	10,879	10,101	1,683	1,086	175	112	3,523	3,475
Dusadh	1,173	895	278	743	213	36	21	34	4
Goala	19,329	10,264	9,065	2,319	1,103	325	260	2,418	2,185
Hari and Mihtar...	3,451	1,822	1,629	849	670	24	21	290	235
Jugi	4,460	2,171	2,289	353	368	49	47	1,043	1,074
Kahar	2,612	1,830	782	854	341	175	84	99	56
Kaibartta	178,155	86,259	91,896	4,577	4,975	936	976	11,133	10,153
Kamar and Lohar	5,327	2,913	2,414	1,004	561	227	155	505	508
Kapali	1,923	969	954	67	39	...	...	249	274
Karanga	2,468	1,312	1,156	68	43	...	..	6	9
Kayastha	17,131	8,866	8,265	3,457	2,221	418	296	936	903
Kumhar	6,693	3,451	3,242	504	380	103	141	1,152	1,056
Kurmi	1,835	1,483	352	1,116	293	83	6	179	17

HUGLI—*concluded.*

Serampur.		Haripal.		Krishnanagar.		Singur.		Chanditala.		Jahanabad.		Goghat.		Khanakul.	
Male.	Female.	Male.	Female.	Male.	Female.	Male.	Female.	Male.	Female.	Male.	Female.	Male.	Female.	Male.	Female.
487	517	476	479	576	630	334	368	419	488	669	714	795	807	952	970
...	...	1	...	13	...	7	...	53	...	17	...	3	...	20	37
30	54	1	...	...	...	...	...	150	147	17	54	5	9	35	55
1,834	929	111	92	116	320	16	2	59	36	548	656	35	32	456	503
868	413	42	46	89	73	50	45	82	100	230	246	92	122	133	190
3,242	3,855	6,671	7,193	5,580	6,665	3,304	3,396	8,344	9,155	6,856	8,559	4,322	5,288	8,910	11,482
450	409	607	684	318	150	360	336	1,412	1,440	154	264	607	770	210	280

HOWRAH.

Jagatballabhpur.		Ulubaria.		Amta.		Bagnan.		Shampur.	
Male.	Female.	Male.	Female.	Male.	Female.	Male.	Female.	Male.	Female.
4,457	4,619	3,831	3,797	7,564	7,995	1,196	1,455	1,576	1,749
50	58	27	18	84	98	24	20	30	11
15	21	64	46	229	230	...	...	...	...
332	323	395	272	328	505	259	240	178	173
197	171	64	32	213	287	127	143	47	32
70	101	131	118	110	117	24	43	20	12
133	176	...	...	911	903	208	260	...	...
2,040	2,323	1,193	1,145	3,141	3,770	2,011	2,268	1,220	1,112
205	175	283	174	373	300	130	90	159	94
295	314	636	753	393	519	304	551	691	790
1,149	1,132	1,174	1,065	1,317	1,163	1,166	1,275	692	793
40	20	32	14	10	6	...	...	...	...
1,678	1,937	911	932	1,424	1,639	575	559	620	450
273	280	105	97	177	184	89	75	15	17
198	225	157	151	69	85	100	139	202	200
294	50	200	25	43	58	82	98	83	70
11,071	11,685	8,724	8,725	19,683	23,654	11,073	12,258	18,457	19,470
221	245	195	188	306	403	240	156	215	198
56	57	549	546	...	...	46	36	2	2
55	13	230	211	15	10	147	149	791	721
713	1,024	690	448	902	1,285	1,139	1,372	611	716
384	369	250	260	661	631	229	232	168	171
28	8	39	20	12	...	25	8	2	...

CASTE OR GROUP.	DISTRICT TOTAL.			HOWRAH.		BALLY.		DOMJUR.	
	Total.	Male.	Female.	Male.	Female.	Male.	Female.	Male.	Female.
Maira and Halwai	3,497	1,997	1,500	837	534	34	14	261	205
Namasudra or Chandal	9,773	4,798	4,975	133	116	60	36	139	99
Napit and Hajjam	11,601	5,631	5,970	869	626	177	160	1,044	1,077
Oraon	1,318	1,166	152	200	65	33	10	662	47
Pod	10,553	8,342	8,211	326	342	115	28	5,302	5,188
Rajput	2,759	1,894	865	397	296	189	52	112	115
Sadgop	19,776	10,742	9,034	1,723	1,266	1,573	1,075	4,309	3,351
Sonar	3,684	1,879	1,805	367	232	42	33	408	344
Sukli	1,828	902	926	45	19	7	4	95	91
Sunri and Kalwar	8,777	1,952	1,825	364	234	69	22	203	257
Sutradhar	1,444	710	734	834	273	17	15	60	54
Tambuli	1,947	916	1,031	216	331	7	6	150	150
Tanti and Tatwa ...	13,644	6,797	6,847	1,666	1,289	90	65	55	49
Teli and Kalu ...	16,622	8,619	8,003	3,544	2,413	241	191	1,542	1,031
Tiyar	18,789	9,515	9,274	199	212	23	8	2,997	2,978
Religious devotees and persons returned by sect.									
Baisnab	11,575	5,452	6,123	1,554	1,679	135	122	466	479
Hindus returned by title or common sub-caste.									
Malik	4,380	2,036	2,344	26	56	...	...	125	175
Hindus returned by actual occupation.									
Dulia	6,840	3,384	3,485	92	84	79	46	1,019	1,012
Jaliya	6,841	3,294	3,547	323	308	39	14	420	308
Mala	1,399	1,050	349	499	202	520	134	15	8
Musalmans. Returned by sect.									
Hanifi	1,200	508	692	75	17	3	4	230	501
Sunni	1,094	570	524	75	17	3	4	492	503
Musalmans returned by title.									
Pathan	8,434	4,566	3,868	1,181	462	160	43	512	418
Sayyid	1,572	872	700	216	113	5	...	12	...
Shaikh	129,055	62,535	66,520	12,512	12,248	631	404	13,283	13,122
Musalmans returned by actual occupation.									
Jolaha	1,418	915	498	252	46	...	...	234	52

HOWRAH—*concluded.*

Jagatballabhpur.		Ulubaria.		Amta.		Bagnan.		Shampur.	
Male.	Female.	Male.	Female.	Male.	Female.	Male.	Female.	Male.	Female.
218	236	247	184	266	243	49	54	85	30
176	172	2,785	2,973	325	839	576	598	604	642
477	594	791	804	773	937	596	675	905	1,007
65	...	106	30	100	...	...	...	...	...
98	87	1,234	1,277	55	20	...	1	1,212	1,268
218	248	516	26	312	92	150	36	...	...
332	359	350	369	680	591	304	306	1,501	1,217
217	333	127	107	409	435	132	256	177	165
79	65	129	164	146	184	400	392	1	7
336	514	295	342	267	220	310	123	108	104
69	113	25	13	93	130	96	118	16	18
50	50	200	150	100	150	160	94	33	100
716	787	1,353	1,348	865	894	581	991	1,191	1,424
876	1,161	334	350	979	1,125	603	589	495	543
1,640	1,438	1,181	1,150	1,776	1,766	1,274	1,236	425	401
275	348	799	813	587	655	781	910	855	1,117
320	290	806	952	245	317	292	265	222	239
641	650	379	448	705	783	259	274	190	188
196	197	351	368	1,180	1,463	354	466	431	428
...	...	9	5	2	...	5	...	...	...
...	...	200	170	...	...	...	...	...	...
...	...	...	...	...	...	...	...	...	...
448	474	187	104	549	654	347	394	1,192	1,299
55	80	150	69	121	137	212	197	101	104
8,462	10,708	11,694	12,990	6,741	6,761	5,352	6,193	3,860	4,09
123	35	...	...	307	365	...	...	...	...

PRESIDENCY

DISTRICT

Caste or Group.	District Total.			Tollygänj.		Baruipur.		Sonarpur.		Bishnupur.		Bhangor.		Budge-Budge.	
	Total.	Male.	Female.	Male.	Female.	Male.	Female.	Male.	Female.	Male.	Female.	Male.	Female.	Male.	Female
Bagdi	87,223	44,480	42,743	2,129	2,018	2,687	2,688	1,244	1,135	2,251	2,171	2,569	2,461	5,412	5,090
Baiti	1,528	859	669	...	...	13	14	...	...	98	51	3	...	2	3
Baniya	16,349	9,512	6,837	1,248	989	243	109	353	296	431	247	173	121	293	227
(i)—Gandha Banik... ...	4,544	2,376	2,168	167	155	18	24	106	137	71	69	45	35	106	134
(ii)—Khatri	5,250	3,503	1,747	333	202	175	50	62	46	91	59	38	17	58	4
(iii)—Subarna Banik ...	3,892	1,998	1,894	248	332	...	3	100	98	...	...	25	34	29	26
Barui	5,859	3,026	2,833	...	...	847	943	127	98	...	...	...	...	...	...
Bediya	5,187	2,693	2,494	...	...	2	1	...	...	45	40	2	...	...	...
Bhar	1,042	643	399	...	...	8	4	...	...	...	...	...	...	...	...
Bhuimali and Mihtar ...	7,951	3,966	3,985	361	421	3	3	14	8	127	118	...	...	2	3
Bhuiya	1,275	765	510	75	75	29	17	36	56	35	25	29	19	...	...
Bhumij	5,306	2,773	2,533	...	...	...	...	...	1	...	...	463	401	...	...
Brahman	89,498	46,393	43,105	720	682	1,390	1,451	1,790	2,008	997	887	507	439	1,175	924
Chamar and Muchi ...	42,189	22,999	19,190	996	1,033	403	357	223	243	715	682	950	894	147	68
Chasa Dhopa	4,530	2,260	2,270	...	...	...	...	...	...	...	...	...	...	...	...
Dhopa	21,135	11,312	9,823	1,124	708	198	158	127	122	736	678	226	245	278	256
Dom and Kaora	60,545	31,189	29,356	1,638	1,645	1,773	1,702	1,155	1,155	1,455	1,199	1,056	982	782	815
Dusadh	2,921	1,816	1,105	1,029	701	...	...	3	...	...	...	...	...	16	11
Goala	59,231	31,741	27,490	1,940	762	428	296	1,974	1,009	1,872	1,783	872	700	393	294
Jugi	15,606	8,135	7,471	1,392	1,218	141	169	280	287	407	378	447	421	91	116
Kahar	3,950	2,427	1,523	88	57	16	18	50	51	12	12	...	...	40	19
Kaibartta	163,970	83,312	80,658	3,276	2,522	2,904	3,655	1,258	1,290	6,955	7,211	408	308	7,104	7,020
Kamar and Lohar ...	16,577	8,196	8,381	478	476	227	227	169	180	150	147	352	345	189	267
Kansari	2,650	1,411	1,239	53	72	...	...	1	9	15	2	...	...	7	...
Kapali	7,114	3,953	3,161	109	127	132	35	1	...	54	50	...	...	240	230
Karanga	6,466	3,576	2,890	73	63	...	...	678	470	...	...	91	81	66	52
Kayastha	46,436	23,580	22,856	1,453	1,400	541	630	733	958	830	710	264	279	462	399
Khandait	2,113	1,145	968	196	278	4	...	18	3	...	...	7	13	...	...
Kairi	1,268	813	455	258	175	...	...	...	...	...	...	...	...	15	2
Kol	6,253	3,268	2,985	19	10	...	...	...	...	1	...	...	...	...	...
Kumhar	14,331	7,492	6,839	520	538	330	335	185	173	358	346	416	444	434	418
Kurmi	5,691	3,356	2,335	406	254	44	3	9	2	...	...	39	13	25	15
Maira and Halwai ...	3,217	1,809	1,318	152	138	7	6	11	...	151	130	4	10	160	111
Malakar	1,275	851	424	97	12	47	27	15	3	42	25	56	21	7	4
Muriari	1,229	650	579	...	...	...	...	1	...	...	...	426	339	...	...
Namasudra or Chandal	21,895	11,187	10,708	450	470	327	305	161	146	1,707	1,553	71	31	1,411	1,385
Napit and Hajjam ...	24,141	12,704	11,437	952	851	599	546	380	327	592	557	401	373	296	220
Pasi	1,685	1,009	676	347	305	...	...	1	4	144	60	19	1	...	...
Pod	236,806	120,334	116,472	7,986	7,403	16,535	17,381	4,528	4,857	4,436	5,302	5,560	5,187	6,229	4,800
Rajput	1,742	867	875	1	...	17	10	68	74	...	...	...	...	...	...
Sadgop	26,373	13,463	12,910	876	637	450	430	396	435	661	689	60	46	410	498
Santal	1,499	795	704	166	159	...	...	...	...	70	53	287	298	...	...
Sonar	8,002	4,240	3,762	81	47	178	165	48	58	161	142	98	114	87	131
Sukli	1,593	916	677	472	184	...	...	...	...	75	61	...	...	...	...
Sunri and Kalwar ...	7,116	4,073	3,043	76	26	199	186	133	123	56	17	66	48	155	180
Sutradhar	1,996	1,074	922	19	5	...	...	1	...	10	9	...	...	38	50
Tambuli	1,471	638	833	1	3	...	...	...	...	...	...	2	...	27	46
Tanti and Tatwa	11,088	6,146	4,942	576	477	35	14	19	14	718	633	8	5	570	488
Teli and Kalu	22,602	12,585	10,017	1,045	651	278	251	253	237	508	575	223	282	86	69
Tiyar	46,512	23,557	22,955	3,030	2,844	307	242	1,492	1,442	1,872	1,859	773	742	444	381
Religious devotees and persons returned by sect.															
Baisnab	23,171	11,971	11,200	1,184	1,056	352	269	175	140	513	447	284	314	626	645

DIVISION.

24-PARGANAS.

Canning Town.		Jainagar.		Baranagar.		Barasat.		Deganga.		Habra.		Naihati.		Dum-Dum.	
Male.	Female.	Male.	Female.	Male.	Female.	Male.	Female.	Male.	Female.	Male.	Female.	Male.	Female.	Male.	Female.
2,046	1,910	2,316	2,270	735	929	1,734	1,746	783	862	1,295	1,228	1,479	1,492	1,008	772
105	103	18	5	2	7	6	12	13	7	76	63	100	85	2	1
351	245	133	100	492	439	211	129	91	93	179	150	630	488	440	282
197	126	6	3	253	238	10	18	40	43	66	47	80	47	73	23
46	40	34	4	145	68	198	110	12	1	57	54	333	166	251	150
8	4	93	93	28	34	3	1	39	49	56	49	117	75	16	9
89	158	38	35	110	82	...	...	1	...	169	160	184	131	54	51
221	226	...	...	1	1	...	...	...	...	...	...	96	54	...	...
...	...	...	...	...	...	...	...	...	...	...	...	106	52	...	...
285	158	112	124	103	92	236	267	52	36	135	176	318	333	162	161
186	92	...	...	...	...	2	...	59	63	...	...	67	54	34	8
112	104	...	...	...	...	...	...	...	...	...	...	...	...	...	...
4,936	3,424	1,959	2,301	3,095	2,978	1,122	1,270	543	524	1,328	1,275	1,753	2,250	1,215	921
468	279	520	459	839	485	2,182	1,808	1,788	1,055	1,690	1,584	2,033	1,301	1,168	921
13	11	...	...	...	...	270	276	...	...	760	741	13	7	...	...
131	47	916	883	176	132	203	201	140	115	347	366	612	466	488	435
1,200	1,047	2,317	2,019	381	361	950	943	704	648	601	576	975	867	1,464	1,368
...	...	...	...	118	47	93	60	8	3	26	43	20	4	103	74
524	314	721	426	510	378	3,319	3,211	1,350	1,306	3,042	2,918	3,265	2,998	1,711	1,400
96	38	34	44	204	301	322	389	125	149	257	363	656	298	172	178
290	230	3	...	118	37	104	19	18	20	92	57	219	117	126	65
1,609	1,210	2,168	2,167	2,091	1,929	1,193	1,212	194	145	922	844	3,137	3,176	775	704
214	208	145	136	60	44	364	310	332	346	379	428	532	545	137	153
30	20	10	14	...	...	...	...	...	...	...	...	87	73	...	...
45	49	2	5	1	1	11	10	37	34	82	72	34	11	...	...
146	168	...	...	..	...	...	...	...	...	...	...	28	23	6	7
1,145	703	1,106	1,324	801	596	463	673	177	200	376	377	754	900	466	333
163	192	48	11	72	46	4	...	...	...	10	8	...	...	14	...
...	...	...	...	64	22	...	...	8	4	53	14	176	146	53	45
211	183	...	...	7	2	6	...	...	...	...	...	...	...	...	...
137	102	309	300	105	107	239	223	298	283	379	428	409	508	279	294
266	219	96	69	139	30	42	1	...	...	79	57	201	126	72	28
181	156	6	4	144	72	11	16	...	...	51	64	190	153	110	41
7	6	21	9	59	30	45	11	23	15	2	1	174	64	17	1
10	8	80	114	...	...	...	...	...	...	...	...	...	...	...	...
420	414	675	620	204	202	347	302	85	67	111	113	991	1,078	132	183
452	338	760	696	229	207	467	405	237	235	346	359	411	431	325	320
...	...	...	...	52	27	1	...	...	...	5	1	74	56	133	108
1,606	1,285	14,003	12,658	20	20	1,271	1,036	892	900	238	241	493	360	3,473	3,327
84	86	56	51	25	21	...	...	...	...	4	10	108	90	39	22
31	17	295	290	636	337	214	221	650	729	946	697	3,200	3,162	403	473
9	12	19	15	...	...	45	27	7	7	...	...	55	33	...	...
290	163	317	382	116	104	51	62	59	66	45	72	408	270	113	118
...	...	...	...	287	345	...	...	...	...	...	...	10	13	4	1
310	133	267	219	146	136	33	38	33	46	65	55	115	42	132	126
...	...	4	5	27	24	...	...	10	...	109	79	174	165	...	...
94	163	...	...	83	117	...	...	...	...	241	407	26	9	3	...
65	60	9	4	996	1,038	7	3	3	...	8	12	250	208	255	68
515	380	722	783	633	570	222	221	254	259	274	264	912	638	202	199
111	...	525	1,156	13	6	225	210	127	128	66	74	2,474	2,088	1,161	1,133
514	325	493	549	34	66	84	37	37	46	162	234	316	188	26	19

Caste or Group.	Barrackpur.		Nawabganj.		Khardaha.		Basirhat.		B.durla.		Haroa.		Husainabad.		Diamond-Harbour.	
	Male.	Female.	Male.	Female.	Male.	Female.	Male.	Female	Male.	Female.	Male.	Female.	Male.	Female.	Male.	Female.
Bagdi	804	1,018	47	55	373	400	475	440	1,058	1,477	1,850	1,754	3,222	2,815	2,089	2,085
Baiti	11	14	30	26	...	...	...	...	30	18	...	...	18	14	332	246
Baniya	635	214	139	45	1	1	358	241	1,496	1,415	265	187	200	118	431	339
(i)—Gandha Banik ...	20	20	30	25	1	1	16	41	684	649	129	126	25	20	90	110
(ii)—Khatri	615	194	94	5	...	...	153	159	107	85	136	61	175	98	203	115
(iii)—Subarna Banik ...	...	...	15	15	...	...	89	41	605	681	...	...	...	...	138	114
Barui	82	62	82	62	...	...	170	141	436	303	...	...	...	...	...	...
Bediya	...	...	...	...	34	33	73	77	20	75	...	...	2,197	1,986	...	...
Bhar	...	...	...	...	...	...	...	...	...	...	...	...	...	...	...	...
Bhuimali and Mihtar ...	66	55	38	27	55	67	1	1	616	798	93	96	11	7	9	2
Bhuiya	38	46	...	...	...	...	...	...	...	...	...	...	...	...	...	...
Bhumij	...	...	...	...	...	...	...	...	...	...	862	800	1,284	1,180	...	...
Brahman	1,059	673	507	511	5,883	5,746	1,651	1,893	1,382	1,306	499	245	1,006	812	4,969	4,698
Chamar and Muchi ...	1,262	733	352	172	81	84	2,429	2,205	811	704	897	598	931	773	279	371
Chasa Dhopa	...	...	...	...	...	...	208	223	129	121	21	1	246	208	...	...
Dhopa	290	207	44	31	76	85	477	420	662	887	344	140	157	155	207	205
Dom and Kaora	159	176	109	109	125	123	870	741	1,180	1,280	943	889	425	343	1,252	1,157
Dusadh	141	83	259	79	...	...	...	...	...	...	...	...	...	...	...	...
Goala	848	718	636	485	828	648	908	1,056	944	1,349	575	487	959	750	148	144
Jugi	5	6	264	169	53	47	255	338	1,036	743	196	74	310	327	474	529
Kahar	235	130	89	31	...	...	328	289	100	40	151	46	...	...	71	84
Kaibartta	918	832	692	697	582	602	515	537	2,364	2,132	1,055	862	3,262	2,663	3,177	3,215
Kamar and Lohar ...	59	62	59	28	24	26	608	775	391	485	310	250	385	321	2,070	2,136
Kansari	...	...	82	81	30	21	...	...	10	8	93	98	...	...	...	...
Kapali	...	...	...	...	...	...	1,408	1,297	442	352	235	215	757	445	123	137
Karanga	...	...	..	...	...	...	...	...	...	...	...	...	1,197	1,109	...	...
Kayastha	485	522	279	140	203	144	1,069	1,272	883	1,216	481	267	919	1,055	4,650	4,486
Khandait	...	...	50	37	3	...	10	66	...	...	218	34	19	17	...	...
Kairi	98	14	36	8	13	4	...	...	...	...	21	17	...	...	...	...
Kol	...	...	...	...	...	...	...	...	...	...	...	...	2,854	2,614	170	176
Kumhar	40	35	103	63	204	188	453	393	771	543	176	76	323	208	53	65
Kurmi	151	62	61	80	...	...	110	95	367	385	413	298	159	133	...	...
Maira and Halwai ...	265	130	101	43	105	79	...	...	...	...	125	85	...	...	...	...
Malakar	21	2	14	12	3	4	18	12	80	83	...	...	20	18	35	20
Muriari	1	...	...	...	...	...	...	...	...	...	132	118	...	...	...	...
Namasudra or Chandal	10	...	...	...	...	...	442	494	388	442	565	576	460	276	214	184
Napit and Hajjam ...	407	390	133	99	176	124	537	431	737	607	463	255	487	398	36	48
Pasi	47	31	36	30	...	...	...	...	...	...	...	...	...	...	...	...
Pod	38	11	6	...	58	56	182	122	1,637	2,304	3,921	3,625	7,319	6,272	2,618	3,046
Rajput	10	3	17	15	...	...	...	...	...	...	53	70	64	95	...	...
Sadgop	79	107	529	539	139	147	1,614	1,855	290	242	160	126	232	205	...	...
Santal	...	...	...	...	...	...	...	...	...	...	...	...	71	59	...	...
Sonar	150	142	53	30	64	45	168	164	622	608	131	98	66	47	193	89
Sukli	...	...	...	...	...	...	...	...	...	...	...	...	...	...	...	...
Sunri and Kalwar ...	114	52	20	35	82	30	232	170	441	344	184	165	100	94	119	118
Sutradhar	120	134	79	101	...	...	...	...	17	27	351	147	...	...	...	...
Tambuli	...	...	8	11	...	...	...	...	31	74	122	4	...	...	...	...
Tanti and Tatwa	2	1	262	77	52	51	...	...	160	164	309	244	262	250	118	108
Teli and Kalu	418	348	282	195	118	123	63	15	2,476	1,651	458	267	67	58	340	333
Tiyar	150	176	839	847	220	207	316	412	783	548	169	158	1,040	946	252	263
Religious devotees and persons returned by sect.																
Baisnab	192	233	2	1	182	152	186	257	1,615	1,229	739	642	699	602	950	1,259

GANAS—*continued.*

Kulpi.		Bankipur.		Debipur.		Mathurapur.		Cossipur-Chitpur M. C.		Maniktala M. C.		Entally.		Calcutta Canals.		Sundarbans.	
Male.	Female.	Male.	Female.	Male.	Female.	Male.	Female.	Male.	Female.	Male.	Female.	Male.	Female.	Male.	Female.	Male.	Female.
1,781	1,476	1,126	1,169	1,211	1,239	1,487	1,524	416	301	698	115	79	103	24	...	119	...
...	...	...	...	...	...	...	...	...	...	...	...	...	...	...	...	...	...
2	...	88	86	109	99	1	1	399	130	117	46	...	...	...	...	3	...
2	...	9	3	48	39	1	1	...	...	80	34	...	...	...	...	3	...
...	...	...	...	...	...	...	...	150	37	37	12	...	...	...	...	...	...
...	...	79	83	61	60	...	...	249	93	...	...	...	...	...	...	...	...
...	...	589	574	...	...	...	...	...	...	48	33	...	...	...	...	...	...
...	...	...	...	2	1	...	...	...	...	...	...	...	...	...	...	...	...
...	...	...	...	1	...	...	...	528	343	...	...	...	...	...	...	...	...
413	373	30	32	100	98	503	427	...	...	126	102	...	...	...	...	...	...
...	...	...	...	...	...	75	15	...	...	100	40	...	...	...	...	...	...
...	...	52	47	...	...	...	...	...	...	...	...	...	...	...	...	...	...
1,336	999	1,694	1,524	621	567	635	489	743	334	1,765	1,855	9	4	15	10	69	55
485	406	244	216	61	54	215	215	720	273	150	117	...	...	...	...	...	...
71	95	...	...	...	...	8	9	521	578	...	...	...	...	...	...	...	...
883	831	497	510	261	268	474	496	904	659	328	111	...	...	3	...	3	6
2,194	2,148	2,891	2,827	848	866	2,595	2,692	596	240	493	438	...	...	1	...	7	...
...	...	...	...	...	...	...	...	...	...	...	...	...	...	...	...	...	...
1,150	842	1,537	1,470	588	610	387	195	557	247	720	695	5	...	26	...	10	...
167	187	153	124	174	194	332	316	27	35	...	...	...	...	8	...	37	33
...	...	...	...	45	66	...	...	195	76	37	59	...	...	...	...	...	...
13,918	12,868	5,461	6,163	7,995	8,379	7,391	7,272	643	485	785	531	33	21	184	6	313	...
221	157	159	165	85	72	93	91	...	...	...	...	2	...	...	...	2	1
...	...	2	...	...	...	1	1	990	840	...	...	...	...	...	...	...	...
...	...	84	79	...	...	...	...	30	...	75	21	...	...	39	...	9	1
84	80	1,132	749	73	88	...	...	...	...	...	...	...	...	...	...	...	...
706	719	767	792	255	239	116	75	970	495	1,860	1,875	37	3	53	6	236	68
...	...	...	...	...	...	...	...	302	263	...	...	...	...	10	...	2	...
...	...	2	...	...	...	1	...	...	...	...	...	10	4	...	...	...	...
...	...	...	...	...	...	...	...	...	...	...	...	...	...	...	...	...	...
193	201	191	197	99	101	51	46	...	...	428	221	...	...	8	...	1	...
61	62	...	...	...	...	...	...	615	403	...	...	...	...	1	...	...	...
...	...	...	...	...	...	...	...	...	...	125	80	...	...	...	...	...	...
48	35	...	...	...	...	...	...	...	...	...	...	...	...	...	...	...	...
...	...	...	...	...	...	...	...	...	...	...	...	...	...	...	...	...	...
886	808	224	211	518	572	207	145	146	87	45	44	...	...	...	...	...	...
848	845	1,062	1,131	336	391	366	386	228	68	420	301	...	...	3	...	10	8
...	...	...	...	...	...	...	...	149	44	1	...	...	...	...	...	...	...
13,787	12,958	14,781	13,802	2,596	2,727	6,815	6,690	16	...	60	40	51	59	95	3	87	...
...	...	...	...	...	...	...	...	241	253	80	75	...	...	...	...	...	...
205	208	164	160	116	118	74	79	98	85	535	438	...	...	...	...	...	...
68	41	...	...	...	...	...	...	...	...	...	...	...	...	...	...	...	...
171	194	191	186	75	74	64	49	105	63	132	56	...	...	...	...	...	...
...	...	...	...	68	73	...	...	...	...	...	...	...	...	...	...	...	...
179	189	272	297	55	60	154	63	267	10	60	41	...	...	...	...	...	...
...	...	...	...	...	...	...	...	...	...	115	176	...	...	...	...	...	...
...	...	...	...	...	...	...	...	...	...	...	...	...	...	...	...	...	...
169	82	80	76	125	125	...	...	619	565	450	180	...	...	...	...	...	...
232	171	546	481	188	57	221	110	994	790	85	44	...	...	...	...	...	...
965	866	3,963	4,041	1,249	1,181	794	910	523	339	204	237	...	...	...	...	...	...
1,018	1,061	356	410	207	236	436	463	196	116	525	209	16	13	...	...	...	...

DISTRICT 24-PAR

Group.	District Total.			Tollyganj.		Baruipur.		Sonarpur.		Bishnupur.		Bhangor.		Budge-Budge.	
	Total.	Male.	Female.	Male.	Female.	Male.	Female.	Male.	Female.	Male.	Female.	Male.	Female.	Male.	Female.
Hindus returned by title or common sub-caste.															
Buna	4,244	2,380	1,864	252	155	33	20	68	5	9	7	267	232	15	13
Dalui	1,586	878	708	...	...	...	...	...	...	...	...	...	...	...	...
Nabasakh	1,347	1,137	210	...	...	...	...	...	...	...	...	...	...	...	...
Nagbansi	1,044	507	537	...	...	...	...	208	195	...	...	...	...	...	...
Hindus returned by actual occupation.															
Jaliya	6,192	3,464	2,728	104	28	71	2	...	...	...	...	37	16	241	254
Mala	2,313	1,449	864	...	...	...	...	...	...	...	...	...	...	...	...
Patni	5,464	2,809	2,655	...	...	...	...	...	...	...	...	...	...	...	...
Hindus returned by locality.															
Uriyas	2,967	2,148	819	250	113	146	64	117	67	89	65	57	28	19	...
Musalmans returned by title.															
Atraf	4,833	2,500	2,333	...	...	...	...	...	...	...	...	245	481	...	...
Chaudhuri	1,269	657	612	...	...	...	...	...	...	...	...	...	...	...	...
Khan	10,344	5,393	4,951	...	...	188	5	...	...	...	...	...	...	6	4
Mir	2,037	1,018	1,019	...	...	...	...	...	...	11	9	...	...	...	...
Moghul	2,614	1,499	1,115	...	...	5	3	...	...	4	5	...	...	...	...
Pathan	32,017	16,240	15,777	419	328	344	427	...	...	69	62	724	414	828	706
Sayyid	31,724	15,966	15,758	97	100	182	207	...	...	151	126	423	230	256	172
Shaikh	562,589	296,515	266,074	9,703	9,762	18,563	13,419	1,317	589	8,686	9,419	19,004	14,941	8,616	8,553
Musalmans returned by actual occupation.															
Badyakar	1,781	851	930	...	...	...	...	...	...	...	...	...	...	...	...
Chunari	2,528	1,508	1,020	...	...	...	...	...	...	...	...	...	...	...	...
Dhawa	2,242	999	1,243	...	...	28	123	...	...	...	...	687	790	...	...
Jolaha	11,952	5,915	6,037	...	...	...	...	1	...	...	...	1	...	...	...
Kalu	11,556	5,320	6,236	...	...	...	...	...	...	...	...	...	...	90	87
Nikari	4,625	2,417	2,208	...	...	...	...	...	...	...	...	4	...	...	...

DISTRICT

Caste.	District Total.			Krishnanagar.		Kaliganj.		Nakasipara.		Chapra.	
	Total.	Male.	Female.	Male.	Female.	Male.	Female.	Male.	Female.	Male.	Female.
Bagdi	31,731	15,951	15,780	3,912	3,755	521	558	1,164	1,073	1,092	1,141
Baidya	1,380	624	756	136	121	23	48	33	64	...	...
Baiti	1,899	958	941	126	110	95	84	9	11	1	...
Baniya	14,237	6,645	7,592	752	875	241	319	742	896	309	457
(i)—Gandha Banik	7,714	3,612	4,102	546	615	153	200	581	648	274	423
(ii)—Subarna Banik	5,214	2,329	2,885	175	228	46	80	142	238	3	3
Barui	3,446	1,693	1,753	211	200	163	98	35	36	68	54

GANAS—*continued.*

Canning Town.		Jainagar.		Baranagar.		Barasat.		Deganga.		Habra.		Naihati.		Dum-Dum.	
Male.	Female.	Male.	Female.	Male.	Female.	Male.	Female.	Male.	Female.	Male.	Female.	Male.	Female.	Male.	Female.
657	673	6	8	44	14	84	31	...	...	49	79	65	30	80	29
47	45	...	...	...	...	...	...	...	...	...	...	...	...	...	...
...	...	17	...	...	...	...	...	...	...	...	...	...	...	...	...
...	...	...	...	...	...	...	...	...	...	...	...	...	...	101	157
239	147	41	32	50	57	263	159	5	2	73	90	523	236	...	...
...	...	...	...	165	182	...	...	...	...	...	...	174	80	3	...
...	...	...	...	...	...	...	...	...	...	...	...	32	73	...	...
256	58	175	63	14	4	23	...	3	1	79	28	186	43	4	...
...	...	...	...	...	...	...	...	...	...	...	...	...	...	...	...
...	...	...	...	...	...	...	...	...	...	...	...	...	...	...	...
...	...	...	...	...	...	...	...	...	...	...	...	...	2	6	...
...	...	...	...	...	...	5	3	...	...	...	...	...	...	...	...
390	341	...	...	56	48	199	146	1	...	1	...	223	81	...	...
960	411	515	425	157	80	539	431	98	102	852	1,063	908	477	...	...
1,196	1,004	414	420	...	...	917	861	54	67	640	650	450	394	18	...
7,086	6,870	12,763	11,957	3,245	1,963	20,602	20,502	28,654	27,930	15,822	14,746	13,664	11,959	758	295
...	...	...	...	...	...	...	...	...	...	...	...	...	...	...	...
...	...	...	...	...	...	...	...	...	...	...	...	...	...	...	...
...	...	...	...	...	...	...	...	134	130	...	...	...	...	...	...
...	...	...	...	11	15	9	...	85	68	784	883	147	146	...	...
...	...	...	...	...	...	86	30	1	1	1,136	1,123	...	...	...	...
...	...	...	...	...	...	...	...	3	1	21	20	...	...	...	...

NADIA.

Krishnaganj.		Hanskhali.		Jibannagar.		Ranaghat.		Santipur.		Chakdaha.		Haringhata.	
Male.	Female.	Male.	Female.	Male.	Female.	Male.	Female.	Male.	Female.	Male.	Female.	Male.	Female.
413	466	811	837	365	444	91	86	1,942	1,958	1,799	1,790	1,226	1,157
110	107	7	...	8	4	62	86	72	101	37	48	3	4
48	49	10	8	52	55	16	24	28	24	5	6	...	...
150	122	105	156	223	248	88	118	558	642	142	104	50	39
118	94	5	...	48	40	33	50	296	324	76	52	36	29
2	...	67	121	140	179	38	43	234	294	26	24	...	...
155	159	3	2	55	57	42	31	9	6	101	99	1	...

DISTRICT 24-PAR

Group.	Barrackpur.		Nawabganj.		Khardaha.		Basirhat.		Baduria.		Haroa.		Husainabad.		Diamond-Harbour.	
	Male.	Female.	Male.	Female.	Male.	Female.	Male.	Female.	Male.	Female.	Male.	Female.	Male.	Female.	Male.	Female.
Hindus returned by title or common sub-caste.																
Buna	193	151	63	44	35	13	...	...	141	93	39	24	156	166	63	24
Dalui	...	...	...	...	...	...	...	...	...	...	...	...	...	...	...	...
Nabasakh	...	...	...	...	...	...	...	...	...	...	...	...	...	...	1,120	210
Nagbansi	...	...	...	...	...	...	71	69	...	...	...	...	124	116	...	...
Hindus returned by actual occupation.																
Jaliya	23	12	...	...	33	38	327	298	640	741	289	289	345	254	...	...
Mala	...	...	302	155	...	...	...	...	...	...	...	...	141	33	...	...
Patni	...	...	...	...	...	...	...	...	2,621	2,381	84	106	...	...	72	95
Hindus returned by locality.																
Uriyas	17	9	39	9	15	3	19	7	...	...	...	...	175	98	76	43
Musalmans returned by title.																
Atraf	...	...	...	...	...	...	2,255	1,852	...	...	...	...	...	...	...	...
Chaudhuri	...	...	...	...	...	...	280	254	...	...	308	289	69	69	...	...
Khan	...	...	...	...	...	...	...	...	5,186	4,926	...	...	...	...	...	...
Mir	...	...	1	...	...	...	...	...	991	1,000	10	7	...	...	...	...
Moghul	8	5	10	...	7	...	...	...	...	...	...	...	...	...	...	...
Pathan	665	505	120	44	96	100	498	864	3,903	5,949	908	219	141	76	875	940
Sayyid	38	9	34	35	20	10	206	199	5,227	5,785	192	52	322	286	3,177	3,603
Shaikh	4,251	3,436	2,596	1,865	3,225	2,996	18,273	19,075	10,108	8,597	13,349	9,905	10,076	8,443	4,336	4,172
Musalmans returned by actual occupation.																
Badyakar	...	...	...	...	...	...	...	...	851	930	...	...	...	...	...	...
Chunari	...	...	...	...	...	...	...	...	1,508	1,020	...	...	...	...	...	...
Dhawa	...	...	...	...	...	...	...	...	150	200	...	...	...	...	...	...
Jolaha	...	...	112	40	...	...	369	363	3,647	4,339	636	116	76	81	...	...
Kalu	...	...	...	...	...	...	143	153	3,168	4,435	446	155	300	252	...	...
Nikari	...	...	...	...	...	...	748	739	1,556	1,384	...	...	85	64	...	...

DISTRICT

Caste.	Kushtia.		Naupara.		Daulatpur.		Bhadalia.		Kumarkhali.		Bhaluka.	
	Male.	Female.	Male.	Female.	Male.	Female.	Male.	Female.	Male.	Female.	Male.	Female.
Bagdi	58	73	218	206	25	19	21	13	66	47	19	19
Baidya	5	7	15	10	...	...	...	...	5	...	9	16
Baiti	...	...	66	54	...	...	...	...	6	6	...	...
Baniya	26	35	381	517	95	82	46	51	130	140	10	11
(i)—Gandha Banik	3	21	38	134	24	37	26	33	34	35	...	...
(ii)—Subarna Banik	5	5	256	351	70	45	12	8	72	78	2	3
Barui	2	2	90	110	1	...	74	88	101	81	1	...

GANAS—*concluded.*

Kulpi.		Bankipur.		Debipur.		Mathurapur.		Cossipur-Chitpur M. C.		Maniktala M. C.		Entally.		Calcutta Canals.		Sundarbans.	
Male.	Female.	Male.	Female.	Male.	Female.	Male.	Female.	Male.	Female.	Male.	Female.	Male.	Female.	Male.	Female.	Male.	Female.
28	19	30	20	...	...	33	14	...	...	...	...	...	...	...	...	...	...
851	663	...	...	...	...	...	...	...	...	...	...	...	...	...	...	...	...
...	...	...	...	...	...	...	...	...	...	...	...	...	...	...	...	...	...
...	...	...	...	...	...	...	...	...	...	...	...	...	...	...	...	...	...
19	...	...	...	1	...	...	...	92	55	17	18	...	...	31	...	...	...
...	...	...	...	...	...	...	...	664	414	...	...	...	...	...	...	...	...
...	...	...	...	...	...	...	...	...	...	...	...	...	...	...	...	...	...
...	...	...	...	...	...	...	...	159	63	230	53	...	...	...	...	...	...
...	...	...	...	...	...	...	...	...	...	...	...	...	...	...	...	...	...
...	...	...	...	...	...	...	...	...	...	...	...	...	...	...	...	...	...
11	10	...	...	...	...	...	...	...	...	...	...	...	...	...	...	...	...
...	...	...	...	...	...	...	...	...	...	...	...	...	...	...	...	...	...
5	1	...	...	4	4	...	...	378	281	203	200	...	...	5	...	...	...
724	661	458	475	573	677	136	132	329	60	320	128	...	...	59	...	22	21
360	291	147	171	139	108	87	109	1,149	810	56	58	3	1	3	...	...	...
9,454	9,363	30,092	30,769	5,235	5,459	5,185	4,848	2,363	1,345	4,092	2,473	13	8	2,405	12	2,909	3
...	...	...	...	...	...	...	...	...	...	...	...	...	...	...	...	...	...
...	...	...	...	...	...	...	...	...	...	...	...	...	...	...	...	...	...
...	...	...	...	...	...	...	...	...	...	...	...	...	...	...	...	...	...
1	1	1	...	33	33	...	...	...	...	...	...	...	...	...	...	2	2
...	...	...	...	...	...	...	...	...	...	...	...	...	...	...	...	...	...
...	...	...	...	...	...	...	...	...	...	...	...	...	...	...	...	...	...

NADIA—*continued.*

Meherpur.		Karimpur.		Gangni.		Tehata.		Chuadanga.		Damurhuda.		Alamdanga.		Kalupol.	
Male.	Female.	Male.	Female.	Male.	Female.	Male.	Female.	Male.	Female.	Male.	Female.	Male.	Female.	Male.	Female.
430	450	146	152	35	28	701	536	64	81	525	554	134	173	173	161
50	86	16	21	...	...	3	...	7	3	10	17	8	13	1	...
124	114	106	106	28	33	143	159	1	...	39	31	52	64	4	3
371	369	444	445	154	140	793	890	96	94	221	241	461	540	57	61
237	233	147	143	38	22	661	746	41	39	60	54	100	100	36	30
87	107	275	279	106	103	92	106	27	24	123	155	313	390	16	21
129	128	76	73	...	...	92	72	11	20	271	337	2	...	...	...

DISTRICT

Caste or Group.	District Total.			Krishnanagar.		Kaliganj.		Nakasipara.		Chapra.	
	Total.	Male.	Female.	Male.	Female.	Male.	Female.	Male.	Female.	Male.	Female.
Bauri	2,467	1,186	1,281	155	187	141	169	23	19	...	...
Bhuimali and Mihtar ...	7,393	3,583	3,810	176	195	278	336	192	169	13	12
Bind	1,421	746	675	...	...	1	1	...	...	...	...
Brahman	49,810	23,692	27,118	4,547	5,071	995	1,302	1,428	1,908	397	373
Chamar and Muchi	44,346	21,551	22,795	1,694	1,902	1,179	1,251	1,577	1,780	1,150	1,203
Dhopa	7,175	3,528	3,647	184	238	173	168	43	67	20	32
Dom and Kaora	2,942	1,445	1,497	158	178	136	100	234	270	25	...
Dusadh	1,485	840	645	87	17	...	...	...	...	1	...
Ganrar	1,442	651	791	87	128	19	28	9	16	2	...
Goala	80,471	40,621	39,850	4,861	5,025	2,690	2,336	2,180	2,188	3,493	3,398
Jugi	9,526	4,883	4,943	1,084	1,221	97	98	100	100	79	67
Kahar	2,894	1,511	1,383	144	131	38	21	1	1	...	...
Kaibartta	99,419	49,574	49,845	1,609	1,578	1,987	1,977	1,232	1,203	1,039	1,080
Kamar and Lohar	12,925	6,366	6,559	482	474	163	144	253	275	276	259
Kansari	1,827	859	968	397	434	...	...	21	17	5	...
Kapali	5,900	2,988	2,912	929	913	...	...	120	104	...	...
Kayastha	33,614	15,103	18,511	1,687	2,155	3,333	3,526	1,327	1,671	227	327
Kumhar	17,577	8,088	9,489	550	718	166	155	218	236	193	219
Kurmi	1,857	1,046	811	123	51	26	18	40	31	5	...
Maira and Halwai	19,856	9,733	10,123	721	890	393	446	378	409	4	4
Malakar	1,457	718	739	68	88	60	69	20	17	2	...
Malo	21,962	10,435	11,527	871	431	37	112	282	234	712	655
Namasudra or Chandal ...	37,858	17,701	20,157	450	414	712	737	607	855	518	653
Napit	16,517	8,127	8,390	596	611	255	294	302	322	316	294
Pod	5,821	2,099	2,822	70	60	142	121	...	...	125	116
Rajput	4,008	1,906	2,102	197	303	165	187	158	260	2	1
Sadgop	13,148	6,485	6,663	1,215	1,235	1	3	347	366	87	104
Sonar	4,366	2,161	2,205	327	351	54	73	151	147	101	85
Sunri and Kalwar	6,423	3,170	3,253	538	608	35	12	19	49	16	1
Sutradhar	9,246	4,490	4,756	160	177	136	147	97	52	29	27
Tambuli	1,202	532	670	25	12	34	46	24	45	4	36
Tanti	7,743	3,812	3,931	441	426	44	35	29	38	23	22
Teli and Kalu	25,061	11,536	13,525	1,357	1,758	648	758	321	405	452	518
Tiyar	2,288	1,241	1,047	55	...	40	56	158	177	42	...
Religious devotees and persons returned by sect.											
Baisnab	17,922	7,306	10,616	1,312	1,693	830	444	220	287	159	230
Hindus returned by title or common sub-caste.											
Buna	16,997	8,266	8,731	685	746	724	819	310	302	380	416
Rajbansi	15,095	7,824	7,271	397	400	733	741	978	810	354	380
Hindus returned by actual occupation.											
Dulia	7,803	3,983	3,820	821	796	28	42	48	40	6	5
Jaliya	4,381	2,266	2,115	9	1	6	7	2	...	...	...
Patni	3,630	1,749	1,881	168	180	6	11	29	25	153	163
Musalmans returned by title.											
Pathan	9,823	4,922	4,901	186	183	185	234	42	22	...	...
Sayyid	5,893	2,842	3,051	111	105	201	128	133	112	58	49
Shaikh	931,376	456,164	475,212	20,594	20,980	12,645	11,005	12,035	10,318	19,016	19,616

NADIA—*continued.*

KRISHNAGANJ.		HANSKHALI.		JIBANNAGAR.		RANAGHAT.		SANTIPUR.		CHAKDAHA.		HARINGHATA.	
Male.	Female.	Male.	Female.	Male.	Female.	Male.	Female.	Male.	Female.	Male.	Female.	Male.	Female.
...	...	...	...	64	68	52	57	816	337	124	115	...	...
33	53	125	134	4	6	873	1,038	94	129	93	101	3	3
...	...	...	...	...	...	...	...	...	...	69	24	...	...
537	658	337	353	88	448	832	957	2,596	3,300	1,400	1,099	614	797
677	661	530	572	932	971	1,405	1,631	712	750	1,596	1,501	1,342	1,316
75	104	31	31	47	49	324	336	121	154	193	139	904	861
...	...	15	13	4	7	94	104	33	22	153	176	225	250
34	29	1	...	...	...	250	150	20	3	4	...	...	...
23	30	2	2	3	4	41	37	1	1	47	57	...	...
1,547	1,476	1,406	1,371	882	916	3,398	3,315	3,727	3,404	2,031	1,795	2,172	2,137
107	159	53	34	148	157	234	262	66	59	135	119	19	24
2	1	52	51	159	158	101	1()	70	60	124	102	1	...
1,671	1,704	903	853	1,664	1,574	2,786	3,008	971	912	2,090	2,045	272	270
135	139	182	185	203	167	329	412	204	242	301	290	184	166
...	3	5	...	84	137	47	70	135	188	35	33	2	...
...	...	...	...	...	...	3	...	238	233	37	35	9	7
608	894	262	416	312	481	851	1,121	509	748	564	681	216	295
146	171	169	158	161	187	397	429	382	435	278	288	103	98
8	1	13	6	5	1	42	16	32	4	59	49	12	2
43	69	83	22	8	6	307	316	779	960	149	118	...	...
9	16	36	23	7	6	10	9	30	25	58	34	15	16
468	610	173	136	287	317	651	658	370	126	109	186	...	...
71	97	231	311	309	358	349	377	283	274	149	120	92	94
148	165	173	176	175	176	365	404	264	258	414	318	141	165
...	...	1	...	108	137	140	116	28	45	473	439	790	744
3	8	4	3	3	2	7	14	6	12	691	517	2	...
21	18	85	76	69	63	850	811	838	868	2,122	2,159	280	303
135	57	44	49	14	11	178	192	145	204	67	48	48	41
3	5	19	8	...	1	68	86	312	332	8	9	...	...
46	51	23	19	106	106	38	56	206	221	14	9	19	17
9	...	...	...	79	87	55	92	19	36	63	61	...	...
122	126	5	3	242	238	45	76	1,659	1,755	155	141	1	3
247	278	229	234	106	91	1,120	1,434	1,178	1,407	423	413	80	77
...	...	1	1	...	...	354	335	54	46	123	118	5	9
134	186	114	143	155	284	125	179	200	336	340	411	104	101
440	479	300	305	170	162	1,119	1,224	711	741	357	377	42	39
226	281	126	130	60	73	150	152	112	41	2	1	...	...
26	27	161	149	...	...	849	826	174	185	1,504	1,420	305	279
102	153	...	...	37	33	133	137	50	13	72	74	57	50
44	55	20	22	9	15	77	111	17	8	6	3	...	...
88	85	...	...	...	...	128	110	545	328	240	159	118	116
155	129	...	...	81	86	304	313	...	...	64	63	148	138
6,767	6,688	11,804	11,833	9,462	9,277	17,009	16,607	9,564	8,251	13,404	11,693	9,225	9,602

Caste or Group.	Kushtia.		Naupara.		Daulatpur.		Bhadalia.		Kumarkhali.		Bhaluka.	
	Male.	Female.	Male.	Female.	Male.	Female.	Male.	Female.	Male.	Female.	Male.	Female.
Bauri	...	...	...	...	...	...	...	...	4	5	6	7
Bhuimali and Mihtar ...	157	111	46	46	57	74	45	49	425	428	54	47
Bind	124	107	177	217	8	6	66	51	179	124	63	91
Brahman	294	408	1,251	1,440	398	460	606	718	953	1,116	430	589
Chamar and Muchi ...	266	200	839	849	632	677	459	553	441	438	225	209
Dhopa	69	98	306	290	122	155	64	92	143	127	36	40
Dom and Kaora	44	51	18	13	20	18	5	...	...	...	...	...
Dusadh	7	...	236	185	31	31	...	...	8	...	...	...
Ganrar	...	...	...	...	97	129	25	26	8	11	...	...
Goala	215	186	1,190	1,148	682	710	415	432	509	553	124	128
Jugi	24	16	58	8	486	471	55	58	30	42	84	88
Kahar	39	80	170	152	...	...	156	144	1	...	393	383
Kaibartta	195	201	1,816	1,893	5,401	5,158	918	876	344	394	163	167
Kamar and Lohar	189	102	452	453	301	301	243	230	575	741	180	184
Kansari	3	4	17	13	...	...	3	...	...	...	6	4
Kapali	5	6	2	2	...	...	69	73	1,283	1,258	272	264
Kayastha	433	392	657	858	191	209	413	481	1,095	1,354	454	589
Kumhar	209	238	787	870	270	361	376	412	546	618	276	297
Kurmi	11	16	91	10	96	88	49	46	6	4	2	1
Maira and Halwai ...	11	13	663	678	453	455	9	4	4,754	4,587	97	83
Malakar	4	2	63	58	32	32	21	22	50	52	17	15
Malo	68	59	788	908	319	494	1,062	1,298	299	317	243	298
Namasudra or Chandal ...	240	280	2,913	3,589	1,576	1,887	571	694	1,276	1,541	1,325	1,523
Napit	164	171	696	770	411	443	844	331	683	676	210	232
Pod	58	39	256	278	40	80	...	...	62	91	...	...
Rajput	1	1	7	7	88	88	54	63	...	4	...	...
Sadgop	127	126	19	7	10	14	134	148	12	13	169	218
Sonar	40	90	57	70	11	3	4	1	...	...	...	1
Sunri and Kalwar	9	38	...	...	4	1	...	...	243	280	24	7
Sutradhar	133	123	420	491	287	310	255	266	407	524	187	196
Tambuli	...	...	27	34	3	4	...	1	...	...	...	...
Tanti	4	3	13	2	82	28	3	2	93	97	2	2
Teli and Kalu	150	148	110	89	67	48	458	497	551	689	109	118
Tiyar	91	61	27	20	17	23	...	...	10	...	...	...
Religious devotees and persons returned by sect.												
Baisnab	194	380	472	814	355	455	239	408	420	710	140	261
Hindus returned by title or common sub-caste.												
Buna	71	90	369	377	47	50	149	160	325	334	30	29
Rajbansi	50	57	610	482	51	59	488	453	834	835	450	357
Hindus returned by actual occupation.												
Dulia	...	...	10	2	3	2	3	...	...	...	...	...
Jaliya	524	444	132	117	7	7	81	93	812	775	106	69
Patni	43	58	207	223	99	100	55	63	129	131	85	96
Musalmans returned by title.												
Pathan	...	...	201	278	80	82	127	133	55	54	31	51
Sayyid	...	...	167	255	74	91	81	109	74	75	41	59
Shaikh	12,135	11,523	47,245	53,680	26,171	28,384	25,967	26,837	31,355	41,346	17,664	18,090

NADIA—*concluded.*

Mihrpur.		Karimpur.		Gangni.		Tehata.		Chuadanga.		Damurhuda.		Alamdanga.		Kalupol.	
Male.	Female.	Male.	Female.	Male.	Female.	Male.	Female.	Male.	Female.	Male.	Female.	Ma'e.	Female.	Male.	Female.
10	7	...	...	43	50	38	36	37	48	87	102	...	...	86	74
173	197	165	131	168	127	200	205	...	1	82	90	58	58	69	75
...	...	...	...	...	...	...	...	...	...	...	...	59	54	...	...
744	929	1,102	1,419	256	255	662	898	249	239	771	920	466	484	350	377
644	718	886	961	655	684	1,193	1,271	249	269	590	737	865	878	783	911
70	83	306	284	26	23	49	62	15	16	64	64	77	71	42	63
29	36	86	89	18	28	35	42	8	15	8	8	91	82	6	...
3	...	41	88	17	12	...	...	7	3	8	12	38	67	47	48
56	73	78	81	78	98	18	12	2	...	...	...	15	16	40	40
1,554	1,719	1,488	1,559	738	646	1,855	1,835	228	272	1,861	1,828	893	953	482	520
291	315	126	100	286	214	264	233	300	205	238	249	403	439	116	115
2	4	5	...	...	...	...	...	22	20	...	...	8	3	23	22
3,294	3,357	3,913	4,202	2,495	2,293	7,354	7,751	135	132	4,574	4,552	1,373	1,261	1,355	1,404
226	215	274	266	193	227	264	287	81	81	241	226	314	357	122	136
26	9	1	...	34	42	...	...	2	...	3	1	22	5	11	8
...	...	...	...	...	...	...	...	...	...	...	1	...	...	21	16
282	330	281	325	82	89	219	256	85	79	308	415	461	586	186	236
209	300	683	734	499	718	237	292	44	75	333	469	641	758	186	253
23	28	145	190	110	113	6	1	3	...	17	9	103	113	14	13
168	212	109	119	4	3	284	218	58	49	119	128	133	152	52	53
29	24	35	63	22	35	32	47	12	7	26	28	34	38	26	23
907	1,092	348	220	157	181	617	713	102	88	1,060	1,224	526	732	419	418
548	564	2,075	2,430	696	717	1,170	1,198	133	107	434	408	587	572	386	358
344	411	448	498	342	359	392	438	87	80	290	258	387	372	190	166
...	...	...	...	165	122	...	...	78	63	304	301	150	121	...	...
50	45	20	19	...	...	10	10	6	3	351	480	81	75	...	...
1	1	2	...	21	9	8	...	...	1	1	1	62	69	...	...
113	121	106	122	123	120	78	27	45	37	145	174	104	109	71	72
158	151	287	209	231	248	17	17	207	213	6	...	966	888	...	...
342	343	206	243	208	211	403	368	79	72	198	199	397	394	105	114
73	90	44	38	3	2	17	22	...	...	51	64	...	...	2	...
242	313	64	41	2	1	160	165	7	6	318	303	103	103	3	2
780	910	175	170	166	180	576	741	318	438	920	1,136	708	673	297	315
...	...	157	182	...	...	97	9	...	...	10	10	...	...	...	...
293	403	285	480	311	308	396	580	56	190	255	365	424	656	265	312
437	417	82	87	470	427	174	175	82	98	386	424	201	235	190	218
183	176	84	87	16	21	823	756	...	1	595	492	433	435	69	71
...	...	...	...	46	47	...	...	...	...	...	...	...	...	...	...
1	2	3	4	1	...	...	...	37	25	...	...	91	80	3	2
89	107	99	98	38	48	129	129	25	20	79	83	113	104	30	28
330	398	1,340	1,465	155	138	345	386	233	258	334	291	159	130	...	...
197	235	221	285	109	130	194	172	...	...	104	109	158	224	167	184
10,067	8,053	33,605	36,882	27,107	28,213	20,966	22,567	6,923	6,760	14,456	14,628	29,799	30,743	11,119	11,018

Caste or Group.	District Total.			Jessor.		Kaliganj.		Baghherpara.	
	Total.	Male.	Female.	Male.	Female.	Male.	Female.	Male.	Female.
Bagdi	16,652	7,825	8,827	419	396	102	101	59	92
Baidya	2,219	1,013	1,206	10	2	3	...	...	...
Baiti	1,676	717	959	132	146	85	106	...	...
Baniya	9,507	4,588	4,919	610	641	302	296	141	186
(i) Gandha Banik	4,466	2,128	2,338	272	271	196	216	120	164
(ii) Subarna Banik	4,300	2,103	2,197	244	270	106	80	21	22
Barui	10,848	5,513	5,335	483	480	361	320	196	174
Bediya	1,314	697	617	17	25	20	15	30	28
Bhuimali and Mihtar ...	1,044	493	551	14	17	8	3	...	...
Brahman	41,149	19,807	21,342	1,262	969	708	708	528	622
Chamar and Muchi ...	53,718	27,010	26,708	1,973	1,939	4,013	3,876	411	301
Dhopa	7,509	3,792	3,717	94	73	85	99	60	63
Dom and Kaora	3,509	1,760	1,749	55	74	2	3	70	64
Goala	30,512	15,232	15,280	1,584	1,815	908	985	128	167
Jugi	11,760	5,914	5,846	843	852	547	423	492	488
Kahar	3,783	1,917	1,866	208	170	88	35	52	43
Kaibartta	50,365	25,417	24,948	1,501	1,426	471	440	384	369
Kamar and Lohar ...	15,224	7,517	7,707	826	718	447	452	206	262
Kapali	26,534	13,442	13,092	177	136	1,315	1,260	1,172	1,156
Kayastha	59,339	27,426	31,913	2,215	1,844	843	910	734	808
Kumhar	17,591	8,628	8,963	724	758	558	543	307	256
Maira and Halwai	2,451	1,337	1,114	134	92	140	133	49	53
Malo	11,622	5,853	5,769	1,257	1,116	464	475	...	...
Namasudra or Chandal ...	172,236	84,847	87,389	3,307	3,290	798	750	3,678	3,943
Napit	22,699	11,315	11,384	1,007	1,072	591	589	386	361
Pod	7,478	3,878	3,600	423	404	82	53	...	...
Sadgop	6,236	2,975	3,261	75	71	41	82	191	236
Sonar	1,575	781	794	34	34	25	16	12	15
Sunri and Kalwar	26,892	13,054	13,838	811	656	554	526	351	335
Sutradhar	10,551	5,150	5,401	801	729	352	361	295	338
Tanti	8,307	4,085	4,222	219	228	183	186	219	220
Teli and Kalu	16,399	8,248	8,151	576	514	80	74	760	738
Religious devotees and persons returned bysect.									
Baisnab	13,662	6,290	7,372	583	666	407	493	397	413
Hindus returned by title or common sub-caste.									
Buna	10,799	5,306	5,493	190	190	127	147	88	108
Hindus returned by actual occupation.									
Jaliya	49,934	24,299	25,635	4	...	470	457	1,111	990
Patni	3,035	1,503	1,532	72	77	91	87	20	20
Musalmans returned by title.									
Pathan	10,392	5,260	5,132	744	817	410	396	370	374
Sayyid	7,085	3,601	3,484	209	158	123	154	103	99
Shaikh	1,091,039	547,801	543,238	53,393	50,529	25,593	24,616	16,418	16,108
Musalmans returned by actual occupation.									
Behara	1,154	598	556	...	...	...	...	...	...
Jolaha	37,839	19,139	18,700	3,391	3,178	584	585	433	396

JESSOR.

GADKHALI.		MANIRAMPUR.		KESHUBPUR.		JHENIDAHA.		SALKOPA.		KOTCHANDPUR.	
Male.	Female.	Male.	Female.	Male.	Female.	Male.	Female.	Male.	Female.	Male.	Female.
105	129	...	...	26	73	724	784	395	424	431	546
13	25	1	...	9	6	42	41	...	...	...	...
2	3	44	40	...	...	94	174	26	19	75	75
79	83	515	524	349	383	306	312	261	333	248	214
20	20	169	193	87	100	160	134	104	134	69	52
59	63	346	331	262	283	145	138	107	166	179	162
112	109	765	776	502	487	43	45	...	...	80	92
46	49	71	52	15	8	100	75	10	15	25	30
...	...	3	3	6	11	28	23	125	101	10	3
645	760	1,260	1,400	1,045	987	1,294	1,352	774	858	307	266
1,873	1,847	1,945	1,917	1,399	1,538	1,910	1,821	728	799	2,629	2,650
282	264	560	549	26	20	191	209	144	175	37	39
49	41	160	159	130	129	28	21	5	2	53	41
417	442	406	499	204	221	907	901	462	355	533	490
489	500	630	651	564	594	360	293	249	277	50	49
91	140	24	24	...	...	237	256	110	78	219	237
1,399	1,269	1,772	1,580	1,289	1,236	1,585	1,525	1,457	1,433	397	500
100	78	659	619	379	363	617	655	533	518	206	199
978	926	580	563	552	571	906	848	176	163	2	...
539	667	1,980	2,237	1,694	2,630	1,305	1,441	1,765	2,241	256	258
177	172	516	537	364	465	569	610	543	522	340	396
27	52	90	...	70	84	177	158	85	83	157	13
148	201	...	...	...	...	1,078	1,123	...	...	947	907
46	37	8,136	7,990	794	556	6,751	6,846	7,061	7,987	75	68
319	320	988	942	535	547	753	801	074	728	272	279
136	130	999	988	620	555	299	281	44	33	34	...
1,780	1,134	562	535	78	62	23	15	11	4	76	68
10	8	28	30	82	45	6	5	...	...	3	3
17	7	186	149	353	254	548	549	1,168	1,166	196	169
85	98	832	368	43	11	571	609	436	423	210	190
25	26	53	71	353	347	126	89	23	10	75	37
252	260	653	618	390	322	837	693	100	120	226	203
102	121	394	457	131	128	851	958	461	580	169	234
32	12	...	...	...	...	684	699	573	638	138	142
340	375	1,445	1,361	795	736	1,014	1,038	1,798	2,299	3,488	3,608
39	46	53	41	96	129	115	128	123	123	18	24
20	39	238	242	400	342	88	102	171	188	177	177
12	90	128	127	100	110	137	139	269	207	22	17
20,504	20,209	48,322	46,078	37,000	25,364	45,890	47,562	37,898	40,333	11,724	11,393
...	...	...	...	...	...	...	...	...	...	...	...
318	219	2,295	2,145	2,000	1,952	1,413	1,402	1,127	1,232	728	696

Caste or Group.	Magura.		Muhamadpur.		Salikha.		Narail.		Lohagara.	
	Male.	Female.	Male.	Female.	Male.	Female.	Male.	Female.	Male.	Female.
Bagdi	504	584	48	48	111	112	184	190	97	109
Baidya	218	255	77	103	5	4	56	45	114	149
Baiti	44	40	7	11	...	...	3	4	59	76
Baniya	246	202	213	265	66	51	320	378	180	217
(i) Gandha Banik	143	102	164	227	16	1	142	187	55	57
(ii) Subarna Banik	3	...	49	38	...	...	178	191	125	160
Barui	81	67	429	438	127	106	1,145	1,041	839	835
Bediya	75	50	49	35	21	9	61	57	...	...
Bhuimali and Mihtar ...	110	67	92	194	...	...	3	...	17	24
Brahman	1,848	1,943	729	818	741	830	2,249	2,293	2,119	2,604
Chamar and Muchi ...	699	709	330	267	255	206	794	773	207	203
Dhopa	223	232	83	90	62	80	368	311	248	249
Dom and Kaora	10	7	19	24	...	...	18	12	14	10
Goala	724	668	267	215	151	233	358	325	616	532
Jugi	14	12	...	...	40	42	285	238	1	...
Kahar	347	323	85	74	53	47	...	...	97	94
Kaibartta	2,095	1,042	149	181	23	17	538	540	568	643
Kamar and Lohar	465	463	142	190	230	230	478	502	348	354
Kapali	560	445	275	289	1,004	1,143	1,068	1,089	118	102
Kayastha	2,943	3,026	2,573	2,740	559	788	4,441	5,197	3,219	3,952
Kumhar	692	670	417	411	404	403	399	416	532	619
Maira and Halwai	58	50	28	40	10	14	10	8	7	9
Malo	...	...	...	...	...	...	340	272	727	668
Namasudra or Chandal ...	14,213	14,747	5,880	5,904	5,500	5,715	5,085	5,067	9,576	9,845
Napit	924	982	466	415	259	315	1,075	1,049	715	718
Pod	21	...	15	24	...	...	5	1	6	...
Sadgop	6	...	63	63	100	89	18	4	100	99
Sonar	87	95	16	12	...	...	108	110	140	185
Sunri and Kalwar	1,860	2,250	705	877	77	72	2,640	2,931	1,192	1,272
Sutradhar	521	592	136	187	178	236	202	204	266	309
Tanti	946	1,083	308	331	347	382	733	704	107	116
Teli and Kalu	495	500	67	56	332	364	1,624	1,627	398	448
Religious devotees and persons returned by sect.										
Baisnab	777	1,001	258	257	119	174	460	476	284	341
Hindus returned by title or common sub-caste.										
Buna	842	785	745	702	24	23	62	70	289	307
Hindus returned by actual occupation.										
Jaliya	493	646	946	1,196	1,598	1,621	3,715	3,742	1,820	1,983
Patni	246	251	51	42	70	68	182	119	94	113
Musalmans returned by title.										
Pathan	507	510	335	254	12	15	440	339	606	610
Sayyid	276	301	258	213	57	55	520	535	742	668
Shaikh	42,764	44,038	27,450	27,597	10,607	11,491	35,046	34,504	29,384	29,360
Musalmans returned by actual occupation.										
Behara	...	...	...	...	...	...	400	389	198	167
Jolaha	1,423	1,528	968	991	393	416	604	665	269	269

JESSOR—concluded.

KALIA.		BANGAON.		MAHESPUR.		GARAPOTA.		SARSA.		GAIGHATA.	
Male.	Female.	Male.	Female.	Male.	Female.	Male.	Female.	Male.	Female.	Male.	Female.
13	3	1,136	1,354	822	925	638	728	918	1,023	1,094	1,206
419	532	12	13	21	21	13	11	...	...	...	...
9	31	2	7	15	22	91	179	11	2	18	24
64	62	105	117	305	315	126	164	112	128	35	48
6	1	90	111	149	159	106	131	28	34	32	44
1	...	15	6	156	156	20	33	84	94	3	4
3	...	19	18	166	179	26	29	85	78	51	61
...	...	...	...	25	24	48	44	84	101	...	...
...	...	27	40	38	40	...	...	6	6	11	19
806	812	966	1,032	1,031	1,241	489	510	523	614	483	623
151	138	1,197	1,176	3,154	3,191	1,143	1,204	1,275	1,270	924	884
256	237	328	321	237	209	52	60	26	23	430	409
23	12	316	380	129	118	97	89	261	230	321	333
400	416	1,572	1,570	2,333	2,429	1,044	1,068	641	640	1,277	1,309
...	...	183	180	268	277	378	418	401	399	140	153
19	6	43	45	156	211	3	...	21	19	64	64
4,462	4,483	747	702	3,089	3,110	1,585	1,555	1,441	2,332	465	556
467	476	262	292	429	562	223	232	340	346	160	196
784	796	348	342	200	163	1,158	1,129	1,665	1,567	404	404
827	826	452	475	591	723	184	210	175	169	120	171
606	644	222	233	494	549	253	278	316	267	195	214
38	36	103	91	113	161	37	31	2	...	2	7
...	...	...	...	874	1,007	...	...	...	...	24	...
11,181	11,728	355	396	1,535	1,647	266	280	487	582	31	11
593	603	272	274	520	504	288	286	379	382	209	217
3	...	42	9	163	152	76	83	739	728	171	150
75	70	114	141	431	413	55	51	171	171	5	3
31	45	74	67	44	37	40	49	8	11	33	27
1,639	1,730	14	...	387	460	262	312	67	78	27	35
51	52	308	279	277	274	71	128	13	8	2	5
4	...	109	62	201	256	53	72	1	...	...	...
22	18	512	579	262	282	354	474	234	225	44	36
115	198	168	184	212	219	226	266	86	104	90	102
236	254	443	446	532	676	299	294	...	...	2	...
1,777	2,145	739	810	493	492	851	815	890	801	512	520
63	56	25	34	60	47	70	67	44	44	21	16
35	3	165	157	312	322	4	...	61	81	165	164
112	70	204	199	199	205	89	97	19	27	22	13
16,416	15,708	15,760	15,334	29,828	29,637	16,260	16,866	23,345	22,770	14,199	13,542
...	...	...	...	...	...	...	...	...	...	...	...
99	70	247	267	1,697	1,577	498	513	456	428	202	169

Caste or Group.	District Total.			Sujaganj.		Gorabazar.		Barhampur Municipality.		Burwan.		Daulatabazar.	
	Total.	Male.	Female.	Male.	Female.	Male.	Female.	Male.	Female.	Male.	Female.	Male.	Female.
Bagdi	39,651	18,938	20,713	469	513	331	435	795	747	3,457	3,552	210	345
Baidya	1,282	594	638	...	...	...	...	110	95	10	10	2	...
Baniya	15,902	7,943	7,959	4	1	15	16	1,132	927	596	645	133	170
(i)—Gandha Banik	7,322	3,489	3,833	1	...	12	13	68	55	339	376	5	4
(ii)—Khatri	3,319	1,917	1,402	2	1	...	...	652	398	...	...	...	...
(iii)—Subarna Banik	3,269	1,570	1,699	1	...	1	...	111	83	244	262	128	166
Barui	1,960	1,017	943	...	...	...	...	45	2	54	61	94	100
Bauri	3,607	1,681	1,926	25	35	...	...	2	6	163	156	...	...
Bhuimali and Mihtar	11,996	5,775	6,221	49	46	20	16	107	126	515	646	25	39
Brahman	31,541	16,068	15,473	564	512	556	414	846	742	1,118	1,151	337	351
Chain	36,686	18,151	18,535	120	154	1,016	1,020	858	720	25	21	18	14
Chamar and Muchi	34,698	17,019	17,679	48	66	143	169	208	171	2,341	2,321	282	293
Chasa Dhopa	6,326	3,129	3,197	...	...	...	...	...	...	85	99	...	...
Chasati	5,173	2,514	2,659	42	54	164	256	...	...	...	...	...	...
Dhanuk	5,357	2,491	2,866	...	...	...	...	78	99	...	...	153	173
Dhopa	4,558	2,173	2,385	5	6	44	50	158	170	384	368	25	24
Dom and Kaora	6,800	3,251	3,549	7	4	38	39	19	9	589	614	31	35
Dusadh	2,721	1,417	1,304	7	6	13	10	225	188	45	28	3	...
Goala	35,516	17,820	17,696	168	148	153	145	546	463	343	319	599	608
Jugi	4,071	2,029	2,042	5	6	34	41	60	70	...	...	17	16
Kahar	2,514	1,347	1,167	1	1	1	...	69	43	28	35	4	...
Kalbartta	91,900	44,417	47,483	307	388	909	947	862	789	684	722	3,421	3,493
Kamar	5,567	2,797	2,770	5	...	35	34	173	166	139	133	75	79
Kayastha	13,566	6,661	6,905	50	54	46	50	712	610	673	720	79	103
Koiri	1,973	1,035	938	8	3	1	2	32	14	...	...	46	34
Kumhar	9,087	4,541	4,546	40	42	15	9	114	118	505	476	108	101
Kurmi	2,061	1,012	1,049	14	13	1	3	12	...	94	52	6	1
Maira and Halwai	3,539	1,649	1,890	...	...	4	9	88	54	228	252	...	...
Mal	13,637	6,615	7,022	...	...	19	5	190	7	104	129	62	75
Malakar	1,454	671	783	1	1	1	2	34	9	96	91	10	13
Malo	5,050	2,798	2,252	6	4	51	64	1,118	12	11	9	148	186
Musahar	1,594	794	800	37	29	686	724	6	9	...	...	...	...
Nagar	2,534	1,192	1,342	...	...	...	...	...	...	...	...	...	...
Namasudra or Chandal ...	24,319	11,695	12,024	74	82	443	441	185	164	5	3	387	393
Napit	13,789	6,705	7,084	126	130	39	49	172	197	574	620	178	170
Pod	13,065	6,395	6,670	...	...	...	...	10	...	33	24	31	36
Rajput	6,695	3,043	3,652	...	...	26	27	232	94	372	458	66	56
Sadgop	36,658	18,114	18,544	13	2	13	7	75	97	5,545	6,080	46	35
Santal	4,879	2,508	2,371	...	...	...	...	40	59	...	...	...	...
Sonar	4,128	2,008	2,120	4	1	2	3	40	36	279	248	101	88
Sunri and Kalwar	10,724	5,185	5,539	53	61	...	...	173	8	86	93	109	123
Sutradhar	8,023	4,016	4,007	5	9	...	...	204	212	403	434	74	70
Tanti	10,854	5,381	5,473	1	2	1	1	146	123	549	619	110	98
Teli and Kalu	19,823	9,806	10,017	46	29	49	42	339	326	1,466	1,530	56	49
Tiyar	15,158	7,340	7,818	10	15	1	...	247	101	12	14	15	17
Religious devotees and persons returned by sect.													
Baisnab	18,381	7,697	10,694	...	...	85	117	624	937	974	1,197	156	266
Hindus returned by title or common sub-caste.													
Buna	5,560	2,697	2,863	18	25	...	...	128	135	156	153	30	29
Gurkha	1,659	839	820	...	...	...	...	450	58	...	...	...	...
Rajbansi	9,159	4,357	4,802	21	24	102	93	66	18	40	45	39	29

SHIDABAD.

Hariharpara.		Nowada.		Goas.		Jalinghi.		Shahnagar.		Manulabazar.		Asanpur.		Lalbagh Municipality.	
Male.	Female.	Male.	Female.	Male.	Female.	Male.	Female.	Male.	Female.	Male.	Female.	Male.	Female.	Male.	Female.
209	254	836	847	130	118	361	316	46	108	40	55	165	193	347	435
2	...	...	...	9	18	52	84	...	...	...	...	2	1	81	90
193	160	317	285	3	...	515	586	14	4	8	...	35	44	1,490	1,359
85	95	277	256	...	...	350	403	...	...	...	...	10	14	40	34
13	9	1	...	...	...	9	10	...	...	2	...	...	...	1,086	889
23	39	36	26	3	...	72	81	11	3	1	...	19	16	100	129
36	24	2	...	18	11	20	14	...	...	...	...	4	...	4	6
12	15	...	...	18	36	...	...	...	...	8	10	18	24	...	...
111	158	212	265	88	59	298	206	6	28	39	60	40	56	84	97
637	685	881	445	79	79	641	661	594	429	684	557	154	103	742	524
34	40	16	35	1,910	2,010	525	526	36	54	26	44	29	40	46	104
510	560	378	410	108	110	1,333	1,340	41	21	244	201	64	49	122	92
...	...	...	...	...	...	7	10	...	...	...	...	...	...	65	71
...	...	...	...	435	454	62	64	...	...	...	...	...	...	2	...
137	188	...	...	...	...	...	...	...	...	...	...	...	...	...	...
39	41	220	218	10	8	60	63	7	7	4	6	5	4	...	...
34	36	...	...	...	...	30	23	14	11	2	4	...	...	22	25
...	...	1	...	...	...	...	...	2	...	3	...	3	5	4	...
2,005	2,148	985	897	165	182	1,597	1,626	247	288	54	40	185	174	577	334
319	325	171	174	89	79	124	119	4	8	...	...	94	84	62	56
119	87	1	...	1	...	...	2	...	...	...	...	30	34	287	207
3,169	3,402	5,173	5,085	1,160	1,145	2,975	2,873	480	519	292	273	161	181	437	402
76	69	324	218	34	56	212	214	18	9	38	51	33	56	59	45
149	172	167	176	24	38	339	425	48	58	241	280	53	47	499	456
35	19	...	...	...	...	69	39	1	1	...	...	3	3	14	13
204	237	118	122	52	41	836	840	40	31	56	41	63	74	115	85
18	10	10	11	...	2	20	6	29	30	68	73	22	22	119	95
164	160	52	61	...	...	86	110	1	2	...	...	3	2	169	209
9	10	37	39	27	26	141	236	17	13	36	39	170	158	...	...
6	8	19	28	5	6	48	44	16	21	...	...	...	...	13	12
246	382	130	175	...	...	339	454	...	...	49	51	11	2	69	73
...	...	...	...	...	...	...	...	...	...	4	...	...	...	32	13
...	...	...	...	...	...	...	...	...	...	...	...	...	...	...	...
599	678	482	667	538	553	3,420	3,796	158	177	179	188	62	118	134	166
393	373	197	248	113	110	533	644	43	47	329	341	246	200	187	177
405	391	6	4	...	...	2	...	276	281	392	890	228	230	...	5
17	14	29	59	...	...	...	...	2	...	...	...	28	30	219	303
48	25	59	30	14	15	9	6	...	...	...	...	36	30	63	64
...	...	...	...	...	...	...	...	14	10	...	...	40	36	...	...
105	116	...	...	18	17	143	174	38	32	47	42	5	4	86	115
133	189	125	126	69	102	162	123	13	9	226	232	156	129	86	80
80	71	105	108	64	31	338	320	22	16	5	...	63	22	...	...
257	256	39	41	56	33	160	146	7	10	44	42	203	145	127	114
301	308	355	346	42	39	240	288	24	11	34	46	104	162	343	219
...	...	20	27	11	9	82	152	...	...	16	24	31	40	5	4
238	312	211	334	93	115	245	455	89	140	48	71	145	181	433	443
17	13	125	143	33	29	276	278	26	33	...	...	560	656	...	...
...	...	...	...	36	43	...	...	...	...	...	...	13	10	15	7
83	96	132	152	25	27	123	125	...	...	19	14	47	48	162	191

Caste or Group.	Bhagabangola.		Sagardighi.		Kaliaganj.		Raghunathganj.		Shamsherganj.		Suti.	
	Male.	Female.	Male.	Female.	Male.	Female.	Male.	Female.	Male.	Female.	Male.	Female.
Bagdi	624	633	727	856	530	617	52	41	101	104	112	134
Baidya	13	13	4	6	14	13	47	40	6	...	50	82
Baniya	22	21	85	72	103	103	270	254	110	93	252	251
(i)—Gandha Banik	9	14	73	63	83	91	114	84	31	19	134	127
(ii)—Khatri	...	...	1	...	...	...	22	7	23	3	36	35
(iii)—Subarna Banik	13	17	11	9	18	12	122	151	3	2	67	75
Barui	10	7	15	24	16	2	15	24	113	101	154	139
Bauri	25	39	135	148	250	259	20	27	24	30	7	5
Bhuimali and Mihtar	43	32	345	408	83	86	18	14	113	156	14	15
Brahman	270	231	463	403	266	253	617	418	461	374	395	386
Chain	...	...	838	820	...	...	1,704	1,820	4,448	4,862	800	960
Chamar and Muchi	210	191	727	738	1,072	1,171	214	293	616	693	1,015	1,075
Chasa Dhopa	...	...	...	...	...	...	...	...	...	...	...	...
Chasati	219	213	...	...	123	154	...	...	...	...	...	...
Dhanuk	...	...	...	...	...	...	...	...	532	632	1,591	1,780
Dhopa	27	45	...	...	13	20	4	2	228	262	52	76
Dom and Kaora...	30	35	231	241	183	201	105	120	85	96	43	43
Dusadh	88	32	10	11	9	2	22	20	617	652	144	155
Goala	673	742	800	782	1,236	1,363	318	373	1,188	1,190	542	493
Jugi	60	79	...	...	52	57	1	2	...	...	1	1
Kahar	9	9	16	...	2	1	70	66	330	320	63	71
Kaibartta	2,518	2,631	676	753	403	500	1,069	1,308	2,256	2,581	5,578	6,367
Kamar	91	84	109	89	60	69	179	194	204	236	70	70
Kayastha	54	46	78	75	26	96	275	217	431	433	174	205
Koiri	11	16	...	...	4	9	2	...	...	...	7	1
Kumhar	80	68	48	51	183	196	200	192	356	372	166	179
Kurmi	77	90	6	5	4	...	52	46	166	191	152	158
Maira and Halwai	...	...	7	9	64	75	...	...	78	95	5	7
Mal	107	106	719	686	776	880	1	13	154	246	155	202
Malakar	34	33	1	1	2	11	6	7	20	42	11	17
Malo	...	...	...	...	45	49	15	18	79	202	81	101
Musahar	...	1	22	20	1	...	...	...	..	...	...	...
Nagar	...	...	...	...	...	...	...	...	1,192	1,342	...	...
Namasudra or Chandal ...	628	664	16	18	284	290	205	133	...	...	3	7
Napit	230	209	177	177	141	159	355	350	588	595	324	335
Pod	235	227	281	303	901	950	...	...	1,361	1,363	35	48
Rajput	35	15	192	305	93	108	209	318	191	245	85	55
Sadgop	9	4	8	13	411	463	42	30	9	9	9	18
Santal	...	...	1,102	1,076	652	548	...	...	577	562	...	...
Sonar	114	116	30	42	76	67	62	95	87	132	35	37
Sunri and Kalwar	118	205	183	155	159	143	285	370	407	481	287	356
Sutradhar	89	81	54	60	185	191	223	232	209	217	306	226
Tanti	209	219	47	32	40	23	297	208	157	185	496	505
Teli and Kalu	234	219	140	177	297	283	192	218	484	604	594	603
Tiyar	8	10	97	114	977	1,030	260	245	576	628	1,486	1,627
Religious devotees and persons returned by sect.												
Baisnab	297	398	93	155	206	258	302	504	295	434	123	218
Hindus returned by title or common sub-caste.												
Buna	1	...	351	351	...	...	6	7	6	3	1	...
Gurkha	...	...	1	...	...	...	...	...	312	696	...	...
Rajbansi	155	207	54	32	17	21	181	222	1,074	1,265	940	1,023

SHIDABAD—*continued.*

Dewansarai.		Mirzapur.		Kandi.		Barwa.		Khargaon.		Bharatpur.		Gokarna.	
Male.	Female.	Male.	Female.	Male.	Female.	Male.	Female.	Male.	Female.	Male.	Female.	Male.	Female.
146	103	300	360	1,742	1,978	1,420	1,674	1,997	2,140	2,685	2,973	1,106	1,188
27	20	16	9	20	10	2	...	46	60	59	80	12	7
103	89	95	97	398	421	244	220	474	546	1,142	1,400	195	195
13	15	82	85	202	223	145	117	335	377	977	1,251	104	117
22	17	2	...	8	...	18	19	20	14	...	...	...	...
84	57	...	...	188	198	62	61	101	141	88	94	83	77
21	29	22	22	31	31	20	27	79	72	207	207	47	40
36	24	2	15	12	14	28	40	20	29	511	564	365	450
61	58	403	440	248	295	622	534	621	666	1,363	1,427	297	238
494	427	512	543	975	780	495	693	1,102	1,207	2,244	2,544	541	621
393	455	4,970	5,311	...	...	213	227	...	...	40	44	26	54
175	204	1,054	1,098	433	461	476	369	1,950	2,005	2,863	3,160	397	418
...	...	...	...	...	...	557	560	...	...	2,415	2,457	...	...
...	...	...	...	...	...	984	953	...	...	239	237	244	274
...	...	...	...	...	...	...	...	...	...	...	...	...	...
7	3	14	19	63	85	79	101	12	16	629	714	84	77
18	12	112	127	250	278	148	194	440	452	565	625	255	325
43	10	25	19	1	...	16	33	2	...	4	3	130	130
521	483	332	361	394	350	1,398	1,498	509	491	1,662	1,705	623	499
27	23	65	69	39	34	364	342	24	16	299	341	109	103
81	66	23	32	6	3	76	63	130	127	...	...	...	...
1,529	1,679	663	706	855	973	4,580	4,851	824	908	2,291	2,282	1,145	6,725
141	139	71	60	64	63	155	169	91	116	281	284	61	67
40	40	86	84	613	500	216	155	516	530	957	1,203	115	123
44	42	2	...	680	688	1	...	...	...	42	30	43	24
13	16	23	42	155	154	136	138	230	234	578	579	109	108
58	43	6	1	25	27	11	134	20	6	...	...	27	31
2	3	16	11	81	98	198	299	177	195	110	121	96	118
23	43	2,970	3,080	56	43	36	59	716	772	46	53	44	52
5	8	7	11	4	6	210	200	...	...	114	113	8	9
27	94	16	23	34	28	125	155	10	7	66	60	122	158
6	4	...	...	...	...	...	...	...	...	...	...	...	...
...	...	...	...	...	...	...	...	...	...	...	...	...	...
63	71	...	...	297	324	1,770	1,833	627	714	248	356	858	898
197	181	131	162	229	233	239	280	268	318	576	648	120	131
250	286	768	830	...	...	1	...	481	480	301	352	403	470
30	31	250	240	92	139	90	81	141	146	405	560	239	365
...	...	256	292	2,409	2,472	215	80	2,844	2,983	4,689	4,795	998	994
...	...	63	49	...	...	...	...	20	31	...	...	...	...
37	34	26	12	80	80	54	93	108	102	383	377	48	57
198	222	145	172	212	220	661	737	211	201	820	894	156	158
19	10	95	89	125	153	318	277	241	305	685	756	104	115
45	39	88	88	109	116	63	91	733	770	1,305	1,476	2	1
52	50	142	134	284	296	816	741	554	617	1,097	2,099	621	575
550	610	375	418	311	321	15	18	1,495	1,583	157	193	553	618
149	283	169	273	484	670	402	548	577	672	1,002	1,360	242	354
...	...	12	18	5	26	56	72	567	606	18	14	305	272
...	...	12	6	...	...	...	...	...	...	...	...	...	...
432	471	36	59	15	13	162	194	68	73	282	266	82	96

DISTRICT MUR

Group.	District Total.			Sujaganj.		Gorabazar.		Barhampur Municipality.		Burwan.		Daulatabazar.	
	Total.	Male.	Female.	Male.	Female.	Male.	Female.	Male.	Female.	Male.	Female.	Male.	Female.
Hindus returned by actual occupation.													
Ghatwal	2,824	1,535	1,289	5	4	7	6	34	21	...	...	...	...
Kotal	1,435	686	749	...	...	...	...	3	1	38	44	...	...
Mala	1,001	688	313	...	...	20	...	348	...	...	...	...	...
Patni	1,745	840	905	...	...	10	10	41	20	...	...	81	82
Hindus returned by locality.													
Hindustanis	4,039	1,853	2,186	...	...	...	...	302	401	...	...	...	...
Musalmans returned by title.													
Pathan	10,404	5,246	5,158	24	26	32	28	268	223	189	157	287	312
Sayyid	7,383	3,483	3,900	6	6	10	6	58	17	551	636	24	30
Shaikh	568,048	270,954	297,094	2,737	2,938	1,604	1,690	3,902	1,739	6,970	7,205	10,723	11,432
Musalmans returned by actual occupation.													
Jolaha	4,175	2,046	2,129	...	...	...	...	4	...	...	...	60	51
Kahar	1,733	762	971	...	...	...	...	...	...	...	...	...	...
Kalu	3,345	1,665	1,680	43	43	...	...	...	...	...	...	241	217

DISTRICT MUR

Group.	Bhagabangola.		Sagardighi.		Kaliaganj.		Raghunathganj.		Shamsherganj.		Suti.	
	Male.	Female.	Male.	Female.	Male.	Female.	Male.	Female.	Male.	Female.	Male.	Female.
Hindus returned by actual occupation.												
Ghatwal	...	...	219	179	42	39	...	...	...	...	9	12
Kotal	...	...	...	...	...	...	...	...	...	...	...	...
Mala	...	...	...	...	...	...	10	...	6	...	...	...
Patni	...	1	3	10	102	89	34	25	3	5	50	46
Hindus returned by locality												
Hindustanis	215	225	...	...	124	262	...	...	21	10	186	135
Musalmans returned by title.												
Pathan	247	248	53	45	53	58	285	380	324	358	323	348
Sayyid	60	70	16	19	90	94	51	88	164	202	37	42
Shaikh	14,957	17,585	5,071	5,320	10,238	10,431	17,537	20,289	19,140	21,656	14,923	16,880
Musalmans returned by actual occupation.												
Jolaha	18	16	1	...	...	...	...	...	43	54	19	25
Kahar	...	...	22	33	59	64	...	...	12	7	...	...
Kalu	305	319	...	...	4	...	9	8	...	...	...	...

SHIDABAD—*continued.*

Barihampara.		Nowada.		Goas.		Jalinghi.		Shahnagar.		Manulabazar.		Asanpur.		Lalbagh Municipality.	
Male.	Female.	Male.	Female.	Male.	Female.	Male.	Female.	Male.	Female.	Male.	Female.	Male.	Female.	Male.	Female.
...	...	...	...	...	...	...	...	...	...	49	19	568	468	531	486
...	...	...	...	...	...	...	...	...	...	...	...	...	...	...	...
...	...	...	...	...	...	15	14	131	106	...	...	1	...	...	...
91	109	95	122	6	9	76	91	13	20	18	16	6	10	2	...
645	686	...	...	46	56	...	...	46	63	20	22	...	...	82	105
491	448	159	154	313	337	311	318	57	74	10	17	18	14	444	345
153	185	37	25	23	36	274	331	15	22	5	4	2	...	573	707
14,334	15,104	11,418	15,157	8,027	9,221	35,949	40,337	3,195	3,460	419	435	1,306	1,351	4,465	4,914
337	396	323	355	...	...	531	905	3	1	...	...	8	11	261	161
114	127	...	...	8	5	217	307	...	...	22	23	...	...	104	136
305	358	43	44	144	139	536	509	...	...	...	...	...	...	...	...

SHIDABAD—*concluded.*

Dewansarai.		Mirzapur.		Kandi.		Barwa.		Khargaon.		Bharatpur.		Gokarna.	
Male.	Female.	Male.	Female.	Male.	Female.	Male.	Female.	Male.	Female.	Male.	Female.	Male.	Female.
...	...	...	...	9	5	38	31	...	...	23	17	1	2
...	...	...	...	59	64	1	2	11	13	550	608	15	17
...	...	...	...	1	...	34	35	...	...	...	...	122	158
45	61	51	74	...	...	59	63	...	...	31	22	23	20
53	63	...	...	12	30	...	...	98	125	1	..	3	3
175	187	137	125	39	43	289	244	214	204	398	378	106	87
27	22	41	43	11	12	429	416	89	113	625	690	103	84
19,843	22,191	7,692	8,429	3,270	3,168	19,880	21,051	7,600	7,822	18,012	19,314	7,734	7,766
16	17	...	...	...	...	23	59	63	70	16	8	...	...
...	...	20	35	...	...	156	179	...	...	...	...	28	56
16	15	...	...	...	...	5	7	4	9	...	...	10	12

Caste or Group.	District Total.			Khulna.		Dumuria.		Baitaghata.		Paikgachha.		Bagherhat.	
	Total.	Male.	Female.	Male.	Female.	Male.	Female.	Male.	Female.	Male.	Female.	Male.	Female.
Bagdi	7,484	4,307	3,177	285	252	...	...	50	25	258	140	206	176
Baidya	2,170	1,118	1,052	381	394	32	28	...	...	...	...	286	313
Baniya	5,078	2,794	2,284	815	684	284	271	30	7	278	252	391	335
(i)—Gandha Banik ...	1,429	806	623	402	332	56	48	...	...	...	...	200	162
(ii)—Subarna Banik ...	2,829	1,488	1,341	291	302	164	160	30	7	188	169	88	53
Barui	14,048	7,219	6,829	3,838	3,694	...	...	...	...	55	53	2,195	2,064
Bediya	1,875	1,012	863	...	...	382	332	196	126	...	...	249	222
Brahman	29,701	15,275	14,426	2,721	2,548	1,174	1,255	190	163	535	385	3,332	3,341
Chamar and Muchi ...	29,154	14,734	14,420	686	965	2,126	2,093	161	133	1,105	672	523	343
Dhopa	2,749	1,483	1,266	242	190	166	156	...	...	93	92	348	297
Dom and Kaora	3,689	1,970	1,719	133	77	181	186	...	...	...	...	12	16
Goala	12,549	6,432	6,117	347	193	482	449	271	154	387	305	269	131
Jugi	11,301	6,040	5,261	361	271	777	813	34	10	488	355	1,646	1,524
Kahar	2,241	1,173	1,068	43	46	...	...	71	68	262	275	351	293
Kaibartta	24,487	12,711	11,776	544	408	685	699	...	...	913	694	1,967	2,036
Kamar and Lohar ...	7,833	4,210	3,623	577	566	356	318	...	...	168	77	380	274
Kapali	16,033	8,375	7,658	632	500	818	782	46	49	180	94	413	373
Kayastha	38,089	19,775	18,314	4,182	3,830	1,646	1,800	320	208	896	811	6,284	6,114
Kumhar	10,749	5,577	5,172	569	612	440	410	197	157	166	170	1,302	1,308
Mal	4,923	2,603	2,320	2,598	2,317	...	...	...	...	...	...	...	...
Malo	7,475	4,228	3,247	1,038	1,013	...	...	127	78	915	842	633	529
Namasudra or Chandal	158,015	82,137	75,878	11,010	10,874	7,183	7,099	6,224	6,148	5,461	4,444	13,582	12,055
Napit and Hajjam ...	17,404	9,058	8,346	787	781	842	831	370	322	691	605	1,276	1,229
Pod	86,030	45,153	40,877	190	105	1,857	1,642	2,214	2,131	12,844	11,453	11	5
Sadgop	5,560	2,859	2,701	55	39	385	434	38	32	41	32	350	313
Sunri	11,171	6,453	4,718	1,184	585	1,028	872	123	2	65	41	2,703	2,264
Sutradhar	1,821	1,051	770	364	270	53	33	...	...	213	143	47	24
Tanti	1,925	1,089	836	399	262	223	198	...	...	...	...	63	27
Teli and Kalu	9,617	5,168	4,440	823	570	660	612	167	151	400	401	920	771
Tiyar	6,857	3,582	3,275	248	141	59	56	..	...	34	1	175	145
Religious devotees and persons returned by sect.													
Baisnab	6,753	3,415	3,338	547	473	290	290	88	93	171	150	683	746
Hindus returned by title or common sub-caste.													
Biswas	1,188	618	570	3	...	73	49	...	...	19	3	5	3
Mandal	3,515	1,867	1,648	...	...	...	...	...	...	267	217	...	...
Hindus returned by actual occupation.													
Jaliya	16,284	8,708	7,576	515	245	42	44	134	...	142	26	929	832
Patni	1,438	726	712	...	...	131	143	27	28	91	110	...	...
Musalmans returned by title.													
Biswas	4,240	2,199	2,041	2	...	...	...	...	...	...	...	...	...
Dafadar	2,950	1,496	1,454	29	36	77	84	...	...	...	...	...	...
Gain	1,727	868	859	...	...	...	...	...	...	...	...	...	...
Ghazi	68,172	34,464	33,708	41	26	951	1,001	...	...	407	365	...	...
Khan	4,125	2,243	1,882	40	37	193	131	...	...	134	88	...	...
Pathan	10,543	5,829	4,714	855	588	581	586	120	83	152	124	966	811
Sardar	53,533	27,235	26,298	3	...	397	366	...	...	277	236	...	...
Sayyid	3,427	1,945	1,482	273	309	141	64	...	...	75	56	540	426
Shaikh	360,167	191,574	168,593	33,551	29,332	26,109	25,605	6,995	5,930	15,434	13,529	32,172	28,869
Shana	3,741	1,837	1,904	331	279	...	...	...	...	...	...	...	...

KHULNA.

Mullahat.		Rampal.		Morrellganj.		Satkhira.		Kalaroa.		Magura.		Asasuni.		Kaliganj.	
Male.	Female.	Male.	Female.	Male.	Female.	Male.	Female.	Male.	Female.	Male.	Female.	Male.	Female.	Male.	Female.
...	...	...	...	29	26	963	744	244	192	91	86	541	330	1,640	1,206
7	...	2	...	53	20	98	89	150	116	...	...	27	14	83	79
...	...	55	...	31	2	72	69	237	240	103	123	201	126	298	175
...	...	22	...	20	2	19	17	47	40	4	9	19	13	17	...
...	...	33	...	11	...	53	52	131	199	92	114	182	113	225	172
...	...	42	1	228	156	110	94	152	155	152	176	203	217	244	219
103	108	58	59	22	16	...	...	...	...	...	...	...	...	...	...
265	210	340	234	873	763	1,087	948	821	853	839	942	773	685	2,096	2,099
68	44	180	82	63	2	3,656	3,856	1,955	2,447	1,113	1,223	1,191	993	1,907	1,567
76	61	28	29	145	106	54	50	84	79	43	36	52	38	152	132
...	...	3	3	...	...	342	315	142	128	60	67	129	150	968	777
40	...	233	167	81	30	701	656	716	1,244	563	714	408	335	1,934	1,739
...	...	396	325	244	177	385	365	120	137	367	363	322	207	901	714
...	...	223	213	...	...	...	...	...	...	...	...	50	55	73	118
24	...	128	10	1,296	1,268	1,816	1,682	1,522	1,546	1,397	1,383	951	768	1,468	1,282
76	76	41	...	206	41	514	559	466	454	355	364	201	140	870	754
419	402	371	291	80	66	973	1,015	862	777	293	275	375	260	2,913	2,774
103	30	320	11	1,805	1,254	756	683	421	516	935	1,108	549	362	1,559	1,578
...	...	1,199	1,015	129	75	431	386	306	291	141	125	106	110	591	513
...	...	...	...	...	...	...	...	...	...	...	...	...	...	5	3
385	318	499	176	...	...	26	19	66	26	169	119	168	45	202	87
10,994	10,239	8,921	7,433	6,353	5,518	3,139	2,840	149	119	445	402	2,739	2,431	5,937	5,276
479	434	424	415	553	449	632	597	470	450	421	399	927	757	1,186	1,077
...	...	867	771	...	...	2,293	2,050	25	1	3,172	2,844	7,948	7,050	13,732	12,825
...	...	...	...	...	...	672	672	200	221	635	551	185	39	448	378
183	...	179	7	...	...	226	229	237	261	218	231	73	35	234	191
...	...	...	...	...	...	16	4	164	184	6	...	8	...	180	112
...	...	13	...	...	...	55	57	276	267	3	4	11	5	40	16
...	...	320	207	214	119	36	26	120	117	274	252	378	351	856	872
...	...	...	...	...	...	384	425	13	10	9	13	244	141	2,416	2,343
58	67	234	198	66	80	153	144	74	78	91	110	302	295	658	613
...	...	...	...	...	...	...	...	...	...	...	...	213	174	305	341
...	...	22	13	...	...	10	5	...	...	456	408	...	...	1,112	1,005
516	507	...	...	...	...	1,100	1,082	478	414	1,565	1,482	1,567	1,200	1,720	1,744
32	30	76	63	8	5	...	...	93	96	53	56	59	33	156	149
...	...	...	...	...	...	618	588	1,067	1,075	292	197	220	181	...	...
...	...	...	...	...	...	342	310	896	849	152	175	...	...	...	...
...	...	...	...	...	...	375	404	250	262	...	...	243	193	...	...
...	...	...	...	...	...	7,958	7,269	5,142	5,566	1,980	1,841	5,654	5,018	12,241	11,932
...	...	...	...	...	...	271	275	735	688	394	289	204	144	272	230
57	59	120	84	1,784	1,297	174	151	299	311	52	67	139	106	530	447
...	...	...	...	...	...	15,931	16,030	...	...	2,264	2,073	4,554	4,013	3,809	3,590
76	53	89	75	231	126	264	103	...	...	60	70	...	...	196	200
23,294	20,421	18,218	11,490	23,781	20,005	2,385	1,679	2,545	2,507	3,985	4,015	1,572	853	6,533	4,858
...	...	...	...	...	...	...	...	760	836	78	68	668	721	...	...

t

DISTRICT

Group.	District Total.			Khulna.		Dumuria.		Baitaghata.		Paikgachha.		Bagherhat.	
	Total.	Male.	Female.	Male.	Female.	Male.	Female.	Male.	Female.	Male.	Female.	Male.	Female.
Musalmans returned by actual occupation.													
Badyakar	1,241	650	591	...	...	264	263	...	...	167	109	...	...
Behara	8,927	4,494	4,433	982	905	...	...	...	...	...	...	551	498
Dai	3,536	1,891	1,645	291	226	359	292	...	...	186	156	129	125
Dalal	1,188	587	601	...	...	...	...	...	...	...	...	...	...
Dhuli	2,194	1,091	1,103	...	...	...	...	...	...	...	...	...	...
Fakir	1,263	672	591	43	42	...	...	...	...	51	39	...	...
Hajjam	1,405	699	706	294	285	206	280	...	...	...	...	99	90
Jolaha	19,477	10,138	9,339	350	257	946	812	103	96	706	623	...	...
Kalu	1,841	946	895	198	219	28	39	...	...	41	29	...	...
Karigar	3,386	1,804	1,582	179	145	399	368	...	...	47	49	...	...
Malik	1,597	805	792	87	79	67	92	...	...	...	...	...	...
Mandal	17,964	9,410	8,554	20	5	740	643	...	...	267	217	...	...
Mullah	7,954	4,226	3,728	280	186	...	...	...	...	...	...	...	...
Nikari	6,015	3,056	2,959	817	905	529	402	...	...	153	152	580	654

RAJSHAHI

DISTRICT

Caste.	District Total.			Dinajpur.		Hemtabad.		Kaliganj.		Bansihari.		Birganj.		Patnitolla.	
	Total.	Male.	Female.	Male.	Female.	Male.	Female.	Male.	Female.	Male.	Female.	Male.	Female.	Male.	Female.
Baniya	10,145	5,324	4,821	1,851	1,653	65	42	22	19	491	455	225	217	215	198
(I) Khatri	8,609	4,461	4,148	1,657	1,494	18	20	2	3	375	341	224	217	118	120
Barui	2,005	1,065	940	35	13	10	12	484	390	40	38	34	37	8	9
Bediya	1,907	989	918	116	128	4	...	24	27	21	14	85	65	9	12
Beldar	1,232	687	545	...	...	337	316	188	186	...	...	...	...	...	...
Bhuimali and Mihtar	34,647	17,576	17,071	1,143	1,032	1,057	1,033	2,035	2,005	1,460	1,442	804	735	911	839
Brahman	11,370	6,798	4,572	1,672	846	317	147	215	263	126	63	209	151	555	428
Chamar and Muchi	5,180	3,378	1,802	359	67	345	313	244	210	122	68	123	46	220	156
Dhopa	1,741	931	810	84	62	19	14	112	99	24	22	6	2	348	314
Goala	8,533	5,147	3,386	715	218	171	193	551	519	234	112	262	189	211	195
Jugi	15,188	8,105	7,083	270	180	301	183	1,751	1,673	240	244	395	276	332	230
Kahar	3,366	2,019	1,347	453	247	48	23	12	8	87	42	250	205	23	3
Kaibartta	39,765	20,707	19,058	1,457	1,377	339	300	436	454	295	292	1,536	1,969	1,872	1,626
Kamar and Lohar	4,359	2,341	2,018	440	411	87	59	56	35	122	110	259	261	275	223
Kandu	1,196	638	558	151	140	...	...	...	...	16	12	...	...	1	4
Kayastha	7,424	4,392	3,032	1,067	881	311	265	209	173	162	182	50	28	45	7
Kochh	481,591	247,810	233,781	49,136	47,585	19,441	16,468	19,929	17,636	7,943	7,657	33,262	32,577	7,074	6,973
Kumhar	9,453	4,870	4,583	280	227	72	67	158	152	37	51	292	262	202	126
Kurmi	1,918	1,465	453	406	37	26	6	28	1	29	22	55	...	299	213
Maira and Halwai	1,208	809	399	143	69	2	2	...	...	45	18	39	19	15	10
Malakar	1,756	977	779	78	27	60	52	91	104	77	59	38	51	31	23
Malo	1,900	999	901	...	...	22	15	196	167	...	...	...	...	197	171
Namasudra or Chandal ...	6,981	3,593	3,388	153	77	381	329	263	242	...	...	146	147	74	51
Napit	11,158	5,915	5,243	961	881	251	221	372	343	269	239	780	676	196	178
Nuniya	3,203	2,128	1,075	15	9	25	21	...	...	319	196	121	6	128	86
Oraon	1,386	700	686	33	29	...	...	6	8	...	...	...	...	...	...

KHULNA—*concluded.*

Mullahat.		Rampal.		Morrellganj.		Satkhira.		Kalaroa.		Magura.		Asasuni.		Kaliganj.	
Male.	Female.	Male.	Female.	Male.	Female.	Male.	Female.	Male.	Female.	Male.	Female.	Male.	Female.	Male.	Female.
...	...	103	106	...	...	96	113	...	...	...	...	...	...	...	...
...	...	...	...	...	...	780	785	1,037	1,217	161	172	983	861	...	...
54	56	...	...	95	117	283	286	168	168	117	106	209	163	...	...
...	...	...	...	...	...	330	342	250	251	...	...	7	8	...	...
...	...	...	...	...	...	458	496	175	160	...	...	458	547	...	...
...	...	...	...	29	15	122	108	132	171	124	94	105	67	66	55
...	...	...	...	...	...	47	58	...	...	...	...	53	43	...	...
301	303	...	...	...	...	2,779	2,798	1,417	1,401	1,168	803	241	231	2,127	2,016
...	...	...	...	...	...	373	376	...	...	245	200	61	32	...	...
...	...	...	...	...	...	82	78	965	881	...	...	131	61	...	...
...	...	...	...	...	...	206	193	136	124	78	79	96	81	135	139
...	...	...	...	...	...	1,939	1,861	3,679	3,435	1,553	1,449	1,212	944	...	...
...	...	...	...	...	...	1,053	1,001	1,022	997	237	209	821	644	813	691
...	...	...	...	...	...	119	112	194	196	190	176	93	61	381	301

DIVISION.

DINAJPUR.

Mahadevpur.		Porsha.		Patiram.		Gangarampur.		Chintaman.		Parbatipur.		Nawabganj.		Thakurgaon.		Ranisankail.		Pirganj.	
Male.	Female.	Male.	Female.	Male.	Female.	Male.	Female.	Male.	Female.	Male.	Female.	Male.	Female.	Male.	Female.	Male.	Female.	Male.	Female.
17	7	206	177	705	647	265	246	164	173	309	265	38	24	285	264	178	194	288	240
8	1	149	145	692	645	241	246	164	173	288	251	4	...	174	168	108	119	241	205
4	...	98	127	4	6	66	45	...	...	...	...	1	...	96	86	194	187	...	...
23	13	13	13	238	209	59	61	63	45	163	165	31	23	67	55	3	2	70	86
...	...	...	...	...	...	...	...	...	...	...	...	...	...	...	...	74	57	88	36
647	615	904	897	1,206	1,273	1,888	1,888	549	469	403	375	408	397	2,600	2,507	817	808	744	763
456	482	241	97	520	355	311	270	530	421	114	37	314	133	735	678	161	69	322	163
189	70	288	206	158	45	259	65	239	121	144	52	163	61	171	104	243	167	146	51
156	146	17	2	16	31	17	12	74	54	3	...	6	1	17	22	25	29	7	...
369	290	224	172	350	271	253	196	163	41	394	119	238	129	508	409	223	191	231	193
459	381	...	...	271	244	186	96	99	81	103	108	100	67	3,019	2,907	498	386	61	27
144	56	26	13	18	...	17	2	50	35	192	111	118	58	369	359	173	174	30	11
3,892	3,748	247	153	2,295	2,443	643	548	1,906	1,198	925	184	2,615	2,530	969	944	818	846	462	449
100	51	128	83	244	232	84	98	160	139	9	5	75	59	147	114	78	66	77	73
16	10	164	123	9	8	128	131	9	6	...	...	1	...	17	...	126	124	...	...
215	155	225	142	420	273	224	295	677	444	91	33	75	24	493	117	78	50	50	13
2,656	2,655	3,308	3,271	8,111	6,576	489	447	3,318	3,222	2,565	2,277	9,859	0,874	38,064	34,926	20,238	19,921	22,452	20,716
254	283	167	135	163	134	1,863	1,881	57	57	74	58	77	47	840	866	265	246	79	61
43	6	116	111	77	1	49	15	50	17	69	6	103	2	3	2	60	13	54	1
23	14	6	4	51	15	26	7	88	34	21	...	8	3	152	84	155	91	34	29
18	17	15	12	14	16	23	28	25	16	1	1	7	4	380	265	79	80	40	24
16	11	90	84	414	438	9	1	1	...	30	8	11	5	...	...	...	...	13	1
963	990	1	...	221	207	205	221	79	76	312	316	179	154	80	78	150	144	396	356
194	259	83	74	229	209	268	243	155	146	222	3	148	125	1,231	1,085	243	227	263	334
83	18	436	226	295	205	134	99	124	53	93	...	54	3	180	76	61	33	60	45
56	82	5	8	376	318	103	178	51	60	16	...	44	34	...	...	...	...	10	9

DISTRICT DINAJ

Caste or Group.	District Total.			Dinajpur.		Hemtabad.		Kaliganj.		Bansihari.		Birganj.		Patnitolla.	
	Total.	Male.	Female.	Male.	Female.	Male.	Female.	Male.	Female.	Male.	Female.	Male.	Female.	Male.	Female.
Rajput	2,865	2,049	816	275	109	49	13	86	84	135	53	55	17	64	10
Sadgop	1,379	703	676	100	126	95	89	192	204	44	35	12	6	54	47
Santal	6,515	3,273	3,242	295	269	24	27	347	383	223	237	41	29	493	527
Sunri and Kalwar	3,628	1,966	1,662	349	298	159	136	234	253	129	98	61	33	60	68
Tanti and Tatwa	6,898	3,749	3,149	676	563	84	72	114	118	51	49	687	558	85	60
Teli and Kalu	3,534	1,837	1,697	233	132	170	165	266	330	57	49	6	1	29	1
Tiyar	1,814	858	956	41	50	30	16	242	216	7	4	...	...	...	...
Religious devotees and persons returned by sect.															
Baisnab	18,106	8,760	9,346	916	1,060	284	275	546	616	439	424	555	555	984	958
Hindus returned by title or common sub-caste.															
Buna	8,904	4,843	4,061	12	1	...	...	2	...	18	5	...	...	1,246	1,035
Hindus returned by actual occupation.															
Ghatwal	1,177	779	398	102	29	105	55	19	8	9	...	...	...	63	61
Jaliya	4,395	2,221	2,174	438	448	137	180	10	9	6	...	812	853	...	...
Mala	1,380	1,084	296	1	...	82	15	...	...	54	14	...	...	...	...
Musalmans returned by title.															
Pathan	3,451	1,940	1,511	251	199	67	53	98	106	49	33	392	305	93	66
Sayyid	2,679	1,434	1,245	227	169	52	51	27	27	79	83	87	79	47	51
Shaikh	792,217	411,332	380,885	57,717	55,048	17,892	15,490	15,407	14,625	19,734	18,891	31,970	28,150	22,412	20,734

DISTRICT

Caste.	District Total.			Boalia.		Tanor.		Godagari.		Putia.		Charghat.	
	Total.	Male.	Female.	Male.	Female.	Male.	Female.	Male.	Female.	Male.	Female.	Male.	Female.
Bagdi	2,881	1,377	1,504	389	485	...	...	337	349	51	51	64	56
Baniya	3,157	1,715	1,442	241	224	100	125	135	124	147	175	169	137
(i) Khatri	1,288	710	578	41	24	100	125	35	...	100	175	69	37
Bhuimali and Mihtar	5,298	2,702	2,596	360	307	102	118	163	51	155	122	58	60
Bhumij	1,118	559	559	...	...	...	...	557	558	...	...	...	...
Brahman	14,965	8,245	6,720	1,093	497	298	212	352	167	629	451	556	566
Chain	8,466	4,183	4,283	472	377	17	99	1,388	1,356	10	11	579	578
Chamar and Muchi	6,698	3,462	3,236	264	242	84	69	214	256	194	184	392	428
Chasa Dhopa	1,767	916	851	711	665	198	175	...	...	7	11	...	...
Chasati	1,608	850	758	526	465	...	...	314	291	...	...	...	...
Goala	8,475	4,476	3,999	233	191	140	124	221	151	202	212	492	532
Jugi	2,348	1,250	1,188	64	49	75	80	9	5	...	...	379	373
Kahar	2,205	1,587	618	213	117	84	1	118	62	...	...	95	97
Kaibartta	50,505	25,570	24,935	872	886	1,165	852	490	427	1,732	1,758	2,363	2,317
Kamar and Lohar	4,743	2,404	2,339	184	256	148	114	97	32	178	169	478	539
Kandu	1,853	967	886	125	130	49	48	57	56	40	42	90	80
Kayastha	6,747	3,691	3,056	601	377	141	111	42	21	182	175	179	185
Kochh...	16,026	8,594	7,432	236	110	568	561	348	341	240	154	122	124
Kumhar	7,945	3,929	4,016	278	216	177	272	161	157	288	266	372	396
Kurmi	2,258	1,367	891	109	58	71	50	623	548	39	12	20	11
Malo	4,699	2,550	2,149	468	261	42	42	102	72	13	14	393	331

PUR—*concluded.*

Mahadevpur.		Porsha.		Patiram.		Gangarampur.		Chintaman.		Parbatipur.		Nawabganj.		Thakurgaon.		Ranisankail.		Pirganj.	
Male.	Female.	Male.	Female.	Male.	Female.	Male.	Female.	Male.	Female.	Male.	Female.	Male.	Female.	Male.	Female.	Male.	Female.	Male.	Female.
63	14	61	6	186	11	264	53	229	164	69	20	52	1	53	21	65	2	343	238
19	...	8	6	66	64	24	22	5	6	...	...	6	1	70	63	2	...	6	7
...	...	107	102	1,007	979	228	206	412	407	25	22	...	...	...	...	...	...	71	64
79	55	134	84	23	18	85	67	40	14	52	34	74	47	312	280	133	137	51	46
23	5	26	10	79	76	236	204	204	119	140	132	134	79	879	836	183	136	143	132
86	64	57	8	101	30	60	22	168	100	8	...	13	8	322	484	219	264	42	39
313	369	66	78	68	143	...	...	...	...	...	...	7	6	15	17	27	24	42	33
717	896	299	311	867	912	493	555	541	628	468	428	328	368	986	915	140	170	247	275
1,261	1,068	472	378	765	657	402	378	235	112	2	2	360	327	4	4	124	94	...	...
...	...	39	11	73	20	61	10	111	121	100	50	14	...	...	...	83	33	...	...
164	131	60	55	50	29	221	219	8	1	162	159	56	41	20	24	6	8	71	67
29	15	745	129	3	3	19	...	...	...	2	1	3	...	...	...	133	118	13	1
115	98	49	29	28	10	132	88	67	54	106	79	32	29	320	245	17	12	124	105
118	130	60	58	74	49	137	103	52	33	77	82	56	37	233	203	10	8	98	82
[illegible]	21,859	17,027	15,964	16,945	15,466	17,761	16,352	16,931	15,422	24,611	23,198	25,026	23,190	63,092	58,983	20,360	18,813	21,595	18,301

RAJSHAHI.

Baghmara.		Naugaon.		Manda.		Panchupur.		Nator.		Singra.		Burigram.		Lalpur.	
Male.	Female.	Male.	Female.	Male.	Female.	Male.	Female.	Male.	Female.	Male.	Female.	Male.	Female.	Male.	Female.
8	...	26	32	...	...	12	21	53	50	...	...	62	56	375	395
45	...	75	44	115	105	17	7	94	46	318	267	113	10	146	178
17	...	19	1	15	5	17	7	68	16	115	27	13	10	101	151
89	80	302	280	366	399	253	274	328	371	351	351	91	102	84	81
2	1	...	...	...	...	...	...	...	...	...	...	...	...	...	...
223	153	602	387	836	269	435	473	2,006	1,885	923	895	464	475	278	290
...	...	22	1	15	1	21	11	904	984	226	247	410	400	119	128
...	...	166	125	305	272	395	426	403	349	363	202	348	334	334	349
...	...	...	...	...	...	...	...	...	...	...	...	...	...	...	...
...	...	...	...	...	...	10	2	...	...	...	...	...	...	...	...
183	132	299	256	182	110	249	130	922	912	532	504	496	436	367	269
93	72	131	119	56	60	263	252	58	46	80	86	26	17	32	30
86	2	183	3	120	59	131	8	233	26	16	...	55	11	281	237
2,765	2,796	2,316	2,222	2,903	2,802	2,836	2,660	2,943	3,088	1,886	1,868	1,118	1,213	2,181	2,046
55	64	46	28	306	351	76	78	369	357	141	140	100	111	171	90
37	46	48	21	34	34	75	76	156	133	74	59	32	36	150	125
69	33	225	82	192	82	182	122	828	837	499	416	422	492	129	123
273	212	625	524	2,982	2,808	358	268	114	114	1,950	1.946	160	188	619	82
239	228	245	296	321	326	404	424	368	306	591	605	234	196	251	238
15	2	66	14	142	117	28	14	109	36	61	13	63	14	21	2
63	60	109	106	80	90	17	5	215	230	182	116	100	100	766	722

Caste or Group.	District Total.			Boalia.		Tanor.		Godagari.		Putia.		Charghat.	
	Total.	Male.	Female.	Male.	Female.	Male.	Female.	Male.	Female.	Male.	Female.	Male.	Female.
Namasudra or Chandal ...	28,528	14,289	14,239	498	472	330	348	587	594	787	641	1,117	1,143
Napit	6,973	3,506	3,467	253	237	137	143	156	133	278	254	437	431
Oraon	1,413	905	508	...	...	18	...	329	347	...	...	...	...
Pod	8,725	4,457	4,268	309	273	...	...	...	...	...	...	2,348	2,297
Santal	1,465	845	620	6	...	15	11	64	64	155	176	...	...
Sunri and Kalwar	6,077	3,260	2,817	218	156	170	189	195	95	360	393	559	522
Sutradhar	4,003	2,038	1,965	81	68	68	66	7	...	60	8	414	419
Teli aud Kalu	7,061	3,575	3,486	141	101	390	303	300	300	228	231	185	188
Tiyar	2,311	1,117	1,194	10	...	128	116	47	32	...	...	78	105
Religious devotees and persons returned by sect.													
Baisnab	14,392	5,823	8,569	544	1,038	431	559	272	353	413	671	480	736
Hindus returned by title or common sub-caste.													
Buna	8,129	4,285	3,844	109	110	151	42	1,006	986	130	136	200	215
Haladhar	1,999	955	1,044	804	880	...	...	...	...	...	...	150	164
Hindus returned by actual occupation.													
Jaliya	7,182	3,568	3,614	75	74	29	83	42	29	225	262	300	164
Matiya	6,863	3,499	3,364	214	240	330	401	350	201	11	14	10	8
Patni	1,529	743	786	30	29	19	26	50	51	68	40	55	72
Hindus returned by locality.													
Uriyas	1,145	484	661	150	145	...	...	...	...	230	245	...	...
Musalmans returned by title.													
Pathan	5,015	2,655	2,360	383	284	314	323	72	70	126	104	169	155
Sayyid	3,207	1,613	1,594	127	84	152	153	33	23	83	89	80	80
Shaikh	1,015,921	501,371	514,550	37,148	37,139	36,775	37,586	12,824	12,774	41,521	41,216	45,014	47,894
Musalmans returned by actual occupation.													
Jolaha	3,385	1,647	1,738	54	...	129	132	26	14	120	130	...	...
Kalu	1,195	579	616	40	50	16	14	...	...	55	52	...	...

DISTRICT

Caste.	District Total.			Rangpur.		Kaliganj.		Mahiganj.		Badarganj.		Mithapukhur.		Pirganj.	
	Total.	Male.	Female.	Male.	Female.	Male.	Female.	Male.	Female.	Male.	Female.	Male.	Female.	Male.	Female.
Baniya	2,553	1,576	977	131	54	37	...	149	84	88	46	67	64	121	105
(i) Khatri	1,058	770	288	87	26	22	...	38	1	75	34	6	...	19	5
Barui	1,323	647	676	55	48	...	...	21	19	1	5	2	...	15	20
Bediya	1,506	751	755	26	29	18	23	...	...	18	10	...	...	...	...

SHAHI—*concluded.*

Baghmara.		Naugaon.		Manda.		Panchupur.		Nator.		Singra.		Burigram.		Lalpur.	
Male.	Female.	Male.	Female.	Male.	Female.	Male.	Female.	Male.	Female.	Male.	Female.	Male.	Female.	Male.	Female.
229	300	1,765	1,777	1,825	1,818	1,180	1,149	1,966	2,142	1,451	1,366	1,812	1,813	792	776
250	256	233	243	164	156	260	272	530	627	269	279	301	337	238	199
29	...	96	13	339	122	78	12	...	...	16	14	...	...	...	...
248	233	...	...	400	417	...	...	...	...	...	...	...	...	1,158	1,048
25	...	100	75	301	266	...	...	104	28	25	...	50	...	...	...
29	27	463	315	80	62	145	125	277	228	454	424	162	141	148	140
48	55	136	125	63	52	70	71	394	355	317	365	186	199	194	187
37	2	81	2	291	264	107	111	746	702	394	489	320	329	405	467
97	81	514	634	253	221	...	...	...	...	10	5	...	...	...	...
215	285	512	699	777	961	478	618	486	980	578	079	331	544	311	452
43	...	115	23	1,991	1,863	149	80	28	69	106	186	157	134	100	...
...	...	1	...	...	...	...	...	...	...	...	...	...	...	...	...
38	43	...	...	206	101	404	426	371	442	674	729	1,047	1,191	157	130
17	16	183	157	...	...	834	824	197	197	1,068	1,028	173	158	112	120
...	...	53	40	...	...	44	64	110	164	121	118	150	137	43	45
...	...	...	...	50	145	...	...	54	126	...	...	...	...	...	...
205	165	116	116	106	107	169	143	294	271	128	138	16	23	557	461
203	187	190	203	105	87	179	174	192	206	150	148	77	85	42	75
53,175	54,033	37,217	37,502	40,796	41,259	33,671	34,003	51,655	55,612	43,159	43,295	47,191	40,414	21,325	22,823
61	65	...	...	75	78	200	·207	52	124	308	337	128	142	494	509
121	115	95	107	26	25	...	...	88	104	138	149	...	...	...	...

RANGPUR.

Dimla.		Jaldhákí.		Nilphamari.		Baradari.		Kurigram.		Nageswari.		Ulipur.		Gobindganj.		Sadullapur.		Sundarganj.	
Male.	Female.	Male.	Female.	Male.	Female.	Male.	Female.	Male.	Female.	Male.	Female.	Male.	Female.	Male.	Female.	Male.	Female.	Male.	Female.
87	69	25	7	...	...	257	240	49	29	19	21	40	24	168	59	151	44	192	131
69	59	21	2	...	...	100	89	2	...	8	10	8	...	145	31	132	29	38	2
...	...	...	...	...	...	159	193	...	...	225	237	...	...	169	154	...	...	...	...
60	51	250	234	130	108	119	145	...	...	19	37	...	...	106	104	...	...	5	4

DISTRICT

Caste or Group.	District Total.			Rangpur.		Kaliganj.		Mahiganj		Badarganj.		Mithapukhur.		Pirganj.	
	Total.	Male.	Female.	Male.	Female.	Male.	Female.	Male.	Female.	Male.	Female.	Male.	Female.	Male.	Female.
Bhuimali and Mihtar	9,580	4,720	4,860	252	227	233	211	113	82	127	130	105	87	77	60
Brahman	8,315	5,103	3,212	1,052	431	327	173	415	242	186	73	172	102	220	249
Chamar and Muchi	4,328	3,071	1,257	241	35	105	40	143	28	140	35	80	9	8	5
Dom aad Kaora	1,317	624	693	18	19	...	...	32	29	57	60	54	63	...	...
Goala	5,850	4,191	1,659	356	50	40	21	619	418	287	15	210	43	337	40
Jugi	6,219	3,122	3,097	252	349	285	257	461	419	77	77	65	47	76	76
Kahar	12,189	6,765	5,424	730	611	489	452	976	854	135	81	390	247	620	474
Kaibartta	28,644	14,199	14,445	2,755	2,846	693	709	260	231	1,045	1,014	1,105	1,014	522	467
Kamar and Lohar	3,059	1,595	1,464	117	93	7	11	85	31	52	33	32	22	48	37
Kayastha	10,020	5,309	4,711	656	295	36	8	444	407	44	10	88	61	139	125
Kochh	522,604	266,151	256,453	12,347	12,131	39,404	37,764	11,250	11,162	7,234	6,933	4,202	3,899	2,023	2,272
Kumhar	4,402	2,215	2,187	154	127	133	155	72	51	70	37	170	143	100	92
Kurmi	2,791	1,927	864	317	36	54	21	194	3	172	5	29	11	100	30
Maira and Halwai	25,933	13,144	12,789	467	400	5	...	825	682	44	...	369	370	239	195
Malakar	1,193	605	588	9	10	...	...	21	19	6	2	...	...	...	...
Malo	1,758	1,184	574	19	4	56	...	1	...	3	...	10	...	6	...
Namasudra or Chandal	30,633	15,164	15,469	766	790	497	428	673	642	438	406	482	413	403	340
Napit and Hajjam	9,083	4,669	4,414	334	307	315	275	228	191	227	194	169	146	149	96
Nuniya	2,915	2,357	558	289	103	72	16	272	57	175	9	82	5	100	13
Rajput	17,823	9,489	8,334	39	10	...	...	22	12	42	10	...	...	38	24
Sunri and Kalwar	7,469	3,916	3,553	101	119	80	76	119	39	154	224	569	547	36	21
Sutradhar	1,398	815	553	9	2	...	...	25	25	89	56	16	14	14	12
Tanti and Tatwa	1,889	1,011	878	43	30	10	7	26	19	18	...	6	4	7	3
Teli and Kalu	1,802	898	904	60	63	...	...	92	60	8	1	3	...	27	20
Religious devotees and persons returned by sect.															
Baisnab	24,402	11,146	13,256	1,487	1,904	2,201	2,583	710	785	611	693	1,008	1,165	644	604
Hindus returned by actual occupation.															
Badyakar	2,647	1,394	1,253	57	48	121	111	203	161	138	136	239	221	71	37
Patni	1,150	669	481	46	36	101	82	13	6	52	44	35	7	23	24
Musalmans returned by title.															
Pathan	6,735	3,692	3,043	271	210	67	74	662	467	334	246	80	75	195	135
Sayyid	1,158	698	550	107	76	...	...	164	110	95	79	12	5	36	20
Shaikh	1,285,875	658,656	627,219	43,557	41,041	31,431	28,359	37,558	35,528	31,177	31,873	40,464	40,118	28,544	27,093

DISTRICT

Caste.	District Total.			Bogra.		Shariakandi.	
	Total.	Male.	Female.	Male.	Female.	Male.	Female.
Bagdi	1,119	544	575	13	18	20	19
Baniya	1,175	764	411	183	65	127	69
Bhuimali and Mihtar	7,781	3,954	3,827	978	928	270	291
Brahman	4,391	2,712	1,679	760	377	202	84

RANGPUR—*concluded.*

Dimla.		Jaldhákí.		Nilphamari.		Barabari.		Kurigram.		Nageswari.		Ulipur.		Gobindganj.		Sadullapur.		Sundarganj.	
Male.	Female.	Male.	Female.	Male.	Female.	Male.	Female.	Male.	Female.	Male.	Female.	Male.	Female.	Male.	Female.	Male.	Female.	Male.	Female.
455	436	357	385	376	421	131	153	49	37	723	833	75	107	761	719	750	813	144	159
273	138	210	150	176	143	358	450	64	52	480	265	56	60	453	223	423	291	234	171
134	77	115	15	374	33	223	226	136	12	171	72	277	236	418	188	382	182	124	64
84	86	23	58	...	...	30	36	...	...	114	127	40	46	119	112	...	...	44	57
63	1	108	25	...	...	232	225	...	...	262	183	102	50	558	116	569	368	394	104
146	156	152	171	451	352	131	99	143	117	151	134	50	90	160	149	117	127	406	477
346	336	779	440	...	...	246	306	...	...	189	56	44	30	365	174	1,096	1,048	411	316
346	219	1,652	1,804	88	99	162	285	140	145	129	98	1,699	1,872	1,640	1,593	940	970	1,121	1,079
467	407	67	67	...	...	216	223	...	...	128	150	114	144	201	193	84	18	37	35
83	53	44	21	1,067	1,012	426	566	388	388	271	215	179	164	732	732	552	541	161	134
28,467	34,065	33,533	33,246	28,128	23,867	17,148	16,350	...	...	21,790	21,928	19,837	18,885	7,688	7,734	14,207	13,715	11,233	12,502
...	...	48	48	...	...	201	257	...	...	73	93	154	158	642	621	187	235	217	170
37	7	53	9	...	...	84	91	...	...	54	...	164	7	238	7	147	461	274	176
13	...	70	83	...	...	125	128	16	12	4,247	4,829	502	574	2,912	2,865	2,991	2,387	320	306
...	...	...	...	...	...	63	89	...	...	103	97	93	60	62	69	237	226	11	14
1	...	1	...	151	110	160	124	...	...	3	...	254	219	173	112	348	5	...	...
290	317	1,148	1,168	176	220	553	789	64	80	2,198	2,741	1,326	1,103	2,674	2,477	2,224	2,213	1,302	1,342
476	432	424	423	418	330	167	203	152	120	267	281	184	259	502	493	458	465	199	200
91	20	21	...	...	...	...	...	...	...	105	18	386	113	236	22	343	151	215	31
21	10	18	7	...	...	30	11	8,493	7,536	16	5	23	4	740	705	...	...	1	...
118	147	96	89	...	...	273	339	...	...	194	179	142	153	573	534	939	774	523	312
4	...	1	...	...	...	...	...	...	...	...	...	61	78	308	239	183	66	105	91
216	207	321	293	...	...	195	231	...	...	38	35	36	9	48	...	...	...	47	40
8	2	9	7	33	44	347	430	83	09	14	25	62	73	52	29	97	76	3	5
...	...	901	999	...	...	248	333	6	2	177	197	213	187	1,099	1,513	1,404	1,675	437	616
...	...	...	...	...	...	212	209	...	...	54	29	88	103	32	39	128	107	51	52
18	12	88	67	...	...	45	70	...	...	27	15	23	9	...	...	187	104	11	5
185	147	461	405	649	649	...	...	236	236	39	15	221	192	241	166	...	...	51	36
37	38	60	67	...	...	...	...	...	...	2	...	26	28	145	126	...	...		1
30,179	28,056	43,322	39,582	46,531	40,814	35,844	32,826	20,298	19,853	36,892	34,334	66,251	66,983	77,840	74,754	61,000	57,858	28,773	28,147

BOGRA.

Sibganj.		Panchbibi.		Khetlal.		Nawabganj.		Adamdighi.		Sherpur.	
Male.	Female.	Male.	Female.	Male.	Female.	Male.	Female.	Male.	Female.	Male.	Female.
19	22	118	129	...	...	86	68	14	17	274	302
98	30	184	93	14	...	49	18	43	3	116	133
361	374	879	806	395	424	369	352	455	456	347	196
164	89	356	217	46	30	237	229	516	388	431	266

DISTRICT

Caste or Group.	District Total.			Bogra.		Shariakandi.	
	Total.	Male.	Female.	Male.	Female.	Male.	Female.
Chamar and Muchi	3,703	1,927	776	398	109	386	101
Goala	2,755	1,643	1,112	367	241	259	195
Jugi	5,038	2,788	2,250	736	599	340	237
Kahar	1,498	1,448	50	291	14	414	19
Kaibartta	18,794	9,632	9,162	1,001	968	1,284	1,050
Kamar	1,832	1,017	815	231	192	75	59
Kayastha	3,829	2,174	1,655	780	520	348	261
Kochh	23,685	11,906	11,779	2,147	2,229	1,037	1,031
Kumhar	4,012	2,113	1,899	661	602	176	140
Kurmi	1,824	1,278	546	234	157	57	...
Maira	1,246	709	537	110	65	8	...
Malo	5,523	2,563	2,960	54	54	1,374	1,632
Namasudra or Chandal	10,183	5,183	5,000	1,202	1,186	1,276	1,385
Napit and Hajjam	5,221	3,147	2,074	979	695	506	343
Nuniya	1,958	1,600	358	688	119	127	4
Rajput	4,618	2,367	2,251	1,480	1,407	573	553
Santal	2,000	1,008	992	...	...	...	...
Sunri	2,086	1,109	977	153	125	111	103
Sutradhar	1,669	971	698	256	212	163	87
Tanti and Tatwa	1,953	1,038	915	79	60	8	2
Teli and Kalu	1,970	1,085	885	126	145	60	18
Religious Devotees and persons returned by sect.							
Baisnab	11,303	5,116	6,187	1,175	1,264	832	453
Hindus returned by title or common sub-caste.							
Buna	6,458	3,413	3,075	...	1	...	...
Hindus returned by actual occupation.							
Jaliya	1,416	725	691	63	66	155	93
Matiya	4,342	2,308	2,034	815	761	73	27
Patni	1,150	567	583	44	42	171	220
Musalmans returned by title.							
Pathan	3,020	1,647	1,373	593	518	112	101
Sayyid	1,950	980	970	304	315	72	58
Shaikh	650,843	328,762	322,081	106,812	107,601	58,610	57,196

DISTRICT

Caste.	District Total.			Pabna.		Chatmohar.	
	Total.	Male.	Female.	Male.	Female.	Male.	Female.
Bagdi	1,549	874	675	270	315	38	1
Baidya	1,216	581	635	77	53	68	54
Baniya	4,990	2,421	2,569	380	355	270	262
(i) Gandha Banik	1,429	648	781	33	47	48	59
(ii) Khatri	1,471	804	667	147	108	22	3
Barui	2,627	1,323	1,304	437	396	4	1
Bhuimali and Mihtar	7,812	3,788	4,024	524	519	240	302
Bind	1,752	912	840	498	493	230	215
Brahman	20,429	10,159	10,270	1,897	1,574	1,119	1,139

BOGRA—*concluded.*

Sibganj.		Panchbibi.		Khetlal.		Nawabganj.		Adamdighi.		Sherpur.	
Male.	Female.	Male.	Female.	Male.	Female.	Male.	Female.	Male.	Female.	Male.	Female.
126	78	226	108	92	47	121	44	238	71	340	223
73	10	146	85	58	31	279	232	194	128	273	190
161	168	310	206	168	173	411	288	584	502	78	77
299	6	30	2	32	...	38	...	58	3	293	6
811	716	2,805	2,742	176	158	1,898	1,815	1,289	1,391	368	322
56	52	178	155	75	55	79	58	273	197	50	52
142	118	187	121	100	106	53	43	272	245	292	241
639	618	3,212	3,077	1,184	1,032	432	438	2,021	2,159	1,234	1,195
156	139	287	268	122	123	179	176	328	284	204	167
67	1	404	302	9	...	129	82	44	...	334	4
319	250	52	60	13	11	20	14	140	107	52	...
19	2	643	728	16	17	63	69	...	...	394	458
219	213	468	322	163	156	345	279	913	920	577	539
268	162	379	194	84	86	159	93	514	301	263	200
152	25	102	21	92	31	93	33	228	106	118	19
267	229	...	...	...	...	...	...	...	...	47	62
...	...	934	912	50	51	...	...	24	29	...	...
176	122	56	79	77	46	144	136	287	250	105	116
72	69	110	45	65	40	56	41	97	79	152	125
44	42	162	121	83	78	78	66	398	395	186	151
23	13	182	80	9	9	9	1	414	353	256	257
392	460	1,037	1,186	231	289	446	555	1,039	1,283	464	697
40	28	647	629	107	53	,597	1,507	252	194	770	665
...	...	...	...	...	...	...	...	126	148	381	384
110	58	150	145	81	66	70	50	390	380	619	547
45	60	149	132	...	...	45	36	32	28	81	65
125	106	77	50	169	169	83	47	312	246	176	136
50	50	87	78	170	176	127	113	96	110	75	75
29,088	28,210	23,254	20,437	19,408	19,376	15,243	14,334	43,283	44,283	33,064	30,644

PABNA.

Dulai.		Mathura.		Sirajganj.		Shahzadpur.		Raiganj.		Ulapara.	
Male.	Female.	Male.	Female.	Male.	Female.	Male.	Female.	Male.	Female.	Male.	Female.
24	30	35	1	72	74	134	87	105	41	136	116
10	15	2	...	232	305	55	51	9	6	128	151
20	274	284	328	520	500	253	255	270	261	238	244
77	60	108	137	233	243	81	141	44	54	24	40
29	14	76	91	218	126	72	114	126	107	114	104
144	143	425	427	161	172	...	...	34	40	118	125
742	754	429	459	720	797	650	648	267	268	216	277
24	17	30	45	95	52	17	18	16	...	2	...
1,740	2,071	1,159	1,390	1,203	888	1,819	2,121	439	266	783	821

DISTRICT

Caste or Group.	District Total.			Pabna.		Chatmohar.	
	Total.	Male.	Female.	Male.	Female.	Male.	Female.
Chamar and Muchi	9,346	4,975	4,371	1,928	1,699	491	435
Dhopa	1,776	920	856	251	278	61	42
Dom and Kaora	1,168	580	588	33	29	18	29
Goala	11,294	5,686	5,608	1,072	1,059	548	652
Jugi	1,224	672	552	84	107	57	1
Kahar	2,614	2,016	598	131	19	39	15
Kaibartta	23,544	11,205	12,339	2,680	2,738	553	583
Kamar and Lohar	6,908	3,369	3,539	437	500	189	209
Kapali	5,815	2,925	2,890	...	...	53	39
Kayastha	32,156	15,414	16,742	1,360	1,265	1,257	1,358
Kochh	2,865	1,351	1,514	19	28	74	74
Kora	1,556	809	747	83	91	92	86
Kumhar	10,992	5,439	5,553	903	835	596	628
Kurmi	1,711	1,389	322	143	21	118	50
Maira and Halwai	1,504	770	734	108	100	203	205
Malakar	1,180	577	603	64	67	42	42
Malo	3,394	1,636	1,758	...	...	...	...
Namasudra or Chandal	51,027	25,062	25,965	1,467	1,522	4,216	4,312
Napit	10,883	5,408	5,475	800	827	406	425
Sunri and Kalwar	26,900	12,495	14,405	1,677	1,933	605	612
Sutradhar	12,643	6,412	6,231	724	713	450	453
Tanti	3,861	1,891	1,970	423	464	45	48
Teli and Kalu	9,293	4,332	4,961	666	737	711	831
Tiyar	2,270	1,182	1,088	45	39	40	46
Religious devotees and persons returned sect.							
Baisnab	8,140	3,087	5,063	639	1,128	458	699
Hindus returned by title or common sub-caste.							
Buna	10,168	5,107	5,061	686	688	404	448
Hindus returned by actual occupation.							
Jaliya	47,152	23,146	24,006	2,799	2,784	2,571	2,982
Matiya	4,726	2,392	2,334	...	...	220	231
Patni	4,315	2,170	2,145	248	241	207	107
Musalmans returned by title.							
Pathan	10,402	5,297	5,105	1,001	904	265	240
Sayyid	2,831	1,431	1,400	195	186	177	165
Shaikh	984,161	489,905	494,256	66,752	69,845	48,949	49,881
Musalmans returned by actual occupation.							
Jolaha	1,420	709	711	232	231	...	...

DISTRICT

Caste.	District Total.			Darjeeling.	
	Total.	Male.	Female.	Male.	Female.
Bhuimali and Mihtar	1,757	1,005	752	254	111
Bhutia	8,899	4,674	4,225	1,675	1,604
Brahman	4,924	3,226	1,698	761	370
Dami	3,460	1,892	1,568	871	791

PABNA—*concluded.*

Dulai.		Mathura.		Sirajganj.		Shahzadpur.		Raiganj.		Ulapara.	
Male.	Female.	Male.	Female.	Male.	Female.	Male.	Female.	Male.	Female.	Male.	Female.
416	380	388	441	482	287	437	377	406	364	427	388
143	158	65	61	148	124	146	117	44	25	68	51
75	62	100	100	199	226	64	68	15	10	76	70
746	783	410	412	877	637	921	1,000	336	181	776	884
84	74	95	80	120	89	114	89	115	110	3	2
166	125	125	43	1,036	355	174	33	41	7	284	1
2,685	2,747	667	910	2,186	2,449	688	967	1,283	1,292	463	663
369	406	380	405	707	677	734	733	97	115	456	494
1,060	1,065	24	2	456	400	832	921	123	101	377	372
3,769	3,284	2,429	2,743	1,826	1,728	3,128	3,535	916	815	1,729	2,014
9	5	30	32	214	265	...	1	162	181	843	928
186	168	50	56	60	54	48	39	125	130	165	124
851	874	571	650	562	581	729	783	536	508	691	694
43	6	44	3	346	35	123	46	439	148	133	13
75	95	60	50	218	184	84	91	17	9	6	...
123	168	67	61	64	61	112	99	26	27	79	78
...	...	...	...	769	911	...	...	149	53	718	794
4,198	4,285	2,624	2,799	1,834	1,824	5,666	6,281	1,100	982	3,937	3,960
907	881	513	595	1,046	953	832	932	242	210	662	652
1,733	2,418	1,336	1,685	3,457	3,487	2,461	2,923	145	118	1,081	1,229
807	786	613	593	1,144	1,093	1,417	1,356	273	245	984	992
29	27	4	3	843	877	144	163	212	173	191	215
761	1,079	526	534	731	731	388	510	115	52	434	487
35	4	34	25	828	810	48	9	64	59	88	96
469	856	209	323	303	489	287	434	347	490	375	643
154	158	41	40	405	446	223	237	2,704	2,557	490	497
4,709	4,607	3,702	3,687	3,046	2,637	3,396	4,241	792	796	2,131	2,402
...	...	...	...	783	738	319	344	574	502	496	519
226	219	266	249	338	363	456	459	245	234	184	183
590	541	431	433	1,752	1,696	620	670	335	297	303	324
243	284	93	87	330	298	177	167	133	127	83	86
62,493	63,576	29,153	29,317	88,651	86,235	88,960	92,935	36,073	33,332	68,874	69,335
...	...	...	...	...	...	...	...	...	...	477	480

DARJEELING.

Kalimpong.		Jor-Bangala.		Kurseong.		Siliguri.	
Male.	Female.	Male.	Female.	Male.	Female.	Male.	Female.
58	25	27	9	127	67	539	540
767	675	1,410	1,406	530	410	292	180
946	747	373	158	644	293	500	130
392	299	182	141	372	304	75	33

DISTRICT

Caste or Group.	District Total.			Darjeeling.	
	Total.	Male.	Female.	Male.	Female.
Gharti	3,138	1,645	1,493	299	227
Gurung	9,232	4,712	4,520	1,348	1,285
Kaibartta	1,419	767	652	187	159
Kami	7,048	3,629	3,419	1,317	1,254
Khambu	29,950	15,239	14,711	5,608	4,837
Kochh	33,472	17,680	15,792	5,238	4,978
Lepcha	9,717	4,741	4,976	1,426	1,564
Limbu	12,812	7,026	5,786	2,906	2,650
Mangar	11,412	6,405	5,007	1,711	1,543
Munda	1,283	699	584	510	411
Murmi	21,636	11,006	10,630	3,691	3,800
Newar	4,953	2,814	2,139	695	492
Oraon	5,323	2,739	2,584	28	27
Rajput	9,123	5,293	3,830	1,616	1,282
Sarki	1,547	920	627	312	214
Sunwar	5,156	2,738	2,418	1,341	1,180
Yakha	1,250	629	621	298	341
Hindus returned by title or common sub-caste.					
Buna	1,390	748	642	30	31
Musalmans returned by title.					
Shaikh	7,918	5,244	2,674	808	268

DISTRICT

Caste.	District Total.			Jalpaiguri.		Rajganj.		Titalya.	
	Total.	Male.	Female.	Male.	Female.	Male.	Female.	Male.	Female.
Baniya	10,775	5,604	5,171	189	107	177	170	746	742
(i)—Khatri	10,150	5,252	4,898	126	42	159	158	671	669
Bhuimali and Mihtar ...	7,173	3,758	3,415	508	482	625	541	328	328
Bhutia	4,001	2,179	1,822	120	91	154	111	7	1
Brahman	3,410	2,622	788	713	264	57	18	161	21
Chamar and Muchi	1,617	1,138	479	246	87	82	29	161	55
Goala	2,694	2,013	681	281	63	121	33	185	12
Jugi	2,946	1,624	1,322	138	125	110	113	68	36
Kahar	1,172	684	488	105	78	4	...	69	29
Kaibartta	3,655	1,847	1,808	485	462	31	20	149	145
Kamar and Lohar	2,565	1,453	1,112	213	174	64	48	29	27
Kami	1,048	639	409	13	13	50	26	63	46
Kapali	1,575	755	820	...	...	463	491	69	85
Kayastha	1,649	1,120	529	408	139	24	22	29	15
Khambu	3,540	1,860	1,680	175	160	219	210	265	219
Kharwar	1,579	831	748	113	109	126	170	75	60
Kochh	297,852	155,893	141,959	18,233	17,686	11,136	10,939	9,366	8,120
Kumhar	7,635	4,275	3,360	530	485	517	398	447	323
Limbu	1,218	807	411	...	...	...	...	...	...
Mangar	2,669	1,857	812	88	79	104	49	45	50
Mechh	21,608	11,246	10,362	481	441	484	463	525	530
Munda	2,732	1,468	1,264	251	231	70	72	40	38

DARJEELING—*concluded.*

Kalimpong.		Jor-Bangala.		Kurseong.		Siliguri.	
Male.	Female.	Male.	Female.	Male.	Female.	Male.	Female.
579	520	153	174	488	469	126	103
702	669	776	726	905	905	981	935
209	189	121	116	56	53	194	135
182	241	521	482	1,236	1,185	373	257
2,209	2,689	1,175	1,111	4,933	4,615	1,314	1,459
3,575	3,302	1,560	1,474	1,188	1,024	6,119	5,014
2,047	2,161	154	188	522	531	592	532
949	926	984	810	1,771	1,292	416	108
534	502	699	623	2,629	1,825	832	514
...	...	...	...	60	47	129	126
1,461	1,361	804	800	4,550	4,167	500	502
228	115	387	323	1,186	1,020	318	189
22	16	...	...	329	269	2,360	2,272
1,009	801	750	474	1,552	1,130	366	143
78	72	85	54	336	245	109	42
598	602	339	328	393	274	67	34
56	26	70	60	172	170	33	24
37	42	...	...	37	43	644	526
61	14	66	11	307	82	4,002	2,299

JALPAIGURI.

Boda.		Patgram.		Mainaguri.		Dam-Dim.		Alipore.		Salbari.	
Male.	Female.	Male.	Female.	Male.	Female.	Male.	Female.	Male.	Female.	Male.	Female.
1,518	1,454	399	349	413	302	1,878	1,752	117	132	167	163
1,473	1,416	358	311	382	280	1,823	1,742	104	118	156	162
1,232	1,145	231	223	842	329	104	57	120	99	268	211
5	1	...	...	183	99	941	780	723	691	46	48
265	72	144	44	399	183	385	108	255	27	243	51
161	15	68	28	147	22	161	103	113	98	69	12
132	66	169	80	346	181	358	115	282	101	189	80
743	553	66	70	181	170	112	109	95	45	111	101
238	213	31	9	12	7	147	106	18	1	60	45
753	735	287	305	17	9	83	80	9	4	33	41
454	427	86	35	159	103	272	139	47	21	179	138
...	...	27	18	49	25	877	255	19	9	41	17
224	244	...	...	...	...	...	...	...	...	...	...
148	104	99	82	266	158	5	3	81	4	60	2
176	181	230	221	301	307	167	125	178	119	127	138
19	16	106	60	146	136	70	95	161	93	15	9
37,352	32,859	15,858	13,369	14,641	13,938	26,973	25,001	6,379	5,708	15,960	14,839
898	601	567	467	188	165	228	181	775	625	125	115
...	...	...	...	317	113	321	233	42	18	127	47
98	47	311	45	470	124	175	110	344	128	216	180
81	70	272	287	910	841	165	150	3,962	3,879	4,366	3,711
90	85	...	...	560	511	12	13	163	128	262	186

DISTRICT

Caste or Group.	District Total.			Jalpaiguri.		Rajganj.		Titalya.	
	Total.	Male.	Female.	Male.	Female.	Male.	Female.	Male.	Female.
Namasudra or Chandal ...	3,844	1,939	1,905	218	216	150	134	...	...
Napit and Hajjam	5,837	3,102	2,735	326	293	257	228	492	377
Oraon	20,051	10,642	9,409	175	78	51	52	...	...
Rajput	4,027	2,417	1,610	343	336	228	113	284	103
Santal	1,409	887	522	2	...	13	9	...	...
Sutradhar	1,294	908	386	98	49	75	48	...	...
Tanti and Tatwa	6,259	3,290	2,969	547	496	91	83	230	218
Teli and Kalu	1,670	977	693	242	217	186	153	265	166
Hindus returned by title or common sub-caste.									
Buna	1,287	717	570	41	24	66	43	...	...
Hindus returned by actual occupation.									
Jaliya	1,694	845	849	230	228	...	...	...	...
Hindus returned by locality.									
Hindustanis	1,934	1,106	828	260	195	35	16	95	60
Musalmans returned by title.									
Pathan	2,126	1,371	755	160	115	147	131	33	39
Shaikh	218,256	115,035	103,221	17,245	15,895	12,649	11,888	5,615	5,353

DACCA

DISTRICT

Caste.	District Total.			Lalbagh.		Kapasia.		Sabhar.		Nawabganj.		Keraniganj.	
	Total.	Male.	Female.	Male.	Female.	Male.	Female.	Male.	Female.	Male.	Female.	Male.	Female.
Bagdi	1,385	743	642	...	...	...	...	82	63	...	...	...	...
Baidya	10,450	4,635	5,815	674	302	141	152	227	296	...	...	81	99
Baniya	14,653	7,233	7,420	2,567	1,900	209	199	721	921	224	256	187	138
(i)—Baisya	2,137	1,093	1,044	646	645	...	...	117	137	...	...	187	138
(ii)—Gandha Banik ...	5,618	2,511	3,107	399	337	136	117	454	626	75	80	...	...
(iii)—Subarna Banik ...	4,052	1,892	2,160	489	403	73	82	57	52	...	...	...	...
Barui	18,968	9,313	9,655	133	13	319	316	...	...	...	...	527	467
Bediya	1,370	712	658	106	101	...	...	...	...	...	...	...	...
Bhuimali	13,263	6,664	6,599	83	74	261	237	347	317	1,054	1,160	365	370
Brahman	60,267	28,294	31,973	2,652	1,279	737	657	1,480	1,537	1,234	1,442	1,263	1,183
Chamar	31,206	15,219	15,987	927	749	379	280	1,959	1,961	1,155	1,520	2,157	2,354
Dhopa	11,308	5,513	5,795	556	565	521	495	226	262	162	196	189	187
Goala	30,166	15,181	14,985	1,496	1,127	649	610	2,221	2,035	1,083	1,433	1,221	1,305

JALPAIGURI—*concluded.*

Boda.		Patgram.		Mainaguri.		Dam-Dim.		Alipore.		Salbari.	
Male.	Female.	Male.	Female.	Male.	Female.	Male.	Female.	Male.	Female.	Male.	Female.
...	...	720	729	272	266	187	176	275	271	117	113
583	429	242	305	306	293	304	248	352	331	240	231
23	46	...	...	...	...	9,154	8,254	37	19	1,202	960
322	202	180	182	287	104	377	226	177	149	219	136
...	...	...	...	...	...	...	...	19	5	853	508
59	10	108	29	133	35	249	93	78	40	108	82
476	464	601	547	970	583	126	93	128	96	121	99
96	67	...	...	56	17	67	22	44	34	21	17
...	...	...	...	124	69	485	434	1	...	...	...
293	288	...	...	322	333	...	...	...	...	...	...
83	31	125	69	213	169	178	169	98	96	20	23
297	166	235	133	94	43	161	38	149	30	95	60
38,361	35,024	12,081	11,253	10,615	9,754	7,350	5,537	2,329	1,852	8,790	6,665

DIVISION.

DACCA.

Naraingani.		Rupganj.		Raipura.		Manikganj.		Jafarganj.		Haribampur.		Munshiganj.		Srinagar.	
Male.	Female.	Male.	Female.	Male.	Female.	Male.	Female.	Male.	Female.	Male.	Female.	Male.	Female.	Male.	Female.
...	...	...	...	...	...	180	144	481	435	...	...	...	...	...	...
150	208	853	1,023	146	143	457	84	59	89	99	145	1,209	1,992	539	782
156	180	476	504	284	260	97	122	135	133	104	125	706	1,008	1,367	1,724
...	...	...	...	...	...	...	...	...	...	...	...	143	124	...	...
...	...	123	121	284	260	97	122	135	130	104	125	232	460	472	729
89	88	353	383	...	...	...	...	...	...	...	...	186	224	645	928
423	494	104	101	83	70	...	...	...	...	...	...	2,561	2,637	5,163	5,557
...	...	...	...	98	40	...	...	100	146	...	...	240	220	168	151
159	155	299	292	382	390	440	461	342	347	268	261	1,086	897	1,578	1,618
1,345	881	1,229	1,277	905	843	1,633	1,781	1,884	2,070	781	860	6,425	8,522	6,726	9,641
676	502	1,171	1,146	818	624	2,230	2,499	991	878	444	536	531	575	1,781	2,413
177	174	238	258	369	317	147	146	200	216	141	167	1,326	1,291	1,272	1,495
874	613	397	351	305	228	996	958	561	625	234	138	1,884	1,811	3,261	3,856

Caste or Group.	District Total.			Lalbagh.		Kapasia.		Sabhar.		Nawabganj.		Keraniganj.	
	Total.	Male.	Female.	Male.	Female.	Male.	Female.	Male.	Female.	Male.	Female.	Male.	Female.
Jugi	18,372	9,106	9,266	343	49	917	896	...	...	88	86	386	415
Kahar	4,057	2,919	1,138	111	54	359	319	...	...	180	42	...	...
Kaibartta	52,689	25,677	27,012	1,079	114	2,505	2,434	1,423	1,709	1,607	2,051	1,294	1,303
Kamar	14,522	6,824	7,693	554	497	541	439	854	906	403	525	481	510
Kandu	1,733	1,120	613	361	101	...	...	...	...	...	...	257	400
Kapali	21,298	10,634	10,664	214	...	...	...	1,769	2,092	162	117	240	248
Kayastha	89,587	42,607	46,980	5,151	2,486	1,476	1,375	2,157	2,575	2,333	3,272	2,418	2,764
Kochh	10,574	5,478	5,096	...	...	3,339	3,045	1,685	1,571	454	480	...	...
Kumhar	19,453	9,825	9,628	141	139	334	290	1,153	1,165	879	835	1,588	1,576
Kurmi	2,702	2,085	617	1,092	281	141	159	...	...	...	...	...	...
Maira and Kuri	2,970	1,738	1,232	392	347	84	75	35	15	104	96	45	25
Mal	2,285	1,788	497	1,310	1	...	...	53	56	...	...	110	83
Malakar	2,487	1,236	1,251	67	59	...	...	180	192	58	61	63	73
Namasudra or Chandal	230,419	112,774	117,645	3,187	322	3,049	3,310	15,305	16,785	10,296	11,526	18,097	19,166
Napit	22,446	11,146	11,300	340	169	702	666	620	685	779	760	549	536
Nuniya	1,535	1,188	347	...	...	65	18	...	...	...	...	509	184
Patial	1,264	575	689	...	...	...	...	...	...	...	...	...	...
Rajput	5,622	3,021	2,601	102	73	371	242	1,219	1,223	...	...	1,087	912
Sankhari	2,913	1,431	1,482	956	1,025	...	...	...	...	...	...	...	...
Sunri and Kalwar ...	60,537	28,788	31,749	3,761	2,368	551	343	3,363	4,436	3,433	4,478	1,544	1,656
Sutradhar	17,276	8,588	8,688	372	319	423	374	1,688	1,819	585	556	281	249
Tanti	13,007	7,362	5,645	3,245	2,577	...	...	1,008	1,069	120	35	179	5
Teli and Kalu	19,107	9,014	10,093	628	345	452	407	267	297	59	42	325	308
Tiyar	3,289	1,893	1,396	809	221	...	...	53	56	134	122	378	455
Religious devotees and persons returned by sect.													
Baisnab	8,972	3,221	5,751	419	464	133	248	168	342	193	406	214	397
Hindus returned by title or common sub-caste.													
Buna	1,444	680	764	...	...	...	...	254	226	...	...	155	135
Sudra	26,317	11,666	14,651	409	160	1,538	1,493	181	256	283	398	1,172	1,432
Hindus returned by actual occupation.													
Dai	1,553	807	746	...	...	617	584	...	...	...	...	...	...
Jaliya	58,939	29,303	29,636	2,092	296	2,298	2,205	3,961	4,054	2,714	3,166	3,252	3,509
Patni	5,296	2,789	2,557	247	26	206	242	169	142	139	141	117	124
Musalmans returned by title.													
Khan	3,509	1,726	1,783	574	436	...	...	...	...	251	327	532	738
Pathan	11,843	5,195	6,648	467	460	356	309	582	981	1,064	1,620	459	633
Sayyid	21,675	10,722	10,953	5,347	5,276	93	94	2,166	2,144	57	60	58	50
Shaikh	1,421,900	709,018	712,076	34,921	19,269	46,636	43,383	48,975	53,283	41,829	45,332	45,770	49,103
Musalmans returned by actual occupation.													
Fakir	1,413	708	705	...	...	...	...	...	...	708	705	...	...
Jolaha	9,736	4,792	4,944	...	...	...	...	1,650	1,789	2,090	2,079	124	112

DACCA—*concluded.*

Naraingani.		Rupganj.		Raipura.		Manikganj.		Jafarganj.		Harirampur.		Munshiganj.		Srinagar.	
Male.	Female.	Male.	Female.	Male.	Female.	Male.	Female.	Male.	Female.	Male.	Female.	Male.	Female.	Male.	Female.
476	462	1,213	1,231	1,617	1,644	124	144	275	293	170	178	2,204	2,258	1,285	1,620
837	136	...	...	...	...	246	55	433	214	419	282	84	33	259	3
440	464	1,839	1,855	1,571	1,603	516	723	7,043	6,990	760	975	961	1,027	4,639	5,765
235	224	456	458	207	213	548	561	463	504	345	335	860	1,086	877	1,350
210	15	...	...	...	...	...	...	...	...	...	...	115	12	177	85
...	...	...	...	72	55	3,308	3,010	1,822	1,888	1,143	1,217	1,148	1,219	756	818
1,837	2,123	3,523	3,928	2,388	2,282	1,871	2,391	1,372	160	3,149	3,967	6,876	9,504	8,066	10,154
...	...	...	...	...	...	...	...	...	...	...	...	...	...	...	...
746	784	272	264	306	291	350	341	407	426	767	637	917	959	1,965	1,971
537	124	...	...	...	...	315	53	...	...	...	...	...	...	...	...
59	16	96	82	597	277	102	90	28	13	53	52	61	61	82	83
...	...	315	357	...	...	...	...	...	...	...	...	...	...	...	...
66	52	40	23	59	48	107	129	65	81	...	...	177	155	354	378
6,063	7,500	5,531	5,493	5,344	4,931	7,754	8,402	5,164	5,318	3,332	3,389	10,377	10,146	18,675	21,357
433	303	729	721	878	869	794	746	829	873	702	685	1,517	1,659	2,275	2,628
...	...	...	...	91	17	216	20	223	58	...	...	84	50	...	...
...	...	...	...	...	...	...	...	...	...	...	...	254	282	321	407
...	...	...	...	159	39	...	...	...	...	83	112	...	...	...	...
56	89	...	...	...	...	...	...	...	...	...	...	64	76	355	342
1,966	1,729	2,199	2,550	1,546	1,684	4,458	5,056	...	...	1,987	2,205	1,234	1,403	2,746	3,841
886	306	582	543	1,008	934	1,312	1,493	787	931	444	425	457	434	263	306
237	43	249	42	...	...	1,144	1,259	283	302	132	128	259	161	506	24
560	423	355	333	521	585	433	412	279	83	716	851	1,916	2,312	2,503	3,690
82	56	...	...	...	...	...	...	...	...	...	...	92	82	345	404
173	306	322	632	162	265	239	429	305	514	243	525	254	470	396	753
65	62	...	...	...	...	66	152	140	189	...	...	...	...	...	...
932	886	1,048	1,259	871	405	239	311	...	...	...	...	1,796	2,426	3,697	5,645
...	...	...	...	190	162	...	...	...	...	...	...	...	...	...	...
761	756	1,772	1,820	2,871	2,968	3,082	3,341	1,909	2,158	1,646	1,952	1,234	1,342	1,711	2,069
189	224	418	375	425	359	194	187	101	119	89	108	213	280	232	221
62	45	...	...	232	148	...	...	...	...	...	...	75	94	...	...
...	...	95	88	...	...	466	820	298	303	1,072	1,050	84	72	252	312
...	...	86	84	273	230	42	58	725	765	1,104	1,107	250	542	512	543
42,559	42,067	68,106	66,618	89,319	84,427	61,992	64,685	45,130	45,885	27,723	29,101	88,226	91,985	67,833	76,993
...	...	...	...	...	...	...	...	...	...	...	...	...	...	...	...
...	...	...	...	...	...	100	106	321	331	...	...	...	...	50	527

DISTRICT

Caste or Group.	District Total.			Faridpur.		Bhusna.		Awanpur.		Bhanga.		Maksudpur.	
	Total.	Male.	Female.	Male.	Female.	Male.	Female.	Male.	Female.	Male.	Female.	Male.	Female.
Bagdi	2,798	1,331	1,467	46	48	75	99	...	...	8	9	...	—
Baidya	5,277	2,332	2,945	248	145	52	79	99	93	105	81	168	229
Baniya	8,598	4,083	4,515	314	298	458	384	277	355	257	315	506	596
(i)—Gandha Banik	3,725	1,724	2,001	166	181	127	151	59	66	122	113	234	237
(ii)—Subarna Banik	3,674	1,628	2,046	148	114	108	119	218	289	135	202	267	359
Barui	8,207	4,189	4,018	99	97	390	348	86	97	322	298	221	157
Beldar	2,589	1,313	1,276	...	...	161	185	84	62	226	282	...	1
Bhuimali and Mihtar ...	5,373	2,638	2,735	84	45	30	40	56	37	282	296	65	48
Brahman	48,535	22,176	26,359	1,026	684	903	1,009	726	783	1,623	1,825	1,861	2,101
Chamar and Muchi	5,995	3,120	2,875	261	346	142	104	164	264	353	339	214	194
Dhopa	9,473	4,651	4,822	161	136	234	238	157	147	263	332	274	301
Goala	7,554	4,171	3,383	221	148	112	75	69	89	377	220	280	106
Jugi	5,405	2,626	2,779	120	127	109	115	74	61	131	178	38	31
Kahar	4,322	2,417	1,905	465	341	185	168	240	213	214	129	192	192
Kaibartta	24,166	11,909	12,257	706	751	429	428	479	477	1,030	1,051	595	556
Kamar and Lohar	8,265	3,823	4,442	..	...	310	367	291	240	457	524	252	307
Kapali	13,349	6,676	6,673	253	242	132	132	378	362	350	319	1,750	1,716
Kayastha	84,470	38,091	46,379	2,676	2,651	2,228	2,536	2,137	2,843	3,181	4,270	2,710	3,439
Kumhar	12,979	6,475	6,504	326	299	220	227	435	448	602	673	487	546
Maira and Kuri	3,049	1,682	1,367	56	32	425	216	247	100	150	186	216	250
Malakar	1,048	528	520	27	27	31	35	24	21	39	35	84	34
Namasudra or Chandal ...	287,242	141,666	145,576	4,443	4,065	4,300	4,583	3,372	3,971	12,854	13,286	27,433	28,688
Napit	20,269	10,104	10,165	...	...	465	490	547	570	1,903	1,900	967	902
Sunri	35,776	16,454	19,322	1,773	1,891	1,677	1,831	1,162	1,432	2,187	2,827	1,408	1,793
Sutradhar	5,858	2,938	2,920	421	552	...	...	299	292	352	345	...	...
Tanti	2,973	1,679	1,294	39	6	28	18	18	10	130	79	18	...
Teli and Kalu	14,981	6,896	8,085	1,196	1,192	973	1,025	321	374	606	649	444	462
Religious devotees and persons returned by sect.													
Baisnab	6,327	2,271	4,056	149	323	365	617	130	229	184	360	169	292
Hindus returned by title or common sub-caste.													
Buna	3,331	1,674	1,657	378	364	566	608	9	...	7	4	171	164
Sudra	3,785	1,712	2,073	95	76	44	48	2	6	21	21	115	139
Hindus returned by actual occupation.													
Jaliya	40,782	20,608	20,174	1,652	1,441	1,917	2,198	1,455	1,443	1,519	1,360	2,109	2,192
Patni	2,635	1,310	1,325	52	...	92	89	61	77	105	97	82	61
Musalmans returned by title.													
Pathan	3,037	1,563	1,474	56	47	198	195	38	34	297	290	113	121
Sayyid	3,667	1,901	1,766	129	110	445	333	208	222	193	193	329	228
Shaikh	1,050,970	530,225	520,745	30,180	28,001	29,434	29,261	33,251	34,555	64,193	56,760	50,397	41,502
Musalmans returned by actual occupation.													
Dai	1,710	864	846	88	92	131	140	...	...	100	106	277	258
Jolaha	2,039	1,027	1,012	667	689	...	...	62	50	25	25	75	75
Karigar	27,004	13,643	13,361	778	932	1,538	1,521	1,983	1,905	5,300	5,084	2,203	2,298
Nikari	1,345	562	783	21	...	265	487	13	32	46	52	36	42

FARIDPUR.

Madaripur.		Gopalganj.		Kotalipara.		Palang.		Sibchar.		Goalunda.		Baliakandi.		Pangsa.	
Male.	Female.	Male.	Female.	Male.	Female.	Male.	Female.	Male.	Female.	Male.	Female.	Male.	Female.	Male.	Female.
...	...	1	2	...	...	...	...	...	3	324	353	455	466	422	487
308	345	55	53	404	601	560	873	73	113	100	121	127	173	33	30
369	297	35	...	9	...	1,165	1,472	182	218	284	339	179	185	48	56
156	164	18	...	6	...	373	526	177	218	210	261	76	84	...	...
91	77	17	...	3	...	525	757	5	...	65	73	4	...	42	56
294	260	21	27	22	12	1,194	1,229	120	117	273	264	616	570	551	522
81	102	85	29	...	...	...	...	210	185	100	79	193	146	173	205
446	538	4	...	11	8	528	612	288	276	343	358	172	168	329	309
2,734	3,410	1,267	1,233	1,851	2,236	5,689	8,180	622	651	1,259	1,006	1,442	1,804	1,183	1,427
242	248	242	46	134	188	216	228	263	252	267	167	262	173	360	326
634	698	220	214	526	498	1,027	1,677	264	279	...	...	193	181	108	113
407	217	187	161	170	141	1,035	1,149	419	400	337	203	335	252	222	270
262	287	2	...	...	...	1,465	1,528	179	196	47	33	133	141	66	82
29	8	23	8	17	8	49	16	34	45	418	294	252	261	299	222
449	522	552	501	1,931	1,819	1,285	1,606	608	644	458	385	1,659	1,721	1,723	1,796
337	341	159	193	562	812	537	686	208	258	316	261	134	171	260	282
2,298	2,397	1,196	1,206	13	1	15	12	117	108	32	34	142	144	...	...
4,733	5,915	1,754	1,902	3,335	3,582	6,975	9,813	717	1,014	3,968	4,017	1,897	2,170	1,780	2,227
591	558	68	71	256	298	1,610	1,679	386	385	649	493	438	420	398	407
33	1	...	...	396	456	30	47	...	...	54	13	67	66	8	...
72	62	...	...	4	...	103	111	36	29	55	43	52	68	51	55
13,025	18,063	20,939	21,576	18,196	18,232	8,991	9,327	6,093	6,176	3,970	3,937	9,884	10,100	3,166	3,573
1,024	1,013	780	780	728	721	2,098	2,169	570	591	...	...	415	585	607	644
1,438	1,644	576	341	938	1,048	1,449	2,030	1,269	1,702	1,400	1,541	744	767	433	475
116	120	17	9	...	...	195	199	100	84	639	509	355	351	454	459
44	8	...	...	...	...	54	...	...	...	216	83	82	83	1,150	1,007
747	834	16	2	7	...	1,691	2,620	195	200	...	...	...	...	700	707
141	260	60	87	32	51	192	353	117	154	267	400	133	308	392	532
15	...	206	193	...	...	...	...	...	...	88	13	...	...	284	311
123	136	47	46	2	1	792	1,122	448	463	20	12	...	...	3	3
1,619	1,280	1,953	1,909	67	23	1,902	1,763	910	943	2,396	1,764	1,528	1,722	1,581	2,136
114	110	28	36	3	...	230	257	229	244	79	67	129	142	136	145
88	82	...	...	...	...	127	143	68	90	369	275	60	48	143	140
136	264	75	67	...	1	172	168	32	47	96	69	33	25	53	39
40,663	56,524	17,992	17,540	10,538	11,701	90,748	91,925	49,725	46,823	44,439	38,843	25,856	25,475	42,809	41,835
75	86	100	51	4	4	14	17	46	64	...	...	9	9	20	19
...	...	...	...	...	...	45	60	...	...	...	...	...	...	123	118
330	107	...	...	243	219	16	9	1,197	1,286	...	...	...	...	...	...
110	144	...	...	25	...	24	3	2	...	...	...	...	...	20	23

DISTRICT

Caste or Group.	District Total.			Katwali (Barisal).		Bakhargan j.	
	Total.	Male.	Female.	Male.	Female.	Male.	Female.
Baidya	12,283	6,078	6,205	928	481	108	5
Baniya	3,101	1,755	1,346	241	228	44	12
(I)—Gandha Banik	1,909	921	988	134	167	1	...
Barui	12,753	6,470	6,283	830	836	355	364
Bhuimali and Mihtar	4,690	2,445	2,245	179	162	222	184
Brahman	47,210	24,011	23,199	3,077	2,652	1,956	2,013
Chamar and Muchi	2,870	1,981	889	139	78	162	42
Dhopa	23,218	12,155	11,063	878	739	909	987
Goala	4,182	2,421	1,761	280	289	164	144
Jugi	22,404	11,756	10,648	444	462	885	869
Kaibartta	11,057	6,071	4,986	160	101	132	69
Kamar	10,970	5,831	5,139	311	251	410	385
Kapali	7,743	3,943	3,800	6	14	17	25
Kayastha	95,922	48,612	47,310	4,889	3,821	4,835	4,651
Kumhar	11,679	5,804	5,875	214	222	1,055	1,109
Malakar	1,564	786	778	72	62	92	99
Namasudra or Chandal	298,306	150,153	148,153	5,131	4,524	5,853	5,529
Napit	38,669	19,531	19,138	1,479	1,325	1,893	1,973
Nat	2,479	1,197	1,282	101	82	159	175
Sunri	18,653	10,979	7,674	855	523	1,393	741
Sutradhar	1,292	707	585	49	37	112	147
Teli	6,172	3,965	2,207	346	271	317	210
Religious devotees and persons returned by sect.							
Baisnab	3,534	1,421	2,113	92	120	88	142
Hindus returned by tittle or common sub-caste.							
Sudra	7,571	3,817	3,754	757	611	76	66
Hindus returned by actual occupation.							
Jaliya	19,807	10,353	9,454	730	489	1,388	1,383
Patni	3,679	1,868	1,811	293	281	178	184
Patua	1,090	552	538	4	...	192	205
Musalmans returned by title.							
Moghul	5,441	2,861	2,580	150	128	313	298
Pathan	84,798	50,045	34,753	4,528	3,204	5,134	4,402
Sayyid	11,534	6,479	5,055	610	472	516	539
Shaikh	1,360,788	690,239	670,549	41,504	40,616	42,552	41,539

DISTRICT

Caste.	District Total.			Nasirabad.		Phulpur.		Gafargaon.	
	Total.	Male.	Female.	Male.	Female.	Male.	Female.	Male.	Female.
Bagdi	1,505	758	747	12	11	3	2	...	...
Baidya	3,099	1,644	1,455	218	119	23	13	56	44

BAKHARGANJ.

Mehndiganj.		Gaurnadi.		Jhalakati.		Nalchiti.		Patuakhali.	
Male.	Female.	Male.	Female.	Male.	Female.	Male.	Female.	Male.	Female.
106	79	1,705	2,556	1,526	1,959	505	620	227	43
131	11	279	367	177	184	178	310	119	7
9	...	215	259	171	184	128	241	21	1
232	184	1,436	1,360	261	239	656	675	32	5
327	231	281	299	255	244	66	57	271	279
937	925	5,641	6,811	2,974	3,106	1,560	1,678	751	298
237	123	242	188	150	58	21	7	235	83
1,166	1,057	1,263	1,245	1,037	978	468	515	1,325	1,236
199	127	204	226	186	444	238	235	38	22
1,080	834	835	880	1,558	1,509	527	571	1,142	1,137
138	53	186	76	188	165	87	13	294	243
101	14	1,039	1,320	784	945	179	146	378	74
101	97	1,519	1,473	63	42	27	28	432	372
1,615	1,332	6,075	7,410	7,031	8,698	3,402	3,925	1,847	927
169	164	534	516	623	622	125	133	121	104
29	28	87	95	59	58	40	47	94	105
6,762	6,235	24,862	26,054	14,690	14,477	2,134	2,034	7,746	7,914
936	929	1,668	1,720	2,174	2,324	864	918	2,139	2,060
54	64	171	210	263	271	101	120	33	3
388	317	993	1,155	1,119	944	478	483	779	245
163	143	195	186	13	5	27	22	7	1
169	9	402	399	488	354	408	262	113	2
90	162	245	423	179	299	86	128	60	83
543	556	378	413	611	753	53	57	158	50
1,438	1,324	1,100	1,135	447	265	159	91	281	262
292	291	129	111	196	151	64	72	268	275
3	...	1	...	224	226	78	65	1	...
67	53	184	140	200	204	134	120	178	159
1,960	1,318	2,161	1,223	4,576	2,543	3,298	2,499	6,794	5,177
415	198	378	287	772	718	376	340	780	669
60,417	57,165	46,218	45,956	38,300	38,046	22,905	22,510	71,971	71,363

MAIMANSINGH.

Iswarganj.		Phulbaria.		Netrokona.		Durgapur.		Kendua.	
Male.	Female.	Male.	Female.	Male.	Female.	Male.	Female.	Male.	Female.
...	...	...	...	1	...	14	10	...	...
153	90	...	...	155	127	98	28	333	225

DISTRICT

Caste or Group.	Bauphal.		Gulsakhali.		Golachipa.		Pirojpur.	
	Male.	Female.	Male.	Female.	Male.	Female.	Male.	Female.
Baidya	124	7	1	...	122	2	136	40
Baniya	72	18	60	18	83	25	47	23
(i)—Gandha Banik	25	1	21	2	12	...	10	2
Barui	131	149	3	...	32	...	1,506	1,597
Bhuimali and Mihtar	58	61	49	42	55	50	281	264
Brahman	319	132	212	30	218	22	1,226	1,061
Chamar and Muchi	24	1	92	10	68	11	36	9
Dhopa	619	637	372	369	271	238	709	857
Goala	65	58	14	2	17	...	476	130
Jugi	401	325	111	2	280	237	464	469
Kaibartta	284	232	104	22	15	8	257	144
Kamar	270	90	190	2	224	2	654	786
Kapali	1	...	1,022	986	329	312	146	153
Kayastha	1,461	1,190	627	11	875	431	3,747	3,757
Kumhar	1,187	1,234	80	1	26	...	919	985
Malakar	48	48	14	15	32	29	45	41
Namasudra or Chandal	4,283	3,973	3,662	3,353	2,019	2,352	12,582	12,597
Napit	1,512	1,480	641	604	593	480	1,477	1,467
Nat	18	13	...	...	6	...	25	24
Sunri	633	341	358	74	477	129	1,588	1,286
Sutradhar	...	...	70	...	6	...	4	...
Teli	131	47	99	3	215	14	647	618
Religious devotees and persons returned by sect.								
Baisnab	20	52	39	69	38	99	96	116
Hindus returned by title or common sub-caste.								
Sudra	121	74	20	...	14	...	86	68
Hindus returned by actual occupation.								
Jaliya	629	673	68	25	321	190	718	859
Patni	177	170	...	...	136	158	12	10
Patua	43	40	...	...	4	1	...	..
Musalmans returned by title.								
Moghul	251	243	95	50	320	298	164	139
Pathan	3,485	2,875	3,241	1,821	2,509	2,046	3,236	2,177
Sayyid	459	318	375	222	137	109	429	300
Shaikh	41,282	41,074	44,563	42,877	32,319	29,207	31,306	31,557

DISTRICT

Caste.	Jamalpur.		Diwanganj.		Sherpur.		Nalitabari.	
	Male.	Female.	Male.	Female.	Male.	Female.	Male.	Female.
Bagdi	170	168	10	16	...	...	...	...
Baidya	...	...	108	126	118	79	...	...

BAKHARGANJ—*concluded.*

Bhandaria.		Sarupkati.		Matbaria.		Bhola.		Barhanuddin.	
Male.	Female.	Male.	Female.	Male.	Female.	Male.	Female.	Male.	Female.
59	4	293	360	96	2	90	43	52	4
16	...	131	136	38	6	90	1	49	...
10	...	124	130	9	...	19	1	12	...
647	654	...	...	...	...	295	146	34	74
64	70	129	134	73	81	27	16	108	71
321	207	3,498	3,775	281	38	536	186	504	265
63	4	18	7	205	97	142	83	147	88
479	555	594	607	480	491	840	...	745	552
80	...	95	51	81	1	127	11	107	21
897	970	1,289	1,358	203	117	987	350	653	558
188	36	448	255	208	32	335	288	3,052	3,249
115	3	705	957	204	5	111	50	206	109
266	294	2	...	1	3	4	1	7	...
1,190	1,170	5,897	7,992	885	209	1,758	778	1,878	1,008
15	...	230	289	54	...	57	...	395	496
83	70	15	17	65	59	3	3	8	2
9,073	8,690	34,588	35,448	11,903	11,264	2,723	2,650	1,542	1,059
831	890	1,303	1,316	698	624	683	546	640	483
17	24	96	165	...	...	...	...	163	151
86	1	1,037	1,184	130	7	331	122	334	122
...	...	...	...	...	...	25	33	36	11
60	2	..	...	130	12	214	4	26	...
26	62	186	148	31	53	64	78	81	79
7	...	666	882	33	1	137	82	155	81
382	453	978	998	125	40	803	677	701	600
27	22	20	16	...	...	...	...	76	70
...	...	...	...	...	...	2	1	...	...
125	109	135	185	164	170	287	215	94	69
2,482	2,167	1,424	619	3,771	2,280	711	99	745	30
243	185	258	224	212	127	295	108	224	149
29,231	30,223	34,145	36,466	42,020	40,871	64,518	60,580	46,998	40,407

MAIMANSINGH—*continued.*

Tangail.		Gopalpur.		Kalihati.		Kisorganj.		Nikli.		Bajitpur.	
Male.	Female.	Male.	Female.	Male.	Female.	Male.	Female.	Male.	Female.	Male.	Female.
2	1	453	500	93	39	...	...	...	...	...	...
255	378	36	27	72	130	...	...	55	69	34	...

Caste or Group.	District Total.			Nasirabad.		Phulpur.		Gafargaon.	
	Total.	Male.	Female.	Male.	Female.	Male.	Female.	Male.	Female.
Baniya	12,896	6,847	6,049	388	225	63	40	74	35
(i) Gandha Banik	4,088	2,021	2,067	68	30	33	40	74	35
(ii) Khatri	5,704	3,192	2,512	86	...	10	...	...	...
(iii) Subarna Banik	2,069	1,050	1,019	142	119	...	...	...	...
Barui	8,859	4,519	4,340	348	297	238	219	4	1
Bediya	2,076	883	1,193	104	150	...	...	30	32
Bhar	1,679	1,606	73	57	18	72	5	39	...
Bhuimali and Mihtar	24,847	12,535	12,312	409	307	4,369	3,726	82	64
Brahman	42,951	22,166	20,785	3,242	2,235	672	627	683	501
Chamar and Muchi	18,312	10,871	7,441	737	578	239	112	605	468
Dhopa	13,876	7,179	6,697	418	363	332	360	220	196
Dom	1,612	848	764	73	53	80	83	5	10
Garo	28,085	14,306	13,779	215	190	5,995	5,814	329	332
Goala	33,209	18,681	14,528	2,208	1,120	472	357	417	208
Gonrhi	2,760	2,511	249	62	13	...	...	506	92
Jugi	40,992	20,830	20,162	1,544	1,315	666	608	387	750
Kahar	9,390	8,768	622	353	45	...	...	661	78
Kaibartta	110,530	55,931	54,599	3,478	3,428	1,672	1,627	11	...
Kamar and Lohar	12,788	6,456	6,332	278	145	165	110	85	55
Kandu	1,022	646	376	7	...	7	10	28	18
Kapali	11,222	5,749	5,473	224	224	989	813	...	...
Kayastha	97,507	48,545	48,962	4,990	3,910	2,892	2,738	1,280	1,315
Koohh	44,338	22,549	21,789	4,255	4,260	355	338	3,326	3,254
Kumhar	22,682	11,976	10,706	618	509	202	171	505	509
Maira and Kuri	6,013	3,258	2,755	161	54	159	97	210	225
Mal	5,955	3,708	2,247	...	...	179	136	21	17
Malakar	9,927	5,009	4,918	12	8	9	...	319	434
Malo	5,711	3,140	2,571	...	...	...	...	...	...
Musahar	1,061	572	489	13	25	...	...	...	...
Namasudra or Chandal ...	159,659	80,757	78,902	3,310	3,137	3,036	2,677	2,609	2,413
Napit and Hajjam	47,402	23,657	23,745	981	709	1,467	1,428	365	344
Nuniya	9,326	7,799	1,527	1,318	298	599	123	406	22
Rajput	7,980	4,181	3,799	124	112	22	1	9	24
Sunri and Kalwar	46,293	23,371	22,922	224	107	287	199	460	401
Sutradhar	29,544	15,165	14,379	269	159	393	328	266	203
Tanti	11,151	5,756	5,395	215	480	216	309	...	...
Teli and Kalu	8,126	4,016	4,110	205	252	...	...	...	...
Tiyar	7,467	4,015	3,452	382	344	31	17	389	144
Religious devotees and persons returned by sect.									
Baisnab	6,775	2,827	3,948	338	315	334	308	110	147
Hindus returned by title or common sub-caste.									
Sudra	15,378	7,732	7,646	580	399	315	293	251	231
Hindus returned by actual occupation.									
Dulia	5,457	2,733	2,724	25	1	294	87	692	721
Jaliya	71,311	35,767	35,544	1,600	1,677	650	592	2,768	2,788
Manjhi	6,497	3,428	3,069	172	163	...	...	7	5
Matiya	1,440	745	695	111	125	3	2	13	35
Mistri	1,048	544	504	...	...	...	...	...	...
Patni	19,425	9,924	9,501	284	270	115	109	...	...

MAIMANSINGH—*continued.*

Iswarganj.		Phulbaria.		Netrokona.		Durgapur.		Kendua.	
Male.	Female.	Male.	Female.	Male.	Female.	Male.	Female.	Male.	Female.
191	116	46	19	158	132	147	67	1,191	727
171	111	20	6	...	...	91	39	226	243
...	...	...	...	72	54	...	...	952	474
20	5	26	13	16	16	2	...	13	10
287	278	2	...	905	883	51	50	234	246
65	72	42	10	141	262	...	...	222	239
68	...	34	...	41	5	18	...	29	...
536	530	...	...	241	231	705	693	261	359
1,809	1,435	262	242	2,257	2,136	1,014	849	1,981	1,897
460	197	377	305	340	128	513	368	252	127
1,306	1,006	122	116	1,798	1,772	507	463	330	526
166	167	...	...	65	55	93	92	57	68
62	41	335	340	193	167	4,045	3,872	...	...
1,525	1,086	269	126	560	247	94	41	1,214	1,183
5	2	21	12	222	40	1	3	...	...
2,559	2,402	441	465	2,721	2,459	887	732	2,167	2,332
323	16	594	52	19	...	250	...	1,524	79
2	1	1,588	1,581	1,587	470	25	22	6,267	4,742
239	205	101	83	404	316	176	240	396	563
...	...	102	92	10	15	...	...	19	5
730	709	...	...	133	120	10	...	460	517
4,204	3,860	555	501	5,943	5,710	3,111	2,772	3,771	4,344
17	13	2,870	2,842	...	...	9	7	4,935	4,950
425	406	113	123	1,039	880	705	600	1,761	1,632
218	199	4	...	4	3	...	...	563	283
...	...	...	...	234	114	...	...	1,481	1,173
122	253	...	...	...	...	2,392	1,502	...	...
...	...	1,237	828	8	...	...	...	11	16
...	...	25	11	...	...	...	...	...	...
5,085	4,815	3,024	3,037	7,047	6,343	2,637	2,127	6,091	5,791
1,419	1,316	1,252	2,254	1,370	1,273	1,485	1,487	1,315	1,220
780	95	388	67	527	155	246	116	440	25
311	292	141	...	90	54	33	2	25	...
1,291	643	272	151	1,914	2,025	1,336	1,310	1,336	1,134
1,325	1,352	175	158	1,589	1,410	299	249	1,915	1,861
114	89	6	...	238	234	...	...	25	9
199	221	3	...	120	220	259	231	297	390
45	49	22	27	27	...	...	...	198	100
198	203	162	186	42	28	26	35	271	181
905	978	6	8	1,205	1,046	...	...	1,175	1,210
112	225	93	88	10	2	116	41	205	323
1,954	2,215	532	489	4,187	3,867	2,483	1,937	4,201	3,504
...	...	563	564	...	...	726	636	501	455
135	90	...	...	...	...	...	...	170	186
3	5	...	...	...	...	...	...	24	24
237	254	1	...	3,255	3,161	2,889	2,571	1,262	1,119

Caste or Group.	Jamalpur.		Diwanganj.		Sherpur.		Nalitabari.	
	Male.	Female.	Male.	Female.	Male.	Female.	Male.	Female.
Baniya	245	385	176	164	1,042	1,052	57	...
(i) Gandha Banik	...	...	13	...	17	1	11	...
(ii) Khatri	115	260	...	...	1,022	1,050	...	...
(iii) Subarna Banik	68	74	59	71	3	1	2	...
Barui	...	...	311	295	149	139	5	...
Bediya	4	...	92	88	..	...	...	...
Bhar	...	...	...	...	16	...	16	...
Bhuimali and Mihtar	401	418	95	107	1,681	1,744	1,440	1,431
Brahman	824	1,210	210	99	511	209	169	81
Chamar and Muchi	514	229	101	50	268	165	112	68
Dhopa	127	99	13	18	71	52	25	17
Dom	...	...	67	83	8	2	29	31
Garo	563	491	24	18	...	...	63	...
Goala	1,966	1,199	338	229	1,539	1,526	274	167
Gonrhi	75	10	62	20	221	17	240	6
Jugi	874	875	367	376	228	191	165	119
Kahar	1,404	66	298	4	391	2	214	...
Kaibartta	1,776	1,865	614	517	7	6	268	273
Kamar and Lohar	208	181	1,197	1,199	48	18	8	...
Kandu	...	...	72	49	61	38	42	9
Kapali	101	28	...	...	...	...	...	...
Kayastha	3,406	3,166	641	502	558	1,533	541	453
Kochh	...	...	76	86	1,257	1,258	2,143	2,229
Kumhar	489	477	40	47	50	32	260	215
Maira and Kuri	317	223	174	154	279	273	169	177
Mal	76	29	360	...	19	3	302	121
Malakar	16	17	4	28	18	18	1	...
Malo	24	...	...	...	...	...	...	...
Musahar	...	...	...	...	...	...	...	...
Namasudra or Chandal ...	1,370	1,180	553	426	1,315	1,662	726	593
Napit and Hajjam	1,553	2,521	1,311	1,295	1,647	1,187	181	172
Nuniya	...	...	225	7	469	138	641	133
Rajput	1,431	1,339	12	...	27	...	...	...
Sunri and Kalwar	487	410	1,210	1,095	286	149	287	185
Sutradhar	508	384	142	125	134	114	95	62
Tanti	858	361	32	40	25	5	2	7
Teli and Kalu	...	...	15	2	210	413	31	...
Tiyar	604	304	102	205	...	...	55	54
Religious devotees and persons returned by sect.								
Baisnab	201	301	..	...	97	121	115	171
Hindus returned by title or common sub-caste.								
Sudra	43	25	...	...	251	252	14	5
Hindus returned by actual occupation.								
Dulia	191	65	185	495	...	...	...	...
Jaliya	903	891	245	261	298	350	305	325
Manjhi	493	644	360	...	...	...	19	...
Matiya	...	...	228	249	...	...	...	...
Mistri	42	87	...	...	3	...	...	...
Patni	68	65	54	50	87	77	24	21

MAIMANSINGH—*continued.*

Tangail.		Gopalpur.		Kalihati.		Kisorganj.		Nikli.		Bajitpur.	
Male.	Female.	Male.	Female.	Male.	Female.	Male.	Female.	Male.	Female.	Male.	Female.
675	721	360	357	608	656	371	375	579	383	476	645
324	362	114	119	154	199	204	232	212	236	269	416
...	...	30	109	385	361	82	98	292	20	146	185
290	349	216	228	18	14	85	45	59	57	33	17
221	193	596	586	...	...	301	290	700	702	167	161
...	...	...	...	...	...	81	45	...	...	106	295
43	2	185	3	...	...	388	39	600	...	2	1
1,312	1,441	597	742	...	...	120	223	...	...	286	296
3,196	2,999	474	649	947	982	1,356	1,207	973	2,278	1,587	1,159
2,366	2,378	1,680	1,392	123	118	116	69	586	101	1,483	588
348	353	187	158	124	95	490	465	386	367	376	271
75	12	49	48	15	2	63	57	...	...	3	1
2	...	180	174	...	...	...	...	...	...	2,300	2,331
1,543	1,385	665	351	1,452	1,475	781	727	1,230	785	2,234	2,316
...	...	...	...	...	...	1,024	30	...	...	72	4
54	53	1,385	1,580	1,278	1,367	1,125	1,083	1,330	1,371	2,152	2,084
609	31	1,354	163	158	1	326	50	241	33	49	2
15,047	16,442	6,477	6,197	2,051	2,422	7	...	664	581	14,390	14,431
1,760	1,834	...	...	586	604	292	267	178	177	335	336
...	...	...	...	...	...	...	...	...	...	298	140
1,922	1,904	...	...	...	...	997	1,025	19	13	144	120
8,463	9,475	578	700	2,024	2,417	2,576	2,551	1,000	1,070	2,012	1,945
806	121	1,967	1,892	534	539	...	...	...	...	...	...
1,358	1,273	1,305	591	1,630	1,647	338	362	508	473	630	699
59	25	62	50	138	180	126	94	136	135	479	583
...	...	104	35	...	...	...	...	392	317	540	302
379	393	524	709	9	...	602	824	...	...	602	732
346	462	74	67	...	...	471	484	392	402	577	312
...	...	...	...	93	49	...	...	...	...	441	404
23,798	26,014	1,823	1,609	1,315	1,344	6,865	6,699	3,963	3,834	5,690	5,201
2,761	2,830	1,956	2,000	2,491	1,614	503	540	551	508	1,049	1,047
533	122	673	171	162	19	200	27	143	5	47	4
189	209	30	10	1,085	1,032	224	109	322	256	106	309
4,517	5,165	3,472	3,565	1,832	2,443	896	930	784	853	2,480	2,157
2,800	2,836	1,227	1,174	906	883	586	508	1,078	1,158	1,868	1,915
1,630	1,606	814	752	758	811	...	...	709	643	114	40
678	437	985	906	476	722	75	45	376	259	75	18
1,116	1,075	...	...	109	131	...	...	700	795	235	207
500	891	414	794	...	...	117	115	102	154	...	...
148	184	198	167	...	...	317	305	1,444	1,640	380	403
369	312	301	259	4	...	...	...	...	...	137	106
3,586	3,936	2,404	2,708	1,494	1,682	1,244	1,432	1,407	1,477	5,446	5,413
204	185	183	174	120	129	65	97	...	...	15	17
...	...	...	...	10	8	27	...	...	...	48	...
107	89	105	165	209	123	...	...	...	...	54	61
222		254	263	364	365	364	473	61	72	383	391

DISTRICT

Group.	District Total.			Nasirabad.		Phulpur.		Gafargaon.	
	Total.	Male.	Female.	Male.	Female.	Male.	Female.	Male.	Female.
Hindus returned by unidentifiable caste.									
Jaraj	3,918	2,013	1,905	27	15	32	29	...	...
Patit	3,491	2,253	1,238	...	...	184	180	...	...
Musalmans returned by title.									
Khan	18,663	10,399	8,264	492	302	1,023	821	1,248	1,103
Mir	1,245	644	601	136	113	101	92	104	98
Moghul	1,288	698	590	91	103	43	29	2	3
Pathan	24,146	12,527	11,619	460	296	206	132	123	102
Sayyid	6,301	3,174	3,127	186	146	74	72	124	101
Shaikh	2,301,365	1,174,412	1,126,953	82,669	80,137	41,429	38,019	50,171	48,640
Musalmans returned by actual occupation.									
Dai	3,578	1,986	1,592	90	95	210	186	264	284
Fakir	1,161	620	541	64	44	126	99	71	67
Jolaha	3,142	1,632	1,510	168	119	2	...	43	...
Kalu	7,480	3,751	3,729	923	809	...	...	298	328

DISTRICT

Group.	Jamalpur.		Diwanganj.		Sherpur.		Nalitabari.	
	Male.	Female.	Male.	Female.	Male.	Female.	Male.	Female.
Hindus returned by unidentifiable caste.								
Jaraj	629	572	...	...	...	...	92	42
Patit	...	...	...	...	1	...	...	...
Musalmans returned by title.								
Khan	437	357	126	84	69	48	85	50
Mir	24	26	...	...	...	...	...	...
Moghul	38	26	...	...	1	...	2	...
Pathan	579	460	574	590	126	97	82	48
Sayyid	153	151	84	67	47	21	71	54
Shaikh	93,839	90,272	55,934	53,769	48,083	46,311	24,426	22,276
Musalmans returned by actual occupation.								
Dai	299	297	23	21	...	...	11	16
Fakir	...	...	5	4	11	9	29	32
Jolaha	384	407	...	...	...	...	3	...
Kalu	370	382	123	120	...	...	11	6

MAIMANSINGH—*continued.*

Iswarganj.		Phulbaria.		Netrokona.		Durgapur.		Kendua.	
Male.	Female.	Male.	Female.	Male.	Female.	Male.	Female	Male.	Female.
59	87	51	...	5	2	85	60	201	242
145	89	42	44	130	37	...	...	...	...
71	74	87	55	1,510	1,273	824	619	2,026	1,064
50	37	16	10	15	13	8	3	8	10
12	1	43	22	27	14	2	2	2	...
732	614	191	122	1,102	891	250	167	1,161	1,106
138	114	12	5	202	140	23	20	421	597
94,281	92,012	32,872	31,107	79,496	73,594	76,931	74,329	88,949	85,774
38	40	21	23	550	185	42	36	251	209
153	159	42	43	64	43	9	12	27	25
...	...	2	...	2	...	1	...	...	...
182	161	746	736	...	...	...	...	...	...

MAIMANSINGH—*concluded.*

Tangail.		Gopalpur.		Kalihati.		Kisorganj.		Nikli.		Bajitpur.	
Male.	Female.	Male.	Female.	Male.	Female.	Male.	Female.	Male.	Female.	Male.	Female.
195	296	...	...	221	205	...	...	...	...	416	355
16	17	1,415	713	3	1	292	150	25	7	...	...
1,220	1,236	422	356	62	56	296	267	131	126	270	383
74	100	59	54	17	18	10	6	4	1	18	20
146	106	174	168	104	109	11	7	...	...	...	...
4,779	5,023	965	793	868	865	245	255	26	21	58	37
759	722	198	202	220	255	94	75	125	115	243	270
115,336	116,410	100,234	100,276	39,784	40,663	28,094	25,075	51,335	39,609	70,549	68,588
6	1	...	...	7	7	168	189	...	...	6	3
1	...	7	...	...	...	7	4	3	2	1	...
655	601	62	57	310	326	...	...	...	...	...	...
366	441	...	...	439	427	141	118	70	116	88	

CHITTAGONG

DISTRICT

Caste or Group.	District Total.			Chittagong.		Mirsharai.		Kumira.		Phatikchari.		Hathazari.	
	Total.	Male.	Female.	Male.	Female.	Male.	Female.	Male.	Female.	Male.	Female.	Male.	Female.
Baidya	5,868	2,941	2,927	434	489	70	57	35	12	36	20	53	79
Baniya	8,738	4,222	4,516	209	198	146	90	177	176	771	729	348	372
(i) Subarna Banik	5,231	2,477	2,754	18	...	105	90	95	104	310	260	293	331
Barui	2,948	1,472	1,476	1	...	114	118	290	299	12	22	102	101
Bhuimali and Mihtar	6,829	3,233	3,596	206	201	176	197	88	67	372	498	204	259
Brahman	23,507	11,700	11,807	743	763	484	398	442	373	544	567	579	599
Dhopa	12,475	6,011	6,464	190	187	1,313	1,348	704	756	610	665	296	283
Dom	12,181	6,002	6,179	555	521	1	...	49	...	44	41	527	570
Jugi	32,723	15,588	17,135	1,153	1,105	2,674	3,089	1,515	1,673	2,816	2,995	1,776	2,075
Kahar	1,029	526	503	61	27	113	109	3	...	7	6	64	69
Kaibartta	6,303	3,122	3,181	283	245	152	140	22	14	220	213	6	6
Kamar	2,863	1,322	1,541	17	13	210	229	74	94	180	178	36	30
Kayastha	74,206	36,153	38,053	3,055	2,412	3,412	3,681	1,227	1,772	2,819	3,288	3,214	3,665
Kumhar	5,931	2,898	3,033	251	298	373	380	142	145	212	254	274	273
Namasudra or Chandal ...	2,469	1,240	1,229	5	...	142	137	97	96	442	459	95	97
Napit	18,124	8,898	9,226	444	468	781	899	622	651	932	1,019	572	624
Sunri	1,196	582	614	13	6	169	189	137	142	196	208	54	65
Sutradhar	1,169	579	590	3	...	139	148	24	35	95	94	21	13
Tanti	2,106	1,040	1,066	56	44	...	...	41	48	5	6	10	1
Teli and Kalu	3,764	1,575	2,189	62	115	206	246	100	127	116	207	64	113
Hindus returned by title or common sub-caste.													
Sudra	56,703	25,898	30,805	481	454	1,531	1,706	39	35	190	161	244	296
Hindus returned by actual occupation.													
Jaliya	9,395	4,684	4,711	606	571	1,175	1,126	1,146	1,003	37	36	...	...
Machhua	1,828	883	945	194	185	33	24	85	90	...	...	...	...
Musalmans returned by title.													
Pathan	2,216	1,120	1,096	225	213	33	31	62	38	72	82	42	47
Sayyid	7,801	3,754	4,047	428	447	56	53	183	226	316	448	296	311
Shaikh	911,411	434,332	477,079	33,136	36,260	30,438	32,590	23,925	26,122	38,664	41,715	32,599	35,318

DISTRICT

Caste.	District Total.			Sudharam.		Hatia.		Bamni.	
	Total.	Male.	Female.	Male.	Female.	Male.	Female.	Male.	Female.
Baidya	1,204	693	511	219	141	11	3	14	3
Baniya	3,947	1,945	2,002	83	78	19	...	46	46
(i) Gandha Banik	1,743	879	864	26	24	8	...	...	...
(ii) Subarna Banik	1,701	781	920	4	...	2	...	8	...
Barui	3,086	1,561	1,525	18	16	15	6	...	...
Bhuimali	3,946	1,981	1,965	147	167	71	75	69	69
Brahman	11,910	6,466	5,444	825	509	164	86	117	106
Dhopa	17,520	9,059	8,461	665	625	522	416	309	278
Dom	1,672	818	854	...	...	...	...	...	...

DIVISION.

CHITTAGONG.

Raujan.		Patia.		Banskhali.		Satkania.		Cox's Bazar.		Chakaria.		Maiskal.		Teknaf.	
Male.	Female.	Male.	Female.	Male.	Female.	Male.	Female.	Male.	Female.	Male.	Female.	Male.	Female.	Male.	Female.
535	628	1,387	1,320	214	265	54	32	53	11	34	14	...	...	6	...
653	726	658	727	495	666	353	438	103	107	212	230	37	25	60	32
311	323	583	659	384	564	230	273	13	...	84	125	17	20	34	5
37	44	197	184	174	185	88	78	281	275	101	102	...	...	75	68
529	696	1,045	1,114	300	310	228	177	78	77	...	...	3	...	4	...
1,817	1,985	4,212	4,294	1,108	1,164	998	1,031	175	107	166	166	136	110	296	250
664	771	793	836	482	518	473	541	110	118	103	117	129	195	144	129
1,032	1,084	1,401	1,403	1,135	1,304	568	661	94	65	438	410	117	100	41	...
1,905	1,987	1,248	1,351	1,131	1,252	1,019	1,247	89	78	103	117	146	165	13	1
46	47	31	41	124	126	...	...	70	74	...	...	1	...	6	4
546	529	470	438	366	380	113	251	...	...	18	25	927	935	...	...
326	397	118	140	92	116	210	269	...	...	58	75	1	...	...	...
3,471	4,045	10,949	11,033	3,285	3,225	4,068	4,501	383	277	161	40	...	...	109	94
389	387	158	175	235	281	245	265	185	190	194	175	165	190	25	20
48	36	104	119	283	275	13	10	17	...	...	...	...	...	..	...
1,180	1,242	1,290	1,342	1,057	1,115	885	876	426	391	306	264	285	251	118	84
...	...	3	...	...	...	10	4	...	...	...	...	...	...	...	...
...	...	250	259	11	8	36	33	...	...	...	...	...	...	...	...
458	473	450	482	7	4	...	...	1	...	12	8	...	...	...	...
207	360	407	497	143	152	46	87	150	163	41	65	33	37	...	...
7,770	9,062	7,529	9,518	4,689	5,981	1,649	1,929	616	547	568	564	539	510	53	42
236	237	8	12	1,219	1,512	...	...	149	124	96	90	12	...	...	...
232	290	...	...	18	12	312	336	1	...	...	...	13	8	...	...
104	92	314	309	191	209	57	69	14	1	1	...	5	5	...	...
677	718	983	1,046	208	180	340	383	95	56	13	14	16	20	143	145
44,335	47,705	57,714	64,550	40,079	47,164	59.468	66,398	26,729	28,102	19,916	2,1254	18,787	16,336	13,542	13,565

NOAKHALI.

Ramganj.		Lakshmipur.		Begamganj.		Sundwip.		Fenny.		Chhagalnaia.	
Male.	Female.	Male.	Female.	Male.	Female.	Male.	Female.	Male.	Female.	Male.	Female.
145	105	48	19	74	55	12	13	159	111	11	1
214	216	111	64	475	486	225	203	368	380	404	529
152	154	56	39	318	309	30	30	148	138	141	170
61	62	15	11	90	96	194	173	180	235	227	343
193	183	317	286	147	100	2	...	380	406	489	463
308	272	245	224	282	303	133	122	307	383	339	350
1,065	920	744	553	1,138	1,115	333	241	780	678	1,300	1,236
1,211	1,114	1,011	938	1,510	1,428	1,255	1,102	1,383	1,402	1,193	1,158
...	...	8	11	...	...	...	...	810	843	...	...

DISTRICT

Caste or Group.	District Total.			Sudharam.		Hatia.		Bamni.	
	Total.	Male.	Female.	Male.	Female.	Male.	Female.	Male.	Female.
Goala	2,216	1,157	1,059	80	82	6	...	36	30
Jugi	45,001	22,277	22,724	1,487	1,543	730	656	1,040	1,121
Kahar	2,295	1,139	1,156	277	321	55	41	70	53
Kaibartta	23,039	11,624	11,415	794	796	1,528	1,384	336	322
Kamar and Lohar	1,853	979	874	68	47	23	4	7	...
Kayastha	45,251	22,903	22,348	2,548	2,567	382	330	266	283
Kumhar	4,900	2,524	2,376	193	185	199	181	16	...
Namasudra or Chandal ...	23,540	12,110	11,430	484	457	126	81	1,461	1,409
Napit	14,866	7,483	7,383	770	759	343	278	357	356
Nat	1,020	431	589	83	103	...	...	16	10
Sunri	7,788	4,055	3,733	688	602	282	226	83	18
Sutradhar	5,016	2,568	2,448	274	248	23	9	50	42
Teli	4,305	2,234	2,071	510	525	8	...	5	...
Religious devotees and persons returned by sect.									
Baisnab	2,530	1,100	1,430	196	256	57	40	60	64
Hindus returned by title or common sub-caste.									
Sudra	3,674	1,824	1,850	371	328	136	147	92	135
Hindus returned by actual occupation.									
Jaliya	11,066	5,743	5,323	595	577	852	770	587	569
Patni	2,623	1,354	1,269	133	138	...	...	100	86
Musalmans returned by title.									
Pathan	1,342	729	613	78	46	14	9	102	88
Sayyid	1,363	710	653	119	112	9	3	25	21
Shaikh	757,665	380,521	377,144	48,259	48,978	21,809	18,130	19,218	20,281

DISTRICT

Caste.	District total.			Comilla.		Muradnagar.		Daudkandi.		Chandina.	
	Total.	Male.	Female.	Male.	Female.	Male.	Female.	Male.	Female.	Male.	Female.
Baidya	4,723	2,343	2,380	365	232	176	221	122	101	164	133
Baniya	6,324	3,297	3,027	454	464	430	371	257	233	231	161
(i) Gandha Banik	2,967	1,530	1,437	231	248	284	269	105	97	92	61
Barui	9,447	4,881	4,566	874	842	685	680	307	301	585	594
Bhuimali	7,540	3,779	3,761	411	432	177	164	441	445	93	107
Brahman	30,970	16,386	14,584	1,818	1,384	1,468	1,346	964	920	901	871
Chakma	1,983	1,198	785	236	180	66	50	198	168	...	...
Chamar and Muchi	6,480	3,566	2,914	202	111	163	129	216	177	228	202
Dhopa	17,636	9,117	8,519	1,121	1,080	647	576	322	286	572	544
Goala	10,984	6,051	4,933	867	589	409	282	384	229	47	50
Jugi	69,441	34,809	34,632	4,395	4,289	5,476	5,775	2,164	2,256	2,157	2,124
Kaibartta	60,547	30,203	30,344	1,817	1,378	1,221	1,358	2,371	2,394	209	176
Kamar and Lohar	5,612	2,881	2,731	628	559	365	354	210	199	55	58

NOAKHALI—*concluded.*

Ramganj.		Lakshmipur.		Begamganj.		Sundwip.		Fenny.		Chhagalnaia.	
Male.	Female.	Male.	Female.	Male.	Female.	Male.	Female.	Male.	Female.	Male.	Female.
190	177	194	176	365	327	10	...	107	89	169	178
2,641	2,608	2,129	2,060	4,733	4,525	1,504	1,492	4,451	4,906	3,562	3,813
43	30	78	68	103	83	15	7	414	447	85	106
63	61	1,254	1,241	507	437	3,266	3,073	2,674	2,700	1,193	1,411
173	178	128	101	176	183	60	53	168	136	176	172
3,941	3,856	2,287	2,020	3,360	3,364	964	880	2,052	2,002	7,108	7,046
160	177	236	189	263	250	141	127	535	455	781	812
598	473	3,143	2,790	2,382	2,316	1,422	1,394	1,732	1,634	762	867
881	834	634	576	1,131	1,095	891	836	1,151	1,269	1 325	1,380
68	63	69	77	79	103	12	...	37	30	67	203
289	291	740	586	910	944	238	191	340	296	535	564
289	250	463	405	775	856	155	156	357	321	182	161
196	183	396	255	406	346	2	...	451	457	260	305
69	73	185	239	345	493	85	86	81	153	22	26
78	68	113	99	582	642	178	134	210	225	64	72
133	120	199	180	213	193	1,602	1,433	1,261	1,221	301	260
...	...	229	226	7	7	464	398	270	270	151	144
76	47	186	156	113	137	33	16	104	90	23	24
46	40	57	41	51	63	254	256	68	52	81	60
35,196	35,977	56,507	53,999	59,538	57,378	37,204	38,015	60,478	62,635	39,610	41,751

TIPPERA.

Chaudagram.		Laksham.		Brahmanbaria.		Kasba.		Nabinagar.		Chandpur.		Hajiganj.	
Male.	Female.	Male.	Female.	Male.	Female.	Male.	Female.	Male.	Female.	Male.	Female.	Male.	Female.
81	54	34	26	542	597	266	353	263	359	264	258	46	46
235	184	396	321	330	334	174	141	402	503	187	200	111	115
129	85	110	81	95	103	119	110	139	109	145	184	81	90
150	132	121	108	414	390	464	422	521	397	654	591	106	109
241	247	187	167	746	747	377	364	319	326	560	542	227	220
948	860	1,090	814	2,706	2,471	1,574	1,500	1,755	1,750	1,613	1,318	1,489	1,350
2	...	4	...	109	76	363	171	...	...	221	200	...	...
114	102	434	234	988	890	327	264	582	501	202	165	130	130
1,142	995	1,008	933	715	764	306	424	355	326	1,847	1,634	1,022	937
212	163	232	199	1,006	1,499	510	512	461	361	988	768	345	281
2,190	2,083	2,574	2,531	4,513	4,510	3,727	3,861	3,078	3,115	2,165	1,867	2,370	1,022
1,058	1,036	874	844	8,107	8,148	2,470	2,427	3,068	3,000	8,975	8,963	533	560
124	112	110	80	466	506	182	185	239	248	390	339	112	91

DISTRICT

Caste or Group.	District Total.			Comilla.		Muradnagar.		Daudkandi.		Chandina.	
	Total.	Male.	Female.	Male.	Female.	Male.	Female.	Male.	Female.	Male.	Female.
Kapali	9,367	4,736	4,631	170	155	14	...	14	...	24	24
Kayastha	72,554	35,208	37,346	3,439	2,796	5,177	6,027	3,549	3,774	3,260	3,246
Kumhar	10,338	5,253	5,085	690	650	316	331	201	177	210	207
Maira and Kuri	1,101	575	526	59	75	41	32	56	33	75	69
Mal	4,764	2,412	2,352	130	131	351	307	551	518	35	28
Malakar	4,290	2,176	2,114	158	121	386	403	163	166	192	187
Malo	3,155	1,652	1,503	246	230	136	171	119	88	202	173
Namasudra or Chandal	96,160	50,122	46,038	3,697	3,424	4,052	3,870	3,130	2,896	4,100	3,680
Napit	22,736	11,576	11,160	1,314	1,248	1,221	1,246	709	706	544	554
Nuniya	1,314	1,122	192	43	12	549	85	23	4	...	...
Rajput	1,204	600	604	171	159	6	...	...	...	8	...
Sunri	38,185	18,650	19,535	1,709	1,582	2,565	2,837	2,590	2,796	387	278
Sutradhar	16,400	8,333	8,067	784	758	694	636	959	989	613	593
Teli and Kalu	7,179	3,661	3,518	665	649	213	229	176	182	85	77
Tippera	3,299	1,680	1,619	789	744	69	60	22	12	...	...
Religious devotees and persons returned by sect.											
Baisnab	3,046	1,331	1,715	383	475	379	479	164	178	...	...
Hindus returned by title or common sub-caste.											
Das	2,524	1,275	1,249	143	149	183	145	200	232	77	79
Sudra	8,162	4,148	4,014	604	549	248	187	11	9	...	...
Hindus returned by actual occupation.											
Jaliya	2,607	1,392	1,215	265	270	...	...	168	123	18	10
Patni	6,537	3,203	3,334	279	269	279	256	383	398	...	...
Musalmans returned by title.											
Pathan	2,677	1,585	1,092	71	36	242	226	38	33	18	19
Sayyid	2,829	1,430	1,399	238	207	76	108	41	44	55	55
Shaikh	1,215,716	622,312	593,404	85,232	81,588	58,951	56,807	66,964	66,053	34,954	33,443

DISTRICT CHITTA

Caste or Group.	District Total.			Chakma Circle.		Mong Raja's Circle.	
	Total.	Male.	Female.	Male.	Female.	Male.	Female.
Chakma	35,288	18,727	16,561	15,618	13,455	2,676	2,737
Kuki	2,471	1,179	1,292	168	192	...	...
Lushai	1,228	586	642	...	...	...	...
Tippera	25,299	13,156	12,143	1,611	1,549	6,691	5,153
Musalmans returned by title.							
Shaikh	3,256	2,968	288	1,569	266	171	...

TIPPERA—*concluded.*

Chaudagram.		Laksham.		Brahmanbaria.		Kasba.		Nabinagar.		Chandpur.		Hajiganj.	
Male.	Female.	Male.	Female.	Male.	Female.	Male.	Female.	Male.	Female.	Male.	Female.	Male.	Female.
5	...	485	492	923	852	1,778	1,786	1,296	1,277	...	...	27	45
2,535	2,640	2,026	1,774	5,645	6,158	2,514	3,047	2,819	3,103	2,150	2,903	2,094	1,878
812	848	196	180	844	810	866	884	781	730	206	156	131	112
14	16	23	20	100	95	6	...	63	61	...	...	108	125
4	...	95	83	38	13	246	261	871	826	45	51	46	39
115	114	134	125	189	206	277	257	279	281	171	147	112	107
74	48	123	134	...	...	196	191	140	162	372	260	44	46
953	820	847	772	11,857	11,310	3,599	3,319	4,069	3,814	11,077	9,736	2,741	2,397
688	644	584	546	1,961	1,858	1,337	1,299	778	794	1,610	1,562	810	703
...	...	18	...	78	...	67	13	230	45	5	...	109	33
30	19	...	...	196	170	...	...	148	210	20	16	21	30
541	499	696	646	3,438	3,800	1,363	1,660	1,745	1,892	2,058	1,989	1,558	1,556
460	454	591	460	1,567	1,602	843	865	740	756	603	514	479	440
87	86	119	153	594	600	214	238	174	176	1,046	921	288	207
...	...	...	...	60	55	...	...	...	...	651	658	89	90
...	...	...	...	122	132	164	217	119	234	...	...	...	...
81	75	113	143	146	119	232	216	...	...	100	101	...	...
99	110	155	164	214	177	1,313	1,307	1,428	1,482	43	26	3	3
64	50	23	19	6	3	252	263	86	79	483	364	27	34
286	285	132	128	907	998	...	...	504	403	369	398	64	79
18	14	25	13	662	408	170	99	86	50	142	98	113	96
58	48	123	165	622	582	24	24	140	129	24	19	29	18
46,937	46,948	43,278	40,308	70,869	68,290	34,588	32,324	41,915	40,029	93,519	88,585	45,085	39,030

GONG HILL TRACTS.

Bhomong's Circle.		Sangu Khas Mahal.		Head-Quarter Khas Mahal.		Forest Reserves.	
Male.	Female.	Male.	Female.	Male.	Female.	Male.	Female.
433	309	...	...	...	...	...	...
1,003	1,100	...	...	8	...	...	...
116	130	470	512	...	...	...	...
5,228	4,822	...	...	620	617	6	2
785	20	11	...	98	2	334	...

PATNA

DISTRICT

CASTE.	DISTRICT TOTAL.			PIRBAHOR.		SULTANGANJ.		ALAMGANJ.	
	Total.	Male.	Female.	Male.	Female.	Male.	Female.	Male.	Female.
Agarwala	1,616	814	802	3	2	1	...	3	1
Agrahari	1,587	753	834	7	6	4	2	...	...
Babhan	158,194	78,875	79,319	1,235	1,264	1,382	1,322	1,123	1,196
Baniya	30,897	14,953	15,944	217	201	188	203	268	324
(i) Barnawar...	1,980	848	1,132	...	...	...	...	...	...
(ii) Jaunpuri	1,339	621	718	...	...	27	37	52	65
(iii) Kasarwani	3,203	1,649	1,554	...	...	13	11	37	34
(iv) Khatri	1,579	760	819	24	21	13	18	3	...
(v) Mahuri	8,180	3,963	4,217	2	...	4	...	4	...
(vi) Raunlar	6,364	3,149	3,215	28	10	101	106	59	89
(vii) Sinduria	1,482	623	859	...	...	2	1	...	...
Barhi	24,555	11,984	12,571	156	143	62	59	497	480
Bari	3,849	1,893	1,956	102	109	103	102	3	...
Barui	3,498	1,670	1,828	85	90	...	...	15	10
Beldar	16,871	8,335	8,536	2	...	39	37	29	46
Bhar	1,391	643	748	3	8	...	...	...	...
Bhat	1,349	755	594	...	...	3	2	18	14
Bind	4,462	1,616	2,846	91	59	2	4	2	6
Brahman	42,462	22,296	20,166	695	274	232	181	517	386
Chain	3,635	1,551	2,084	19	28	677	990	24	40
Chamar	57,314	27,659	29,655	335	312	116	98	194	334
Dhanuk	36,443	17,415	19,028	20	2	94	94	725	781
Dhopa	12,984	6,429	6,555	173	192	87	84	154	129
Dom	4,639	2,299	2,340	30	28	21	32	56	61
Dusadh	98,931	48,737	50,194	273	284	183	204	392	271
Gareri	8,524	4,157	4,367	26	25	35	10	68	81
Goala	220,340	112,771	107,569	1,248	1,293	1,078	1,059	1,172	1,152
Gonrhi	8,775	4,238	4,537	272	261	304	369	...	...
Hajjam	26,374	12,703	13,671	207	184	156	161	245	255
Halwai	9,108	4,467	4,641	203	194	100	82	243	247
Hari and Mihtar	2,103	1,048	1,055	86	92	26	26	...	...
Jugi	1,635	785	850	...	...	1	...	11	12
Kahar	82,816	39,760	43,056	1,041	1,012	325	369	544	800
Kalwar and Sunri	14,977	7,133	7,844	328	350	134	139	737	989
Kandu	29,148	14,144	15,004	243	247	107	90	353	329
Kasera	6,214	3,032	3,182	302	323	...	...	9	8
Kayastha	28,064	13,740	14,324	1,243	582	357	270	264	239
Koiri	80,222	40,386	39,836	990	1,026	739	768	795	877
Kumhar	23,971	11,877	12,094	181	181	133	160	261	309
Kurmi	200,791	98,261	102,530	233	152	122	104	482	656
Lohar and Kamar	8,113	3,937	4,176	60	73	77	83	147	156
Malakar	5,323	2,622	2,701	57	41	38	34	58	51
Musahar	37,210	18,738	18,472	98	92	5	10	19	10
Nuniya	13,207	6,545	6,662	6	6	1	...	44	91
Pasi	35,495	17,382	18,113	138	142	195	237	406	388
Rajput	67,830	33,851	33,979	406	323	337	300	358	262
Rajwar	4,260	2,016	2,244	...	...	...	...	...	...
Sonar	21,682	10,718	10,964	102	105	94	110	177	203
Tambuli	3,569	1,740	1,829	55	56	19	19	46	51
Tatwa and Tanti	20,818	9,797	11,021	9	6	12	14	144	175
Toli	57,623	27,932	29,691	413	382	260	303	910	1,024
Thathera	2,041	963	1,078	26	34	82	98	41	50
Tiyar	1,705	520	1,185	26	34	15	55	2	10

DIVISION.

PATNA.

Khwaja Kalan.		Chauk Kalan.		Malsalami.		Bankipur.		Bikram.		Masaudhi Bazurg.	
Male.	Female.	Male.	Female.	Male.	Female.	Male.	Female.	Male.	Female.	Male.	Female.
87	89	321	357	...	...	11	6	4	7	42	47
20	22	38	42	325	364	...	...	...	...	29	33
1,117	1,185	106	254	182	207	2,835	2,865	19,133	19,591	3,115	2,889
399	411	645	595	161	322	641	602	1,239	1,320	1,193	1,176
25	28	77	98	73	235	...	...	...	...	...	3
87	107	27	27	9	2	25	28	77	85	...	...
76	84	322	306	...	...	74	82	308	284	161	152
43	55	...	...	...	...	7	...	38	49	5	4
25	2	59	...	...	...	3	3	1	5	5	4
50	33	78	76	...	...	121	115	399	425	609	582
11	4	4	2	2	2	...	...	55	75	70	82
348	370	286	288	207	165	470	458	1,302	1,287	489	544
21	23	...	...	280	310	...	...	135	119	23	23
35	5	109	103	83	110	35	20	13	10	210	236
33	35	48	54	31	31	102	115	357	323	765	762
...	...	...	...	...	...	...	...	...	...	...	...
20	15	...	...	147	103	7	20	...	...	38	28
...	...	142	117	72	103	123	355	...	...	10	9
646	435	990	825	313	191	1,012	657	3,470	3,688	811	901
...	...	61	2	5	9	668	944	...	...	5	5
219	222	227	228	539	601	1,663	1,703	3,750	4,091	2,193	2,201
264	298	249	246	48	44	152	169	...	...	28	24
180	238	161	164	106	117	56	103	585	602	358	313
109	102	29	28	25	29	142	128	180	175	155	161
289	226	535	297	765	890	2,703	2,891	5,035	5,144	3,363	3,019
55	88	23	14	44	71	292	319	590	628	409	432
1,308	1,412	1,936	1,453	3,902	3,854	10,044	10,139	11,868	11,081	11,495	11,088
466	491	133	157	144	160	...	...	342	330	881	898
313	314	241	227	320	303	943	939	1,344	1,409	991	1,042
300	282	161	140	141	139	536	545	652	695	138	143
84	37	77	71	112	133	15	23	50	57	30	31
20	10	13	15	2	9	168	216	87	105	70	71
1,643	1,572	974	1,189	429	588	1,752	2,009	5,204	4,928	2,296	2,608
384	426	153	143	778	876	196	209	284	318	24	35
294	283	107	148	374	426	817	905	2,448	2,387	672	725
338	369	148	133	30	41	...	...	1,392	1,460	...	...
856	863	540	525	192	154	901	642	909	1,212	565	666
783	745	893	928	1,438	1,390	3,413	3,720	8,328	7,824	1,021	1,601
123	131	219	230	788	729	1,029	1,058	431	506	330	400
953	1,658	824	913	616	230	5,790	6,174	2,696	2,768	13,783	14,336
506	521	116	118	77	67	415	506	682	744	269	275
100	88	43	55	56	50	109	168	261	294	142	155
37	3	26	14	49	56	1,092	1,065	1,393	1,379	2,367	2,248
36	42	23	19	52	58	212	255	471	409	262	231
320	348	77	82	442	462	1,462	1,696	1,042	991	1,247	1,327
336	361	559	485	991	1,044	2,362	2,211	2,511	2,286	1,801	1,735
...	...	2	10	...	...	...	...	126	186	...	...
531	608	317	316	180	183	428	402	552	539	485	457
356	389	56	57	65	75	86	96	232	211	68	83
184	192	192	195	308	304	104	102	158	130	14	17
464	495	389	380	626	600	1,139	1,193	2,140	2,106	1,107	1,102
14	10	19	25	31	31	15	3	73	90	122	141
1	...	...	...	2	...	149	403	...	...	...	...

DISTRICT

Caste.	Dinapur.		Maner.		Barh.		Fatuha.	
	Male.	Female.	Male.	Female.	Male.	Female.	Male.	Female.
Agarwala	91	63	...	...	74	70	4	1
Agrahari	...	...	...	...	273	308	57	57
Babhan	1,085	2,069	2,990	3,277	10,187	9,987	5,127	4,195
Baniya	1,638	1,776	482	539	1,338	1,306	425	424
(i) Barnawar	50	106	...	...	481	527	...	...
(ii) Jaunpuri	120	149	129	148	...	...	15	19
(iii) Kasarwani	169	159	43	48	86	42	...	2
(iv) Khatri	252	273	2	...	161	161	22	16
(v) Mahuri	2	4	...	...	217	189	203	219
(vi) Rauniar	1,027	1,059	85	98	23	21	4	...
(vii) Sinduria	...	...	23	29	13	16	3	...
Barhi	797	857	357	424	1,546	1,825	891	437
Bari	...	...	13	11	...	...	2	1
Barui	31	45	84	129	202	173	111	164
Beldar	20	37	57	66	1,233	1,261	601	638
Bhar	626	724	...	...	...	...	14	16
Bhat	77	64	41	19	29	14	128	94
Bind	62	138	294	722	283	341	18	26
Brahman	1,202	962	1,275	1,387	2,143	1,872	1,179	1,424
Chain	...	...	...	...	...	...	54	57
Chamar	1,863	2,114	1,280	1,487	2,602	3,049	1,523	1,628
Dhanuk	17	20	1	...	4,900	5,428	363	363
Dhopa	316	421	200	270	711	742	568	515
Dom	127	150	98	92	280	240	208	253
Dusadh	1,299	1,444	1,695	1,951	7,670	8,078	2,756	3,058
Gareri	196	239	229	290	303	321	100	68
Goala	5,049	4,992	13,604	13,521	10,445	10,307	6,278	6,103
Gonrhi	563	580	110	107	1	...	365	488
Hajjam	419	498	743	853	1,478	1,644	532	625
Halwai	360	342	312	385	201	120	146	209
Hari and Mihtar	338	318	30	29	123	116	14	8
Jugi	24	18	8	11	16	8	8	11
Kahar	980	1,220	1,182	1,462	5,840	5,493	1,992	1,933
Kalwar and Sunri	382	416	529	657	911	1,004	685	662
Kandu	546	622	1,443	1,554	2,669	2,991	626	582
Kasera	54	37	251	233	12	13	27	31
Kayastha	382	392	666	853	1,129	1,195	485	522
Koiri	2,425	2,424	2,230	2,314	1,959	1,894	1,547	1,702
Kumhar	503	507	487	549	1,253	1,282	516	536
Kurmi	2,091	2,945	3,398	3,866	10,453	10,731	4,495	4,591
Lohar and Kamar	350	364	396	455	75	57	85	84
Malakar	69	82	187	187	294	280	148	159
Musahar	350	379	316	383	2,165	2,198	132	151
Nuniya	33	43	107	110	1,014	895	158	122
Pasi	771	852	...	...	1,582	1,703	808	868
Rajput	332	368	2,519	2,741	9,420	9,348	1,964	2,803
Rajwar	...	...	...	...	7	4	...	...
Sonar	608	620	461	469	1,416	1,440	455	482
Tambuli	88	96	64	73	80	90	84	74
Tatwa and Tanti	165	164	98	136	1,608	1,816	974	995
Teli	896	949	1,537	1,601	3,172	3,379	1,837	1,889
Thathera	19	19	...	...	...	...	68	51
Tiyar	...	4	10	38	132	292	15	36

PATNA—*continued.*

Mukameh.		Bihar.		Hilsa.		Chandi.		Islampur or Athasarai.		Silao.	
Male.	Female.	Male.	Female.	Male.	Female.	Male.	Female.	Male.	Female.	Male.	Female.
119	94	3	...	33	36	...	...	15	29	3	...
...	...	...	...	...	...	...	...	...	...	...	...
7,812	8,481	6,753	6,275	4,957	4,642	2,906	2,796	2,490	2,298	4,340	4,526
463	480	1,517	1,947	897	935	424	442	1,803	1,905	1,016	1,036
17	10	40	47	10	10	...	...	15	13	60	55
...	...	...	...	53	51	...	...	...	...	...	...
15	18	3	2	109	112	18	10	215	208	...	...
42	54	24	27	8	5	37	53	43	44	36	39
48	53	1,091	1,282	577	604	93	98	900	988	729	766
6	...	12	12	4	3	103	123	440	463	...	...
32	32	265	494	42	51	41	23	16	11	44	37
745	748	1,874	1,965	682	727	536	546	1,087	1,096	152	152
...	...	445	463	...	...	144	134	418	428	204	233
120	192	65	69	33	32	43	48	373	370	23	23
580	602	1,248	1,342	1,210	1,228	963	997	523	504	494	458
...	...	...	...	...	...	...	...	...	...	...	...
69	87	...	...	...	...	69	35	54	47	55	52
508	956	...	...	...	...	...	...	...	...	9	10
1,215	915	2,090	1,864	1,091	993	1,064	947	952	952	1,399	1,342
30	...	...	...	3	3	...	...	6	6	...	...
1,333	1,369	2,919	3,105	1,817	1,827	1,314	1,490	2,544	2,543	1,228	1,253
6,578	6,902	2,667	3,206	376	387	371	430	288	294	274	340
468	449	962	913	323	308	308	285	311	338	412	372
126	151	298	254	94	125	105	97	104	125	122	100
5,416	5,806	7,788	7,185	2,640	2,596	2,693	2,844	1,791	1,946	1,451	1,460
358	416	189	186	238	241	78	83	229	249	701	657
4,440	4,364	10,769	9,570	8,097	7,136	4,496	4,196	1,455	902	4,092	3,947
201	251	227	213	4	...	33	81	192	201	...	...
700	748	2,002	2,366	...	...	777	744	636	621	656	738
161	170	279	308	148	163	76	80	206	256	114	141
31	18	3	3	14	16	30	33	4	3	31	41
...	...	169	146	40	32	1	5	82	119	56	62
2,133	2,395	4,140	5,050	2,547	2,699	2,334	2,670	2,104	2,364	2,300	2,695
166	133	716	788	130	119	438	448	63	59	95	73
1,156	1,266	1,016	1,124	442	470	555	554	...	...	276	292
5	...	353	408	...	...	...	...	69	76	42	50
333	224	2,575	3,468	600	744	547	536	580	659	616	578
402	332	7,753	7,568	561	544	391	352	2,282	2,042	1,836	1,785
2,308	2,355	1,286	1,117	610	579	500	471	387	406	532	588
3,260	2,991	18,477	18,897	9,460	9,489	9,042	9,308	5,516	5,451	6,561	7,270
71	64	151	153	113	136	42	43	153	126	152	151
83	69	326	322	128	123	152	154	159	147	152	242
1,993	1,982	4,098	3,614	1,062	1,152	1,434	1,590	607	632	1,495	1,514
721	787	1,820	1,527	521	552	1,074	1,100	103	103	387	362
436	453	4,783	4,856	1,014	1,012	614	609	866	871	1,179	1,196
738	577	3,348	3,495	994	759	1,289	1,217	1,537	1,460	2,049	2,204
26	84	225	233	...	...	43	48	32	38	1,555	1,601
1,085	1,018	1,503	1,507	711	728	692	682	536	560	385	445
139	116	115	116	57	78	33	45	36	36	56	69
1,877	2,094	2,733	3,394	308	310	299	284	202	259	348	344
1,144	1,134	7,979	8,867	1,254	1,393	752	831	1,271	1,345	643	718
6	5	209	251	68	79	84	99	74	74	12	18
3	4	165	309	...	...	...	...	...	...	...	...

DISTRICT

Group.	District Total.			Pirbahor.		Sultanganj.		Alamganj.	
	Total.	Male.	Female.	Male.	Female.	Male.	Female.	Male.	Female.
Religious devotes and persons returned by sect.									
Atith	1,218	472	746	...	...	2	...	6	13
Fakir	1,733	763	970	1	...	5	9	...	...
Gosain	3,438	1,682	1,756	7	12	...	...	7	5
Hindus returned by actual occupation.									
Machhua	1,269	562	707	238	290	3	3	40	60
Mala	15,633	7.654	7,979	65	95	31	88	118	142
Patua	1,436	658	778	2	6	41	51	12	16
Hindus returned by unidentifiable caste.									
Barnasankar	1,318	598	720	15	9	8	13	5	9
Musalmans returned by title.									
Moghul	1,573	796	777	8	13	6	6	27	33
Pathan	12,392	5,958	6,434	274	297	179	160	388	436
Sayyid	14,297	6,941	7,356	485	495	116	106	169	213
Shaikh	67,862	38,556	29,306	1,954	1,231	1,279	1,050	1,480	1,264
Musalmans returned by actual occupation.									
Churihar	1,169	546	623	...	...	...	...	9	7
Darzi	1,338	632	706	15	18	13	9	19	22
Dhunia	5,549	2,527	3,022	49	34	44	57	48	32
Hajjam	2,050	958	1,092	10	10	7	11	6	...
Jolaha	38,293	17,241	21,052	159	207	319	472	461	527
Kalal	1,063	497	566	1	1	23	29	67	55
Kunjra	7,491	3,613	3,878	...	...	64	63	29	13
Pasi	2,177	1,059	1,118	...	...	...	...	...	...
Sayin	2,465	1,101	1,364	2	1	...	...	5	4

DISTRICT

Group.	Dinapur.		Maner.		Barh.		Fatuha.	
	Male.	Female.	Male.	Female.	Male.	Female.	Male.	Female.
Religious devotees and persons returned by sect.								
Atith	26	56	129	354	1	...	6	3
Fakir	...	...	53	47	86	80	78	62
Gosain	7	6	...	...	283	306	76	65
Hindus returned by actual occupation.								
Machhua	178	233	3	6	...	...	14	33
Mala	101	250	424	486	1,080	1,061	344	411
Patua	4	13	9	6	5	3	344	420
Hindus returned by unidentifiable caste.								
Barnasankar	85	58	15	30	66	72	19	35
Musalmans returned by title.								
Moghul	28	32	1	...	28	29	1	...
Pathan	631	658	178	225	430	550	121	165
Sayyid	214	223	176	275	385	479	215	266
Shaikh	3,137	2,676	1,756	1,234	2,609	1,464	1,247	1,424
Musalmans returned by actual occupation.								
Churihar	7	9	41	45	1	...	46	50
Darzi	75	61	15	12	34	40	28	22
Dhunia	80	114	132	206	275	327	147	221
Hajjam	23	33	...	...	26	137	5	2
Jolaha	1,016	1,318	1,393	1,696	1,569	1,970	266	36
Kalal	35	40	61	60	37	22	...	...
Kunjra	76	88	96	121	402	744	184	288
Pasi	...	...	1,058	1,117	...	...	...	...
Sayin	42	81	83	44	91	108	57	55

PATNA—*continued.*

Khwaja Kalan.		Chauk Kalan.		Malsalami.		Bankipur.		Bikram.		Masaudhi Bazurg.	
Male.	Female.	Male.	Female.	Male.	Female.	Male.	Female.	Male.	Female.	Male.	Female.
...	...	16	7	3	4	53	24	99	88	115	190
1	1	...	...	...	...	8	5	...	...	6	3
13	35	...	...	...	...	17	18	276	295	49	63
27	27	28	18	15	16	12	16	4	5	...	...
254	347	188	99	89	154	475	427	668	604	620	604
30	30	...	...	...	...	...	...	9	14	14	18
20	23	85	98	8	15	11	26	70	88	19	39
178	114	26	25	70	88	3	6	16	21	115	124
751	850	274	287	63	55	270	300	294	345	117	99
1,153	1,147	244	190	88	94	464	339	242	258	280	366
3,657	2,203	1,781	1,259	867	827	2,519	1,335	793	883	1,665	1,590
62	54	38	41	8	4	73	74	118	145	86	114
3	1	22	25	7	6	8	13	77	118	26	31
91	91	20	16	44	56	154	207	246	295	172	124
1	6	...	...	...	...	26	21	16	28	22	18
1,105	13,53	...	...	163	216	942	1,370	2,666	2,941	2,858	3,733
9	14	20	25	...	...	...	...	119	155	108	150
35	44	15	6	10	17	47	59	195	198	34	20
1	1	...	...	...	...	...	...	...	...	...	...
...	...	...	...	...	...	55	53	412	572	57	59

PATNA—*concluded.*

Mukameh.		Bihar.		Hilsa.		Chandi.		Islampur or Athasarai.		Silao.	
Male.	Female.	Male.	Female.	Male.	Female.	Male.	Female.	Male.	Female.	Male.	Female.
...	...	10	7	...	...	6	...	...	...	...	...
160	222	233	399	...	...	...	...	3	...	129	148
50	53	400	360	146	151	88	95	180	196	83	96
...	...	...	...	...	...	...	...	...	...	...	...
1,008	1,041	503	505	402	383	567	549	217	216	510	517
...	...	3	3	8	9	...	...	43	83	134	156
45	56	66	78	5	9	18	85	28	25	10	4
...	...	258	260	...	...	1	...	26	18	4	8
175	135	1,059	1,059	164	200	181	212	218	237	187	164
274	816	1,490	1,582	411	408	128	120	239	233	168	142
1,522	845	6,186	5,311	924	1,009	1,421	1,157	2,397	1,584	862	961
...	...	45	50	...	...	12	16	...	...	10	14
10	9	139	172	55	57	63	45	11	17	27	21
113	122	306	449	197	224	157	151	41	46	211	250
...	...	5	6	811	820	...	...	...	...	...	...
354	413	1,868	1,977	638	806	543	628	107	250	820	800
8	8	...	...	...	...	...	...	9	12	...	...
...	...	1,914	1,824	...	...	149	137	...	...	273	256
...	...	...	...	...	...	...	...	...	...	...	...
30	36	1	7	240	264	...	...	38	83	38	47

Caste or Group.	District Total.			Gaya Town.		Mufassal Gaya.		Atri.		Tikari.		Sherghati.	
	Total.	Male.	Female.	Male.	Female.	Male.	Female.	Male.	Female.	Male.	Female.	Male.	Female.
Agarwala	3,243	1,449	1,794	286	269	80	96	...	...	366	473	58	47
Babhan	165,578	84,128	81,450	841	212	3,142	2,949	6,283	6,176	11,249	10,963	2,577	2,725
Baniya	45,547	22,102	23,445	2,682	2,481	1,552	1,604	1,036	961	1,449	1,567	1,428	1,883
(i) Adrakhi	5,494	3,033	2,461	...	...	167	9	...	...	...	...	...	...
(ii) Barnawar	3,071	1,497	1,574	72	27	378	450	...	...	...	...	...	...
(iii) Kasarwani	3,175	1,658	1,517	261	223	...	...	95	98	245	259	83	128
(iv) Mahuri	11,921	5,680	6,241	535	422	564	680	628	550	517	535	114	111
(v) Nichondia	3,257	1,416	1,841	...	...	137	179	...	...	152	178	773	1,042
(vi) Raunlar	9,134	4,385	4,749	1,687	1,696	114	107	222	209	360	414	315	407
(vii) Sinduria	1,968	938	1,030	99	82	69	62	...	...	86	69	104	140
Barhi	37,289	18,166	19,123	447	427	1,906	2,225	874	900	1,864	1,986	1,419	1,601
Bari	2,751	1,345	1,406	112	110	13	21	24	25	63	50	...	...
Barui	5,121	2,463	2,658	258	269	21	33	...	...	138	150	148	120
Beldar	17,181	8,742	8,439	54	113	672	634	619	556	697	721	291	303
Bhat	5,468	2,625	2,843	72	69	145	186	109	111	588	509	134	150
Bhuiya	91,110	44,460	46,650	839	853	9,007	9,905	3,535	3,596	3,556	3,471	14,251	15,675
Brahman	73,503	36,721	36,782	3,037	1,862	1,951	1,700	1,359	1,381	3,470	3,105	1,579	1,639
Chamar	84,015	40,371	43,644	617	464	3,248	3,454	2,952	3,193	3,274	3,470	3,304	3,469
Dhanuk	2,949	1,412	1,537	...	...	...	...	...	...	...	...	...	...
Dhopa	18,444	9,130	9,314	401	414	518	569	310	310	980	979	846	816
Dom	7,429	3,708	3,721	356	386	187	163	95	90	134	154	232	219
Dusadh	110,192	54,747	55,445	571	564	4,876	4,805	3,152	3,456	6,144	6,225	4,813	5,126
Gareri	14,607	7,075	7,532	138	145	757	780	144	146	353	351	221	268
Goala	323,294	161,834	161,460	1,524	1,285	16,054	15,868	9,444	8,864	14,925	14,349	11,624	11,770
Hajjam	35,135	16,976	18,159	968	998	1,399	1,669	861	897	1,420	1,576	1,119	1,110
Halwai	13,559	6,790	6,769	705	741	547	531	173	151	988	1,158	657	733
Hari and Mihtar	1,474	702	772	116	145	19	38	43	56	27	38	49	62
Jugi	2,828	1,237	1,591	69	85	63	87	80	74	175	245	56	68
Kahar	125,770	59,767	66,003	3,710	4,505	3,616	4,623	2,201	3,013	5,214	6,009	2,315	2,933
Kalwar and Sunri	9,136	4,254	4,882	183	180	50	54	88	112	77	100	152	176
Kandu	22,088	10,628	11,460	749	527	336	357	357	375	1,021	990	383	402
Kasera	4,751	2,299	2,452	146	131	594	595	63	54	114	189	...	...
Kayastha	44,212	21,246	22,966	2,560	1,648	1,396	1,429	850	971	1,789	2,027	1,242	1,529
Koiri	149,351	76,179	73,172	949	783	7,018	6,643	7,741	7,538	9,903	9,522	6,331	6,338
Kumhar	25,995	12,911	13,084	752	894	839	845	503	518	1,136	1,067	960	1,109
Kurmi	44,261	21,862	22,390	1,338	1,734	541	594	338	384	932	965	468	606
Lohar and Kamar	18,299	8,981	9,318	155	171	657	768	346	333	780	804	817	860
Malakar	6,160	3,080	3,080	247	233	102	114	170	145	341	294	156	168
Musahar	58,280	29,057	29,223	...	...	14	7	3,266	3,530	432	459	496	519
Nat	1,216	544	672	26	29	16	27	22	36	47	53	12	15
Nuniya	16,323	8,078	8,245	242	210	116	121	416	359	554	554	88	73
Pasi	39,867	19,812	20,055	482	519	2,136	2,053	1,912	1,672	1,420	1,552	1,207	1,283
Rajput	113,234	56,612	56,622	926	546	7,136	6,899	2,987	3,091	3,831	3,880	2,575	2,494
Rajwar	42,269	20,293	21,976	73	175	457	463	1,059	967	...	...	...	...
Sonar	17,266	8,427	8,839	961	960	394	413	392	472	658	670	381	388
Tambuli	5,482	2,776	2,706	55	21	164	106	58	65	163	178	94	132
Tatwa and Tanti	5,545	2,691	2,854	649	714	264	259	100	97	57	68	197	213
Teli	59,246	28,834	30,412	1,579	1,908	1,891	1,883	1,225	1,136	2,191	2,292	1,801	1,863
Thathera	2,175	967	1,208	77	85	29	49	83	73	107	218	93	108
Turi	1,131	519	612	...	...	...	...	...	...	...	...	...	...
Religious devotees and persons returned by sect.													
Atith	1,228	613	615	...	...	...	...	...	...	...	...	...	...
Baisnab	1,850	1,003	847	...	...	...	...	...	...	...	...	...	...
Gosain	2,561	1,423	1,138	119	100	154	145	218	207	319	234	93	46

GAYA.

Barachati.		Nawada.		Pakribarawan.		Rajauli.		Jahanabad.		Arwal.		Aurangabad.		Daudnagar.		Nabinagar.	
Male.	Female.	Male.	Female.	Male.	Female.	Male.	Female.	Male.	Female.	Male.	Female.	Male.	Female.	Male.	Female.	Male.	Female.
...	...	95	139	...	...	56	84	44	102	...	...	210	320	79	93	175	171
1,446	1,269	19,322	18,998	3,243	3,002	822	718	19,546	19,233	6,650	6,630	3,890	3,497	4,171	4,288	946	790
1,327	1,359	4,190	4,445	716	715	656	654	2,113	1,977	981	1,004	1,470	1,870	1,228	1,550	1,274	1,455
450	428	2,099	1,736	...	...	317	288	...	...	...	...	...	...	...	...	...	...
293	274	...	...	484	483	...	...	68	61	...	...	...	...	202	279	...	...
180	105	52	66	...	...	...	...	539	460	203	178	...	...	...	...	...	...
221	260	1,751	2,292	79	83	295	317	870	845	2	1	100	139	2	1	2	5
...	...	...	...	...	...	...	...	...	...	...	...	224	278	130	164	...	...
63	37	18	29	153	149	18	31	226	190	256	277	28	37	843	1,080	84	86
79	109	102	67	...	...	...	...	149	155	...	...	126	188	51	26	73	132
1,075	1,078	1,859	1,918	612	580	610	541	2,222	2,256	1,160	1,141	1,939	2,264	1,230	1,261	940	942
...	...	...	...	...	...	...	...	738	580	...	...	188	192	107	324	100	95
...	...	...	...	656	772	...	...	106	118	64	63	994	1,050	78	83	...	...
234	213	2,502	2,373	567	486	255	256	2,118	2,033	269	269	351	398	52	27	41	37
80	95	175	308	56	53	105	96	291	303	319	364	484	526	1	...	66	73
4,546	5,980	...	...	...	...	...	...	3,742	2,101	...	...	4,132	4,204	...	...	853	865
863	991	4,913	5,103	665	661	700	770	5,181	5,831	2,025	2,067	5,297	6,143	2,700	2,168	2,891	3,351
1,289	2,036	3,260	3,729	1,121	1,123	1,284	1,407	5,512	5,758	2,329	2,437	6,078	7,074	2,427	2,646	2,976	3,384
...	...	797	791	480	587	...	...	135	159	...	...	...	...	...	...	...	...
297	286	1,066	1,099	288	294	202	201	1,047	1,056	724	668	1,200	1,347	610	644	641	651
46	50	991	915	279	305	21	35	414	418	141	184	470	460	169	137	221	205
2,265	2,381	2,968	2,728	1,762	1,679	720	707	7,450	6,872	3,748	3,911	7,717	8,494	3,536	3,138	4,935	5,359
134	159	392	332	112	155	51	54	1,118	1,106	651	538	1,897	2,139	61	66	1,056	1,237
15,714	15,369	18,533	18,074	6,280	6,156	8,291	8,162	21,576	22,641	7,367	7,241	18,789	20,239	7,887	7,721	3,826	3,721
848	1,048	1,773	1,749	755	802	642	767	2,271	2,201	961	1,063	1,869	2,099	1,158	1,157	932	1,023
161	175	473	502	90	138	37	30	585	441	367	410	842	847	936	636	229	276
38	43	25	33	28	23	11	13	59	59	10	13	198	169	9	12	70	79
63	58	222	318	27	39	50	54	200	280	45	59	91	147	70	37	36	40
1,568	2,229	7,237	8,475	1,912	2,177	897	1,194	10,728	10,142	5,148	5,491	7,552	8,504	3,327	2,571	4,342	4,137
77	106	231	327	150	73	75	112	194	112	589	602	1,351	1,641	444	526	593	761
179	195	1,037	1,072	330	324	126	174	1,415	1,496	1,334	1,419	1,488	1,647	1,179	1,482	694	700
230	120	...	...	...	...	...	...	631	820	156	130	104	35	209	302	52	76
797	821	3,050	3,606	552	531	560	589	3,188	3,535	814	917	2,462	3,042	1,082	1,091	964	1,230
2,429	2,398	10,401	9,764	2,448	2,378	1,595	1,512	15,163	14,254	410	551	5,730	5,857	3,351	3,065	2,650	2,569
697	610	1,533	1,415	584	543	413	423	1,769	1,747	918	896	1,569	1,704	606	697	602	625
184	209	2,727	2,786	1,112	970	344	387	5,544	5,429	3,905	3,745	1,636	1,722	2,164	2,353	568	565
407	403	714	780	172	131	261	264	1,000	1,252	556	568	1,530	1,646	897	644	689	694
88	107	450	491	51	50	4	6	530	466	196	200	406	484	170	151	175	171
...	...	11,008	10,871	6,305	6,177	3,045	3,135	3,970	4,012	521	513	...	...	...	...	...	...
11	8	11	9	...	...	...	...	181	205	22	32	138	195	16	17	42	46
667	762	1,455	1,348	612	713	274	248	1,331	1,873	128	145	1,067	944	188	13	880	892
1,020	1,010	3,974	4,235	548	526	1,046	1,037	2,030	2,033	778	752	1,904	1,783	802	1,058	553	542
1,175	987	1,978	1,563	607	567	1,140	1,072	3,786	3,837	1,519	1,421	15,626	16,094	1,811	2,572	11,526	11,599
987	998	9,727	10,656	518	605	4,676	5,120	...	...	1,027	997	659	591	690	981	430	493
193	232	1,258	1,245	527	497	280	834	1,410	1,272	275	276	800	1,033	480	512	469	535
35	9	1,108	1,106	25	10	31	13	520	320	153	160	143	203	36	49	191	235
21	20	774	834	12	13	234	210	213	256	51	60	15	16	66	52	38	43
1,165	1,381	4,076	4,698	1,283	1,382	1,355	1,470	4,225	4,270	1,675	1,703	3,152	3,475	1,746	1,337	1,470	1,614
20	41	52	50	21	38	35	57	154	157	29	37	172	186	39	57	41	52
147	168	124	156	...	...	173	204	51	52	...	...	...	...	24	32	...	...
...	...	...	...	...	...	...	...	82	62	162	233	87	109	123	132	159	79
...	...	319	195	60	47	63	54	51	37	65	81	265	335	119	37	61	61
29	39	50	55	90	99	75	70	25	30	...	...	181	113	...	...	...	...

DISTRICT

Group.	District Total.			Gaya Town.		Mufassal Gaya.		Atri.		Tikari.		Sherghati.	
	Total.	Male.	Female.	Male.	Female.	Male.	Female.	Male.	Female.	Male.	Female.	Male.	Female.
Hindus returned by title or common sub-caste.													
Banpar	6,082	2,985	3,097	781	782	...	...	148	174	...	...	368	386
Hindus returned by actual occupation.													
Ghatwal	5,091	2,483	2,608	...	...	3	4	...	...	...	...	...	...
Mala	10,246	4,749	5,497	169	187	84	73	167	179	583	542	629	646
Patua	3,128	1,623	1,505	687	738	38	49	21	12	114	114	71	67
Musalmans returned by title.													
Pathan	29,491	13,713	15,778	1,403	1,307	887	1,061	1,335	1,215	462	597	2,383	3,555
Sayyid	13,076	5,927	7,149	1,001	906	396	432	267	296	525	718	441	547
Shaikh	153,611	66,799	86,812	5,352	6,030	5,468	6,919	2,759	2,793	7,918	9,916	6,979	8,936
Musalmans returned by actual occupation.													
Jolaha	11,535	4,861	6,674	300	354	804	1,051	522	756	...	...	94	115
Kalal	2,202	973	1,229	225	203	25	39	76	105	...	...	...	...

DISTRICT

Caste.	District Total.			Arrah.		Belauti.		Piru.		Baxar.	
	Total.	Male.	Female.	Male.	Female.	Male.	Female.	Male.	Female.	Male.	Female.
Agarwala	1,466	599	867	187	164	83	96	...	...	1	...
Agrahari	2,035	1,073	962	...	...	...	...	1	...	29	31
Babhan	90,397	52,304	38,093	7,755	7,909	9,708	5,717	8,135	8,100	3,411	2,470
Baniya	23,120	11,317	11,803	1,257	1,428	1,011	1,254	1,092	1,225	1,497	1,200
(i) Kasarwani	11,546	5,518	6,028	1,165	1,335	581	658	336	345	993	1,056
(ii) Kasojan	1,003	469	534	14	18	8	10	9	13	15	20
(iii) Khatri	1,361	668	693	15	13	...	...	15	8	...	...
(iv) Raunlar	8,643	4,322	4,321	63	62	422	586	732	859	489	124
Barhi	12,984	6,290	6,694	1,023	1,835	...	...	1,259	1,356	292	360
Bari	7,174	3,375	3,799	340	379	222	261	235	368	212	230
Barui	5,855	2,636	3,219	63	34	...	...	...	...	292	360
Bhar	11,608	6,075	5,533	9	6	195	257	256	223	1,509	1,591
Bhat	5,774	2,855	2,919	31	23	...	...	...	...	101	122
Bind	20,583	9,248	11,335	1,676	3,197	534	833	322	320	475	565
Brahman	210,413	98,928	111,485	12,173	18,434	9,874	12,577	6,062	7,408	12,536	12,083
Chamar	105,311	47,375	57,936	4,863	4,641	3,443	3,933	5,346	6,280	5,692	7,164
Dhanuk	1,704	810	894	442	488	345	395	...	...	12	3
Dhopa	17,924	8,042	9,882	812	953	798	927	817	863	485	515
Dom	7,595	3,741	3,854	68	65	127	115	198	226	476	351
Dusadh	85,058	40,696	44,362	6,423	7,303	3,414	4,408	4,459	5,138	2,324	3,047
Gareri	22,174	10,382	11,792	830	1,054	565	742	1,120	1,206	1,022	1,372
Goala	273,037	131,205	141,832	27,154	24,830	289	297	16,866	16,936	9,325	9,581
Gonrhi	12,540	5,891	6,649	432	501	815	921	558	641	105	147
Hajjam	29,194	14,073	15,121	2,524	2,999	1,259	1,479	2,000	2,051	1,316	1,693

GAYA—*concluded.*

Barachati.		Nawada.		Pakribarawan.		Rajauli.		Jahanabad.		Arwal.		Aurangabad.		Daudnagar.		Nabinagar.	
Male.	Female.	Male.	Female.	Male.	Female.	Male.	Female.	Male.	Female.	Male.	Female.	Male.	Female.	Male.	Female.	Male.	Female.
193	174	919	991	...	...	494	494	...	...	...	...	82	96	...	...	...	...
113	140	368	106	937	1,041	1,073	1,317	...	...	...	...	...	...	...	...	...	...
31	30	212	211	89	84	27	25	687	746	642	893	796	992	464	642	169	257
67	15	156	171	56	27	62	31	39	25	58	31	50	29	39	25	165	171
585	963	1,722	2,040	617	604	417	616	631	537	381	326	1,393	1,161	931	1,448	296	349
88	73	498	612	81	76	73	83	1,086	1,475	298	372	921	1,217	137	119	116	173
1,368	2,658	6,580	9,004	2,791	3,210	2,465	3,212	7,435	9,226	3,486	4,300	9,302	14,772	1,883	2,105	3,113	3,731
334	470	1,230	1,668	145	131	...	...	216	277	...	...	730	1,252	486	600	...	...
96	125	303	404	3	7	2	12	173	225	5	6	8	35	55	63	2	5

SHAHABAD.

Dumraon.		Sasaram.		Kharghar.		Dhangain.		Dehri.		Bhabhua.		Mohania.	
Male.	Female.	Male.	Female.	Male.	Female.	Male.	Female.	Male.	Female.	Male.	Female.	Male.	Female.
...	...	94	353	3	2	...	...	...	...	119	172	112	80
...	5	75	92	41	36	55	46	39	41	225	232	608	479
2,434	1,806	5,316	2,105	4,191	2,949	670	740	3,894	1,046	3,340	2,567	3,460	2,684
879	962	746	765	913	1,028	1,645	1,528	294	197	1,262	1,387	721	831
763	816	224	282	201	214	...	...	210	135	650	784	395	403
24	29	10	15	11	17	20	25	18	11	239	261	101	115
2	6	512	468	8	7	11	3	8	5	97	183	...	...
90	111	...	...	693	790	1,274	1,271	58	46	276	159	225	313
156	165	1,192	1,115	56	75	1,116	1,229	532	528	...	...	64	31
73	110	396	486	110	149	616	408	198	255	555	686	418	377
772	1,007	212	374	164	186	444	376	31	46	461	497	197	339
3,149	2,008	233	230	7	...	439	29	...	...	33	13	1,245	1,146
165	177	881	878	...	...	329	376	...	...	510	677	888	666
715	958	1,141	939	...	...	...	...	242	672	2,517	2,327	1,626	1,535
13,135	20,263	6,097	5,370	6,600	7,174	6,818	6,915	2,808	2,632	7,437	3,272	9,738	10,367
4,563	6,256	3,446	3,335	3,644	4,524	1,470	1,982	3,973	4,855	5,782	9,481	5,153	5,485
...	...	3	3	...	...	8	5	...	...	...	...	...	...
1,075	2,150	968	1,182	483	503	829	675	248	259	783	972	744	883
197	199	671	656	139	137	578	966	256	83	565	613	471	443
5,060	5,818	4,348	4,257	2,676	2,890	4,523	5,300	2,249	2,390	2,755	1,037	2,465	2,712
464	590	30	44	1,232	1,298	1,556	1,352	368	762	997	1,111	2,198	2,261
35,071	39,372	1,818	1,187	3,958	3,884	14,476	16,537	7,341	7,777	14,963	11,472	9,046	9,959
1,358	1,507	38	25	67	73	...	...	410	228	1,362	2,368	246	238
2,414	1,963	997	1,064	782	807	204	212	356	354	1,240	1,392	981	1.057

Caste or Group.	District Total.			Arrah.		Belauti.		Piru.		Baxar.	
	Total.	Male.	Female.	Male.	Female.	Male.	Female.	Male.	Female.	Male.	Female.
Hari and Mihtar	3,570	1,574	1,996	229	269	135	151	160	138	147	181
Jugi	2,160	997	1,163	156	211	87	113	113	133	...	...
Kahar	61.089	29,064	32,025	3,893	4,853	1,578	1,908	2,834	2,951	589	385
Kalwar and Sunri	39,152	18,170	20,982	957	649	691	885	5,651	6,188	1,059	1,281
Kandu	63,967	30,939	33,028	6,417	7,199	4,263	3,964	2,998	3,098	2,505	3,025
Kayastha	51,297	24,260	27,037	4,552	4,749	1,761	2,300	2,586	3,470	2,423	2,523
Kharwar	7,464	3,854	3,610	15	...	...	...	56	40	...	...
Koiri	147,096	71,597	75,499	8,541	9,033	12,501	12,701	6,655	6,924	7,971	8,655
Kumhar	24,798	11,595	13,203	1,038	1,034	1,079	1,511	1,088	1,527	933	968
Kurmi	59,039	28,778	30,261	2,006	2,377	2,469	2,744	2,236	2,327	1,293	1,320
Lohar	28,463	14,125	14,333	1,489	1,380	1,815	1,886	1,051	938	1,435	1,500
Malakar	5,573	2,551	3,022	516	579	337	819	173	319	75	65
Musahar	16,909	8,625	8,284	2,318	2,294	1,168	1,163	1,352	1,195	493	601
Nat	2,455	1,114	1,341	93	155	15	19	169	150	39	45
Nuniya	22,474	10,908	11,566	434	396	857	893	693	430	1,047	1,109
Pasi	11,230	5,650	5,580	924	857	338	363	687	671	156	200
Rajput	280,963	138,724	142,239	34,995	34,849	10,814	11,462	10,177	11,051	7,856	8,771
Rajwar	7,187	3,439	3,748	...	...	...	...	935	1,005	...	...
Sonar	20,797	10,116	10,681	3,022	3,467	1,061	1,166	770	812	637	644
Tambuli	5,589	2,679	2,910	911	1,077	575	571	44	48	53	64
Tatwa and Tanti	9,087	4,144	4,943	659	800	516	464	950	1,340	33	20
Teli	47,444	21,095	26,349	3,582	4,162	2,137	2,683	2,376	2,940	1,896	2,333
Thathera	2,099	1,174	925	...	...	...	...	66	21	65	18
Turaha	4,239	1,998	2,241	...	...	652	852	164	153	112	122
Religious devotees and persons returned by sect.											
Atith	7,141	3,405	3,736	253	340	318	386	549	593	208	158
Hindus returned by title or common sub-caste.											
Buna	1,230	616	614	...	...	...	...	...	...	...	...
Hindus returned by actual occupation.											
Kamkar	10,023	4,543	5,480	...	...	1,539	2,107	63	75	1,396	1,599
Mala	15,194	5,916	9,278	764	1,327	284	585	430	587	744	1,290
Patua	1,967	799	1,168	43	80	66	95	59	54	10	9
Musalmans returned by title.											
Pathan	21,310	9,668	11,642	603	761	854	1,340	956	1,027	707	621
Soyyid	6,222	3,050	3,172	469	410	179	281	344	267	366	315
Shaikh	30,766	13,694	17,072	4,586	5,442	2,090	2,538	364	452	764	946
Musalmans returned by actual occupation.											
Bhat	1,513	743	770	29	45	...	...	...	...	99	112
Bhathiara	1,060	450	610	59	103	...	...	...	...	...	...
Churihar	2,968	1,417	1,551	119	145	38	28	218	237	104	167
Dafali	1,761	855	906	92	115	20	26	37	64	103	113
Darzi	4,619	2,301	2,318	324	345	236	253	113	118	127	150
Dhopa	1,186	589	597	...	...	...	...	...	...	140	139
Dhunia	9,615	4,265	5,350	698	907	254	331	605	592	199	416
Hajjam	3,533	1,694	1,839	33	47	...	2	56	54	171	183
Jolaha	47,073	2,1082	25,991	3,400	4,692	877	1,028	1,963	2,446	1,267	2,560
Kasai	1,145	512	633	5	4	34	39	82	107	5	...
Kunjra	3,305	1,581	1,724	480	409	...	...	64	39	100	123
Pawaria	1,531	750	781	81	98	15	21	41	51	39	45
Bangres	1,825	846	979	54	67	99	97	189	210	63	84

SHAHABAD—*concluded.*

Dumraon.		Sasaram.		Kharghar.		Dhangain.		Dehri.		Bhabhua.		Mohania.	
Male.	Female.	Male.	Female.	Male.	Female.	Male.	Female.	Male.	Female.	Male.	Female.	Male.	Female.
63	83	319	543	23	33	35	38	49	65	159	175	256	301
6	2	41	47	...	...	128	140	...	...	138	139	328	378
3,461	3,900	3,497	3,776	2,601	2,490	3,652	4,543	1,809	1,782	2,761	2,826	2,399	2,611
1,455	2,962	209	288	156	178	475	570	44	73	2,845	3,584	8,628	4,324
4,271	4,783	1,525	1,684	1,791	1,749	2,938	3,041	1,572	1,468	1,058	981	1,601	2,036
2,307	2,986	2,610	3,216	933	1,012	1,842	2,253	1,178	728	2,165	2,287	1,413	1,513
...	...	378	321	...	...	...	...	1	2	3,404	3,247	...	...
3,897	3,469	2,848	3,862	4,202	3,891	7,117	10,294	5,149	4,998	3,456	2,285	4,260	4,387
756	781	...	...	56	57	3,850	4,096	343	340	1,294	1,646	1,158	1,243
4,331	4,905	2,803	1,958	6,273	6,856	3,850	4,096	469	348	2,045	2,177	1,104	1,153
1,600	1,774	846	897	920	866	1,475	1,294	513	456	1,503	1,912	1,478	1,435
154	137	223	243	116	128	180	188	126	251	337	338	314	465
758	878	649	485	80	104	556	209	126	151	561	560	564	644
5	6	103	117	60	85	95	113	14	27	413	391	108	233
354	1,065	1,285	1,411	1,344	1,414	1,760	1,805	492	481	1,167	1,273	975	1,289
355	257	1,107	1,268	116	128	701	446	383	398	893	992	...	...
15,368	17,067	10,291	11,588	5,575	5,743	9,947	10,908	5,404	4,516	13,725	11,950	14,672	14,334
307	225	1,035	1,222	223	211	605	737	384	348	...	...	...	...
1,388	1,337	504	741	327	364	921	446	309	481	533	563	684	665
35	48	852	823	60	83	40	49	45	67	38	44	26	36
584	667	277	317	505	670	500	560	98	83	22	22	...	...
2,230	3,140	1,514	2,213	1,350	1,364	1,775	2,375	966	1,822	1,595	1,280	1,624	1,087
106	86	30	20	46	27	4	...	665	665	31	31	161	57
901	943	...	...	49	76	120	95	...	...	...	...	...	...
408	621	80	198	213	215	760	635	65	23	265	272	286	295
1	1	444	437	...	...	...	...	11	11	142	161	18	4
1,315	1,434	11	14	15	24	14	30	23	45	...	...	267	152
609	1,423	1,038	1,626	45	33	...	...	698	1,090	508	472	796	845
8	20	243	263	56	84	130	272	54	109	62	82	68	100
983	1,362	1,785	2,417	96	51	1,222	1,343	345	460	1,424	1,500	693	760
196	386	416	548	57	29	182	225	98	132	291	308	352	271
2,615	3,186	1,105	1,646	83	75	784	1,131	526	388	492	47	355	621
161	170	...	...	...	...	...	...	...	...	169	157	235	286
...	...	149	191	...	...	...	...	...	...	66	99	176	217
153	175	282	207	53	82	89	91	19	27	165	170	187	222
41	22	47	89	59	73	...	...	140	24	175	173	141	208
156	96	118	128	244	268	103	113	113	93	374	377	343	377
...	...	108	113	...	...	...	...	79	26	144	173	118	146
417	618	251	320	156	140	534	604	175	190	510	560	466	603
187	303	694	544	184	115	104	212	58	34	257	346	...	...
2,460	2,917	2,436	3,842	1,077	1,248	1,348	1,566	2,074	2,372	1,718	1,063	1,442	1,357
...	...	219	275	8	2	132	133	...	...	27	73	...	...
32	44	108	156	179	177	...	...	45	45	237	207	336	435
283	264	75	92	50	58	56	44	41	26	41	43	59	39
46	89	208	223	43	43	29	40	36	43	57	63	23	20

Caste.	District Total.			Darbhanga.		Bahera.		Rosera.		Madhubani.	
	Total.	Male.	Female.	Male.	Female.	Male.	Female.	Male.	Female.	Male.	Female.
Agarwala	1,116	608	508	425	354	...	...	...	...	96	69
Amat	42,232	20,752	21,480	1,770	1,874	1,420	1,516	2,839	2,797	3,745	3,974
Babhan	143,699	71,417	72,282	9,796	9,668	7,883	7,573	7,528	7,522	7,267	8,236
Baniya	36,160	17,823	18,337	1,344	1,291	3,053	3,189	2,625	2,674	719	747
(i).—Bais	12,195	5,954	6,241	482	322	...	...	1,844	1,911	106	131
(ii).—Barnawar	3,000	1,467	1,533	...	...	368	424	—	...	36	55
(iii).—Jaunpuri	2,264	1,159	1,105	320	300	656	655	...	...	...	...
(iv).—Kath	2,001	968	1,033	133	133	22	24	79	98	153	176
(v).—Khatri	4,260	2,171	2,089	141	186	257	259	270	267	74	45
(vi).—Raunlar	5,714	2,782	2,932	...	...	1,433	1,477	...	...	...	...
(vii).—Sinduria	1,644	815	829	150	145	67	80	75	70	100	90
Bantar	5,492	2,668	2,824	498	515	...	...	1,109	1,241	508	500
Barhi	33,061	15,661	17,400	2,330	2,664	1,976	2,021	1,676	1,870	1,333	1,288
Bari	1,090	515	575	150	155	190	260	...	...	75	55
Barui	17,395	8,554	8,841	2,166	2,167	653	701	177	186	2,581	2,000
Beldar	7,751	3,577	4,174	369	383	227	329	195	225	217	288
Bind	5,031	2,369	2,662	88	59	...	...	...	...	13	22
Brahman	200,194	99,673	100,521	9,599	8,456	19,948	20,023	7,767	7,864	13,844	14,930
Chamar	101,002	47,991	53,011	6,258	6,479	4,725	5,057	3,133	3,254	3,318	3,590
Dhanuk	142,521	67,970	74,551	10,290	10,339	7,365	7,940	6,050	6,098	8,145	9,021
Dhopa	24,657	11,988	12,669	1,835	1,873	1,098	1,159	1,044	967	879	975
Dom	5,316	2,640	2,676	296	300	300	290	244	356	196	224
Dusadh	214,039	105,328	108,711	15,669	15,924	13,954	13,755	9,150	9,290	9,389	96,93
Gareri	10,019	4,877	5,142	866	740	955	1,007	606	452	...	...
Goala	368,612	185,435	183,177	20,726	20,802	20,566	20,868	19,915	16,974	13,184	12,111
Gonrhi	12,988	6,232	6,756	866	740	955	1,007	460	446	787	871
Hajjam	32,017	15,541	16,476	2,277	2,368	1,730	2,103	1,563	1,538	989	934
Halwai	39,736	19,558	20,178	3,419	3,714	3,498	3,541	905	909	1,920	1,904
Hari	3,503	1,676	1,827	488	492	206	233	73	101	249	267
Kahar	6,433	3,085	3,348	419	474	160	142	382	390	271	373
Kalwar and Sunri	42,337	20,985	21,352	4,562	4,009	1,568	1,644	1,815	1,971	2,181	2,404
Kandu	33,511	16,232	17,279	1,231	1,265	669	705	2,553	2,220	393	258
Kayastha	40,681	19,368	21,313	4,947	4,952	2,252	2,749	1,628	1,585	2,135	2,612
Kewat	68,284	32,516	35,768	2,199	3,065	3,782	3,998	2,191	2,117	6,717	7,425
Khatbe	61,880	29,919	31,961	5,676	5,878	2,803	3,078	5,050	5,388	3,216	3,363
Khatik	1,194	561	633	319	379	...	...	...	...	...	...
Koiri	125,701	61,103	64,598	3,082	2,963	1,742	1,709	6,550	6,734	2,165	2,293
Kumhar	34,378	17,024	17,354	1,983	1,971	4,408	4,565	1,377	1,380	883	879
Kurmi	55,325	26,775	28,550	2,291	2,282	1,573	1,603	7,301	7,569	3,030	3,236
Lohar and Kamar	14,517	7,243	7,274	826	855	639	613	826	953	432	417
Malakar	6,538	3,074	3,464	318	620	304	313	274	279	366	388
Musahar	73,531	36,365	37,166	4,255	4,180	6,539	6,653	5,831	6,210	3,686	3,742
Nat	2,041	932	1,109	180	300	43	59	...	...	46	66
Nuniya	28,016	12,656	15,360	3,144	3,425	100	100	915	978	722	871
Pasi	11,407	5,555	5,852	1,647	1,826	528	552	209	210	214	224
Rajput	85,729	45,446	40,283	6,042	4,789	6,673	5,721	5,514	4,508	3,827	3,337
Sonar	15,599	7,865	7,734	1,373	1,388	817	854	667	606	1,016	1,136
Tambuli	4,955	2,437	2,518	303	307	...	...	...	...	461	547
Tatwa and Tanti	72,047	35,201	36,846	5,115	5,638	4,259	4,501	5,932	6,208	1,494	1,607
Teli	81,619	39,627	41,992	6,253	6,447	4,325	4,478	3,490	3,401	2,726	2,863
Thathera	3,275	1,541	1,734	273	316	141	144	194	269	53	62
Turaha	5,939	2,606	3,333	50	83	...	...	77	106	698	685

DARBHANGA.

Benipati.		Khajauli.		Phulparas.		Samastipur.		Maniarpur.		Dalsingsarai.	
Male.	Female.	Male.	Female.	Male.	Female.	Male.	Female.	Male.	Female.	Male.	Female.
...	...	...	...	...	...	87	85	...	...	...	...
2,048	2,131	2,155	2,311	3,662	3,763	154	185	126	132	2,839	2,797
6,835	6,639	-4,881	4,665	3,107	3,126	9,583	9,669	7,117	7,382	7,430	7,802
1,645	1,597	1,554	1,523	1,513	1,402	1,545	1,727	1,891	2,021	1,934	2,166
...	...	109	121	458	433	1,199	1,344	739	824	1,017	1,155
...	...	96	71	408	353	146	141	...	...	413	489
92	79	91	71	...	...	...	...	...	...	...	...
...	...	300	317	...	...	...	...	...	...	281	285
639	477	383	338	...	...	...	...	385	382	122	135
753	788	175	215	...	...	...	...	421	452	...	...
134	133	150	140	...	...	43	58	96	113	...	...
...	...	97	100	60	69	406	400	...	...	...	...
1,773	1,831	...	...	1,354	1,348	2,039	2,631	’910	874	2,270	2,873
100	105	...	...	...	...	...	...	...	...	...	...
568	589	105	105	978	999	229	238	147	157	1,000	1,729
274	315	980	1,139	1,232	1,387	83	110	...	...	...	...
894	889	355	393	...	...	142	183	...	...	883	1,116
12,551	13,200	5,965	5,915	6,455	6,823	13,779	13,672	4,098	4,046	5,672	5,592
3,316	3,554	3,257	4,123	8,239	8,620	6,838	8,500	4,044	4,448	4,183	5,392
6,357	6,798	3,286	3,538	12,915	13,749	3,559	4,027	3,115	3,264	6,888	9,777
939	953	1,136	1,121	1,355	1,394	1,334	1,563	797	853	1,571	1,813
214	196	216	239	308	290	312	321	244	232	310	228
8,899	9,274	8,629	0,119	5,575	5,965	12,743	14,260	7,537	7,033	13,783	13,498
...	...	...	...	...	...	731	1,037	1,221	1,348	408	558
14,601	15,201	19,203	19,656	25,879	25,047	8,212	8,099	18,630	19,866	24,569	24,553
573	500	177	257	250	243	731	1,037	985	1,097	498	558
958	1,045	1,516	1,563	1,535	1,561	1,828	1,983	1,133	1,184	2,016	2,247
2,415	2,617	2,123	2,167	3,725	3,801	302	180	863	918	388	487
94	106	137	145	146	148	219	241	64	74	...	...
250	230	150	175	161	143	461	469	208	223	608	729
1,792	2,012	3,450	3,847	1,464	1,454	547	427	2,328	1,920	1,278	1,604
118	92	327	377	72	72	4,729	5,185	1,573	1,794	4,567	5,291
2,041	2,500	1,128	1,242	1,237	962	1,909	2,391	921	1,131	1,170	1,239
4,800	5,200	4,375	4,520	6,720	7,506	871	965	510	581	351	391
2,921	3,117	2,915	3,044	5,606	6,108	1,006	1,063	228	205	594	717
...	...	...	...	...	...	...	...	205	218	37	36
3,464	3,627	12,805	13,107	5,693	5,659	14,420	15,441	570	278	10,612	10,787
1,809	1,268	1,628	1,642	1,330	1,349	1,798	1;867	794	865	1,514	1,574
877	835	1,958	2,120	1,028	995	4,259	4,836	1,768	2,018	2,695	3,056
729	663	773	771	1,050	1,070	959	938	516	526	403	468
322	319	315	310	261	277	383	403	184	196	347	369
2,375	2,429	2,423	2,401	5,896	0,179	2,308	2,286	1,184	1,163	1,868	1,923
144	148	166	174	223	222	74	95	56	63	...	...
...	...	512	573	2,428	3,283	3,514	2,654	1,250	1,326	1,071	1,150
156	123	94	91	167	184	1,039	1,083	459	499	1,065	1,060
1,717	1,508	4,029	3,507	4,110	3,800	2,629	2,400	3,357	3,186	7,548	7,527
705	742	520	457	960	797	779	646	251	249	777	859
...	...	98	93	...	...	1,160	1,092	260	323	155	157
2,967	3,099	3,474	3,474	2,289	2,398	6,117	6,124	3,554	3,797	...	...
4,327	4,461	3,609	3,717	6,407	6,323	3,629	4,478	2,034	2,131	2,827	3,693
109	115	105	126	68	63	280	295	166	200	152	144
...	...	93	23	...	...	589	854	383	460	716	1,112

DISTRICT

Group.	District Total.			Darbhanga.		Bahera.		Roshra.		Madhubani.	
	Total.	Male.	Female.	Male.	Female.	Male.	Female.	Male.	Female.	Male.	Female.
Religious devotees and persons returned by sect.											
Fakir	1,492	706	716	427	415	...	...	...	...	100	93
Sanyasi	7,542	3,557	3,985	381	369	130	129	337	350	375	356
Hindus returned by actual occupation.											
Laheri	2,926	1,441	1,485	11	...	170	151	91	73	300	316
Mala	115,836	54,713	61,123	10,523	11,619	9,724	10,353	6,616	6,998	3,865	4,112
Patua	3,722	1,765	1,957	411	403	1,195	1,386	...	...	21	36
Musalmans returned by sect.											
Sunni	1,636	808	828	...	...	...	...	...	...	313	317
Musalmans returned by title.											
Moghul	1,293	747	546	299	388	148	158	75	...	125	...
Pathan	13,819	6,802	7,017	2,536	2,640	1,681	1,776	380	369	295	363
Sayyid	9,020	5,410	3,610	2,317	1,466	121	96	530	579	257	238
Shaikh	148,494	69,601	78,893	23,912	27,882	10,842	11,518	2,338	2,869	5,538	5,839
Musalmans returned by actual occupation.											
Chamar	2,646	1,181	1,465	9	1	...	...	...	...	...	...
Dafali	1,019	593	426	50	14	42	30	48	43	90	77
Darzi	6,083	3,096	2,987	342	309	1,564	1,526	148	171	350	337
Dhopa	3,656	1,759	1,897	84	70	100	75	161	160	89	75
Dhunia	38,206	18,975	19,231	3,429	3,269	2,224	2,323	1,356	1,400	1,363	1,314
Fakir	6,638	3,224	3,414	578	637	406	443	274	262	445	418
Hajjam	3,589	1,728	1,861	589	629	184	178	161	146	118	109
Jolaha	45,166	22,022	23,144	6,781	7,709	1,423	2,120	121	131	3,972	3,670
Kasai	1,524	728	796	501	536	...	...	...	...	62	40
Kunjra	34,384	16,820	17,564	2,965	2,933	2,851	2,938	785	835	1,874	1,924
Laheri	2,225	1,165	1,060	116	177	162	147	...	...	107	82
Mukeri	1,138	521	617	248	271	...	...	...	...	69	90
Sikalgar	1,070	506	564	174	174	107	155	...	...	79	80

DISTRICT

Caste.	District Total.			Muzaffarpur.		Paru.		Katra.		Sitamarhi.	
	Total.	Male.	Female.	Male.	Famale.	Male.	Female.	Male.	Female.	Male.	Female.
Agrahari	1,618	806	812	114	122	116	132	97	99	86	87
Amat	5,326	2,455	2,871	...	...	...	...	376	439	578	675
Babhan	176,323	87,106	89,217	7,812	7,927	17,769	17,964	7,653	10,083	7,810	7,518
Baniya	21,909	10,717	11,192	885	1,021	540	664	556	642	1,162	1,123
(i)—Kasarwani	1,533	800	733	15	18	27	24	15	8	584	502
(ii)—Kath	2,005	811	1,194	80	77	97	86	65	151	70	69
(iii)—Raunlar	6,735	3,331	3,404	146	138	216	305	146	144	1,096	1,104
Barhi	15,728	7,785	7,943	320	412	416	476	1,141	839	1,331	1,330
Bari	2,069	997	1,072	25	26	83	102	38	40	57	68
Barui	19,672	9,491	10,181	535	646	1,032	1,093	1,071	903	1,475	1,482
Bediya	1,525	683	843	78	95	64	88	103	111	96	107

DARBHANGA—*concluded.*

Benipati.		Khajauli.		Phulparas.		Samastipur.		Maniarpur.		Dalsingsarai.	
Male.	Female.	Male.	Female.	Male.	Female.	Male.	Female.	Male.	Female.	Male.	Female.
...	...	...	...	...	...	179	208	...	...	...	...
188	177	133	157	109	77	1,197	1,590	192	179	515	571
157	145	...	...	62	71	226	270	175	188	249	271
4,043	4,126	2,763	2,727	3,617	3,896	4,850	5,566	5,666	7,264	3,050	4,463
66	72	...	...	72	60	...	...	...	...	...	...
495	511	...	...	...	...	...	...	...	...	...	...
...	...	...	...	...	...	100	...	...	...	...	...
409	412	...	...	287	291	638	602	284	339	202	225
123	116	1,055	52	...	...	450	438	373	388	184	237
8,898	9,626	1,813	1,840	4,641	4,897	6,306	8,050	2,906	3,444	2,315	2,928
788	1,080	384	384	...	...	...	...	...	...	...	...
75	50	92	89	85	...	46	56	...	...	65	67
225	208	156	139	81	77	152	137	78	83	...	...
187	197	200	160	201	204	331	357	206	214	200	305
1,652	1,700	1,647	1,636	2,491	2,610	2,219	2,586	919	983	1,175	1,410
491	504	420	436	330	340	113	164	84	103	74	107
378	447	...	...	134	144	164	208	...	...	...	...
2,726	2,694	1,432	1,026	2,635	2,380	1,662	1,853	525	557	745	1,005
165	220	...	...	...	...	...	...	...	...	...	...
2,180	2,292	1,342	1,336	2,950	3,076	474	642	409	449	990	1,139
196	213	312	250	210	119	...	...	...	...	62	72
73	78	131	178	...	...	...	...	...	...	...	...
146	155	...	...	...	...	...	...	...	...	...	...

MUZAFFARPUR.

Siuhar.		Pupri.		Belsand.		Hajipur.		Lalganj.		Mahua.	
Male.	Female.	Male.	Female.	Male.	Female.	Male.	Female.	Male.	Female.	Male.	Female.
46	35	88	84	56	65	69	61	59	44	75	83
...	...	1,011	1,188	499	569	...	...	...	...	...	...
8,509	9,612	6,745	5,647	6,531	6,582	6,640	6,780	9,987	10,781	7,650	6,323
1,203	2,087	1,634	904	884	929	1,016	1,050	1,620	1,687	1,217	1,085
20	22	10	4	12	16	18	16	30	28	69	95
89	174	96	80	88	166	120	169	36	29	70	193
248	256	225	213	658	699	187	189	135	141	274	215
260	364	1,205	1,394	615	709	456	642	1,080	1,155	961	1,122
15	18	610	631	6	9	24	20	30	36	107	122
486	500	1,431	1,857	1,038	1,040	384	530	661	719	1,378	1,321
76	89	56	65	40	65	69	78	29	35	71	110

Caste or Group.	District Total.			Muzaffarpur.		Paru.		Katra.		Sitamarhi.	
	Total.	Male.	Female.	Male.	Female.	Male.	Female.	Male.	Female.	Male.	Female.
Beldar	4,549	2,381	2,168	185	194	134	204	206	195	389	401
Bhat	2,824	1,339	1,485	94	134	204	162	84	96	53	76
Bind	20,154	10,092	10,062	649	784	829	980	455	273	2,132	2,120
Brahman	98,021	42,537	55,484	5,423	7,228	6,104	7,961	1,255	3,154	2,266	3,754
Chain	1,325	540	785	56	98	32	41	28	36	55	81
Chamar	127,130	60,234	66,896	6,620	7,512	9,790	10,940	3,710	4,179	7,942	6,823
Dhanuk	58,159	28,499	29,660	564	682	792	778	4,371	4,857	6,252	6,524
Dhopa	29,141	14,535	14,606	646	784	1,823	2,030	1,212	1,590	2,726	3,149
Dom	7,486	3,205	4,281	234	328	564	591	138	255	335	424
Dusadh	188,124	94,015	94,109	8,440	8,510	11,349	14,823	8,979	6,879	17,720	11,962
Gareri	10,439	4,872	5,567	85	94	136	186	67	86	94	108
Goala	328,874	164,987	163,887	17,369	21,228	14,625	15,409	24,425	14,854	20,199	19,889
Gonrhi	8,923	4,383	4,540	58	64	78	85	49	56	56	63
Hajjam	43,792	20,730	23,062	856	924	3,023	3,594	1,320	1,558	2,521	2,699
Halwai	10,093	4,989	5,104	88	17	86	94	1,401	1,486	1,008	1,076
Hari and Mihtar	3,385	1,720	1,665	112	103	135	197	147	138	136	125
Jugi	1,568	635	933	34	40	130	190	26	35	195	212
Kahar	25,658	11,473	14,185	...	...	4,212	4,873	1,369	1,614	1,491	1,604
Kalwar and Suuri	73,196	34,920	38,276	1,664	1,780	2,826	2,048	4,443	5,697	14,101	13,664
Kandu	93,412	44,353	49,059	4,644	5,812	6,027	6,931	2,436	2,441	5,040	5,177
Kayastha	48,159	22,911	25,248	2,460	2,940	4,670	5,098	1,399	1,498	2,333	1,437
Kewat	8,091	3,711	4,380	127	104	...	...	491	1,057	1,383	1,446
Khatbe	6,736	3,211	3,525	104	95	56	78	1,433	1,668	970	1,049
Khatik	1,902	828	1,074	64	98	134	198	88	104	78	64
Koiri	121,907	59,494	62,413	3,443	5,690	8,680	10,679	1,949	3,517	15,589	17,501
Kumhar	42,311	19,593	22,718	1,846	2,045	2,747	3,193	1,663	2,268	2,800	2,911
Kurmi	117,568	52,807	64,761	5,322	6,579	7,881	10,353	1,561	1,962	5,894	5,923
Lohar and Kamar	57,917	27,537	30,380	6,128	5,545	2,858	3,758	1,053	1,096	2,393	2,427
Malakar	11,862	5,648	6,214	890	944	717	716	346	541	586	623
Musahar	45,670	22,076	23,594	4,640	4,720	828	942	2,137	2,287	2,060	2,181
Nat	1,404	690	714	45	50	255	225	54	68	36	50
Nuniya	52,888	24,883	28,005	884	940	7,135	7,890	1,859	2,045	2,027	3,278
Pasi	10,936	4,951	5,985	338	350	214	210	804	470	201	199
Rajput	170,571	87,247	83,324	4,560	6,846	17,926	16,030	9,474	9,414	10,371	6,663
Sonar	24,284	11,124	13,160	1,094	1,344	1,118	1,236	521	578	1,953	2,034
Tambuli	3,008	1,472	1,536	156	169	163	184	102	111	188	104
Tatwa and Tanti	51,760	26,049	25,711	3,560	3,340	3,381	4,029	1,952	1,502	3,666	3,551
Teli	79,115	35,219	43,896	4,335	5,612	4,446	4,816	261	2,702	7,618	7,613
Thathera	1,694	875	819	73	84	254	97	56	59	212	220
Turaha	13,110	6,183	6,927	826	1,036	695	798	886	853	183	188
Religious devotees and persons returned by sect.											
Atith	3,226	1,381	1,845	145	140	372	404	60	99	96	84
Sanyasi	4,270	2,109	2,161	284	309	85	61	64	73	238	200
Hindus returned by title or common sub-caste.											
Banaudhia	1,639	795	844	46	63	101	187	60	50	93	105
Hindus returned by actual occupation.											
Kabari	10,884	5,299	5,585	69	84	2,239	2,308	1,268	1,156	167	150
Laheri	8,773	4,153	4,620	646	685	564	589	121	136	117	196
Mala	83,216	40,452	42,764	5,486	5,794	5,590	6,832	4,868	4,734	1,818	1,966
Hindus returned by locality.											
Marwaris	3,212	1,590	1,622	145	164	204	177	184	246	118	144

MUZAFFARPUR—*continued.*

Siuhar.		Pupri.		Belsand.		Hajipur.		Lalganj.		Mahua.	
Male.	Female.	Male.	Female.	Male.	Female.	Male.	Female.	Male.	Female.	Male.	Female.
226	274	195	234	481	47	336	367	85	76	94	176
235	198	209	292	67	85	54	96	159	186	130	160
346	389	2,695	2,268	653	643	536	684	956	980	841	941
7,238	8,844	2,079	2,457	3,594	3,565	7,324	8,450	2,668	4,231	4,586	5,840
72	90	63	88	91	90	35	69	20	44	88	148
6,759	9,292	3,247	3,655	4,509	4,125	4,150	6,637	3,838	4,441	9,669	9,292
780	940	5,343	5,483	4,478	4,896	720	854	146	174	5,053	4,472
434	694	759	961	1,976	2,039	596	684	972	1,540	3,401	2,135
386	518	189	270	294	302	444	570	268	353	353	670
6,302	3,980	7,094	7,318	9,087	7,130	5,605	4,785	9,464	8,689	9,975	20,033
63	69	99	115	86	119	93	164	3,673	4,183	477	443
19,539	16,340	28,320	34,429	8,990	8,992	10,428	22,213	4,587	4,959	16,507	5,574
46	43	35	39	25	34	18	27	44	60	3,974	4,069
1,464	1,796	1,498	2,048	1,602	1,719	2,453	2,673	1,356	1,923	4,587	4,128
120	244	1,573	1,443	275	265	278	286	56	79	104	115
188	172	149	120	288	270	267	211	142	189	156	140
45	77	69	190	86	104	22	28	16	29	12	28
...	...	202	456	916	890	...	...	853	1,114	2,430	3,634
1,873	1,961	3,489	2,923	2,822	4,029	1,502	1,616	913	2,088	1,287	2,470
5,420	6,390	2,540	1,615	5,588	5,802	3,812	4,640	4,059	4,631	4,787	5,620
3,450	4,480	1,478	1,859	2,009	1,932	1,105	1,812	1,297	1,649	2,650	2,603
135	130	724	733	230	300	27	40	...	...	594	570
88	74	28	29	45	44	94	86	35	52	358	350
46	59	98	116	59	78	75	89	48	75	138	193
2,604	4,252	3,644	3,905	3,485	3,486	3,485	5,812	4,771	5,056	11,844	2,515
2,144	2,812	2,024	2,363	1,715	1,705	1,984	2,025	844	1,107	1,826	2,289
4,140	6,038	4,989	6,526	5,301	5,386	6,380	8,360	4,288	5,703	7,051	7,931
5,230	4,566	1,030	1,076	1,639	1,704	3,100	3,484	1,129	1,517	2,979	5,212
745	894	397	367	411	428	735	784	330	368	491	540
3,330	4,516	2,002	2,090	1,521	1,515	3,648	3,207	501	544	1,409	1,592
35	45	52	48	63	75	54	46	50	57	46	50
645	786	2,150	2,154	3,081	3,425	756	894	2,431	3,063	3,315	3,540
684	789	255	139	284	386	415	734	530	550	1,226	2,158
3,884	4,437	7,161	2,075	11,654	9,359	2,385	5,192	10,335	8,046	9,497	15,262
1,446	2,384	923	1,403	958	892	1,138	1,556	727	814	1,241	919
184	183	154	148	168	174	153	184	90	132	109	147
2,515	1,935	1,896	1,885	2,604	3,246	3,505	3,112	1,030	1,317	1,940	2,294
2,640	4,887	3,016	3,031	3,598	3,655	3,612	5,816	2,016	2,380	3,677	3,384
55	96	...	...	...	...	89	99	...	...	136	164
843	829	523	549	565	742	905	1,025	193	241	615	666
206	195	15	106	68	94	93	5	209	449	117	179
239	286	144	122	176	179	296	815	263	213	320	403
109	117	178	125	58	84	45	9	46	64	66	60
82	89	...	...	...	...	63	95	...	...	1,411	1,703
584	602	116	174	494	546	609	784	778	798	124	110
4,634	4,884	3,371	2,165	4,573	4,682	3,884	2,944	1,844	2,642	4,444	6,131
275	184	48	59	98	115	156	178	98	146	264	209

DISTRICT

Group.	District Total.			Muzaffarpur.		Paru.		Katra.		Sitamarhi.	
	Total.	Male.	Female.	Male.	Female.	Male.	Female.	Male.	Female.	Male.	Female.
Musalmans returned by title.											
Pathan	11,864	6,170	5,694	991	726	197	228	358	470	928	823
Sayyid	5,303	2,486	2,817	546	506	215	246	123	220	121	118
Shaikh	1,69,118	78,191	90,927	7,540	8,890	3,999	4,490	10,998	10,162	9,070	8,089
Musalmans returned by actual occupation.											
Darsi	4,576	2,172	2,404	346	445	268	284	...	...	175	155
Dhopa	7,159	3,806	3,353	148	271	1,073	971	213	253	631	657
Dhunia	35,503	16,637	18,866	2,846	2,976	1,848	2,944	826	1,127	3,151	2,029
Fakir	6,016	2,878	3,138	176	148	306	307	244	305	374	543
Hajjam	4,043	1,903	2,140	266	264	155	173	147	187	164	159
Jolaha	69,661	32,971	36,690	...	...	3,599	3,532	1,168	2,040	6,115	5,096
Kunjra	7,414	3,413	4,001	344	384	182	234	286	465	126	136
Laheri	2,737	1,341	1,396	46	47	133	272	56	77	512	478

DISTRICT

Caste.	District total.			Chapra.		Manjhi.		Parsa.		Mashrak.	
	Total.	Male.	Female.	Male.	Female.	Male.	Female.	Male.	Female.	Male.	Female.
Agrahari	1,124	528	596	266	301	84	96	...	...	...	...
Babhan	127,026	60,838	66,188	8,963	9,137	3,030	3,604	8,024	9,631	8,053	8,334
Baniya	27,639	12,202	15,437	1,081	1,296	644	911	830	985	629	937
(i)—Barnawar	5,620	2,690	2,930	...	...	290	335	...	...	...	...
(ii)—Kasarwani	1,802	842	960	59	68	114	146	20	9	9	3
(iii)—Rastogi	1,266	615	651	104	151	64	77	20	23	250	332
(iv)—Raunlar	9,727	4,437	5,290	823	975	155	171	362	450	130	150
(v)—Sinduria	1,145	514	631	95	102	25	35	47	78	52	73
Barhi	17,619	8,556	9,063	1,588	1,887	683	1,079	392	433	99	138
Bari	7,495	3,478	4,017	272	336	244	307	185	225	58	43
Barui	12,155	5,837	6,318	911	982	355	397	223	243	275	280
Bediya	1,139	515	624	124	130	54	48	43	46	19	22
Bhar	12,536	5,860	6,676	403	503	245	331	...	...	...	...
Bhat	3,993	1,653	2,340	326	528	340	442	77	169	...	...
Bind	20,208	7,924	12,284	1,570	3,212	264	712	727	1,067	373	533
Brahman	164,675	78,430	86,245	11,209	11,701	7,418	8,831	5,010	6,056	3,845	4,731
Chamar and Muchi... ...	127,214	55,001	72,213	6,042	8,981	2,827	3,813	4,689	7,352	2,761	4,434
Dhanuk	19,063	8,562	10,501	1,525	1,928	1,554	1,980	289	337	97	109
Dhopa	20,810	9,726	11,084	658	823	283	326	605	729	267	342
Dom	9,499	4,611	4,888	707	690	263	295	460	455	270	287
Dusadh	84,879	39,209	45,670	6,525	8,577	2,259	2,746	3,239	4,190	1,898	2,520
Garerí	10,730	5,222	5,508	1,077	1,201	150	164	247	298	210	227
Goala	307,820	145,945	161,875	24,085	26,185	5,831	6,444	19,892	23,001	13,095	14,259
Gonrhi	30,974	12,627	18,347	3,786	5,502	632	926	325	447	123	195
Hajjam	34,350	15,718	18,632	2,544	3,109	1,113	1,403	1,557	2,069	1,066	1,369
Halwai	1,104	528	576	108	111	34	49	22	30	9	6
Hari and Mihtar	4,050	1,829	2,221	257	315	101	195	123	172	58	86
Jugi	1,038	465	573	98	126	12	20	6	10	...	...
Kahar	42,641	18,168	24,473	2,742	3,723	932	1,512	1,831	1,732	335	530
Kalwar and Sunri	24,395	10,855	13,540	2,336	3,008	721	981	316	470	197	255

MUZAFFARPUR—*concluded.*

Sitamarhi.		Pupri.		Belsand.		Hajipur.		Lalganj.		Mahua.	
Male.	Female.	Male.	Female.	Male.	Female.	Male.	Female.	Male.	Female.	Male.	Female.
848	624	847	998	464	525	946	553	267	420	324	327
273	239	122	333	142	130	486	450	131	183	327	392
9,858	18,464	13,894	14,676	5,142	5,325	9,694	10,446	1,581	2,174	6,415	8,211
446	544	227	204	148	134	398	426	164	212	...	...
454	289	416	448	159	154	335	246	...	...	377	64
2,795	2,448	1,409	1,697	1,173	1,127	1,145	1,448	630	875	1,814	2,195
265	259	457	543	287	292	318	384	68	80	183	297
238	167	151	274	149	176	311	316	86	119	236	306
...	...	13,237	14,216	1,691	1,694	...	...	2,031	2,922	5,130	7,190
456	495	672	653	367	404	333	494	91	112	556	634
28	34	160	9	221	251	35	38	80	109	70	81

SARAN.

Sonpur.		Gopalganj.		Mirganj.		Sewan.		Darauli.		Basantpur.	
Male.	Female.	Male.	Female.	Male.	Female.	Male.	Female.	Male.	Female.	Male.	Female.
...	...	...	...	...	...	178	199	...	...	...	...
4,499	4,985	4,559	5,072	6,436	6,830	5,143	5,864	3,104	3,608	9,027	9,128
936	1,170	1,142	1,373	2,685	3,130	1,318	1,901	1,333	1,706	1,604	2,193
...	...	362	426	740	753	580	626	718	790	...	...
18	10	...	...	403	451	199	265	12	4	8	4
16	19	...	...	11	9	17	23	...	...	133	17
285	336	448	510	996	1,020	432	579	422	579	384	520
20	23	65	64	37	46	90	108	23	47	60	55
390	453	1,191	1,092	1,563	1,268	1,624	1,430	351	419	766	864
166	200	334	447	1,211	1,247	309	400	306	348	393	464
826	917	963	1,061	439	463	768	846	656	704	421	425
59	66	29	43	45	42	124	204	...	...	18	21
53	21	76	90	1,930	2,031	821	955	2,210	2,619	122	126
...	...	51	53	528	633	69	65	...	...	262	445
523	1,053	1,761	2,033	718	733	1,053	1,428	379	674	536	834
2,024	2,570	9,378	10,078	17,194	18,520	8,864	9,767	13,324	13,781	169	810
1,283	2,041	6,771	8,478	12,638	13,735	7,502	9,973	6,480	7,544	4,008	5,862
154	172	2,072	2,344	335	351	563	694	...	...	1,974	2,586
500	584	948	1,082	2,496	2,540	1,218	1,421	1,245	1,376	1,506	1,861
214	232	410	452	833	901	686	724	308	349	460	503
1,709	3,135	5,982	6,674	5,045	5,506	5,487	6,883	3,283	3,680	3,782	3,760
24[illegible]	225	696	693	1,067	1,166	700	699	386	403	440	443
7,888	9,723	17,644	17,977	18,045	18,688	16,457	17,326	10,567	10,687	12,441	17,585
514	718	74	98	126	182	6,310	9,170	96	136	642	973
812	1,067	1,761	1,960	2,199	2,330	1,364	1,469	1,422	1,649	1,880	2,187
73	87	...	...	30	35	133	134	79	64	40	60
150	162	199	213	114	123	332	444	270	290	135	216
19	28	26	34	74	91	54	84	129	95	47	85
1,104	1,724	3,280	4,164	3,553	5,450	2,482	2,557	1,151	1,558	1,258	1,514
99	109	1,818	1,979	1,425	1,757	1,507	1,822	1,108	1,317	1,283	1,847

Caste or Group.	District Total.			Chapra.		Manjhi.		Parsa.		Mashrak.	
	Total.	Male.	Female.	Male.	Female.	Male.	Female.	Male.	Female.	Male.	Female.
Kandu	95,633	43,191	52,442	7,544	9,678	1,164	1,564	5,105	6,436	3,759	3,727
Kayastha	50,770	23,348	27,422	4,844	4,640	1,574	2,200	1,810	2,530	1,180	1,677
Khatik	1,791	861	930	106	107	12	15	18	25	...	...
Koiri	169,856	82,718	87,138	10,414	11,649	4,264	4,798	4,569	5,209	3,443	3,698
Kumhar	26,355	11,515	14,840	1,917	2,232	1,698	2,543	815	1,478	806	1,114
Kurmi	124,604	56,596	68,008	5,662	7,133	2,061	2,756	9,773	11,888	1,274	1,806
Lohar	47,470	22,270	25,200	3,088	3,095	1,010	1,332	3,000	3,034	1,455	1,854
Malakar	6,393	2,941	3,452	464	564	119	134	478	529	185	262
Musahar	5,893	2,588	3,305	176	284	12	13	109	158	131	215
Nat	2,486	1,158	1,328	132	192	120	142	140	120	...	...
Nuniya	79,348	34,646	44,702	4,304	5,738	1,847	2,693	3,826	5,270	3,030	4,119
Pasi	4,655	2,289	2,366	975	1,040	138	152	127	124	...	...
Rajput	266,720	125,916	140,804	24,702	27,563	12,259	14,385	12,163	14,901	15,275	17,640
Rajwar	1,078	530	548	75	77	23	25	55	61	57	49
Sonar	23,588	10,863	12,725	2,059	2,453	874	1,153	949	1,208	507	622
Tatwa and Tanti	8,472	3,634	4,838	1,102	1,529	68	106	375	547	324	477
Teli	70,798	32,672	38,126	4,981	6,399	1,839	2,137	2,576	3,230	1,883	2,474
Tiyar	1,376	333	1,043	85	321	9	23	...	...	13	39
Turaha	19,851	7,727	12,124	1,586	2,696	336	505	480	769	437	763
Religious devotees and persons returned by sect.											
Atith	22,766	9,214	13,552	1,717	3,059	1,617	2,748	1,144	1,899	330	464
Baisnab	2,579	1,516	1,063	405	242	188	133	59	48	33	44
Fakir	1,161	527	634	165	207	...	...	32	26	65	82
Hindus returned by actual occupation.											
Baid	1,418	674	744	134	150	70	75	83	92	56	59
Mala	23,353	9,265	14,088	1,173	2,067	503	1,417	784	1,161	547	830
Musalmans returned by title.											
Pathan	19,061	8,511	10,550	1,888	2,687	517	733	250	387	444	672
Sayyid	5,817	2,576	3,241	532	433	117	195	52	59	45	69
Shaikh	69,107	30,948	38,159	5,005	7,726	635	883	1,406	1,915	777	1,018
Musalmans returned by actual occupation.											
Bhat	1,903	797	1,106	39	56	30	45	48	92	45	75
Churihar	3,565	1,669	1,896	46	67	58	107	28	23	29	31
Dafali	1,338	637	701	51	60	35	46	45	52	23	35
Darzi	7,187	3,064	4,123	442	722	212	295	290	469	191	294
Dhopa	12,745	5,865	6,880	1,042	1,303	567	659	610	804	666	799
Dhunia	19,470	8,345	11,125	1,034	1,473	444	617	794	1,137	541	743
Fakir	9,828	4,500	5,328	393	497	274	319	256	327	222	301
Hajjam	10,815	4,902	5,913	779	1,172	111	144	172	247	87	137
Jolaha	1,07,744	48,536	59,208	5,859	6,735	2,012	2,982	4,597	5,299	2,035	2,793
Kasai	1,057	501	556	265	278	...	...	49	58	...	...
Kunjra	6,711	3,094	3,617	600	727	96	109	179	249	296	392
Laheri	1,749	690	1,059	127	186	58	102	151	235	63	112
Mali	1,993	928	1,065	133	144	56	72	...	...	12	18
Pawaria	1,421	638	783	50	80	30	33	62	76	27	35
Rangrez	1,461	675	786	163	160	35	46	25	33	19	30

SARAN—*concluded.*

Sonpur.		Gopalganj.		Mirganj.		Sewan.		Darauli.		Basantpur.	
Male.	Female.	Male.	Female.	Male.	Female.	Male.	Female.	Male.	Female.	Male.	Female.
2,640	3,633	5,199	5,966	4,409	4,672	6,667	7,447	3,060	3,268	4,644	6,051
908	1,373	2,357	2,725	2,848	2,964	3,687	4,576	2,053	2,416	2,087	2,321
23	18	...	...	683	742	10	11	...	...	10	12
2,048	2,313	6,959	7,036	23,061	23,347	13,170	13,983	7,543	7,926	7,227	8,179
516	687	821	985	2,212	2,310	15	38	1,657	1,694	1,059	1,759
3,594	4,676	7,112	8,193	6,048	7,357	11,983	13,896	3,738	4,233	4,451	6,070
775	814	2,092	2,642	3,045	3,333	3,033	3,555	2,522	2,981	2,250	2,560
289	314	213	268	365	449	198	200	295	334	315	398
15	16	418	574	1,460	1,592	122	209	13	14	132	230
120	155	163	150	84	93	68	62	203	294	128	130
743	1,021	5,390	6,867	4,596	5,089	4,839	6,013	2,620	3,251	3,451	4,641
186	209	134	132	115	136	373	371	96	75	147	127
9,793	13,532	13,305	13,681	6,519	6,188	7,062	7,114	13,700	13,980	11,138	11,820
62	58	15	28	59	72	76	69	65	59	43	50
739	988	975	1,316	1,411	1,445	1,605	1,571	777	835	967	1,134
394	547	922	1,138	142	152	62	57	144	163	101	117
1,170	1,021	3,381	3,869	5,670	5,942	4,982	5,350	3,420	3,477	2,770	3,627
67	103	2	11	...	...	...	...	157	546	...	...
214	232	1,436	1,797	591	703	1,210	2,309	666	925	771	1,425
73	78	1,017	1,201	844	1,022	1,733	2,291	739	790	...	...
48	51	243	136	87	64	326	236	...	...	127	59
23	35	45	54	6	9	119	133	19	23	53	65
18	23	32	35	...	...	201	222	29	32	51	56
571	865	2,680	3,009	551	777	373	617	1,812	2,971	271	348
153	184	345	418	1,512	1,678	1,971	2,282	922	967	509	642
28	64	211	228	123	126	742	980	392	533	334	474
603	818	4,607	5,123	3,639	3,915	9,840	12,134	1,313	1,461	2,523	3,166
43	57	100	108	197	246	156	206	100	149	39	72
34	43	239	250	654	725	244	253	172	195	155	202
39	40	85	109	173	158	78	81	32	31	76	89
110	171	453	572	340	362	457	538	206	169	363	531
...	...	1,245	1,397	517	527	1,004	1,254	115	137	...	...
367	580	1,065	1,407	1,400	1,514	1,213	1,740	684	804	803	1,110
42	54	766	908	673	720	1,553	1,829	282	314	39	59
101	128	548	621	1,315	1,368	1,406	1,673	375	407	8	16
1,204	1,749	5,552	6,739	8,597	9,127	11,750	11,316	3,745	4,489	3,185	7,980
...	...	...	...	...	...	187	220	...	...	...	...
41	73	418	455	412	468	430	466	243	202	379	336
20	25	85	123	16	18	67	88	16	21	87	149
...	...	274	335	180	186	250	290	14	20	...	...
40	43	85	52	85	121	236	255	35	29	38	59
47	63	24	22	136	168	76	80	78	108	72	76

Caste or group.	District Total.			Motihari.		Govindganj.		Kesaria.	
	Total.	Male.	Female.	Male.	Female.	Male.	Female.	Male.	Female.
Agrahari	1,569	815	754	254	186	5	1	36	36
Babhan	28,496	13,016	15,480	1,682	2,745	3,307	3,354	2,761	2,915
Baniya	32,219	16,061	16,158	870	1,570	927	1,005	1,879	1,873
(i)—Barnawar	2,704	1,388	1,316	...	...	113	115	...	...
(ii)—Kasarwani	1,561	805	756	82	78	71	79	148	250
(iii)—Raunlar	12,784	6,445	6,339	510	467	473	497	1,057	1,040
Barhi	8,077	4,067	4,010	676	548	1,014	969	508	606
Bari	1,955	971	984	42	40	114	144	85	99
Barui	11,736	5,799	5,937	644	734	37	12	446	50
Bhar	8,219	4,235	3,984	388	379	84	84	...	...
Bhat	8,173	4,073	4,100	502	601	59	62	48	23
Bind	27,331	13,567	13,764	1,249	1,222	675	731	602	642
Brahman	84,493	44,093	40,400	2,954	2,285	4,405	4,870	8,225	9,259
Chamar and Muchi	126,997	63,166	63,831	5,725	5,799	5,292	5,320	5,092	5,365
Dhanuk	11,460	5,795	5,665	978	955	922	980	341	347
Dhopa	21,355	10,528	10,827	818	770	574	580	1,006	1,199
Dom	8,154	4,040	4,114	386	384	343	353	358	330
Dusadh	91,452	44,553	46,899	4,938	5,057	4,531	4,688	4,805	5,560
Gareri	7,441	3,688	3,753	264	226	287	343	224	185
Goala	183,732	93,143	90,589	9,845	9,776	6,659	6,240	10,027	10,522
Gonrhi	32,205	16,099	16,106	4,534	4,558	1,245	1,234	1,445	1,497
Hajjam	27,239	15,126	12,113	1,334	1,010	2,422	1,318	1,611	1,677
Halwai	3,639	1,870	1,769	133	138	160	142	156	149
Hari and Mihtar	3,077	1,500	1,577	205	171	146	196	250	290
Jugi	1,235	655	580	99	61	...	...	46	102
Kahar	5,816	2,901	2,915	329	337	209	195	539	521
Kalwar and Sunri	33,796	17,125	16,671	2,340	2,168	1,558	1,968	860	863
Kandu	68,588	34,529	34,059	3,815	3,695	3,478	3,341	3,055	3,318
Kayastha	27,624	14,738	12,886	1,454	1,073	1,569	1,691	2,865	2,328
Kewat	5,714	2,945	2,769	61	50	...	...	103	134
Koiri	108,877	56,344	52,533	4,747	4,415	5,759	5,664	6,793	4,954
Kumhar	24,954	12,738	12,216	1,064	1,509	838	888	1,263	1,487
Kurmi	96,145	48,108	48,037	3,994	3,555	4,242	4,544	3,414	3,881
Lohar and Kamar	28,193	14,154	14,039	1,020	1,006	1,190	1,171	2,241	2,291
Malakar	5,418	2,753	2,665	259	212	225	182	468	406
Musahar	40,206	20,032	20,174	2,369	2,346	1,218	1,214	854	1,023
Nuniya	52,903	26,281	26,622	2,787	2,827	3,146	3,433	2,287	2,409
Pasi	2,297	1,162	1,135	120	110	89	96	104	101
Rajput	86,440	45,034	41,406	3,855	3,435	4,270	3,960	8,115	8,361
Sonar	14,525	7,692	6,833	983	767	569	591	804	931
Tambuli	2,424	1,242	1,182	120	139	517	784	...	...
Tatwa and Tanti	32,301	15,898	16,403	1,147	1,136	1,620	1,654	2,183	2,457
Teli	58,916	29,509	29,407	2,796	2,447	1,906	1,964	2,656	2,972
Tharu	27,620	13,810	13,810	...	...	...	...	...	...
Turaha	26,775	13,033	13,742	2,197	2,315	1,804	2,006	1,294	1,309
Religious devotees and persons returned by sect.									
Atith	11,946	6,301	5,645	550	440	735	732	859	794
Baisnab	1,167	693	474	77	109	63	41	84	74
Hindus returned by title or common sub-caste.									
Buna	8,541	4,319	4,222	95	110	118	110	96	53

CHÁMPARAN.

Madhuban.		Dhaka.		Adapur.		Bettiah.		Hardi.		Bagaha.	
Male.	Female.	Male.	Female.	Male.	Female.	Male.	Female.	Male.	Female.	Male.	Female.
239	260	101	115	5	5	174	151	...	...	1	...
845	406	1,087	1,500	1,200	1,723	1,514	2,359	354	328	266	150
804	772	2,033	2,079	3,103	2,062	2,460	2,815	2,699	2,644	1,280	1,338
183	166	314	315	71	70	544	487	...	...	163	163
60	65	164	36	100	110	86	39	84	99	...	...
352	347	571	601	1,571	1,488	652	631	451	388	880	880
50	56	122	123	146	149	1,367	1,398	92	87	92	74
42	26	41	39	...	...	280	278	181	194	186	164
511	498	536	550	991	952	1,229	1,203	959	936	446	480
100	125	...	...	41	82	157	146	1,457	1,313	2,008	1,855
291	314	820	820	446	507	223	147	1,205	1,339	485	297
104	87	1,817	1,678	1,176	1,302	3,870	3,870	667	679	3,407	3,493
2,412	2,323	4,411	4,127	2,744	2,001	7,241	6,276	4,945	4,251	6,756	4,913
3,597	4,612	6,637	6,145	6,010	5,833	11,612	11,974	8,653	8,174	10,548	10,609
125	115	658	663	1,339	1,317	1,090	1,077	243	215	99	56
867	910	2,290	2,387	1,964	1,964	1,173	1,222	669	658	1,167	1,146
280	300	388	410	498	495	648	763	640	672	499	407
2,427	2,630	8,351	8,678	4,517	4,751	6,674	7,126	5,652	5,594	2,658	2,815
251	306	168	149	125	139	937	1,002	802	768	630	635
6,943	7,184	14,040	13,766	10,055	10,177	13,480	12,937	6,869	6,017	16,325	13,970
724	596	1,462	1,427	1,803	1,418	1,244	1,216	1,929	1,986	2,213	2,174
707	917	1,658	1,666	2,144	1,466	3,183	2,101	959	896	1,108	1,062
170	164	223	202	113	52	332	316	146	118	535	536
...	...	150	106	300	304	329	357	...	...	120	153
73	67	55	50	76	61	68	52	180	144	56	43
329	316	533	556	411	404	245	181	154	226	152	179
1,384	1,218	3,024	3,156	1,717	1,651	2,625	2,566	1,829	1,562	1,788	1,519
1,772	1,927	5,021	5,165	3,231	3,182	8,596	8,631	2,880	2,570	2,631	2,230
796	682	2,386	2,425	1,005	888	2,471	1,875	1,804	1,419	888	505
...	...	55	51	95	99	262	274	2,141	1,971	228	190
5,698	5,899	6,943	6,304	3,646	3,624	14,642	13,960	3,614	3,401	4,497	4,312
935	770	1,898	1,939	1,800	1,620	1,769	1,672	1,598	1,489	978	842
3,155	3,269	7,998	8,163	5,034	5,901	9,937	9,065	4,397	3,972	5,337	5,067
906	894	2,654	2,762	1,485	1,432	1,929	1,859	1,355	1,266	1,374	1,358
230	219	235	559	354	390	394	330	311	219	277	148
851	837	1,314	1,229	829	811	3,325	3,333	4,860	4,846	4,412	4,535
1,131	1,255	2,782	2,772	2,148	2,214	4,630	4,515	3,955	3,795	3,415	3,402
342	349	105	108	80	73	226	220	...	...	87	78
3,666	3,322	11,772	10,708	4,324	4,128	4,877	4,208	2,063	1,561	2,072	1,724
459	430	1,136	1,019	634	472	1,613	1,513	867	603	625	517
49	67	106	122	151	120	...	...	...	...	...	...
1,617	1,766	2,661	2,719	1,464	1,375	3,040	3,148	1,350	1,311	816	837
2,196	2,340	6,266	6,487	3,239	2,959	4,491	4,516	2,855	2,806	3,014	2,896
...	...	835	1,148	...	...	...	...	8,165	7,748	4,810	4,914
620	680	2,368	2,441	563	607	2,784	2,827	722	844	681	713
284	293	815	726	633	600	1,048	922	953	786	424	352
200	100	178	104	...	...	91	46	...	...	...	...
284	293	359	384	136	138	509	582	483	496	2,244	2,167

DISTRICT

Group.	District Total.			Motihari.		Govindganj.		Kesaria.	
	Total.	Male.	Female.	Male.	Female.	Male.	Female.	Male.	Female.
Hindus returned by actual occupation.									
Bardai	1,378	755	623	...	...	...	...	...	...
Kamkar	11,392	5,705	5,687	202	203	804	888	650	577
Mala	63,070	31,116	31,954	4,207	4,085	3,635	3,836	2,822	3,075
Musalmans returned by title.									
Pathan	13,545	6,750	6,795	588	580	561	559	532	638
Sayyid	3,516	1,806	1,710	140	146	183	204	130	146
Shaikh	62,459	30,322	32,137	4,998	5,138	543	514	1,187	1,579
Musalmans returned by actual occupation.									
Barhi	1,958	965	993	300	314	...	...	...	...
Churihar	5,353	2,906	2,447	146	165	367	336	216	215
Darzi	5,272	2,720	2,552	290	297	230	231	229	267
Dhopa	11,210	5,442	5,768	920	964	805	848	216	215
Dhunia	26,994	13,443	13,551	1,212	1,226	1,352	1,432	957	1,093
Fakir	11,036	5,579	5,457	486	527	230	331	355	478
Gadi	4,753	2,883	2,370	67	68	...	...	121	113
Hajjam	4,926	2,439	2,487	347	341	53	49	121	116
Jolaha	80,358	41,437	38,921	4,123	3,831	3,633	3,629	2,314	2,518
Kalu	3,161	1,517	1,644	145	220	112	128	52	75
Kunjra	7,452	3,644	3,808	566	576	84	83	1,000	1,500
Lahori	1,153	523	630	...	...	...	...	...	...
Mukeri	1,352	673	679	...	...	...	...	...	...
Rangrez	1,002	541	461	...	...	...	...	165	160

BHAGALPUR

DISTRICT

Caste.	District Total.			Bhagalpur.		Sultanganj.		Kolgong.		Bihipur.	
	Total.	Male.	Female.	Male.	Female.	Male.	Female.	Male.	Female.	Male.	Female.
Amat	9,499	4,745	4,754	210	242	75	80	173	162	...	...
Babhan	37,048	18,935	18,113	2,180	2,063	1,442	1,487	1,245	1,040	5,065	5,202
Baniya	51,579	25,551	26,028	1,497	1,854	2,812	2,672	1,557	1,686	2,567	2,675
(i)—Baisya	10,539	5,270	5,269	215	236	420	342	130	165	185	109
(ii)—Barnawar	2,312	1,154	1,158	153	182	302	200	...	...	...	...
(iii)—Kasojan	1,638	731	907	60	75	71	80	40	82	80	70
(iv)—Khatri	12,587	6,169	6,418	255	79	513	560	513	561	413	558
(v)—Rauniar...	8,062	3,987	4,075	120	114	820	807	188	195	1,203	1,255
Bantar	17,098	8,411	8,687	...	...	972	930	...	...	...	...
Barhi	3,093	1,898	1,707	425	496	...	...	...	...	...	...
Barui	6,678	3,259	3,419	696	733	301	287	712	757	452	517
Beldar	8,632	4,054	4,578	...	...	801	864	493	541	55	64
Bhar	1,658	847	811	37	41	...	...	...	...	...	...
Bhat	2,360	1,193	1,167	85	73	115	90	81	88	149	194
Bhuiya	29,602	13,646	15,956	...	...	151	184	1,090	1,272	...	...

CHAMPARAN—*concluded.*

Madhuban.		Dhaka.		Adapur.		Bettiah.		Hardi.		Bagaha.	
Male.	Female.	Male.	Female.	Male.	Female.	Male.	Female.	Male.	Female.	Male.	Female.
...	...	...	...	...	...	...	...	...	...	755	623
130	137	112	116	327	262	1,416	1,463	1,463	1,489	590	552
4,321	4,708	2,588	2,737	1,073	1,113	5,871	5,557	2	2	6,597	6,841
337	320	1,282	1,332	703	651	1,461	1,542	707	697	579	476
183	205	281	297	79	77	227	216	583	419	...	...
1,167	1,281	8,915	9,977	2,870	2,869	4,945	5,108	4,694	4,817	1,003	854
...	...	...	...	...	...	466	455	81	125	118	99
31	41	174	190	301	309	1,073	612	852	345	256	234
56	64	454	427	292	233	474	368	311	347	384	323
109	130	477	490	147	197	1,483	1,402	876	1,047	409	415
649	728	2,111	2,092	1,809	1,802	2,361	2,327	1,691	1,565	1,301	1,286
300	339	843	533	761	784	852	803	1,452	1,290	300	372
...	...	381	326	...	...	1,276	1,263	40	50	498	550
76	102	304	362	...	...	608	709	523	530	283	278
1,457	1,610	4,096	4,203	6,429	5,289	9,293	9,305	5,358	5,089	4,685	4,447
596	672	...	...	510	503	102	46	...	...	...	...
23	28	161	169	696	418	524	565	230	103	360	366
42	71	115	141	366	418	...	...	...	...	...	...
...	...	...	...	...	...	362	401	279	247	32	31
66	7	53	53	70	46	65	75	122	120	...	...

DIVISION.

BHAGALPUR.

Supul.		Pratabganj.		Bangaon.		Madehpura.		Kishanganj.		Banka.		Amarpur.		Katuria.	
Male.	Female.	Male.	Female.	Male.	Female.	Male.	Female.	Male.	Female.	Male.	Female.	Male.	Female.	Male.	Female.
2,867	2,909	...	...	685	657	206	185	130	126	52	102	315	239	32	43
1,136	796	1,223	1,420	809	906	580	423	725	564	1,003	1,052	1,659	1,370	1,778	1,800
2,586	2,430	2,234	2,490	2,396	2,446	2,433	2,451	2,173	2,232	1,174	1,329	2,579	2,714	1,553	1,549
75	88	604	572	599	691	1,204	1,100	830	866	...	...	1,008	1,100	...	...
...	...	...	...	...	...	...	...	52	62	...	...	247	283	400	431
70	57	50	100	90	40	30	110	45	63	75	80	25	90	95	60
813	558	517	550	874	957	513	558	560	558	413	566	613	558	372	355
1,142	1,044	367	585	147	75	...	...	...	...	...	...	...	...	...	...
5,721	5,988	...	...	...	...	1,718	1,709	...	...	...	...	...	...	...	...
556	490	...	...	654	612	...	...	...	...	...	...	...	...	263	199
...	...	...	...	330	337	323	337	...	...	261	269	184	182	...	...
214	226	40	39	178	193	480	530	840	948	539	645	414	528	...	...
80	69	...	...	...	...	555	538	...	...	87	74	...	...	88	89
202	106	25	32	90	110	46	52	96	102	30	60	184	175	90	85
893	834	...	...	...	...	...	...	...	...	5,910	7,122	1,238	1,498	4,365	5,046

Caste or Group.	District Total.			Bhagalpur.		Sultanganj.		Kolgong.		Bihipur.	
	Total.	Male,	Female.	Male.	Female.	Male.	Female.	Male.	Female.	Male.	Female.
Bind	2,883	1,488	1,395	263	275	...	...	869	846	101	56
Brahman	65,799	33,551	32,248	1,151	1,423	2,804	2,639	2,930	2,481	2,326	2,455
Chain	2,756	1,320	1,436	421	459	...	...	526	607	294	339
Chamar and Muchi	88,129	43,129	45,000	5,467	5,938	2,306	2,466	3,327	3,510	1,125	1,270
Dhanuk	106,477	51,081	55,396	4,901	5,155	4,304	4,752	4,348	4,874	3,122	3,634
Dhopa	18,806	9,418	9,388	717	800	360	370	967	976	244	285
Dom	25,480	11,947	13,533	296	296	133	135	228	228	163	136
Dusadh	74,694	36,673	38,021	3,826	3,903	2,042	2,279	3,344	3,608	1,090	1,165
Gangauta	67,379	32,531	34,848	13,127	12,990	2,144	2,255	13,588	15,942	3,274	3,612
Gareri	4,299	2,079	2,220	266	352	114	161	144	206	130	146
Goala	376,088	185,655	190,433	9,411	9,708	3,729	3,784	7,205	7,532	4,268	4,462
Gonrhi	40,121	18,968	21,153	536	877	1,253	1,232	2,227	2,458	1,748	1,970
Hajjam	33,894	16,956	16,938	1,180	1,155	682	726	1,604	1,674	838	854
Halwai and Maira	22,511	11,489	11,022	708	694	326	331	773	798	546	620
Hari and Mihtar	3,968	1,807	2,161	52	73	122	159	229	298	71	74
Kadar	10,743	5,118	5,625	...	...	...	...	...	...	...	...
Kahar	24,612	11,815	12,797	1,505	1,553	1,130	1,283	819	797	485	430
Kalwar and Sunri	39,615	19,507	20,108	1,379	1,429	707	817	1,507	1,442	1,771	1,865
Kamar and Lohar	25,401	12,998	12,403	751	802	658	779	1,038	919	1,001	1,002
Kandu	20,545	9,925	10,620	950	1,026	586	620	1,237	1,392	1,136	1,366
Kapali	2,259	1,108	1,151	501	624	78	105	...	...	...	...
Kayastha	19,843	10,498	9,345	3,197	2,772	449	547	778	642	231	254
Kewat	55,214	27,223	27,991	120	139	87	23	603	674	...	...
Kharwar	6,873	3,171	3,702	...	...	...	...	3,096	3,616	...	...
Khatbe	9,855	4,907	4,948	...	...	...	...	...	...	...	...
Khatik	1,032	484	548	130	116	36	62	...	...	82	111
Koiri	77,125	38,659	38,466	2,522	2,621	2,598	2,834	2,510	2,635	1,697	2,084
Kol	12,966	6,420	6,546	857	897	...	...	1,428	1,509	236	253
Kumhar	30,428	15,046	15,383	901	922	410	462	1,323	1,404	634	693
Kurmi	20,114	10,011	10,103	...	...	2,785	3,007	1,481	1,467	...	...
Malakar	2,685	1,388	1,297	...	...	...	...	...	...	118	131
Markande	3,658	1,781	1,877	184	205	...	...	655	755	324	368
Muriyari	1,340	653	687	...	...	...	...	623	655	...	...
Musahar	86,288	43,053	43,235	556	576	1,524	1,613	2,425	2,471	242	219
Nagar	5,504	2,797	2,707	...	...	...	...	...	...	1,331	1,419
Naiya	2,905	1,463	1,442	375	346	...	...	...	...	...	...
Nat	2,454	1,223	1,231	85	91	46	51	60	71	177	92
Nuniya	4,584	2,212	2,372	...	...	...	...	228	197	...	...
Pargha	7,032	3,200	3,832	...	...	...	...	...	...	...	...
Pasi	5,051	2,404	2,647	915	1,051	260	271	297	328	...	...
Rajput	61,485	33,463	28,022	1,573	1,066	1,672	1,372	2,068	1,408	1,201	1,067
Santal	50,063	24,876	25,187	20	3	3	1	8,718	8,734	...	...
Sonar	10,842	5,470	5,372	664	714	221	234	549	511	422	497
Tambuli	1,081	613	468	4	5	12	7	27	19	1	...
Tatwa and Tanti	12,853	6,210	6,643	100	117	191	184	109	99	1,008	1,375
Teli	74,106	36,825	37,281	2,588	2,879	1,272	1,276	2,634	2,881	869	1,019
Thathera	3,717	1,797	1,920	252	273	92	99	138	144	171	208
Tiyar	4,479	2,195	2,284	...	...	...	...	378	357	361	463
Religious devotees and persons returned by sect.											
Gosain	2,433	1,237	1,196	194	186	115	115	331	338	134	105
Hindus returned by title or common sub-caste.											
Banpar	1,411	558	853	...	...	...	...	558	853	...	...

BHAGALPUR—*continued.*

Supul.		Pratabganj.		Bangaon.		Madhepura.		Kishanganj.		Banka.		Amarpur.		Katuria.	
Male.	Female.	Male.	Female.	Male.	Female.	Male.	Female.	Male.	Female.	Male.	Female.	Male.	Female.	Male.	Female.
...	...	...	...	...	...	...	...	...	...	179	117	...	...	76	101
3,618	3,646	1,684	1,177	5,387	5,735	1,862	1,546	3,336	3,374	3,069	2,839	4,015	3,910	1,369	1,023
...	...	...	...	...	...	...	...	...	...	...	...	...	...	79	31
5,336	5,336	4,432	4,492	2,508	2,499	4,318	4,541	1,983	1,952	3,380	3,438	5,753	6,208	3,189	3,350
12,089	13,157	4,529	4,712	2,751	2,802	3,560	3,800	3,072	2,928	3,275	3,695	4,097	4,624	1,133	1,063
905	880	2,253	2,097	545	555	1,177	1,196	568	510	492	527	730	728	460	464
455	446	5,481	6,804	173	152	444	444	226	195	1,669	1,751	540	629	2,139	2,317
6,518	6,633	4,729	4,658	3,464	3,585	3,950	4,096	2,041	2,068	1,728	1,864	3,429	3,614	512	548
91	45	...	...	...	...	...	...	307	4	...	...	...	...	...	...
683	703	...	...	353	362	178	169	...	...	211	121	...	...	...	...
33,793	34,660	16,091	16,571	16,258	16,914	50,679	53,273	9,693	8,700	10,366	10,706	9,097	9,628	14,405	14,495
2,912	3,025	1,307	2,070	1,777	1,773	2,327	2,307	1,591	1,223	2,531	3,454	167	69	592	695
2,017	1,885	760	740	977	972	2,385	2,376	1,050	1,021	1,271	1,257	1,313	1,312	2,879	2,966
3,126	2,518	785	786	1,619	1,623	1,794	1,760	772	762	340	343	340	411	300	376
212	241	...	...	213	229	...	...	85	102	50	72	518	610	255	303
...	...	...	...	...	...	...	...	...	...	4,636	5,112	482	513	...	...
186	186	...	...	...	...	479	458	513	503	2,126	2,470	2,275	2,564	2,357	2,548
3,602	3,735	1,602	1,589	1,843	1,846	2,124	2,180	580	569	2,375	2,600	1,252	1,299	765	737
1,749	1,695	459	622	468	409	2,420	2,248	1,145	932	828	822	1,092	1,118	1,389	1,155
335	318	526	509	552	574	1,166	1,255	859	784	646	676	1,301	1,435	632	665
241	310	288	112	...	...	...	...	...	...	...	...	...	...	...	...
1,060	772	929	955	779	687	962	669	417	362	716	726	688	776	302	200
14,373	14,614	950	943	1,725	1,793	7,940	8,394	1,146	1,228	...	...	155	68	115	115
...	...	...	...	...	...	...	...	...	...	75	86	...	...	...	...
4,550	4,575	...	...	...	...	357	373	...	...	...	...	...	...	...	...
...	...	121	93	...	...	...	...	...	...	46	57	70	109	...	...
8,513	8,369	3,577	3,221	89	15	3,545	3,195	2,301	2,062	3,375	3,206	6,152	6,783	1,480	1,441
...	...	502	579	...	...	...	...	2,480	2,411	262	233	5	6	590	658
2,484	2,799	1,968	1,820	806	833	1,859	1,875	842	743	1,057	1,044	693	730	2,068	2,058
180	67	1,431	1,319	313	346	156	90	429	400	482	523	2,630	2,753	124	131
281	223	351	360	154	142	326	324	158	117	...	...	...	...	...	...
...	...	42	33	...	...	...	...	391	297	185	219	...	...	...	...
...	...	...	...	...	...	30	32	...	...	...	...	...	...	...	...
7,626	7,737	4,310	4,205	4,761	4,790	12,110	12,128	5,068	4,079	1,328	1,380	1,810	1,817	1,284	1,311
...	...	...	...	...	...	...	...	1,466	1,278	...	...	...	...	...	...
...	...	298	313	...	...	...	...	...	...	404	481	61	70	235	232
205	157	...	...	39	58	65	101	413	461	...	...	...	...	133	149
606	860	766	765	47	63	264	262	...	...	100	102	92	107	109	16
83	58	...	...	...	...	...	...	15	...	2,753	3,344	297	368	52	62
...	...	49	49	162	183	57	40	70	61	206	251	205	197	183	207
3,176	2,585	4,281	4,318	3,603	3,075	3,837	2,800	3,752	3,187	2,709	2,523	4,050	3,423	1,547	1,198
3	5	718	885	...	...	12	10	...	...	7,652	7,746	291	276	7,459	7,527
477	454	352	309	134	80	461	409	220	193	1,481	1,444	200	237	289	291
211	207	189	107	23	9	5	1	33	21	19	5	80	33	50	54
927	890	486	496	1,114	1,233	673	657	542	593	225	179	85	118	744	702
8,636	8,164	3,673	3,465	4,453	4,546	5,610	5,833	2,130	2,224	2,043	250	1,6[illegible]	1,764	1,300	1,180
343	346	81	89	129	134	92	95	...	...	160	154	179	226	170	152
822	850	...	...	521	540	...	...	113	74	...	...	...	...	...	...
...	...	...	...	...	...	...	...	...	...	157	136	233	263	73	53
...	...	...	...	...	...	...	...	...	...	...	...	...	...	...	...

DISTRICT

Group.	District Total.			Bhagalpur.		Sultanganj.		Kolgong.		Bihipur.	
	Total.	Male.	Female.	Male.	Female.	Male.	Female.	Male.	Female.	Male.	Female.
Hindus returned by actual occupation.											
Ghatwal	4,250	1,983	2,267	...	...	...	...	130	157	...	...
Laheri	1,160	581	579	127	143	...	...	139	130	54	51
Mala	7,933	3,995	3,938	...	...	...	...	108	24	...	...
Hindus returned by locality.											
Bengalis	3,738	1,835	1,903	...	...	...	...	...	...	1,672	1,693
Hindus returned by unidentifiable caste.											
Kalar	1,326	651	675	71	62	44	50	41	43	73	69
Musalmans returned by title.											
Pathan	10,228	5,251	4,977	957	1,056	600	639	352	325	125	132
Sayyid	12,439	6,023	6,416	654	720	98	88	92	84	...	...
Shaikh	28,088	14,002	14,086	1,081	1,009	501	605	553	442	1,000	1,210
Musalmans returned by actual occupation.											
Bhat	1,166	603	563	76	86	...	...	...	...	...	...
Dhopa	3,278	1,627	1,651	270	250	320	360	...	...	165	214
Dhunia	22,758	11,088	11,670	793	829	578	677	786	832	561	715
Fakir	2,847	1,437	1,410	178	167	129	157	91	87	128	171
Jolaha	86,719	42,189	44,530	12,313	13,914	2,317	2,593	4,921	4,924	2,227	2,760
Kalal	1,415	677	738	70	88	...	...	...	...	...	...
Kunjra	20,734	10,029	10,705	425	621	505	659	949	1,094	832	960
Mohifarash	1,711	880	831	49	43	37	31	101	107	51	59

DISTRICT

Caste.	District Total.			Monghyr.		Gogri.		Jamalpur.		Surajgarha.	
	Total.	Male.	Female.	Male.	Female.	Male.	Female.	Male.	Female.	Male.	Female.
Agarwala	1,511	757	754	175	276	71	51	97	98	318	261
Babhan	236,252	116,871	119,381	2,652	2,425	6,234	6,113	343	272	14,168	19,438
Baniya	39,655	19,117	20,538	979	1,140	4,332	4,407	471	494	1,157	1,335
(i)—Baisya	8,544	4,179	4,365	81	124	2,319	2,207	64	79	206	357
(ii)—Barnawar	6,119	2,983	3,136	157	206	9	16	16	13	114	138
(iii)—Kasarwani	8,022	3,824	4,198	342	384	1,198	1,310	43	19	197	198
(iv)—Mahuri	1,262	611	651	...	...	...	...	1	...	9	7
(v)—Rauniar	1,517	744	773	15	16	318	353	26	13	28	27
(vi)—Sinduria	3,184	1,531	1,653	197	201	251	274	...	...	398	404
Barhi	29,806	14,362	15,444	1,374	1,584	1,388	1,418	178	181	1,308	1,401
Barui	12,187	6,184	6,003	809	810	71	56	766	760	490	401
Beldar	14,649	7,287	7,362	248	270	694	879	54	74	546	563
Bhuiya	4,946	2,329	2,617	...	...	...	...	...	...	...	...
Bind	5,374	2,499	2,875	516	547	879	945	...	...	891	873
Brahman	72,048	35,138	36,910	2,164	1,716	2,849	2,464	834	693	1,828	1,783
Chain	2,567	1,283	1,284	968	1,074	141	36	...	...	84	79

BHAGALPUR—*concluded.*

Supul.		Pratabganj.		Bangaon.		Madehpura.		Kishanganj.		Banka.		Amarpur.		Katuria.	
Male.	Female.	Male.	Female.	Male.	Female.	Male.	Female.	Male.	Female.	Male.	Female.	Male.	Female.	Male.	Female.
...	...	190	140	...	...	...	...	...	...	1,122	1,294	...	...	541	676
...	...	85	63	...	...	...	...	...	...	95	97	81	95	...	...
2,330	2,434	...	...	883	804	188	269	304	295	...	...	...	...	182	112
...	...	...	...	...	...	...	...	...	...	...	...	163	211	...	...
54	58	112	119	4	53	51	57	38	46	13	15	21	27	86	76
1,123	926	420	372	610	670	277	100	166	133	180	179	384	402	57	43
4,794	5,125	90	49	59	42	64	58	66	79	...	...	176	171	...	...
3,800	2,500	300	106	2,647	2,699	2,800	2,750	1,420	1,600	500	605	180	398	220	102
96	93	115	82	44	69	...	...	...	...	211	201	...	...	61	32
632	624	...	...	60	63	...	...	...	...	...	...	...	...	180	140
2,349	2,396	542	659	817	854	1,572	1,633	598	548	284	304	1,007	1,059	1,201	1,102
403	378	...	...	151	141	133	112	...	...	83	67	141	130	...	...
1,212	1,332	1,492	1,802	6,027	6,271	742	659	2,239	1,060	4,570	4,858	2,090	2,317	2,039	2,051
124	119	68	29	...	...	132	132	...	...	52	55	169	226	62	89
...	...	...	...	2,269	2,362	3,498	3,523	1,024	963	...	...	...	...	527	523
37	24	179	181	99	97	41	55	47	38	71	59	82	83	86	54

MONGHYR.

Kharakpur.		Begusarai.		Teghra.		Jamui.		Shaikhpura.		Sikandra.		Chakai.	
Male.	Female.	Male.	Female.	Male.	Female.	Male.	Female.	Male.	Female.	Male.	Female.	Male.	Female.
23	23	...	...	61	34	...	...	...	...	5	8	7	
1,383	1,086	45,259	33,834	23,443	30,326	1,434	1,192	10,190	12,851	9,560	9,316	1,388	2,478
1,476	1,726	593	742	2,714	2,891	1,892	1,909	1,608	1,751	2,025	2,334	1,870	1,809
90	107	81	105	1,010	1,080	4	1	...	...	324	305	...	...
135	229	...	...	353	349	710	693	153	153	232	255	1,104	1,084
342	357	...	...	606	686	319	349	206	207	458	570	113	108
...	...	...	...	...	...	...	...	321	386	...	...	280	258
20	24	1	...	46	53	39	40	...	...	215	210	36	37
14	10	30	52	...	...	248	273	117	130	173	195	103	114
1,846	1,071	711	800	2,652	3,255	868	896	1,711	1,563	972	971	1,352	1,384
400	400	,401	1,400	1,226	1,229	...	...	668	603	342	328	11	16
2,956	3,228	9	10	141	36	1,796	1,395	137	109	686	683	20	15
196	180	...	...	...	...	512	534	...	...	...	...	1,621	1,903
...	...	132	182	681	928	...	...	...	...	...	...	...	...
3,461	3,246	12,750	15,253	3,039	4,721	2,786	2,352	2,266	2,136	1,220	1,140	1,951	1,401
6	1	...	...	77	99	...	...	7	2	...	...	...	...

Caste or Group.	District Total.			Monghyr.		Gogri.		Jamalpur.		Surajgarha.	
	Total.	Male.	Female.	Male.	Female.	Male.	Female.	Male.	Female.	Male.	Female.
Chamar	56,997	26,626	30,371	1,767	1,908	5,074	5,217	436	318	2,090	2,846
Dhanuk	122,551	56,473	66,078	4,208	4,542	10,572	11,675	440	476	6,839	7,234
Dhopa	18,360	9,087	9,273	569	704	2,050	1,986	116	106	897	1,200
Dom	11,945	5,961	5,984	423	328	455	447	52	48	1,064	1,042
Dusadh	128,796	62,499	66,297	2,748	3,314	6,790	7,249	536	438	4,609	5,734
Gangauta	9,496	4,597	4,899	2,202	2,424	2,274	2,277	...	...	...	...
Gareri	4,557	2,234	2,323	163	204	1,313	1,250	...	...	138	148
Goala	237,469	118,004	119,465	7,094	8,273	29,786	27,663	3,672	3,909	4,883	4,997
Gonrhi	17,323	8,243	9,080	484	669	3,680	4,009	4	5	725	895
Hajjam and Napit	46,376	23,090	23,286	1,596	1,634	3,649	3,998	101	102	1,423	1,607
Halwai	16,840	8,249	8,591	729	766	2,553	2,819	106	118	747	713
Hari and Mihtar	4,196	2,010	2,186	170	176	190	197	174	178	144	140
Kahar	50,520	25,339	25,181	1,374	1,405	2,292	2,295	662	485	4,158	4,159
Kalwar and Sunri	17,652	8,800	8,852	833	912	2,432	2,440	332	352	406	400
Kamar and Lohar	8,914	4,380	4,534	297	351	1,494	1,595	256	158	91	87
Kandu	56,930	27,679	29,251	1,462	2,002	4,457	4,874	182	150	2,021	3,373
Kayastha	34,239	17,079	17,160	1,343	1,389	1,121	1,080	294	219	1,302	1,375
Kewat	3,878	1,561	2,317	273	638	554	677	1	...	43	103
Khatik	2,061	910	1,151	600	808	20	21	14	11	182	212
Koiri	84,027	41,640	42,387	2,184	2,214	3,708	3,020	325	321	1,700	1,687
Kora	2,615	1,284	1,331	615	663	...	...	...	...	...	...
Kumhar	27,073	13,093	13,980	770	846	2,302	2,493	125	135	978	1,037
Kurmi	31,238	15,418	15,820	1,765	1,857	1,718	1,802	101	98	4,063	4,541
Malakar	7,748	5,348	2 400	73	57	528	520	182	105	118	106
Markande	3,015	1,386	1,629	107	120	1,279	1,509	...	...	...	...
Musahar	118,858	59,264	59,594	2,850	2,564	8,814	8,201	184	349	4,883	5,088
Nagar	8,465	4,036	4,429	...	...	3,897	4,280	...	...	...	...
Nuniya	6,833	3,399	3,434	244	249	575	582	682	707	1	...
Pargha	1,070	485	585	...	...	...	...	...	...	...	...
Pasi	13,750	6,752	6,998	839	863	540	520	51	50	494	528
Rajput	57,974	30,658	27,316	3,139	2,927	6,910	6,078	189	155	946	846
Santal	18,827	9,232	9,595	1,122	1,270	29	21	...	...	203	245
Sonar	14,596	7,718	6,878	536	621	584	589	86	83	1,082	1,107
Surahiya	3,998	1,793	2,205	164	196	1,297	1,552	3	3	118	120
Tambuli	5,537	2,662	2,875	75	76	1,644	1,807	4	5	251	346
Tatwa and Tanti	38,131	18,009	20,122	2,894	3,508	6,002	6,998	989	1,134	1,698	1,797
Teli	71,882	29,584	42,298	2,217	3,869	5,199	6,274	287	876	2,525	3,706
Thathera	2,523	1,208	1,315	177	241	297	286	...	...	112	122
Tiyar	17,737	8,363	9,374	492	744	7,669	8,340	...	...	76	85
Turaha	1,027	418	609	235	318	...	...	48	47	...	...
Religious devotees and persons returned by sect.											
Baisnab	1,442	656	786	392	510	...	...	...	...	...	...
Gosain	2,759	1,227	1,532	...	...	340	382	30	73	110	137
Hindus returned by actual occupation.											
Ghatwal	5,508	2,600	2,908	81	124	...	...	...	...	...	...
Laheri	2,035	1,024	1,011	59	59	73	50	19	13	157	162
Mala	11,812	5,061	6,751	409	296	614	433	225	285	...	...
Poddar	1,777	868	909	...	...	854	894	...	...	...	...
Musalmans returned by title.											
Pathan	11,036	5,244	5,792	864	983	930	975	123	110	286	350
Sayyid	10,539	4,793	5,746	522	612	464	569	77	45	604	666
Shaikh	64,870	31,265	33,605	4,699	4,586	7,715	7,357	741	665	1,993	2,330

MONGHYR—*continued.*

Kharakpur.		Begusarai.		Tegra.		Jamui.		Shaikhpura.		Sikandra.		Chakai.	
Male.	Female.	Male.	Female.	Male.	Female.	Male.	Female.	Male.	Female.	Male.	Female.	Male.	Female.
2,311	2,574	3,982	4,883	2,613	3,947	2,241	2,256	2,157	2,317	1,340	1,491	2,615	2,615
4,841	4,607	9,922	14,993	8,813	10,028	3,605	4,195	4,116	4,779	2,299	2,679	818	870
543	589	991	803	1,371	1,305	546	616	745	734	562	531	697	699
637	633	576	581	368	399	584	609	311	385	148	165	1,363	1,347
3,275	3,587	19,877	16,333	12,396	16,945	2,493	2,562	5,090	5,214	2,545	2,720	2,140	2,201
76	85	17	8	29	105	...	...	...	...	...	...	...	...
30	48	96	150	71	86	121	165	170	129	41	35	91	108
9,898	10,775	15,923	17,876	5,926	6,112	9,342	9,214	10,325	9,789	8,479	8,375	12,676	12,482
181	251	2,391	2,368	81	159	28	35	565	534	37	56	67	109
1,046	1,355	6,370	5,343	1,904	2,220	1,662	1,567	1,565	1,658	1,113	1,161	2,661	2,621
645	685	2,017	2,087	768	783	139	117	291	256	132	111	122	121
279	322	218	291	157	149	168	172	285	311	107	104	118	146
1,749	1,765	1,794	1,735	772	783	2,738	2,781	4,731	4,752	3,073	3,048	1,996	1,973
1,356	1,447	1,256	1,042	267	302	619	640	582	536	476	542	241	239
1,223	1,397	35	42	90	109	283	258	170	129	235	217	217	191
935	1,028	8,383	8,451	5,205	5,266	1,421	1,349	1,147	1,197	994	999	572	562
1,129	1,188	3,217	3,092	2,103	2,136	2,029	2,054	1,177	1,234	1,843	1,877	1,521	1,516
125	220	310	330	248	349	...	...	...	...	...	...	7	...
43	54	...	...	4	3	...	...	...	...	47	42	...	...
5,485	5,855	9,863	10,608	3,750	4,063	2,678	2,813	5,026	4,720	4,279	4,380	2,643	2,706
162	161	...	...	136	131	...	...	117	119	107	121	147	136
921	1,028	2,637	3,028	1,624	1,733	819	923	1,265	1,241	630	606	1,021	910
873	891	333	332	175	242	46	20	6,145	5,853	21	3	178	181
171	142	3,577	669	363	407	88	83	127	128	117	100	54	63
...	...	...	...	...	...	...	...	...	...	...	...	...	...
1,604	1,163	14,787	14,829	837	988	7,103	7,601	8,798	9,146	7,417	7,881	1,987	1,784
2	...	...	...	136	149	...	...	1	...	...	...	...	...
34	36	11	10	384	382	19	17	1,158	1,142	268	289	23	20
293	356	...	...	...	...	145	172	...	...	47	57	...	...
406	472	849	867	682	714	231	252	1,954	2,033	620	609	86	84
3,885	3,063	3,406	3,027	2,894	2,595	3,827	3,687	1,518	1,370	1,884	1,605	2,060	1,963
1,427	1,526	...	...	...	...	1,743	1,864	...	...	...	...	4,648	4,669
447	440	1,561	605	588	618	294	288	1,536	1,533	626	613	358	375
...	...	...	...	211	334	...	...	...	...	...	...	...	...
64	63	...	...	216	154	24	21	208	223	134	137	42	43
208	210	502	426	1,439	1,782	2,069	1,991	929	953	902	979	387	344
2,403	4,042	4,848	5,706	2,646	3,868	1,887	3,218	3,759	4,847	2,348	2,906	1,465	2,986
98	117	32	31	177	162	82	70	74	112	97	104	62	70
14	16	...	...	112	189	...	...	...	...	...	...	...	...
...	...	...	...	120	236	...	...	...	...	15	8	...	...
33	34	179	214	...	...	7	...	...	...	45	28	...	...
230	348	...	...	17	26	188	231	29	26	121	113	162	196
226	246	...	...	...	...	860	954	5	2	27	19	1,401	1,563
94	86	220	244	171	144	73	86	106	124	40	31	12	12
...	...	2,106	3,179	1,591	2,354	...	...	116	204	...	...	...	...
...	...	...	...	14	15	...	...	...	...	...	...	...	...
606	708	107	148	408	405	329	331	1,017	1,132	450	551	124	109
205	213	101	183	700	831	62	39	1,942	2,470	108	115	8	3
2,830	3,470	4,651	5,150	2,208	2,307	781	715	2,924	3,925	1,483	1,737	1,240	1,363

DISTRICT

Group.	District Total.			Monghyr.		Gogri.		Jamalpur.		Surajgarha.	
	Total.	Male.	Female.	Male.	Female.	Male.	Female.	Male.	Female.	Male.	Female.
Musalmans returned by actual occupation.											
Dhobi	4,757	1,227	3,530	69	398	166	658	...	...	...	...
Dhunia	10,789	4,986	5,803	268	314	1,396	1,526	125	184	193	226
Fakir	1,931	924	1,007	30	31	552	558	25	23	18	17
Jolaha	35,410	16,545	18,865	152	164	1,453	1,735	559	601	1,095	1,257
Kalal	5,118	2,387	2,731	269	320	291	306	38	42	219	258
Kunjra	25,125	10,837	14,288	767	1,149	2,922	3,505	310	507	915	1,508
Mukeri	2,550	1,186	1,364	...	...	...	...	...	...	...	...

DISTRICT

Caste.	District Total.			Purnea.		Amur Kasba.		Dhamdaha.		Gondwara.		Kadwa.	
	Total.	Male.	Female.	Male.	Female.	Male.	Female.	Male.	Female.	Male.	Female.	Male.	Female.
Amat	10,033	5,042	4,991	359	304	...	...	103	121	...	...	481	537
Babhan	5,366	3,176	2,190	441	361	53	46	540	371	388	207	127	85
Baniya	27,772	14,222	13,550	3,266	3,328	127	125	992	858	2,107	1,987	2,040	1,838
(i)—Baisya	6,781	3,357	3,424	2,932	3,074	...	...	75	44	...	...	...	...
(ii)—Khatri	3,546	1,882	1,664	43	35	...	...	...	...	180	121	...	...
Barhi	21,319	10,611	10,708	317	334	2,329	2,610	67	33	421	298	4,732	4,881
Barui	4,633	2,381	2,252	606	620	249	307	322	223	99	62	165	155
Bauri	3,082	1,512	1,570	9	7	181	253	...	...	...	...	115	117
Beldar	9,047	4,631	4,416	647	674	238	234	421	407	607	594	844	762
Bhat	2,862	1,482	1,380	97	92	...	...	70	52	83	84	62	63
Bind	9,562	4,924	4,638	1,894	1,819	309	266	623	619	497	409	341	324
Brahman	28,306	14,257	14,049	1,191	1,043	228	180	2,916	2,798	1,628	1,538	551	597
Chain	2,161	1,183	978	68	18	36	10	14	8	160	187	...	...
Chamar	18,342	9,144	9,198	929	906	339	222	1,827	2,025	989	1,083	865	821
Chapual	6,960	3,474	3,486	...	...	735	731	...	...	...	...	1,156	1,142
Dhanuk	43,634	21,753	21,881	2,479	2,263	...	...	4,056	3,860	3,279	3,465	3,462	3,707
Dhopa	10,789	5,342	5,447	1,101	1,110	171	163	486	451	496	503	419	434
Dom	5,712	2,926	2,786	429	395	53	46	276	263	197	195	96	79
Dusadh	27,008	13,968	13,040	2,345	2,278	...	...	2,754	2,606	1,809	1,714	487	431
Gangauta	51,287	25,973	25,314	385	335	1,692	1,778	820	428	3,178	3,362	1,438	1,388
Gareri	5,419	2,725	2,694	141	148	263	255	898	831	159	116	159	267
Goala	134,110	67,774	66,336	7,911	10,068	2,538	2,916	13,498	10,829	4,876	5,060	3,089	3,202
Gonrhi	27,382	13,544	13,838	7,673	8,296	...	...	2,677	2,350	961	918	75	75
Hajjam and Napit	18,191	9,342	8,849	787	760	581	533	772	728	757	737	291	292
Halwai and Maira	8,270	4,265	4,005	562	520	149	114	628	528	281	178	222	224
Hari and Mihtar	66,160	34,921	31,239	607	585	3,394	2,790	355	309	103	101	4,449	3,902
Jugi	14,674	7,577	7,097	...	...	...	...	3,777	3,688	...	...	68	74
Kahar	9,644	5,112	4,532	405	351	132	93	534	422	634	543	450	410
Kaibartta	58,724	28,976	29,748	2,241	2,279	3,194	3,269	643	645	4,804	5,108	3,802	4,199
Kalwar and Sunri	18,863	9,690	9,173	578	497	621	717	757	629	914	683	855	920
Kamar and Lohar	16,358	8,781	7,577	856	770	419	370	796	760	923	844	561	530
Kandu	5,566	3,014	2,552	550	507	63	69	1,155	1,056	245	141	177	173
Kayastha	12,751	6,823	5,928	838	615	182	186	473	364	582	467	344	356
Kewat	17,849	9,058	8,791	897	868	135	133	1,551	1,588	227	40	287	258
Khanjar	1,838	977	861	...	...	...	...	...	...	...	...	335	319
Kharwar	7,632	3,820	3,812	120	96	...	...	...	...	...	...	452	469
Khatbe	1,755	920	835	...	...	...	...	...	...	441	336	...	...
Kochh	136,558	69,598	66,960	...	...	1,392	1,504	99	80	...	...	81	59

MONGHYR—*concluded.*

Kharakpur.		Begusarai.		Tegra.		Jamui.		Shaikhpura.		Sikandra.		Chakai.	
Male.	Female.	Male.	Female.	Male.	Female.	Male.	Female.	Male.	Female.	Male.	Female.	Male.	Female.
38	223	...	...	886	1,946	...	...	...	...	70	306	...	...
41	53	1,573	1,697	690	967	266	315	170	232	205	218	59	72
...	...	25	29	96	152	13	29	52	48	109	118	4	2
2,245	2,399	3,471	4,112	1,822	2,093	943	1,019	2,018	2,349	1,206	1,495	1,581	1,641
29	37	...	...	19	12	354	376	222	290	483	560	463	530
361	691	3,400	3,872	1,307	1,646	852	446	153	381	250	343	100	240
1,186	1,364	...	...	...	...	...	...	...	...	...	...	...	...

PURNEA.

Balarampur.		Manihari.		Araria.		Matiari.		Raniganj.		Kishenganj.		Bahadurganj.		Kaliaganj.	
Male.	Female.	Male.	Female.	Male.	Female.	Male.	Female.	Male.	Female.	Male.	Female.	Male.	Female.	Male.	Female.
...	...	59	30	1,143	1,055	1,115	1,223	550	568	...	...	1,232	1,153	...	...
39	27	61	27	316	174	581	441	450	352	63	85	45	35	72	29
1,523	1,400	364	359	562	691	1,112	1,062	470	474	247	198	363	372	1,049	858
...	...	...	...	103	108	...	...	...	...	247	198	...	...	...	...
1,384	1,263	45	34	...	...	230	211	...	...	...	...	...	...	...	...
623	602	39	52	70	32	261	236	...	...	533	469	617	607	602	534
115	111	32	36	267	219	286	282	163	156	77	81	...	...	...	...
163	164	...	...	130	143	...	...	...	...	...	...	200	209	714	677
553	487	41	35	639	612	286	282	49	33	16	19	253	242	37	35
...	...	72	37	62	75	...	...	...	...	1,036	977	...	...	...	...
33	19	164	106	69	67	367	356	308	440	252	169	25	17	42	27
208	230	561	559	2,639	2,614	1,601	1,695	1,284	1,282	324	382	500	553	626	578
102	9	363	393	80	69	66	67	...	...	294	217	...	...	...	...
236	175	411	426	581	639	1,287	1,392	1,043	1,082	249	121	251	194	137	112
144	154	59	43	...	...	50	58	...	...	...	...	1,068	1,110	262	248
118	121	663	639	1,829	1,834	3,535	3,411	2,203	2,455	129	126	...	...	...	...
61	74	244	252	698	687	433	446	793	923	111	104	149	161	180	139
65	33	167	159	382	364	948	919	86	75	65	33	53	35	109	188
...	...	1,245	1,265	2,547	2,146	241	203	2,079	2,002	249	176	212	159	...	...
...	...	634	739	2,947	3,124	...	...	204	190	835	320	8,627	8,377	5,718	5,276
46	39	257	267	85	29	46	37	...	...	624	622	83	79	19	4
1,167	1,205	8,316	7,089	9,524	10,766	3,017	2,797	8,763	7,466	580	697	3,187	3,236	999	1,005
...	...	...	...	1,111	1,157	...	...	871	858	...	...	176	189	...	...
270	261	333	376	1,081	972	936	874	361	355	471	415	1,044	987	1,658	1,559
57	55	488	512	621	610	174	235	288	297	206	168	269	240	320	324
4,141	3,656	356	298	4,946	4,542	287	359	334	386	2,826	2,251	6,372	6,107	6,751	5,863
214	198	...	...	...	...	...	...	1,560	1,303	493	450	514	492	951	912
347	313	34	33	294	232	689	642	195	193	336	339	679	612	383	340
674	689	505	469	7,003	6,972	169	89	1,641	1,716	1,733	1,815	932	930	1,635	1,561
372	404	450	512	676	590	1,278	1,166	1,600	1,330	553	501	585	673	456	551
385	204	467	371	819	767	775	664	553	487	753	573	868	712	601	519
55	40	133	137	39	47	161	55	159	108	118	96	65	33	94	90
77	85	155	101	313	250	3,207	2,996	271	262	222	195	104	80	55	21
106	115	44	61	3,742	3,831	41	44	1,842	1,746	63	33	53	45	70	29
...	...	...	...	...	...	...	...	...	...	...	...	642	542	...	...
...	...	1,743	1,646	...	...	...	...	835	760	...	...	670	641	...	...
...	...	...	...	...	...	...	...	479	479	...	...	...	...	...	...
27,877	27,550	2,480	1,143	1,928	1,784	...	...	119	124	4,700	4,737	9,377	8,708	21,545	21,271

Caste or Group.	District Total.			Purnea.		Amur Kasba.		Dhamdaha.		Gondwara.		Kadwa.	
	Total.	Male.	Female.	Male.	Female.	Male.	Female.	Male.	Female.	Male.	Female.	Male.	Female.
Koiri	22,471	11,704	10,767	3,825	3,708	370	366	1,296	1,081	1,851	1,778	679	631
Kol	2,991	1,528	1,463	...	...	...	...	192	168	...	...	569	548
Kumhar	10,910	5,492	5,418	428	421	217	231	379	356	771	795	260	278
Kurmi	6,489	3,942	2,547	537	399	53	13	1,323	950	284	103	114	57
Malakar	3,089	1,628	1,461	97	117	61	65	91	71	81	53	75	65
Markande	8,741	4,229	4,512	94	77	...	...	2,971	3,079	945	1,099	...	...
Muriyari	3,436	1,699	1,737	...	...	...	...	74	78	888	943	254	246
Musahar	48,607	25,501	23,106	3,800	3,677	289	238	10,777	10,107	3,285	3,289	511	511
Nagar	3,002	1,498	1,504	...	...	...	...	357	349	...	...	269	296
Namasudra or Chandal ...	18,340	9,188	9,152	75	75	...	...	...	...	...	...	...	...
Nat	1,974	823	1,151	...	...	...	...	...	...	151	194	...	...
Nuniya	8,337	4,730	3,607	222	155	115	91	382	288	413	401	99	65
Rajput	13,575	8,026	5,549	806	601	100	33	2,090	1,443	801	389	543	393
Sadgop	5,768	2,976	2,792	45	36	135	138	...	...	...	...	...	...
Sonar	4,639	2,579	2,060	203	140	205	162	201	142	282	206	301	212
Tatwa and Tanti	15,602	7,887	7,715	1,217	1,114	109	112	585	561	1,254	1,395	257	253
Teli	36,805	18,518	18,287	1,935	1,735	843	922	2,240	1,934	1,235	1,102	1,175	1,214
Thathera	2,351	1,170	1,181	140	118	74	69	86	96	144	167	153	156
Tiyar	17,579	8,538	9,041	356	383	32	31	43	46	1,914	2,124	2,380	2,500
Turaha	1,240	673	567	273	195	...	...	...	...	...	...	233	252
Religious devotees and persons returned by sect.													
Baisnab	2,085	1,019	1,066	...	...	...	...	...	...	63	49	80	88
Fakir	4,029	2,167	1,862	159	172	...	...	...	...	102	131	103	92
Gosain	1,077	546	531	99	110	...	...	145	146	104	80	...	...
Sanyasi	1,436	743	693	...	...	...	...	...	...	...	...	...	...
Hindus returned by title or common sub-caste.													
Buna	9,578	5,272	4,306	293	257	...	...	1,251	1,233	1,573	1,498	898	901
Singh	3,317	1,880	1,437	1,880	1,437	...	...	...	...	...	...	...	...
Hindus returned by actual occupation.													
Bakali	1,120	534	586	43	50	151	154	43	51	...	...	...	...
Kabari	2,516	1,290	1,226	57	43	...	...	1,233	1,183	...	...	...	...
Kawali	1,938	963	975	38	43	74	42	63	34	...	...	...	...
Lahori	1,391	735	656	169	121	159	162	...	...	54	46	...	...
Mala	6,491	3,728	2,763	...	...	389	353	190	141	397	153	372	281
Manjhi	4,548	2,368	2,180	...	...	189	194	...	...	...	...	...	...
Hindus returned by unidentifiable caste.													
Kalar	1,219	604	615	74	71	...	...	184	164	...	...	63	63
Musalmans returned by title.													
Mir	1,092	540	552	25	17	...	...	...	...	...	...	168	147
Pathan	9,352	4,994	4,358	464	505	253	235	187	26	283	229	338	301
Sayyid	9,398	4,665	4,733	56	56	168	191	88	48	105	93	209	207
Shaikh	710,012	360,400	349,612	20,584	19,909	36,007	35,931	2,037	2,435	4,534	4,453	18,846	19,196
Musalmans returned by actual occupation.													
Dafali	5,050	2,605	2,445	38	33	...	...	...	...	...	...	...	...
Darzi	1,002	512	490	154	182	...	...	21	17	...	...	...	...
Dhunia	9,761	4,874	4,887	739	763	13	10	622	611	303	302	662	663
Fakir	1,807	860	947	49	60	...	...	213	305	...	...	63	21
Jolaha	39,958	20,454	19,504	3,668	4,070	1,782	1,814	478	465	1,555	1,504	3,395	3,014
Kunjra	10,894	5,476	5,418	610	416	58	81	1,233	1,183	437	340	300	319

NEA—*concluded.*

Balarampur.		Manihari.		Araria.		Matiari.		Raniganj.		Kishenganj.		Bahadurganj.		Kaliaganj.	
Male.	Female.	Male.	Female.	Male.	Female.	Male.	Female.	Male.	Female.	Male.	Female.	Male.	Female.	Male.	Female.
125	68	223	167	707	567	1,393	1,304	882	791	60	46	140	123	153	137
178	180	9	10	247	237	196	204	...	...	...	...	...	...	137	126
227	238	285	232	688	668	497	454	182	180	461	428	662	726	435	411
49	18	55	37	634	556	260	97	154	109	287	164	101	12	91	32
175	184	27	22	182	180	106	51	86	78	77	67	172	141	398	367
...	...	69	65	...	...	150	192	...	...	...	...	...	...	...	...
...	...	252	189	...	...	...	...	...	...	236	281	...	...	...	...
...	...	664	675	870	785	1,963	1,497	2,842	1,941	321	280	81	47	98	59
...	...	159	180	...	...	16	17	697	662	...	...	...	...	...	...
619	746	1,743	1,846	...	...	4,789	4,736	...	...	843	896	232	250	687	601
...	...	177	201	271	346	112	213	43	98	...	...	13	14	56	85
208	163	18	9	852	705	401	511	680	591	340	248	667	843	333	37
309	228	368	299	575	436	875	590	1,039	852	102	40	306	214	119	31
149	152	...	...	...	...	...	...	...	...	...	...	1,818	1,736	829	730
29	15	90	127	277	175	304	265	107	86	193	248	107	140	220	142
152	110	...	...	509	472	1,600	1,558	58	74	178	121	981	897	987	1,043
506	453	627	628	3,073	3,314	2,916	3,013	1,131	1,064	577	539	1,122	1,240	1,136	1,129
...	...	...	...	255	232	157	171	88	104	...	...	73	69	...	...
809	781	1,155	1,253	730	813	357	324	366	423	396	363	...	...	...	...
...	...	81	53	...	...	86	67	...	...	...	...	...	...	...	...
465	502	...	...	...	...	...	...	...	...	...	...	209	197	202	230
...	...	92	90	656	541	122	119	169	67	126	142	464	380	174	128
...	...	58	37	...	...	2	1	92	103	...	...	46	54	...	...
...	...	88	45	87	84	395	352	110	111	...	...	63	71	...	...
...	...	744	153	...	...	405	177	108	87	...	...	...	...	...	...
...	...	...	...	...	...	...	...	...	...	...	...	...	...	...	...
...	...	...	...	130	128	19	28	...	...	...	...	148	166	...	...
...	...	...	...	...	...	...	...	...	...	...	...	...	...	...	...
...	...	106	96	471	477	162	242	...	...	...	...	49	41	...	...
...	...	78	83	72	44	174	170	...	...	...	...	29	30	...	...
576	508	546	213	349	320	115	51	...	...	...	...	420	407	374	336
...	...	80	56	256	247	...	...	...	...	325	298	581	553	937	832
213	226	...	...	70	91	...	...	...	...	...	...	...	...	...	...
...	...	118	157	26	24	...	...	...	...	...	...	...	...	203	207
99	72	285	275	385	356	423	374	117	120	1,441	1,316	326	237	393	313
24	28	2,726	2,093	463	303	44	36	147	107	394	371	57	48	164	162
26,089	25,137	3,217	3,386	42,271	42,325	6,826	6,480	6,680	5,718	55,730	52,484	62,623	61,255	74,056	70,903
...	...	2,497	2,348	...	...	70	64	...	...	...	...	...	...	...	...
...	...	78	41	...	...	21	15	...	...	243	235	...	...	...	...
2	1	714	681	880	868	303	377	500	512	108	91	10	3	18	5
...	...	45	60	35	64	271	234	97	109	...	...	87	94	...	...
122	112	1,685	1,503	3,109	2,658	1,926	1,871	1,577	1,529	144	128	411	408	512	428
100	181	805	850	204	209	400	460	888	886	83	72	208	231	150	190

Caste or Group.	District Total.			Malda.		Kharba.		Ratua.	
	Total.	Male.	Female.	Male.	Female.	Male.	Female.	Male.	Female.
Baniya	6,848	3,327	3,521	259	318	440	366	860	928
Barhi	3,046	1,513	1,533	...	...	139	126	864	889
Barui	1,940	1,054	886	127	70	616	643	114	51
Beldar	2,247	1,143	1,104	...	...	757	756	218	173
Bind	10,395	5,034	5,361	149	125	80	34	1,407	1,655
Brahman	8,318	4,620	3,698	289	210	568	365	1,042	1,016
Chain	41,213	20,093	21,120	243	180	494	552	7,373	8,380
Chamar and Muchi	5,982	2,978	3,004	89	108	176	169	524	575
Dhanuk	7,302	3,557	3,745	127	137	709	771	610	637
Dhopa	4,097	2,002	2,095	117	137	226	212	450	414
Dom	1,924	934	990	15	17	54	48	109	98
Dusadh	3,957	1,998	1,959	...	...	...	...	527	541
Gangauta	3,125	1,539	1,586	195	223	350	362	218	231
Goala	15,291	7,928	7,363	385	255	1,573	1,449	2,040	2,051
Gonrhi	3,871	1,892	1,979	173	165	333	414	648	708
Hajjam and Napit	6,950	3,439	3,511	151	143	458	449	607	602
Hari and Mihtar	15,067	7,504	7,563	283	259	3,873	3,964	72	57
Jugi	13,398	6,656	6,742	116	95	5,877	5,375	1,052	1,164
Kahar	3,367	1,656	1,711	240	219	...	...	457	517
Kaibartta	37,744	18,164	19,580	291	208	1,174	1,144	7,603	8,462
Kalwar and Sunri	4,125	2,090	2,035	554	490	442	485	336	285
Kamar and Lohar	5,293	2,633	2,660	227	224	281	274	274	306
Kandu	1,773	955	818	72	81	252	251	117	117
Kayastha	2,702	1,438	1,264	111	99	150	142	212	279
Kewat	3,121	1,368	1,753	...	...	...	...	326	459
Kharwar	6,413	3,099	3,314	...	...	791	811	2,114	2,329
Koch	62,975	32,127	30,848	5,375	5,004	1,166	818	4,942	5,236
Kol	3,227	1,630	1,597	177	153	356	353	75	76
Kumhar	4,158	2,155	2,003	167	197	...	...	272	245
Kurmi	2,199	1,352	847	207	31	...	...	68	10
Mahili	1,165	576	589	...	...	70	75	...	...
Malo	5,662	2,915	2,747	361	320	231	255	84	35
Muriyari	2,220	1,051	1,169	85	105	85	49	65	60
Nagar	18,878	8,790	10,088	57	60	...	...	960	1,108
Namasudra or Chandal	4,669	2,329	2,340	412	496	474	478	368	450
Pod	9,574	4,691	4,883	485	540	...	...	67	60
Rajput	2,871	1,743	1,128	145	63	212	132	...	...
Sadgop	1,024	517	507	142	112	...	...	61	19
Santal	20,989	10,897	10,092	5,301	4,871	121	116	7	30
Sonar	2,056	1,045	1,011	412	464	...	...	104	120
Surahiya	2,257	1,651	606	172	8	184	196	131	84
Tatwa and Tanti	5,445	2,741	2,704	659	706	77	63	83	126
Teli and Kalu	8,195	3,871	4,324	182	106	906	989	771	813
Tiyar	14,301	7,060	7,241	191	113	1,313	1,303	2,952	3,235
Turi	1,256	647	609	...	...	...	...	202	195
Religious devotees and persons returned by sect.									
Baisnab	6,508	2,572	3,936	225	339	509	656	119	156
Hindus returned by title or common sub-caste.									
Buna	4,732	2,378	2,354	554	585	...	...	149	164

MALDA.

Gajol.		English Bazar.		Kaliachak.		Sibganj.		Gumashtapur.		Nawabganj.	
Male.	Female.	Male.	Female.	Male.	Female.	Male.	Female.	Male.	Female.	Male.	Female.
52	62	600	662	207	191	164	106	663	811	82	77
81	68	363	380	208	190	217	203	76	96	65	81
...	...	...	...	...	...	69	63	128	59	...	...
46	39	122	136	...	...	...	...	...	...	...	...
139	110	328	338	1,368	1,572	578	540	285	265	700	722
159	56	1,127	871	581	575	322	289	400	230	132	86
555	431	522	403	8,352	8,989	1,067	1,236	913	470	574	529
72	66	760	784	331	381	365	331	455	312	206	278
49	49	1,155	1,187	429	477	...	...	478	487	...	...
64	42	379	413	417	475	249	256	100	116	...	...
56	68	82	72	75	76	405	486	87	66	52	59
226	187	58	80	248	281	503	552	436	318	...	...
...	...	182	160	524	577	...	...	...	...	70	33
202	126	1,117	1,046	1,382	1,337	589	592	540	356	100	151
125	82	124	110	300	200	121	183	...	...	108	117
195	170	373	379	679	687	455	552	222	233	299	296
1,379	1,389	1,100	1,215	64	47	360	342	80	87	293	213
111	108	...	...	..	...	...	...	...	...	...	...
54	46	404	379	391	421	110	129	...	...	...	...
253	154	1,070	2,029	5,516	6,313	822	841	314	264	221	145
86	108	19	16	99	95	222	208	199	189	133	159
269	268	238	277	315	292	265	250	292	320	472	449
59	62	176	140	77	73	42	12	51	30	109	52
106	107	312	248	189	161	178	151	80	81	100	43
...	...	282	383	636	840	...	...	...	...	124	71
149	141	...	...	...	...	...	...	45	33	...	...
13,661	12,720	66	75	857	897	1,496	1,703	2,175	2,112	2,369	2,263
42	51	75	82	103	120	83	75	387	328	332	359
140	143	283	258	196	180	166	146	779	735	152	99
...	...	157	57	...	...	...	...	...	...	920	749
...	...	...	...	...	...	...	...	106	112	400	402
113	48	535	649	125	82	365	354	403	354	698	644
55	89	84	95	12	18	201	219	322	345	142	189
119	55	5,304	6,119	1,716	1,989	343	432	291	325	...	...
55	63	283	299	246	152	231	214	58	56	202	137
...	...	3,294	3,376	601	627	160	185	...	...	84	95
540	432	319	292	...	...	...	...	527	209	...	...
81	73	88	125	...	...	93	124	...	...	52	54
4,845	4,583	569	437	10	8	2	3	42	44	...	...
78	61	196	184	255	242	...	...	...	...	...	...
199	23	...	...	487	101	159	...	319	194	...	...
478	504	139	101	523	472	293	317	175	169	314	244
37	8	461	530	739	753	473	498	156	259	146	368
410	414	1,351	1,323	347	427	140	132	209	142	147	152
143	143	...	...	...	...	...	...	171	163	131	108
288	279	528	936	243	348	216	467	294	276	200	479
182	174	362	862	111	109	288	318	557	539	175	183

DISTRICT

Group.	District Total.			Malda.		Kharba.		Ratua.	
	Total.	Male.	Female.	Male.	Female.	Male.	Female.	Male.	Female.
Hindus returned by actual occupation.									
Dulia	1,716	812	904	243	225	...	...	321	388
Patni	1,126	554	572	29	117	...	...	42	46
Hindus returned by locality.									
Bengalis	1,961	897	1,064	128	139	130	142	261	385
Musalmans returned by title.									
Pathan	5,259	2,618	2,641	116	91	239	226	450	526
Sayyid	2,600	1,311	1,289	57	82	180	188	155	160
Shaikh	360,903	173,241	187,662	7,646	8,131	21,755	23,323	11,096	11,771
Musalmans returned by actual occupation.									
Dhunia	2,658	1,253	1,405	77	70	...	...	402	464
Jolaha	7,457	3,519	3,938	182	185	165	131	317	378
Kunjra	1,904	912	992	145	150	55	59	359	373

DISTRICT SAN

Caste.	District Total.			Deoghar.		Madhupur.		Sarath.		Godda.		Mahagama.		Poreya.	
	Total.	Male.	Female.	Male.	Female.	Male.	Female.	Male.	Female.	Male.	Female.	Male.	Female.	Male.	Female.
Babhan	6,420	3,386	3,034	933	717	1,096	1,122	1,028	970	43	26	34	32	...	...
Bagdi	3,812	1,830	1,982	132	163	68	64	...	...	25	3	...	...	...	...
Baniya	33,049	16,456	16,593	935	980	933	968	1,024	955	667	754	1,090	1,177	568	600
(i)—Gandha Banik	3,123	1,573	1,550	24	18	147	183	178	159	...	...	...	...	...	...
(ii)—Khatri	14,933	7,250	7,683	...	...	425	427	313	191	376	437	624	689	218	234
(iii)—Rauniar	3,502	1,815	1,687	114	87	175	184	173	180	126	118	99	113	102	105
Barhi	5,604	2,845	2,759	501	536	268	273	161	153	177	177	113	113	363	302
Barui	1,036	511	525	45	44	37	43	56	73	...	...	31	38	78	93
Bauri	33,396	16,643	16,753	263	274	669	633	831	837	238	231	3,392	3,360	65	70
Bhuiya	26,351	12,528	13,823	1,902	1,772	...	...	...	...	276	353	...	...	352	281
Bind	1,409	699	710	...	...	...	...	...	...	...	...	...	...	...	...
Brahman	30,122	16,283	13,839	4,022	3,363	1,504	1,366	873	765	1,852	1,593	1,184	1,063	651	919
Chain	13,425	6,335	7,090	...	...	...	...	...	...	...	...	...	...	...	...
Chamar and Muchi	31,621	15,931	15,690	3,752	3,378	1,012	1,163	1,080	1,086	1,937	1,968	1,805	1,936	476	520
Dhanuk	13,024	6,422	6,602	1,720	1,861	180	201	367	362	909	842	1,321	1,392	...	...
Dhopa	7,890	3,877	4,013	447	466	175	194	107	116	312	331	351	355	87	99
Dom	32,445	16,247	16,198	2,657	2,638	1,338	1,352	1,230	1,100	1,279	1,280	794	765	1,438	1,472
Dusadh	11,540	5,626	5,914	1,285	1,347	113	118	19	21	769	873	1,236	1,320	39	49
Goala	99,685	50,251	49,434	13,581	13,804	3,897	3,710	3,109	2,922	4,484	4,598	3,020	3,072	2,202	2,165
Gonrhi	2,372	1,214	1,158	...	...	...	...	...	...	52	61	...	...	245	221
Hajjam and Napit	17,102	8,392	8,710	1,225	1,288	561	581	465	449	789	822	560	570	509	273
Halwai and Maira	15,222	7,736	7,486	262	247	327	304	478	403	1,294	1,143	363	371	843	833
Hari and Mihtar	7,207	3,316	3,891	289	342	153	155	162	187	275	371	176	185	178	311
Jugi	1,588	762	826	99	103	88	97	53	56	22	27	61	62	...	...
Kadar	6,215	2,995	3,220	...	...	...	...	...	...	1,149	1,278	86	101	1,087	1,110
Kahar	17,533	8,626	8,907	1,873	2,037	1,697	1,728	554	578	1,183	1,319	663	696	193	199
Kaibartta	2,945	1,396	1,549	11	5	41	42	97	97	281	314	...	...	...	...
Kalwar and Sunri	27,652	14,000	13,652	1,082	1,006	358	323	577	597	2,067	2,065	748	770	795	881

MALDA—*concluded.*

Gajol.		English Bazar.		Kaliachak.		Sibganj.		Gumashtapur.		Nawabganj.	
Male.	Female.	Male.	Female.	Male.	Female.	Male.	Female.	Male.	Female.	Male.	Female.
...	...	...	...	248	291	...	...	...	...	...	...
133	109	...	...	...	...	338	282	...	...	22	18
...	...	75	94	...	...	...	...	74	80	229	224
82	23	473	450	825	883	197	217	92	81	144	144
71	59	129	88	212	217	111	105	195	199	201	241
7,507	6,467	16,988	18,106	28,189	30,289	40,715	45,866	16,693	17,844	22,652	25,864
...	...	326	371	383	414	...	...	70	66	...	...
...	...	679	869	2,176	2,355	...	...	...	...	...	...
...	...	229	269	59	71	...	...	65	70	...	...

TAL PARGANAS.

Portion of Daminikoh (Godda Subdivision).		Pakaur.		Maheshpur.		Portion of Daminikoh (Pakaur Subdivision).		Rajmahal.		Sahibganj.		Portion of Daminikoh (Rajmahal Subdivision).		Dumka.		Portion of Daminikoh. (Dumka Subdivision).		Jamtara.	
Male.	Female.	Male.	Female.	Male.	Female.	Male.	Female.	Male.	Female.	Male.	Female.	Male.	Female.	Male.	Female.	Male.	Female.	Male.	Female.
43	29	...	...	...	...	...	...	27	34	...	...	...	...	47	4	...	...	135	100
31	34	...	...	...	...	46	51	100	102	8	6	243	303	721	766	...	...	455	490
338	385	1,073	992	1,095	844	576	523	662	661	297	302	834	803	4,023	4,196	235	221	2,106	2,232
...	...	86	72	95	82	38	34	73	80	15	4	105	93	298	293	...	...	515	532
94	147	105	75	151	107	179	144	208	240	72	131	371	355	2,797	2,986	18	1	1,399	1,519
114	112	4	...	157	102	227	212	112	89	103	99	154	147	43	38	112	101	...	...
192	180	263	250	...	...	1	...	...	...	397	372	28	23	839	353	...	...	42	37
8	5	6	4	...	...	3	8	95	86	87	78	...	...	50	48	...	...	15	...
1,430	1,339	571	619	30	20	647	645	140	144	365	442	243	270	1,704	1,745	139	139	5,907	5,985
340	390	105	124	138	141	271	202	...	...	2,049	2,651	173	184	5,475	6,202	...	...	1,447	1,443
...	...	...	...	...	...	...	...	421	462	269	243	...	...	9	5	...	...	...	...
377	365	442	275	195	110	663	563	353	244	355	300	125	86	1,944	1,437	412	216	1,331	1,084
...	...	197	203	169	152	...	...	5,673	6,529	306	206	...	...	...	...	...	...	...	...
88	88	549	483	482	442	...	...	521	547	179	156	205	219	2,393	2,272	...	...	1,452	1,435
17	10	460	528	35	20	330	381	180	157	45	36	61	53	506	480	...	...	291	279
8	14	160	128	27	15	661	669	267	289	110	105	110	118	404	535	11	6	550	573
886	846	1,034	1,087	738	745	634	683	546	560	87	122	692	624	...	...	269	299	2,625	2,625
40	34	75	68	9	9	93	87	617	707	854	832	67	54	335	325	57	57	18	13
126	183	621	562	326	326	344	328	1,437	1,326	663	438	577	479	8,757	8,575	6	8	7,001	6,838
386	303	...	...	...	...	195	192	...	...	302	281	27	31	8	9	...	...	...	...
394	378	396	500	225	247	133	156	430	426	164	270	321	304	1,359	1,524	50	31	911	891
186	197	389	343	287	319	169	99	202	213	150	156	303	319	1,244	1,265	44	44	1,205	1,230
25	23	156	252	210	224	200	232	91	89	78	76	80	100	780	889	454	455	...	...
74	70	35	45	38	41	8	7	10	8	...	...	33	40	139	140	3	...	99	112
49	50	1	...	...	...	118	99	126	130	...	...	19	18	364	434	1	...	...	...
266	251	50	45	304	211	341	353	286	264	208	190	31	28	734	712	...	...	243	296
...	...	432	568	23	28	119	149	190	205	105	75	...	...	96	71	1	...	...	...
183	188	758	696	86	103	241	162	380	334	217	187	743	716	3,023	9,354	99	76	2,684	2,674

Caste or Group.	District Total.			Deoghar.		Madhupur.		Sarath.		Godda.		Mahagama.		Poreya.	
	Total.	Male.	Female.	Male.	Female.	Male.	Female.	Male.	Female.	Male.	Female.	Male.	Female.	Male.	Female.
Kamar and Lohar	29,733	14,723	15,010	906	904	302	308	322	334	830	809	485	501	359	410
Kandu	1,952	1,065	887	276	257	117	102	...	...	73	56	16	18	64	23
Kayastha	6,457	3,484	2,973	506	423	417	402	190	202	231	187	268	254	83	70
Kewat	3,022	1,513	1,509	157	158	69	61	86	79	50	58	...	...	...	...
Khaira	1,690	867	823	7	9	...	...	6	13	...	...	...	...	...	...
Kharwar	1,314	691	623	...	...	...	..	...	...	23	31	...	...	38	30
Koiri	10,158	5,132	5,026	1,036	1,147	423	447	527	517	854	879	604	612	...	...
Kol	14,449	7,228	7,221	1,021	1,005	1,006	1,031	765	729	...	...	...	...	157	145
Kora	4,095	1,968	2,127	...	...	...	...	35	48	30	32	226	231	...	...
Kumhar	21,676	10,858	10,818	1,528	1,444	508	519	713	702	1,160	1,200	629	666	378	422
Kurmi	18,169	9,036	9,133	345	369	90	83	469	481	3,830	3,812	1,868	1,853	190	229
Mahili	17,237	8,506	8,731	496	494	289	338	453	490	212	187	...	...	306	289
Mal	7,837	3,804	4,033	502	590	42	48	268	279	68	53	...	...	73	102
Malakar	1,732	854	878	50	44	13	8	47	49	...	...	78	78	...	...
Malo	2,749	1,329	1,420	...	...	...	...	...	...	...	...	...	...	...	...
Mal Paharia	17,068	8,349	8,719	260	275	340	325	126	169	285	270	315	380	506	504
Markande	2,902	1,373	1,529	...	...	...	...	...	...	585	702	...	...	184	195
Musahar	20,963	10,340	10,623	1,704	1,775	1,061	1,056	927	991	1,629	1,693	2,069	2,197	13	8
Naiya	17,937	8,691	9,246	1,049	1,031	991	991	807	787	...	...	33	38	...	...
Namasudra or Chandal ...	2,184	1,006	1,178	125	130	7	4	...	...	175	170	...	...	...	...
Nuniya	1,593	823	770	...	...	...	...	...	...	149	151	...	...	11	19
Pargha	6,703	3,202	3,501	309	315	19	18	...	...	699	782	...	...	...	...
Pasi	2,623	1,402	1,421	720	684	92	88	17	5	21	22	56	68	270	320
Rajput	34,456	17,101	17,355	995	976	419	384	426	435	1,211	1,231	1,005	1,040	298	293
Rajwar	12,508	6,124	6,384	335	368	489	555	1,345	1,313	522	525	44	67	23	24
Sadgop	1,737	863	874	30	34	4	4	...	...	...	...	...	...	...	...
Santal	617,158	307,282	309,876	3,222	3,209	5,083	5,132	9,981	9,002	11,743	11,671	5,939	5,966	11,049	11,978
Sonar	3,837	1,983	1,854	215	220	110	100	154	136	85	70	213	182	87	94
Tambuli	2,709	1,381	1,328	30	27	10	5	58	53	127	139	...	...	79	70
Tatwa and Tanti	6,597	3,265	3,332	550	569	128	166	19	32	126	151	15	15	22	29
Toli and Kalu	38,698	19,315	19,383	1,613	1,648	1,335	1,322	1,060	1,080	2,282	2,286	1,679	1,651	490	424
Turi	1,331	645	686	...	...	...	...	...	...	...	...	...	...	...	...
Religious devotees and persons returned by sect.															
Baisnab	4,668	2,145	2,523	45	42	15	19	107	121	31	34	51	60	28	24
Gosain	1,998	1,082	916	391	354	167	141	298	255	25	24	...	...	42	26
Hindus returned by title or common sub-caste.															
Buna	6,284	3,092	3,192	...	...	2	4	...	...	1	...	848	823	...	...
Mandal	1,949	905	1,044	...	...	...	...	...	...	...	...	...	...	...	...
Rajbansi	1,604	752	852	...	...	...	...	...	...	...	...	...	...	...	...
Hindus returned by actual occupation.															
Ghatwal	101,285	47,322	53,963	4,243	4,681	2,526	2,792	2,498	2,893	4,089	4,623	2,808	3,346	2,915	3,813
Kawali	2,459	1,217	1,242	...	...	...	...	...	...	...	...	...	...	...	...
Mala	1,029	497	532	15	...	...	...	...	...	...	...	...	...	...	...
Hindus returned by locality.															
Paharias	111,592	55,433	56,159	1,399	1,382	862	899	982	983	1,100	1,120	1,810	1,819	2,123	2,241
Musalmans returned by title.															
Shaikh	82,586	38,864	43,722	2,235	2,662	1,706	1,885	975	960	4,464	4,434	4,153	4,904	1,209	1,616
Musalmans returned by actual occupation.															
Jolaha	3,222	1,559	1,663	248	261	...	...	...	...	191	217	400	339	166	226

PARGANAS—*concluded.*

Portion of Daminikoh (Godda Subdivision).		Pakaur.		Mahespur.		Portion of Daminikoh (Pakaur Subdivision.)		Rajmahal.		Sahibganj.		Portion of Daminikoh (Rajmahal Subdivision).		Dumka.		Portion of Daminikoh (Dumka Subdivision).		Jamtara.	
Male.	Female.	Male.	Female.	Male.	Female.	Male.	Female.	Male.	Female.	Male.	Female.	Male.	Female.	Male.	Female.	Male.	Female.	Male.	Female.	Male.	Female.
1,164	1,175	1,368	1,381	921	960	156	152	785	845	81	64	863	898	4,230	4,312	348	342	1,603	1,615
7	...	41	25	24	15	163	156	40	31	121	93	21	18	70	54	...	...	39	39
14	22	133	121	44	31	155	144	147	99	163	95	56	41	540	422	13	3	482	457
7	2	149	173	15	14	117	129	183	120	...	...	67	82	405	436	49	45	159	152
...	...	58	63	...	...	...	...	4	3	...	...	...	...	689	622	5	...	98	108
11	8	37	40	26	20	...	...	98	91	50	38	364	322	15	14	...	...	29	29
...	...	13	3	29	16	300	264	102	91	47	26	223	233	852	715	17	10	106	68
253	253	264	244	596	641	...	...	37	41	...	...	375	417	1,305	1,350	438	423	1,011	942
196	236	101	103	501	551	42	51	...	...	91	92	11	7	505	508	...	...	231	269
491	469	...	...	434	443	77	71	841	904	113	101	570	582	2,101	2,001	89	84	1,226	1,210
110	115	104	95	164	182	52	46	554	560	220	223	78	61	224	216	183	205	546	603
839	874	515	566	416	443	155	156	349	399	22	28	829	838	2,433	2,433	551	558	636	638
193	225	...	...	610	646	...	...	325	358	21	...	58	60	1,044	1,093	13	18	588	631
...	...	...	...	268	264	341	365	38	42	6	6	7	6	11	16	...	...	...	...
...	...	439	433	888	987	...	...	...	...	...	...	...	...	...	...	...	...	2	...
894	896	905	959	349	391	610	620	990	980	174	181	826	860	424	481	690	750	659	669
1	3	66	69	...	...	77	89	88	104	20	13	27	26	164	165	...	...	161	163
11	11	272	289	...	...	187	193	1,454	1,445	417	409	437	425	53	40	...	...	106	121
...	...	277	279	557	598	...	...	251	220	...	...	131	135	3,540	3,618	412	890	643	659
...	...	119	121	190	236	...	...	206	266	...	...	...	...	103	172	...	...	81	79
...	...	...	...	...	...	...	...	...	...	...	...	73	62	590	538	...	...	...	...
1	...	...	...	...	...	154	187	932	1,037	...	...	119	126	926	998	12	10	31	28
...	...	...	...	...	...	16	18	63	76	46	57	...	1	87	74	1	...	11	8
871	891	615	611	228	221	146	135	703	704	400	471	1,604	1,646	6,496	6,524	870	875	814	818
153	181	466	482	33	37	867	954	480	484	27	33	252	257	582	595	33	42	468	467
...	...	14	14	90	110	49	65	38	36	...	...	...	...	387	363	...	...	251	248
[illegible]	31,989	31,436	31,970	29,353	29,970	2,837	2,887	20,831	20,965	1,842	1,822	8,612	8,780	100,543	101,134	9,797	9,801	23,113	22,700
7	3	...	...	124	139	49	29	145	146	104	90	54	66	370	373	...	...	264	206
46	38	84	62	15	24	16	10	7	4	21	10	23	31	419	380	70	65	376	412
39	49	161	112	98	93	24	18	359	377	482	591	168	127	543	512	184	180	347	311
608	629	1,214	1,258	392	380	739	779	768	814	928	987	695	696	2,890	2,861	160	136	2,408	2,363
...	...	...	...	...	...	...	...	400	423	...	...	211	228	34	35	...	...	...	...
39	60	135	193	125	184	91	149	98	104	27	40	86	94	680	717	14	18	564	664
...	...	11	20	...	...	...	...	51	36	...	...	5	1	92	59	...	...	...	...
3	2	12	17	...	...	258	255	1,099	1,125	...	...	491	490	220	284	...	...	160	192
...	...	...	...	3	5	42	49	23	38	837	952	...	...	...	...	...	...	...	...
10	18	565	600	4	6	152	206	13	11	...	...	8	11	...	...	...	...	...	...
[illegible]	704	1,418	1,584	2,465	2,839	87	86	1,389	1,676	119	104	2,478	2,901	14,440	16,157	1,349	1,532	3,869	4,232
...	...	...	...	...	...	518	515	205	222	...	...	...	...	494	505	...	...	...	...
...	...	...	...	...	...	...	...	244	246	238	286	...	...	...	...	...	...	...	...
11,388	11,502	9,671	9,610	1,584	1,633	2,112	2,211	2,700	2,737	969	1,038	8,634	8,776	7,158	7,172	1,659	1,764	1,282	1,272
1,626	1,932	4,298	4,809	3,257	3,571	2,484	2,892	4,025	4,398	1,861	2,167	816	813	1,709	2,472	268	242	3,728	4,180
...	...	...	...	...	...	...	...	141	164	6	1	13	18	394	437	...	...	...	...

ORISSA

DISTRICT

Caste or Group.	District Total.			Cuttack.		Banki.		Salepur.		Tirtol.	
	Total.	Male.	Female.	Male.	Female.	Male.	Female.	Male.	Female.	Male.	Female.
Bagdi	5,422	2,887	2,535	37	48	79	98	11	...	...	...
Baniya	23,524	11,518	12,006	1,444	1,240	510	481	1,440	1,584	474	470
(i)—Baisya	8,609	4,270	4,339	863	764	63	46	453	442	305	294
(ii)—Khatri	7,600	3,588	4,012	308	258	96	79	335	482	106	107
Barhi	21,426	10,777	10,649	1,513	1,393	218	208	1,612	1,680	1,078	999
Barui	1,732	853	879	139	133	...	...	314	325	4	...
Bauri	69,234	34,000	35,234	8,297	8,517	616	609	5,995	6,401	3,111	3,151
Bhandari	38,251	18,788	19,463	1,968	1,803	582	619	2,537	2,782	1,904	1,935
Bhumij	3,277	1,640	1,637	...	...	...	...	...	...	...	...
Brahman	183,909	89,518	94,391	8,351	8,605	2,904	2,976	13,208	14.724	6,328	6,057
Chamar and Muchi	15,778	7,402	8,376	419	437	147	107	2,219	2,672	589	630
Chasa	132,432	65,050	67,382	12,252	12,932	6,087	6,042	11,149	11,829	5,291	5,855
Dhopa	37,319	18,083	19,236	1,970	1,942	461	426	2,774	2,821	2,093	2,171
Dom	3,498	1,759	1,739	172	175	23	29	196	168	339	352
Goala	131,642	63,139	68,503	7,160	6,799	1,604	1,630	6,411	6,988	5,452	5,364
Gokha	11,628	5,826	5,802	239	236	275	279	274	345	332	302
Gola	5,370	2,989	2,381	318	265	22	23	400	307	12	13
Guria	71,818	34,720	37,098	2,929	3,063	894	997	7,123	7,598	3,224	3,236
Hari	6,573	3,057	3,516	540	501	801	893	209	452	158	187
Jugi	6,733	3,334	3,399	103	173	37	58	263	267	522	523
Jyotis	8,817	4,313	4,504	963	927	12	9	84	120	335	299
Kachra	5,261	2,618	2,643	176	153	...	...	369	365	1	3
Kahar	1,093	553	540	162	123	23	19	8	6	59	46
Kaibartta	4,828	2,233	2,595	76	95	28	32	...	...	156	186
Kamar	14,626	7,258	7,368	977	922	216	226	1,010	1,028	774	769
Kandra	84,347	42,015	42,332	1,874	1,915	180	192	6,198	6,436	4,646	4,566
Kunsari	6,214	3,207	3,007	141	132	18	14	493	482	380	299
Kayastha and Karan ...	61,428	27,778	33,650	4,493	3,661	670	607	3,943	4,309	2,829	3,831
Kela	2,651	1,321	1,330	87	81	108	102	228	238	55	77
Kewat	69,355	33,380	35,975	4,440	5,033	1,735	1,979	3,899	4,407	3,835	3,733
Khandait	404,919	195,952	208,967	10,722	11,017	8,825	8,781	20,336	21,895	23,987	26,310
Kumhar	22,999	11,424	11,575	1,303	1,399	304	335	1,249	1,356	995	1,001
Malakar	5,683	2,859	2,824	259	255	729	748	294	286	168	170
Niyari	1,720	774	946	30	34	25	54	85	96	20	39
Pan	94,754	46,698	48,056	3,685	3,752	1,037	992	6,455	7,073	624	673
Rajput	6,930	3,223	3,707	949	1,051	145	249	348	369	426	546
Raula	1,236	582	654	6	5	...	...	348	369	114	137
Sankhari	1,426	663	763	110	119	7	7	55	61	...	...
Savar	25,322	12,463	12,859	4,101	4,179	1,448	1,465	460	513	20	22
Sonar and Kamila	12,772	6,212	6,560	918	953	38	45	1,191	1,331	639	675
Sunri	3,866	1,818	2,048	450	481	164	170	101	141	103	190
Tambuli	2,369	1,063	1,306	268	276	2	1	108	104	43	34
Tanti	59,363	29,907	29,456	2,514	2,406	1,494	1,539	6,731	6,300	1,756	1,889
Thathera	3,959	1,983	1,976	297	333	...	...	803	780	207	206
Teli	63,070	29,206	33,864	4,444	4,624	1,743	1,896	3,743	4,611	1,747	1,760
Thoria	3,305	1,264	2,041	268	396	123	202	391	515	...	...
Tiyar	1,407	681	726	124	123	129	132	161	172	...	...
Religious devotees and persons returned by sect.											
Baisnab	16,660	8,559	8,101	538	494	479	451	1,463	1,441	1,375	1,366
Sanyasi	1,087	994	093	66	58	...	...	100	91	109	108

DIVISION.

CUTTACK.

Jagatsinghpur.		Kendrapara.		Patamundi.		Aul or Rajabari.		Jajpur.		Dharmsala.	
Male.	Female.	Male.	Female.	Male.	Female.	Male.	Female.	Male.	Female.	Male.	Female.
...	...	11	9	...	...	14	17	720	754	2,015	1,609
1,566	1,555	982	1,095	447	406	606	582	1,830	2,222	2,219	2,362
818	828	12	14	41	38	339	324	781	944	615	645
195	187	580	694	96	97	244	230	701	890	927	988
1,934	1,926	1,175	1,120	530	537	416	397	992	1,096	1,309	1,294
7	4	10	17	...	...	...	...	209	219	170	161
13,948	14,411	1,538	1,680	126	91	18	10	23	21	333	343
3,056	3,055	2,313	2,370	959	1,051	733	655	2,316	2,580	2,420	2,613
...	...	...	...	...	...	...	...	...	...	1,640	1,637
12,888	13,331	10,296	11,129	4,638	5,187	3,395	3,335	14,586	15,885	12,924	13,162
847	967	668	769	296	387	139	115	1,481	1,628	597	664
9,401	9,525	4,317	4,350	3,707	3,656	3,922	3,737	2,423	2,756	6,502	6,700
2,715	2,675	1,836	1,940	1,209	1,263	1,088	1,171	2,004	2,687	1,933	2,140
506	494	140	153	30	37	56	52	161	148	136	131
8,706	8,628	6,184	6,755	6,276	8,056	4,981	5,869	8,445	9,977	7,920	8,437
124	102	982	949	987	963	1,022	1,042	1,463	1,472	128	112
36	39	338	277	6	3	50	49	1,369	1,210	406	196
4,489	4,519	5,310	5,816	1,453	1,507	968	1,018	2,844	3,491	5,486	5,853
287	347	406	472	197	191	57	70	181	226	131	177
556	528	701	697	340	367	80	41	630	657	102	88
789	795	937	961	273	257	248	229	457	664	215	243
552	570	391	379	243	251	175	156	469	470	242	296
34	39	28	35	7	9	84	93	35	27	123	143
...	...	81	74	1,892	2,228	...	...	...	...	...	...
1,306	1,342	646	631	387	379	246	321	636	700	1,060	1,050
5,838	5,715	8,225	8,146	4,886	5,038	2,687	2,671	5,888	5,998	1,593	1,655
50	32	144	134	695	782	350	232	653	642	283	258
5,130	8,012	2,902	3,859	922	1,044	1,272	1,320	8,263	4,433	2,354	2,574
143	133	81	92	66	56	71	86	300	292	182	173
3,050	3,385	4,321	3,964	5,627	6,429	1,279	1,492	1,968	1,975	3,226	3,578
14,781	14,902	29,914	31,774	15,526	17,821	19,820	18,607	24,105	27,748	27,936	30,112
1,504	1,449	1,330	1,260	782	779	670	611	1,608	1,614	1,679	1,762
259	258	142	158	189	198	51	68	377	362	391	321
...	...	...	...	27	38	421	481	145	176	21	26
838	812	2,478	2,591	901	795	1,558	1,696	11,465	12,046	17,657	17,626
312	363	283	300	161	158	214	231	114	114	271	326
26	83	87	105	...	...	...	...	...	...	1	5
104	187	76	68	...	...	36	39	132	130	143	146
193	203	2	...	...	...	...	...	154	195	6,085	6,282
974	968	532	567	381	408	146	129	717	808	676	676
323	366	126	149	36	49	46	46	176	151	293	305
58	68	53	40	175	251	73	81	162	262	121	189
2,172	2,182	3,746	3,653	1,329	1,232	1,034	1,061	4,469	4,502	4,662	4,742
248	238	72	62	...	...	2	1	118	118	236	238
3,746	3,873	2,466	2,650	862	906	864	846	4,444	5,817	5,145	6,872
462	928	...	...	...	...	...	...	...	...	...	...
...	...	...	...	...	...	...	...	3	...	264	299
1,005	742	529	414	235	201	324	348	1,912	2,098	699	546
143	108	82	98	195	194	26	32	131	131	142	173

DISTRICT

Group.	District Total.			Cuttack.		Banki.		Salepur.		Tirtol.	
	Total.	Male.	Female.	Male.	Female.	Male.	Female.	Male.	Female.	Male.	Female.
Hindus returned by title or common sub-caste.											
Mahanti	1,127	480	647	178	148	105	209	6	10	47	57
Naik	2,510	1,228	1,282	40	38	69	80	987	1,045	37	31
Patra	15,533	7,245	8,288	1,037	1,080	129	123	1,440	1,710	441	426
Pradhan	20,142	10,178	9,964	1,440	1,494	480	420	320	280	1,880	1,848
Sudra	32,975	16,708	16,267	1,745	1,739	96	102	1	...	812	783
Hindus returned by actual occupation.											
Darji	1,235	624	611	230	160	12	13	91	105	38	58
Mala	1,040	427	613	6	8	...	...	17	...	...	...
Siyal	2,307	1,112	1,195	323	349	10	...	327	387	73	45
Tulabhina	1,177	574	603	60	43	105	105	150	142	7	10
Hindus returned by locality.											
Bengalis	1,576	749	827	202	178	...	...	8	14	9	3
Madrasis	1,629	884	745	619	542	2	...	4	1	23	18
Hindus returned by unidentifiable caste.											
Shagirdpesha	25,035	11,133	13,902	539	316	13	9	1,486	2,246	1,424	1,753
Musalmans returned by title.											
Maghul	1,397	677	720	188	107	...	...	232	331	4	8
Pathan	22,299	10,533	11,766	1,923	2,177	...	...	2,099	2,011	438	481
Sayyid	2,920	1,425	1,495	588	880	...	...	391	572	97	142
Shaikh	15,470	7,110	8,360	1,958	2,316	...	...	1,921	2,509	574	802

DISTRICT

Caste.	District Total.			Thana Puri.		Town Puri.	
	Total.	Male.	Female.	Male.	Female.	Male.	Female.
Baniya	11,094	5,384	5,710	694	758	277	395
(I)—Baisya	1,522	733	789	143	167	66	67
Barhi	12,842	6,568	6,274	1,163	1,105	747	683
Bauri	78,821	39,721	39,100	7,827	7,606	...	...
Bhandari	20,964	10,610	10,354	2,222	2,176	532	282
Brahman	94,930	46,495	48,435	11,318	12,738	3,731	3,043
Chamar and Muchi	1,303	656	647	240	235	38	41
Chasa	273,715	137,119	136,596	48,173	49,042	1,995	2,512
Dhopa	14,265	7,820	6,445	1,844	427	136	132
Dom	2,496	1,258	1,238	424	395	22	23
Goala	59,141	29,720	29,421	4,249	4,259	559	293
Gola	8,236	4,083	4,153	881	859	239	224
Guria	24,503	12,425	12,078	2,485	2,425	309	238

CUTTACK—*concluded.*

Jagatsinghpur.		Kendrapara.		Patamundi.		Aul or Bajabari.		Jajpur.		Dharmsala.	
Male.	Female.	Male.	Female.	Male.	Female.	Male.	Female.	Male.	Female.	Male.	Female.
8	16	12	14	25	69	14	12	73	97	13	15
...	...	70	68	25	20	...	...	...	...	...	...
1,008	947	1,151	1,290	350	346	146	209	609	834	934	1,323
78	60	2,930	2,884	2,169	2,119	376	333	264	281	241	245
13,641	13,241	49	51	272	257	...	...	...	...	93	94
111	150	39	26	23	25	8	2	56	59	16	13
4	...	...	...	...	...	302	506	...	...	98	99
216	250	18	16	1	1	9	12	88	90	47	45
29	35	38	42	...	...	...	...	34	47	151	179
13	16	74	122	8	7	37	24	209	307	129	156
33	27	42	51	40	33	14	14	27	4	80	55
2,251	2,556	929	1,296	333	421	496	549	2,827	3,685	835	1,071
26	22	134	175	10	5	...	...	78	69	5	3
786	901	1,084	1,144	335	349	236	214	1,998	1,991	1,634	1,898
27	31	183	233	2	...	29	25	80	88	28	24
121	122	840	845	51	51	82	85	937	986	626	644

PURI.

Gop.		Pipli.		Khurda.		Banpur.	
Male.	Female.	Male.	Female.	Male.	Female.	Male.	Female.
343	316	1,870	1,859	1,884	1,972	316	410
73	68	242	253	166	203	43	31
1,021	999	1,440	1,351	1,592	1,559	605	577
9,259	9,115	14,976	14,678	6,769	6,842	890	859
1,563	1,561	2,672	2,726	2,490	2,507	1,131	1,102
5,305	5,446	12,200	12,990	8,355	8,548	5,586	5,670
45	47	320	321	13	3	...	...
17,633	17,445	32,474	32,240	18,261	16,982	18,583	18,366
1,282	1,327	2,071	2,028	1,879	1,896	608	635
238	244	413	418	90	94	71	64
6,940	6,654	5,754	5,613	9,957	10,205	2,261	2,397
177	223	265	294	1,865	1,864	656	689
1,187	1,157	3,588	3,462	3,959	3,976	897	830

Caste or Group.	District Total.			Thana Puri.		Town Puri.	
	Total.	Male.	Female.	Male.	Female.	Male.	Female.
Hari	9,412	4,620	4,792	474	438	333	342
Jugi	1,292	642	650	272	287	10	...
Jyotis	3,572	1,852	1,720	762	729	58	64
Kachra	2,269	1,129	1,140	78	54	9	8
Kaibartta	5,458	2,793	2,665	160	125	...	...
Kamar	8,016	4,032	3,984	664	680	222	230
Kandh	2,229	1,132	1,027	5	5	...	...
Kandra	18,663	9,665	8,998	2,845	2,711	93	76
Kansari	5,154	2,618	2,536	313	268	158	126
Kayastha and Karan	35,016	17,407	17,609	3,351	3,798	1,867	1,535
Kela	1,696	802	894	246	309	4	2
Kewat	26,258	13,060	13,198	3,850	3,807	154	148
Khandait	8,193	4,292	3,901	531	475	263	111
Khatia	1,366	626	740	201	277	14	25
Kumhar	7,709	4,001	3,708	1,097	1,010	296	291
Kumuti	1,739	876	863	123	97	173	184
Malakar	12,969	6,567	6,402	1,776	1,743	36	99
Naliya	2,554	1,239	1,315	590	640	373	375
Pan	7,107	3,614	3,493	402	369	30	10
Rajput	6,372	3,310	3,062	1,139	1,072	163	128
Savar	18,887	9,297	9,590	1,224	1,234	259	324
Sonar	5,276	2,638	2,638	762	729	245	237
Tanti	15,695	7,885	7,810	1,068	1,031	63	53
Teli	35,253	17,460	17,793	2,367	2,247	445	376
Thoria	3,493	1,529	1,964	4	1	3	1
Tiyar	1,249	627	622	224	170	...	...
Religious devotees and persons returned by sect.							
Baisnab	3,970	2,191	1,779	301	241	108	54
Hindus returned by title or common sub-caste.							
Buna	2,055	1,047	1,008	402	369	...	...
Mahanti	2,048	1,037	1,011	209	175	...	...
Naik	1,252	581	671	...	...	...	...
Patra	4,926	2,453	2,473	371	373	166	66
Sudra	42,471	21,480	20,991	293	300	107	276
Hindus returned by actual occupation.							
Paik	4,853	2,380	2,473	141	139	36	22
Siyal	4,073	2,100	1,973	1,177	1,080	18	7
Hindus returned by unidentifiable caste.							
Shagirdpesha	3,849	2,146	1,703	172	196	155	133
Musalmans returned by title.							
Pathan	9,934	5,021	4,913	318	218	138	87
Shaikh	4,050	1,994	2,056	182	156	76	11

PURI—*concluded.*

Gop.		Pipli.		Khurda.		Banpur.	
Male.	Female.	Male.	Female.	Male.	Female.	Male.	Female.
44	54	280	282	2,270	2,432	1,219	1,244
96	84	...	...	194	206	70	73
264	214	617	577	...	...	151	136
453	404	451	535	131	139	7	...
...	...	37	35	228	284	2,378	2,221
903	845	933	937	1,013	989	297	303
...	...	...	...	...	...	1,127	1,092
1,765	1,578	3,829	3,515	920	900	213	218
86	71	1,284	1,190	534	552	243	319
1,765	1,748	3,658	4,457	4,292	4,481	1,574	1,590
54	69	207	265	51	65	211	184
2,355	2,265	3,159	3,127	3,542	3,851	...	...
458	393	747	720	1,448	1,407	845	795
...	...	29	33	...	...	382	405
425	402	1,057	1,008	962	885	165	112
...	...	...	...	15	2	565	580
317	284	1,601	1,527	1,846	1,807	991	942
140	152	88	90	48	56	...	2
238	245	1,063	980	872	894	1,009	995
222	297	518	401	1,015	983	253	181
396	401	3,201	3,156	4,058	4,287	159	138
325	335	899	984	338	293	69	60
816	882	2,601	2,506	2,848	2,842	489	497
2,343	2,286	4,661	5,070	6,484	6,668	1,160	1,146
114	118	693	1,000	697	838	18	6
...	...	...	...	54	56	349	396
596	544	367	310	492	357	327	273
180	162	373	379	85	81	7	17
39	32	59	32	504	517	226	255
...	...	155	161	426	510	...	...
12	11	747	825	1,119	1,156	38	42
15,759	15,439	1,406	1,376	2,882	2,435	1,033	1,166
53	59	2,122	2,228	28	25	...	...
192	166	685	689	24	25	4	...
425	301	704	573	430	348	260	153
687	701	1,338	1,262	2,053	2,194	487	501
656	715	462	501	461	550	137	123

Caste or Group.	District Total.			Balasor.		Soro.		Jaleswar.	
	Total.	Male.	Female.	Male.	Female.	Male.	Female.	Male.	Female.
Bagdi	1,236	600	636	5	6	250	252	67	80
Baniya	5,842	2,868	2,974	323	332	422	515	284	279
(i)—Baisya	1,303	622	681	113	121	149	175	4	5
(ii)—Gandha Banik	1,687	801	886	111	133	86	101	17	17
Barhi	6,871	3,234	3,637	184	207	1,191	1,295	16	9
Barui	6,681	3,314	3,367	164	174	270	258	49	56
Bhandari	17,087	8,275	8,812	866	915	1,773	1,762	406	409
Bhumij	3,274	1,671	1,603	82	84	209	112	505	520
Brahman	119,289	58,259	61,030	6,721	6,131	16,485	17,586	1,115	976
Chamar and Muchi	8,189	3,942	4,247	379	340	2,429	2,624	22	20
Chasa	20,672	9,953	10,719	1,287	1,484	5,219	5,514	596	605
Dhopa	22,625	10,665	11,960	1,058	1,075	2,360	2,734	569	578
Dom	1,787	899	888	115	113	235	264	49	56
Goala	73,463	33,966	39,497	3,149	3,256	8,082	9,068	1,889	1,974
Gokha	27,147	13,119	14,028	1,640	1,669	3,041	3,308	91	73
Gola	33,820	17,078	16,742	3,432	3,322	2,475	2,485	600	646
Guria	13,190	6,268	6,922	617	709	1,311	1,317	132	109
Hari	4,792	2,264	2,528	208	207	346	477	345	356
Jugi	1,578	793	785	51	73	127	121	109	99
Jyotis	3,876	2,006	1,870	207	194	546	540	47	53
Kachra	1,463	732	731	...	...	240	235	2	...
Kadma	1,974	993	981	3	2	...	...	81	87
Kaibartta	17,905	8,879	9,026	1,611	1,547	762	893	400	416
Kamar	11,194	5,560	5,634	1,052	1,056	1,182	1,180	369	390
Kandra	31,619	15,605	16,014	3,302	3,494	1,271	1,246	1,582	1,552
Kansari	2,019	980	1,039	4	4	354	357	10	16
Karanga	1,299	673	626	87	72	6	4	96	75
Kayastha and Karan ...	26,832	13,434	13,398	1,800	1,339	2,258	2,332	1,233	1,198
Kela	1,453	706	747	38	49	70	...	9	7
Kewat	26,110	12,284	13,826	1,184	1,321	2,894	3,166	295	274
Khadal	8,348	4,214	4,134	1,120	1,102	863	840	212	179
Khandait	185,852	88,697	97,155	10,034	10,190	20,698	21,847	367	329
Kumhar	11,248	5,482	5,766	905	964	675	717	374	349
Pan	54,319	25,964	28,355	2,003	2,219	6,132	6,679	77	99
Rajput	2,512	1,272	1,240	121	120	263	311	23	6
Raju	40,757	20,325	20,432	263	243	246	229	6,126	6,389
Santal	4,593	2,253	2,340	8	3	1	...	1,906	2,031
Sonar and Kamila	8,746	4,203	4,543	1,030	1,091	1,308	1,347	53	51
Sunri	1,831	922	909	114	116	161	149	59	63
Tambuli	2,412	1,189	1,223	502	552	233	242	25	26
Tanti	56,767	27,649	29,118	2,742	2,793	8,028	8,429	1,417	1,386
Teli	46,890	22,805	24,085	1,808	2,127	5,081	5,304	2,298	2,228
Religious devotees and persons returned by sect.									
Baisnab	14,647	7,161	7,486	573	618	597	626	739	757
Bhartari	1,068	499	569	3	2	163	175	...	...
Hindus returned by actual occupation.									
Jaliya	1,140	586	554	...	...	...	...	...	...
Manjhi	2,301	1,117	1,184	...	...	...	...	1,058	1,134
Ujia	3,766	1,845	1,921	770	814	20	15	72	77

BALASOR.

Balliapal.		Basta.		Bhadrak.		Basudebpur.		Dhamnagar.		Chandbali.	
Male.	Female.	Male.	Female.	Male.	Female.	Male.	Female.	Male.	Female.	Male.	Female.
189	187	35	37	1	...	...	...	51	69	2	5
185	208	151	142	572	629	270	255	381	309	280	215
17	45	...	...	92	100	65	45	154	151	28	39
67	64	...	1	243	295	105	110	84	82	88	83
55	53	9	11	639	789	311	308	539	680	290	265
1,382	1,363	198	214	397	498	44	45	782	743	28	16
881	874	632	626	1,258	1,490	757	859	1,205	1,381	497	496
238	232	473	440	115	114	...	1	49	50	...	...
2,100	1,876	1,513	1,393	11,813	13,555	5,853	6,027	9,537	11,115	2,822	2,391
16	8	34	13	681	790	61	64	300	355	20	24
395	418	11	14	1,942	2,122	137	184	9	8	357	370
1,057	1,028	760	804	1,834	2,139	793	990	1,537	1,929	697	683
236	209	86	85	146	134	1	...	25	19	6	8
1,487	1,459	1,026	1,092	6,262	8,077	3,718	4,686	4,892	6,316	3,459	3,569
231	215	772	835	2,196	2,512	1,911	1,892	1,680	2,010	1,557	1,514
4,060	4,001	5,001	4,794	1,486	1,491	...	1	12	1	12	1
215	219	330	374	1,249	1,463	499	556	1,286	1,582	629	593
552	559	279	271	282	376	74	71	105	161	73	50
257	248	15	6	...	...	107	118	4	...	123	120
159	134	94	92	486	556	183	167	161	32	123	102
...	...	3	...	112	145	23	24	255	234	97	93
886	871	22	21	...	...	...	...	1	...	...	...
797	695	1,380	1,347	596	705	480	639	1,519	1,785	1,334	999
601	609	367	309	978	1,085	324	310	512	560	175	142
1,561	1,486	3,727	3,625	1,212	1,351	597	717	866	945	1,487	1,598
...	...	55	68	302	313	171	209	54	45	30	27
324	313	158	158	2	4	...	...	...	...	...	...
1,943	2,008	842	678	1,906	2,350	1,377	1,439	1,245	1,430	830	630
11	10	89	131	243	289	9	10	91	88	146	163
953	883	847	901	2,336	2,901	755	375	2,721	3,210	299	295
875	820	293	283	580	636	174	144	95	137	2	...
3,212	3,194	5,604	5,633	16,678	20,680	8,726	9,800	13,815	15,986	9,563	9,496
497	503	518	536	864	958	636	691	706	765	307	293
25	16	720	756	8,541	9,355	1,660	2,008	6,193	6,613	613	610
18	15	284	255	844	361	4	...	130	133	85	39
10,852	10,777	2,837	2,893	...	1	1	...	...	...	...	...
258	234	72	72	8	...	...	...	...	...	...	...
177	168	15	...	551	596	557	633	475	634	42	23
50	57	242	209	68	105	23	33	120	127	65	50
38	42	86	77	109	105	40	42	89	91	67	46
1,662	1,573	1,359	1,330	5,307	5,835	2,084	2,270	4,156	4,656	894	846
3,313	3,192	2,379	2,372	3,114	3,519	1,548	1,633	2,035	2,566	1,229	1,144
2,494	2,701	978	980	735	897	520	608	241	281	284	18
...	...	...	...	87	110	12	19	187	221	47	42
70	62	148	129	368	373	...	...	...	...	...	...
...	...	57	50	...	...	...	...	1	...	1	...
562	571	421	444	...	...	...	...	...	...	...	...

DISTRICT

Group.	District Total.			Balasor.		Soro.		Jaleswar.	
	Total.	Male.	Female.	Male.	Female.	Male.	Female.	Male.	Female.
Hindus returned by locality.									
Bengalis	1,187	556	631	12	8	35	47	1	...
Uriyas	5,798	2,885	2,913	...	...	1	...	446	463
Hindus returned by unidentifiable caste.									
Shagirdpesha	6,043	2,604	3,439	106	126	149	207	157	231
Musalmans returned by title.									
Pathan	8,052	4,069	3,983	984	1,079	361	288	117	99
Sayyid	1,872	912	960	67	55	117	146	23	28
Shaikh	13,409	6,769	6,640	1,475	1,542	840	768	228	205

NOTE.—For District Angul with Kandh Mahals,

CHUTIA NAG

DISTRICT

Caste.	District Total.			Hazaribagh.		Barhi.		Bagodhar.		Tandwa.		Ramghar.		Jageswar.	
	Total.	Male.	Female.	Male.	Female.	Male.	Female.	Male.	Female.	Male.	Female.	Male.	Female.	Male.	Female.
Agaria	1,824	841	983	20	21	50	55	80	95	1	3	78	99	375	442
Agarwala	1,979	992	987	8	4	10	5	50	45	15	10	30	25	22	...
Babhan	25,727	14,032	11,695	1,109	1,079	276	260	236	208	298	211	193	166	1,550	1,045
Bandawat	6,835	3,245	3,590	212	200	...	...	6	4	...	...	2	...	11	10
Baniya	29,098	14,115	14,983	1,345	1,414	795	971	544	602	489	490	288	807	1,161	1,170
(i)—Barnawar	6,434	3,182	3,252	11	7	51	59	387	426	...	...	...	1	...	...
(ii)—Khatri	1,986	970	1,016	180	197	132	159	54	61	15	25	4	1	61	74
(iii)—Mahuri	3,670	1,714	1,956	135	182	100	250	3	15	4	12	72	100	76	70
(iv)—Sinduria	1,239	592	647	19	28	12	13	...	...	370	373	12	5	24	26
Barhi	20,360	10,017	10,343	1,365	1,665	710	1,043	320	300	745	792	4	2	84	64
Bauri	1,557	755	802	...	...	...	...	2	2	...	...	41	16	...	...
Bediya	10,886	5,216	5,670	...	...	...	...	...	...	...	...	4,102	4,517	737	770
Beldar	1,154	566	588	17	8	17	16	59	54	...	...	...	...	5	7
Bhat	1,411	745	766	59	60	16	9	41	32	6,	7	30	21	68	63
Bhogta	32,668	15,929	16,739	673	768	3	5	7	10	2,166	2,294	661	707	518	501
Bhuiya	99,031	43,589	55,442	7,536	9,655	1,896	2,197	665	843	3,250	3,802	820	857	1,287	1,410
Brahman	31,013	17,158	13,855	2,350	1,318	587	711	572	498	963	963	506	442	1,278	708
Chamar and Muchi ...	39,230	18,772	20,458	2,031	2,095	985	1,050	1,180	1,253	475	1,082	...	...	657	745
Chasa	1,008	493	515	...	...	...	...	...	...	...	...	...	...	...	...
Dhanuk	1,453	735	718	1	...	...	...	3	4	64	66	404	411	13	7
Dhobi	10,568	5,013	5,555	273	437	264	306	288	305	245	248	209	228	125	148
Dom	7,576	3,758	3,818	59	60	7	5	216	218	50	54	123	125	437	437
Dusadh	25,252	12,122	13,130	1,636	1,938	880	944	786	908	516	584	147	155	368	496
Ghasi	3,942	1,963	1,979	42	50	...	...	157	148	74	85	900	893	92	118
Goala	133,805	64,947	68,858	3,809	4,302	3,216	4,217	3,355	3,504	1,155	1,169	446	399	1,736	1,639

BALASOR—*concluded.*

Baliapal.		Basta.		Bhadrak.		Basudebpur.		Dhamnagar.		Chandbali.	
Male.	Female.	Male.	Female.	Male.	Female.	Male.	Female.	Male.	Female.	Male.	Female.
21	18	1	...	279	289	57	81	142	188	8	...
...	...	1	...	75	59	...	...	2,016	2,033	346	378
163	196	14	11	958	1,215	19	22	1,023	1,433	16	8
445	376	274	262	1,100	1,271	120	91	407	382	261	135
43	49	40	28	459	521	59	53	80	73	25	7
530	494	446	396	2,038	2,380	243	209	615	577	354	65

... Imperial Table XVI, pp. 95 to 101, vol. V.

PUR DIVISION.

HAZARIBAGH.

Kasmar.		Chauparan.		Hunterganj.		Chatra.		Simaria.		Giridih.		Gawan.		Kodarma.		Kharakdiha.		Dumurhi.	
Male.	Female.	Male.	Female.	Male.	Female.	Male.	Female.	Male.	Female.	Male.	Female.	Male.	Female.	Male.	Female.	Male.	Female.	Male.	Female.
...	...	77	82	...	...	...	...	86	119	50	45	...	...	...	...	...	...	24	22
...	...	19	11	20	28	78	76	10	5	108	96	234	288	...	...	277	276	111	119
950	540	1,302	788	532	535	444	381	496	458	852	731	752	705	156	133	4,549	4,237	248	212
...	...	2,680	3,006	26	13	42	30	6	1	...	...	5	4	88	83	264	239	3	...
493	479	831	832	652	673	1,238	1,263	124	128	1,029	932	690	687	1,000	944	1,773	1,947	1,663	2,149
...	...	69	89	1	2	...	...	1	...	194	146	425	432	832	780	751	830	460	480
43	34	79	68	...	...	...	...	1	1	159	173	38	25	12	6	35	43	157	149
50	45	137	122	24	36	200	210	5	...	176	113	27	30	38	29	479	565	188	177
...	...	46	53	27	35	38	53	17	22	...	...	...	...	18	29	8	9	1	1
5	...	1,234	1,209	26	22	860	923	264	310	979	972	410	409	1,634	1,734	1,119	713	229	185
184	203	...	...	...	...	...	...	...	...	407	475	29	20	...	...	...	...	92	86
...	...	...	...	345	374	2	...	...	...	...	...	2	...	1	5	26	4	1	...
...	...	...	...	61	49	43	70	2	3	181	207	5	4	70	65	29	23	77	82
72	72	59	34	27	25	72	70	17	3	29	23	15	18	91	79	116	118	27	32
29	19	169	192	3,402	3,512	863	1,972	4,006	4,777	1,717	1,913	1	...	64	16	3	4	36	49
394	381	5,198	5,749	8,128	8,563	5,868	6,345	3,515	3,871	2,786	3,073	3,335	4,055	262	313	2,571	3,280	980	1,058
797	697	1,051	1,033	577	566	1,249	1,193	312	302	2,100	1,094	796	544	831	847	2,591	2,468	598	471
125	121	990	1,030	918	1,028	806	844	2,072	2,202	2,270	2,321	939	1,083	4,271	4,606	63	78	940	920
...	...	...	...	...	...	...	...	...	...	...	2	...	...	493	513	...	...	...	...
...	...	...	...	32	30	...	...	5	6	55	37	9	7	1	...	141	147	7	3
186	163	376	415	163	178	...	...	203	206	397	515	175	180	680	709	1,071	1,125	358	392
192	190	46	61	32	23	122	115	25	25	1,571	1,041	57	...	27	16	681	750	111	98
17	20	813	835	939	1,037	512	586	312	341	605	587	167	150	1,342	1,464	2,955	3,082	127	7
399	366	1	...	83	27	79	87	18	12	12	23	4	6	...	...	23	27	129	117
575	569	5,071	5,453	5,200	5,230	4,368	4,809	1,590	1,580	4,616	4,855	6,179	6,416	10,821	11,390	11,244	12,311	1,569	1,425

DISTRICT

Caste or Group.	District Total.			Hazaribagh.		Barhi.		Bagodhar.		Tandwa.		Ramghar.		Jageswar.	
	Total.	Male.	Female.	Male.	Female.	Male.	Female.	Male.	Female.	Male.	Female.	Male.	Female.	Male.	Female.
Gulgulia	13,885	6,478	7,407	4,044	4,930	1,587	1,705	137	148	4	...	76	71	114	89
Hajjam and Napit	25,635	12,722	12,913	1,332	1,380	702	777	859	891	421	458	555	509	533	544
Halwai and Maira ...	2,704	1,375	1,329	333	327	317	285	46	43	56	68	32	37	40	36
Hari and Mihtar	2,655	1,310	1,345	408	437	...	...	...	...	...	...	...	...	13	15
Jugi	1,129	512	617	62	77	...	...	37	45	21	16	60	70	2	1
Kahar	31,977	14,997	16,980	2,066	2,307	859	960	755	767	489	562	166	155	536	574
Kalwar and Sunri	18,046	8,826	9,220	570	612	464	534	1,564	1,726	325	355	274	269	735	774
Kandu	5,520	2,586	2,934	488	613	111	106	139	152	107	114	3	4	103	93
Kayastha	9,413	4,779	4,634	854	717	311	283	154	165	119	125	105	109	131	113
Kewat	2,002	996	1,006	5	...	...	...	5	13	...	...	196	203	58	69
Koiri	44,700	42,110	22,590	3,008	3,140	146	156	589	609	1,754	1,835	1,106	1193	391	421
Kol	10,239	5,063	5,176	125	123	286	244	45	23	397	467	282	294	309	327
Kora	1,698	798	900	90	80	...	...	50	65	150	165	23	25	...	...
Kumhar	21,322	10,535	10,787	886	935	63	43	738	753	504	539	511	597	588	584
Kurmi	71,065	34,243	36,822	284	272	146	149	5,131	5,674	2,710	3,030	9,787	10,265	4,706	5,183
Lohar and Kamar	15,166	7,578	7,588	256	230	38	31	481	490	356	437	1,897	1,894	959	1,002
Mahili	3,774	1,858	1,916	2	1	238	232	81	84	6	...	297	324	103	120
Malakar	1,377	650	727	57	77	...	...	49	41	58	68	134	148	61	50
Munda	13,654	6,596	7,058	250	260	320	329	150	175	310	421	511	610	712	769
Musahar	5,704	2,795	2,909	38	45	...	...	60	63	...	...	1	...	10	12
Nuniya	1,053	507	546	33	31	35	25	5	7	9	5	182	188	24	26
Pasi	3,353	1,730	1,623	109	113	39	37	6	1	106	109	3	3	8	4
Rajput	34,183	18,346	15,837	2,991	1,593	596	508	494	517	357	394	496	440	1,319	1,326
Rajwar	9,160	4,333	4,827	39	46	64	71	140	178	6	4	526	578	363	376
Santal	69,245	34,497	34,748	3,118	3,210	579	596	1,037	1,053	480	465	2,095	2,156	5,978	6,105
Sonar	6,558	3,171	3,387	483	587	109	100	409	438	129	201	178	183	117	109
Tatwa and Tanti	2,109	1,085	1,024	70	49	5	...	3	...	12	10	94	94	398	441
Teli	44,372	21,609	22,763	1,853	2,116	1,375	1,462	1,660	1,881	2,187	2,405	993	1,036	748	750
Turi	20,778	10,005	10,773	637	761	302	308	635	738	352	419	247	302	499	548
Religious devotees and persons returned by sect.															
Gosain	3,763	1,863	1,900	135	155	190	245	73	80	37	45	30	27	45	54
Hindus returned by title or common sub-caste.															
Ganjhu	4,851	2,340	2,511	42	25	...	...	270	272	281	339	575	641	...	...
Jaiswar	1,061	504	557	...	...	17	17	37	53	...	6	18	22	46	66
Hindus returned by actual occupation.															
Ghatwal	40,256	18,616	21,640	2,191	2,802	4	...	2,103	2,686	5	2	214	233	682	816
Jolaha	3,070	1,416	1,654	1,363	1,595	...	...	...	...	...	...	...	...	...	...
Mala	1,891	931	960	37	38	13	11	8	6	27	35	2	...	...	...
Musalmans returned by title.															
Pathan	6,289	3,225	3,064	211	137	150	155	81	102	149	156	95	104	250	260
Sayyid	1,179	581	598	82	141	...	...	...	...	...	...	...	...	150	110
Shaikh	68,837	34,124	34,713	2,438	2,939	1,425	1,430	2,359	2,486	1,160	1,210	2,224	2,232	956	948
Musalmans returned by actual occupation.															
Jolaha	28,287	13,448	14,844	430	576	950	900	640	634	804	789	543	572	836	823
Kalal	3,822	1,873	1,949	200	224	...	...	...	...	52	51	...	...	108	100

HAZARIBAGH — *concluded.*

KASMAR.		CHAUPARAN.		HUNTERGANJ.		CHATRA.		SIMARIA.		GIRIDHI.		GAWAN.		KODARMA.		KHARAKDIHA.		DUMURHI.	
Male.	Female.	Male.	Female.	Male.	Female.	Male.	Female.	Male.	Female.	Male.	Female.	Male.	Female.	Male.	Female.	Male.	Female	Male.	Female.
7	1	340	306	22	6	20	26	5	7	47	63	50	45	5	...	14	11	6	...
539	514	880	874	437	476	691	682	332	308	1,274	1,210	444	476	1,063	1,128	1,815	1,847	864	839
1	4	15	20	101	117	76	70	19	20	129	112	18	20	21	14	38	48	133	108
113	103	...	...	...	...	...	..	...	...	413	381	83	69	1	...	154	190	128	150
47	42	40	50	2	...	17	30	...	...	86	75	3	52	49	67	41	38	45	54
106	102	1,203	1,280	780	964	911	1,201	859	388	1,577	1,641	650	749	919	1,056	3,264	3,900	362	374
394	353	150	179	93	91	107	108	434	527	1,296	1,247	208	237	310	339	1,378	1,388	524	486
67	74	201	223	10	5	142	202	32	27	219	219	143	152	576	450	310	370	165	130
129	108	373	519	224	231	300	323	85	38	611	395	200	170	203	199	906	1,057	124	89
246	264	2	..	2	...	2	...	...	...	229	213	3	...	...	...	...	...	248	244
410	457	1,156	1,168	362	328	2,049	2,134	440	448	2,719	2,751	208	185	804	764	6,156	6,302	810	699
596	580	250	225	328	409	107	100	44	52	450	470	609	599	220	208	500	555	521	500
...	...	18	35	140	150	46	14	107	134	...	...	...	...	79	132	...	...	95	100
765	759	571	595	314	355	429	484	149	153	1,162	1,179	327	325	964	983	1,753	1,773	810	800
2,985	2,917	29	6	64	56	166	169	162	188	100	65	7,812	8,635	25	8	47	36	89	119
910	904	178	151	194	218	129	133	194	149	589	600	277	262	141	124	280	279	699	694
507	500	...	...	...	...	6	4	...	...	302	348	...	...	...	...	78	71	238	232
...	...	42	34	27	44	37	43	20	21	51	47	14	17	25	27	65	101	10	9
910	999	250	275	327	369	512	499	200	310	950	995	840	250	250	225	154	100	450	472
76	79	13	21	...	...	...	...	...	...	868	824	1,270	1,375	256	249	55	60	146	181
1	1	8	11	...	...	40	45	1	2	72	94	25	30	16	12	55	69	1	...
7	2	72	56	126	112	...	...	1	2	275	237	390	348	129	140	458	459	1	...
1,615	1,606	81	65	547	546	1,134	1,176	231	239	1,886	1,387	1,807	1,689	1,849	1,808	2,457	2,087	468	454
1,168	1,250	...	...	95	106	4	9	21	28	1,209	1,436	407	421	80	71	72	77	139	181
2,150	2,210	2,350	2,406	3,446	4,500	5,999	5,876	317	280	30	32	1,994	1,068	142	134	2,232	2,182	2.550	2,476
45	47	148	152	63	78	105	163	18	10	299	275	86	107	204	227	414	380	669	335
180	177	1	...	8	5	9	8	...	...	182	146	36	21	...	1	87	72	...	...
955	945	120	112	560	575	1,328	1,339	1,812	1,826	1,341	1,365	1,005	929	2,040	2,075	2,418	2,740	1,214	1,207
396	404	209	181	152	145	141	156	266	325	1,446	1,460	765	875	529	533	1,695	1,793	1,734	1,825
[illegible]	52	55	63	57	68	18	12	13	12	237	241	...	...	304	292	483	480	129	79
269	254	497	532	10	13	...	...	7	6	...	...	...	...	1	2	...	...	388	427
147	147	126	138	...	...	...	...	9	1	3	3	...	...	101	104	...	...	...	...
1,412	1,502	464	521	18	24	1	3	22	29	2,352	2,543	696	779	2,902	3,458	1,816	2,176	3,734	4,066
...	...	44	41	...	...	9	18	...	...	...	...	...	...	...	...	...	...	...	...
81	68	4	...	227	228	44	49	8	13	14	19	287	290	1	...	172	186	6	
280	180	169	82	253	292	161	156	158	177	175	131	161	172	607	672	211	204	114	84
...	...	...	...	...	...	81	111	...	...	161	143	...	...	...	...	107	93	...	...
1,261	1,208	1,962	1,730	1,575	1,570	1,246	1,607	124	131	4,942	4,774	135	118	3,271	3,302	5,794	5,846	3,212	3,092
743	706	872	760	367	442	1,602	1,947	924	939	461	461	1,225	1,390	142	108	1,658	2,566	1,246	1,[illegible]
...	...	...	...	204	271	101	126	76	54	207	175	502	506	...	...	423	442	...	...

DISTRICT LOHARDAGA.

Caste.	District Total.			Ranchi.		Sili.		Tamar.	
	Total.	Male.	Female.	Male.	Female.	Male.	Female.	Male.	Female.
Agaria	1,616	830	786	84	79	12	8	...	...
Asur	2,303	1,170	1,133	252	263	...	...	101	93
Babhan	7,272	3,557	3,715	...	...	...	...	25	11
Baidya	1,035	501	534	4	2	...	...	...	...
Baniya	24,740	12,503	12,237	673	618	127	128	36	36
(i) – Kasarwani	2,032	1,049	983	21	25	109	111	...	...
(ii) – Khatri	2,157	1,211	946	191	150	...	...	...	...
(iii) – Raunier	5,424	2,861	2,563	280	210	...	...	33	30
Barhi	8,668	4,241	4,427	831	849	99	65	...	...
Barui	1,876	925	951	111	113	104	102	9	8
Bediya	5,419	2,655	2,764	2,444	2,620	...	...	...	...
Bhat	6,437	3,143	3,294	20	12	2	1	174	166
Bhogta	29,177	14,680	14,497	2,387	2,132	81	73	2	3
Bhuiya	77,936	39,233	38,703	3,433	3,430	1,961	1,873	2,327	2,381
Binjhia	2,653	1,453	1,200	278	278	...	...	...	...
Brahman	43,946	22,085	21,861	1,101	1,002	925	837	1,106	1,197
Chamar and Muchi	28,389	14,121	14,268	150	153	67	56	347	345
Chero	14,111	7,001	7,110	2	3	...	...	...	...
Chik	20,822	10,430	10,392	189	210	75	85	11	15
Dhanuk	2,497	1,198	1,299	...	1	...	...	...	...
Dhopa	10,310	4,997	5,313	458	476	266	258	406	433
Dom	5,122	2,602	2,520	23	4	30	22	3	3
Dusadh	26,835	13,642	13,193	219	215	45	22	49	46
Gareri	5,597	2,649	2,948	76	68	28	18	...	...
Ghasi	18,687	9,348	9,339	1,719	1,722	1,115	1,064	1,229	1,210
Goala	80,733	40,265	40,468	3,352	3,259	4,048	3,998	2,598	2,376
Gond	1,760	996	764	64	79	3	2	41	45
Gulgulia	1,995	982	1,013	...	...	95	126	...	...
Hajjam and Napit	15,206	7,111	8,095	1,198	1,390	525	635	821	991
Halwai and Maira	3,216	1,709	1,507	151	160	13	15	9	12
Hari and Mihtar	1,744	930	814	159	123	25	30	99	98
Jhora	2,430	1,238	1,192	5	13	...	...	7	3
Kahar	29,615	14,050	15,565	604	624	47	51	37	41
Kalwar and Sunri	11,107	5,474	5,633	328	321	488	533	140	165
Kandu	7,020	3,536	3,484	69	74	10	1	1	...
Kansari	1,092	550	542	80	90	...	...	...	...
Kayastha	6,332	3,441	2,891	444	314	55	50	38	15
Kewat	1,303	669	634	39	33	55	44	...	...
Kharia	39,362	19,519	19,843	27	3	8	19	28	28
Kharwar	56,242	27,692	28,550	...	...	2	1	1,526	1,523
Koiri	28,892	14,430	14,462	746	792	635	599	157	168
Korwa	9,710	4,912	4,798	...	...	...	...	151	143
Kumhar	19,801	10,002	9,799	1,401	1,373	755	767	280	254
Kurmi	60,382	29,869	30,513	290	318	12,832	12,387	5,932	5,963
Lohar and Kamar	35,294	16,357	18,937	336	501	701	643	1,370	1,493
Mahili	10,773	5,494	5,279	543	566	1,668	1,584	58	87
Malakar	2,055	1,060	995	35	27	42	33	...	...
Munda	221,552	108,366	113,186	14,699	14,757	4,273	4,316	...	...
Nagesia	3,145	1,516	1,629	15	3	2	...	...	...
Nuniya	2,222	1,089	1,133	267	250	...	...	...	...
Oraon	350,095	165,070	185,025	25,850	28,141	1,533	1,459	10,218	12,205
Parhaiya	6,370	3,199	3,171	2	...	...	...	1	...
Pasi	1,189	587	602	14	3	...	...	6	7
Rajput	42,466	21,038	21,428	1,131	1,139	451	444	625	668

INCLUDING PALAMAU.

Karra.		Mandar.		Khunti.		Lohardaga.		Chainpur.		Toto.	
Male.	Female.	Male.	Female.	Male.	Female.	Male.	Female.	Male.	Female.	Male.	Female.
...	...	272	254	...	...	22	17	2	3	...	...
...	...	...	...	17	9	...	...	337	370	...	...
65	41	...	...	...	...	110	109	1,442	1,572	...	...
8	1	...	...	17	19	...	...	4	21	221	224
494	451	1,398	1,344	933	927	1,222	1,219	232	192	858	865
...	...	394	342	...	...	101	91	11	13	181	171
303	251	...	...	21	13	113	85	221	179	...	...
191	200	3	3	41	37	701	675	...	...	91	101
71	68	59	64	35	38	550	530	89	87	125	132
181	187	43	40	...	...	63	61	25	23	45	49
...	...	...	...	...	...	...	...	...	...	...	...
21	27	4	2	...	...	577	515	1	1	...	...
...	...	...	...	845	840	4,673	4,683	85	89	45	49
516	514	881	891	13	21	5,663	5,656	1,999	1,989	8,888	8,768
58	49	...	...	38	48	...	...	99	89	54	13
1,338	1,026	1,610	1,557	1,106	1,106	1,506	1,504	1,119	1,101	898	936
279	261	392	432	48	37	262	155	1,144	1,192	231	121
...	...	2	1	...	...	...	...	6	9	10	5
675	676	19	20	379	566	192	186	862	832	874	892
4	5	...	...	...	...	...	...	...	...	...	...
142	175	157	140	49	54	188	179	53	38	151	161
252	248	341	331	157	143	51	58	3	2	97	75
21	17	28	19	9	...	159	169	39	40	186	204
36	62	35	30	2	2	67	82	1	...	1	...
383	357	346	362	563	576	279	300	476	525	268	273
2,999	3,001	1,958	2,112	3,635	3,538	2,519	2,609	2,058	2,150	1,159	1,160
...	...	...	...	41	29	...	...	11	16	16	19
75	74	48	37	129	128	59	60	37	38	74	72
55	65	30	85	257	256	78	66	52	97	619	827
45	39	66	64	39	26	164	138	53	59	44	26
25	30	90	72	21	18	95	74	...	...	...	...
5	7	...	...	36	46	...	1	...	...	231	239
121	134	53	61	62	28	605	608	147	137	116	130
111	115	480	478	29	45	420	425	191	149	122	183
2	1	99	112	14	1	50	61	7	6	3	2
8	10	24	21	...	...	21	22	...	...	92	97
136	132	56	57	57	32	112	102	55	48	40	50
...	...	...	...	1	...	18	20	104	133	142	122
...	2	...	...	2	...	10	3	281	256	403	413
73	82	...	...	166	147	2,136	2,126	989	985	1,938	1,937
178	172	232	206	...	...	559	531	3	3	276	251
282	285	1	...	1	...	35	34	1,029	947	187	217
1,032	1,009	...	...	618	586	553	602	332	312	371	402
517	516	4,263	4,245	206	204	338	425	210	206	107	105
420	498	745	798	1,778	1,865	1,340	1,394	710	882	1,529	1,588
36	23	267	289	42	31	426	449	666	541	185	182
7	12	28	19	...	...	3	5	16	11	546	581
10,040	12,890	3,354	3,910	24,267	24,932	1,381	1,614	1,725	1,795	2,497	2,575
...	...	...	...	2	...	489	485	70	84	45	48
21	27	...	...	18	14	177	181	...	...	57	68
27,573	26,040	14,748	19,448	964	893	12,294	15,165	9,576	9,441	24,021	28,156
...	...	...	...	...	...	23	8	1	...	...	...
...	...	...	...	19	5	28	25	38	30	...	...
1,055	1,140	774	817	404	351	674	634	682	622	1,210	1,333

DISTRICT LOHARDAGA,

Caste.	Palkot.		Kochdaga.		Basia.		Daltonganj.		Garhwa.	
	Male.	Female.	Male.	Female.	Male.	Female.	Male.	Female.	Male.	Female.
Agaria	...	...	4	6	363	350	71	69	...	...
Asur	91	101	...	...	3	2	...	...	...	...
Babhan	3	7	...	...	41	43	57	51	54	40
Baidya	...	...	84	89	...	...	...	...	75	77
Baniya	121	129	2,109	2,301	565	478	619	585	473	480
(i)—Kasarwani	...	...	...	...	21	19	111	113	...	...
(ii)—Khatri	...	...	86	68	23	15	131	83	...	...
(iii)—Rauniar	...	...	...	...	400	325	...	...	...	...
Barhi	352	371	61	59	145	156	363	402	14	17
Barui	63	61	...	...	...	...	201	207	4	3
Bediya	211	144	...	...	...	...	...	...	...	...
Bhat	...	...	...	...	30	19	198	182	23	16
Bhogta	99	101	...	...	...	...	1,001	991	355	360
Bhuiya	571	564	908	916	2,321	2,222	3,691	3,487	607	654
Binjhia	278	273	...	...	388	187	156	158	...	...
Brahman	918	837	1,506	1,509	1,305	1,206	608	598	1,009	1,099
Chamar and Muchi	1,796	1,790	127	128	59	55	2,095	2,002	58	41
Chero	...	...	3	1	2	2	3,178	3,347	69	59
Chik	2,438	2,278	2	...	1,159	1,226	1,070	1,658	2	...
Dhanuk	...	...	6	1	...	...	669	720	...	...
Dhopa	155	146	84	52	83	99	374	538	579	685
Dom	510	536	70	62	23	31	118	105	65	62
Dusadh	21	16	274	245	22	26	2,037	1,897	1,879	1,895
Gareri	7	12	...	...	2	5	421	545	512	588
Ghasi	607	632	344	354	792	784	32	34	53	47
Goala	1,898	1,936	500	569	1,301	1,397	2,516	2,618	2,410	2,359
Gond	2	3	153	152	323	212	262	116	69	88
Gulgulia	88	90	59	60	100	101	90	98	23	29
Hajjam and Napit	370	365	43	45	75	60	125	100	419	482
Halwai and Maira	34	34	6	4	30	24	300	256	39	55
Hari and Mihtar	98	96	5	9	11	10	52	40	19	16
Jhora	174	176	611	546	155	139	14	22	...	...
Kahar	156	131	16	38	37	13	2,751	3,694	2,688	2,735
Kalwar and Sunri	253	262	57	53	162	204	300	344	443	525
Kandu	...	...	1	...	25	17	485	511	416	420
Kansari	36	33	...	...	...	...	54	54	59	46
Kayastha	67	56	536	428	58	30	553	609	255	256
Kewat	59	61	137	139	89	69	...	...	1	...
Kharia	...	...	7,497	7,718	...	...	5,739	6,465	...	...
Kharwar	158	151	282	183	28	22	195	162	2,086	2,073
Koiri	133	107	360	362	36	42	1,137	1,315	777	850
Korwa	...	...	2	6	11	10	480	423	45	42
Kumhar	552	478	488	466	606	590	669	540	564	598
Kurmi	102	100	110	110	120	200	453	538	429	488
Lohar and Kamar	1,081	2,234	347	463	1,415	1,678	537	551	602	644
Mahili	...	...	93	124	102	50	229	121	181	216
Malakar	2	3	70	17	1	...	37	44	31	27
Munda	...	...	1,037	1,032	17,401	18,088	93	92	...	...
Nagesia	690	798	191	210	3	5	...	...	...	...
Nuniya	90	100	...	...	4	7	6	8	96	102
Oraon	6,020	10,227	6,437	7,051	2,037	2,052	2,277	2,016	1,066	1,123
Parhaiya	...	...	...	...	...	...	693	675	533	535
Pasi	...	...	90	90	5	2	39	50	19	23
Rajput	552	615	348	302	305	320	1,571	1,536	619	586

INCLUDING PALAMAU—*continued.*

Banka.		Chhatrapur.		Patan.		Husainabad.		Latihar.		Mahuadanr.		Balumat.	
Male.	Female.	Male.	Female.	Male.	Female.	Male.	Female.	Male.	Female.	Male.	Female.	Male.	Female.
...	...	...	...	...	...	...	...	...	...	...	...	...	...
201	193	69	33	...	...	66	40	33	29	...	...	...	...
855	902	...	...	8	6	4	3	10	10	883	911	...	...
...	...	...	...	...	...	...	...	93	101	...	...	...	...
124	132	186	187	545	521	898	842	193	201	91	93	606	508
...	...	93	89	...	...	7	9	...	...	...	...	...	...
3	2	4	5	111	89	4	6	...	...	...	...	...	...
...	...	...	...	161	163	479	410	...	...	...	...	501	409
259	260	21	27	32	31	200	204	76	89	656	639	203	289
...	...	15	19	...	...	41	61	...	...	13	11	7	6
...	...	...	...	...	...	...	...	...	...	...	...	...	...
...	...	...	...	4	6	2,083	2,344	6	3	...	...	...	...
3,440	3,430	235	215	169	155	472	563	175	185	563	555	63	73
275	215	1,080	983	2,003	2,023	991	983	231	260	471	468	403	405
...	...	...	...	...	...	...	...	...	...	104	106	...	...
1,125	1,206	525	624	817	816	1,142	1,079	506	509	809	901	1,106	1,211
537	566	109	91	296	327	3,311	3,399	464	524	1,629	1,903	720	690
17	9	43	44	1,219	1,275	487	484	1,921	1,834	31	33	11	4
...	...	...	...	12	1	1,868	1,743	1	...	2	4	...	...
...	...	...	...	513	572	...	...	6	...	...	...	...	...
80	78	224	219	364	416	890	926	98	96	27	29	169	156
49	88	302	286	111	120	6	11	71	64	...	...	320	269
273	276	1,228	1,290	1,738	1,838	4,722	4,318	304	377	33	37	266	246
18	4	62	46	465	547	898	938	12	...	...	...	6	1
101	110	217	174	25	29	20	9	167	156	317	329	305	292
1,817	1,918	1,854	1,815	656	859	1,659	1,557	973	922	290	205	106	110
6	3	...	...	2	...	...	...	...	...	1	...	2	...
...	...	28	30	31	38	25	16	19	16	...	...	...	...
580	587	45	35	164	180	980	1,077	275	305	23	15	387	432
30	23	140	141	104	73	180	131	125	105	53	58	84	64
25	18	45	16	...	...	32	32	18	25	72	64	39	38
...	...	...	...	...	...	...	...	...	...	...	...	...	...
312	310	728	795	1,783	1,852	3,255	3,786	253	221	48	39	231	137
137	121	325	291	266	201	522	581	341	301	42	28	317	308
65	56	219	214	609	577	1,314	1,291	3	1	1	...	143	139
19	12	5	...	39	62	66	79	...	...	32	15	15	1
22	20	118	72	146	128	510	412	26	38	36	3	112	39
...	...	...	...	23	13	1	...	...	...	...	...	...	...
...	...	...	...	...	...	5,517	4,036	...	...	...	...	2	...
1,041	954	5,122	5,712	...	...	5	7	5,957	6,358	1,239	1,274	4,719	4,653
24	30	369	328	4,193	4,169	4,355	4,352	57	...	2	...	201	185
...	...	4	2	313	319	2,174	2,150	194	220	3	...	...	...
68	74	224	236	561	566	745	760	89	91	94	91	...	...
260	266	2,302	2,388	279	291	600	653	202	300	304	300	513	510
225	246	341	354	619	602	846	845	428	581	305	316	682	761
61	44	...	...	76	59	8	8	1	1	852	904	...	...
13	10	25	16	16	19	135	161	2	...	2	...	49	10
1,003	1,002	...	...	23,473	23,642	8	6	7	8	46	56	2,372	2,471
...	...	...	...	...	...	...	...	...	...	...	...	3	1
165	163	46	34	21	19	98	142	3	2	...	...	21	16
1,811	1,838	2.210	2,194	1,695	1,711	1,112	1,121	2,359	2,470	2,989	2,104	8,280	10,170
561	522	273	294	224	246	163	153	493	472	107	119	125	147
10	23	142	142	8	15	149	147	5	4	2	1	20	26
61	32	1,638	1,378	2,108	2,362	5,824	5,931	249	343	284	282	573	543

DISTRICT LOHARDAGA,

Caste or Group.	District Total.			Ranchi.		Sili.		Tamar.	
	Total.	Male.	Female.	Male.	Female.	Male.	Female.	Male.	Female.
Rajwar	3,935	2,293	1,642	306	291	296	211	2	1
Rautia	22,345	9,456	12,889	38	15	86	59	101	274
Sarak	5,033	2,482	2,551	908	912	125	145	28	30
Sonar	3,991	1,888	2,103	173	186	198	229	45	40
Tatwa and Tanti	2,745	1,315	1,430	5	11	207	226	208	204
Teli	35,780	17,040	18,740	2,255	2,354	468	477	213	246
Thathera	1,128	431	697	8	1	19	27	...	...
Turi	10,258	5,134	5,124	168	187	198	114	104	102
Religious devotees and persons returned by sect.									
Baisnab	1,245	688	557	125	136	12	14	18	36
Gosain	5,667	2,900	2,767	152	131	143	102	517	566
Hindus returned by title or common sub-caste.									
Baraik	4,692	2,404	2,288	285	238	348	357	58	56
Ganjhu	2,938	1,435	1,503	58	79	55	59	386	375
Jaiswar	1,141	521	620	62	70	171	223	...	...
Patar	1,919	1,010	909	...	...	231	251	713	600
Hindus returned by actual occupation.									
Gorait	8,745	4,365	4,380	645	680	2	10	10	5
Krishan	4,681	2,448	2,233	...	...	...	...	...	...
Mala	9,426	4,541	4,885	50	48	...	1	12	11
Manjhi	3,906	2,128	1,778	3	2	1,647	1,348	32	36
Paik	2,155	1,018	1,137	20	25	222	295	...	...
Hindus returned by locality.									
Hindustanis	3,304	1,591	1,713	623	622	266	282	...	...
Uriyas	6,008	3,070	2,938	...	...	...	...	...	...
Musalmans returned by title.									
Pathan	8,688	4,331	4,357	229	244	37	28	25	13
Sayyid	3,933	1,927	2,006	1,068	1,148	12	...	7	6
Shaikh	68,409	34,849	33,560	6,297	6,132	309	143	214	166
Musalmans returned by actual occupation.									
Jolaha	2,591	1,292	1,299	46	72	...	...	...	...

INCLUDING PALAMAU—*continued.*

KARRA.		MANDAR.		KHUNTI.		LOHARDAGA.		CHAINPUR.		TOTO.	
Male.	Female.	Male.	Female.	Male.	Female.	Male.	Female.	Male.	Female.	Male.	Female.
...	...	1	12	...	...	133	102	...	...	113	103
125	114	8	9	2,006	3,085	8	4	207	300	136	342
36	45	125	129	98	96	15	19	40	39	...	4
43	63	54	94	30	31	99	95	20	11	81	67
49	25	189	222	70	85	4	7	...	...	31	42
1,064	1,109	654	657	1,272	1,276	967	926	83	101	1,096	1,065
125	196	88	116	6	5	16	25	...	...	8	...
209	205	173	114	328	322	297	346	235	243	223	234
4	5	45	36	...	...	98	92	...	...	95	48
148	172	162	153	146	140	172	174	38	35	227	198
65	62	...	...	184	168	180	175	265	256	...	...
...	...	106	104	...	...	...	...	...	...	...	...
47	33	5	2	16	12	2	6	6	10	79	74
...	...	...	...	...	...	...	...	...	...	...	...
814	829	909	920	120	87	1,220	1,180	25	30	375	383
18	21	2	1	12	12	...	...	7	4	...	...
9	9	32	44	7	4	7	9	54	...	...	...
11	9	268	266	55	51	...	...	...	...	...	...
118	108	...	...	392	397	...	...	3	2	13	14
...	...	169	229	53	65	83	74	...	...	7	8
...	...	...	...	...	...	...	...	3	3	...	...
94	148	194	194	25	21	240	217	42	36	129	132
40	55	31	43	12	8	44	54	12	10	80	66
1,044	988	2,145	1,991	247	134	2,649	2,763	277	242	1,002	931
...	...	...	...	...	...	...	...	...	...	...	...

DISTRICT LOHARDAGA,

Caste or Group.	Palkot.		Kochdaga.		Basia.		Daltonganj.		Garhwa.	
	Male.	Female.	Male.	Female.	Male.	Female.	Male.	Female.	Male.	Female.
Rajwar	1	...	...	...	61	25	105	104	339	501
Bautia	1,674	2,050	987	1,602	4,009	4,919	68	107	...	...
Sarak	96	92	78	76	95	99	105	106	372	376
Sonar	81	85	2	6	72	91	287	292	237	299
Tatwa and Tanti	...	...	...	...	4	2	4	1	...	...
Teli	1,086	2,640	249	242	1,223	1,175	912	949	1,169	1,063
Thathera	...	...	...	...	2	2	30	187	65	92
Turi	352	375	788	863	464	451	189	177	155	115
Religious devotees and persons returned by sect.										
Baisnab	99	47	...	...	...	...	...	...	100	70
Gosain	103	99	146	18	229	254	317	232	3	4
Hindus returned by title or common sub-caste.										
Baraik	101	98	42	62	16	11	4	10	18	25
Ganjhu	...	...	...	...	5	9	5	...	...	...
Jaiswar	25	34	15	40	2	13	5	19	2	2
Patar	...	...	...	...	...	...	...	...	...	...
Hindus returned by actual occupation.										
Goraït	38	40	44	47	60	77	19	25	27	15
Krishan	7	...	...	...	176	157	88	94	44	34
Mala	4	2	822	863	9	11	937	978	1,663	1,749
Manjhi	3	2	...	...	...	...	...	...	36	20
Paik	92	100	10	12	...	...	...	...	...	...
Hindus returned by locality.										
Hindustanis	5	...	...	...	...	...	105	110	81	79
Uriyas	5	3	3,039	2,906	23	26	...	...	...	...
Musalmans returned by title.										
Pathan	284	150	86	33	38	29	510	473	672	742
Sayyid	19	9	58	64	11	11	105	93	20	29
Shaikh	250	223	150	127	214	231	2,161	2,357	4,590	4,650
Musalmans returned by actual occupation.										
Jolaha	...	...	...	...	...	...	621	647	525	489

INCLUDING PALAMAU—*concluded.*

RANKA.		CHHATRAPUR.		PATAN.		HUSAINABAD.		LATIHAR.		MAHUADANR.		BALUMAT.	
Male.	Female.	Male.	Female.	Male.	Female.	Male.	Female.	Male.	Female.	Male.	Female.	Male.	Female.
3	3	151	154	282	136	...	...	...	...	...	...	...	...
...	...	...	9	...	...	...	...	...	...	...	...	3	...
216	215	10	20	19	16	30	39	6	7	44	48	36	38
17	14	44	31	102	125	253	336	42	26	13	12	45	20
211	199	...	...	91	101	139	172	...	...	...	...	103	133
260	274	525	551	1,015	1,006	1,472	1,649	331	347	66	43	660	570
3	3	15	14	3	...	6	22	...	...	...	...	42	7
81	68	105	106	220	205	15	11	162	221	82	95	566	570
...	...	87	66	...	...	...	...	...	...	5	7	...	...
3	1	8	3	284	217	59	56	10	14	5	5	26	16
49	51	88	85	85	75	68	78	12	15	536	466	...	...
28	30	...	...	...	...	...	...	...	...	...	...	792	847
28	36	4	...	...	...	...	...	1	...	...	...	51	46
66	58	...	...	...	...	...	...	...	...	...	...	...	...
...	...	5	...	34	37	...	...	...	...	...	...	18	15
278	271	...	...	1	...	...	...	...	...	1,820	1,639	...	...
4	...	1	...	402	448	937	1,113	21	28	70	62	...	...
43	20	...	...	8	5	2	...	7	14	13	5	...	...
...	...	...	...	...	...	...	...	...	..	148	184	...	...
...	...	...	...	...	...	...	...	6	6	...	...	194	238
...	...	...	...	...	...	...	...	...	...	...	...		...
37	28	32	8	313	367	1,137	1,316	79	89	61	27	117	112
4	2	15	1	24	8	813	361	23	13	19	19	10	6
833	779	968	1,003	3,103	3,101	4,956	4,539	1,390	1,348	375	418	1,675	1,294
...	...	...	...	...	...	...	...	100	91	...	...	...	...

Caste or Group.	District Total.			Purulia.		Jhalda.		Baghmundi.		Chandil.		Barabhum.	
	Total.	Male.	Female.	Male.	Female.	Male.	Female.	Male.	Female.	Male.	Female.	Male.	Female.
Bagdi	5,105	2,391	2,714	528	612	418	437	...	...	...	...	86	116
Baidya	2,411	1,235	1,176	176	120	157	109	...	...	6	6	...	...
Baniya	20,751	10,538	10,213	1,801	1,710	895	755	337	378	786	388	357	492
(i) Baisya	2,069	1,122	947	232	212	116	118	...	...	9	2	...	...
(ii) Gandha Banik	9,827	5,056	4,771	464	354	163	119	99	120	444	65	248	387
(iii) Khatri	1,552	796	756	140	135	17	20	38	58	55	46	28	13
(iv) Subarna Banik	4,946	2,271	2,675	465	509	306	334	...	...	278	275	81	92
Barui	1,591	837	754	65	14	18	22	24	10	13	2	6	...
Bauri	88,510	42,776	45,734	6,581	6,975	2,509	2,569	2,079	2,068	2,013	2,002	2,413	2,434
Bediya	1,750	851	899	52	47	743	801	35	39	21	12	...	...
Bhat	2,309	1,194	1,115	99	92	175	161	118	162	18	2	55	52
Bhuiya	33,851	16,408	17,443	1,113	1,123	1,940	1,926	828	898	600	647	640	712
Bhumij	106,437	51,746	54,691	9,625	9,431	3,674	3,768	5,123	5,385	2,540	2,100	2,890	2,650
Brahman	51,639	26,761	24,878	5,144	4,779	1,094	989	384	291	429	307	447	540
Chamar and Muchi	8,191	5,048	3,143	941	656	317	196	164	67	...	...	350	221
Dhobi	10,334	5,138	5,196	833	881	592	597	452	294	107	187	750	717
Dom	19,293	9,600	9,693	1,797	1,863	1,356	1,328	406	400	625	610	701	752
Dusadh	1,339	734	605	85	65	...	...	...	...	12	7	70	11
Ghasi	4,487	2,244	2,243	306	299	751	747	478	490	623	622	83	83
Goala	31,151	16,013	15,138	2,933	2,818	878	862	294	287	1,013	960	920	928
Gond	1,416	746	670	150	145	50	45	35	40	55	40	46	40
Hajjam or Napit	17,194	8,703	8,491	1,560	1,564	795	783	273	277	596	536	838	779
Halwai and Maira	12,596	6,341	6,255	619	633	217	206	200	90	114	128	351	339
Hari and Mihtar	12,261	6,041	6,220	1,572	1,683	172	161	10	25	210	205	919	940
Ho	2,342	1,080	1,262	150	165	50	65	45	60	30	39	25	30
Jugi	1,781	879	902	117	155	55	50	...	...	43	78	50	60
Kahar	6,915	3,385	3,530	248	252	373	383	472	481	3	10	264	275
Kaibartta	3,867	1,777	2,090	154	162	178	207	...	...	270	573	59	52
Kalwar and Sunri	23,648	11,892	11,756	879	871	758	779	148	137	900	877	533	494
Kandu	1,001	545	456	50	45	242	200	...	...	...	...	60	17
Kayastha	7,391	3,550	3,841	644	617	156	98	125	200	715	737	223	212
Kewat	2,834	1,389	1,445	229	222	100	111	34	50	19	24	56	59
Khaira	4,120	2,047	2,073	145	147	125	137	165	167	220	239	25	10
Koiri	4,211	2,104	2,107	106	120	591	493	282	281	...	...	...	...
Kora	12,736	6,215	6,521	1,237	1,261	114	130	629	638	839	856	501	537
Kumhar	27,847	13,898	13,949	63	53	3,526	3,636	1,661	1,648	835	879	1,255	1,273
Kurmi	226,034	111,235	114,799	30,731	31,987	15,730	16,095	2,628	2,566	4,800	4,900	16,672	16,727
Lohar and Kamar	30,291	15,250	15,041	2,563	2,367	1,999	1,926	840	856	1,832	1,794	911	971
Mahili	10,794	5,236	5,558	1,143	1,235	601	609	178	214	729	801	546	563
Mal	2,149	1,012	1,137	215	235	188	147	...	...	123	103	78	89
Malakar	1,131	543	588	59	86	106	119	...	...	2	1	...	...
Rajput	14,773	7,577	7,196	1,045	1,024	884	904	240	235	300	224	736	757
Rajwar	29,598	14,214	15,384	3,681	3,986	797	801	207	183	123	163	255	281
Santal	181,374	89,935	91,439	11,562	11,929	3,504	3,595	1,859	1,664	5,456	5,891	6,084	5,543
Sarak	11,264	5,639	5,625	493	399	449	468	511	523	322	341	229	265
Sonar	2,736	1,343	1,393	160	158	150	145	50	60	50	45	108	116
Sutradhur	1,235	623	612	220	217	45	56	58	54	39	46	40	41
Tambuli	3,802	2,060	1,742	1,156	983	308	234	...	...	46	4	185	156
Tatwa and Tanti	12,911	6,472	6,439	425	422	429	436	691	650	2,073	2,021	1,160	1,169
Teli and Kalu	33,356	16,882	16,474	3,002	3,007	1,212	1,152	600	609	1,250	1,022	1,316	1,250
Religious devotees and persons returned by sect.													
Baisnab	10,952	5,201	5,751	797	870	840	940	177	187	699	735	463	496

MANBHUM.

Manbazar.		Raghunathpur.		Gaurandi.		Para.		Chas.		Gobindpur.		Nirsa.		Topchanchi.	
Male.	Female.	Male.	Female.	Male.	Female.	Male.	Female.	Male.	Female.	Male.	Female.	Male.	Female.	Male.	Female.
...	...	388	427	88	66	321	359	116	131	150	175	246	266	50	125
...	...	532	659	65	67	117	66	...	...	75	93	107	56	...	...
540	415	1,387	1,591	717	691	600	605	1,416	1,387	789	886	674	666	239	249
...	...	8	3	184	118	...	...	336	294	179	144	58	58	...	...
407	390	1,093	1,211	345	390	144	130	631	647	452	406	471	453	95	99
5	45	70	80	97	90	61	47	85	67	50	55	50	65	50	35
78	80	216	597	91	93	95	128	264	379	108	281	95	92	94	116
...	...	283	299	11	...	12	...	19	15	138	120	31	52	217	211
3,565	3,882	2,283	2,299	5,930	6,956	3,435	3,893	3,050	3,251	1,868	1,882	4,154	4,518	2,896	8,005
...	...	...	...	...	...	...	...	...	...	...	...	...	...	...	...
110	56	30	35	119	116	...	...	110	112	153	162	40	20	167	145
760	931	596	540	899	977	2,077	2,254	2,605	2,866	1,066	1,737	1,684	1,825	1,000	1,008
4,396	4,645	2,245	2,713	1,075	1,168	1,547	2,498	661	706	14,687	15,406	2,560	2,728	823	1,403
1,257	1,079	4,147	4,172	1,324	1,180	1,617	1,572	5,456	6,125	3,252	2,823	1,032	895	1,178	1,126
375	102	...	...	105	105	175	175	959	564	479	329	585	260	598	468
313	262	230	269	116	256	165	172	691	710	449	494	72	63	318	294
267	249	1,041	1,085	219	168	217	218	1,154	1,162	945	961	256	201	616	606
...	...	25	16	108	80	55	41	88	85	291	300	...	...	...	...
...	...	3	2	...	...	...	...	...	...	...	...	...	...	...	...
1,306	1,367	1,011	495	926	752	882	975	1,850	1,786	1,841	1,822	728	694	1,426	1,392
30	25	49	48	50	49	45	46	55	50	49	30	79	70	54	42
670	656	809	807	316	304	308	324	984	945	665	687	320	315	569	514
197	207	1,000	950	373	368	936	908	231	244	1,032	1,037	550	636	521	509
367	379	283	303	162	160	102	190	563	585	872	879	291	290	458	461
54	60	60	80	29	30	100	180	180	235	175	196	40	35	82	87
101	106	132	130	100	50	45	50	124	110	...	...	...	...	112	113
363	345	13	10	475	355	80	95	239	390	375	387	200	209	280	318
100	88	109	98	71	60	257	235	233	235	64	63	289	317	...	...
536	540	840	825	782	810	103	94	706	650	3,854	3,813	1,241	1,278	592	588
...	...	...	...	45	50	35	40	25	20	88	84	...	...	...	...
168	151	142	95	225	465	108	111	280	254	112	148	449	464	203	289
90	104	75	113	63	64	130	115	77	73	201	209	20	35	296	266
340	309	135	167	169	203	235	236	111	126	175	160	...	...	182	170
145	144	...	...	...	...	141	221	390	381	240	242	...	...	209	225
72	83	727	776	580	507	485	631	348	365	161	171	314	296	208	290
907	925	800	970	510	514	289	224	2,046	1,975	1,232	1,209	369	341	405	382
8,525	8,618	4,042	4,076	2,509	2,469	3,102	3,203	9,070	10,038	7,417	7,754	752	733	5,257	5,633
1,067	1,070	1,635	1,622	807	840	63	78	802	771	749	753	1,531	1,529	451	464
292	303	199	184	197	259	68	71	231	246	544	560	112	112	396	401
38	55	116	127	111	121	86	104	66	59	53	97	...	...	...	...
...	...	152	175	...	...	...	...	...	...	96	77	128	130	...	...
626	503	96	101	97	53	101	147	798	796	892	862	326	234	1,536	1,356
366	397	398	452	245	278	1,453	1,610	3,471	3,592	2,396	2,667	114	99	708	880
10,589	11,071	8,183	10,070	7,209	7,278	701	825	3,603	3,586	17,690	16,388	11,140	11,221	2,215	2,378
388	396	290	286	385	359	1,482	1,451	521	533	163	178	345	356	61	70
80	75	55	40	75	72	101	128	120	103	123	175	135	35	136	181
68	31	...	...	72	82	...	...	...	...	...	...	81	85	...	...
118	72	71	76	58	98	...	...	57	65	...	...	66	54	...	...
372	387	739	782	220	225	88	85	87	65	54	47	134	150	...	...
552	564	2,391	2,394	776	800	637	646	213	161	1,946	1,901	1,269	1,281	1,718	1,687
214	286	577	616	223	208	101	110	205	215	217	224	256	293	432	563

DISTRICT

Group.	District Total.			Purulia.		Jhalda.		Baghmundi.		Chandil.		Barabhum.	
	Total.	Male.	Female.	Male.	Female.	Male.	Female.	Male.	Female.	Male.	Female.	Male.	Female.
Hindus returned by title or common sub-caste.													
Malik	4,460	2,160	2,300	49	54	436	499	...	...	385	387	...	...
Hindus returned by actual occupation.													
Bagal	2,180	1,067	1,113	90	110	103	100	155	165	102	108	453	459
Ghatwal	1,266	600	666	125	155	...	...	...	...	55	45	...	...
Mudi	8,073	3,904	4,169	1,219	1,176	207	219	79	80	...	...	864	891
Poddar	1,774	931	843	127	158	141	152	...	...	102	103	57	58
Musalmans returned by title.													
Pathan	2,301	1,288	1,013	224	212	102	63	51	50	12	...	86	54
Sayyid	1,196	643	553	119	101	7	8	15	13	5	4	31	16
Shaikh	45,331	23,514	21,817	4,753	4,340	1,919	1,191	361	283	659	514	1,248	1,115
Musalmans returned by actual occupation.													
Jolaha	3,621	1,786	1,835	101	102	104	104	141	143	141	128	172	279

DISTRICT

Caste.	District Total.			Chaibasa.	
	Total.	Male.	Female.	Male.	Female.
Bagdi	1,117	546	571	108	105
Baniya	1,585	838	747	75	63
Bhuiya	12,546	6,335	6,211	1,332	1,353
Bhumij	51,050	25,046	26,004	868	857
Brahman	3,635	2,003	1,632	148	55
Chamar and Muchi	1,184	615	569	198	203
Dhobi	2,682	1,316	1,366	273	297
Dom	2,280	1,137	1,143	243	194
Ghasi	3,416	1,728	1,688	376	393
Goala	46,855	22,433	24,422	13,420	12,712
Gond	2,212	1,083	1,129	46	56
Hajjam or Napit	2,365	1,207	1,158	105	100
Hari and Mihtar	1,694	811	888	45	35
Ho	131,287	63,959	67,328	50,712	53,495
Kalwar and Sunri	1,673	852	821	50	45
Kayastha and Karan ...	2,352	1,302	1,050	161	75
Kewat	1,472	751	721	223	286
Kharia	3,865	1,936	1,929	50	54
Kharwar	1,413	757	656	50	45
Kol	57,989	28,322	29,667	26,539	27,976
Kumhar	6,979	3,453	3,526	1,292	1,294
Kurmi	12,400	6,333	6,067	650	504
Lohar and Kamar	10,731	5,299	5,432	1,495	1,460
Mahili	2,821	1,445	1,376	150	147
Mal	2,200	1,045	1,155	20	25
Munda	21,365	10,718	10,647	5,718	5,647

MANBHUM—*concluded.*

Manbazar.		Raghunathpur.		Gaurandi.		Para.		Chas.		Gobindpur.		Nirsa.		Topchanchi.	
Male.	Female.	Male.	Female.	Male.	Female.	Male.	Female.	Male.	Female.	Male.	Female.	Male.	Female.	Male.	Female.
267	293	...	...	121	123	287	297	55	69	560	578	...	...	...	...
52	59	...	...	...	...	112	112	...	...	...	...	...	...	...	...
45	55	...	...	...	...	...	...	330	352	45	59	...	...	...	...
420	475	...	...	296	473	...	...	819	855	...	...	...	...	...	...
203	189	...	...	207	99	...	...	94	84	...	...	...	...	...	...
19	14	120	92	75	45	137	87	54	45	123	108	222	189	63	54
70	42	87	60	15	19	101	125	22	30	114	92	24	6	33	27
670	641	1,661	1,800	555	435	1,407	1,589	2,807	2,815	3,469	3,507	1,831	1,537	2,144	2,050
106	104	110	109	157	207	200	210	217	209	123	131	107	107	105	102

SINGHBHUM.

Chakradharpur.		Manoharpur.		Ghatsila or Dhalbhum.	
Male.	Female.	Male.	Female.	Male.	Female.
131	119	192	186	115	161
58	75	244	167	461	442
1,202	1,190	1,899	1,778	1,802	1,890
2,915	2,890	749	499	20,514	21,758
403	303	130	23	1,322	1,251
100	59	120	90	202	217
93	97	86	42	864	930
98	95	60	40	736	814
570	529	283	250	499	516
5,010	7,910	785	622	3,268	3,178
331	344	223	271	483	458
95	100	62	11	945	947
40	30	...	...	726	818
6,361	7,300	6,720	6,376	166	157
50	16	50	55	702	705
364	315	108	16	609	644
210	160	190	160	128	135
76	82	61	53	1,740	1,740
50	55	24	26	633	530
655	682	796	664	332	345
310	332	154	150	1,697	1,750
1,939	1,913	679	632	3,065	3,018
1,470	1,404	145	123	2,189	2,426
150	101	81	80	1,064	1,048
29	25	...	...	996	1,105
740	680	1,210	1,320	3,050	3,000

DISTRICT SINGH

Caste or Group.	District Total.			Chaibasa.	
	Total.	Male.	Female.	Male.	Female.
Oraon	3,220	1,584	1,636	649	935
Pan	1,057	516	541	333	356
Rajput	3,008	1,565	1,443	284	299
Santal	81,808	42,084	39,724	9,234	5,974
Tatwa or Tanti	25,174	12,644	12,530	5,810	5,770
Teli and Kalu	3,644	1,884	1,760	302	200
Religious devotees and persons returned by sect.					
Baisnab	2,827	1,406	1,421	96	87
Hindus returned by title.					
Mahto	1,166	613	553	...	...
Hindus returned by actual occupation.					
Bagal	6,179	3,053	3,126	...	...
Manjhi	4,416	2,176	2,240	...	...
Musalmans returned by title.					
Shaikh	2,150	1,232	918	312	303

FEUDATORY

KUCH

Caste or Group.	Total.			Phulbari.		Kuch Bihar or Kotwali.	
	Total.	Male.	Female.	Male.	Female.	Male.	Female.
Brahman	6,129	4,220	1,909	317	50	1,832	934
Chamar and Muchi	1,295	1,074	221	172	35	417	75
Garo	1,261	628	633	380	420	90	89
Goala	1,666	1,123	543	54	21	549	171
Hajjam or Napit	2,999	1,624	1,375	147	126	416	318
Hari	3,172	1,617	1,555	212	193	524	525
Jugi	4,972	2,604	2,368	289	293	706	576
Kaibartta	3,204	1,628	1,576	102	104	652	609
Kayastha	2,605	1,646	959	47	β	928	534
Koch	352,409	180,302	172,107	24,692	22,683	43,990	41,084
Kumhar	1,100	630	470	99	88	267	189
Mech	3,778	1,962	1,816	321	245	302	223
Namasudra or Chandal ...	4,486	2,160	2,326	209	223	345	383
Nuniya	1,187	893	294	156	21	215	115
Tanti and Tatwa	1,657	891	766	187	180	178	166
Hindus returned by actual occupation.							
Jaliya	1,159	583	576	126	100	1	1
Hindus returned by locality.							
Morangias	2,480	1,266	1,214	...	...	40	33
Musalmans returned by title.							
Shaikh	168,493	88,158	80,335	10,150	9,074	16,168	14,456

BHUM—*concluded.*

Chakradharpur.		Manoharpur.		Ghatsila or Dhalbhum.	
Male.	Female.	Male.	Female.	Male.	Female.
100	161	597	340	238	200
50	55	57	47	76	83
402	287	435	420	444	437
2,080	2,131	2,536	2,439	28,234	29,180
1,777	1,735	589	514	4,468	4,511
170	165	98	50	1,314	1,345
115	100	90	92	1,105	1,142
...	...	...	...	613	553
176	184	...	...	2,877	2,942
93	69	...	...	2,083	2,171
383	243	235	78	302	294

STATES.

BIHAR.

Matabhanga.		Haldibari.		Mekliganj.		Dinhata.	
Male.	Female.	Male.	Female.	Male.	Female.	Male.	Female.
658	305	205	131	285	74	923	415
219	46	75	13	75	10	116	36
4	1	50	45	54	50	50	28
172	164	83	7	133	162	132	18
377	310	111	99	195	179	378	343
185	165	164	176	231	229	301	267
40	77	59	53	37	37	1,473	1,333
140	100	117	114	25	17	592	632
153	77	57	10	198	111	263	224
50,880	49,025	6,958	6,565	14,626	13,436	39,226	38,709
106	70	18	24	90	46	50	53
227	223	446	485	237	229	429	411
655	642	220	240	78	81	653	802
190	40	31	35	143	35	149	39
2	8	228	142	293	268	3	2
110	106	110	130	212	230	15	9
1,226	1,181	...	...	...	...	...	...
17,520	15,998	9,260	8,467	9,245	8,589	25,815	23,761

Caste.	Total.			Athgarh.		Talcher.	
	Total.	Male.	Female.	Male.	Female.	Male.	Female.
Bagdi	16,796	8,591	8,205	...	...	...	...
Baniya	10,622	5,210	5,412	62	45	52	43
(i) Baisya	1,220	668	552	48	55	41	39
(ii) Subarna Banik	1,422	684	738	12	9	...	...
Barhi	6,126	3,130	2,987	108	97	104	91
Bathudi	39,807	19,989	19,818	...	...	...	...
Bauri	2,002	989	1,013	214	203	62	58
Bhandari	16,008	7,966	8,042	300	298	352	330
Bhuiya	52,280	26,254	26,026	1	...	...	...
Bhumij	60,322	29,996	30,326	839	806	...	1
Brahman	68,550	34,332	34,218	962	995	1,197	1,505
Chamar and Muchi	3,115	1,510	1,605	1	...	36	39
Chasa	201,156	98,095	103,061	3,376	3,288	3,896	3,976
Dhopa	20,974	10,510	10,464	236	226	196	213
Dom	7,074	3,963	3,111	38	36	32	40
Ghasi	3,323	1,633	1,690	...	...	...	...
Goala	154,083	77,238	76,845	1,245	1,138	1,162	1,175
Gokha	1,712	847	865	41	47	42	46
Gola	9,935	5,066	4,869	2	5	7	6
Gond	16,569	8,396	8,173	1	...	3	...
Gulgulia	3,118	1,448	1,670	...	...	48	53
Guria	20,992	10,531	10,461	528	523	458	417
Hari and Mihtar	19,332	9,401	9,931	116	121	398	397
Jhora	9,495	1,278	1,217	...	...	4	...
Juang	9,173	4,697	4,476	46	51	...	...
Jugi	1,457	721	736	10	6	1	...
Jyotis	1,854	919	935	41	39	15	18
Kachra	1,068	525	543	5	1	...	...
Kaibartta	1,226	610	616	...	...	...	...
Kalita	1,116	525	591	...	...	...	...
Kamar and Lohar	25,980	11,877	14,103	210	208	63	65
Kandh	52,890	26,433	26,457	4	...	681	655
Kandra	5,516	2,761	2,755	194	199	185	194
Kansari	4,114	2,053	2,061	24	33	32	37
Karanga	2,521	1,256	1,265	2	2	...	...
Kastha	1,139	559	580	2	...	8	4
Kayastha and Karan	14,764	8,202	6,562	208	170	173	156
Kewat	41,292	21,209	20,083	699	691	970	993
Khadal	2,940	1,480	1,460	...	...	...	...
Khaira	20,621	10,163	10,458	...	...	4	1
Khandait	63,205	31,513	31,692	253	228	417	409
Kharia	1,141	582	559	...	...	...	...
Kol	90,537	45,419	45,118	...	...	...	...
Kora	3,606	1,855	1,751	68	51	312	353
Kumhar	21,970	11,035	10,935	143	134	175	199
Kumuti	1,204	589	615	...	...	...	...
Kurmi	39,989	20,360	19,629	...	...	...	...
Mahili	1,934	927	1,007	...	...	...	...
Mali	11,633	5,865	5,768	119	187	285	265
Munda	38,596	19,209	19,387	56	21	2	1
Oraon	8,888	5,443	3,445	982	643	5	3
Pan	150,373	75,035	75,338	1,917	1,896	1,482	1,483
Rajput	7,581	3,883	3,698	62	63	58	67

TARY STATES.

Moharbhanj.		Nilgiri.		Keonjhar.		Pal Lahara.		Dhenkanal.		Athmalik.	
Male.	Female.	Male.	Female.	Male.	Female.	Male.	Female.	Male.	Female.	Male.	Female.
2,665	2,524	33	36	5,490	5,294	62	52	...	...	...	...
560	551	21	12	2,686	2,710	7	1	531	691	11	5
74	72	4	...	47	37	6	...	136	115	11	5
310	325	...	...	162	159	1	...	86	108	...	...
72	87	129	143	218	203	...	...	990	960	4	4
12,989	13,029	1,123	1,184	5,877	5,605	...	...	...	...	...	...
114	119	35	46	56	69	25	20	6	4	6	...
1,171	1,147	305	301	868	862	30	39	1,421	1,434	116	110
12,543	12,740	112	126	12,385	11,997	916	921	24	19	3	...
25,912	26,237	1,862	1,996	1,332	1,246	51	40	...	...	...	...
3,786	3,271	2,572	2,500	5,661	5,918	124	103	5,073	5,116	309	219
236	238	31	40	132	132	22	23	382	431	8	7
158	145	4,027	4,097	2,210	2,051	1,823	1,692	21,979	23,685	3,322	2,985
1,995	1,923	466	449	2,125	2,140	181	184	1,426	1,444	285	293
1,617	1,211	287	212	637	481	1	1	749	565	21	14
1,080	1,127	...	...	3	2	33	30	...	...	...	...
14,282	14,387	1,609	1,683	19,942	19,591	865	867	8,141	8,153	2,686	2,513
6	3	554	562	157	153	...	...	...	...	...	...
2,020	1,942	498	488	582	572	...	1	112	50	...	...
55	52	2,342	2,345	301	315	562	549	1,879	1,824	1,696	1,617
...	...	...	...	182	230	5	8	755	840	5	5
353	355	215	214	928	881	26	19	2,510	2,574	53	11
1,393	1,448	121	143	967	1,024	97	117	2,011	2,246	207	242
270	208	...	...	168	138	60	67	527	526	5	11
232	296	...	...	2,954	2,722	...	...	1,465	1,407	...	...
125	140	25	25	121	118	...	...	265	275	8	...
84	78	26	31	269	308	10	13	89	80	6	9
6	...	...	...	105	137	...	...	364	384	3	...
317	287	21	15	3	14	...	...	269	300	...	...
64	112	...	...	...	...	...	...	3	1	...	...
5,598	6,548	303	250	2,610	3,826	210	201	1,128	1,225	98	101
2	1	...	...	220	185	462	488	1,538	1,599	1,004	982
270	287	407	391	50	47	...	...	61	69	1	...
25	15	...	1	306	318	127	122	606	594	5	2
113	116	...	...	1	...	...	...	35	33	...	...
274	361	18	18	16	17	...	..	16	18	2	...
1,630	1,061	424	271	896	802	11	2	970	810	41	16
1,176	1,263	718	764	1,721	1,941	84	94	5,799	4,841	538	495
232	213	340	343	139	137	...	...	156	155	43	45
4,815	4,865	...	...	102	130	21	25	2,734	2,867	297	302
6,310	6,184	3,261	3,281	13,265	13,883	8	1	5,854	5,837	13	1
163	164	53	53	1	...	176	164	...	...	4	1
28,879	28,806	1,359	1,297	9,274	8,938	348	377	412	376	149	136
253	254	...	...	231	236	...	...	530	413	...	...
3,724	3,694	453	480	1,286	1,256	108	100	1,175	1,142	205	189
...	...	...	...	4	9	...	...	2	...	...	...
14,174	13,778	307	295	5,323	4,998	19	16	121	111	22	21
926	1,007	...	...	...	...	...	...	...	...	1	...
296	310	4	4	227	174	17	18	670	642	306	271
5,410	6,805	7	10	10,833	10,008	19	16	10	9	90	83
1,454	956	...	...	47	50	...	...	106	100	...	...
9,965	10,254	818	899	13,972	13,834	1,518	1,456	20,036	20,079	1,251	1,340
365	295	142	132	379	343	164	203	864	738	134	127

Caste.	Hindol.		Narsinghpur.		Baramba.		Tigaria.	
	Male.	Female.	Male.	Female.	Male.	Female.	Male.	Female.
Bagdi	...	...	...	...	...	...	...	...
Baniya	340	417	81	56	93	100	132	173
(i) Baisya	2	...	62	44	38	38	61	61
(ii) Subarna Banik	51	62	...	...	...	...	...	...
Barhi	70	74	161	139	49	49	96	97
Bathudi	...	...	...	...	...	...	...	...
Bauri	10	...	6	7	13	8	61	61
Bhandari	163	180	314	301	252	253	253	260
Bhuiya	...	...	9	7	...	...	...	..
Bhumij	...	...	...	...	...	...	...	...
Brahman	1,334	1,470	1,232	1,304	1,121	1,194	683	696
Chamar and Muchi	139	164	84	104	335	331	13	15
Chasa	4,769	4,847	3,774	7,662	7,348	7,211	2,818	2,774
Dhopa	153	175	864	326	377	414	118	126
Dom	163	122	40	34	...	...	83	87
Ghasi	...	...	...	...	...	...	517	531
Goala	800	851	1,326	1,489	1,483	1,406	399	423
Gokha	...	...	...	...	...	...	...	...
Gola	...	2	119	113	3	4	...	...
Gond	1	...	94	81	348	324	221	212
Gulgulia	...	...	...	...	442	514	11	20
Guria	293	286	561	533	401	390	271	335
Hari and Mihtar	287	306	393	406	154	141	196	198
Jhora	...	...	8	...	236	267	...	...
Juang	...	...	...	...	...	...	...	...
Jugi	...	...	3	...	17	16	...	...
Jyotis	19	18	20	21	19	14	3	1
Kachra	11	...	...	...	16	...	2	...
Kaibartta	...	...	...	...	...	...	...	...
Kalita	...	...	2	2	...	...	...	...
Kamar and Lohar	101	110	138	128	288	299	61	65
Kandh	951	988	725	723	406	383	48	55
Kandra	7	...	319	336	174	138	1	...
Kansari	33	18	44	49	98	118	76	88
Karanga	40	43	1,008	1,036	...	...	...	...
Kastha	4	...	3	2	...	...	2	2
Kayastha and Karan	296	268	143	89	419	376	126	130
Kewat	449	472	1,057	1,047	646	598	512	575
Khadal	...	...	...	2	74	70	...	...
Khaira	340	344	5	...	311	343	...	...
Khandait	977	897	9	1	159	133	100	87
Kharia	...	...	...	...	...	...	...	...
Koi	...	...	21	21	2	1	...	...
Kora	...	...	16	9	..	...	...	...
Kumhar	181	157	223	240	426	446	140	125
Kumuti	...	...	...	...	...	...	...	...
Kurmi	...	...	...	...	110	138	...	...
Mahili	...	...	...	...	...	...	...	...
Mali	168	192	313	344	228	203	166	144
Munda	56	42	201	216	304	321	18	16
Oraon	...	...	...	...	14	17	8	10
Pan	2,664	2,768	1,420	1,532	4,140	4,060	810	833
Rajput	233	239	86	33	940	975	54	57

STATES—*continued.*

Kandhpara.		Nayagarh.		Ranpur.		Daspalla.		Boad.	
Male.	Female.	Male.	Female.	Male.	Female.	Male.	Female.	Male.	Female.
340	299	...	...	...	...	1	...	...	...
418	397	95	94	17	16	51	54	53	47
60	34	42	32	8	7	1	3	27	30
56	73	...	...	...	...	6	2	...	...
348	275	489	514	191	162	106	92	9	...
...	...	...	...	...	...	...	...	...	...
2	...	18	...	181	191	1	...	170	227
675	686	936	992	304	321	230	262	276	266
2	1	...	...	14	16	200	166	45	33
...	...	...	...	...	...	...	...	...	...
2,914	2,673	4,247	4,386	1,379	1,384	735	722	983	
16	20	48	37	8	9	2	1	17	1
12,709	12,977	16,585	16,760	4,932	5,003	2,379	2,203	1,900	1,705
217	241	1,263	1,226	224	231	222	220	662	633
33	29	177	175	33	37	47	66	...	1
...	...	...	...	...	...	...	...	...	...
1,890	1,763	4,555	4,677	1,559	1,549	1,878	1,969	13,517	13,211
13	16	34	38	...	...	...	...	...	...
20	19	1,539	1,531	146	127	10	9	8	...
26	23	175	141	...	1	23	18	669	671
...	...	...	...	...	...	...	...	...	...
872	911	2,016	2,057	611	588	338	319	97	48
587	587	1,475	1,502	456	461	875	413	168	179
...	...	...	...	...	...	...	...	...	...
...	...	...	...	...	...	...	...	...	...
77	74	60	79	...	1	9	2	...	...
102	99	143	140	22	33	24	16	27	17
9	19	2	1	1	...	1	1	...	...
...	...	...	...	...	...	...	...	...	...
...	...	48	32	...	...	407	444	...	...
233	231	298	319	113	104	137	153	288	270
766	779	4,269	4,250	669	674	5,697	5,835	8,991	8,860
430	435	551	566	40	37	49	42	22	14
162	160	228	208	142	136	97	98	58	64
24	15	14	13	1	...	10	8	8	...
3	...	146	135	20	18	5	5	38	...
359	362	1,453	1,222	672	506	171	117	210	144
1,362	1,207	875	878	340	345	833	791	3,430	3,088
...	...	302	308	...	...	28	19	166	168
4	2	106	116	...	...	1,128	1,147	296	316
13	13	463	422	248	223	59	44	104	43
...	...	...	...	179	168	...	...	6	9
4,823	5,045	6	3	...	...	94	85	52	33
318	319	...	...	...	...	25	16	102	100
314	365	687	697	224	188	385	383	1,186	1,140
...	...	396	396	89	109	98	101	...	...
3	...	116	126	...	...	146	139	19	7
...	...	...	...	...	...	...	...	...	...
556	574	839	843	347	337	319	300	1,015	1,010
1,792	1,425	...	...	2	3	409	412	...	...
2,292	1,197	112	89	404	370	...	...	19	1
1,540	1,434	4,937	4,863	774	763	3,181	3,212	4,615	4,623
55	59	50	33	164	171	26	26	157	137

Caste or Group.	Total.			Athgarh.		Talcher.	
	Total.	Male.	Female.	Male.	Female.	Male.	Female.
Raju	2,800	1,440	1,360	...	...	...	...
Santal	95,267	48,152	47,115	...	...	...	...
Savar	45,770	22,884	22,886	2,644	2,525	695	673
Sunri	9,637	4,919	4,718	188	158	36	42
Tanti	31,543	15,810	15,733	300	318	330	326
Taula	11,939	5,698	6,241	410	445	594	635
Teli	44,698	22,646	22,052	587	627	751	865
Thoria	2,157	985	1,172	4	...	29	41
Tiyar	1,474	752	722	6	2	2	...
Religious devotees nd persons returned by sect.							
Baisnab	5,613	2,916	2,697	75	64	5	...
Hindus returned by title or common sub-caste.							
Mahanti	3,834	1,918	1,916	157	136	67	77
Naik	1,013	585	428	28	29	85	99
Patra	6,855	3,450	3,405	16	16	114	126
Sudra	25,890	12,939	12,951	2,348	2,436	68	82
Hindus returned by actual occupation.							
Kapuria	1,101	550	551	...	...	...	...
Manjhi	2,998	1,855	1,143	...	...	...	...
Matiya	3,017	1,513	1,504	12	14	12	13
Tulabhina	1,359	666	693	39	40	41	35
Ujia	1,718	837	881	17	20	...	...
Hindus returned by locality.							
Telingas	1,448	749	699	8	2	6	2
Uriyas	4,731	2,376	2,355	3	...	19	21
Hindus returned by unidentifiable caste.							
Shagirdpesha	2,071	1,086	985	10	10	...	...
Musalmans returned by title.							
Pathan	4,364	2,409	1,955	64	57	47	40
Shaikh	1,363	711	652	25	23	6	6

STATES—*continued.*

Moharbhanj.		Nilgiri.		Keonjhar.		Pal Lahara.		Dhenkanal.		Athmalik.	
Male.	Female.	Male.	Female.	Male.	Female.	Male.	Female.	Male.	Female.	Male.	Female.
1,008	874	259	256	12	...	...	...	...	...	...	...
46,236	45,254	167	167	900	826	2	2	...	...	...	...
1,412	1,468	289	304	3,103	2,957	801	806	10,512	10,654	6	13
1,173	1,155	305	295	163	145	14	11	690	708	76	62
1,963	1,907	1,085	1,123	2,722	2,696	2	1	4,272	4,319	81	65
29	31	13	8	129	114	219	236	1,334	1,485	523	587
2,499	2,226	790	787	4,013	4,066	147	82	4,602	4,288	343	119
9	13	...	...	39	47	72	75	189	136	15	...
...	...	...	...	...	...	...	...	162	155	10	18
1,525	1,487	116	104	237	204	55	64	296	229	67	49
284	225	...	...	52	44	19	15	194	210	1	1
14	15	30	28	14	11	11	16	256	84	1	...
1,098	1,130	64	66	349	333	2	1	447	367	7	...
10	14	1	1	2	...	50	55	184	204	2,663	2,707
34	29	259	268	39	61	...	...	57	72	...	...
1,798	1,076	9	15	34	35	...	...	...	...	...	...
3	...	308	367	90	101	11	15	849	763	...	...
175	183	...	...	60	50	...	...	156	172	...	...
733	752	87	109	...	...	...	...	...	...	...	...
3	5	12	17	39	39	2	...	44	36	...	...
313	323	1	...	24	27	26	27	11	8	26	35
17	19	12	15	10	11	1	2	32	53	8	2
1,098	946	22	6	182	168	...	...	243	139	51	40
411	415	...	...	58	47	...	...	86	50	4	1

Caste or Group.	Hindol.		Narsinghpur.		Baramba.		Tigaria.	
	Male.	Female.	Male.	Female.	Male.	Female.	Male.	Female.
Raju	1	1	...	...	...	...	...	...
Santal	...	...	...	...	...	...	...	...
Savar	106	109	2	...	869	936	626	625
Sunri	47	38	137	115	253	249	34	24
Tanti	375	384	441	454	182	219	192	197
Taula	1,034	1,213	239	278	...	...	190	214
Teli	325	308	973	1,048	649	519	469	657
Thoria	18	48	16	16	52	67	1	...
Tiyar	92	75	90	91	10	15	59	58
Religious devotees and persons returned by sect.								
Baisnab	15	8	34	17	90	102	36	39
Hindus returned by title or common sub-caste.								
Mahanti	...	...	25	29	269	274	44	51
Naik	35	33	4	10	30	83	51	44
Patra	9	...	16	10	87	24	...	...
Sudra	702	712	2,038	1,826	504	510	18	19
Hindus returned by actual occupation.								
Kapuria	161	121	...	...	...	...	...	...
Manjhi	13	16	1	1	...	...	...	...
Matiya	117	131	89	44	7	4	...	...
Tulabhina	29	35	6	3	...	...	28	37
Ujia	...	...	...	...	...	...	...	...
Hindus returned by locality.								
Telingas	12	1	4	...	6	4	...	...
Uriyas	2	...	5	6	...	...	...	...
Hindus returned by unidentifiable caste.								
Shagirdpesha	6	17	117	54	57	61	26	21
Musalmans returned by title								
Pathan	87	84	2	...	54	76	114	98
Shaikh	2	2	...	...	5	4	73	76

STATES—*concluded.*

Kandhpara.		Nayagarh.		Ranpur.		Daspalla.		Boad.	
Male.	Female.	Male.	Female.	Male.	Female.	Male.	Female.	Male.	Female.
117	173	43	56	...	...	...	...	...	...
847	866	...	...	...	...	...	...	...	...
624	628	42	40	773	782	5	...	375	376
242	260	683	670	200	191	270	247	408	348
569	584	1,396	1,344	459	406	97	81	1,344	1,309
234	235	217	220	24	27	389	395	120	118
1,289	1,312	2,470	2,508	903	961	667	717	1,169	1,012
431	617	2	2	...	1	91	109	17	...
51	45	163	162	37	39	27	36	43	26
103	101	47	49	67	69	31	25	117	86
421	463	286	272	17	39	57	66	15	14
...	...	21	17	...	...	5	9	...	...
725	766	261	316	179	178	48	44	78	28
47	45	252	272	1,152	1,141	500	515	2,400	2,412
...	...	...	...	...	...	...	...	...	...
...	...	...	...	...	...	...	...	...	...
4	3	20	17	4	3	27	23	10	6
...	...	60	75	35	33	35	29	2	1
...	...	...	...	...	...	...	...	...	...
4	2	446	494	88	72	42	1	33	24
89	93	1,133	1,149	102	114	194	188	428	364
705	622	46	51	40	45	3	1	1	1
31	14	244	149	115	106	11	3	44	29
...	...	17	4	21	13	...	...	6	6

Caste or Group.	Total.			Chang Bhukar.		Korea.		Sirguja.	
	Total.	Male.	Female.	Male.	Female.	Male.	Female.	Male.	Female.
Agaria	36,592	18,418	18,174	1,243	1,223	2,283	2,235	1,547	1,537
Babhan	13,566	6,852	6,714	70	57	314	304	2,990	3,016
Baniya	3,113	1,513	1,600	34	21	25	18	577	631
Barui	1,405	727	678	89	87	125	106	95	99
Bhat	1,283	734	549	56	33	18	12	102	82
Bhuiya	44,867	23,306	21,561	26	27	4	...	3,702	3,678
Bhumij	14,030	6,966	7,064	...	...	...	...	...	...
Binjhia	2,074	1,077	997	...	...	144	120	577	527
Brahman	9,309	4,910	4,399	159	122	301	215	1,993	1,904
Chamar and Muchi	9,019	4,552	4,467	278	234	363	324	2,390	2,377
Chasa	1,092	594	498	...	...	...	...	...	...
Chero	4,856	2,447	2,409	523	506	634	692	550	594
Chik	6,267	3,237	3,030	...	...	...	...	744	675
Dhopa	5,737	2,915	2,822	14	16	181	128	932	947
Dom	2,599	1,283	1,316	9	8	6	5	85	80
Ghasi	6,659	3,347	3,312	12	9	348	368	132	138
Goala	55,653	27,872	27,781	765	648	1,649	1,568	17,904	17,933
Gond	125,176	65,012	60,164	2,945	2,927	4,962	4,809	38,904	35,617
Hajjam and Napit	3,375	1,821	1,554	18	13	82	44	796	633
Hari	1,212	672	540	90	38	96	85	55	60
Ho	16,013	8,044	7,969	775	685	...	...	125	115
Jhora	1,259	631	628	78	69	21	31	22	19
Kahar	9,098	5,168	3,930	633	430	775	552	1,039	831
Kaibartta	1,604	904	700	42	39	12	10	106	96
Kalita	2,185	1,135	1,050	...	...	55	50	...	...
Kamar and Lohar	25,940	13,010	12,930	100	105	1,062	964	3,902	3,733
Kaur	11,290	5,738	5,552	90	70	217	199	2,233	2,147
Kayastha and Karan	1,452	809	643	15	3	17	...	229	173
Kewat	5,267	2,684	2,583	72	61	32	24	1,139	1,077
Khandait	1,346	702	644	...	...	105	100	...	...
Kharia	4,442	2,255	2,187	...	...	...	...	436	441
Kharwar	2,793	1,417	1,376	97	79	246	241	337	318
Koiri	2,431	1,275	1,156	54	37	188	182	700	620
Kol	40,476	20,184	20,292	370	278	224	115	3,064	2,889
Kora	9,843	5,157	4,686	16	14	25	23	2,020	1,696
Kumhar	23,828	11,945	11,883	97	63	1,260	1,232	2,927	2,840
Kurmi	27,944	13,544	14,400	5	...	35	37	2,555	2,530
Mahili	1,201	600	601	...	...	10	9	54	63
Munda	55,720	28,056	27,664	2,960	2,899	3,540	3,601	3,973	3,933
Oraon	83,663	42,015	41,648	863	860	106	91	11,394	11,520
Pan	9,009	4,719	4,290	563	547	569	547	934	878
Rajput	6,632	3,469	3,163	229	204	293	224	1,099	1,015
Rajwar	16,379	8,252	8,127	...	...	1,694	1,665	6,140	6,010
Rautia	11,640	5,908	5,732	54	42	5	8	490	440
Sadgop	29,292	14,729	14,563	1,856	1,859	2,254	2,302	1,998	1,878
Santal	42,022	20,959	21,063	1,500	1,400	473	461	1,835	1,787
Savar	3,672	1,965	1,707	220	205	211	204	396	336
Sunri and Kalwar	5,016	2,600	2,416	510	495	151	123	371	317
Tambuli	4,851	2,386	2,465	17	21	425	429	1,051	1,099
Tanti and Tatwa	7,145	3,600	3,545	44	24	25	19	52	40
Teli	13,204	6,747	6,457	41	36	109	79	1,020	888
Turi	2,551	1,351	1,200	...	...	...	...	566	535
Religious devotees and persons returned by sect.									
Baisnab	1,005	499	506	...	...	6	4	175	188
Gosain	1,411	756	655	...	...	...	...	239	166

TRIBUTARY STATES.

Udaipur.		Jashpur.		Gangpur.		Bonai.		Kharsawan.		Seraikela.	
Male.	Female.	Male.	Female.	Male.	Female.	Male.	Female.	Male.	Female.	Male.	Female.
2,148	2,128	2,295	2,541	2,879	2,523	2,250	2,398	1,995	1,869	1,778	1,717
193	207	1,122	1,139	947	851	809	799	309	308	98	33
122	186	375	379	160	138	40	36	14	9	166	182
78	69	52	49	95	76	68	60	62	68	63	64
5	6	133	87	204	166	176	127	17	13	23	18
15	26	793	788	12,263	10,511	3,706	3,611	760	852	2,037	2,068
...	...	...	...	803	761	133	118	1,196	1,166	4,834	5,019
...	...	...	...	356	350	...	...	...	...	...	...
42	35	237	196	645	609	444	408	291	212	798	698
505	506	468	471	256	224	113	166	37	33	142	132
174	128	...	...	...	...	420	370	...	...	...	...
417	326	3	1	75	60	198	195	47	35	...	...
764	776	1,045	1,003	634	576	...	...	...	...	...	...
461	341	235	297	513	507	183	164	142	155	254	267
70	51	387	394	185	187	44	46	144	143	353	402
1,071	1,070	438	415	305	349	19	17	225	264	797	652
1,023	1,215	2,167	2,119	463	402	514	448	1,595	1,648	1,792	1,800
1,993	1,894	1,263	1,233	10,664	9,896	2,316	2,108	976	1,010	989	670
35	21	76	78	368	352	34	35	210	194	202	184
155	106	98	86	72	69	55	52	2	2	50	42
...	...	...	...	...	...	...	...	7,050	7,128	94	41
12	11	109	109	186	178	118	125	13	13	72	73
608	405	855	646	543	535	432	305	168	85	115	112
259	150	99	76	89	78	30	44	42	41	225	166
236	205	198	190	266	248	195	182	120	118	65	57
3,531	3,820	1,247	1,212	1,802	1,736	182	168	319	291	865	899
1,578	1,534	834	834	786	768	...	...	...	...	...	...
91	64	39	29	41	30	3	4	324	289	50	51
55	52	64	84	891	847	223	229	17	13	191	196
53	52	...	...	193	173	1	...	127	119	223	200
53	52	599	578	958	905	73	75	136	136	...	...
...	...	454	483	251	217	...	...	23	24	9	14
...	...	6	8	310	282	10	19	...	...	7	8
693	792	45	51	5,695	5,613	3,370	3,372	3,186	3,452	3,537	3,730
326	290	2,180	2,100	460	467	...	...	...	...	110	96
156	145	629	629	1,921	1,854	1,788	1,848	1,263	1,278	1,904	1,994
11	9	920	681	445	636	1,387	1,309	2,270	2,235	5,916	6,963
137	140	146	107	63	47	64	63	92	76	34	36
2,428	2,426	3,611	3,668	5,070	4,718	3,147	3,124	2,209	2,107	1,118	1,098
847	773	17,426	16,821	10,678	10,855	293	284	253	295	155	149
931	913	415	421	597	358	604	545	66	44	40	37
360	365	411	373	457	418	215	181	244	227	161	156
9	...	122	133	284	315	...	...	...	...	3	4
890	864	2,457	2,236	1,890	2,023	46	41	22	22	54	56
1,925	1,940	1,180	1,197	1,559	1,599	1,578	1,537	1,491	1,498	888	753
1,852	1,794	2,500	2,600	575	578	1,842	1,660	1,567	1,024	8,815	9,159
211	156	117	120	239	226	251	184	118	82	203	194
258	202	322	313	353	347	152	102	94	101	389	416
27	29	120	140	...	...	702	691	16	15	28	41
23	21	...	...	65	65	170	153	819	818	2,402	2,405
20	14	110	130	1,045	957	363	348	185	187	3,855	3,818
...	...	452	430	329	231	4	4	...	...	...	...
14	16	48	39	...	...	40	39	67	68	140	152
51	44	235	223	231	222	...	...	...	...	...	...

Group.	Total.			Chang Bhukar.		Korba.		Sirguja.	
	Total.	Male.	Female.	Male.	Female.	Male.	Female.	Male.	Female.
Hindus returned by title.									
Ganjhu	1,108	511	597	...	...	334	402	...	...
Mandal	1,316	670	646	...	...	...	...	...	...
Nagbansi	8,508	4,258	4,250	105	105	875	861	1,125	1,125
Hindus returned by actual occupation.									
Darsi	1,138	622	516	14	13	109	101	117	109
Manjhi	3,035	1,616	1,419	...	...	...	...	256	223
Musalmans returned by title.									
Shaikh	1,769	916	853	8	3	28	12	115	132
Musalmans returned by actual occupation.									
Jolaha	1,887	996	891	123	120	108	108	333	329

NOTE :—For Hill Tippera State, see Imperial

TRIBUTARY STATES—*concluded.*

Udaipur.		Jashpur.		Gangpur.		Bonai.		Kharsawan.		Seraikela.	
Male.	Female.	Male.	Female.	Male.	Female.	Male.	Female.	Male.	Female.	Male.	Female.
75	86	...	...	80	22	...	...	41	53	31	34
...	...	...	...	...	...	...	...	121	109	549	537
949	946	117	119	190	182	281	275	616	637	...	...
85	70	17	14	111	109	...	...	75	55	94	45
957	798	...	...	295	288	...	...	...	...	108	110
2	3	174	164	67	80	12	3	162	164	348	292
273	225	24	15	43	35	45	29	...	...	47	30

Table XVI, pages 121 to 125, Vol. V.

2 *d*

C. A. P. & others—Reg. No. 1219J—1,503—21·8·93.